*Heralds and Heraldry
in Shakespeare's England*

Frontispiece (overleaf): Portrait of William Camden,
Clarenceux King of Arms, in his tabard.
London, Worshipful Company of Painter-Stainers.

HERALDS AND HERALDRY IN SHAKESPEARE'S ENGLAND

Edited by

NIGEL RAMSAY

SHAUN TYAS
DONINGTON
2014

© the contributors, 2014

Typeset from the files of the editor
and designed by the publisher

Published by

SHAUN TYAS
1 High Street
Donington
Lincolnshire
PE11 4TA

ISBN
978-1-907730-35-1

Arms of The Heraldry Society (see page vi).

Printed and bound in the Republic of San Marino by Fotoedit s.r.l.

Contents

	The Heraldry Society	vi
	Preface	vii
	Notes on Contributors	vii
	Editorial Note	ix
	Abbreviations	x
1	The Heralds and the Elizabethan Court: Robert Dudley, Earl of Leicester as Deputy Earl Marshal, by Simon Adams	1
2	William Smith, Rouge Dragon Pursuivant, by Nigel Ramsay. With an Edition by Ann Payne of Smith's MS Tract on Abuses Committed by the Painters and Others to the Detriment of the Heralds	26 / 45
3	Grants and Confirmations of Arms, by Clive Cheesman, Richmond Herald	68
4	"A herald, Kate? O put me in thy books." Shakespeare, the Heralds' Visitations, and a new Visitation Address, by Adrian Ailes	105
5	Tudor Pedigree Rolls and Their Uses, by Sir John Baker	125
6	Colours of Continuity: The Heraldic Funeral, by Roger Kuin	166
7	Heraldry and the Gentry Community in Shakespeare's England, by Richard Cust	190
8	"Wanting Arms": Heraldic Decoration in Lesser Houses, by Tara Hamling	204
9	Heraldry in Tudor and Jacobean Portraits, by Karen Hearn	220
10	Heraldic Language and Identity in Shakespeare's Plays, by Beatrice Groves	236
11	Literary and Dramatic Heraldry, by Kathryn Will	266
12	Heraldry and Alternate Emblematic Forms in the Age of Shakespeare, by Alan R. Young	283
	Afterword: From the Late Seventeenth Century to the Present Day, by Peter O'Donoghue, York Herald	308
	Further Reading	322
	Illustration Credits	330
	Index	331

THE HERALDRY SOCIETY

The publication of this book has been supported by a generous grant from The Heraldry Society. The Society's coat of arms is displayed above, with a different artist's interpretation from that on p. iv.

The aim of The Heraldry Society is to further the understanding and knowledge of heraldry and related subjects such as chivalry and genealogy. It publishes a quarterly newsletter, *The Heraldry Gazette*, and a twice-yearly journal, *The Coat of Arms*. Every two years it organizes a Congress, with lectures and excursions. It also runs a programme of lectures throughout the year, and it has for sale a variety of heraldic publications, new and secondhand. Details of the Society's activities, and of how to join it, are available on its website: theheraldrysociety.com

Preface

A research fellowship which the Folger Shakespeare Library (in Washington DC, USA) awarded me in 2009 opened my eyes to the scholarly value of its holdings of heraldic manuscripts. For the armorist, these are unsurpassed save by those of the British Library, the College of Arms and the Bodleian Library. Later, the planning for an exhibition in 2014 of part of the Folger's heraldic collection led me to realise that a systematic scholarly treatment of the main elements of the heraldic world in the late sixteenth and early seventeenth centuries was long overdue. That this book is now being published, and in such handsome form, is entirely thanks to generous grants from The Heraldry Society and the Marc Fitch Fund.

My personal thanks are due to the authors, not just for their essays but also for their suggestions for illustrations that I hope have resulted in an integrated combination of texts and images. It has also been a pleasure to work with the publisher, Shaun Tyas, who has enthusiastically met the challenge of designing the book to show these images to their best advantage.

I owe, too, a host of debts of gratitude to those who have helped at every stage of the book's genesis. Professors Vanessa Harding and Grace Ioppolo were its first readers, as referees for grant applications. Dr Lynsey Darby, the Archivist at the College of Arms, and Caryn Lazzuri and Natalie Zmuda at the Folger Shakespeare Library, all helped on dozens of occasions in the obtaining of suitable images, as well as providing information. (The reader's attention might be drawn here to the Folger's excellent LUNA website, with its extensive stock of high resolution images, all available *gratis*.) At the Victoria and Albert Museum, special help was given by Judith Crouch, Dr Kirstin Kennedy and Gill Saunders. Dr Jane Eade of the National Portrait Gallery helped particularly in the obtaining of images of paintings held in private collections, and Pippa Shirley expedited matters at Waddesdon Manor. Dr Julian Litten provided a photograph of an engraving in his own collection. At a critical stage in the book's preparation, Peter O'Donoghue, York Herald, went out of his way to help with an invaluable series of suggestions and pictures.

My warmest thanks go, as ever, to my wife who has nobly tolerated the almost endless series of intrusions into our domestic life that have resulted from the whole undertaking.

Nigel Ramsay

Notes on Contributors

Simon Adams, formerly Reader in History at the University of Strathclyde, retired in 2011 and is happily completing his biographies of Elizabeth I and Robert Dudley. His published works include *Leicester and the Court* (2002) and *Household Accounts of Robert Dudley, Earl of Leicester* (1995). He was Associate Editor of *The Oxford Dictionary of National Biography* for the Elizabethan Court and his work in press includes the introductory essay to *The Elizabethan Garden at Kenilworth* (English Heritage, 2013).

Nigel Ramsay is a Senior Research Fellow in the School of Law, Exeter University, and an Honorary Research Associate of the History Department, University College London. He is at present engaged in preparing an edition and translation of the medieval records of cases brought in the Court of Chivalry (the court of the Constable and Marshal); this is to be published by the Selden Society.

Ann Payne retired in 2001 as Keeper of the Department of Manuscripts at the British Library. Her main fields of research are in medieval and early modern history, with a particular interest in heraldic, antiquarian and topographical manuscripts. She co-authored *Medieval Pageant. Writhe's Garter Book. The Ceremony of the Bath and the Earldom of Salisbury Roll* (Roxburghe Club, 1994), and she contributed the chapter 'Heraldry and Genealogies' to *The Lumley Inventory and Pedigree: Art Collecting and Lineage in the Elizabethan Age*, ed. Mark Evans (Roxburghe Club, 2010).

Clive Cheesman is Richmond Herald of Arms; he was formerly a curator in the Department of Coins and Medals at the British Museum. He is joint editor of *The Coat of Arms*, journal of The Heraldry Society.

Adrian Ailes is Principal Record Specialist, Early Modern Records, The National Archives. He is an Honorary Research Fellow of Bristol University and a member of the Académie Internationale d'Héraldique. He wrote 'The Development of the Heralds' Visitations in England and Wales, 1500–1600' in *The Coat of Arms*, 3rd ser., vol. 5 (2009), and is currently editing Elias Ashmole's Church Notes taken on his visitation of Berkshire 1665–66.

Sir John Baker is Emeritus Downing Professor of the Laws of England, University of Cambridge). His most recent books are *Oxford History of the Laws of England*, vol. 6, *1483–1558* (2003), and *The Men of Court, 1440 to 1550: A Prosopography of the Inns of Court and Chancery and the Courts of Law*, 2 vols (Selden Soc., 2012).

Roger Kuin is Professor Emeritus at York University, Toronto. He has published an edition of the Correspondence of Sir Philip Sidney (2012), *Chamber Music: Elizabethan Sonnet-Sequences and the Pleasure of Criticism* (1989) and an edition of Robert Langham's *Letter* (1983), as well as numerous articles, mainly on Sidney. A 2012 paper at the Renaissance Society of America, 'Colours of Continuity', presented the first systematic decoding of the heraldic elements in Sidney's funeral procession. Sidney's funeral and its details are the subject of his continuing research.

Richard Cust is Professor of Early Modern History at the University of Birmingham. He researches and writes on the political, social and cultural history of early Stuart England and has carried out extensive research in the archives of the College of Arms. His recent publications include *Charles I. A Political Life* (2005) and *Cases in the High Court of Chivalry 1634–1640*, edited with Andrew Hopper (Harleian Soc., new ser. 18, 2006). He has a forthcoming book on *Charles I and the Aristocracy 1625–1642* (to be published by Cambridge University Press).

Tara Hamling is Senior Lecturer in the History Department at the University of Birmingham. She is author of *Decorating the Godly Household: Religious Art in Post-Reformation Britain* (2010), and editor (with Catherine Richardson) of *Everyday Objects: Medieval and Early Modern Material Culture and its Meanings* (2010) and (with Richard L.

NOTES ON CONTRIBUTORS

Williams) *Art Re-formed: Reassessing the Impact of the Reformation on the Visual Arts* (2007). Her current projects include a monograph co-authored with Catherine Richardson, provisionally entitled *A Day at Home in Early Modern England: The Materiality of Domestic Life* (forthcoming with Yale University Press, 2016).

Karen Hearn was Curator of 16th and 17th Century British Art at Tate Britain, 1992–2012, and is now an Honorary Professor at University College London. In 1995 she curated the Tate exhibition *Dynasties: Painting in Tudor & Jacobean England 1530–1630*. Her final Tate shows, with accompanying books, were *Van Dyck & Britain* (2009) and *Rubens and Britain* (2011–12). She co-edited *Lady Anne Clifford: Culture, Patronage & Gender in 17th Century Britain* (2009); other publications include 'The English Career of Cornelius Johnson', in *Dutch & Flemish Artists in Britain 1550–1700*, ed. J. Röding *et al.* (2003); and 'The Full-Length Portrait in Early 17th-Century Britain', in *The Suffolk Collection*, ed. Laura Houliston (Swindon: English Heritage, 2012). Karen lectures, writes and teaches on British art between 1500 and 1710.

Beatrice Groves is Research Lecturer in Renaissance English at Trinity College, Oxford. She has published widely on Shakespeare and early modern drama, including *Texts and Traditions: Religion in Shakespeare, 1592–1604* (2006) and two forthcoming essays for Cambridge University Press's Shakespeare series. Her current projects include a monograph on the theme of the destruction of Jerusalem in early modern literature.

Kathryn Will recently received a doctorate from the Department of English Language and Literature Department at the University of Michigan. Her dissertation explores the historical and literary roles of heralds and heraldry in Elizabethan and Jacobean England by analyzing their portrayal in prose manuals, ballads, and popular drama.

Alan Young is Professor Emeritus at Acadia University (Wolfville, Nova Scotia). He has published extensively on the Early Modern period and is the author of *Tudor and Jacobean Tournaments* (1987), *The English Tournament Imprese* (1988), *Emblematic Flag Devices of the English Civil Wars 1642–1660* (1995), and *Henry Peacham's Manuscript Emblem Books* (1998). His most recent books are *Hamlet and the Visual Arts, 1709–1900* (2002) and *Punch and Shakespeare in the Victorian Era* (2007).

Peter O'Donoghue is York Herald of Arms, and Librarian of the College of Arms, as well as joint editor of *The Coat of Arms*, journal of The Heraldry Society. He has written and lectured on various aspects of the institutional history of the College and its records, with particular focus on the eighteenth and twentieth centuries, as well as on post-medieval heraldic and genealogical topics.

Editorial Note

The editorial aim with the various manuscript texts that are printed or excerpted in this volume has been to present them in the clearest and most readable form. Contractions have accordingly been expanded, 'u' and 'v' have been printed in their present-day form, and the long 'i' has been printed as 'i', not 'j'.

Citations of folio numbers are to be taken as being of rectos, unless the verso is indicated. Likewise, references to signatures (or gatherings) in printed books are to be assumed as being to the recto unless the verso is indicated.

Abbreviations

Baker, *Men of Court* John Baker, *The Men of Court, 1440 to 1550. A Prosopography of the Inns of Court and Chancery and the Courts of Law*, 2 vols (Selden Soc., Supplementary Ser., 18, 2012).

Bodleian Library Oxford, Bodleian Library, Department of Western Manuscripts

Cal. Pat. Rolls *Calendar(s) of the Patent Rolls Preserved in the Public Record Office*, variously published by the Public Record Office and the List and Index Society.

Cal. S. P. For. *Calendar(s) of State Papers, Foreign Series, of the Reign of Edward VI* [etc.] ... *Preserved in the ... State Paper Office* [etc.] (London, 1861 etc.).

Godfrey and London, *College of Arms* W. H. Godfrey, assisted by A. R. Wagner, *The College of Arms, Queen Victoria Street; with A Complete List of the Officers of Arms*, by H. S. London, London Survey Committee, Monograph 16 (London, 1963).

Hasler, *Commons, 1558–1603* P. W. Hasler, *History of Parliament: The House of Commons, 1558–1603*, 3 vols (London, 1981).

Heralds' Commemorative Exhibn. Cat. *Heralds' Commemorative Exhibition, 1484–1934* (London, 1930; reprinted 1970).

Hist. MSS Commn. Historical Manuscripts Commission, also known as the Royal Commission on Historical Manuscripts

Jnl. *Journal*

ODNB *Oxford Dictionary of National Biography*, ed. H. C. G. Matthew and Brian Harrison, 60 vols (Oxford, 2004); also online.

PRO The National Archives [of England and Wales]: Public Record Office

Proc. *Proceedings*

Ramsay, *Robert Glover* (forthcoming) N. L. Ramsay, *Letters and Papers of a Tudor Scholar and Herald: Robert Glover, Somerset Herald* (Harleian Society, forthcoming)

Rymer, *Foedera* T. Rymer and others, *Foedera, Conventiones, Literae et Cuiuscunque Generis Acta Publica*, 20 vols (London, 1704–35); 2nd edn., 20 vols (London, 1727–35); 3rd or Hague edn., 10 vols (The Hague, 1739–45).

Scott-Giles, *Shakespeare's Heraldry* C. W. Scott-Giles, *Shakespeare's Heraldry* (London, 1950)

Ser. Series

Soc. Society

Trans. *Transactions*

Wagner, *Heralds of England* A. R. Wagner, *Heralds of England: A History of the Office and College of Arms* (London, 1967).

Woodcock and Robinson, *Oxford Guide to Heraldry* T. Woodcock and J. M. Robinson, *The Oxford Guide to Heraldry* (Oxford, 1988).

The Heralds and the Elizabethan Court: Robert Dudley, Earl of Leicester, as Deputy Earl Marshal

SIMON ADAMS[1]

'In the time of Q[ueen] Elizabeth when the Earls of Warwick and Leicester powerful men in their day did flourish most learned and expert genealogists of that age spared not their endeavours to magnifie that family whence these great men did by a younger son derive their descent'. Thus Sir William Dugdale introduced a particular genealogical controversy, the Anglo-Saxon origins of the Suttons, Lords Dudley, in *The Baronage of England*.[2] He singled out William Hervey and his successor as Clarenceux King of Arms, Robert Cooke, as the chief magnifiers of the Dudleys, but his remarks have been read as a commentary on a wider venality among the Elizabethan heralds. For Dugdale as for other royalists, Leicester was a notorious figure, whose patronage of the Puritans had sowed the seeds of the Great Rebellion.[3]

The power and influence that Leicester enjoyed, thanks to Elizabeth's misplaced favour (as the Royalists saw it), also included the College of Arms. During most of the 1570s and 1580s he served as deputy to the Earl Marshal, George Talbot, sixth earl of Shrewsbury. Absent from the court owing to his custody of the Queen of Scots, Shrewsbury has been dismissed as an ineffectual earl marshal.[4] But his absence generated a considerable body of correspondence – with Leicester in particular – that sheds an unprecedented light on the politics of the College.[5] On one level Leicester was a good

---

[1] I should like to thank His Grace the Duke of Norfolk, the Most Honourable the Marquess of Bath and the College of Arms for their kind permission to cite manuscripts in their possession. I should also like to record my thanks to the College's former archivist Mr Robert Yorke for his assistance in my research at the College many years ago. I owe an especial debt to the editor of this volume not only for his forbearance over the delay to this contribution, but also for putting the materials he assembled for his forthcoming Harleian Society volume on Robert Glover at my disposal. A fuller discussion of a number of wider issues will be found in my forthcoming biography of Elizabeth I.

[2] 2 vols (London, 1675–6), II, p. 214. The subsequent discussion of this issue here is based on ' "Because I am of that Countrye & mynde to Plant myself there": Robert Dudley, Earl of Leicester, and the West Midlands', in S. Adams, *Leicester and the Court: Essays on Elizabethan Politics* (Manchester, 2002), pp. 310–73.

[3] The Royalist view of Leicester was derived from the Catholic tract *Leicester's Commonwealth* (see below), which strongly influenced the High Anglican explanation of 'the rise of Puritanism'; see Adams, 'Baronial Contexts? Continuity and Change in the Noble Affinity, 1400–1600', in Adams, *Leicester and the Court*, pp. 374–410, at 387.

[4] Wagner, *Heralds of England*, p. 12.

[5] A few items are mentioned in passing by Wagner; see *Heralds of England*, p. 200. Both men's correspondence has been radically dispersed. For Leicester's, see Adams, 'Because I am of that Countrye', pp. 350–1, n. 5. The Talbot family papers were saved by the 17th-century antiquary

choice as deputy, for he had a genuine interest in matters historical and heraldic and in the College's work. On another, however, his position at the centre of government did not provide him with extensive spare time to devote to the College and he did have controversial personal causes to pursue.[6]

Among these causes was the Anglo-Saxon origin of the Lords Dudley, ostensibly an example of what a series of historians have labelled the Elizabethan 'obsession' with pedigree and lineage. But thanks to their ideological preconceptions they have failed to appreciate that 'the ancient nobility' was one of the major political issues of the reign.[7] It was also an issue that the College was not institutionally equipped to address.

From the 1560s Catholic polemic emphasised that Catholicism was the religion of 'the ancient nobility' and the new religion the work of low-born new men.[8] The argument was made explicit by the rebels of 1569, particularly in their proclamation at Darlington: 'Whereas divers newe set upp nobles ... go about to overthrow and put downe the ancient nobilitie of this realme'.[9] A more notorious exposition was the tract defending the executed fourth Duke of Norfolk, *A Treatise of Treasons against Q. Elizabeth* published in 1573. Lord Burghley was so upset by its aspersions on his gentility that he began preparing a reply.[10] The equally notorious *Leicester's Commonwealth* of 1584 did not disparage Leicester's origins as strongly as one might expect; it merely dismissed them: 'he hath not ancient nobility, whereby men's affections are greatly moved'.[11] The issue

---

Nathaniel Johnston, who then dispersed them. He gave a large number of the most interesting to the 6th duke of Norfolk, who deposited most in the College of Arms, but the equivalent of a further volume remains at Arundel Castle ('Autograph Letters, 1513–1585'). Two volumes were obtained by the 1st Viscount Weymouth and are now at Longleat House ('Original Letters [of the] Earls of Shrewsbury'). A further large collection went to Lambeth Palace Library, and there are smaller groups in the Sheffield Central Library and the Folger Shakespeare Library. The Talbot Papers at the College of Arms were purchased by Lambeth Palace Library in the 1980s, and their present pressmarks are employed here. The Historical Manuscripts Commission has calendared both the College of Arms and the Lambeth collections in *A Calendar of the Shrewsbury and Talbot Papers*, 2 vols (1966–71) and the Longleat Original Letters in *Manuscripts of the Marquess of Bath*, V (1982).

[6] For examples of the pressures on his time, see Adams, 'Because I am of that Countrye', pp. 343–4.

[7] To be fair, when I first addressed this subject twenty-odd years ago in 'Favourites and Factions at the Elizabethan Court', in Adams, *Leicester and the Court*, pp. 46–67, I did not fully understand it either.

[8] There was an obvious Henrician background, but the case was not made then.

[9] *The Rising in the North: The 1569 Rebellion, being a reprint of the Memorials of the Rebellion of the Earls of Northumberland and Westmoreland edited by Sir Cuthbert Sharp 1840*, ed. Robert Wood (Durham, 1975), p. 42.

[10] This is not the place to discuss the vexed question of the authorship of this tract. For Cecil's reaction, see his correspondence with Archbishop Parker, 11 Sept. 1573, in *Correspondence of Matthew Parker D.D. Archbishop of Canterbury*, ed. J. Bruce and T. T. Perowne (Parker Soc., xlii, 1853), artt. 337–8.

[11] *Leicester's Commonwealth. The Copy of a Letter Written by a Master of Art of Cambridge (1584) and Related Documents*, ed. Dwight C. Peck (Athens, Ohio, 1985), p. 314; see also Adams,

was not simply one of evil ministers; the Queen's own legitimacy was questionable. The running debate over the claim of the Queen of Scots had made Henry VIII's manipulation of the succession a public issue. Behind it lurked Philip II's claim as heir of John of Gaunt, a claim that challenged the legitimacy of the Tudor dynasty itself.[12]

If the cause of the ancient nobility served as a polemical means of deflecting attacks on a foreign church, it survived into the seventeenth century. The earliest 'family history' was John Smyth of Nibley's *Lives of the Berkeleys* (written between 1618 and 1630), a saga of the tribulations (frequently self-inflicted) of a family of the ancient nobility.[13] *Leicester's Commonwealth* supplied Smyth with his overall narrative for Elizabeth's reign. By then the attack on the ancient nobility also implied some form of social revolution, which gave Stuart High Churchmen an explanation for the rise of Puritanism. The theme of the destruction of a medieval nobility in a social revolution was extremely attractive to twentieth-century historians of the Left, beginning with R. H. Tawney, as they sought to explain both the causes of the Civil War and the birth of capitalism. Tawney's intellectual heir, Lawrence Stone, first explored 'the obsession with lineage'; he explained it as a product of the social insecurity of *nouveaux riches* seeking to bolster their status by elaborate pedigrees, and he has been followed by subsequent *annaliste*-inspired historians.[14]

Modern British social history is notoriously obsessed with social class, but the sixteenth-century nobility was not a class.[15] It was an order that underwent a major political transformation in the century before Elizabeth's accession. The late medieval peerage was divided effectively into upper and lower divisions by the royal family. Junior male members of the royal family (the royal dukes) and English husbands of royal daughters were the only peers the Crown was obliged to create. But there was also 'the extended royal family': male relations of English queens, and bastard lines, the Beauforts in particular. There was a particularly controversial aspect to the royal peers. Endowment of senior peers on a large scale was a heavy drain on the Crown estate and

---

'Because I am of that Countrye', p. 352 n. 20.

[12] Since Mary Stuart's claim to the English succession was as heir to Henry VII, she could not challenge the legitimacy of the Tudor dynasty, and, to the extent that she hoped Elizabeth would recognise her as successor, it was not in her interest to challenge her either. The wider challenge arose after Mary's death, thanks chiefly to the Jesuit Robert Persons.

[13] Published in *The Berkeley Manuscripts*, ed. J. Maclean, 2 vols (Gloucester, 1883–5).

[14] L. Stone, *The Crisis of the Aristocracy, 1558–1641*, reprinted with corrections (Oxford, 1979), pp. 23-7; cf. Wagner, *Heralds of England*, pp. 205, 209; Mervyn James, 'English Politics and the Concept of Honour, 1485–1642', in his *Society, Politics and Culture: Studies in Early Modern England* (Cambridge, 1986), pp. 308–415; Felicity Heal and Clive Holmes, *The Gentry in England and Wales, 1500–1700* (Basingstoke, 1994), ch. 1; Daniel Woolf, *The Social Circulation of the Past: English Historical Culture, 1500–1700* (Oxford, 2003), esp. p. 88; Jan Broadway, *'No Historie so Meete': Gentry Culture and the Development of Local History in Elizabethan and Early Stuart England* (Manchester, 2006), ch. 5.

[15] Stone's *Crisis of the Aristocracy* is dominated by his obsession with social class (e.g. the section on 'Class Attitudes', pp. 39-49) and his quasi-republican hostility to his subject.

it was the two notoriously weak monarchs, Richard II and Henry VI, who were most generous to the extended royal family. The royal peers were also the main victims of the Wars of the Roses and of Henry VIII's campaign against potential White Rose claimants.[16]

The lower peerage was dominated by the cadet lines of existing great families, Howards, Nevilles and Greys in particular. Henry VIII's policy in creating new peers (at least in the early part of his reign) was to promote wealthier members of lower rank, regardless of their political significance – a policy that Elizabeth largely followed.[17] Only in Edward VI's reign can one detect an intent to replenish the peerage by 'those who have been most useful to the King and the realm as leaders in war and counsellors in peace' – as the patent of Lord Darcy of Chiche's creation in 1551 put it.[18] Mary I created a few barons (not all of whom were strong Catholics) for their service in 1553 and against Wyatt's rebellion in 1554, but otherwise she was more concerned to restore older peerages than establish a new Catholic nobility.[19]

As a result, by Elizabeth's accession the extended royal family was virtually extinct. Only a few peers could claim any royal blood: the Duke of Norfolk, the Earl of Huntingdon, the Lords Stafford and – thanks to their marriages to Brandon women – the children of the Earl of Hertford and the fourth Earl of Derby. By a curious coincidence the leading members of the royal family who were resident in England during her reign were Scots: the Lennox Stewarts and the Queen of Scots herself. There was one survivor from the old extended royal family, William Somerset, third earl of Worcester, and there were two relatives of Henry VIII's wives: Jane Seymour's nephew, Edward Seymour, earl of Hertford, and Catherine Parr's brother William, marquess of Northampton (who died heirless in 1571).[20] Elizabeth's additions to the extended royals from her Boleyn kinsmen were limited: Henry Carey and Thomas Sackville became barons, but neither Sir Francis Knollys (though holding several court offices) nor his numerous sons became peers in her reign.

The absence of an extended royal family distinguished the Elizabethan peerage from its predecessors.[21] The gap in the higher peerage was filled by 'the ancient nobility', though only the Duke of Norfolk (a fifteenth-century creation), two earls (Arundel and Oxford) of extended lineage, two of fourteenth-century (Northumberland and

---

[16] It is worth noting *en passant* that the prominence of the royal peers in the Wars of the Roses explains the paradox of the neutrality of so many peers in an apparent 'baronial war'.

[17] See Adams, 'The Patronage of the Crown in Elizabethan Politics: The 1590s in Perspective', in Adams, *Leicester and the Court*, pp. 68–94, at 73–5.

[18] *Cal. Pat. Rolls, 1550–3*, p. 135, quoted in Stone, *Crisis of the Aristocracy*, p. 66.

[19] A number of Mary's restorations are referred to below.

[20] The first Somerset earl of Worcester was an illegitimate son of Henry Beaufort, duke of Somerset.

[21] The Stuart and Hanoverian preference for foreign marriages limited the subsequent royal peers. After 1603 they comprised only the Lennox Stewarts, to be followed later by the dukedoms granted to Charles II's bastards and then the male members of George III's and Victoria's large families.

Westmorland) and two of fifteenth-century creation (Shrewsbury and Derby), together with a handful of barons could claim to be members of it. The majority of the peerage was of Tudor creation, even if some of the original baronies of the earls were older. Elizabeth did not create a 'new peerage'; those of her creations who were not existing peers promoted in rank comprised only the Dudleys, William Cecil and a handful of barons, and the Dudleys could be considered an Edwardian restoration.[22] She was also very conservative in recognising claims through the female line, and a number of them were outstanding on her death, to be resolved by James I. James I's dramatic expansion of the peerage was ultimately driven by fiscal demands, but initially it was an attempt to pacify old English disputes.

Nor was the connection between the old Church and the 'the ancient nobility' straightforward. Some of the staunchest Catholic peers of the reign were of Tudor creation – notably the second Earl of Southampton and the third Lord Paget. If the events of 1569–72 could be portrayed in retrospect as a defeat of an old order, the incoherence of Northumberland's, Westmorland's and Norfolk's various statements still makes it difficult to explain precisely why they were alienated.[23] But they had allies – who for reasons equally unexplained survived the years unscathed – in particular the Earl of Arundel and his son-in-law Lord Lumley, who took their status as members of the ancient nobility seriously. After 1572 they were joined by Norfolk's younger brother Lord Henry Howard (created earl of Northampton by James I), who certainly saw his brother as a martyr. Despite being reconciled to Rome in 1576, Howard also enjoyed a charmed life, despite being the most obvious contributor to the ancient nobility polemic.[24]

Those Elizabethan peers who considered themselves members of the ancient nobility could (at best) claim a Norman creation. But the reign also saw a novel reinterpretation of the ancient nobility: the tracing of genealogies back to the Anglo-Saxon monarchy.[25] Leicester's interest in the origins of the Suttons was not a unique example; Burghley and a number of members of the gentry also took their Anglo-Saxon descent seriously.[26] However historically suspect Anglo-Saxon pedigrees might be, the political context is significant. Thanks to the fourteenth-century *Modus Tenendi Parliamentum*, there was

[22] Elizabeth offered Burghley a promotion from the baronage in 1588, but he declined it on the grounds that having two sons to endow, his estate could not support it.
[23] The case is strongest for Northumberland, the most openly Catholic of the three. Norfolk always claimed to be a Protestant, and Westmorland was married to his sister Jane, who was also a Protestant.
[24] He has been advanced as the author of *A Treatise of Treasons* and in January 1581 was questioned about his possession of what appears to have been a copy of it. He may have had a role in the preparation of *Leicester's Commonwealth*.
[25] When I first explored this development during the early 1990s in 'Because I am of that Countrye' (see p. 317), I was not entirely clear of its significance. Subsequent discussions (Heal and Holmes, *Gentry in England and Wales, 1500–1700*, pp. 36–7; Woolf, *Social Circulation of the Past*, pp. 122–6; and Broadway, 'No Historie so Meete', p. 100) have provided further examples.
[26] For Burghley, see Stone, *Crisis of the Aristocracy*, pp. 23–4.

an established belief in legal circles that there was an 'Ancient Constitution' of Anglo-Saxon origin that included Parliament.[27] One version of the *Modus* was sometimes included in a collection of texts related to the Earl Marshal and may have originated in the College of Arms.[28] Elizabeth's reign saw a new interest in the Anglo-Saxon kingdom, stimulated in part by Archbishop Parker's sponsorship of the collecting and publishing of Anglo-Saxon documents in an attempt to prove the historic continuity of the English church.[29] The Norman Conquest also had uncomfortable contemporary resonances, particularly the issue of governing the kingdom by right of conquest. The threat of Philip II employing right of conquest had emerged as early as his marriage to Mary, most notoriously in the so-called 'Machiavellian treatise'.[30] An Anglo-Saxon pedigree became both a patriotic statement and an implicit challenge to an 'ancient nobility' of Norman origin.

The gentry were as affected by the wider political issues as the nobility. The concomitant to the ancient nobility was a network of established gentle families who governed the counties under them. The earliest 'county history' was the 'View of Staffordshire', by the combative recusant Sampson Erdeswicke.[31] There was, however, a significant practical difference between noble and gentle concerns: the novel demand made in the Elizabethan heraldic visitations for documentary evidence of claims to gentility.[32] Visitations, together with funerals, comprised the bulk of the work of the members of the College during her reign, because, despite the legends, Elizabeth's reign saw only a few major royal ceremonial occasions.[33] Elizabeth regarded her progresses as essentially private relaxation.[34] She was obliged to entertain only four major foreign embassies: those from France to ratify or negotiate treaties in 1559, 1564, 1572 and 1581. There were two other major public ceremonies: the funeral of Sir Philip Sidney in February 1587 and the thanksgiving for the defeat of the Armada in November 1588. The heralds' principal diplomatic activity was in embassies to invest foreign monarchs

---

[27] See J. G. A. Pocock, *The Ancient Constitution and the Feudal Law* (Cambridge, 1957), pp. 42–5, and Nicholas Pronay and John Taylor, *Parliamentary Texts of the Later Middle Ages* (Oxford, 1980), esp. p. 80.

[28] The so-called B Recension. Leicester owned a copy of the English text: British Library, Add. MS 15091. According to Pronay and Taylor (p. 206) he also owned a Latin text, BL, Add. MS 38139, but I can find no evidence of this in the manuscript itself.

[29] Brief discussions can be found in V. J. K. Brook, *A Life of Archbishop Parker* (Oxford, 1965), esp. pp. 321–5, and Retha M. Warnicke, *William Lambarde: Elizabethan Antiquary, 1536–1601* (Chichester, 1973), esp. ch. 4.

[30] See P. S. Donaldson, *A Machiavellian Treatise by Stephen Gardiner* (Cambridge, 1973).

[31] See M. W. Greenslade, 'Erdeswick, Sampson (*c.* 1538–1603), in *ODNB*, 18, pp. 495–6.

[32] Woolf hints strongly at this in *Social Circulation of the Past*, ch. iv, 'The Genealogical Imagination', but is not explicit.

[33] Wagner drew the opposite conclusion (*Heralds of England*, p. 205); but he exaggerated the extent of the ceremonial occasions.

[34] On this point see my article ' "The Queenes Majestie ... is now become a great huntress": Elizabeth I and the Chase', in *The Court Historian*, 18 (2013), pp. 143–64, at 157–9.

who had been elected to the Order of the Garter. Nor did Elizabeth involve the College in the leading heraldic issue of the day – the claim of the Queen of Scots – with the limited exception of the judgement in June 1559 as to whether Mary had the right to include the arms of England in her coat of arms in France.[35]

The visitations brought to the fore the institutional weakness of the College of Arms, for it was not equipped to serve as an impartial learned adjudicator of the tendentious issues of the day. On one level the Elizabethan College was similar to the lesser bureaucracies created by the expansion of central government in Henry VIII's reign. Offices initially attached to the court department known as the Chamber, the Household above Stairs, or later the Lord Chamberlain's Department (often held by a single officer), became mini-bureaucracies. The most dramatic example is the way the Clerk of the Ships became the Navy Board in 1546, but the Revels was another. The model for these new bureaucracies appears to have been the Board of Green Cloth that administered the Hall, the Household below Stairs and later the Lord Steward's Department. While there was considerable variation in structure (often shaped by dominating personalities), the offices all shared three general characteristics. Firstly, financial 'independence': that is to say, they were funded directly by, and accounted to, the Exchequer. Secondly, they were ultimately responsible to one of the Great Officers of State: the Board of Green Cloth to the Lord Steward, the Navy Board to the Lord Admiral, and the Revels to the Lord Chamberlain. Lastly, they tended to function collegially, with internal promotion by seniority, often effectively independent of their presiding officer.[36]

The College of Arms was an uneasy amalgam of three entities: the individual officers of arms or heralds, the Order of the Garter and the earl marshalcy. The heralds were personal servants of the Crown, and their individual salaries were paid directly by the Exchequer throughout the century. It has been argued that they were originally part of a third department of the court, the Courtyard, presided over by the Constable of England and the Earl Marshal, from which they derived their later relationship to the Earl Marshal.[37] However, as a branch of the Court the Courtyard disappeared relatively

---

[35] Neville Williams, *Thomas Howard, Fourth Duke of Norfolk* (London, 1964), pp. 32-3, based on *Cal. S. P. For., 1558-9*, art. 868. The arms issue is more complicated than Williams allowed for. Mary began displaying the arms of England at the time of Elizabeth's coronation, but in the treaty of Cateau-Cambrésis (2 April 1559) Henry II effectively recognised Elizabeth as queen of England and nothing was said about Mary's claim; it was the revival afterwards that caused the controversy. The College's judgement was not published and the matter was pursued discreetly. The issue was only raised publicly (and then obliquely) in the proclamation justifying Elizabeth's military intervention in Scotland on 24 March 1560 and directing Mary to cease displaying the arms *Tudor Royal Proclamations*, ed. P. L. Hughes and J. F. Larkin, 3 vols (New Haven, 1964-9), II, no. 467). The issue is discussed in more detail in my *Elizabeth* (Yale UP, forthcoming).

[36] An early Elizabethan set of ordinances for the Navy Board made specific provision for internal promotion: PRO, SP 12/15, art. 4, printed in *Elizabethan Naval Administration*, ed. C. S. Knighton and D. M. Loades (Navy Records Soc., 160, 2013), doct. 2.

[37] Wagner, *Heralds of England*, p. 125.

early, to be replaced by the lesser Stables. Nevertheless the Earl Marshal continued to share with the heralds the regulation of certain ceremonies (particularly coronations), while he and the Constable shared the presidency of the High Court of Chivalry, which had jurisdiction (*inter alia*) over misuse of arms.

The earl marshalcy and the constableship of England were among the few Great Offices of State to survive as hereditary into the sixteenth century. The constableship came to an end with the execution of the third Duke of Buckingham in 1521. Possibly as a result, both Henry VIII and Elizabeth took an autocratic line towards the earl marshalcy, manipulating it or leaving it vacant for substantial periods of time.[38] The earl marshalcy was held by the heirs of the twelfth-century John FitzGilbert the Marshal (even by the female line), and these by the fifteenth century were the Mowbray and then Howard dukes of Norfolk. However, Henry VIII granted the office to his brother-in-law the Duke of Suffolk, after the death of the second Howard duke of Norfolk in 1522. In 1533 the third Duke demanded it as part of his inheritance and Suffolk yielded only on compensation as Lord President of the Council.[39] Norfolk lost the office on his attainder in 1546, and under Edward VI it was held first by the Protector Somerset and then (from 17 April 1551) by the Duke of Northumberland. Mary restored it to Norfolk on his release in 1553, and on his death in 1554 it was inherited by his grandson, the fourth Duke.

Early in the fifteenth century an issue had emerged that was to dominate the College during the following century. Since the mid fourteenth century there had been two provincial kings of arms, Norroy and Clarenceux, whose jurisdictions followed the established administrative geography of the kingdom, north and south of the River Trent.[40] However, in 1417 Henry V created Garter King of Arms to serve the Order of the Garter, and – although the Order was a separate institution based at Windsor Castle – also designated him 'Principal Officer within the Office of Arms'.[41] He omitted, however, to define Garter's relationship to the two existing kings of arms. Garter's primary responsibility was the Order and in practice this was extended to the peerage and the House of Lords, leaving the rest of the armigerous to the other heralds. The issue was not considered worthy of resolution in the incorporation of the Officers of Arms by Richard III (2 March 1484), which only gave it a permanent legal status and a residence. The residence that Richard granted was reclaimed by Henry VII – a serious loss since it meant that a central library and archive could not be established. Each herald created his own library, and possession of materials became an issue of dispute.

---

[38] Elizabeth also dispensed with a Lord Privy Seal for all but a few months of her reign, and with a Lord Steward for long periods.
[39] S. J. Gunn, *Charles Brandon, Duke of Suffolk, 1484–1545* (Oxford, 1988), p. 121.
[40] Another example is the division of the administration of the Forests.
[41] Elias Ashmole, *The Institution, Laws and Ceremonies of the Most Noble Order of the Garter* (London, 1672), p. 252.

The issue of Garter's status came into the open in 1530.[42] Clarenceux King of Arms claimed that Garter was conducting visitations under his own authority when they were reserved to the two other Kings of Arms, and he asserted that Garter was too liberal in the granting of arms to unworthy persons – a standard charge in subsequent heraldic disputes.[43] Henry VIII intervened, but resolved it idiosyncratically by declaring that the granting of arms was a prerogative of the Crown and that the heralds were merely his agents. They had no independent authority and should follow such rules as he laid down.[44] Subsequent visitations were undertaken under commissions by letters patent from the Crown – although few appear to have been carried out after the mid-1530s, until a fresh series in the 1560s.

The College was incorporated as a separate institution on 18 July 1555.[45] The new incorporation established the complement for the next century and a half: the three kings of arms, six heralds (Chester, Lancaster, Richmond, Somerset, Windsor and York) and four pursuivants (Bluemantle, Portcullis, Rouge Croix and Rouge Dragon).[46] It also gave them a permanent residence (Derby House), which in turn finally made possible a central library – 'for the preservation of our books' as Robert Glover (Somerset Herald 1570–88) later noted.[47] The fourth Duke of Norfolk has been credited with obtaining the second incorporation, but if Glover is to be believed the process began under Edward VI and he gave the Duke of Northumberland credit for it.[48]

Even if Glover was deliberately complimenting Leicester by the reference to his father, it was during Northumberland's earl marshalcy that the statutes of the Order of the Garter were reformed. This was a complicated process that began early in Edward VI's reign and was only completed by the new statutes published on 17 March 1553, a few months before the King died – but repealed by Mary I immediately after her accession.[49] Edward VI himself played a large role, particularly in severing the Order's

---

[42] The fullest account of the incident is by Wagner (*Heralds of England*, pp. 161-5), who notes that the only record of it is that left by Clarenceux.

[43] Cf. Wagner, *Heralds of England*, p. 204. The charge of overly liberal grants has strong similarities to those of peculation of stores in disputes within the Navy Board,

[44] James, *Society, Politics and Culture* (cit. in n. 14), pp. 335-6, sees the incident as initiating 'the intervention of the state', which may be an exaggeration. Gunn credits Suffolk with a role in the settlement: *Charles Brandon, Duke of Suffolk*, p. 123.

[45] *CPR, 1555–57*, p. 31.

[46] In 1484 the complement had been four kings of arms, four heralds and four pursuivants.

[47] 'A Brief Rehersall of the Causes of the Disorder in the Office of Arms', British Library, Cotton MS Titus C. i, f. 426ᵛ, printed in Ramsay, *Robert Glover*, ch. 3; Ramsay notes that this important source for the disputes within the Elizabethan College survives in numerous versions, which can be dated between 1580 and 1586.

[48] *Ibid*. The case for Norfolk is made by Williams, *Thomas Howard, Fourth Duke of Norfolk*, pp. 40-3. Wagner accepts it (*Heralds of England*, pp. 182–3), while noting Glover's claim for Northumberland.

[49] The main revision of the statutes appears to have taken place in 1551–2. In 1560 a new reform of the statutes was agreed but nothing appears to have transpired; see Roy Strong, 'Queen Elizabeth

association with the cult of St George.[50] One aspect of the 'Protestantising' of the Order was the provision that its chancellor should henceforth be a layman, a provision that Mary retained.[51]

Whatever the fourth Duke of Norfolk's role in 1555, he was unquestionably the most interventionist earl marshal of the century, despite being absent from court for long periods thanks to his mourning for his second and third wives in 1564–5 and 1567–8, while his tenure of office effectively came to an end in 1569. The first stage was the revival of visitations by the two provincial Kings of Arms; it is possible that they began in 1558, and they were certainly underway by 1561.[52] As a result Elizabeth's reign saw the most intensive series of visitations to date, and, as noted above, these need to be taken into account in any discussion of contemporary private concern over pedigrees. In February 1565 the College took up residence in Derby House and on the 4th Norfolk issued orders that anyone whose claim to arms had been disclaimed in a visitation was to be fined and that no new grants of arms were valid unless allowed by him, or in his absence by Cecil or Leicester.[53] Norfolk's major legacy was the 'constitutions' of 8 July 1568.[54] He proclaimed the earl marshal's authority in uncompromising form: he alone had the power to nominate heralds for appointment by the monarch and to make orders for the College. Otherwise the constitutions were a worthy attempt to square the circles of the College's existing tensions. He confirmed Garter as the presiding office of the College responsible to the earl marshal and with authority over funerals of the nobility, but he also confirmed the visitational powers of Clarenceux and Norroy over their provinces.[55] He reiterated the necessity of the earl marshal's consent for the granting of new arms but relegated the issuing of pedigrees to the kings of arms. He also tried to strengthen the preservation of the College's records and to arrange a limited common treasury from consulting fees.

I and the Order of the Garter', in Strong, *The Tudor and Stuart Monarchy: Pageantry, Painting, Iconography*, 3 vols (Woodbridge, Suff., 1995–8), II, pp. 55–86, at 60.

[50] See E. Maunde Thompson, 'The Revision of the Statutes of the Order of the Garter by King Edward VI', *Archaeologia*, liv (1893), pp. 173–98, and Diarmaid MacCulloch, *Tudor Church Militant: Edward VI and the Protestant Reformation* (Harmondsworth, Middx., 1999), pp. 30–5.

[51] Ashmole, *Institution, Laws and Ceremonies of the Garter*, p. 239.

[52] Wagner, *Heralds of England*, p. 185. There is a question whether William Hervey (Clarenceux, 1557–67) deserves the credit.

[53] There is a dispute over whether the order should be dated 1565 or 1566. Wagner, *Heralds of England*, pp. 185–7, accepts 1565, but Ramsay, *Robert Glover*, appx. vi, suggests 1566. Norfolk was certainly at court in late January 1566.

[54] Printed in *Munimenta Heraldica*, ed. G. D. Squibb (Harleian Soc., new ser. iv, 1985), pp. 97–105; see also the comments of Wagner, *Heralds of England*, pp. 188–97.

[55] Norfolk had in fact confirmed the authority of Garter over funerals of the nobility and knights on 10 June 1563: *The Diary of Henry Machyn, Citizen ... of London, A.D. 1550 to A.D. 1563*, ed. J. G. Nichols (Camden Soc., orig. ser., xlii, 1848), p. 309. One beneficial result was the creation of that invaluable source, 'Sir William Dethick's Book of Funeralls of the Nobility, 1585–1603' (MS at the College of Arms).

However this was to be the limit of Norfolk's involvement with the College. His implication in the 1569 rebellion, his imprisonment and then his involvement in the Ridolphi Plot effectively terminated his career as earl marshal in early 1569.[56] It is worth surveying the position at this point. The 1555 incorporation had not defined the College's internal structure, leaving it to the heralds to agree among themselves 'for the good estate and rule of their faculty' and for the keeping of any relevant records. Unlike similar offshoots of the Court, there was neither a treasurer nor a chancellor to administer the College. Norfolk's constitutions had supplied only a limited internal structure and if the College was to act as a disinterested expert body, the financial aspect remained a real weakness. As with so many branches of the Court, the heralds earned fee income from performing their duties. Since the late fourteenth century their functions (and fees) at various major ceremonies had been established – but, as noted above, these were not plentiful. A particular issue was Garter's role in organising the obsequies of the nobility, which (it was claimed) caused him to encourage overly-lavish funerals. Norfolk's efforts to regulate the granting of arms ran against the financial interest of the heralds in the fees for new grants. There was also the issue of any private work that individual heralds undertook.

Norfolk's constitutions also created a new area of internal tension. There was an established understanding that promotion within the College should be by seniority. However, the constitutions implied that the earl marshal could override seniority. The struggle over promotions now came to dominate the College, thanks in large part to the dominant position of the Dethicks. Sir Gilbert Dethick (Garter from 1550 until his death in 1584) was the principal officer of the College, and was followed by his two sons, Sir William (Rouge Croix Pursuivant 1567, York Herald 1570 and Garter 1586), and Nicholas (Bluemantle Pursuivant 1564, Windsor Herald 1583). Robert Glover later claimed that the 1568 constitutions were effectively a plot by Dethick to revive the claims of Garter against the provincial kings of arms.[57]

On 2 January 1573 Elizabeth appointed George Talbot, the sixth earl of Shrewsbury, as earl marshal, declaring that Norfolk's attainder had left the office at her disposal.[58] He was not the senior earl, as Arundel and Oxford were older creations. But Arundel, whom Elizabeth had retained as Lord Steward on her accession, had resigned that office in mysterious circumstances in 1564 and was compromised by his association with Norfolk in 1569. Oxford was young and, if clever, was soon to become notorious for bizarre behaviour. Shrewsbury was reliable and uncontroversial, and may have been acting informally in the office earlier – he presided as Lord Steward over Norfolk's trial in January 1572.[59] But he had no particular interest in heraldry or history and he was

---

[56] There is, however, some evidence that he conducted business for the College during his house arrest in the winter of 1570–1.
[57] 'Brief Rehersall', f. 426; printed by Ramsay, *Robert Glover*, ch. 3.
[58] *Cal. Pat. Rolls, 1572–75*, art. 290.
[59] Elizabeth and Leicester addressed letters to Shrewsbury as earl marshal in October and December

already serving in another major – if also informal – role, as guardian of the captive Queen of Scots. Although no one at the time would have expected his guardianship to have continued until 1584, he had not been a regular attendant at Court prior to 1569 either. The best explanation for the appointment, apart from his reliability, is that Elizabeth intended it as a gesture of confidence, similar to his appointment to the Privy Council when he was named Mary's guardian. Shrewsbury had approached his appointment as Mary's guardian with understandable trepidation, but when the occasion of replacing him arose during the 1569 rebellion, he took it as a serious slight to his honour.

Given his absence, there was no question of Shrewsbury exercising the earl marshalcy in the interventionist way that Norfolk had exemplified. He was forced to follow Norfolk's earlier example and appoint a deputy of authority, and he chose the Earl of Leicester. The earliest reference is a letter from Leicester dated only as 5 July that has been calendared to 1571. In it he complains that in the absence of a full commission from Shrewsbury he is unable to satisfy 'the gentlemen that do desire in your absence to have had their causes heard'.[60] The suggested date appears too early, but the content is not specific enough to clarify the year. Shrewsbury's choice of Leicester, on the other hand, is not surprising. They had been friends since Edward VI's reign if not earlier and on 26 May 1571 Leicester had appointed Shrewsbury High Steward of all his lands in England.[61]

Unlike Shrewsbury, Leicester was a known quantity in the College. Although it is not clear how actively he performed as Norfolk's deputy, he was commissioned by Norfolk in 1569 together with the Marquess of Winchester to resolve a long-running dispute between the College and the dean and chapter of Westminster Abbey over rights to the funeral furniture of peers buried there.[62] Moreover, one leading herald, Robert Cooke (d. 1593), had been his servant. Over Cooke's initial appointment there is some confusion. Henry Machyn recorded in his diary on 25 January 1562 that Cooke was appointed Blanche Rose Pursuivant. He noted that Cooke was Dudley's servant, and added the derisive comment 'the which he never served in no place a-for'. On 8 February Machyn recorded the appointment of William Flower, Chester Herald, as Norroy King of Arms and further that Cooke then succeeded him as Chester – a dramatic promotion.[63] A similar story, that Cooke was created Blanche Rose Pursuivant extraordinary by the Queen's special favour and twelve days later Chester Herald, was cited in 1580 as evidence that strict seniority had never been followed in the College.[64] However, the

---

1572: Lambeth Palace Library, MS 3197, ff. 41, 73.
[60] *Ibid.*, f. 17.
[61] *Ibid.*, f. 13.
[62] Wagner, *Heralds of England*, p. 115. Leicester and Winchester delivered their report on 6 April and Norfolk ruled against the dean and chapter on the 29th.
[63] *Diary of Henry Machyn*, ed. Nichols, pp. 275–6.
[64] Letter of Glover to unknown recipient, 14 Mar. 1580, printed in Ramsay, *Robert Glover*, ch. 3.

Patent Rolls tell a more complicated story. No letters patent for Cooke's appointment as Blanche Rose are enrolled, but those of his as Chester are dated 25 January and Flower's as Norroy (on the death of Laurence Dalton) are dated 29 January.[65] The obvious sequence is reversed, though this may be a consequence of Chancery clerical delays. Furthermore, Dudley's household account for 1559–61 records a payment of £10 to Robert Cooke, herald, on 22 December 1560.[66] This may be a consequence of silent amendment, but the possibility remains that Cooke had been a pursuivant prior to January 1562.[67] In his biography of Norfolk, Neville Williams states that Norfolk considered Cooke's appointment 'an unwarrantable intrusion into his province', but does not supply a source.[68]

It was not Cooke himself, however, who created Leicester's connection with the College; it was established by Leicester's father, John, duke of Northumberland, and the Dudley family's complicated genealogy. Leicester's grandfather, Henry VII's notorious minister Edmund Dudley, was the son of John Dudley of Atherington (Suss.), the second son of John Sutton, first Baron Dudley of Dudley Castle.[69] Edmund's wife Elizabeth was a far greater heiress. She was the youngest daughter of Edward Grey, created Viscount Lisle in 1483, who was a descendant of Margaret, eldest daughter of Richard Beauchamp, earl of Warwick by his first marriage, and wife of John Talbot, first earl of Shrewsbury. Beauchamp's first wife was the sole daughter of the fourth Lord Berkeley, who was also Baron de Lisle and Teyes. Thanks to the fact that the dispute lasted until the nineteenth century, the Lisle barony (originally the lordship of the Isle of Wight), became the source of the greatest of all the disputes between heirs general and heirs male.[70] Elizabeth Dudley remarried in 1515. Her second husband was Edward IV's illegitimate son, Arthur Plantagenet, to whom Henry VIII granted the Lisle viscountcy in the right of his wife in 1523. Plantagenet's death in 1542 without male heirs was followed by John Dudley's rise to the peerage, when Henry VIII created him Viscount Lisle in the right of his mother. In the initial Edwardian distribution of peerages in 1547, he claimed the earldom of Warwick by descent and adopted the Beauchamp device of the bear and ragged staff, which his sons revived flamboyantly in Elizabeth's reign. In the meantime

---

[65] *Cal. Pat. Rolls, 1560–3*, pp. 265, 305.

[66] *Household Accounts and Disbursement Books of Robert Dudley, Earl of Leicester, 1558–1561, 1584–1586*, ed. S. Adams (Camden 5th Ser., vi, 1995), p. 126. There is no further reference to Cooke in Dudley's accounts for this period.

[67] The two surviving copies of Dudley's early household accounts are fair copies drawn up for audit sometime after the originals concluded. There is evidence that the clerks amended personal details to reflect subsequent changes of circumstance.

[68] Williams, *Thomas Howard*, p. 81; his only reference is to the entry in the Patent Rolls. Williams has been followed by Wagner, *Heralds of England*, p. 189 n.

[69] The descent from Lord Dudley was challenged, by Sampson Erdeswick among others, but it is genuine; see Adams, 'Because I am of that Countrye', p. 315.

[70] The 19th-century phase was the claim to the barony by Sir John Shelley Sidney in the 1820s.

he had also bought Dudley Castle from the poverty-stricken third Lord Dudley.[71]

Leicester and the other three surviving children of John Dudley (his elder brother Ambrose and his sisters Mary Sidney and Katherine Hastings) were restored in blood by the Parliament of 1558, but they forfeited any claim of right to his lands or offices. Thus anything granted to them by Elizabeth I was by grace – including Ambrose Dudley's 'restoration' to the earldom of Warwick and the barony of Lisle at Christmas 1561.[72] Nevertheless, two aspects of John Dudley's rise were shared by his sons. The first was the near-antiquarian way in which they pursued their claims by descent.[73] The second was the fact that the main claims were by descent through the female line. This was a wider contemporary issue for it also affected the royal family, since Henry VII's only royal blood came from his mother, and she in turn was an illegitimate Beaufort descendant of John of Gaunt. Henry VIII's Yorkist blood also came from his mother. Female line claims ran counter to two medieval attempts to strengthen male lines: the determination that certain baronies could only descend through the male line and the making of entails in tail male. They were the source of recurrent disputes between heirs general (i.e., through the female line) and heirs male. Ultimately, however, in the absence of a clear male heir, recognition depended on monarchical grace, and all monarchs (Henry VIII in particular) were prepared to bend the rules in favour of their friends.

So far as Robert Dudley is concerned, the immediate issues arising from the Beauchamp descent were resolved by Elizabeth's grant to his elder brother, Ambrose, of the Lisle barony and the earldom of Warwick at Christmas 1561. His own creation as earl of Leicester posed no questions, except for the still unexplained one of why Elizabeth delayed granting the earldom for a year after the grant of Kenilworth Castle. There were, however, two further issues, one obscure, the other one of the controversies of the reign. The obscure issue is the origin of the Suttons, Lords Dudley, and specifically the claim that they were descended from an Anglo-Saxon lord of Sutton in Holderness. It was the dispute over this issue that sparked Dugdale's comments. What makes it of more than antiquarian interest is that in March 1561 Elizabeth granted to Dudley lands in Holderness and the East Riding (some of which had belonged to Northumberland) – raising the question of whether there was an ultimately superseded intention of creating him lord of Holderness.

The celebrated issue was the final stage of the 'Great Berkeley Lawsuit', the central subject of Smyth of Nibley's 'History of the Berkeleys', which he began writing in 1618

---

[71] The discussion here is based on that in Adams, 'Because I am of that Countrye', pp. 315–22. On 4 November 1554, Mary granted the lordship of Dudley Castle to the 5th Lord Dudley for his service (*CPR, 1554–55*, pp. 22–3), a good example of her effective restoration of the 'ancient nobility'.

[72] Despite Robert Dudley referring to it as restoring his house, in a letter to Shrewsbury at the time (Adams, 'Because I am of that Countrye', p. 321).

[73] For Northumberland's connection to William Hervey (appointed Norroy King of Arms in 1550), see Adams, 'Because I am of that Countrye', p. 316. It should be noted that the 1553 Dudley pedigree referred to there was incorrectly cited as College of Arms, Muniment Room, 61/5; it should be 16/5. A detail is illustrated below, Fig. 26.

to celebrate the 'final settlement' of 1609.[74] It centred on the Lisle barony and began on the death of the fifth Lord Berkeley in 1417. The fifth Lord held both the Honor of Berkeley Castle, which had been entailed in 1349, and the Lisle barony, which was not subject to an entail. The substantive issue was whether Berkeley had included in the entailed estate certain Gloucestershire manors that actually belonged to the Lisle barony. The issue was taken up by his niece Margaret, countess of Shrewsbury, and then by her son and grandson the Talbot Viscounts Lisle and led to the so-called 'battle of Nibley Green' (20 March 1470) in which the second Viscount Lisle was killed.[75]

Following Lisle's death, the seventh Lord Berkeley regained the manors in question, but then had to compromise in 1482 following a revival of the Lisle claim by Elizabeth Dudley's father, Edward Grey, created Viscount Lisle in the right of his wife, the second Talbot Viscount's sister Elizabeth. However, in 1489 Berkeley settled the Berkeley Castle estate on Henry VII and his heirs in exchange for a marquessate and in order to injure his brother and heir. The Crown retained possession of the Berkeley estate, thus rendering further dispute dormant, despite the subsequent creations of the Plantagenet and Dudley Viscounts Lisle. However, on 11 November 1554, on the ground that the death of Edward VI had extinguished the male heirs of Henry VII, Mary recognised the right of Henry, 12th Lord Berkeley as heir to the Marquess.[76] But thanks to the Duke of Northumberland's attainder the Lisle claim had also reverted to the Crown, and according to Smyth the Crown intended to revive it at the end of Mary's reign.

Smyth's account has dominated discussion of Leicester's revival of the Lisle claim in 1572. However, Smyth (1567–1640) did not become Lord Berkeley's steward until 1596 and therefore was not an eyewitness to the events themselves, though he regularly refers to conversations with those who were. What complicated it was the fact that thanks to the terms of their restoration in blood the Dudleys had lost any claim of right and the lawsuit was pursued in Elizabeth's name, with the lands in question being granted to Leicester and Warwick afterwards.[77] This added a political dimension, supplied by the execution of Norfolk, whose sister Katherine was Berkeley's wife. Smyth followed *Leicester's Commonwealth* in insinuating that Leicester had destroyed Norfolk, who had hitherto protected Berkeley. But Smyth also assumed that Elizabeth's willingness to help Leicester was the result of an animus between her and Lady Berkeley over Norfolk's death. However, he then introduced two popular if contradictory issues. One is how Berkeley's supposed friends abandoned him once 'the Court' was involved. The other is the Tacitean 'women's wars', in this instance how strong-willed women – Lord Berkeley's mother as well as his own wife – prevented Berkeley from accepting the compromises

---

[74] The 'final settlement' was made between the 12th Lord Berkeley and Robert Sidney, Viscount Lisle, as heir to both Leicester and Warwick.

[75] There is a recent account of the 15th-century phase: Peter Fleming and Michael Wood, *Gloucestershire's Forgotten Battle: Nibley Green 1470* (Stroud, 2003).

[76] *Cal. Pat. Rolls, 1554–5*, pp. 9–10. This is another example of Mary's restoration policy.

[77] There were actually two stages, the first in 1573, the second in 1580.

that in some cases his former friends had tried to arrange.[78]

The Berkeley lawsuit was legal rather than genealogical, in that no one disputed the descents of the claimants. What makes it relevant here is the way in which Leicester approached the suit. Smyth recounts a story that in 1570 when Leicester was preparing his case he lured the unsuspecting Berkeley into allowing 'one Harvey a herald' access to his evidences on the pretext of compiling a genealogy showing how Leicester 'discended from his ancient house', but also to remove evidence relevant to the suit.[79] Unfortunately for this anecdote, William Hervey, Clarenceux, had died on 27 February 1567. On the other hand, on 10 December 1572 Leicester asked Shrewsbury to search his archives for 'certain evidences which might greatly please me and my brother of Warwick', i.e. anything relating to the Berkeley lands during the life of the first Earl of Shrewsbury: 'Good my lord, cause some that hath skill make diligent search for any of these things, specially petitions, offices, or awards or surveys of the lands and I shall think myself not a little beholding unto you.'[80]

Leicester's ability and willingness to assemble evidences raises questions about his exploitation of the College to advance his own ends. He was the recipient of some of the grander surviving Elizabethan heraldic manuscripts and a number of these were by Cooke. The earliest is a pedigree of 1564, presumably to celebrate his creation.[81] Three years later (November 1567) William Bowyer, keeper of the Records in the Tower, produced another elaborate celebration of his descent, the 'Heroica Eulogia' (Figs 2a–b).[82] The College of Arms presently holds an elaborate pedigree of Leicester, compiled in the mid-1570s, probably by Cooke (although it is by Glover's hand), that lists among its sources 'an old petigre' of the earls of Warwick formerly belonging to George, duke of Clarence, now in Leicester's possession, and an old pedigree of the earls of Shrewsbury, also in Leicester's possession.[83] At some point after 1581, Cooke presented Leicester with a lavishly illustrated 'Book of Petegrees', which he noted was based on evidences both in the College and in Leicester's possession (Fig. 1).[84] However, the two are not directly related: the earlier emphasises the Sutton descent, the later the Beauchamp.

Cooke received a further promotion, to Clarenceux King of Arms on 21 May 1567,

---

[78] The most famous 16th-century English example of a 'women's war' is the clash between the widowed Catherine Parr and Anne, duchess of Somerset, in 1547.
[79] Smyth, *Lives*, II, pp. 292–3. As in so many of these lawsuits, possession of the evidences was a key issue.
[80] Lambeth Palace Library, MS 3197, f. 73. Leicester also included a brief account of the various marriages.
[81] Sotheby sale catalogue, 13 July 2000, lot 207, information kindly sent to me by Dr Peter Beal.
[82] Now San Marino (Calif., USA), Huntington Library, MS HM 160. Cf. Wagner, *Heralds of England*, p. 206.
[83] College of Arms, MS 13/1. Although Cooke is not named as compiler, his books are listed among the sources
[84] Longleat House, MS 249. This work can be dated by the fact it contains the sole record of the birth of Leicester's son, Robert, lord of Denbigh, on 6 June 1581.

1. Guy of Warwick: Robert Cooke portrayed the legendary Anglo-Saxon hero as the first earl of Warwick in the 'Book of Petigrees' presented to Robert Dudley, earl of Leicester, *c.* 1581. Longleat House, MS 249, p. 11 (detail).

following the death of Hervey on 27 February.[85] Cooke was undoubtedly considered Leicester's man in the College, not least by the Dethicks.[86] But he was not the only herald to receive Leicester's support, the other was (as the editor of this volume describes him) 'the herald's herald', Robert Glover (*c.* 1544–88), appointed Portcullis Pursuivant on 24 March 1568.[87] About this time Glover married Elizabeth, the daughter of William Flower, Norroy, and his and Norroy's careers became intertwined. On 29 December 1570 Glover was appointed Somerset Herald.[88] More controversial was what happened ten years later. Flower, now elderly, obtained a place as a Poor Knight of Windsor in January 1580. He surrendered his 1562 patent as Norroy on 8 March and on the 9th a new one was issued to him and Glover in survivorship, a standard device to evade the restrictions on inheritance of office.[89] In June Glover went to conduct the visitation of Cheshire with a letter from Leicester to Shrewsbury praising him as 'very honest, skillfull in his profession and one that will I doubt not every way endeavour to deserve the favours if it shall pleas your Lordship to do him.' Leicester also mentioned that Shrewsbury 'at my request gave your consent lately for that office'.[90] However, in January 1582 he reminded Shrewsbury that the new patent for Flower and Glover had been 'gotten without your knolege or myne ether by Mr Secretary Walsingham ii yere synce', though he still considered Glover 'the most suffycyent man euery way among them all'.[91] Walsingham's involvement should not necessarily be considered an external intervention. He had been appointed Chancellor of the Order of Garter on 8 October 1577, in succession to Sir Thomas Smith.[92]

In 1581 Shrewsbury and Leicester were drawn into a major dispute within the College, caused by the death of Richard Turpin, Windsor Herald, on 17 October. On the 23rd Shrewsbury asked the officers of the College for their views on the claim of Nicholas Dethick (then Bluemantle) 'by ancient custom' – i.e., by seniority. He referred them to Leicester, to whom he had given a signed bill in favour of Dethick.[93] But there appear to

[85] *Cal. Pat. Rolls, 1566–69*, art. 823. For the date of Hervey's death see Ann Payne, 'Harvey, William (d. 1567)', in *ODNB*, 25, pp. 677–8.
[86] Wagner, *Heralds of England*, p. 209.
[87] *Cal. Pat. Rolls, 1566–69*, art. 1410.
[88] *Cal. Pat. Rolls, 1569–72*, art. 1932
[89] *Cal. Pat. Rolls, 1578–80*, art. 1584. The most famous example of this practice is the patent obtained by Benjamin Gonson shortly before his death at the end of 1577 for his treasurership of the Navy to be held in survivorship with his son-in-law John Hawkins.
[90] Longleat House, Original Letters, I, f. 13, 19 June 1580.
[91] Lambeth Palace Library, MS 701, f. 181^v, 14 Jan. 1582.
[92] *Cal. Pat. Rolls, 1575–78*, art. 2587. This corrects Conyers Read's date of 22 Apr. 1578 in *Mr Secretary Walsingham and the Policy of Queen Elizabeth*, 3 vols (Oxford, 1925), III, p. 417. In April 1587 Walsingham surrendered the chancellorship to Sir Amyas Paulet when appointed Chancellor of the Duchy of Lancaster. Paulet died in September 1588 and Walsingham may have resumed the office, for the Patent Rolls contain a note that he did not finally surrender it until 6 June 1589.
[93] *Calendar of the Shrewsbury and Talbot Papers*, II, *Talbot Papers in the College of Arms*, comp. G.

have been strong internal objections to Dethick, and less than a fortnight later Shrewsbury wrote to Leicester admitting he knew nothing about the Dethicks' 'disability', but then went on to say 'marry I would that order were in placing of the officers there, for that they have not come in heretofore by the queen's majesty's letters patents as I am now informed, but the gift of those offices hath been always in the gift of the earl marshal' and asked Leicester to intercede with Elizabeth.[94] This assumption appears to have been based on Norfolk's 1568 constitutions, but the heralds had always been appointed by letters patent.

On 14 January 1582, Leicester sent Shrewsbury a very informative commentary on the dispute.[95] He admitted he had delayed carrying out Shrewsbury's instruction to appoint Dethick as Windsor Herald until he had been able to inform him of the situation.[96] Although he wished seniority to be respected, he had been informed that the other officers of the College were unhappy with the Dethicks holding three heralds' posts and had requested him to appoint Richard Lee, then Portcullis Pursuivant, as Windsor Herald – an appointment that Leicester supported, considering Lee 'a gentleman born and very skilfull'. Moreover Gilbert Dethick had previously attempted to circumvent both him and Shrewsbury by obtaining appointments for his friends directly from the Queen. Leicester had successfully complained to her, but as a result they were now denouncing Shrewsbury. He then suggested a compromise. Since William Flower was now a Poor Knight of Windsor, he should resign his office as Norroy to Glover, thus making that of Somerset free for Nicholas Dethick if Shrewsbury still wanted him made a herald. There would then be two pursuivants' places open (Lee's and Dethick's) and for one he recommended Humphrey Hales, 'an honest gentleman, he ys altogether geven to matters of petygres and very well sene aledy in them. He doth drawe and paynt eccellently well …' Hales had been suing for a pursuivancy for two years.

It may have been in consequence of this letter that Shrewsbury delegated to Leicester the power to appoint two new pursuivants.[97] However, Leicester's compromise appears to have been still-born. Instead, Nicholas Dethick was appointed Windsor Herald in April 1583. Hales now renewed his suit for Bluemantle, this time employing Sir Thomas Heneage as suitor to the Queen, and was successful. On 3 March 1584 Shrewsbury complained to Leicester about the further infringement of his rights as Earl Marshal and

---

R. Batho (Hist. MSS Commn. and Derbys. Archaeological Soc. Record Ser., 1971), p. 116.
[94] British Library, Cotton MS Otho E. viii, f. 101, 2 Nov. 1581.
[95] Lambeth Palace Library, MS 701, ff. 181–182ᵛ, printed in Ramsay, *Robert Glover*, ch. 3.
[96] The instruction has not survived but was presumably about 23 October, when Shrewsbury informed the College of his bill in favour of Dethick. It should be noted that these months saw the trial of Edmund Campion and the second visit of the Duke of Anjou. The disputes in the College were not Leicester's most pressing concern.
[97] Longleat House, Dudley Papers XX, 'A Generall View of the Evidences' [a posthumous index to Leicester's muniments of title and other major personal documents], f. 73. The delegation (undated) is the only item concerning the College in the volume.

asked him to take it up with Elizabeth.[98] Leicester replied a week later that he had been delayed by sickness but had 'on this day' taken up Shrewsbury's complaint, and Elizabeth 'did promise that none should pass her hand, but such as be commanded and placed by your lordship'.[99] He then hinted at a reason 'and some fault is in the party that will seek the assigning of their bills by the masters of requests and that way the lack often groweth of their good dispatch' which would appear to suggest that Shrewsbury's nominees were pipped at the post by others. He also assured Shrewsbury that 'whilst I am here and may have knowledge of any matter concerning your office, I will carefully and faithfully look to it as anything within my own office', which again raises the question whether given his other responsibilities he was the best choice for a deputy.

It is probable that Glover was Leicester's main source during the disputes over Nicholas Dethick.[100] Glover had first submitted his 'Brief Rehersall' to Shrewsbury in July 1580 but subsequently to Leicester, possibly on Shrewsbury's advice. It rehearsed the dispute between Garter and the two Kings of Arms and recommended repealing Norfolk's constitutions of 1566 and 1568. Glover then attended Lord Willoughby d'Eresby on his embassy to confer the Garter insignia on Frederick II of Denmark in the summer of 1582.[101] On his return he was the subject of several political attacks. William Dethick was later charged with accusing Glover of being a supporter of the Stuart succession.[102] At the beginning of 1584 Glover defended himself to Leicester against charges of Catholic allegiance for keeping company with papists and specifically his conduct during the funeral of the openly Catholic second Earl of Southampton.[103]

However, the real crisis in the College was caused by the death of Sir Gilbert Dethick in 1584 and the ambition of his son William to succeed him. Nothing related to this survives in the Leicester-Shrewsbury correspondence, possibly because both were engaged in more pressing matters. It appears that Cooke served as Garter in an acting capacity and Leicester may have hoped that he would in time be appointed. At the end of 1585 Leicester departed for the Netherlands and it was probably not coincidental that it was during his absence in the Netherlands that Dethick was appointed Garter, on 21 April 1586, with a clause enabling him to override the other kings of arms, apparently obtained by bribery.

By 1585 Leicester had gained a further protégé, William Segar (c. 1564–1633), who ended his career as Garter King of Arms. Before he became a herald Segar enjoyed a

---

[98] Lambeth Palace Library, MS 3198, f. 241.
[99] Arundel Castle, Autograph Letters 1513–1585, art. 103. Dated only 11 March.
[100] In January 1582, Glover dedicated to Leicester the 'Brevis Enumeratio', a survey of the outstanding dynastic disputes in Europe: College of Arms, MS Vincent 76.
[101] He subsequently presented to Frederick II an armorial of the English nobility, now Manchester, John Rylands University Library, MS Eng. 6.
[102] 'Causes why Sir William Dethick should be put from his Office' (c. 1603), printed in Ramsay, *Robert Glover*, ch. 3.
[103] British Library, Cotton MS Titus B. vii, f. 14, 24 Jan. 1583/4.

2a. Shield of arms and crest (bear and ragged staff) of Robert Dudley, earl of Leicester; with script by the writing-master John de Beauchesne. From the lavishly illustrated *Heroica Eulogia* compiled by William Bowyer for Leicester in 1567. San Marino (Calif.), Huntington Library, MS HM 160, f. 11.

reputation as a portrait painter, and Leicester employed him in this capacity in 1584–5.[104] Following the promotion of Richard Lee to Richmond Herald on 2 June 1585, Segar was appointed Portcullis Pursuivant on the 4th.[105] Segar's appointment presumably had Leicester's approval, but Thomas Lant later credited it to Sir Thomas Heneage. Segar left an account of Leicester's celebration of the St. George's Day Garter ceremony at Utrecht on 23 April 1586 and it has been assumed he accompanied Leicester to the Netherlands in December 1585. The reality is more complex. When he left for the Netherlands, Leicester took John Coxe, Lancaster Herald, with him. As he informed Walsingham later, he had also asked Segar but 'he made sute a day before I came away to tarry at [home] with xx excuses'. He still needed a pursuivant and told Walsingham to ask Robert Cooke to nominate a fit man.[106] Two months later Segar arrived in the Netherlands in attendance on Heneage in his mission to Leicester over the governor-generalship – but he was not expected to stay. On 16 April Coxe died of a stroke, and Leicester wrote immediately to Burghley to send Glover over together with a pursuivant – adding that knowledge of the armouries of the Netherlands would increase their skill.[107] If Segar superintended the St George's Day ceremony, it was purely by coincidence.[108]

The last promotional issue that Leicester dealt with followed the death of Glover on 8 April 1588. Leicester nominated Segar, as senior pursuivant, to succeed him. Walsingham wanted Thomas Lant to succeed Segar as Portcullis, and Leicester agreed.[109] Both appointments were made, though Segar's letters patent were not issued until 4

2b (opposite). 'De fratre hypochritico'. William Bowyer included records of the various estates held by Leicester in 1567 in the *Heroica Eulogia*. Those of lands once held by religious houses are accompanied by anti-clerical illustrations. A hypocritical friar, who happily dons secular dress, heads the records of the hospital of Burton Lazars (Leicestershire). San Marino (Calif.), Huntington Library, MS HM 160, f. 130.

[104] His accounts record two payments to Segar, described as a painter or picture drawer, on 10 April 1584 and 20 May 1585: *Household Accounts of Robert Dudley*, ed. Adams, pp. 177, 255. Precisely what work Segar undertook for him then is unknown. Elizabeth Goldring has been able to identify only one Segar portrait in Leicester's collection, of Leicester himself as Lord Steward, which can only date from the spring of 1588; see her forthcoming *Painting and Patronage at the Elizabethan Court: Robert Dudley, Earl of Leicester and his World*.
[105] *Draft Cal. Pat. Rolls, 27 Elizabeth I* (List and Index Society, 241, 1990), pp. 19–20. The signet warrant for Segar's appointment is dated 27 May, PRO, SO 3/1/20.
[106] *Correspondence of Robert Dudley, Earl of Leycester, during his Government of the Low Countries*, ed. John Bruce (Camden Soc., orig. ser., xxvii, 1844), p. 32, to Walsingham, 26 Dec. 1585.
[107] *Cal. S. P. For.*, 1585–6, p. 560, 17 Apr. 1586; see also p. 557.
[108] Segar was paid £30 for attending Heneage between 13 February and 9 June 1586: British Library, MS Harley 1641, f. 27.
[109] Hist. MSS Commn., *Bath MSS*, V, p. 89, Leicester to Shrewsbury, 11 April, and Walsingham to Shrewsbury, 10 April. Lant is best-known as the designer of the engraved funeral roll of Sir Philip Sidney.

De fratre hypochritico.

Non enim in conspectu eius venit omnis hypochrita. Iob. 13. v 16.

Diuinæ mentes hominis miserentur egeni:
    Afflictisque viuis, munera nulla negant.
Quamuis pauperibus nil confert vilis auarus:
    Cuius mens nullis, est satiata bonis:
Hunc pudor atque metus, faciunt impendere multa:
    Cum se commoueat, nil pietatis opus.
Hac spe commoti, quam raro fallere constat:
    Illico nos inopes, finximus esse viros.
Quare contulerant proceres, terrasque domosque:
    Rustica plebs nobis, munera larga dedit.

February 1589. His final intervention with Shrewsbury (30 May) was over an issue relevant more to the Court of Chivalry than the College, outstanding claims to baronies through the female line.[110] Elizabeth, as noted above, had strong views on this subject, but Leicester does appear to have been influential in one of the few occasions when she conceded, the recognition of Peregrine Bertie as Lord Willoughby d'Eresby at the end of 1580.[111]

Leicester's death in September 1588 was followed by Shrewsbury's on 18 November 1590. Of the heralds whom Leicester had patronised, Glover had predeceased him and Cooke was to follow in 1593, although Richard Lee succeeded him as Clarenceux. The ending of an era was further emphasised by Elizabeth putting the earl marshalcy into a commission of her most reliable privy councillors: Burghley, the Lord Admiral (Howard of Effingham) and the Lord Chamberlain (Hunsdon). However, to pacify the Earl of Essex at the end of 1597, she granted the earl marshalcy to him on 18 December. Whatever motives may have inspired Essex to demand the office, his Irish expedition and subsequent political demise limited his effective tenure to the first half of 1598.[112] When he took office, Henry Howard drafted a 'Discourse' for him on the powers of the earl marshalcy. Howard was convinced that the venality of the heralds had led to the widespread granting of arms to unworthy persons, and he recommended returning to Norfolk's constitutions and calling in all arms granted subsequently – a policy he himself followed as one of the lords commissioners of the earl marshalcy under James I. He included a typically snide comment on Shrewsbury: 'he could make no other use of the [Earl Marshal's] staff than by measuring the breadth of his fat oxen between the horns'.[113] The office then remained vacant from 1601 until the Queen's own death. The commissioners proved no more successful than Shrewsbury and Leicester in resolving the disputes within the College. However, the commission years saw the most famous – and yet oddest – appointment to the Elizabethan College. On the death of Richard Lee in 1597 Burghley apparently engineered the appointment of William Camden as Clarenceux on 23 October, an entry into the College more blatant than Cooke's in 1562, Camden having been appointed Richmond Herald only the previous day. It is difficult not to see it as an inducement to Camden to agree to Burghley's request

---

[110] *Ibid.*, p. 91.
[111] PRO, SP 12/147, f. 51r-v, Richard Bertie to Leicester, 11 Nov. 1580.
[112] His motives are explored in P. E. J. Hammer, *The Polarisation of Elizabethan Politics: The Political Career of Robert Devereux, 2nd Earl of Essex, 1585–1597* (Cambridge, 1999), pp. 386-8. For his conduct in office see Alexandra Gajda, *The Earl of Essex and Late Elizabethan Political Culture* (Oxford, 2012), pp. 175–8.
[113] All that is known of the origin of the 'Discourse' comes from Howard's letter to Essex, 30 Dec. 1597, printed in Thomas Birch, *Memoirs of the Reign of Queen Elizabeth*, 2 vols (London, 1754), II, pp. 365–7. This is obscure about whose idea it was; it is also the source of the comment on Shrewsbury. Howard's views on the College are discussed by L. L. Peck, *Northampton: Patronage and Policy at the Court of James I* (London, 1982), pp. 14, 156–9.

to undertake the history of the reign. But Camden had little interest in heraldry or even modern history. His answer to a request from Sir Edward Cecil for information about the military history of the Dutch Revolt is revealing:

> The proposition you make is out of the reach of my profession and not of antiquitie but of late memorie. By reason of Sir Robert Cottons absence I can imparte nothing from him as yeat and for my owne observation it is verye slender.[114]

The mixture of personal and jurisdictional clashes that dogged the College throughout Elizabeth's reign can be found elsewhere in her bureaucracy.[115] From this perspective the relatively co-operative atmosphere in the Privy Council prior to the mid-1590s is impressive. The Queen bears the major responsibility, for she could easily have settled the jurisdictional conflict between the three Kings of Arms had she wanted. Her style of government was highly non-interventionist: she expected those nominally in charge to deal with their subordinates. But she did not delegate the administration of the College to a powerful earl marshal either. She inherited Norfolk, whom she never really trusted, and by appointing Shrewsbury in a gesture of political support, followed by a commission of senior privy councillors, she revealed her enduring dislike of bureaucracy, which meant that her government was chronically understaffed and various key members were grossly overworked.

At the end of the day, Elizabeth was not greatly interested in ceremonial matters and the College was low on her list of priorities. Like many other monarchs, she kept politically sensitive matters – notably, the succession and the composition of the peerage – tightly under her own control and made no use of the College's expertise. Catholic claims about the destruction of the ancient nobility were not considered worthy of answer. Shrewsbury himself appears to have had little real interest in the work of the College, other than to maintain the dignity of the earl marshalcy. That left Leicester, who, if he may have had his own interests to pursue, was at least concerned to see that heralds with the requisite skills were appointed.

---

[114] British Library, Cotton MS Julius F. vi, f. 464, undated minute.
[115] The Navy Board is again the most obvious example.

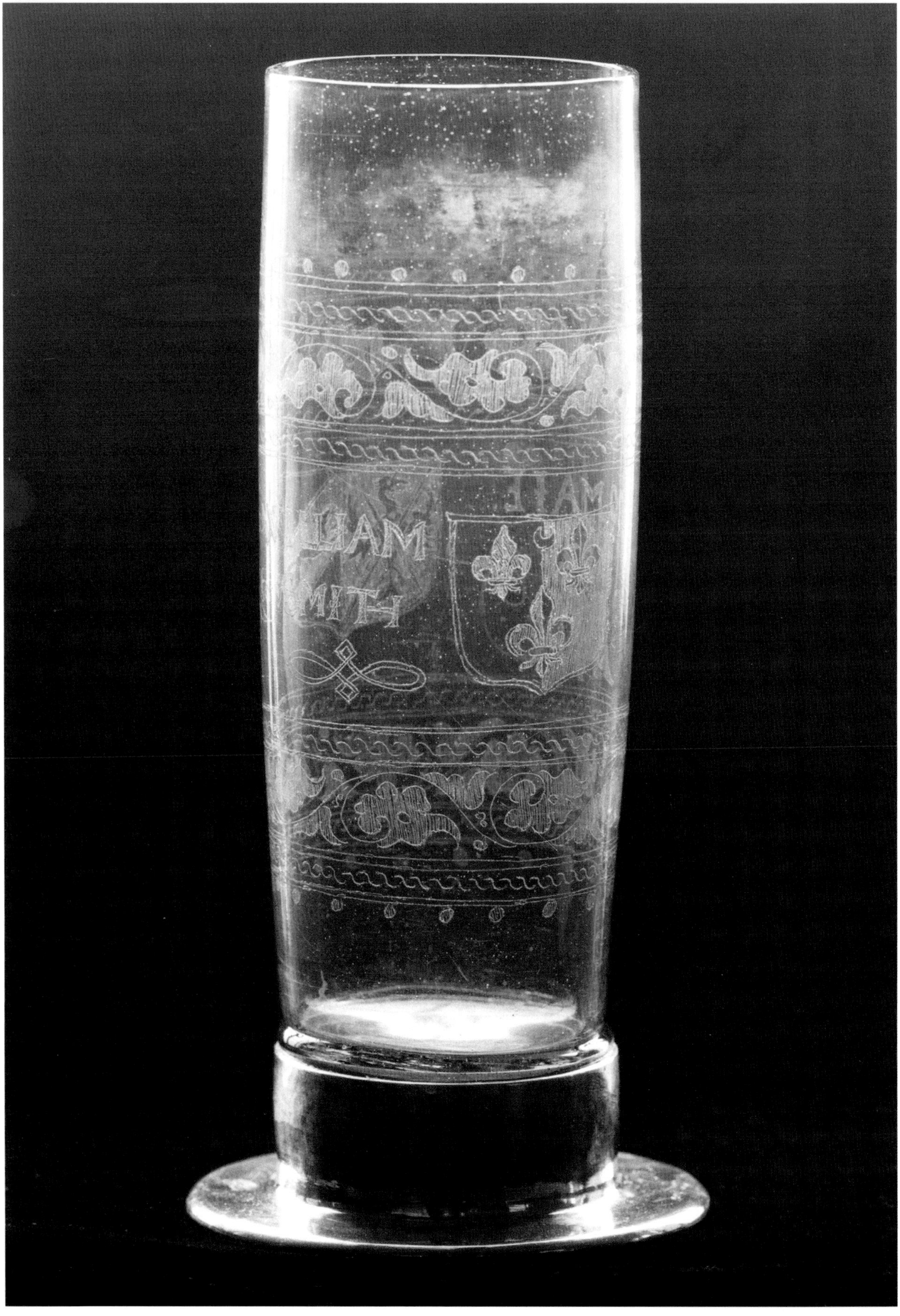

William Smith, Rouge Dragon Pursuivant

NIGEL RAMSAY

William Smith was a Cheshire man by birth, the son of Randal Smith, of Old Hough (in Warmingham), and Jane, daughter of Ralph Bostock.[1] Both parents were of armigerous families, but Randal was a younger son and so too, it seems, was William.[2] Randal's elder brothers and their sons all seem to have died before the end of the century, and so William in later life was able to bear the family coat of arms without any differencing. That was clearly something that mattered enormously to him, even before he became one of the Crown's pursuivants at arms and thus a member of the College of Arms. In most of the many manuscripts that he wrote, he included the coats of arms of the Smiths of Oldhaugh and of the Bostocks. He was also no less conscious of his Cheshire origins, returning to the county in his writings if not much in reality.

The actual date of his birth is unknown; it is generally put as *c.* 1550, but this seems rather too late for someone who made a cartographic survey of a town in 1568, as well as heraldic notes in around 1565. Nothing is known, either, about his schooling and formative years. Whether or not he was a younger son, he will have had to expect to make his own way in the world. Anthony Wood claimed that he studied 'for a time' at Oxford; if that is true, he is presumably identifiable as the William Smith who was admitted BA at Oxford in 1567.[3] It is likelier, however, that after his schooling he was bound apprentice: this will have been to a London haberdasher, since he was certainly a member of the London livery company of the Haberdashers. He was presumably free of his apprenticeship by 1571, since he in this year took up residence in Nuremberg, in Bavaria. The city had adopted Protestantism in the 1520s, and had become a centre for English merchants who imported cloths from England. Smith later wrote of his abode in Germany as being 'Twentie yeares and two monthes, To say, from the xii[th] of August, Anno 1571: Till the xv[th] of October, Anno 1591.'[4]

---

1. General accounts of Smith's life include those by H. S. London, in Godfrey and London, *College of Arms*, pp. 220–1, and by David Kathman, 'Smith, William (*c.* 1550–1618)', in *ODNB*, 51, pp. 358–9. Valuable information about his German connexions is given by Wolf-Rüdiger Baumann, *The Merchants Adventurers and the Continental Cloth-Trade (1560s–1620s)* (Berlin and New York, 1990), esp. pp. 176–8 and 359–61 – as Ann Payne kindly informed me.
2. See *The Visitation of Cheshire in the Year 1580, Made by Robert Glover, Somerset Herald*, ed. J. P. Rylands (Harleian Soc., xviii, 1882), pp. 210–11; *Pedigrees Made at the Visitation of Cheshire, 1613*, ed. G. J. Armytage and J. P. Rylands (Record Soc. Lancs. & Ches., lviii, 1909), pp. 214–15.
3. A. Wood, *Athenae Oxonienses*, ed. P. Bliss, 4 vols (London, 1815), II, col. 233, guessing that he was at Brasenose College, 'where several of his sir-name and time studied'; *Register of the University of Oxford*, I, ed. C. W. Boase (Oxford Historical Soc., orig. ser., i, 1885), p. 265; cf. J. Foster, *Alumni Oxonienses*, Early Ser., *1500–1714*, IV, p. 1384.
4. College of Arms, MS Philipot b. 42, title-page. Quoted in *Heralds' Commemorative Exhibn. Cat.*, p. 51, no. 40.

---

3 (opposite). William Smith's drinking glass, engraved with his arms, 1582. The metal stand is modern. London, Victoria and Albert Museum, C 460–1928.

The heraldic historian John Anstis (d. 1744) recorded that Smith 'is said to have kept an Inn at the Sign of the Goose in Nuremberg'.[5] This seems most improbable, but it is certainly the case that before 1580 he was living – like most of the English merchants who were then resident in the city – in the Gulden Gans ('Golden Goose') inn, the oldest and most important Nuremberg inn of the day.[6] On 10 October 1580 he married Veronica Altensteig, widow of Hans Kentz. She had lived on the Alter Rossmarkt and it was not the case that she owned the Gulden Gans. She was, however, a woman of means, and she was young enough to bear Smith three sons and two daughters over the next ten years. Marriage had made her property subject to the Nuremberg property tax, and to escape this Smith renounced his English citizenship and became a citizen of Nuremberg. As if to mark the event, he commissioned a drinking-glass, engraved with his name, the date 30 May 1582 (just a fortnight after his citizenship had been entered in the Neubürgerbuch) and a shield of arms on which his own coat is impaled with that of his wife.[7] He retained his Nuremberg citizenship until 1591, when he renounced it and accordingly he was made liable to pay a tax on his movable goods. These were assessed as worth 160 Gulden, ten per cent of which he now had to pay.

Smith the Draughtsman, Cartographer and Chorographer

As early as 1568, when he was perhaps still only in his teens, Smith surveyed and drew a plan of Bristol. He recorded that this was 'Measured and laid in Platforme [*i.e.*, in form of a 'plat' or map], by me, W. Smith, at my being at Bristow, the 30 and 31 July, Anno Domini 1568.'[8] This is in fact the only map or plan of which he specifically claims to have been the surveyor; certain of his other maps and plans were derived from other people's work, but for most it is not known how he came to draw them.[9] Unquestionably, the making of maps and plans and the sketching of views or prospects were activities that he continued to engage in for the rest of his life: they were a passion that he can hardly have expected to benefit from financially, but which he shared with a growing, if still select, number of his contemporaries. Robert Glover, Somerset Herald from 1570 until his death in 1588, is known to have drawn a map of Kent, and a number of painter-stainers – such as Ralph Treswell (d. 1616/17), father of the herald Robert Treswell – combined armorial painting with surveying. In or after 1573, when Smith had perhaps only recently learned German, he made an English translation of the German text of the

---

[5] College of Arms, MSS Officers of Arms, II, p. 145, and III, p. 145.
[6] It was located at what is today 15 Winklerstrasse.
[7] Remarkably enough, this is still extant; it is now in the Victoria and Albert Museum and is illustrated above, Fig. 3. See Wilfred Buckley, *Diamond Engraved Glasses of the Sixteenth Century* (London, 1929), pp. 21–4, reprinting from the *Burlington Magazine*, Feb. and Mar. 1929, an article by B. Rackham and a letter from himself.
[8] See *The Particular Description of England, 1588 ... by William Smith, Rouge Dragon*, intro. H. B. Wheatley and E. W. Ashbee (London, 1879), plate xxv.
[9] See R. A. Skelton, 'Tudor Town Plans in John Speed's *Theatre*', *Archaeological Jnl.*, cviii (1952, for 1951), pp. 109–20, at 111–12; the whole of the present paragraph is indebted to this article.

first modern atlas, Abraham Ortelius's *Theatrum oder Schawplatz des Erdbodems* (Antwerp, 1572[–3]).[10] Nuremberg, where he was then based, was the cartographic and printing centre of southern Germany, and Smith got to know such men as the cartographer Paul Pfinzing. It has been suggested that it was through such means that he became familiar with the latest cartographic practices, such as including roads on maps and having a key to the conventional signs or symbols; he may also have been the source of knowledge of these for English cartographers, like John Norden – another of his acquaintances.[11] It must also have been through his Nuremberg experiences that he learned how to distinguish between true and magnetic north and how to show both on a map's compass-rose.

One way or another, Smith must have gained a reputation for his cartographic skills, since it was he who was chosen to be the intermediary for a venture to adapt Christopher Saxton's maps of English counties (made in the 1570s) for an atlas of such maps: this seems to have been projected by a Dutch or Flemish mapseller in the years around 1600. Smith was perhaps responsible for gathering information from Norden, William Burton of Leicestershire, and others. He himself drew at least four updated maps for the atlas: Hertfordshire, 1601; Worcestershire, 1602; Warwickshire, 1603; and Cheshire (undated). Unfortunately for him, the atlas was never completed; its publisher doubtless abandoned the scheme when John Speed's series of county maps began to be engraved and sold, c. 1603.[12] Speed also came from Cheshire, and the two men seem to have been friends and even, to a degree, collaborators; but the glory of publication belongs to Speed.

Smith liked to combine the making of surveys and maps with the drawing of bird's-eye views or plans of towns and also with the making of prospects or perspective-drawings of towns; and he did this in Germany as well as England. Indeed, his ideal account of a place would seem to have been a text that presented its political structure (perhaps with a certain amount of history) together with a plan of the place and perhaps a map of its county or region, and certainly also with one or more prospect-drawings. For his native Cheshire, for instance, he wrote a description rather like the chorographies (outline topographical, geographical and historical accounts) that were written by several other topographers in the late sixteenth century, and he embellished this with both a map of the county, a bird's-eye plan of Chester, and a coloured wash drawing of Chester seen from across the river Dee. At least three versions of this work survive, each by his hand;

[10] Sotheby's sale of English Literature and History, London, 10–11 July 1986, lot 359; cf. P. Barber, 'Mapmaking in England, ca. 1470–1650', in *The History of Cartography*, vol. 3, *Cartography in the European Renaissance*, ed. David Woodward (Chicago and London, 2007), pp. 1589–669, at 1634–5.

[11] E. M. J. Campbell. 'The Beginnings of the Characteristic Sheet to English Maps', *Geographical Jnl.*, cxxviii (1962), pp. 411–15, at 412–13, 414; Catherine Delano-Smith and Roger J. P. Cain, *English Maps: A History* (London, 1999), pp. 71–5, 186–8.

[12] See further R. A. Skelton, 'Four English County Maps, 1602–3', *British Museum Quarterly*, xxii (1960), pp. 47–50. Smith's four MS maps were among those that had been printed (engraved by Jodocus Hondius in Amsterdam) before the scheme was abandoned.

4. Map of Lancashire, drawn by William Smith, Rouge Dragon Pursuivant. Included in Smith's transcript, 1598, of the Visitation of Lancashire, 1567. British Library, MS Harley 6159, ff. 3*v–4.

in two, the drawing of Chester is dated September 1585.[13] He seems to have realised that the work merited publication, but he could not achieve this, as one copy has a rueful comment by him, added to its title-page: 'A work deserving to be better Handled. But want of Cunning in the Author, was the cause.'[14] Printed it ultimately was, but not until 1656, and then as a mere part of Daniel King's *Vale Royal of England, Or the County Palatine of Chester Illustrated*; in this, Smith's alphabetically arranged collection of coats of arms was omitted, although some other coats were substituted.[15] County histories

[13] British Library, MS Harley 1046 (with map of Cheshire and view of Chester from across the river Dee, both dated Sept. 1585), and Bodleian Library, MSS Ashmole 765 (with view of Chester from across the Dee, dated 7 Sept. 1585) and Rawl. B. 282* (undated; possibly derived from Ashmole 765). In the last, he has endorsed the bird's-eye plan as 'The Cittie of Chester. In platforme', and the wash drawing as 'The Cittie of Chester. In perspective'—indicating his own terminology.
[14] Bodleian Library, MS Rawl. B. 282.
[15] Extensive portions of Smith's work were reprinted in G. Ormerod, *History of the County Palatine and City of Chester*, 2nd edn, ed. T. Helsby, 3 vols (London, 1882), I, pt. 1, pp. 119–42.

illustrated with hundreds of coats of arms were not an attractive proposition for contemporary publishers. For instance, the 'General Description of the County of Dorset' written by Thomas Gerard (d. 1634), with 295 coats of arms, was printed only in 1732.[16]

In 1588, he completed what is today his best-known work: 'The Particuler Description of England. With the Portratures of certaine of the Cheiffest Cities and Townes.'[17] Here he set out, county by county, summary notes about the location and history of the towns of each county, together with lists of parliamentary boroughs, fairs (in date-order, beginning at January 6), and the distances (in miles) between London and many other towns. He also included dozens of painted coats of arms, of peers above the rank of baron, and several bird's-eye plans and perspective drawings (Fig. 5). The illustrations are attractive, but the text is less appealing, being more like that provided in some sort of ready reckoner. In any case, its completion came just a couple of years after the publication of William Camden's *Britannia*, the success of which put paid to all rivals for a good many years to come. Smith's 'Particuler Description' had no hope of competing with Camden's far more extensive and more richly historical compendium.

More than a decade earlier, in 1575, he had put together a 'Breff Description of the Famous Cittie of London'. This was a much more discursive, analytical work: it includes a list (with some notes) of the London livery company halls and accounts of the Court of Orphans and of the mayor, sheriffs and City officials (in a section headed 'Of the Estate and Pollicie of London'), although half of the book is taken up with an annotated list of the mayors and sheriffs of London, year by year, from 1190 to 1575 – very much in the manner of a medieval London chronicle. He was only in his twenties when he wrote it, but it is a perfectly coherent and well set out account of the City's governance and of such institutions as its hospitals, prisons, markets and fairs, ports and shambles. He must have felt satisfied with it himself, as he both added the names of later mayors and sheriffs to his own copy, and he also wrote out a copy of the entire work in 1588.[18]

Following the general arrangement of this account of London, Smith produced in 1594 an account of Nuremberg. By its subject-matter, however, this was bound to be novel to almost any English reader.[19] Indeed, in the dedication copy that was addressed to Lord Burghley he said as much, remarking that he knew how well supplied Burghley already was with heraldic books.[20] It is a more interesting and more ambitious work than

[16] [T. Gerard], *Coker's Survey of Dorsetshire*, with an Afterword by Rodney Legg (Sherborne, 1980). Gerard's work had been miscredited to another author.

[17] Printed as *The Particular Description of England*, intro. Wheatley and Ashbee (cit. in n. 8), from Smith's original MS, Sloane 2596 in the British Library. A much shorter, preliminary version, in Latin, is British Library, MS Add. 10620, dated 1580.

[18] The 1575 version, which has additions down to the 1610s, is now London Metropolitan Archives, Guildhall Library MSS, CLC/262/MS2463; the 1588 copy is British Library, MS Harley 6363.

[19] Printed by K. Goldmann and W. Roach, with a German translation, as 'William Smith: "A Description of the Cittie of Noremberg" (Beschreibung der Reichsstadt Nürnberg) 1594', *Mitteilungen des Vereins für Geschichte der Stadt Nürnberg*, 48 (1958), pp. 194–245, at 203–45.

[20] The book survives in three copies, the first of which is seemingly the dedication copy for Lord

CANTERBVRY.

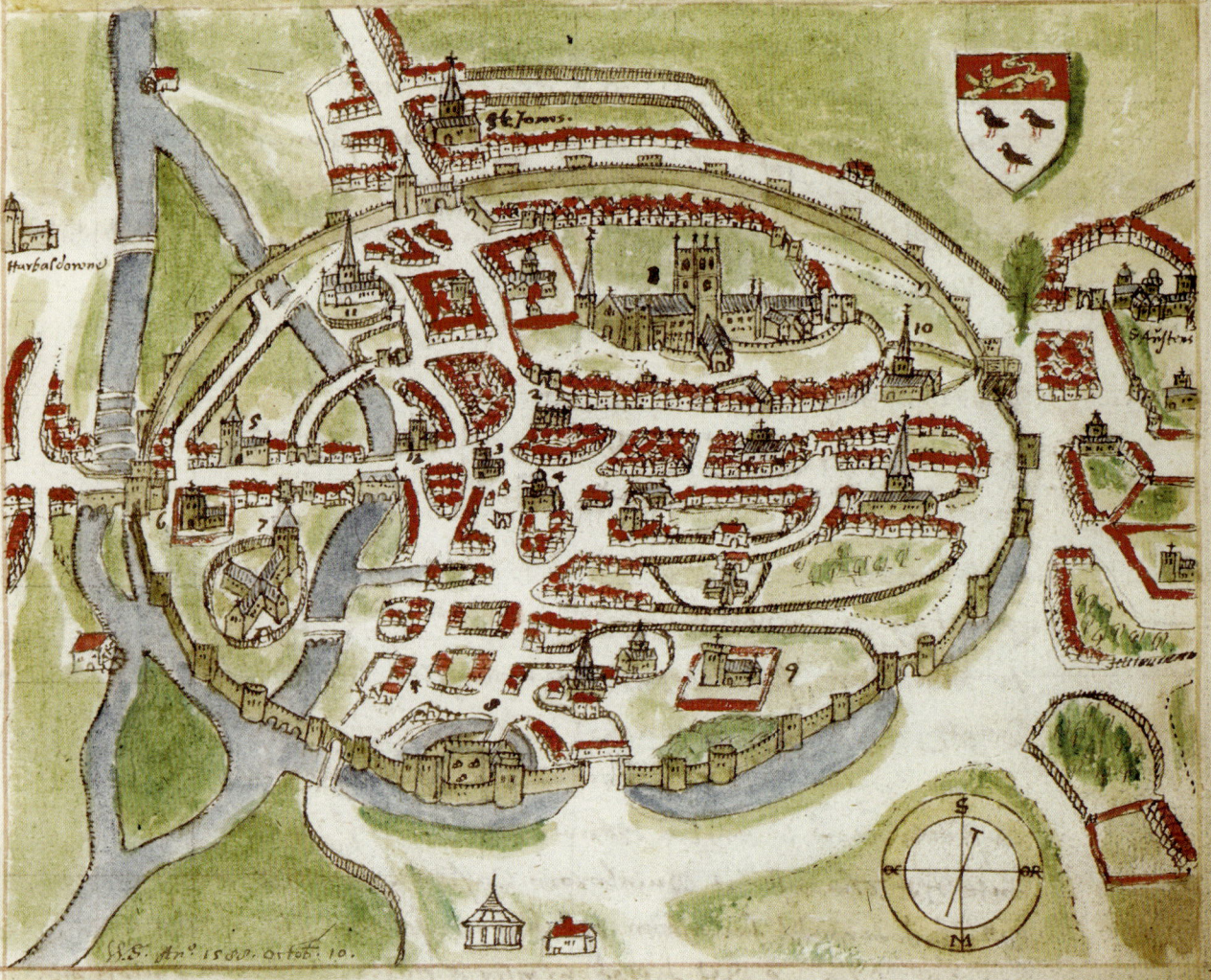

1. Chrifts church.
2. ý market place.
3. our Lady.
4. St. Andrewes.
5. St. Peter.
6. Weftgate church.
7. St. mildred.
8. The caftell.
9. our Lady.
10. St. george.
11. the freeres.
12. Alhalows.

5. Bird's-eye view of Canterbury by William Smith, dated 10 Oct. 1588. British Library, MS Sloane 2596, f. 15. Perhaps derived from – and certainly closely related to – the view of Canterbury printed in the same year by Georg Braun and Franz Hogenberg in their *Civitates Orbis Terrarum*.

its model, in that it provides far more extensive descriptions of what might be called the social anthropology and political economy of the city ('their Government [*sic*], Customes, and Ceremonies', as he puts it), with a good deal of information about the civic administration of Nuremberg, as well as descriptions of burial-practices, weddings and christenings, the treatment of crime, and the maintenance of public health. It concludes with a list of all the town magistrates (councillors) from 1477 down to 1591, and a collection of 202 painted coats of arms of 'the gentility of this Cittie', past and present, in rough alphabetical order.

Smith the Playwright

A good many of the heralds in late Tudor and early Stuart England were men of accomplishments that ranged far beyond their own profession's needs, which were for skill in interpreting medieval records and particularly in understanding documents written in Latin and the French of late medieval England (today often called 'Anglo-Norman'), as well as familiarity with the laws of inheritance (part of the common law) and of arms (part of the civil law). For instance, John Hart (d. 1574) was the author of books on pronunciation and orthography, including a system of phonetic spelling; Thomas Lant (d. 1600 or 1601), who had served under Sir Philip Sidney, made a remarkable drawing of Sidney's funeral procession. A few heralds, like Henry Lilly (d. 1638) and Edward Norgate (d. 1650), were accomplished miniaturists; Sir William Segar (d. 1633), Garter King of Arms, was both a portrait painter, a miniaturist and a fine calligrapher.[21] William Camden, brought into the Office of Arms as Clarenceux King of Arms at the same time as Smith was created Rouge Dragon, was a scholar with a European reputation,[22] and even the disagreeable Sir William Dethick, Garter King of Arms, played a large part in organising the first English 'society of antiquaries' in the 1580s and 1590s.[23]

Smith's range of talents was thus far from exceptional in the College of Arms of his day; equally, it may be said that he hardly needs a further string to his bow. It is quite possible, however, that he was also a playwright. A play called 'The Hector of Germanie, or The Palsgrave, Prime Elector', which was written in 1613 to celebrate the marriage of

---

Burghley (British Library, MS Add. 78167); two other copies each include two or more dedications and so were perhaps reference copies for Smith's own use: Lambeth Palace Library, MS 508 (includes dedication to Sir George Carey) and Nuremberg, Stadtbibliothek, Nor. H. 1142 (includes dedication to Edward la Zouche, Lord Zouch).

[21] Details of all these men's heraldic offices are given in Godfrey and London, *College of Arms*; they are also included in *ODNB*. The regard in which Segar's contemporaries held him for his writing skills is shown by his having been chosen to be one of the judges for a calligraphy competition, in which the prize was a golden pen worth £20: H. R. Woudhuysen, *Sir Philip Sidney and the Circulation of Manuscripts, 1558–1640* (Oxford, 1996), p. 34. For Segar as painter, see Erna Auerbach, *Nicholas Hilliard* (London, 1961), pp. 271–81.

[22] See e.g. W. H. Herendeen, *William Camden: A Life in Context* (Woodbridge, 2007).

[23] See May McKisack, *Medieval History in the Tudor Age* (Oxford, 1971), Ch. vii.

Princess Elizabeth (the 'Winter Queen') to Frederick V, the Elector Palatine, is known to have been the work of one W. Smith; it was produced by a group of London tradesmen. 'W. Smith' was for long identified by scholars as a London scrivener named Wentworth Smith, but the possibility that he might in fact have been William Smith the herald has recently come to be widely accepted.[24] There are arguments to advance both for and against the proposition: the herald did indeed write some verses in ballad metre, in his account of 'The XII Worshipfull Companies or Misteries of London' (1605), and of course he had all manner of German connexions (although he had perhaps hardly been in Germany since the mid 1590s); but it might have been expected that a play written by him would have been produced by the King's Players, the company previously patronised (as the Lord Chamberlain's Players) by his own patron, George Carey, Lord Hunsdon. That he inveighed against the granting of arms to playwrights (in his 'Breff Discourse') might also seem a telling point. Temperamentally, too, the herald seems to have been a man who dealt in facts and figures, and not the literary conceits requisite for the stage. Attractive as the idea of his being a playwright naturally is – even if *The Hector* has been described as containing 'little to recommend itself as literature'[25] – it is safer to regard it as no more than an intriguing possibility.

Smith the Armorist and Herald

Smith was already an enthusiastic armorist when living in Nuremberg. He had doubtless been aware since childhood that his own family was armigerous, being a younger branch of the Smiths of Cuerdley (Lancs.).[26] In 1605 he mentions consulting 'some notes of my owne gathering 40 yeares ago' – that is to say, made in 1565.[27] In Germany he began to put together collections of English and Continental genealogies and coats of arms. The earliest surviving such collection (Bodleian Library, MS Rawl. B. 141) has rather crudely drawn pedigrees, in tabular form, mostly dated 1578; at this stage he had not discovered the value of red ink for highlighting title-words and so forth. The book contains pedigrees of the ruling houses of Europe, and is distinctive for its inclusion of several families of the higher German nobility. By about this date he was also putting together a collection of Continental coats of arms (College of Arms, MS Philipot b. 42).[28] In 1586 he began

---

[24] E.g. by David Kathman, in *ODNB*, 51, pp. 378–9: 'the circumstantial evidence for William Smith's authorship is overwhelming'. The herald's authorship is also accepted *faute de mieux* by Hans Werner, '"The Hector of Germanie, or The Palsgrave, Prime Elector" and Anglo-German Relations of Stuart England: The View from the Popular Stage', in *The Stuart Court and Europe. Essays in Politics and Political Culture*, ed. R. M. Smuts (Cambridge, etc., 1996), pp. 113–32. The standard edition of the *The Hector of Germanie* remains that by L. W. Payne (Philadelphia, Pa., 1906), who considered the possibility that the herald was the author but concluded (p. 10): 'It is very improbable that as an old man he should have turned to the writing of plays.'

[25] Donald W. Foster, *Elegy by W.S.: A Study in Attribution* (Newark, London and Toronto, 1989), p. 268.

[26] H. S. London, in Godfrey and London, *College of Arms*, p. 220.

[27] Bodleian Library, MS Top. gen. e. 29 (*S.C.* 25534), f. 6.

[28] See f. 11, where the arms of the duke of Brunswick are painted 'at this Present', to which Smith has

compiling a collection of heraldic texts, very much like one of the precedent-books that every professional herald tended to write for his own reference. The title that he gave to this collection suggests that he was well aware of how close he was getting to being an interloper in the heralds' private world: 'The Image of Heraldry: shewinge divers Secrett Matters and Secrettes touching Heraldrye: Wherein is described the true Path-waye to obtaine that excellent Science.'[29]

In the course of the 1590s he produced a whole series of heraldic books, all in manuscript. He by now wrote a very clear, neat and rather individual script, combining both secretary and italic elements. Characteristically, though not invariably, he used bright red ink for titles (e.g., the family name, for a pedigree) and, sometimes, for the lines that link up names on a tabular genealogy. Like the herald Robert Glover just a few years earlier, he drew wavy lines to indicate illegitimate parenthood. He also liked to write a full-page title for all of his works, often including his own and other coats of arms. In 1593 he completed both a substantial collection of German arms (with over 1,500 painted coats, on pages that had been printed in Germany with outline shields and mantling) and a shorter book of the 'Armes of the Nobilitie in Polonia'.[30] He may have continued to trade and to act as a factor, but within the next few years he had set his mind on becoming a herald and joining the English Crown's Office of Arms, as a member of the College of Arms.

In the early to mid 1590s, the College of Arms was in a state of corporate disarray, as its records and library were not kept up to date and its regular functions (such as maintaining a roster of duty officers to answer general enquiries) were not carried out. On the other hand, its individual members still had the opportunity to prosper mightily, thanks to the heralds' monopoly on the conducting of heraldically-ordered funerals and what approached being a monopoly in related armorial and genealogical activities, such as the researching and production of elaborately written pedigrees, often presented in roll format. The heralds were paid what was little more than a token salary by the Crown (£40 for Garter King of Arms, £20 for the two other kings of arms, £13 6s. 8d for a herald of arms and £10 for a pursuivant),[31] supplemented by the Crown's regular 'largess' (distributions made at the principal feasts of the year) and payments made by each new peer and knight. However, by their own energies they could build up a substantial professional practice which would yield many tens and perhaps hundreds of pounds a year. It was a competitive world, and not for the faint-hearted; and it was accordingly difficult to gain admission to it.

---

added 'anno 1577'. The work as a whole is stated by Smith in its title to have been 'gathered' between 1571 and 1591, while he headed its title-page with the date 1593.

[29] Bodleian Library, MS Rawl. B. 120.

[30] College of Arms, MS Philipot c. 16; perhaps unfinished and incomplete, and lacking a title-page. There are about 292 coats, some in outline only and unblazoned.

[31] Wagner, *Heralds of England*, p. 99. In March 1618 Smith was granted an extra £10 a year by James I – a rare mark of favour. Rymer, *Foedera*, original edn., XVII, pp. 73–4.

Smith, however, set about demonstrating his worth, and secured support from two sides. On the one hand, he persuaded the entire Office of Arms to write a letter in support of his candidature to the commissioners for the office of Earl Marshal (who acted in the Earl Marshal's stead from after the death of George Talbot, earl of Shrewsbury, in 1590, until the appointment of Robert Devereux, earl of Essex, in December 1597). 'May it please your lordships', they wrote, 'that besydes our certeyn knowledge of his honest lyfe and conversation we fynde him to be both learned and langwaged and able to serve her Majesty in the sayd Office [of pursuivant] and therfore worthy to be of our society.'[32] Crucially, too, Smith had the support of Sir George Carey, Lord Hunsdon, who was one of the commissioners for the Earl Marshalcy and, being also Lord Chamberlain from April 1597, as well- placed a patron at Court as could be wished for.[33] In 1594 Smith had demonstrated his heraldic credentials in the classic way, by dedicating to Carey one of the copies of his account of Nuremberg and its heraldry. It was then perhaps not such a surprise that on 23 October 1597 Smith was one of a whole group of heralds and pursuivants who were formally created officers of arms, his office being that of Rouge Dragon Pursuivant. His actual patent (that is, the letters patent of the Crown formally appointing him), followed several years later, on 20 March 1603. Such an extremely long delay seems to have been unprecedented and cannot now be explained.

The various manuscript books of which Smith was the author or compiler have survived more-or-less in their totality. We know this, thanks to his having made a list of them in one of his notebooks: every one of the eleven that are listed here is extant in his own handwriting.[34] He put together several books of genealogical tables or pedigrees and of coats of arms. Rather as if heraldry was a field that cried out for order to be introduced to it, Smith set to work, both casting his net as widely as he could and then sorting and systematising his catch. Given that he began his armorial researches as early as 1565, it is perhaps unsurprising that he was so successful in his haul; but he no doubt drew on the work of other heraldic compilers rather than just seeking out individual coats of arms wherever he went.

[32] The letter is given in full by Thomas Lant, Portcullis Pursuivant, in College of Arms, MS Arundel 40, f. 37, on a page headed 1596; the letter itself is undated but is probably datable to after the death of Nicholas Dethick, Windsor Herald, which occurred in Jan. 1596. Nicholas Dethick would otherwise be conspicuous by his absence. The date can probably be narrowed down further to in or after May 1596, since Smith is said to have been a suitor for office for two years, and the death of Richmond Herald in May 1594 had created the expectation of a vacancy at pursuivant level. Lobbying for a pursuivant's post would have begun the moment that any herald's death was reported.

[33] L. L. Peck, *Northampton: Patronage and Policy at the Court of James I* (London, 1982, pp. 157–8. See also the account of Carey by W. T. MacCaffrey, in the entry on 'Carey, Henry, first Baron Hunsdon (1526–1596)', in *ODNB*, 10, pp. 75–9, at 78–9. As Lord Chamberlain, George Carey became patron of the Lord Chamberlain's Players – as his father had been before him.

[34] British Library, MS Harley 6601, ff. 4v, 8. The MS, which dates from the late 1590s or a little later, has had its 16 leaves bound in the wrong order.

The most essential work for any professional herald to have in his hands is an ordinary of arms (often called simply an ordinary), in which coats of arms are classified and grouped on a systematic basis according to their design and subject-matter; the name and perhaps place or county of the bearer is given, but no further information. Only by resort to an ordinary can a herald be sure whose a particular coat is: it is the one reliable way to identify a coat's historic bearer. Smith completed an ordinary in 1599:[35] this is a substantial collection, with several thousand carefully drawn coats, and it is no criticism of Smith that he seems to have derived some of its material from the ordinary which had been compiled by Robert Glover (d. 1588), Somerset Herald.[36] Glover was the most capable and reliable herald of recent years, and it may even be that Smith had known him, for he refers in his 'Breff Discourse' (discussed below) to Glover's father-in-law, William Flower, Norroy King of Arms, in terms that suggest that he was acquainted with Flower.

An ordinary of arms is a work of a wholly conventional or traditional sort: other heralds had compiled, and would for centuries to come continue to put together, very comparable collections. Smith struck out in some unexpected ways, however. He had an unusually well ordered approach to armory, and produced what no other contemporary managed to achieve: a comprehensive collection of coats of arms arranged alphabetically (by the first two letters of the alphabet).[37] He evidently aimed for completeness, and in his own manuscript[38] of this 'alphabet of arms' (as such works later came to be called) he recorded that he began the task on 20 October 1594 and finished it on 30 October 1597. Later, on 10 July 1602, he totted up how many coats he had entered: 10,969. This was a remarkable achievement, especially given the fact that for all save the last week of its preparation he had not had the advantage of being a member of the College of Arms. The ordinary of arms which was completed in 1584 by the formidably thorough Robert Glover, contained no more than 8,982 different coats.[39] Smith had left little room in his book for additions, and he subsequently worked on a further alphabet, which he finished on 20 July 1604.[40]

Wholly without precedent – and with very few successors – was another armorial category that he presented in book form: a collection of the arms of families called Smith.[41] It is not a large piece of work, containing just 92 shields of arms (and no crests);

[35] College of Arms, MS EDN 22.
[36] See H. S. London, 'John Philipot, M.P., Somerset Herald, 1624–1645', *Archaeologia Cantiana*, 60 (1948, for 1947), pp. 24–53, at 49.
[37] Ralph Brooke, York Herald, did produce a relatively large alphabet of arms, but arranged on a county-by-county basis (Folger Shakespeare Library, MS V.b.144, pp. 2–112); it drew on an earlier one, by Sir Christopher Barker (d. 1550), Garter King of Arms.
[38] Folger Shakespeare Library, MS V.b.217.
[39] This ordinary was in the Milner-Gibson-Cullum collection at Bury St Edmunds Library until it was lost in about the last fifty years. See Ramsay, *Robert Glover*, forthcoming, Appx. iii. Glover also produced an alphabet of arms, but this has long been lost.
[40] College of Arms, Misc. MSS, 'Smith's Alphabet'.
[41] London, Society of Antiquaries, MS 429, at ff. 12–23v.

THE VISITACION OF
LANCASHIRE, &c:
Made in Anno. 1567. Ano⁹ 9ᵒ Rᵉ Eliz.

DVCAT' LANCASTRIAE.

Visitacio ista Lancastriæ, transcripta et augmentata fuit, in Anᵒ 1598. p̱ me Wᵐ Smith (als) Rougedragon, Prosecutorem ad Arma.

at least eight of the coats are for Smith (or perhaps Schmidt) families of different parts of Germany. His own arms are given, near but not at the beginning, as those of Sir Thomas Smith of Cuerdley (Lancs.). A few of the coats are quartered; none is dated.

In his gathering together of pedigrees, Smith lit upon a source that very few other heralds drew on even in an occasional way, and that no one save a member of the College of Arms could ever have considered: funeral certificates. The Earl Marshal's orders of 18 July 1568 required each officer of arms who served at a funeral to bring into the Office 'a true and certain certificate under the hands of the executors and mourners that shall be present at the said funeral, containing the day of the death, the place of burial of the person so deceased, and also to whom he or she married, what issue they had, what years they were of at the time of the said burial ... to the intent that the said certificate may be registered and so remain as a perpetual record in the said Office for ever'. By Smith's time, these certificates had lengthened into considerable texts, where siblings and grandparents were sometimes also recorded: it certainly made sense to treat the certificates as genealogical source-material. Perhaps soon after he had become an officer of arms and thus gained access to the certificates, he produced a whole volume of pedigrees derived from them, presented in chronological order, 1567–96.[42]

For slightly less obvious reasons, he also set about transcribing complete texts of recent heraldic visitations of different English counties. Each original visitation pedigree – which almost invariably included a drawing in trick (that is, in plain ink, but with a written indication of the colours) of each family's coat of arms – was in principle deposited in the library of the College of Arms by the king of arms who was responsible for making it. Smith as a pursuivant of arms was one of the privileged few who had ready access to the library: to a careful and thorough compiler like himself, this was a godsend, since the visitation books amounted to the largest as well as the most reliable collection of systematically grouped modern pedigrees in existence. Beginning in the very year of his appointment as Rouge Dragon, he set about making his own copies of visitations, and several of these are extant today: Lancashire, 1567 (copied in 1598);[43] Cheshire, 1566 and 1580 (both also 1598);[44] Suffolk, 1561, and Norfolk, 1563 (both 1600);[45] Berkshire, 1566 (1602);[46] and Dorset, 1562 (1612).[47] Today, it is easy to admire him for his industry and, perhaps, for not re-ordering the visitation-books' contents (as was done by some of the arms-painters and others who managed, more or less surreptitiously, to get hold of the originals for commercial copying purposes). That he found his transcripts useful is shown by his having sometimes added to the individual pedigrees in them. One

[42] Folger Shakespeare Library, MS V.b.194.
[43] British Library, MS Harley 6159 (Fig. 6, opposite); Smith has added to it, and has also painted the arms, many of which contain several quarterings.
[44] Birkenhead, Wirral Archives, Misc. Accessions, YPX/91/1.
[45] College of Arms, MSS Philipot 41 Suffolk and Philipot 34 Norfolk.
[46] College of Arms, MS Philipot 3.2.1 Berks. & Beds.
[47] British Library, MS Harley 2186.

6 (opposite). Title-page of William Smith's transcript, 1598, of the Visitation of Lancashire, 1567. British Library, MS Harley 6159, f. 2*.

may, however, wonder: would he have made all these copies if he had known that he would never be entrusted with taking a visitation himself?

Works of historic heraldry seem to have interested Smith far less. Only one transcript by him of a medieval roll of arms has been traced: a copy made of the names and blazons of the knights who appear in the 'Parliamentary Roll'.[48] These excerpts, made in 1597, are rather carelessly written, even his title for the work having a mistake in it.[49] There survives, too, one manuscript which he filled with transcripts of medieval charters and pedigrees of medieval families (British Library, MS Harley 245); but these – as his own headings make clear – were copied not from original charters but from two of the volumes compiled by the scholar-herald Glover.[50] For once, moreover, Smith's usual industriousness left him, and he only copied excerpts from Glover's substantial works; he did, however, add a few other transcripts drawn from other sources.[51]

'Breff Discourse of the Causes of Discord amongst the Officers of Armes'

At some point before October 1606, Smith produced the most outspoken piece of writing of his entire life.[52] In its draft form, he gave it the title 'A Breff discourse of the causes of Discord amongst the officers of Armes: And of the great Abuses and absurdities committed by Painters, to the great preiudice and hindrance of the same office.' It is in two parts, the first being a discussion of what Smith sees as wrong within the Office of Arms, and the second being about the harm that is being done by painters and other unskilled artificers who paint or engrave incorrect coats of arms for their customers. The discord within the Office is presented quite summarily: it is in effect a complaint from the lower ranks, that posts within the Office are not being offered according to the seniority of existing office-holders (that is, years of service as a professional) and that the heraldic officers' 'droits' (rights to a share in certain customary payments, such as those given by newly made knights and peers) are not being allocated in the customary way. Smith also asserts that attempts are being made to deprive the pursuivants of their due turns in the allocation of funeral-taking commissions. All this has led, he avers, to a decline in the attraction of holding office as a pursuivant, as those who seek a post in the Office now aim to become a herald of arms straightaway, without first serving as a pursuivant. Here one may suspect that Smith has in mind such instances as the recent

---

48 British Library, MS Harley 4628, ff. 260–271.
49 Other copies of the Parliamentary Roll are listed, along with the roll that was perhaps Smith's original (British Library, Cotton MS Caligula A. xviii, ff. 3–21v; once owned by William Camden) by A. R. Wagner, *Catalogue of English Mediaeval Rolls of Arms*, Aspilogia I (Oxford, 1950), pp. 42-50.
50 Smith's sources were College of Arms, MSS Glover A and B.
51 E.g., Smith included transcripts of 18 charters belonging to the antiquary Joseph Holland, with careful drawings of their armorial seals: MS Harley 245, ff. 68v–73v.
52 Mention of 'within these nine years' since he became a pursuivant dates it to within nine years of 23 October 1597, i.e. to before 23 October 1606. At f. 18 (below, p. 66) Smith refers to the funeral of Sir George Harvey as 'the last funeral I served': this was in Sept. 1605.

appointments of Richard St George and Francis Thynne. As he himself had recorded in one of his notebooks, on the eve of St George's Day 1602 these two men had each been made a pursuivant and then, immediately afterwards, had been elevated to a full herald's post.[53] It was clearly seen by Smith as a wounding insult that outsiders should enter the College at his junior level in what was so obviously a mere formality, as the prelude to their becoming his seniors.

Smith's points are no doubt at least correct, but his lack of self-restraint may have rather marred the effect: it was perhaps foolish to refer to the lack of linguistic competence of four recent kings of arms, and it was surely a serious mistake to denigrate one of his fellow pursuivants, Philip Holland.

Smith was on safer ground in the second part of the Discourse, where he looks at the faults committed by the painters and seal-engravers. Here, he is curiously guarded in his criticism, choosing to mention those customers who have been the victims of the painters' armorial ignorance, rather than identifying the perpetrators: he merely names one coach-painter, Estgrigg, and gives the approximate address of two painters. Perhaps he did not wish to fall out with the Painter-Stainers' Company, to which the arms-painters who were based in London would doubtless all have belonged.

When he moves on, to consider – at even greater length – the way in which heraldic funerals in the country are being conducted, he is franker and gives names throughout. The irony is, however, that the encroachment on the heralds' lucrative funeral-taking business by inexpert locally-based arms painters was a problem with which many people were already familiar. The heralds had for years been combatting such interlopers, and had often settled for the admittedly unsatisfactory compromise of giving a measure of deputed authority to these men, in return for a fairly small share of the fees paid. Realistically, there was not much alternative for the heralds: if funerals needed to be taken in, say, Devon or Cheshire, the distances and consequently the time needed to arrange matters were such as to generally rule out the heralds from being directly involved. For the Office of Arms, the appointment of 'deputy heralds' was a necessary evil.[54]

Smith concludes his 'Discourse' with a short attack on certain of the City companies for getting above themselves, heraldically speaking. He blames Robert Cooke (d. 1593), Clarenceux King of Arms (and thus with arms-granting authority in London) for granting new coats of arms to people and institutions that already had a coat; still more, he blames 'base' (or 'inferior') companies, such as the Leathersellers, Pewterers, Waxchandlers and Saddlers, for acquiring supporters for their arms. Smith's own company, the Haberdashers, was one of the Twelve 'Great' livery companies, and it is hard not to feel that he was being unduly partisan in this part of his tract. The point was nevertheless a fair one in principle; the Office of Arms has over the last five centuries been

---

[53] Bodleian Library, MS Gough Berks. 12 (S.C. 17726), f. 13.
[54] See further A. R. Wagner and G. D. Squibb, 'Deputy Heralds', in *Tribute to an Antiquary. Essays Presented to Marc Fitch by Some of his Friends*, ed. F. Emmison and R. Stephens (London, 1976), pp. 229–64.

troubled from time to time by uncertainty as to how far it is acceptable to grant supporters to non-noble persons and institutions. Smith was a sharp-eyed observer of all matters heraldic in the City companies, and took seriously any failure to measure up to the standards that he knew to be requisite.

Smith was not a man to give up a campaign, once he had embarked on it. In 1605 he had already attacked certain of the City of London companies for setting up incorrect coats of arms in their halls. His armorial collection, entitled 'The XII Worshipfull Companies, or Misteries of London. With the Armes of all them that have bin Lord Mayors, for the space almost of 300 yeares ... Also most part of the Sheriffes, and Aldermen', includes in its dedicatory Epistle a whole section on the mistakes that he found in their halls.[55] Smith had been told of the Mercers' series of coats of arms of their members who had been mayors, 'painted upon Targetts and Pavises, for the furnishing of their hall'. When he looked at these, he found various of them 'to be false, erronious, and absurd. And great Iniury offred by the Painters (and those that did sett them on Work) aswell to those Gentlemen deceased: as to others that be yet living'. He then looked elsewhere: 'I found the lyke abuses committed in the Grocers hall. ... The lyke in other halls also, But especially in the Fishmongers.' He thereupon resolved to complete the collection, and presented it to the then Lord Mayor, Sir Thomas Low, who was a Haberdasher. Neither this nor the 'Breff Discourse' ended the campaign, however: in 1609 he returned yet again to the fray, with further copies of the collection.[56] Smith was nothing if not persistent, and his membership of the Haberdashers' Company no doubt made him take a particularly close interest in the doings of the City Companies.

Conclusion

On 19 December 1617, Smith made his last will and testament.[57] Its religious tone is wholly conventional. Smith requests burial in the church of St Alphege, London, as near as possible to his wife and children. His specific bequests are more revealing. He bequeaths 20*s*. to his friend Arthur Squibb, to make himself a ring. This legatee must surely be the Exchequer clerk, later a Teller of the Exchequer, who in 1646 was appointed Clarenceux King of Arms, thanks to his son-in-law, who was one of the Parliamentary commissioners for carrying out the heraldic duties of the earl marshalcy.[58] Smith also leaves £5 to Robert Winchell, citizen and painter-stainer of London: this probably reveals Winchell as the arms-painter who had been Smith's preferred collaborator or contractor

---

[55] Bodleian Library, MS Top. gen. e. 29 (S.C. 25534). A copy, also by Smith's hand and dated 1605 (but added to in subsequent years), is London Metropolitan Archives, Guildhall Library MSS, CLC/262/MS2464.

[56] Both British Library, MS Harley 1349, and London Metropolitan Archives, Guildhall Library MSS, CLC/262/MS2077 are both by Smith's hand, 1609. A further version is British Library, MS Harley 6860, made a few years later and brought down to 1624.

[57] PRO, PROB 11/133, f. 94r–v; proved 12 Feb. '1618'. I owe my knowledge of this will, and a copy of it, to the kindness of Ann Payne.

[58] See the account of Squibb by H. S. London, in Godfrey and London, *College of Arms*, p. 88.

in the handling of funeral commissions. The direction that these sums be paid within one year of his death, and the fact that his only other specific legacy is of 20*s*. to his cousin Ralph Smith, while he leaves all the residue of the estate to another cousin, Mary Smith, 'nowe dwelling with mee', makes it fairly certain both that he had outlived all his immediate family and that he anticipated leaving only a very modest estate. Smith adds that he would have bequeathed something to Humfrey Dyson, notary public (better known today as a book-collector on a prodigious scale),[59] whose acquaintance he has long had, but Dyson is unwilling to receive any legacy; and so he simply asks Dyson to aid and assist Mary Smith in her role as executrix. The will gives no hint that he was in other than reasonable health at the time, and indeed he lived for another nine months, dying on 1 October 1618.

In some ways, Smith's career might be seen as a disappointment. In none of the activities that he engaged in did he rise to the top. He does not appear to have made himself wealthy by his mercantile activities, and it was perhaps symptomatic of his status that he was always just a member of the Haberdashers' Company of London and not of the more cosmopolitan Merchant Adventurers' or Mercers' Companies.[60] As a cartographer and topographical draughtsman he is overshadowed by his contempor- aries, men such as Christopher Saxton, John Norden, Abraham Ortelius and John Speed: his work remained unprinted until modern times. As a herald, he never advanced beyond being a pursuivant. Did he lack the right patron, or was he simply not seen as sufficiently worthy to merit promotion? All had augured well at the beginning, when his appointment was so encouraged by the officers of arms. Did he lose friends by his outspoken attacks on named individuals in his 'Breff Discourse'?

One plausible explanation may be that he did not aspire to more. He could perfectly well have continued as a merchant in Nuremberg, but chose to leave this line of activity in mid-career, despite being well positioned in local society by his marriage. He may well have made his maps and bird's-eye views of towns principally for his own amusement – as is suggested by his inclusion of maps in certain of his transcripts of heraldic visitations, which can only have been intended for his own use. He must always have been well aware that the high cost of making engraved plates made it almost certain that his books of a heraldic sort or with armorial illustrations could never be printed.

---

[59] See N.L. Ramsay, 'Dyson, Humfrey (d. 1633)', in *ODNB*, 17, p. 513.

[60] Smith himself in his account of the Twelve Great Livery Companies asserted that 'no Company in London, hath so many marchants in it, as this of Haberdashers': British Library, MS Harley 6363, f. 20. It is true that in Smith's time the Haberdashers' Company was much less a company of importers and retailers of haberdashery than it had been, and had become much more a general mercantile company. Smith himself claimed that no other London Company had so many members, and it was indeed perhaps only exceeded in size by the Merchant Tailors. In the 1590s the Haberdashers' Company may have had as many as 1500 members. See Ian W. Archer, *The History of the Haberdashers' Company* (Chichester, 1991), pp. 18–20.

7. A herald in his tabard, the letters HERALD being expanded to show his requisite qualities: Humble, Expert, Righteous, Advysed, Learned and Dutifull. Drawn by William Smith, 1597, and perhaps intended as a self-portrait. Washington (DC), Folger Shakespeare Library, MS V.b.217, opening leaf.

Nevertheless, as a herald Smith must surely have hoped for more. A sense of grievance is an undercurrent that surfaces at more than one point in the 'Breff Discourse'. His remarkably numerous armorial and genealogical compilations and transcripts suggest a herald with boundless ambitions. On the other hand, his physical energy must surely have been waning by 1606, when he was approaching the age of sixty. Would he at this date still have wanted the potentially more arduous post of a herald of arms, with its constant travelling around the country? Was his appetite for travel perhaps now sated, and even if he was not rich, had he perhaps made sufficient money to live a perfectly comfortable life?

Heraldry had begun for Smith as a private hobby, back in the 1560s, and it is perfectly possible that he now lacked the requisite zeal for promotion. It may even be that his writing of the 'Breff Discourse' marked in some sense his abandonment of expectations of advancement for himself, and that he was indeed writing for the greater good of the Office of Arms as a whole (while not overlooking the needs of the pursuivants in particular). Like Robert Glover, Somerset Herald, he was temperamentally industrious and, it seems, independent in spirit. It may not have struck him that his brother-officers of arms would prefer to battle with the Painter-Stainers' Company rather than find fault with the kings of arms for an over-readiness to grant arms and supporters, mistaken though the kings may have been. The embattled years before 1597 had left their mark on the College of Arms. On the other hand, Smith's years of foreign travel – which included time in France as well as Germany – must have given him a fresh perspective on English affairs, and the Discourse is certainly striking for its sketching out (with much specific evidence) a national framework or picture. Smith had a remarkable ability to stand back and survey, figuratively or actually. Whatever prompted his writing of the Discourse, we may be glad that someone so centrally placed in the early-seventeenth-century heraldic world chose to set out so clearly and precisely his well-informed view of everything in its activities that was under threat or needed correction.

APPENDIX

Ann Payne

Autograph fair copy by Smith of his treatise on the causes of discord among the officers of arms and the abuses committed by arms-painters, addressed to Henry Howard, earl of Northampton, commissioner for the office of the Earl Marshal. Datable to 1606. Folger Shakespeare Library (Washington, DC), MS V.a.199.[61]

The manuscript is a fair copy by Smith of his autograph draft of this work, Folger MS V.a.157,[62] incorporating all the additions made by him to the draft and lacking only the draft's title, 'A Breff discourse of the Causes of Discord amongst the officers of Armes:

---

[61] Numbered 1186.1 in Seymour de Ricci's *Census of Medieval and Renaissance Manuscripts*.
[62] Numbered 423.2 in de Ricci's *Census*.

8. Peter le Neve (d. 1729), painted after 1704, when he became Norroy King of Arms; attributed to George Vertue. College of Arms.

And of the great Abuses and absurdities committed by Painters, to the great preiudice and hindrance of the same office', and the dedication 'To the Right honorable Henry Erle of Northampton, Baron Marnhill, knight of the most honorable ordre of the Garter and one of his Ma[iesties] Commissioners, for the office of the Erle Marshall' (Folger, MS V.a.157, f.1v). The autograph copy bears the title 'Abuses committed by Painters and others to the præiudice of the Officers of Armes' (f. 1), in the italic hand of the collector Sir Robert Cotton (1571–1631), although this heading correctly relates only to the second part of the text. Peter le Neve (d. 1729), Norroy King of Arms, mistakenly claimed in a note on the flyleaf that this copy was addressed to Lord Burghley as Earl Marshal. The date of 1606 (for which see below) precludes this. William Cecil, Lord Burghley, died in 1598, and his son Thomas who inherited the title would not have continued to use it after he was created earl of Exeter in 1605. There is no reason to suppose that this is other than a direct copy of the draft addressed to Henry Howard, earl of Northampton. The only substantial modern work to draw at length upon Smith's tract is that of A. R. Wagner: *Heralds of England* (London, 1967).

Provenance
As well as inserting an abbreviated title, Sir Robert Cotton has signed the manuscript at the foot of the first page (f. 1) and added the attribution 'By William Smith Rouge Dragon' on the last (f. 19).[63] The manuscript subsequently belonged to Peter Le Neve, herald and antiquary[64] whose ownership inscription 'Liber Petri Leneve alias Norroy AD 1704' is on the flyleaf and whose annotations occur throughout. A faded, almost illegible, ink title on the front cover of the binding, 'Account of officers of Armys | Will. Smith | Rouge Dragon [written(?)] | about the year 1614' may also be in Le Neve's hand. Nothing more is known of the volume's provenance until it was acquired by William Augustus White (1843–1927), of Brooklyn; his pencil note on the flyleaf records 'W A White |11 April 1905'. The number '15' on the binding and printed sale-catalogue label on the pastedown inside the front cover have not been identified.[65]

Text
The copy is on paper with a flyleaf and nineteen leaves (measuring 19×14 cm). The contemporary binding is of limp vellum with gilt decoration. The manuscript is written throughout in William Smith's own careful italic hand, and in this differs from the more cursive secretary hand of his autograph draft (Folger, MS V.a.157). Characteristically,

[63] Cotton's ownership of the volume is briefly discussed by C. G. C. Tite, "'Lost or Stolen or Strayed': A Survey of Manuscripts Formerly in the Cotton Library", in *Sir Robert Cotton as Collector: Essays on an Early Stuart Courtier and his Legacy*, ed. C. J. Wright (London,1997), pp. 262–306, at 275 and 300, n. 86.
[64] Cf. T. Woodcock, 'Le Neve, Peter (1661–1729)', in *ODNB*, 33, pp. 341–3, and see Fig. 8.
[65] A further pencil note on the flyleaf, in a twentieth-century hand, claiming that 'This famous manuscript is quoted and discussed in [Sir Sidney] Lee's *Life of William Shakespeare*, 1916, pp. 285 and 286', has been amended with the note 'not this one – one belonging to Mr H. C. Folger' [i.e. the draft, Folger MS V.a.157].

Smith makes much use of red ink with the black; he has foliated the manuscript and given marginal rulings to each page in red, with rubrics, highlighted passages, and some initial letters in the same colour. Text printed here in bold corresponds to this rubrication. Catch words, present in the manuscript, have been omitted, and annotations by Peter Le Neve (mostly underlinings and marginal notes of contents) are not recorded unless they give additional information. Only substantial differences in the draft copy are noted.

The text begins opposite the blank verso of the flyleaf, where it may have been intended to have the title and dedication inserted.

/f. 1/ Abuses committed by Painters and others to the præiudice of the Officers of Armes[66] Right honorable, my very good Lord: considering your honorable Inclynation, And knowing the lyke endevor, for the erecting upp of the poore decayd office of Armes: I thought it my Dutie to Impart unto your Lordshipps favorable acceptance, what I have noted and observed in many yeares, but especially within these ix. yeares, since I was one of the same Society.[67] For although a body which is full of sores, be fully cured of the greatest and most apparant: yet if but one or two litle-ones be left, the same may peradventure trouble the Patient, as much as all the rest. And even so, although there be never so many good orders made, for the establishing of this said Office: yet if one thing[68] /f. 1v/ be not taken away, there wilbe no unitie, or agreement amongst us. And that is **Discord**, which proceedeth cheifly of Discontentment: And that is for two sundry causes. The first is, for want of due preferment: The second, Unequall Parting of Droites. Of which two causes (with your Lordshipps honorable favor) I will say somwhat, and as breefly as I can.

First, touching preferment. It hath bin alwais an ancient use and order in the said office, to preferre the most ancient and eldest officer, from a Poursuyvant, to a herold, and so from a Herold, to be a King of Armes. Which order hath bin observed (except very seldome) till of late yeares, within mans remembrance. That some have bin preferred /f. 2/ and overleaped their fellowes, more by favor then for skill. And it must needes seeme strange that a man shall study all the dayes of his lyffe: shall travaile many yeares in strange Countreis, for obtayning of skill and languages: shall sue long for the Place

---

[66] This heading – inserted, in italic, in the top margin – is in the hand of Sir Robert Cotton (d. 1631).

[67] MS V.a.157: office *deleted*. William Smith was created Rouge Dragon Pursuivant in the College of Arms on 23 Oct. 1597; the reference to nine years in which he has been of that society therefore indicates a date before October 1606 for the manuscript. The earl marshalcy was vacant at this time and its powers vested in a commission of six peers of whom the earl of Northampton (named as the dedicatee in the autograph draft) was one. See P. Croft, 'Howard, Henry, earl of Northampton (1540–1614)', in *ODNB*, 28, pp. 366–74. For Northampton's attempts to regulate the Office of Arms and reform the Earl Marshal's office, see Peck, *Northampton* (cit. in n. 33), pp. 14, 156–60, 245–8, with a discussion of this tract at pp. 156–7; see also P. H. Hardacre, 'The Earl Marshal, the Heralds and the House of Commons, 1604–1641', *International Review of Social History*, ii (1957), pp. 106–25, at 111.

[68] *Signature of Sir Robert Cotton (d. 1631), in the lower margin*: Robert Cotton: Bruceus.

beffore he gett it: shall serve long in the place beffore he have the fees and proffitts of it: And yet shalbe overleaped by his Inferiors in skill, and those which peradventure have not sued a month, nor yet served a day for it.

I wryte not this to taxe any of my Lordes now commissioners:[69] neither do I meane any of the office at this present lyving, although I have good cause.[70] For I have knowne in my tyme, foure Kinges of Armes, to say, Clarencieux Cook, Clarencieux Lee, Norrey Floure, and Norrey Knight. And none of these 4. could either wryte, or speak, true Latin, true French, or true English.[71] Yet had they their preferment when it fell, /f. 2v/ saving Cook, who was pursyvant extra ordynary, herold, and Clarenseaux, and all in the space of one yeare. Yet (as I said beffore) more by favor then for skill. Which his absurdities do witnes, aswell in geving of so many Hundrethes of new Armes: as also his erronious Pedegrees, and those cheifly for want of Learning. For how can he sett downe any trew matter of Antiquity: who cannot either read, or understand, an ancient Record, or peece of evidence.[72] Therfore I would not wish any one to be taken in, to be a pursuyvant: except his skill be sufficient to be a King of Armes. As at this present I dare presume to say (without arrogancy be it spoken) There is never a Poursuyvant of Armes (one yong man only excepted)[73] but they surpass in skill, any of the said foure kinges whilest they lived: And comparable with any of the herolds which be now in office. In the tyme of Clarencieux Cook, and Norrey Flowre, lived Sir Gilbert Dethick, who /f. 3/ was as Ignorant as the best, yet he came in orderly, as first Hams,[74] then Rouge Cross, then Richmond, then Norrey, and lastly Garter. This was Orderly succession, and so likewise divers others. Yet for the Place of a King (if the partie be not found sufficient) good reason another should have it. But I meane those that wilbe Heroldes at the first dash, (although they be but yong in yeares), and also some others that I know, who following ill presidents: meane to come in as others have attempted to do. The reason is, the Pursyvantes are kept so bare from their due fees by the heroldes, And sitt still without removing: That no man desireth to be a Pursyvant, as hereafter in another Place, shalbe declared.

The second cause of Discontent (as I said beffore) is the unequall Particion of mony, to say, fees and Droites, belonging to the same officers.

[69] MS V.a.157 : that are now commissioners.
[70] MS V.a.157: although I have good cause *inserted*.
[71] Cf. Wagner, *Heralds of England*, p. 207. Robert Cooke, Clarenceux King of Arms 1567–93; Richard Lee, Clarenceux King of Arms 1594–7; William Flower, Norroy King of Arms 1562–88; Edmund Knight, Norroy King of Arms 1592–3. For biographical details, see H.S. London, in Godfrey and London, *College of Arms*.
[72] Wagner, *Heralds of England*, p. 207.
[73] The young man can only be Philip Holland, Portcullis Pursuivant (patent of office: Dec. 1606) who was born in March 1576, the eldest son of the antiquary Joseph Holland; he had been the servant or assistant of Camden, Clarenceux. See H. S. London, in Godfrey and London, *College of Arms*, pp. 204–5.
[74] Dethick held the post of Hampnes Pursuivant (an 'extraordinary' pursuivant, not a member of the body corporate) from 1536 until 1540, when he became Rouge Croix Pursuivant.

¶ The Officers of Armes greatly
    hindred by Paynters.
And of a nomber of Absurdities comitted
by them (& other Artificers) aswell in
    London, as in the Countrey.

The greatest hindrance & Inconvenience
that the Officers of Armes do at this day sustaine:
is through the manifold errors and abuses
dayly comitted by Painters, & sundry other
persons, taking vppon them ye office of herolds.
Whereby great Indignitie is offred vnto the
kings ma^{tie}. his Subiectes mightely abused:
And ye officers of Armes fallen into y^t decay, & hindrance: that they are not able to maintayne
them selues according to their calling.
For every Painters shopp, is now become
an office of Armes. They take many for
serching for Armes, do forge and devise
                                    both

Painters shop an office of Armes.

9a. 'The Officers of Armes greatly hindred by Paynters': two pages from William Smith's 'Breff Discourse of the Causes of Discord amongst the Officers of Armes'. Washington (DC), Folger Shakespeare Library, MS V.a.199, ff. 6v–7. Approximately actual size.

both cotes, Creasts, and make Pedegrees.
Not long ago, A Gentleman came into a
Painters shopp in fletestrete, to serch for
his Armes. And fynding y̔ same, demanded
what he must geve, to have it drawne in
coulers: The paynter told hym, that y̔ serch
was ten grotes, besydes y̔ making.

¶ A Gentleman named m̔. Pantolf, died
in Turnbull strete, and was buried with
Scutcheons. thither went I (being sent
by m̔. Clarenseaux) to see what warrant
they had for his Armes: I was answered by
two gentlemen, that y̔ Armes was right,
for they had it, at y̔ herolds office, in fletestrete.

¶ Another named Leigh, came to a Painter
dwelling in Siluerstrete, to serch for Armes.
Which Painter shewed hym xvj sundry
cotes, by the name of Leigh: And did mar=
shall them all in one Escutcheon for him.

¶ The Painters do sett vp Achevements in
churches,

[marginalia:]
Paunters doo forge coats make Pedigrees

Pantolf

Herolds office in fletestrete

Leigh 16 cotes by the hand marshalld all in one Escucheon for one man

Embrotherers comitt faultes in making of
Badges wthout consent of ye herold, as is to be seene
on ye Erle of Arundells footmen, who haue a
Dukes Coronet over the whyte horse: The Erle
of Sussex men, haue a Marques Coronet over
their starre: Sr wm Cicells men, haue a Peacock
(the Erle of Rutlands badge): Sr frances fanes
footmen, wt a pyed bull, the L. of Burgavenies
badge. But this last is of silver, and therfore
Goldsmiths work.

But Gravers of Sealls, their faultes are Jnumerable
in graving of Armes: yet haue they their direct=
ions from ye Painters. As Sr Ric. Musgraves Armes
could not haue bin graven, except a Painter had
first drawne them. ¶ Phillipps ye Player had
graven in a gold Ring: ye Armes of Sr wm Phillipp
L. Bardolff, wt ye said Lord Bardolffs cote quartred,
as J shewed mr York, at ye Seall gravers in fuster
Lane. ¶ Pope ye Player, would haue no
other Armes: But ye Armes of Sr Tho. Pope,
Chancelor of the Augmentations.

¶ Abuses

Badges for footmen imbroidered

Seal gravers

Sir Richard Musgrave

Phillipps ye Player.

Pope, the Player.

9b. Two pages from William Smith's 'Breff Discourse of the Causes of Discord amongst the Officers of Armes'. Washington (DC), Folger Shakespeare Library, MS V.a.199, ff. 9v–10. Approximately actual size.

¶ Abuses Comitted by Painters, in the Countrey.

There is never a Shyre Towne in England, yt hath not a Painter or ij, yt playeth yͤ herold. Do bury Esquires to Barons (as if they were Barons) and let their herses stand in yͤ Churches, in some places a whole yeare together. Of these, I will speak but of some ij or iij Shyres. wherby a man may gess, what is done, in other Countreis of yͤ Realme. And because I will not seeme Partiall: I will beginne wt yͤ Countrey wherein I was borne, which is Cheshyre.

Cheshyre is devyded into ij partes by the Riuer of weever, to say, vpper Cheshyre, & Lower Cheshyre. And ech of these parts, hath his Painter, who playeth yͤ Provinciall herold. As first, in higher Cheshyre, is one Henry Oberton, (comonly called Harry Painter) who amongst dyvers others, hath buried these men of worship. ¶ Sr. Piers Legh of Lyme. ¶ Sr. Edmūd Trafford. ¶ Sr. John

[marginalia: Esqrs buriedas Barons Horses stand in Churches in this country]
[marginalia: H. Overton]
[marginalia: Legh of Lyme Trafford]

/f. 3v/ **Every** Poursuyvant of Armes, hath of the king yearly x $^{li.}$ standing fees. A herold xx$^{ti.}$ markes, and a King of Armes xx $^{li.}$ (which is twise so much as a Pursyvant) and this is indiffrency. And so I could wish, that in all other particions, the lyke Order were observed. That if a Poursuyvant had xii ^{d} a herold should have xviii ^{d}, and a king of Armes ii ^{s}. But the ancient custome hath bin, that a king hath had twise so much as a herold, and a herold twise so much as a Pursyvant. Which although it may seem unequall dealing: yet if it were generally observed in all other fees and partitions, it were somwhat tollerable. But some of our captious herolds, when they read the bookes of ancient presidents, for fees due to the Officers of Armes, for knights of the Bath, and others, and fynding there written, **which garments shalbe fees to the Heroldes:** do straight waies take hold of the wordes, and not of the meaning, saying. **Here** /f. 4/ **be no Pursyvantes named.** no indeed, neither is there any kinges named. Nay, the heroldes do deny the pursyvants to be of their Corporation. Taking advantage of the wordes in the lettres Patents of Q. Mary, for the gift of Darby house, where all the Kinges and Herolds, are named by their christian and surnames, concluding thus, **with the rest of the Herolds and Pursyvants, that now be, or hereafter shalbe**, and not naming the Pursyvants at all. By couler whereof, they exclude them, from all Particions of all Knights Fees, which the said pursivants had, during all the Raigne of K. Henry. 8. They exclude them also from their fees, for making knights of the Bath, (which they ever had):[75] And make a question, whether they ought to have any thing for Knightes of the Garter.

Touching knights fees, the same was wont to be but xx $^{s.}$ a knight, which was not passing viii ^{d} ob' a Pursyvant, which small somme they litle regarded. But since the Kings coming,[76] /f. 4v/ (through his gratious bountifulnes) the same knights fees have bin advanced from xx $^{s.}$ to V. poundes, after the maner of Scotland (as dyvers other officers also have fees of newe made knights, which in tymes past had nothing). But the Pursivants of Armes are in worse case, then the very Gromes of the kings chamber.

Our Herolds are content to receave v $^{li.}$ of every new made knight, after the maner of Scotland: But they will not make particion of the same after the maner of Scotland, which is, to lett every Pursivant have halfe so much as a herold, as in all other droits. But our herolds do kepe even reakoning with the Poursuyvants: for they lett them have iust nothing.

And not only for Knights fees: but also for the Creations of Noble men. As for iii Erles and viii Barons, created at Hampton Court, on Thursday the 21. July. 1603: The Pursuyvants spent their mony there, and lay at charges both for horse and man, but yet hitherto have /f. 5/ had nothing. The Herolds have no excuse for this, but that some of the mony is not yet receaved, And therfore will not part that which they have. But I know not what they can alleage for the xx $^{li.}$ \which/ they have receaved for Creation of the Erles of Northampton, and of Dorcet: of which the Pursivants have not yet had one

---

[75] Peter le Neve comments: (*above the line*) 'a lye'; (*right margin*) 'and justly for they never had them'.
[76] James I succeeded Elizabeth I in 1603.

peny.[77] This matter is worth the examining: But more worthy of redress.

Thus much were matter enough to cause variance: yet the Herolds are not thus content, but seek to hinder the pursivants of their turnes at Funeralls, which they have not, somtymes not one in a whole yeare and more, Alleaging, that for serving of a funerall, a Pursivant ought not to have as much as a herold. And I see no reason, but that he ought to have no less, it falling out to be his turne, And he performing the same in all respectes as well as the herold, being nothing Inferior unto him in skill. And that a Pursivant /f. 5v/ may serve as a herold, and weare a herolds cote: As a herold to serve for a King, and to weare a Kinges cote. Neither can it be any hindrance to the herold, who hath nothing the less for his turne when it falleth. And if Pursyvantes shall have less then heroldes for their funeralls: I thinck Gentlemen wilbe content to be served for the least mony.

Thus may your Lordshipp see the causes of the variance[78] and brablements[79] of this troublesome office, consisting only of xiii persons: or <u>Monster with iii heads vi bodies, and iiii Legges (</u>I speak **ex mœrore animi**)[80] Neither do I thinck it wilbe otherwise, except by your Lordshipps meanes some remedy may be provyded: or ells that it please his Ma[iestie] to make them all alyke (as I heare say they be in France).

This is the cause that now adaies, euery \one/ that sueth, wilbe a Herold at the first. And so the Pursyvants (being the kinges servants) may serve all the dayes of their Lyves, without preferment. As at this present I know them, which meane to sue for the next herolds place that falleth (some but /f. 6/ very yong youths)[81] who say playnly they scorne the place of a Pursyvant. The Imbrothered cotes which the heroldes procured for themselves, and excluded the pursyvantes: is sufficient cause if there were nothing ells.

But being fully persuaded, your Lordshipp conceaveth these matters, better than I am able[82] to sett them downe: I will here make an end. And with your honorable favor, say somwhat of Paynters, and others. By whom not only great Iniury is offred to the Officers of Armes: But also great Indignity to his Ma[iestie], and all sortes of Nobilitie.

/f. 6v/ ¶The Officers of Armes greatly hindred by Paynters. And of a nomber of Absurdities committed by them (and other Artificers) aswell in London, as in the Countrey.

The greatest hindrance and Inconvenience that the Officers of Armes do at this day sustaine: is through the Manifold errors and abuses dayly committed by Painters, and

---

77 On 13 March 1604, Thomas Sackville, Lord Buckhurst (d.1608), was created earl of Dorset, and Lord Henry Howard (d. 1614), was created Baron Howard of Marnhill and earl of Northampton.
78 MS V.a.157 : dissensions.
79 'Cavilling, quibbling' [*OED*].
80 'Out of sadness of the heart.'
81 MS V.a.157 : beardlesse boyes *deleted*; very yong youthes .
82 MS V a.157: The remainder of this paragraph in the draft was given on a slip formerly pasted in at the foot of f. 6 and now interleaved between ff. 13 and 14. One line of text, 'to sett ... with your', is lacking in the draft, having been cut off.

sundry other persons, taking uppon them the office of herolds. Whereby great Indignitie is offred unto the Kings Ma[iestie] his Subiectes mightely abused: And the Officers of Armes fallen into that decay, and hindrance: that they are not able to maintayne them selves according to their calling.

For every Painters Shopp, is now become an Office of Armes. They take mony for serching for Armes, do forge and devise /f. 7/ both Cotes, Creasts, and make Pedegrees.[83] Not long ago, A Gentleman came into a Painters shopp in Fletestrete, to serch for his Armes. And fynding the same, demanded what he must geve, to have it drawne in coulers: The Paynter told hym, that the serch was ten grotes, besydes the making.

¶ A Gentleman named Mr Pantolf, died in Turnbull strete, and was buried with Scutcheons. Thither went I (being sent by Mr Clarenseaux)[84] to see what warrant they had for his Armes: I was answered by two gentlemen, that the Armes was right, for they had it at the <u>herolds Office in Fletestrete</u>.

¶ Another named Leigh, came to a Painter dwelling in Silverstrete, to serch for Armes. Which Painter shewed hym xvi sundry Cotes, by the name of Leigh: And did Marshall them all in one Escutcheon for him.

¶ The Painters do sett up Achevements in /f. 7v/ churches, perswading men not to use any Herold. And yet they them selves (without consent of any Officer of Armes) do bury Gentlemen with false Armes, as it shall hereafter appeare.[85]

¶ Sergeant Wetnall, was buried at S\t Clements without Temple barr, with a cleane contrary Armes.[86]

¶ One Mathew, buried at S\t Dunstons within Temple barr, the Armes in wrong couler, and not right marshalled.

¶ One Hawkins, buried at the same church with the Armes of Sir John Hawkins, who died sanz issu: The Armes being granted to the said Sir John, and to his posteritie.[87]

¶ Another Hawkins was buried at Alhalows on London Wall, with the Armes of Hawkins of Kent: he being come from Hawkins of the West Countrey, who gave a Contrary Armes, but not so good as the other.

---

[83] Quoted hence by Wagner, *Heralds of England*, p. 238.

[84] William Camden, historian and herald, Clarenceux King of Arms from 1597 to 1623.

[85] The examples that follow of burials set up with false achievements of arms in London churches are also mentioned by Henry Howard, earl of Northampton, in his treatise 'A Certeyne Forme of Orders to bee prescribed to the Officers of Armes For Reformation of Abuses and Prevention of Corruptions deepely rooted and not easy to bee removed' [1604×14]; British Library, MS Add. 23747, ff. 9–37v, at 32. For other examples of Northampton drawing on Smith's tract for this treatise, see notes 101, 106, 109 below.

[86] John Whetenhall, the Queen's serjeant-at-arms in ordinary, d. by Aug. 1600: *Cal. Pat. Rolls, 42 Elizabeth* (List and Index Soc., 332, 2010), no. 1129.

[87] 'One Hawkins' was in fact Katherine, the wife of Sir John Hawkins, Treasurer of the Navy, to whom the Queen herself had granted arms; their only child, Sir Richard Hawkins (*c.* 1560–1622) was perhaps born a few years before their marriage. See B. Morgan, 'Sir John Hawkins (1532–1595)', in *ODNB*, 25, pp. 919–27.

¶ Doctor Balgay, was buried at the Temple, for whose funerall, his wyffe and frendes were /f. 8/ willing to have Armes.[88] And brought a Painter to the said Doctors Chamber, being in the Inner Temple, In the glass windowes whereof, was the Armes of Gerard Leigh, somtyme owner therof.[89] Which Armes were iiii cotes quartred. The first, for Leigh: The second for Baguley: The third for Leach: and the fourth for Levensham. The Painter made two dozen of these Armes in Escutcheons, <u>Putting the second cote of Baguley, in the first quarter for Balgay</u>. I had understanding of it, and went to the Gentlewoman, telling her, that it would be neither Worshipp nor Credit for her, to have her husband buried with those Armes. She was mightely offended at the Painter, and Asked hym, Why he did not go to the heroldes, as she willed him: He answered (in my hearing) that he did it, to save her a fee, which the heroldes did look to have.[90]

¶ This Painter is he, whom your Lordshippes lately committed, who also about a yeare past, made a Penon of silk, to be sent into the Countrey. I was sent to him by /f.8v/ Mr Clarencieux, to know for whom it was, and whither it went: He answered me, that he knew not for whom it was, or whither it went, neither did he care. For he was paid for his work, and would make more, for as many as came to hym. Neither did he care either for Clarencieux or me, It was his Trade, he was brought upp to nothing ells. **So may every Cutpurse say.**

These and a nomber such lyke abuses, are committed by Painters here in London, whereof I could make a whole volume, if I should go to all the churches in the cittie: but especially in the halles of Companies, where the faultes are intollerable. The Wardens of some Companies have bin tould of it. they lay all the blame on the Painters, Who ought not to medle with Armes, without consent of the Herold: no more then An Apothecary to minister Phisik without Consent of the Doctor.

/f. 9/ ¶ **Abuses committed by Painters of Coaches, Marblers, Glasiers, Embrotherers, and Gravers of Sealls.**

Beffore I go in hand with the Painters in the Countrey: I must say somwhat of Painters of Coaches, Marblers, Glasiers, Embrotheres, and Gravers of Sealles. **And first for Coaches:** There is one Estgrigg, who Painteth Coaches, over against Durham house, where my Lord of Devonshyrers Coach standeth, with iiii Cotes only within the Garter, and ii of them wrong. There have I seene the Visc[ount] Montacutes whole Armes, with an Erles Coronet over them, and dyvers others, which I told the Painter of: Who answered me, that he did them, as he was comaunded, by them that paid him for his Work.[91]

¶ Marblers and Glasiers, if they committ any absurdities: It is comonly long of the

---

[88] Nicholas Balgay, DD, Master of the Temple from 1591, died in August 1601: J. Foster, *Alumni Oxonienses, 1500–1714*, 4 vols (Oxford and London, [1891-2]), I, p. 61.
[89] Gerard Legh (d. 1563), lawyer and author of *The Accedens of Armory* (London, 1562); *ODNB*. A note by Peter le Neve on the flyleaf of the MS asserts: 'Gerrard Leigh of the Inner Temple 8. fol. was A bastard'
[90] Smith has written in the margin: This is worth noting.
[91] This passage is cited by Wagner, *Heralds of England*, p. 238.

Painter, from whom they have their directions. As lately at Christes Church in London, where a monument is sett upp, for one Roger Brook. And neither Armes or Inscription true. /f. 9v/ **Embrotherers** committ faultes in making of Badges without consent of the herold, as is to be seene on the Erle of Arundells footmen, who have a Dukes Coronet over the Whyte horse: The Erle of Sussex men, have a Marques Coronet over their Starre: Sir William Cicells men, have a Peacock, (the Erle of Rutlands badge): Sir Frances Fanes footmen, with a pyed bull, the Lord of Burgavenies Badge. But this last is of silver, and therfore Goldsmiths work. **But** Gravers of Sealls, their faultes are Inumerable in graving of Armes: yet have they their directions from the Painters. As Sir Richard Musgraves Armes could not vhave bin graven, except a Painter had first drawne them. ¶ Phillipps the Player had graven in a gold Ring: the Armes of Sir William Phillipp Lord Bardolf, with the said Lord Bardolfs cote quartred, as I shewed Mr York,[92] at the Seall gravers in Foster Lane. ¶ Pope the Player , would vhave no other Armes: But the Armes of Sir Thomas Pope, Chancelor of the Augmentations.[93]

/f. 10/ ¶**Abuses Committed by Painters, in the Countrey.**

There is never a shyre Towne in England, which hath not a Painter or ii, that playeth the herold. Do bury Esquires with Baners (as if they were Barons) and let their herses stand in the Churches, in some places a whole yeare together. Of these, I will speak but of some ii or iii Shyres. Wherby a man may gess, what is done, in other Countreis of the Realme. And because I will not seeme Partiall: I will beginne with the Countrey wherein I was borne, which is Cheshyre.

Cheshyre is devyded into ii partes by the River of Weever, to say, Upper Cheshyre, and Lower Cheshyre. And ech of these parts, hath his Painter, who playeth the Provinciall herold. As first, in higher Cheshyre, is one Henry Overton, (comonly called Harry Painter)[94] who amongst dyvers others, hath buried these men of worshipp. ¶ Sir Piers

---

[92] Ralph Brooke, York Herald from 1592 until his death in 1625.

[93] This passage in Smith's text has been discussed in print many times, thanks to its mention of the players, Augustine Phillips and Thomas Pope. The latter (who d. 1603×4) was among those listed in the 1590s as being a member of the Lord Chamberlain's Company (and thus under the patronage of George Carey, Lord Hunsdon); Phillips and Pope were each shareholders – like William Shakespeare– in the Globe theatre, from 1599. For Pope, see E. K. Chambers, *The Elizabethan Stage*, 4 vols (Oxford, 1923), II, pp. 344–5, and E. Nungezer, *Dictionary of Actors ... in England before 1642* (New Haven and London, 1929), pp. 285–7; for Phillips, see P. Thomson, 'Phillips, Augustine (d. 1605)', in *ODNB*, 44, pp. 97–8. Thomson comments that 'the wording of [Phillips's] will makes it clear that he considered himself a gentleman.'

[94] Henry Overton of Dunham (Ches.) owed his appointment as a deputy to the noted forger William Dakins, posing as Norroy King of Arms. Dakins appointed him on 2 Nov. 1579 to be his deputy in Cheshire and Lancashire; the licence with a list of fees for funerals has been printed from Bodleian Library, MS Ashmole 845, f. 157, by W. H. Rylands, 'Some Lancashire and Cheshire Heraldic Documents', *Trans. Historic Soc. of Lancs. & Ches.*, 63 (1912, for 1911), pp. 217–18; see also G. D. Squibb, 'The Deputy Heralds of Chester', *Jnl., Chester Archaeological Soc.*, 56 (1969), pp. 23–36, at 26. For Dakins see further below, p. 143.

WILLIAM SMITH ROUGE DRAGON PURSUIVANT: APPENDIX

Ligh of Lyme.[95] ¶ Sir Edmund Trafford.[96] /f. 10v/ ¶ Sir John Radcliff.[97] ¶ Sir William Bouth of Dunham.[98] And Sir Hugh Cholmley. For this last he had xxiiii $^{li.}$ [99] He hath also made a nomber of Pedegrees.

In Lower Cheshyre atthe Cittie of Chester) was Thomas Chalenor, lately dead (his man <u>Randoll Holme</u>, supplyeth now his Place).[100] This Chalenor had a lettere of Deputacion from W. Dethik late Garter, by couler whereof, he played the herold,[101] the best that ever I heard of (Dakins the great counterfaict herold excepted). As first, Sir Robert Salesbury of Denbighshyre, was buried with viii Banerolls, as if he had bin a Duke.[102] But the funerall of Sir John Savage was so magnificent: That I never knew any nobleman buried with the lyke Pompe. The proceeding wherof I will here set downe, only to be wondred at, (according to the note written with Chalenors owne hand).[103] And so will make an end with Cheshyre.

[95] Sir Piers (Peter) Legh (d. 1590), of Lyme (Ches.).

[96] Sir Edmund Trafford d. 14 May, and was buried in Manchester collegiate church on 21 May, 1590: Hasler, *Commons, 1558–1603*, III, p. 522.

[97] Sir John Ratcliffe, of Ordsall (Lancs.), was buried in Manchester collegiate church on 11 Feb. 1590: Hasler, *Commons, 1558–1603*, III, p. 278.

[98] Sir William Booth d. 8 Nov. 1579: Hasler, *Commons, 1558–1603*, I, p. 456.

[99] Sir Hugh Cholmondleigh (d. 1601) was buried at Malpas (Ches.); cf. *Ches. & Lancs. Funeral Certificates*, ed. J. P. Rylands (Record Soc. of Lancs. & Ches., vi, 1882), pp. 59–60; Hasler, *Commons, 1558–1603*, I, p. 606.

[100] On Thomas Chaloner (d. 1598), painter-stainer and antiquary, see A. R. Wagner and G. D. Squibb, 'Deputy Heralds', in *Tribute to an Antiquary: Essays Presented to Marc Fitch*, ed. F. G. Emmison and R. Stephens (London, 1976), pp. 229–64, at 233, 253-4. Robert Tittler, in *Portraits, Painters and Publics in Provincial England, 1540-1640* (Oxford, 2012), pp. 112–13, n. 38, refers to Chaloner's wider interests as a painter, poet and actor, through his association with the local magnate Henry Stanley, 4th earl of Derby (including performance with the earl's players). Chaloner took as apprentice Randle Holme (1571–1655), the first of a four-generation dynasty of arms-painters of that name; see *ODNB*. Holme's subsequent marriage to his master's widow gained him the business. He was appointed deputy herald for Cheshire, Lancashire and North Wales by William Segar, Norroy King of Arms, on 1 March 1601 (British Library, MS Lansdowne 879, f. 1), and was reappointed in 1603 and 1606: *Ches. & Lancs. Funeral Certificates*, p. vi.

[101] According to his memorial inscription, Chaloner was officially appointed a deputy herald only on the day of his death in 1598; but he had been employed as a deputy on an *ad hoc* basis as early as 1591: see Wagner and Squibb, 'Deputy Heralds', p. 233. Northampton asserted (British Library, MS Add. 23747, f. 31) that Chaloner had a patent from Garter Dethick for three years, renewed for a similar term on expiry.

[102] Cited by Northampton; British Library, MS Add. 23747, f. 32. Salesbury died in Wales on 14 July 1599: Hasler, *Commons, 1558–1603*, III, p. 334.

[103] Sir John Savage (d. 5 Dec. 1597), of Rock Savage (Ches.). Another account of this extravagant funeral, by the first Randle Holme, includes the names of mourners and friends and a note that the funeral work cost £57 10s. 8d: British Library, MS Harley 2129, ff. 64v–65v, printed in *Ches. & Lancs. Funeral Certificates*, pp. vii–x. Holme's version is discussed with details of Savage's career by W. Walters-DiTraglia, 'Death, Commemoration and the Heraldic Funeral in Tudor and Stuart Cheshire and Lancashire: Part II', *Coat of Arms*, 3rd ser., iii (2007), pp. 103–16, at 110–16 and Plate 2.

/f. 11/ ¶ **A copy of the progression, for the funerall of the Right and Most Wo[rshipful] Sir John Savage knight, Lieutenant of the County and Citty of Chester. Buried at Maxfeld** [*i.e.*, Macclesfield], **24. January 1597, anº 40. Elizab[eth].**

First, a Trompetor with a baner of his Armes in silk, sounding a dolefull note.
Secondly, Two yeomen with black staves, for Conductors to the poore: and in one hand a whyte handkercher.
Thirdly, so many poore men, as he was yeares of age, passing by 2. and 2. together orderly, two yardes betwene ech couple. In ech mans hand a Pensell, with his creast on the one syde, some with lyons pawes for Savage: Some with unicorns heads for Daniell: Some with beares heads for Bostock: Some with bores heads for Vernon. And on the other syde of the pensell, the yeare of our Lord he died in, 1597, which pensells afterwards, must be placed about the herse, and in the Chapell, where his body lyeth.
Then another Trompetor, with lyke baner of his Armes, Sounding also some lamentable note.
Then ii yeomen Conductors to his servants, with black staves, and in the one hand, a white handkercher.
Then the Ensigne of his coulers, caried, and somtymes trayled, by a tall yeoman, in a mourning cote.
/f. 11v/ **Then** his yeomen retayners, and houshold servantes, passing orderly by 2. and 2. three yardes betwene ech couple. Ech man witha white handkercher in his hand.
Then a squarbrode baner of his Armes in metall, in token he was her Ma[iesties] Lieutenant, and generall of his Countrey: to be borne by a tall gentleman in a cloke.
Then his gentlemen, reteyners and servantes, by 2. and 2. passing iii yardes asunder, in a moderate pace, with whyte handkerchers in their handes.
Then his Guidon, in respect he was Lieutenant, somtymes borne, and somtymes trayled, by a tall gent. in a cloke, with sundry Creasts thereon, as also his poesy [*i.e.*, motto].
Then the choristers and singing men, in whyte surplesses.
Then the Chapleins and Ministers.
Then the Steward of his house, Clark of his kitchin, and other officers, in their degree.
Then the gentlemen of his bloud and alyances, 2. and 2. bearing baners, whereon was wrought on silk with metall: the cotes of all his Matches Impaled, to say.
First. Sir John Savage knight Lord of Staynsby, in Com. Darby: and Avice, d[aughter] and heire of Walkington.
Secondly Sir John Savage Knight: and Margret doughter and heire of Sir Thomas Daniell, Impaled in metall, on silk.
/f. 12/ **Thirdly** Sir John Savage knighted at Agincourt: and Maud, d[aughter] and heire of Sir Robert Swinerton, Impaled.
Fourthly Sir John Savage knight, who maried Elizabeth d[aughter] to Sir William Brereton of Brereton, also Impaled.

Fyftly Sir John Savage knight, that maried Katherin d[aughter] to Thomas Lord Stanley, steward of house to K. H. 6: sister to Thomas Erle of Darby, high Constable of England.
Sixtly, Sir John Savage k[night] of the garter, that maried Doroty d[aughter] and heire to Sir Raff Vernon knight, Lord of Shipbroke.
Seventhly Sir John Savage knight, who maried Anne doughter and heire of Raff Bostocke Esquire (Sonne and heir of Sir Adam Bostock knight) all on silk, fringed about, wrought on both sydes in metall.
Eightly Sir John Savage knight, that maried Elizabeth d[aughter] to Charles Somerset Erle of Worcest[er], and of Elizabeth d[aughter] and heir to William Herbert Erle of Huntington, and of Mary Woodvile etc. which Charles was naturall sonne to Henry Duke of Somerset, discended from John of Gaunt, Duke of Somerset, father to K. H. 4.
Ninthly Sir John Savage k[night] now deceased, who maried to his first wyff, Elizabeth doughter to Thomas Erle of Rutland.
Tenthly thesame Sir John Savage, and Elenor d[aughter] and heire to John Cotgrave of Chester, gent.
/f. 12v/ **Foure** of these last discents, shalbe placed at the iiii corners of the Corpes: the other vi, in places beffore shewed.
Then an Esquire in a mourning gowne, to carry a playne white staff, in regard he was her Ma[iesties] Lieutenant of the Cittie of Chester: which must be broken, and throwne into the vault with the Corps.
Then a penon, with his Creast and mot [*i.e.*, motto], written.
Then a gent. that shall trayle his lance, made black.
Then his horse covered with black cloth, and Scutcheons of his Armes thereon, beffore and behind, on both sydes, ledd by a gentleman of his Stable.
Then his Word or Mot, caried by a gent.
Then his gilt Spurres, caried by a gent.
Then his Gantletts, caried by a gent.
Then his Helm, Creast, and Mantells, by a gent.
Then his Sword and Targe, caried also by a gent.
Then his Cote of Armes, borne also by a gent., passing a fayre distance, betwene every one.
Then the Preacher, and Phisetion
Then his gentleman usher, bareheaded.
Then Buckram Scutcheons on the horses, that draw the Corps.
Then the Corps, with his owne Armes at ech end, and on both sydes Impaled with both his Ladies, /f. 13/ fayre wrought in gold, silver and other coulers, and about the 4. Corners of the Corps, 4. banerells as afforsaid.
Then the principall mourner by hym self.
Then his children, and sonnes in law.
Then gent. of his bloud, knights, Esquires, and alyances.
Then Frendes and well willers.

Then Tenants, and servants of worshippfull men.

And thus till they came into the Church. Where a place was rayled about the Corps with formes, during the Sermon tyme. On which all the baners were placed. The other monuments heald by the bearers. And so ech bearer offred their severall monuments, **to the Marshall, the King of Armes his Deputie**, to be advanced in their due places, for those purposes made, and erected.

Thus much was sett downe and performed accordingly, by this counterfait herold. But I was told by one which saw this funerall: That after all was done, this Painter took the sheild of the Defunct, shewing the same uunto the people, pointing to every severall Cote, and telling them, by what name, every cote was borne.

/f. 13v/ ¶ **Abuses comitted in Yorkshyre, and Nottinghamshyre.**

William Dakins (the great Counterfait herold)[104] besydes a great number of Armes, which he had granted by Patent, and lyke number of false Pedegrees which he had forged: Confessed of one Swichgaile, to have solemnised, and served as herold, these funeralls following. Edward Bincks,[105] Richard Anyson, and Robert Farebank of York, being Painters for the same work.

The Names of the Gentlemen, and the somes of mony, that the said Counterfait herold had.

Sir William Babthorp, of Osgodby	xvi$^{li.}$		
Sir Marmaduke Constable, of Everingham, and his lady	xxi$^{li.}$	vi$^{s.}$	viii^{d}
Sir Edward Gower and his lady	xxi$^{li.}$	vi$^{s.}$	viii^{d}
Mr Cheek, Secretary of York	xx$^{li.}$		
Mr Meres of York	xviii$^{li.}$		
Mr Haynes of York	xiii$^{li.}$	vi$^{s.}$	viii^{d}
The Lady Beckwith of York	xiii$^{li.}$	vi$^{s.}$	viii^{d}
Mr Ask of Aughton	xxi^{li}		
/f. 14/ Mr Stapleton, of Carleton	vi$^{li.}$	vi$^{s.}$	viii^{d}
Sir Thomas Gray, of Chillingham	xx$^{li.}$		
Mr Crathorne, of Cleveland	viii$^{li.}$		
Mr Wombwell, of Erkingfeld	ii$^{li.}$		
The Lady Malory, of Studley	iiii$^{li.}$		
Sir Thomas Bointon, and his Lady	xxii$^{li.}$		
The Lady Dawney, of Sesey	vi$^{li.}$		
Sir Thomas Dawney	xii$^{li.}$		

---

[104] Le Neve notes in the top margin: 'See the copy of the proceedings at length against him in the Star Chamber dated 13 of Febr. 22 Elizab. [1580] in Mr Hares M:S:S: the thickest with red leaves fol. 215B: 216A'; this MS is now College of Arms, R.36. For a vivid account of Dakins's fraudulent activities, see Wagner, *Heralds of England*, pp. 237–8.

[105] See Wagner and Squibb, 'Deputy Heralds', pp. 243, 248–9, 253. Edward Binks was appointed deputy herald for Yorkshire in 1600 and 1612.

Mr Aclam, of Moreby .... iiii$^{li.}$
Sir Thomas Danby of Cave .... x^{li}
Mr Girlington, of Hackford .... vi$^{li.}$ xiii$^{s.}$ iiii^{d}
Sir Richard Cholmley .... xiii$^{li.}$ vi$^{s.}$ viii^{d}
Mr Witham, of Ledsom .... vi$^{li.}$ xiii$^{s.}$ iiii^{d}
Mr Witham of York... iii$^{li.}$
Mr Estoftes, of Craven .... xiii$^{li.}$ vi$^{s.}$ viii^{d}
Sir Thomas Gargrave and his lady,
    and Sir Cotton Gargrave his sonne .... xxxiii$^{li.}$ xiii$^{s.}$ iiij^{d}
Gervis Cressy of Birkin Esquire... xiii$^{li.}$ vi$^{s.}$ viii^{d}
Mris Grimston, of Smeton .... v^{li}
Mris Metham, of Metham .... v$^{li.}$
Mris Saltmarsh, of Saltmarsh .... iiii$^{li.}$
Richard Barnes, Bishopp of Durham .... xiii$^{li.}$ vi$^{s.}$ viii^{d}
Francis Metham, of Wigginthorp .... v$^{li.}$
Thomas Gower, of Stidnam.. viii$^{li.}$
/f. 14v/ Captaine Bambrough .... xxi$^{li.}$
Captayne Gurley .... ix$^{li.}$
Mr Hutchinson, of Wickham Abbay.................................... iii$^{li.}$ vi$^{s.}$ viii^{d}
Mr Wivell, of Caton.. iij$^{li.}$ vi$^{s.}$ viii^{d}
Mr Wentworth, of Wodersom.. viii$^{li.}$

    ¶ **Funeralls done by Melchor Apsyne, and Samuell his sonne.**
The Lady Geffrey .... x$^{li.}$
Frances Cholmley Esquire .... viii$^{li.}$
Mr Leggard, of Risnam .... vi$^{li.}$ vi$^{s.}$ viii^{d}
Mr Holme, of Paulholme... v$^{li.}$
Mr Ellerker, of Risby... vi$^{li.}$

    ¶ **Funeralls done by Frances Edwards, of Doncaster**
Mr Boswell, of Gouthwate.. xiii$^{li.}$ vi$^{s.}$ viii^{d}
Mr Boswell, of Newhall .... vi$^{li.}$ v$^{s.}$ viii^{d}
Mr Gamelion Drax.. iii$^{li.}$ vi$^{s.}$ viii^{d}
Mr Rockley, ... vi$^{li.}$ xvi$^{s.}$ viii^{d}
Mr Wortley .... viii$^{li.}$
Mr Thornhill, ... x$^{li.}$

/f. 15/¶ **Funeralls done by John Mathew of Nottingham, and Nathan his sonne.**
Mr Sidney of Hull .... xx$^{li.}$
The Lady Ogle .... iiii$^{li.}$
Mr Rookby .... iiii$^{li.}$
Sir Tho. Cokain, of Darbyshire .... xx$^{li.}$
Mr Wentworth .... viii$^{li.}$
Mr Cowper, of Thurgarton .... xiii$^{li.}$ xiii$^{s.}$ iiii^{d}

Mr Siddenham ………………..……………………………………………… xiii^li. vi^s. viii^d

Sir Thomas Stanhopp, of Shelford. **This** funerall was made redy by John Mathew, who had made two Cotes of the defunct, one to be caried, and the other for hym self to weare lyke a herold:[106] But he was prevented by Richard Lee Clarencieux, who ridd to Shelford (standing on this syde the Trent) and served the turne.[107]

¶ **Funeralls done in Lincolnshyre, by Richard Haselwood, of Lincolne.**
¶ Mr Markham, of Sedgebrook.
¶ Mr Tirwitt, of Stanfeld.

Summa totalis of all the mony.   580^li. 5^s. 8^d

Garret Clough of Halifax, a great meddler, and Intruder, in Heroldry. /f. 15v/ William Hilton of Durham: Hardcastle of Newcastle: and John Mathews man, of Nottingham. These Painters presumed at the first to play the herolds, under couler of <u>Mr Garters Letteres of Deputation</u>: But since almost all the Painters in England, have followed their stepps, without any authority at all.

All these funeralls beffore named, (the ii last in Lyncolnshyre \excepted, and Stanhope Nott./)[108] were served in the Province of Norrey. Therfore very fitt, that he, or his Deputy (one of the office) should lye at York, and another at Chester, with authority to correct these Painters.

And now I must say somwhat of the Province of Clarencieux: Least it might be thought, the same were cleere of these Absurdities. /f. 16/

Funeralls Painted by the direction of John Hooker alias Vowell, Chamberlain of Excester. And also by him ordred and served, as if he had byn a Herold, or King of Armes, hymself bearing the Defuncts Cote, and his sonne (or some other by his appointment) to beare the helm and Creast. As is to be proved, aswell by sufficient witnesses: as also by his owne Confession.[109]

¶ Mr Brett, of Whitstanton, in Somersetshyre, buried with these Achevements, following. Helm and Creast, Cote and Penon, **ordynary.** vi Pensells, **extraordinary.**
¶ Mr Strangwaies of Melbury, in Com. Dorset: buried in lyke maner, as Mr Brett was.
¶ Mr Baunfeld of Poltmore, in Com. Devon. Helm and Creast, Cote and Penon, **ordinary.**

---

[106] Sir Thomas Stanhope of Shelford (Notts.), MP for Nottinghamshire, died 1596; see Hasler, *Commons, 1558–1603*, III, pp. 495–6. Mathew's conduct of the funeral was cited by Northampton in his treatise 'A Certeyne Forme of Orders', British Library, MS Add. 23747, ff. 30v–31.

[107] Richard Lee, Clarenceux King of Arms 1594–7; see Godfrey and London, *College of Arms*, pp. 84–5.

[108] Peter le Neve has added to the insertion above the line: 'and Stanhope Notts'.

[109] John Hooker alias Vowell of Exeter, antiquary and civic administrator. For his public career, see S. Mendyk, 'Hooker [Vowell], John (*c.* 1527–1601)', in *ODNB*, 27, pp. 960–3; no mention is made of his predilection for playing the herald. British Library, MS Harley 1567, f. 64^v, has notes by Ralph Brooke, York Herald, taxing Hooker with devising, giving and setting up coats without authority, and his case is among examples of such abuse cited by the earl of Northampton in 'A Certeyne Forme of Orders', British Library, MS Add. 23747, f. 31.

Two Pensells, **extraordinary.**

¶ Mr Kirkham
¶ Mr Popham
¶ Mr Maunsell } These vi. were buried, as Mr Baunfeld was.
¶ Mr Court.
¶ Mr Mallett.
¶ Mr Luttrell.

/f. 16v/ ¶ Sir Robert Denys of Bocton, in Com. Devon. Buried with these Achevements.

Standard, and Penon.
Helme and Creast. } **ordynary.**
Sword and Targett.
Cote of Armes.

A great Baner
A Penon of St George. } **extraordynary**
iiii Pensells

¶ Sir George Siddenham, of Coomb Siddenham, in Com. Somerset, buried lyke Sir Robert Denis.

¶ Sir John Clifton, of Barington, co. Somerset.

Standard and Penon.
Helm and Creast. } **ordynary.**
Sword and Targett.
Cote of Armes.

A great Baner
Two Banerolls } **extraordynary**
A Penon of St George
Two Pensells.

/f. 17/ ¶ Sir John Gilbert, of Greenway, in Com. Devon. Buried in the Cathedrall Church of Excester.

Standard and Penon.
Helm and Creast. } **ordynary.**
Sword and Targett.
Cote of Armes.

A great Baner, of his owne Armes
A baner of St George, with a rose in the cross } **extraordynary**
A Penon of St George
Two Pensells

And for hym was sett upp a Barons hearse, in the Chapell where he was buried, all covered with Searge downe to the ground, The valance having a deepe black silk fringe, all full of Scutcheons, which stood so, a whole yeare.

This Hooker named him self Excester Herold, and did weare a Cote of Armes. He hath made above xl. gentlemen, by geving them Armes belonging to their name: Although

nothing to their Famely.

/f. 17v/ There is a Painter named Tyler, dwelling at Radcliff, who hath the Painting of the Shipps in the Thames.[110] Which Tyler is no workman him self: But setteth other men on work. And they make the Kinges Armes on the Sterne of the shipps, with Silver helmetts (somtymes but with Steele Helmetts) The Mantells Redd and Whyte. Which helme ought to be gold: as also the Mantells of gold, lyned with ermin. This is both a disgrace to the Armes, and also an indignitie to his Ma[iestie] to have his Armes so painted on Shippes, which go into strange and farr Countreis. I told the painter of it: Who answered me, that the owners would not go to the charges, to have them done with gold.

There are also some Gentlemen in the countrey (that I do know) who make Pedegrees, Devise and Confirme, both Cotes and Creasts. And do kepe Painters in their houses, for the same purposes.

/f. 18/ **The** Provinciall Kinges of Armes, have heretofore had commission to visitt in their Provinces. And to correct and controll, all Armes, Creasts and Pedegrees. with these wordes of prohibition for workmen, <u>That no Painter, Graver, Goldsmith, Marbler, nor Glasier shall medle with Armes, Creastes, Cognizances, or Pedegrees, without consent of the King of Armes of the Province: or of his Deputie, or Deputies.</u> **But** now a dayes so soone as any Gent. is dead: The Painter getteth the work, beffore any herold knoweth of it. And so, if the Armes be not right: the herold hath the blame. As at this present, Scarlet (the Arch painter of London for Armes)[111] had the funerall of Sir Francis Gawdy to make, vi weekes beffore any composition was made with Mr Clarencieux.[112] And so, the last funerall I served (which was <u>Sir George Harvy, Lieutenant of the Tower, buried at Rumford</u>), The painter had made the worke without consent of any herold, as appeared by 2. or 3. Cotes not right Marshalled, and in wrong coulers. Yet must it Pass for currant, because he was buried with heroldes.[113]

Whensoever it shall happen the said Kinges of Armes to make their Visitacions: They shall fynd many more Abuses and Absurdities, then I have here /f. 18v/ noted, especially in the churches. As in S^t. Mary Abchurch in London, one Mansbridge a Draper is Buried only with a Baneroll, and a Penon of his Armes slitt at the end, lyke a Standerd. **And** amongst the Companies (or Corporations in London) they shall fynd many abuses.

[110] Tyler has not been identified; the riverside hamlet of Ratcliff was in Stepney (Middx.).

[111] Richard Scarlett (d. 1607), prominent London painter-stainer, antiquary and collector of manuscripts. See L. Campbell and F. W. Steer, *Catalogue of Manuscripts in the College of Arms*, I: *Collections* (London, 1988), pp. 240–2 and 245–6. His name is recorded in royal accounts for those undertaking work for the Court in 1578, 1580 and 1605: Susan Foister, 'Foreigners at Court; Holbein, Van Dyck and the Painter-Stainers Company', in *Art and Patronage in the Caroline Courts: Essays in Honour of Oliver Millar*, ed. David Howarth (1995), pp. 32–50, at 35 and 46 n. 20.

[112] Sir Francis Gawdy, judge, died of apoplexy on 15 December 1605 but was not buried until 27 February 1606; see D. Ibbetson, 'Gawdy, Sir Francis (d. 1605)', in *ODNB*, 21, pp. 663–4.

[113] Sir George Harvy (Harvey), Lieutenant of the Tower, died 10 August 1605; the funeral was 5 Sept 1605.

WILLIAM SMITH ROUGE DRAGON PURSUIVANT: APPENDIX

For first, xii of the cheiffest thereof: are named **The xii. Worshippfull Companies.** Because the Lord Maior, must be alwais one of the same xii. And therfore some reason to have supporters. But here I must blame Clarencieux Cook, for geving of Supporters to base Companies. As a Roe Buck and a Ramme to the Lethersellers: Two Sea Horses to the Pewterers: Two Buckes to the Whyte Bakers: Two Unicornes to the Waxchandlers: Two Whyte Horses to the Sadlers: A golden Buck, and a Silver Gote to the Curriers (supporters beseeming a nobleman of great estate): Two Dragons to the Plasterers. And yet the cheiffest Company (which is the Mercers) hath none. Neither yet the Iremongers, nor Vintners, being also of the xii. Therfore do I see no reason, why these Inferior Companies /f.19/ ought to have any supporters at all. It was but the corruption of the said Clarencieux, who would never suffer a man to enioy his ancient Armes: if he could perswade hym to a new. The lyke blame also, for geving away the Armes of ancient gentlemen: to new startup fellows.

They shall also fynd them, that use other mens Armes in steed of their owne: yea some Aldermen lately knighted. As this last yeare, one did sett upp in sundry places of his house, and on the Table of the officers names: his wyves Armes. And writt underneath the same, **Sir Thomas Hayes knight, and Sheriff of London.**[114]

And so fearing I have bin over tedious: I do humbly crave pardon. Beseeching your good Lordshipp that some good course may be taken, for the quietnes of the said Office of Armes. Or some act of parliament established, for restraint of these Painters from Playing the herold. And we all (according to our bounden duties) shall dayly pray unto Almighty God, for the happy estate of your good Lordshipp long to endure.

FINIS[115]
By William Smith. Rouge Dragon[116]

---

[114] V.a.157. *The sentence beginning* 'As this last yeare' *crossed through with a marginal note*: 'Leave this quyte out'. 'Sir Thomas Hayes knight' *deleted*. Smith appears to have changed his mind about whether he ought to include this passage concerning a prominent City of London worthy. Sir Thomas Hayes (d. 1617), a merchant and member of the Drapers' Company, was elected an alderman and knighted in 1603, and was subsequently Sheriff of London, 1604–5, and Mayor, 1614–15. Peter le Neve annotates: 'Hayes, Sir Tho. set up his wifes arms for his own Posted to He[nry] Pecham,1633 page 195. See his son ment[ioned] in the visitation of Northamptonshire'.

[115] V.a.157 *ends*: 'your Lordships Most humble in all dutie | W. S. R. Dragon'.

[116] Written in the italic hand of Sir Robert Cotton (d. 1631).

Grants and Confirmations of Arms

CLIVE CHEESMAN

Before 1673, the three senior heralds of England – known since their medieval origins as kings of arms – operated as independent agents of the Crown. Each was individually empowered upon his appointment to issue patents concerning heraldry to the Crown's subjects, both personal and corporate, under the nominal supervision of the Earl Marshal. Some patents granted new coats of arms, while some confirmed the recipient's right to existing arms; they also dealt with rank and status, purporting to confer or confirm gentility or (to use a word still regarded as interchangeable with it at the start of the sixteenth century) 'noblesse'. Patents were also issued to foreigners, and it appears that arms were sometimes granted or confirmed by means of other instruments such as certificates. The kings of arms might act in concert, but more often did so singly – indeed, they were frequently in open, even hostile, competition with each other. The records at the College of Arms of patents and certificates from this period, today known collectively but misleadingly as 'Old Grants', are a confused and disparate mass, but they have an as yet unmined potential for the social and cultural history of late medieval and early modern life in England, Wales and beyond.

The year 1673 saw the then Earl Marshal impose a degree of order and co-operation on the system of granting and recording arms; with relatively few modifications this system prevails to the present day. This chapter looks at the preceding era, the era of 'Old Grants' – and particularly at the central phase, from the accession of Henry VIII to the death of James I.

Ramping to Gentility

Two well-known passages from different genres of Elizabethan literature, history and drama, characterize the granting of arms in the period. Both will bear looking at again, for both, in co-operative and contrasting ways, assist in giving form and direction to a survey of the phenomenon.

In his densely learned 'Historicall Description', prefaced to the 1577 and 1587 editions of Holinshed's *Chronicles*,[1] the historian and antiquary William Harrison wrote:

> Who soever studieth the lawes of the realme, who so abideth in the universitie giving his mind to his booke, or professeth physicke and the liberall sciences, or beside his service in the roome of a capteine in the warres, or good counsell given at home, whereby his

---

[1] William Harrison, 'A Historicall Description of the Island of Britain', in Raphael Holinshed, *Chronicles* (London, 1587), book 1, p. 162. Quoted at greater length, from F. J. Furnivall, *Harrison's Description of England in Shakspere's Youth* (London, 1877), by Wagner, *Heralds of England*, p. 187.

commonwealth is benefitted, can live without manuell labour, and thereto will bear the port, charge and countenance of a gentleman, he shall for monie have a cote and armes bestowed upon him by heralds (who in the charter of the same doo of custome pretend antiquitie and service, and manie gaie thinges) and thereunto being made so good cheape be called master, which is the title that men give to esquiers and gentlemen, and reputed for a gentleman ever after.

Harrison was a serious student of universal history.[2] Drawing parallels with ancient civilizations, he approved the general principle by which learned men, physicians and servants of the state were elevated to the state of gentility; but his description of how it was achieved in the England of his own day has an unmistakably ironic, even sardonic, flavour.

The second passage is the scene in which the clownish Sogliardo, in Jonson's *Every Man Out of His Humour* (1599),[3] displays his new coat of arms to his carping friends:

> SOG: [...] by this Parchment Gentlemen, I have ben so toil'd among the Harrots [Heralds] yonder, you will not beleeve, they doe speake the straungest language, and give a man the hardest termes for his money, that ever you knew.
> CARLO: But ha' you armes? ha' you armes?
> SOG: Yfaith, I thanke God I can write myself Gentleman now, here's my Pattent, it cost me thirtie pound by this breath.

Jonson's characters confirm what is suggested by Harrison, that a grant of arms was in some way a conferment of gentility. Like Harrison, furthermore, they draw attention – repeatedly – to the exchange of money that accompanied the grant. Where Harrison smiled knowingly, Jonson calls for open laughter. That wealth accompanied status was customary and natural; but the traditional pattern had been for money to accrue to dignity. Too obvious an inversion of this pattern, as when money is scraped together to purchase dignity, was a source of humour. It was the very stuff that satire was made of.

The view that a grant of arms conferred gentility is often encountered in this period, not least in the grants themselves and in other writings of the kings of arms and the heralds who worked with them. Indeed, not long before, it had been possible for a grant of arms to be spoken of as a 'graunt of noblesse'.[4] Now grants of arms had sometimes been made in the context of an ennoblement – that was to be the usual context in some continental jurisdictions – but it has been argued that the two things were always distinct and separate in England, and that the kings of arms did not have power to confer rank.[5] That may have been technically so, and certainly the subsequent doctrine was that a grant of arms was a recognition of gentility (or higher rank) rather than a bestowal of it: a man needed to be a gentleman to qualify for arms, he did not become one by virtue of the

---

[2] Since Wagner wrote, the 'genially prolix' Harrison conjured up by Furnivall's 'selective mining of the picturesque, "Merry England" sections' of his work has been questioned: Glyn Parry, 'Harrison, William (1535–1593)', in *ODNB*, 25, pp. 538–9.
[3] Act III, scene i.
[4] By Thomas Benolt, Clarenceux King of Arms, 1531: PRO, SP 1/73/187.
[5] Sir George Sitwell, 'The English Gentleman', *The Ancestor*, i (April 1902), pp. 58–102, at 80–1.

grant of arms. But the fact is that even if this distinction held in the sixteenth century, the language used to speak of grants of arms frequently obscured it, and throughout the period that concerns us, debate about the subject is coloured by the notion that a grant of arms was in some measure the attainment of a social status. Whether they were bestowing gentility itself or (in Harrison's more sophisticated, but perhaps in practical terms not very different construction) a visible mark of its 'repute', the kings of arms were conferring something beyond mere legal rights of ownership in a graphic design.

However, the question of the graphic design cannot easily be sidelined. If we return to Sogliardo and his friends, we find them examining the arms on his patent.

> PUNTAROLO: A very faire Coat, well charg'd and full of Armorie.
> SOG: Nay, it has as much varietie of colours in it, as you have seene a Coat have, how like you the Crest, Sir?
> PUNT: I understand it not well, what is it?
> SOG: Marry, Sir, it is your Bore without a head rampant.
> PUNT: A Bore without a head, that's very rare.
> CARL: I, and Rampant too: troth I commend the Heralds wit, he has deciphered him well: A Swine without a head, without braine, wit, any thing indeed, Ramping to Gentilitie. You can blazon the rest signior? can you not?
> SOG: O, I, I have it in writing here of the purpose, it cost me two shillings the tricking.
> PUNT: It is the most vile, foolish, absurd, palpable, and ridiculous Escutcheon that ever eye survis'd. Save you good Master *Fastidius*.
> CARL: Silence good knight: on, on.
> SOG: GYRONY of eight peeces, AZURE and GULES, betweene three plates a CHEV'RON, engrail'd checky, OR, VERT, and ERMINES; on a cheefe ARGENT between two Ann'lets, SABLES, a Bores head, PROPER.

Jonson has deliberately described a truly awful piece of heraldry, overloaded with elements and, in its unharmonious colours, purposefully resembling a clown's motley.[6] But Puntarolo may have exaggerated: it is not so outlandish that it might not have been inspired by genuine grants from earlier in the century and therefore be intended to satirize newly-bought coats of arms. The point is that the design is shown as mattering, as being something that people looked at. The visual side of a patent of arms, and of the arms that it granted or confirmed, is something that needs to be taken seriously too. It was, after all, serious enough to be open to satire in its own right.

The Prerogative of the Kings of Arms

In the Early Modern period, as subsequently, the right to issue patents granting or confirming arms was understood as being delegated to kings of arms. But long and intricate disputes impeded clarity as to which kings of arms had this prerogative and to what extent each one's rights were qualified by those of the others; these typically collegiate disputes were complicated further by temporary agreements and the deaths or absences of the parties, all the while being subject to the intermittently exercised authority of the Earl Marshal, and exacerbated by a vituperative, irrational and

[6] '... of as many colours, as e'er you saw any fooles coat in your life'.

damagingly competitive spirit that practically constitutes a College of Arms tradition.

Thus while it was clear that the rights of two kings of arms, Clarenceux and Norroy, were, in relation to each other, exclusive in their 'provinces' (south and north of the river Trent respectively), it was not certain what powers of granting arms, if any, were inherent in the senior office of the three, Garter king of arms. A practical solution to this uncertainty was found by Thomas Wriothesley, who was appointed to the Gartership on his father's death in 1505. Wriothesley (born Writhe) made agreements with successive provincial kings of arms to share their duties of granting and indeed visiting (though he never undertook a visitation); his powers to grant were further strengthened by new statutes of the Order of the Garter in 1522 and he made abundant use of them, issuing numerous coats of arms in a distinctive new style of design. For most of his period in office Wriothesley's colleague as Clarenceux was Thomas Benolt, who until 1530 was largely occupied with foreign missions and therefore issued patents relatively rarely. Wriothesley's busy staff kept records of the arms he granted, alongside (and frequently intermixed with) the records of pre-existing arms that he was also keen to compile; as a result, his grants are sometimes hard to disentangle and have not always figured as prominently in the statistics as they should – but it is clear that for two decades or more he dominated the process of granting arms (Fig. 10).[7] He might even be suspected of having given it – for good or ill – the form and the character that it was to retain throughout the Early Modern period.

Wriothesley's contractual arrangement with Benolt did not last. In 1530 Clarenceux successfully asserted his right to conduct visitations on his own; the visitation commission issued by the king also permitted him, in the course of visitations, to grant arms within his province.[8] Norroy did not receive such a commission, but went on to act as though he had. Wriothesley, excluded from this new enterprise, responded bitterly that the right to grant arms had always been Garter's alone, exercised by provincial kings on his sufferance and on condition that they submit records of their grants to him. The dispute escalated and continued beyond the deaths of Wriothesley and Benolt in 1534. But the tide of royal opinion had turned against the Gartership and in 1539 Wriothesley's successor, Christopher Barker, signed an agreement in Chapter whereby only the provincial kings would make grants, and any gentleman seeking arms from Garter would be redirected to the relevant one of the two, Garter retaining a fee of two marks.[9] This sum was one fifth of the fee then recommended for a wealthy gentleman, so it was not a negligible sum; but the agreement still represented a considerable concession by Garter.

In fact, however, Barker continued to issue patents after 1539. It may be that he frequently drafted his patents as confirmations and thereby avoided infringing the letter

---

[7] Wagner, *Heralds and Heraldry*, 2nd edn. (London, 1956), pp. 83–7; idem, *Heralds of England*, pp. 159–66.
[8] Wagner, *Heralds and Heraldry*, pp. 9–11.
[9] College of Arms, MS R. 36, ff. 148v–150. Summarized by Wagner, *Heralds of England*, pp. 179–80.

10. Page from a vellum armorial compiled in the office of Sir Thomas Wriothesley (Garter King of Arms, 1505–34), showing coats of arms confirmed or granted by Wriothesley himself. Several of the shields and crests show the distinctively intense design style that he favoured. One shield is quartered: this will be a case in which Wriothesley issued a confirmation of male-line arms and the right to quarter different arms inherited in a female line. College of Arms, MS L.10, f. 92v.

of his agreement. But in some cases, where the full text of the patent survives, we can see that he did openly grant arms in both provinces: for instance, his patents to John Aylworth of Somerset in 1546[10] and Robert Stanysby of County Durham in 1543.[11] In other cases we know that he granted arms only because they were subsequently revised or replaced by later kings of arms.[12]

The continuing activity of Barker and his successor in the Gartership, Gilbert Dethick, certainly led to further friction and drew the Earl Marshal – the heralds' overseer and protector – into the fray. Before the mid sixteenth century, the Earl Marshal's control over the exercise by the kings of arms of their prerogative to grant arms seems to have been general, rather than specific: as we will see, he laid down fees, and he also ruled that Clarenceux and Norroy should not grant arms outside their respective provinces. Within these limits the kings' discretion seems to have been unfettered. But early in the reign of Elizabeth, Thomas Howard, 4th duke of Norfolk and Earl Marshal since 1554 (who had engineered the grant of Derby House to the heralds under Mary, and whom Wagner describes as the 'real founder' of the College of Arms[13]), set about trying to change this (Fig. 11). The first move seems to have been in 1561, the same year that saw the visitations re-established on a methodical basis. According to Dethick, at a Chapter held at Christ Church (the old Greyfriars church, in Newgate) on 22 April that year, in the presence of the Earl of Sussex, the Earl Marshal commanded that the kings were to issue no patent of arms without his consent, and were to submit to him a list of the grants they had made since the start of the reign.[14] Writing in 1563 or 1564, Dethick claimed that he had complied – and in fact we have his list of grants for the first two and a half years of the reign, a rather paltry sixteen in number[15] – but that Clarenceux, William Hervey, had never submitted any list and had simply carried on granting regardless, without the Earl Marshal's permission. The Earl Marshal had evidently foreseen the possibility of disobedience: the patent of appointment of a new Norroy king of arms, William Flower, in January 1562, had for the first time ever contained a term limiting the appointee's right to grant arms, with the words *'cum consensu et assensu Comitis Marescalli'*.[16] But Hervey was bound by no such clause.

[10] College of Arms, MS EDN 56, f. 2. Original patent: British Library, Add. Charter 8661.
[11] College of Arms, MS Old Grants, 2/118. Original patent: private collection.
[12] Grant of new arms and crest by Clarenceux and Norroy to Sir Ralph Sadleir, 1576; discussed below, p. 99.
[13] Wagner, *Heralds of England*, p. 182.
[14] College of Arms, MS Vincent 92, pp. 482–5. Discussed and transcribed, P. L. Gwynn-Jones, 'Tudor Enigmas', *Coat of Arms*, 3rd ser., i (2005), pp. 73–104, at 79–82 and 98–103. The document and the Chapter of 22 April 1561 seem to have been unknown to Wagner.
[15] College of Arms, MS Vincent's Old Grants 1 (= MS Vincent 157 or 178), f. 219. Gwynn-Jones, 'Tudor Enigmas', pp. 81, 103–4.
[16] Wagner, *Heralds of England*, p. 120. Flower's list of grants made between his appointment and the end of the fourth year of the reign is at PRO, SP 12/35, art. 35; printed in 'Grants of Arms', *Yorkshire Archaeological Jnl.*, xviii (1905), pp. 342–52, at 351–2.

11. Thomas Howard (d. 1572), duke of Norfolk, Earl Marshal. Unknown Anglo-Dutch artist, oil on panel. A poorly preserved inscription dates the picture to 1565, the year in which Norfolk successfully asserted his control over the heralds and they moved into Derby House, which he had procured for them. He was 27 years old; seven years later he was executed. National Portrait Gallery.

GRANTS AND CONFIRMATIONS OF ARMS

Perhaps as a result of Dethick's complaint, the Earl Marshal reasserted his authority in February 1565, just as the heralds were (after many delays) moving into Derby House. He declared once again that the kings were to make no grant or gift of new arms to any person, by patent or otherwise, without his consent, or – in his absence – that of the Earl of Leicester, Sir William Cecil or some other appointed deputy.[17] In May 1567 he ensured that the appointment of Robert Cooke as Clarenceux included a clause similar to the one in Norroy's patent. And in July 1568, more orders followed. Of wide import for establishing once and for all the Marshal's authority over the officers of arms, these contained further provisions as to grants. They ordained that all new grants or confirmations of arms and crests must be made by all three kings acting together, and that all grants of arms (though not of crests, or confirmations) needed his consent; every December the kings were to bring him a register containing copies of all the patents granted in that year.[18]

The Earl Marshal's provisions of 1561, 1565 and 1568 as to grants did not have the intended lasting effect. For a short period grants were indeed made by all three kings, and cited 'the assent and consent of the high and mighty Prince Thomas Duke of Norfolk Erle Mareschall of Englande'.[19] But a desire not to have to seek consent may, in fact, have led the kings to draft their patents as confirmations (or as confirmations of arms and grants of a crest); the confirmation, already a tempting option for the way it flattered the recipient, was now attractive for procedural reasons. And it seems to have been decided soon, if not at once, that where consent was not needed, a king of arms could act alone. Grants by the kings acting in concert soon became – as they had been before – a rarity.

Other events were, in any case, to intervene. In October 1569 Norfolk was imprisoned; in June 1572 he was executed. The marshalcy passed to the much less interventionist (and generally absentee) Earl of Shrewsbury and it was doubtless felt that the ordinances of the 1560s no longer applied.[20] Nonetheless, the Earl Marshal's consent does seem to have been sought on occasion. In 1587 Robert Cooke, as Clarenceux, stated in a grant of arms to Sir Christopher Wray that he was making the grant on the instructions of the Earl Marshal (*præceperit ut ... insignia quædam honorabilia ... assignarem*).[21] At about the same time, Robert Glover (Somerset Herald) appears to have drafted a letter of reference to the Earl Marshal recommending one William Farrand of Skipton for a grant.[22] A patent confirming arms and a quartering was duly issued.[23]

---

[17] College of Arms, MS Heralds III, p. 1224. Wagner, *Heralds of England*, p. 187.

[18] College of Arms, MS 4/3; printed by G. D. Squibb, *Munimenta Heraldica* (Harleian Soc. Publications, n.s. 4, 1985), pp. 97–105; discussed by Wagner, *Heralds of England*, p. 197.

[19] To quote the grant to Thomas Kitson, 13 February 1569: Cambridge University Library, MS Hengrave 65.

[20] Although Shrewsbury did, in 1585, express displeasure about the state of the record-keeping of the kings of arms, and may have asked for a list of recent patents: Ramsay, *Robert Glover*, forthcoming, Appces iv and vi.

[21] Bodleian Library, MS Ashmole 834, ff. 66v–67.

[22] College of Arms, MS Glover A, f. 184; printed by Ramsay, *Robert Glover*, forthcoming, Chapter

Glover's letter on behalf of Farrand, addressing Shrewsbury as *ex officio* 'the Princes eye, to take knowledge of well desearvinge persons' and asking him to interpose his authority with Norroy, is all the more striking for its recipient's noted lack of interest in the heralds' activities. Norroy at this time was Glover's father-in-law, William Flower, and it is inconceivable that the letter could have been drafted other than at his instigation. Presumably, for some reason we cannot now guess, Flower needed or wanted especially authoritative back-up for this grant, in case its propriety or his jurisdiction were challenged, and the Earl Marshal was a convenient source to draw it from. We cannot know how often this practice was followed (the text of the patent as issued to Farrand makes no reference to the Earl Marshal) but it most probably remained exceptional.

On Shrewsbury's death in 1590 the marshalcy went into commission and for much of the next eighty years it flowed back and forth between commissioners and brief tenures by great nobles with relatively little interest in the day-to-day business of the heralds – a rhythm interrupted only by the long *fermata* of the Interregnum. However, the attempts by the Earl Marshal to impose order in the 1560s, and the methods adopted by the kings to sidestep those attempts, are revealing, and really only make sense if one takes seriously the notion that the process concerned the conferment or grant of gentility. Not only does it explain the gravity of the procedure as a whole and the need to control it.[24] It also accounts for the different treatment consistently accorded to confirmations, by all parties including the Earl Marshal. On the face of it, grants and confirmations are very similar productions. As physical documents they require very similar resources and preparation, and both represent formal acts of a king of arms made by the authority of his patent of appointment. So why did the Earl Marshal consistently exempt confirmations from his attempts to exert control? It seems odd (especially given the ease with which kings of arms could redraft a grant as a confirmation). But if it was seriously believed that gentility was actually being conferred by virtue of a grant – but not by a confirmation – the distinction becomes clear. If, on the other hand, a grant of arms had been merely something that could be issued to someone who was already a gentleman, it would itself be little more than a confirmation; to subject the one to control, the other not, would be irrational.

For the kings of arms, by contrast, the confirmation of a person's right to arms was a way to establish their arms without implying that they had not hitherto been of gentle status. The vagaries of record keeping – as we shall see – and the simple historical reality that many coats of arms had been self-assumed by undoubted gentry made it easy to claim that a coat of arms had long been in use already. Confirming arms, rather than granting them, now relieved the kings of a tedious procedural obligation. The attractions were clear.

4, item (f).
[23] Bodleian Library, MS Ashmole 844, f. 68v: 20 March 1587.
[24] Wagner, *Heralds of England*, p. 164, with reference to Lawrence Stone on Henry VIII's serious concern for the maintenance of hierarchy.

GRANTS AND CONFIRMATIONS OF ARMS

The Patent of Arms

What was it exactly that patentees paid for? And indeed how much did they pay? The evidence is that a sliding scale was used, reflecting the grantee's wealth. At some point between 1524 and 1533 an order from the Earl Marshal laid down both who was entitled to a grant and what they should pay.[25] A man (not a clergyman) with property in land or feudal incidents over £100 was to pay £6 13s. 4d (ten marks). If he was worth less than that sum in land, but was still of substance, or if he had 1,000 marks in movable property, £6; if his worth was still less, £5. The higher clergy (bishops, abbots and priors of great possessions) were to pay £10, abbots and priors of mean possessions ten marks, and lower clergy (beneficed to a value not below £100) £5. The fee of £10 was also set down for incorporated 'crafts' – the merchants' and tradesmen's livery companies of the city of London and elsewhere.

By 1637, it seems, the sums had risen considerably. The Garter of the day seems to have charged not less than £20 for a coat of arms; for supporters (the animal or human figures shown flanking the arms of noblemen or great corporations), the sum was £10.[26] And in 1673 the standard fee for a new grant was £30, with £10 being charged for a crest alone and £10 for an alteration to arms. Importantly, it is noted that these were fees intended for the kings of arms; the scrivening, painting and recording of the grant were charged separately, and will have added to these sums.[27] We do not know the details of the inflationary curve between the 1530s and the 1670s, but Sogliardo, 'well charg'd' £30 in 1599, may not in fact have paid too much over the odds.

Clearly patents of arms were meant to be eye-catching documents from the outset. Done on vellum, surviving examples are large (rarely less than fifteen inches in breadth) and usually have generous borders. The coat of arms being granted or confirmed is always painted and given a prominent position. In the continental tradition, where grants of arms usually emanated from rulers' chancelleries rather than from heralds or kings of arms, the arms being granted stood in the centre of the document, with the text around.[28] This is seen even in grants made by foreign sovereigns to English subjects: thus the imperial patent to Matthew Trystram in 1467, given at London, places the granted arms in the middle of the dense block of text.[29] This practice was still observed in English patents of arms issued directly by the Crown in the fifteenth century, such as Henry VI's grants to Eton and King's College Cambridge in 1449 and Edward IV's grant to Louis

[25] College of Arms, MS R. 36 (= Hare 1), ff. 179v–180: transcript made by Richard Lee, Clarenceux, 1591. Printed by J. Dallaway, *Inquiries into the Origin and Progress of the Science of Heraldry in England* (Gloucester, 1793), pp. 170–1; discussed by Wagner, *Heralds of England*, pp. 119–20, 166–7.
[26] College of Arms, MS Heralds VI, f. 357; Wagner, loc. cit.
[27] College of Arms, MS I. 25, ff. 125, 148v. Wagner, loc. cit.
[28] See e.g. *Wappen und Kleinod. Wappenbriefe in öffentlichen Archiven Südtirols*, ed. G. Pfeifer, Veröffentlichungen des Südtiroler Landesarchivs, 11 (Bolzano, 2001), p. 18; Ghislain Brunel, *Les chartes décorées des Archives Nationales, XIIIe – XVe siècle* (Paris, 2005), pp. 30–2.
[29] British Library, MS Add. 37687A.

de Bruges, earl of Winchester in 1472.[30] Patents from the kings of arms, however, from the outset consistently have the arms in the left or upper left margin, sometimes in earlier cases actually within the initial letter of the text: thus the elegant tracery T of the opening phrase 'To alle nobeles and gentiles' in a 1468 patent from William Hawkeslowe, Clarenceux, encloses the arms that the document is granting to one John Parys.[31] I have seen only one exception to the general rule: a very elegant patent from Gilbert Dethick, Garter, confirming arms and granting a new crest to Edward Hoby in 1570 rather strikingly has the arms and crest in question in the middle of the text.[32] But the normal practice was so generally observed that by the seventeenth century even royal grants were placing the arms in the upper left margin.[33]

The borders, as noted, were usually generous; they were also frequently decorated, with an increasingly standardized repertoire of scroll work, floral motifs, ribbons (sometimes bearing mottoes) and occasional architectural features such as obelisks or pillars and capitals. By the start of the seventeenth century, when grants were being made in great numbers, the same basic border designs recur often; it is probable that kings had stocks of vellums with ready done borders, awaiting the insertion of the text of the grant and a painting of the arms being granted. From time to time, however, something special could be provided. William Dethick's grant of arms to the town of Eye (Suff.) in 1592 has the arms of thirteen members of the town corporation in the margins.[34] A patent of 1598 from Dethick and Camden, confirming arms to the brothers Robert and William Herick (and purporting to replace one originally drafted by Clarenceux Lee years earlier but lost before it could be issued or recorded) has in the border the arms of the brothers' father and mother and the latter's parents.[35] The grant by all three kings in 1621 to Augustine Vincent, Rouge Croix Pursuivant, is surrounded by an armorial pedigree showing his kinship with Sir Francis Vincent, Bt.[36] This sort of thing was risky: including arms for decorative purposes in the border of a grant of arms inevitably gave the

---

[30] Original patents at Eton and King's respectively. Bruges: British Library, MS Egerton 2830; printed by W. H. St J. Hope, 'On a Grant of Arms Under the Great Seal of Edward IV to Louis de Bruges', *Archaeologia*, lvi (1898–9), pp. 27–38.

[31] Original grant, private collection. Patents in French (beginning *A tous presens et advenir* or similar) did not have this option, since the barred A was not roomy enough; but an early Latin patent commencing *Universis Christi fidelibus* does manage to insert the arms being granted to Peter Hellard in the initial U: British Library, MS Add 37687B, Thomas Holme, Norroy, to Peter Hellard, 1 October 1469; printed [by H. B. McCall(?)], 'Grants of Arms', *Yorkshire Archaeological Jnl.*, xviii (1905), pp. 109–22, at 110–11.

[32] Original grant: private collection.

[33] Thus (e.g.) the royal patents to Sir Martin Tromp, 1642 (The Hague: Nationalarchief), Sir Arnulph L'Isle, 1646 (British Library, Add. Ch. 4115) and Colonel William Carlos, 1658 (at College of Arms).

[34] Original patent: Ipswich, Suffolk Record Office, EE2/C/1. Draft at College of Arms, MS Vincent Old Grants 1 (Vincent 157 or 178), f. 234.

[35] Original patent: Leicestershire Record Office, DG9/2572.

[36] Original patent at College of Arms.

impression of confirming their validity, and Dethick was to be upbraided for the marginal heraldry in the Herick document by his colleagues, who presumably rejected the story of the earlier, lost patent.[37]

Often present in the upper border of a patent of arms from the mid sixteenth century were symbols indicative of the ultimate authority by which it was issued: the arms of the sovereign, or a selection of royal badges, usually crowned and often surrounded by the Garter. The granting kings of arms might also ensure that they were themselves represented, by their own arms of office, sometimes impaled with their personal arms (or occasionally their personal arms alone); there might also be a portrait of the king of arms within the opening initial of the text, usually full-length and gesturing with his wand towards the arms he was granting or confirming.

The king of arms issuing the patent was of course responsible for the text of the document, though it is clear that some farmed the drafting work out to colleagues or juniors who, in some cases, developed a specialism in the area: one expert draftsman in this period was Robert Glover, Somerset Herald from 1570 to 1588, who seems to have been involved in many formal acts by both his father-in-law Flower, Norroy King of Arms, and also Robert Cooke, the prolific Clarenceux of the same era. The oldest English grants of arms were in French; but by the early sixteenth century the majority were in the vernacular, and French virtually died out as an option.[38] From the middle of the sixteenth to the later seventeenth a sizable minority of grants were in Latin, though not all heralds had equal mastery of the language, and men like Glover were probably quite widely called on to draft grants in it. Even for specialists, however, blazoning in Latin (or rather in jargon-rich neo-Latin) presented a challenge; some saw this as an interesting intellectual puzzle, while others sidestepped it – for instance, Camden generally turned to French when he got to the blazon.[39] And even leaving aside the technicalities of the blazon, the choice of language did not usually reflect or determine the drafting, which generally proceeded along fairly traditional lines. On rare occasions a Latin grant might be drafted with more than usual attention to classical idiom, and this could prompt a radically different approach; the remarkable and little studied 1598 grant by Camden and Segar in memory of John Foxe is a case in point, beginning with a lengthy and rhetorical preamble on the theme of the ephemeral character of glory.[40] In this case and a very few others, language, idiom and style informed and reinforced each other; in most cases the linguistic choice seems arbitrary, and nothing in Glover's papers or in John Gibbon's chatty essay *Introductio ad Blasoniam Latinam* tells us why some grants were

---

[37] College of Arms, MS R. 21, f. 284.
[38] A late instance is the grant by Bysshe as Parliament-appointed Garter (calling himself Edoüard de la Biche) to Sir John Wittewronge, 27 November 1648: Hertfordshire Archives, D/ELW/F14.
[39] As noted by John Gibbon, *Introductio ad Blasoniam Latinam* (London, 1682), p. [i].
[40] College of Arms, MS Camden's Grants 2, f. 55 (transcript from patent by Henry St George, 1692), and MS R. 22, f. 322 (draft and correspondence). Among its eccentricities are the complete lack of a blazon and of any reference to the petitioner.

done in this language, others not. Most likely it was up to the grantee.

As for the traditional content of a patent of arms, it can be characterized as follows. It is drafted in the name of the king of arms issuing it and starts with a salutation, which (as befits letters patent) is to all and singular rather than a named party such as the grantee. The granting king identifies himself by his office and (if his authority is provincial) the area of the kingdom for which he has jurisdiction. In this period, a preamble then gives the background to the practice of heraldry and the granting of arms, justifying the practice in terms of ancient, well-founded custom – the 'manie gaie things' mentioned by Harrison. These preambles follow some fixed lines – the oldest ones regularly start with an invocation of equity and reason as the twin sponsors of social distinction – but they also display interesting variations indicating that thought was given to them. A standard example, from a Cooke patent of 1576, but closely resembling the phrasing of grants by Hervey and Flower, follows:[41]

> Whereas aunciently from the beginning the valiant and virtuous actes of worthie persons have ben comendid to the worlde with sondry monuments and remembrances of their good desertes Emongst the which the chiefest and most usuall hath ben the bearing of signes in Shilds called Armes : which are evident demonstracions of prowes and valoir, diversly distributed, according to the qualities and deserte of the persons, which order as it was most prudently devised in the beginning, to stirre and kindell the hartes of men to the imitac'on of virtue and noblenesse : Even so hath the same ben, and yet is continually observed, to thende that such as have don commendable service to their Prince, or Contry, eyther in warre or peace, may both receave due honor in their lives, and also derive the same successively to their posteritie for ever.

Some kings seem to have had a penchant for recounting antique precedent at still greater and more elaborate length (see Fig. 12).

Then, in the case of a grant, the patentee is introduced, as a specific example of birth and personal merit deserving the distinction of arms and gentility. Thus, in a 1543 patent by Barker:[42]

> ... he hath deserved and is well worthie from hensforthe evermore to be in all places of worshippe admitted reno'med accompted nowmbred accepted and received into the nowmbre and of the Company of other Aunciant gentill and noble men ...

The king of arms then invokes his authority to grant arms by his own patent of appointment, and proceeds to 'devyse, ordeyne, assign, gyve and graunt' (or similar) a coat of arms, which he describes, to the grantee and his descendants; the document then concludes with a dating clause. The document is signed and sealed by the king of arms, often with two seals – one displaying his personal arms, the other his arms of office. Where the patent is issued by more than one king of arms acting together, the text is adjusted accordingly and all the kings sign and seal at the foot.

[41] Confirmation of arms and grant of crest to Peter Temple by Cooke, Clarenceux, 10 November 1576. Original patent at College of Arms, MS 11/23.
[42] Grant of arms and crest to Robert Stanysby by Christopher Barker, 1543. See above, p. 73.

GRANTS AND CONFIRMATIONS OF ARMS

In the case of a confirmation, however, where the patentee has in theory already inherited arms and is already fully accepted into the number of the gentry, he is said to have required the king of arms 'to make searche in the registers and recordes of myne Office for the auncient armes belonging to him from his auncesters'; finding proper arms, the king proceeds, citing his authority, to 'verefie and ratefie' or 'ratifie, confirm and allow', before concluding in like manner as in a grant.[43]

Similar formulae were used when – as was frequently the case – the patent was a grant of a crest alone, or a confirmation of a quartering indicative of descent in the female line. Some of the most splendid productions of the sixteenth and seventeenth centuries were, in fact, of this nature. Adding further quarterings to existing arms by means of a patent became, in fact, an addictive process for some (Fig. 13).[44]

Many of these things could in practice be accomplished by a less imposing form of act, generically referred to as a declaration or certificate. Possibly these were very frequent, but they survive only rarely. They are also (and must have been at the time) hard to distinguish on the one hand from the certificates issued at a visitation by or on behalf of a king of arms and, on the other, from certified paintings of recorded arms issued, down to the present day, by officers of arms of all ranks. Certificates issued by kings of arms did, however, embody a prerogative act, and junior officers of arms were simply not competent to issue equivalent documents.[45] By way of example, here is the text of a certificate issued by Segar as Garter in 1623:

> Theis Armes, that is to saye *Argent between two Cheverons Azure, three Leaves vert, with the Crest being an Hynds head couped of the first charged with the like Cheverons*: doe belong to Richard Peirson, the Sonne of Thomas Peirson of Olney in the Countye of Buckingham: which Armes, and Creast I Sir William Segar Knight principall King of

12 (following two pages). Original patent of Lawrence Dalton (Norroy King of Arms, 1557–61), 'ratifying and confirming' arms and a crest to William Partryche of Sisseter (Cirencester, Glos.), 20 April 1561. The vellum document has a decorated border typical of the period, with royal badges in a floral setting. The motto *Plustot la mort qu'offence de foy* is recorded elsewhere as Partryche's. The text of the document has a particularly elaborate and prolix preamble locating heraldry in a tradition of recognising valour and worth dating back to the Greeks. College of Arms, MS 1/1.

[43] Examples quoted from Hervey's confirmation of quarterly arms to Christopher Wilkenson and Gilbert Dethick's confirmation of arms and grant of crest to John Bridges, both 1562: Essex Record Office, D/DU/290/1 and D/DGe/F1 respectively.

[44] For discussion of an acute case, see C. E. A. Cheesman, 'Penniston, Hatton and Three English Kings of Arms in Search of Quarterings', in *Genealogica et Heraldica. St Andrews MMVI: Myth and Propaganda in Heraldry and Genealogy*, Proc. of the XXVII International Congress of Genealogical and Heraldic Sciences, St Andrews, 21–6 August 2006, 2 vols (Edinburgh, 2008), I, pp. 207–28.

[45] Cf. a Latin declaration or certificate issued by William Dethick as York Herald to the brothers Thomas and Cuthbert de la Lynde, 20 Feb. 1577, surviving as a transcript and translation at College of Arms, MS Old Grants [cross paty], f. 71/73v. The attestations by three witnesses to the veracity of the transcript suggest that it was copied as potential evidence against Dethick.

PLVS TO LA...

o all and singuler ... whiche these present shall see ... Heralde of the Easte weast and ... commendacions with greatnge ... equitie and reason, it hath byn ... lerning and knowledge, or of noble ... valiaunt Actes, shulde with sundr... the Greekes by the Inscripcion of ... appellacions of honour accordingly... Signes and tokens of honour called ... that to euerie man according to th... might appeare in estimation and h... and by renowmed Princes allowed ... in warre or peace or by their woor... valiaunce lerning and wisedome ... successiuelie to their posteritie. Howbeit no worldelie thinge as it is ... remaine alweys in remembraunce without forgetfulnes And seing it ... honour shoulde be assigned (Therefore emong other thinges) Officers ... to kepe in Register and recorde the armes Pedegrees and descentes of ... power and auctoritie to set furthe ratifie and allowe vnto the woorth... saide woorthines whearby the desertes of the saide woorthye and ... with some token or remembraunce for that their woorthines the rat...
It knowen that I Norrey kinge of Armes abouesaide ...
of John whiche was the sonne of william who was the sonne of Roc... haue long continued in noblenes bearing armes tokens of honour not o... his saide Predecessours but also to ratifie them vnder Seale whose r... bo checke siluer and sable a bende verre for the Creste on the Helmet ... buttoned and tasseled goulde as more plainelie appearith by the pictu...
Norrey by power and auctoritie to myne Office annexed and t... confirmed and by these presentes do ratifie and confirme vnto and ... ordrelye to vse beare or shewe in Shilde Cote Armour or otherwise ... wheareof I haue signed these presentes with my hande an... Aprill in the thirde yeare of the reigne of our soueraigne Lad... of the faith &c And in the yeare of our Lorde God 1561.

[o] nobles and Gentles as all kinges Heraldes and Officers of Armes with others
[t]o heare Laurence Dalton Esquyer alias Norrey kinge of Armes and Princypall
[t]he parties of Englonde from the Ryver of Trent northwarde Sendith due and humble
asmuche as aunciently from the begynninge, not without greate deliberacion
most noble and famous Prynces constituted and ordeyned, that men of vertue wisedome
and courage, whiche haue ben notoriouslie commended to the worlde by their vertious and
[mo]numentes and tokens of honour accordinge to their desertes be had in remembraunce, as among
[pla]ces, among the Romaines by the erection of Statues Images and arces with titles and
[in] more latter dayes also amongest the most parte of all nations, by bearing of Shieldes with
[armes] whiche be the demonstracions and Evidence of noblenes vertue learning and woorthines
[ver]tues be diuerslie distributed, whearby the vertuouse lerned woorthie faithfull and couragious
[are knowen] before the vnworthie Cowarde and Ignoraunt, Even so yt is yet iudged right and reasonable
[and ob]seruyd that suche as haue don commendable seruyce to their Prince and Countrey either
[in goo]d laudable liefe demenour or learninge euerye man in his vocation by dailie increase in vertue
[dothe] yte well, shoulde receyue due woorshipp and honour in their lyues, and to deryue the same
[well co]nsidered can possiblie continewe without alteracion nor woorthie vertue or valiaunt acte
[forgot]ten and yet is not without greate consideracion and prouidence ordeyned that for menes desertes
[Her]aldes of Armes weare and appointed to whose Office it shoulde be appropriate not onlie
[nobles] and Gentles with their woorthie, vertious and valiaunte actes but also shoulde haue
[some] aduauncement augmentacion token or remembraunce of honour and noblenes for their
[actes] might not be forgotten nor drowned in the bottomlys pytt of oblivion but rewarded
[to mo]ue and styrre others to the imitacion of life vertue lerning and woorthynes **Be**
[yt de]syred by william Partryche of Sisseter in the Countie of Gloucester Gentleman sonne
[of par]tryche sometyme of kendall in the Countie of yorke Gentleman whose Auncestours
[to] make search in the recordes of myne Office for the said armes belonginge to hym and
[it] being so iuste and reasonable I coulde not lawfullie denye the same but founde them to
[be a wreathe] siluer and sable a Castor syluer, pelletted, langyd mantled gules doubled siluer
[where]of in this margent Whiche Armes and Creste with thappurtenaunces **I the said**
[have gr]aunted and attributed by lres patent vnder the greate Seale haue ratifeed and
[to the] saide william Partryche and his posteritie with their dewe differencye the same
[theyr ar]men to be reuested at his and their libertie and pleasure foreuermore **In wytnes**
[I haue] hereunto the Seale of my Office and the Seale of my Armes the twentith day of
[Eliz]abeth by the grace of God Quene of Englonde Fraunce and Irelande Defendour

By me Lawrence Dalton als
Norrey kinge of Armes

> Armes Garter doe confirme unto the said Richard Peirson and his yssue, and testifye the same under my hand and seale of Office, the 18 of October an° Dni. 1623.

Above the text appears a painting of the arms (oddly not conforming to the blazon given) and crest, without helmet or mantling; below appears Segar's signature.[46]

A certificate could, however, achieve more than merely confirming existing arms, and one issued by Segar a few years previously to Peirson's father-in-law is in effect a grant of a crest:

> This Coat of Armes, that is to saye, *Ermyn, on a pale Sables three crosses formy fitchy gould*, belonge to Edmond Criche the Thirde Sonne of Edmond Criche, alias Creiche of Oxfordshire gentleman: And wanting further for an ornament thereunto a convenient Creast, or Cognisance fitt to be borne, Hath requested mee Sir William Segar Knight, alias Garter principall King of Armes to grant and assigne hym one which hee maye lawefully beare: The which his request I have accomplished, and graunted, vizt forthe of a wreathe of his colours, *a Demy Lion ermyn crowned Or supporting a Crosse formy fichey of the same*. All which Armes and Creast, I the saide Garter, doe confirme to hym the saide Edmond Criche, and to his yssue, and testifye the same under my hande and Seale of Office this present xxix^th daye of Maij An° Dni. 1619.

Again the arms, together with the newly granted crest appear above the text.[47] In other cases it appears that the text of a certificate might approach even more closely the form of a grant: one issued to William Cawthorne on 20 August 1648 by William Ryley, the Parliament-appointed Norroy King of Arms, commences 'To all and Singular' in the manner of a patent; it proceeds to 'signifie and declare' that Cawthorne bears a particular coat of arms, crest and motto, 'which I the said William Ryley ... do by these presents assigne grant and confirm'.[48] There is no illustration of the arms, but the document still manages to be a curious hybrid of a grant and a confirmation. Possibly the explanation lies in the disrupted circumstances of the time. What is clear is that certificates could vary considerably in form and style, and they may well account for large numbers of the arms that were in some way given or granted by the kings of arms in this period.

Finally, it is worth noting that although in later ages the roles of king of arms, herald, artist and scrivener were to become clearly distinct, and few if any modern officers of arms have had the penmanship or artistic skill necessary to produce a patent or certificate, there were several in our period who could. William Segar, Garter King of Arms from 1606, was an accomplished limner and a fine penman. Glover also wrote a fine hand and there are surviving patents of arms that can be ascribed to him with confidence.

---

[46] College of Arms, MS Old Grants O, p. 13 (transcript of original; made in 1837; editor's italics); ibid., p. 14 is the certificate issued to Peirson by Henry St George, Richmond, at the 1634 Visitation of London. This corrects the blazon, but gives a completely different crest from the one certified in 1623.
[47] College of Arms, MS Old Grants O, p. 12 (transcript of original, made in 1837; editor's italics).
[48] Original certificate: private collection.

13. Patent of Robert Cooke (Clarenceux King of Arms, 1567–93), confirming arms and 29 quarterings, together with thirteen crests, to Thomas Penyston of Dean (Oxon.), 25 April 1575. This was Penyston's second patent from Cooke and at least his third from the College of Arms. Each patent confirmed more quarterings and crests than its predecessor, and each was accompanied by an elaborate roll pedigree setting out the (largely bogus) genealogy that supported the heraldry. Original patent at College of Arms.

Surviving Records

Relatively few original sixteenth- and seventeenth-century patents of arms remain. To study individual grants and indeed the phenomenon as a whole one must turn to the records maintained by the kings of arms themselves. But, as might be expected, the records left behind by such a discordant and unco-operative group of men are far from uniform in nature or function. They are preserved in a wide range of locations, many having passed with other heraldic papers into the great antiquarian collections of the seventeenth and eighteenth centuries and thence into the British Library, the Bodleian Library and other repositories. Many, however, were retained in or acquired by the College of Arms, which has probably the largest collection of such materials; those that the modern-day heralds have decided, in a sometimes arbitrary way, to treat as official records of 'Old Grants' are housed together in a single press in the College record room, and indexed in a standard, unrefined index of nineteenth-century date (Fig. 14).

This press houses a disparate collection of about fifty original manuscript volumes, varying greatly in size and character, supplemented by later nineteenth- and even

twentieth-century transcripts of relevant manuscripts held elsewhere. The volumes contain much material that is clearly not in any sense a record of grants of arms and in some cases this material constitutes the main or primary contents of the volume. When they do record a grant or confirmation they may do so in a number of ways: as a full and precise transcript of the text with the arms in question painted in the margin, or drawn in black and white with the colours 'tricked' or annotated by means of standard abbreviations; or as a simple note of the surname of the recipient of the grant, with a scribbled sketch of the arms or a brief blazon, with no indication of the date; or some intermediate version between these two extremes. Some volumes also contain draft texts of grants, with alterations and corrections, and very occasionally there is supporting correspondence or background material. It can be hard to be sure, when looking at the shorter entries, that one is seeing the record of a formal act by a king of arms, and not merely a note of arms in use.

Looked at with a view to classification, Old Grants records can be very roughly grouped as follows:

1. Full-text copies of patents, as issued: for instance College of Arms, MSS Miscellaneous Grants 2, 3.
2. Bound-up masses of miscellaneous drafts and related materials, sometimes including approval sketches or correspondence: for instance College of Arms, MSS R. 21 and Vincent's Old Grants 1 and 2.
3. Methodical abstracts of grants or confirmations issued by a particular king or in a particular period, to an internally uniform standard – so-called 'docquets': for instance College of Arms, MSS Dethick's Gifts and Bysshe's Grants.
4. Informal and often very scrappy notebooks recording the acts of a particular king: for instance, College of Arms, MSS Camden's Grants 1, 2 and 3, or F. 13 ('Cooke's Grants').
5. Simple 'rolls' of arms in book form, presumed to contain, for the most part, arms granted or confirmed by a particular king of arms, drawn in trick and labelled with little more than a name, or a name and a date: for instance, College of Arms, MSS EDN 56 and Vincent 161.

These are the main categories; there are others, represented by only one or two volumes, and there are many volumes that combine elements of more than one of these classes – volumes in the Miscellaneous Grants series are cases in point. The same act, furthermore, can appear many times in the Old Grants records; but, because (as we shall see) different kings of arms frequently granted arms to the same grantees, it can be hard to distinguish between separate records of the same act, and records of quite separate acts. Evidently these very difficulties beset Early Modern heralds, and quite a large proportion of the 'Old Grants' records seem to be the attempts of later heralds to get to grips with and make sense of what had actually been granted or confirmed by earlier ones.

14. College of Arms Record Room, press 19: the 'Old Grants' press. Apart from the top shelf, which holds painters' work books, the entire cupboard contains books designated as official records of the College and all containing, to some extent, entries recording grants and confirmations of arms made before 1673. The volumes are in many cases drawn from other collections in the College's possession – most notably the collections of the several kings of arms making the grants and confirmations, but also other heralds such as Augustine Vincent.

Sometimes there were ulterior motives in this. The slim, vellum-bound notebook entitled 'Dethick's Gifts X', for instance, is not a neutral record of the acts of either of the two Garter kings of arms called Dethick. On the first page is the fuller title: 'A Noate of some few Coates and Creasts lately come to my hands. Geven by William Dethick, when he was York Herald and sithence he hath executed the Office of Garter King of Armes'.[49] On each page is a rather crude drawing of a coat of arms granted or confirmed by Dethick, with notes of the fees received and increasingly arch comments, until on folio 10 the full character of the compilation comes out:

> These 3 Crests with the Armes of Parr and the other 4 forged Coats were given to Parr the Embroderer whose father was a Pedler by occupacion and not able to prove his sirname to be Parr, for which Armes and a forged Pedigree to mayntayne the same Garter had 10 li.

The booklet is clearly a weapon of war, for use in the campaign waged against Dethick, which ultimately resulted in his loss of the Gartership in 1604. Throughout, it rather disingenuously applies trade designations to grantees as a way of undermining their status. On its penultimate page appears (with several others) a very rough sketch of a coat of arms labelled 'Shakespeare the player by Garter' (see Fig. 15a). It was in response to the accusations founded on documents like this that Dethick and Camden compiled 'The Answere of Garter & Clarentieux Kings of Armes to a Libellous Scrowle against certein Arms supposed to be wrongfully given' (see Fig. 15b).[50]

But the Old Grants Press does not represent the whole story. It is clear that (just as the volumes that it holds contain much extraneous matter) there are other volumes in the College records and collections that undoubtedly preserve grants of arms. In particular, some of these relate to the early years of the sixteenth century, a period when we have reason to believe that Wriothesley, acting in concert with or on behalf of his fellow kings, issued a great many grants, but few that show up in the designated records of Old Grants. The fine vellum manuscript L. 10, for instance, contains for the most part sections of an early sixteenth-century armorial and ordinary compiled by Wriothesley, giving late medieval heraldry, including the arms of many religious houses; but intermingled with these are between 450 and 500 coats of arms that are clearly of Tudor date, and mostly (from their design) of early Tudor date (see Fig. 10, above, p. 72). The majority are doubtless grants by Wriothesley himself, while the later insertions are likely to be ascribed to William Hervey.[51] Hervey's grants also figure in L. 9, another vellum volume containing portions of Wriothesley's great armorial; on folios 24 to 29 appear 125 coats of arms that clearly postdate both the late medieval heraldry of Wriothesley's armorial

---

[49] College of Arms, MS Dethick's Gifts X, f. 1.
[50] College of Arms, MS WZ, ff. 276–277v. Another version of this is in Bodleian Library, MS Ashmole 846, f. 50.
[51] On the manuscript, see L. Campbell and F. Steer, *Catalogue of Manuscripts in the College of Arms. Collections*, I (London, 1988), pp. 46–9. The entries in question run, interspersed with older heraldry, from f. 58 to f. 110v.

GRANTS AND CONFIRMATIONS OF ARMS

and the grants made by Wriothesley himself in his Gartership; partial overlaps with other records show that they are probably mostly arms granted or confirmed by Hervey in his early years as Clarenceux (1557 onwards).[52] Most of these entries appear in a volume of grants by Hervey in the British Library,[53] as well as in another manuscript in the College of Arms 'L' series,[54] though frequently with quite significant variations, while the crests are copied into a manuscript in the Old Grants Press, without supporting information beyond the surname.[55] Only their presence in the last named manuscript brings them into the orbit of the main collection of 'Old Grants'; and it does so very imperfectly.

Numbers of Patents Issued

Contemporary accounts of how many patents the kings of arms issued in the Early Modern period are essentially unreliable, almost always being offered in the midst of some dispute over the propriety of a specific king's conduct. Large numbers, in the context of such a discourse, led naturally on to the claim that patents had been given indiscriminately. We will examine such claims shortly; they are not without value, but cannot be used uncritically. One would like to be able simply to count the grants and confirmations from the records. Unfortunately, this is notoriously hard.[56] No-one has yet counted all the entries in the various volumes in the 'Old Grants' Press, since to do so would entail a full-scale study of the records themselves; and the index to such a disparate collection must itself be disparate and inconsistent. Though it contains several thousand entries, many acts are represented more than once, and it makes no attempt (or only a very half-hearted one) to reconcile or match up equivalent entries; while many clearly relate to entries in the collection that have nothing to do with the granting or confirming of arms. It is, essentially, the combined (but unconsolidated) index to a particular set of manuscript volumes. It therefore cannot offer a shortcut to an analysis, however superficial, of the Old Grants period.

In default of anything better, and with due exercise of caution, one can turn to Joseph Foster's *Grantees of Arms named in Docquets and Patents to the end of the Seventeenth Century*, which W. H. Rylands edited for publication by the Harleian Society in 1915. Compiled from manuscripts in the British Library, the Bodleian and other prominent repositories, it lists alphabetically a large number of grants and confirmations made in the Old Grants period. Some of its entries do not seem to be directly represented among the College 'Old Grants', and there are also many entries in

---

[52] Campbell and Steer, *Catalogue*, pp. 42–5. For a discussion and edition of ff. 24–29, with apparatus giving cross-references to other records of the arms, see Gwynn-Jones, 'Tudor Enigmas' (cit. in n. 14), pp. 77–8, 84–97.
[53] British Library, MS Add. 16940.
[54] College of Arms, MS L. 6, ff. 86–128v, a miscellaneous compilation; see Campbell and Steer, *Catalogue*, p. 39. All the Hervey grants explicitly ascribed to Londoners in L. 9 also appear in MS M. 11, ff. 27v–29v (Campbell and Steer, *Catalogue*, p. 136).
[55] College of Arms, MS Vincent 161, ff. 21–24.
[56] Wagner, *Heralds of England*, pp. 187–8.

Capull the wife of Anderley of the Robes. (30)

Wotham of Norff: given to Sotherton of London. (31)

Soake & Caunder (32)

Pethouse of Norwich it is Petit Coate in Glovings booke fol: 82. (33)

Shakespeare the Player by Garter (34)

Hagar gave to one ?? a Crest and had to the same

Poake a Coate a Crest

Calvert a patent by Garter
Coy a hosier a patent
Cooley a Marchant in Lymstreet
?? Hadnal of Surrey

Mostratrot Steward to the Bishop of Cant:
Hall of Kent

15a, b. Documents in the controversy between Sir William Dethick, Garter King of Arms from 1587 to 1606, and his fellow officers, over his granting of what they regarded as inappropriate arms to unsuitable persons.

(a) (opposite). Page from a booklet apparently prepared by Mercury Patten (Bluemantle Pursuivant, 1597–1611), illustrating arms granted or confirmed by Dethick, frequently with added critical comments. Illustrated as no. 34 is the coat of arms granted to 'Shakespeare the player by Garter'. College of Arms, MS Dethick's Gifts X, f. 29.

(b) (above). Part of the fair-copy response to the accusations by Dethick, together with William Camden (Clarenceux King of Arms, 1597–1623, and implicated in some of Dethick's controversial grants). The entry shown is the specific response to the charges relating to the grant to John Shakespeare, addressing the doubts raised over the design and the grantee's social status. The text states that the spear on the bend constitutes 'a patible difference' with respect to the arms of Lord Mauley (illustrated in their various forms in the right-hand margin), and recites Shakespeare's credentials. College of Arms, MS WZ, ff. 276–277v.

the index to that series that do not appear in Foster. However, it was argued by Edward Elmhirst, who used a sample from it for a brief statistical survey in 1956, that Foster's list is likely to be an acceptable approximation of the true picture.[57] Responding, Wagner pointed out that early Tudor grants – those made by Wriothesley and his fellow kings – are probably under-represented in Foster, as indeed they are in the College index of Old Grants; but he broadly accepted the list as a useful source.[58] In particular it is of value because it makes a serious effort (not always successful, it is true) to avoid duplication and to resolve separate records of the same act into one. In doing so it may have incorrectly merged together separate grants that had been made to the same individual. But the fact remains that it is at least an attempt – the only one so far – at a synthetic listing of grants and confirmations of arms in the period.

Elmhirst was reticent about the size of his sample and how he made it. Furthermore, he was examining a much longer period of English heraldry than we are concerned with, down to the end of the nineteenth century, and he plotted his figures against demographic data to reflect the rising population of England and Wales. In the narrower period under consideration here, this is not necessary; population estimates for the early modern period are in any case unreliable, and furthermore it is not clear that the *total* population of England (or England and Wales) is a relevant datum, as opposed to (say) the population of London and the South East, or the gentry and mercantile classes. It has therefore seemed sensible to carry out a new survey, with a view to estimating not the coverage that grants and confirmations achieved across the population but their absolute numbers, as an index of the activity of the kings of arms. This survey has taken as a sample the letters C, M and R in Foster's list, which between them yield 1,076 entries, and suggest that the total number of entries in Foster's list is 5,250 to 5,400. Of the 1,076 examined, about 880 can be dated to a particular monarch's reign, and about 830 can be ascribed to a specific decade. If we ignore acts dated to decades prior to the 1480s (before the incorporation of the Office of Arms) and later than 1700 (when Foster's list ceases) we are left with 807. These are broken down by decade in Table 1.

If we take these percentages and apply them to a conservative estimate of the number of acts in Foster's list for the period 1480 to 1700, say 5,000, we can propose the figures presented in Table 2 as the minimum decade-by-decade totals. The low numbers for the first four decades of the sixteenth century are doubtless, for the reasons explained above, misleading. Thereafter, we are on surer ground, though of course it remains a very rough-and-ready set of figures. To a certain extent they mirror those of Elmhirst. He noted a spike in the 1570s, which this study recognises but reconfigures as a surge starting in the 1550s and peaking in the 1580s. A second surge, unnoticed or uncommented on by Elmhirst, appears in the 1610s; and a third is very visible in the Restoration period.

---

[57] E. Elmhirst, 'The Fashion for Heraldry', *Coat of Arms*, 1st ser., iv (1956), pp. 47–50.
[58] A. R. Wagner, 'The Fashion for Heraldry. Dr Elmhirst's View Reviewed', *ibid.*, pp. 119–20.

Table 1: Grants, datable by decade, from Foster, *Grantees of Arms* (C, M and R)

Decade	Grants	%	Decade	Grants	%
1480s	3	0.4	1590s	49	6.1
1490s	9	1.1	1600s	56	6.9
1500s	3	0.4	1610s	80	9.9
1510s	14	1.7	1620s	36	4.5
1520s	8	1.0	1630s	41	5.1
1530s	10	1.2	1640s	27	3.4
1540s	24	3.0	1650s	20	2.5
1550s	54	6.7	1660s	67	8.3
1560s	77	9.5	1670s	24	3.0
1570s	75	9.3	1680s	32	4.0
1580s	85	10.5	1690s	13	1.6

Table 2: Estimated numbers of grants, by decade, 1480 to 1700

Decade	Estimated grants	Decade	Estimated grants
1480s	20	1590s	305
1490s	55	1600s	345
1500s	20	1610s	495
1510s	85	1620s	225
1520s	50	1630s	255
1530s	60	1640s	170
1540s	150	1650s	125
1550s	335	1660s	415
1560s	475	1670s	150
1570s	465	1680s	200
1580s	525	1690s	80

Wagner's account of the peak discerned by Elmhirst in the 1570s doubtless still holds for the slightly more enduring phenomenon of the three decades from 1560 seen here:

> In 1555 the heralds were incorporated and were given the predecessor of the present College building. In 1564 they moved into that building. In 1568 the Earl Marshal inaugurated a new era with his regulations for the conduct of the College and between 1568 and 1592 Hervey, Clarenceux, and Cooke, Clarenceux, completed a cycle of Visitations of unprecedented thoroughness.

The surge represented the fruits of this labour and the benefits of a newly settled and organized approach to business.[59] In part, furthermore, the explanation also holds for the 1610s, the decade in which Camden as Clarenceux and Richard St George as Norroy commenced a new cycle of visitations; and even for the more modest rise in numbers of the 1680s, when Henry St George conducted the final round of visitations in the southern counties as Clarenceux. It would seem that activity and order brought dividends.

The proposed trends seem realistic enough. Whether or not the actual numbers proposed are near the truth is another matter entirely. Some writers have argued that they

---

[59] Wagner, 'The Fashion for Heraldry', p. 120. The year 1564 in the quoted passage in fact refers to early 1565.

should be pitched rather higher. Samples of arms ascribable to Hervey and Cooke outside the main College collection of Old Grants led a recent Garter king of arms to conclude, by extrapolation, that each king may have been responsible for considerably more grants and confirmations than usually appreciated. Suggesting a yearly rate of 50 formal acts to Hervey's decade as Clarenceux (1557 to 1567), Gwynn-Jones proposed a total near 500. Now this figure, according to Ralph Brooke (Rouge Croix Pursuivant from 1580 to 1592, then York Herald until his death in 1625), was the total number made by Cooke in his time as Clarenceux. This was meant to sound a scandalously large number; and Cooke was Clarenceux for twenty-five years. For Cooke himself, Gwynn-Jones proposed a total of a higher order of magnitude – a hundred a year, pushing up towards 3,000 in total.[60]

This is an interesting hypothesis, and it is salutary to be invited to consider that the Elizabethan College of Arms maintained a much higher rate of output than we have been accustomed to imagine. It could be the case, as noted above, that large numbers of formal acts were accomplished by certificate rather than patent, making these totals much more attainable. But the method of extrapolation adopted is unreliable in the extreme. And it seems unlikely that the turbulent, caustic and, above all, eagle-eyed Brooke would have so far underestimated a figure that served his argumentative purpose. Other estimates of Cooke's grant rate are less dramatic. In a very valuable declaration made by Sir Gilbert Dethick in 1585, he estimated Cooke's singlehanded output of patents between 1573 and 1583–4 as about 40. His own, for the period 1571–2 to 1583–4, he estimated as about 80.[61] Though not as hostile as Brooke, Dethick was no friend of Cooke's and is unlikely to have been understating things. The figures in Table 2, far from being underestimates, begin to look likely only if most acts recorded in Foster's list were achieved not by patent, but by certificate.

Who were the New Gentry?
As noted by Harrison, anyone who could maintain the port, charge and countenance of a gentleman – and pay the fees demanded by the kings of arms – could have a grant. This naturally called for an element of judgment or discretion on the part of the kings of arms; it was inevitable that Early Modern kings were often accused by their colleagues of granting too often, and (explicitly, or by implication) to inappropriate persons. Thus, in 1530, Benolt accused Wriothesley of granting to 'bound men, to vile persons not able to uphold the honour of nobless'. Wriothesley denied the charge, claiming to have granted only to appropriate individuals, whom he conveniently defines:

> ... that every person being of good name and fame and good renown, and not vile born

---

[60] Gwynn-Jones, 'Tudor Enigmas', pp. 82–3; cf. J. F. R. Day, 'Cooke, Robert (d. 1593)', in *ODNB*, 13, pp. 160-1.
[61] British Library, MS Add. 14294, f. 56v. See further Ramsay, *Robert Glover*, forthcoming, Chapter 4, n. 130.

or rebels, might be admitted to be ennobled to have arms, having lands and possessions of free tenure to the yearly value of £10 sterling, or in moveable goods £300 sterling.

He added that he always sought a reference from some noble or notable personage, and that all his grantees were at least as worthy of a grant as Benolt himself.[62] And indeed, in specifying any quantifiable threshold for grantees to clear, Wriothesley seems to be more demanding than the roughly contemporary guidance on fees from the Earl Marshal, discussed above, which does not actually state a minimum limit.

Similar disputes arose whenever any king granted arms in large numbers. We have already encountered Ralph Brooke's criticism of Robert Cooke for granting indiscriminately as Clarenceux. After Cooke's death, William Segar commented that he 'confirmed and gave Armes and Creastes without number to base and unworthy persons for his private gaine onely without the knowledge of the Erle Marshall'.[63] In 1597 Brooke again was part of a group of heralds who denounced William Dethick, Garter, to the Commissioners for the Marshalcy on a similar basis.[64] This denunciation has attracted much attention, since the acts complained of included the grant that Dethick had recently made to John Shakespeare, father of the playwright.[65] Like others in the list, the Shakespeare grant was objected to on two grounds: the grantee was unworthy of a grant; and the design granted was too close to an existing coat of arms – in this case the old, simple coat of the thirteenth-century baron, Piers Mauley. There is perhaps also the faint suggestion that the two points had a combined force: that the similarity to the Mauley arms was particularly objectionable *because* the grantee was of lowly status. Dethick had a satisfactory answer on the two principal points, and did not need to address the third (see Fig. 15b, above, p. 91).[66]

Disputes of this nature continued throughout our period and beyond; in 1616 Segar himself, now Garter, was notoriously tricked by the ever fractious Brooke into passing a grant to the common hangman, Gregory Brandon. For this infringement of the principles of gentility – evidently a strict-liability offence – he would be imprisoned in the Marshalsea even after Brooke's deceit was known.[67] He did, however, have Brooke for company.

A hangman was clearly beyond the pale; but John Shakespeare – an alderman and magistrate in a respectable borough – probably represents fairly well the status of many personal grantees in this era, though there were plenty of others with greater wealth, higher rank and stronger metropolitan connections; he probably ended up in the anti-Dethick dossier only because of an unlucky combination of relative provincial

[62] PRO, SP 1/73/187, 204. Discussed by Wagner, *Heralds of England*, pp. 164–5.
[63] College of Arms, MS Arundel 40 (Lant's Observations), f. 29.
[64] Folger Shakespeare Library, MS V.a.156 (formerly 423.1), Ralph Brooke's account of arms granted by William Dethick, 1591–4; College of Arms, MS WZ, ff. 276–277v.
[65] E. K. Chambers, *William Shakespeare*, 2 vols (Oxford, 1930), II, pp. 18–32; K. Duncan-Jones, 'Shakespeare among the Heralds', *Times Literary Supplement*, no. 5116 (20 April 2001), p. 23.
[66] Wagner, *Heralds of England*, p. 203.
[67] College of Arms, MS Heralds VIII, f. 147.

obscurity and a design that caught Brooke's malicious eye. Awareness (and disapproval) of the son's theatrical associations may also have played a part; in the notebook mentioned above, 'Dethick's Grants X', the scribbled trick of the arms is as we saw captioned not for the supposedly humble Stratford alderman but rather for 'Shakespeare the player'. But no accusation could be built on that prejudice; the grant was to the father, not the son.

Among the grantees who *did* have metropolitan associations, many had a flavour of the Court and royal service. In the late 1550s, for instance, we have Thomas Huys, a Gloucestershire man and Physician to Queen Mary;[68] George Webster, 'master cooke to the quenes maiestie';[69] Thomas Lamb 'of the wardrope';[70] 'Kays sergent porter'.[71] 'Thomas Percy of London skynner' turns out on investigation to have been the Queen's Skinner or 'Serjeant of the Peltry'.[72] City office holders recur, with not just lords mayor and aldermen (though there are plenty of these) but men like Thomas Smythe, 'customer of London' and William Blackwell, 'town clerke of London';[73] while many others are described in the Old Grant records merely by reference to the trade or craft of which they were free within the City. The law, predictably, is represented strongly, with clerks and Masters in Chancery, serjeants at law, and all ranks of justices up to the highest; country gentlemen of course figure among the magistrates, the commissioners for Oyer and Terminer and the local receivers-general. Such persons were comfortably off; but they might well seek and benefit from visible marks of gentility.

It is interesting to note the relatively large number of women being granted arms in the sixteenth century, a great many (particularly in the 1550s) being wives of lord mayors or other office holders in the metropolis. Foster lists a total of 127 grants or confirmations made to women (occasionally together with men); of these, 105 can be dated to a decade within the Old Grants period, as presented in Table 3.

Once again the caution necessary when dealing with Foster's data needs emphasizing; the low numbers in the early decades of the sixteenth century should be regarded with particular care. It needs to be noted, for instance, that of the grants that cannot be dated to a decade, nine were by Barker, and therefore made in the period 1536–50. But what is striking is that while the overall surge in grants between 1550 and 1590 is visible here, the later spikes in the 1610s and 1660s leave no trace.

[68] College of Arms, MSS L. 6, f. 87ᵛ, L. 9, f. 25a, and M. 11, f. 28. See A. B. Emden, *Biographical Register of the University of Oxford, A.D. 1501 to 1540* (Oxford, 1974), pp. 285–6 ('Hewes, Thomas').
[69] College of Arms, MSS L. 6, f. 88v, L. 9, f. 25b, M. 11, f. 28v.
[70] College of Arms, MSS L. 9, f. 27b, Misc. Grants 1, f. 243; and elsewhere. He was of Trimley (Suff.).
[71] College of Arms, MSS L. 6, f. 89v, L. 9, f. 26b, M. 11, f. 29v.
[72] College of Arms, MSS L. 6, f. 86v, L. 9, f. 24b, M. 11, f. 27v; *Cal. Pat. Rolls, 1558–60*, p. 91.
[73] Respectively College of Arms, MSS F. 1, f. 204v; and L. 6, f. 96, L. 9, f. 28a, and M. 11, f. 31. For 'Customer Smythe', see B. Dietz, 'Smythe [Smith], Thomas (1522–1591)', in *ODNB*, 51, pp. 468–9.

Table 3: Grants to women, datable by decade, from Foster, *Grantees of Arms*

Decade	Grants	Decade	Grants
1480s	0	1590s	6
1490s	0	1600s	3
1500s	0	1610s	5
1510s	1	1620s	2
1520s	2	1630s	1
1530s	1	1640s	1
1540s	3	1650s	1
1550s	24	1660s	4
1560s	11	1670s	3
1570s	10	1680s	10
1580s	15	1690s	2

More on this interesting phenomenon cannot be said here. Also full of interest would be research into grants and confirmations of arms to clergy. We saw that the scale of fees laid down for grants in Wriothesley's day, on the eve of the Reformation, catered for the full range of greater and lesser clergy, and Wriothesley himself not only took great pains in recording the arms of religious houses and cathedrals but granted arms to many of the ecclesiastics who ruled over them. Later on in the century – perhaps unsurprisingly – we find fewer such cases, though Gilbert Dethick seems to have had a line in granting arms to bishops. Was the attraction of having personal arms to 'impale' with those of the diocese a selling point?

The fact is, however, that relatively little has been done on the question of who the Tudor and early Stuart kings of arms issued their patents to; and yet it is an area where much fascinating and rewarding work is possible. Whatever the ratio of surviving records of grants and confirmations to those actually made, we still have several thousand names of Early Modern individuals who decided to pay a king of arms a hefty fee for a patent or certificate; many of these individuals can be identified – or are expectantly awaiting identification – in other sources, particularly the central, local and family archives that in this very period begin to blossom into richly intricate life. Understanding their lives in greater detail, including their other financial and social commitments, their connections and associations and backgrounds, will illuminate the question of what benefit they hoped to gain from a grant or confirmation of arms; it may even shed light on the obscure question of whether a grant was constitutive or reflective of gentility. Connections between or among grantees would undoubtedly emerge, though care would need to be taken that these were significant: among the gentry of any county, and even to an extent on the national level, links of kinship, alliance and friendship will necessarily emerge and before long enmesh the whole class.

Finally, research could well assist with understanding the artefactual side of heraldry and its uses. Did grantees, more than others, reside in armorially decorated houses or rest in heraldically splendid tombs; did their wills distribute rings with their arms on them, as opposed to the standard death's head *memento mori*? When a gentleman whom we know to have had a grant of arms requests burial without the 'pomp

or sumptuous funeral' that his status allows him,[74] is he regretting the expensive folly of only a few years previously?

Repeat and Replacement Grants

Mention of the artefactual aspects of heraldry brings us back to the design and visual impact of the arms. This, as stated at the outset, was a significant point. A specific accusation made against Clarenceux Cooke was that he 'would never suffer a man to enjoy his ancient Armes: if he could perswade hym to a new'.[75] And it is certainly true that a very marked feature of Cooke's practice and of that of his colleagues is the number of patents issued to persons who had already had grants from earlier kings.

Sometimes, there is no obvious reason for the new patent. In 1562 Hervey apparently granted or confirmed Simon Edulph the same arms and crest that Gilbert Dethick had granted him in 1559.[76] Hervey might have argued that Dethick's grant was invalid, under the agreement signed by Barker in 1539, and not yet (in 1559) superseded. No such explanation seems to avail in the case of Cooke's grant of arms and crest to Robert Grove of Donhead St Andrew (Wilts.) in 1576, which confers exactly the same design granted by Hervey in 1560.[77]

But in many cases the client's second patent grants a new or altered coat of arms; and here we need to engage with the visual features of the fashion for heraldry, which cannot in reality be divorced from the other aspects under which it might be studied. It has often been observed that the sixteenth century saw a clear stylistic swing in the design of newly granted arms. At the start of the century, for instance, Wriothesley grants are immediately recognisable, displaying new arrangements, new elements and more complex, even superabundant, compositions. Wagner described them as having 'a crowded coarse virility of design which is rich and not unpleasing … A charged chevron between other charges and on a chief a charge between two more is a characteristic early Tudor form.'[78] Arms granted by Barker, Hervey and their mid-century colleagues are less heavily laden than Wriothesley's, but still notably more complex than medieval heraldry. From the 1560s, however, we see a return to a simpler style.[79] May it be that the phenomenon of repeat or replacement grants can be explained by grantees (or their

---

[74] Thus John Raymond of Little Dunmow (Essex), granted arms by Dethick, 15 November 1555: College of Arms, MS Grants 1, f. 224. Will, dated 7 March 1560, printed in F. G. Emmison, *Elizabethan Life*, 5: *Wills of Essex Yeomanry & Gentry* (Chelmsford, 1980), pp. 111–12.

[75] William Smith, Rouge Dragon, 1603 or later, in Folger Shakespeare Library, MS V.a.199, f. 19 (printed above, p. 67).

[76] College of Arms, MSS Vincent 163, f. 173 (Dethick, 1559), and Vincent 161, f. 2 (Hervey, 1562).

[77] College of Arms, MS Old Grants (facsimiles) 2, pp. 30–3.

[78] A. R. Wagner, *Heraldry in England* (Harmondsworth, 1946), p. 26.

[79] Thus W. H. St J. Hope, *Grammar of English Heraldry* (Cambridge, 1913), p. 89; 2nd edn., revised A. R. Wagner (Cambridge, 1953), p. 73; W. H. St J. Hope, 'On the Armorial Ensigns of the University and Colleges of Cambridge, and of the Five Regius Professors', *Archaeological Jnl.*, 51 (1894), pp. 299–324, at 320–1; Wagner, *Heraldry in England*, p. 27.

GRANTS AND CONFIRMATIONS OF ARMS

children) returning to the College to have simpler designs when the style changed?

Certainly a subsequent grant of arms sometimes explicitly states that the motive behind it was a desire to simplify over-complicated arms granted previously. Thus the 1576 grant by Cooke and Flower to Sir Ralph Sadleir, Chancellor of the Duchy of Lancaster and a Privy Councillor, refers to the arms previously granted him (by Barker, Garter, in 1542) as 'beinge found to be overmuch intricate with the confuse mixture of to many things in one shylde, contrary to the commendable and best allowed maner of bearing Armes'.[80] The new design is indeed simple (*Or a lion rampant per fess azure and gules armed counterchanged*) but unfortunately we do not know what the arms granted by Barker were. In another similar case, the earlier grant has likewise disappeared, but it has left a trace for a comparison between old and new to be made. In 1587 Cooke granted arms to Charles Morysin (Morison) of Cashiobury (Herts.), to replace arms granted to his father Sir Richard (who had died in 1556). The Latin text of the 1587 grant, apparently drafted by Robert Glover, is very similar to that of Sadleir's second grant, stating that the older design was *confusa ac ex rerum multa varietate uno eodemque clypeo coactarum intricata nimis*, and going on to grant the enviably simple design *Or on a chief gules three chaplets or*.[81] Although, as stated, we know nothing of the earlier grant, it is highly likely that it is represented by a design ascribed to 'Morysine of London' in the mid-sixteenth century alphabet of arms L. 2 (whence it has entered all later alphabets and armorials under the name 'Morison'): *Per saltire gules and or two pelicans vulning themselves in pale and two lions faces in fess all counterchanged on a chief or three chaplets gules*.[82] Cooke simply, and boldly, removed the clutter from the field, leaving only the chief and its chaplets (see Figs 16a, b).

Even in the absence of similarly explicit motivation, it is not hard to find what look suspiciously like parallel cases. In 1559 the London goldsmith Robert Trapes or Trappes was granted arms and crest by Hervey.[83] Complex in design, but clearly carefully thought out, both elements made punning reference to the grantee's name by way of the 'caltrap' or spiked horse-laming device: arms: *Argent between two flaunches azure on each three crosses formy or a lions face azure between six caltraps sable three and three*; crest: *Two wyverns heads erased and addorsed the dexter or the sinister azure langued gules gorged with a single collar charged with three caltraps counterchanged*.

By 1568 Trappes seems to have been granted a different crest,[84] and in 1570 he received from Cooke a grant of a far simpler shield: arms: *Argent three caltraps sable*. It is this coat of arms that continued to be borne by Trappes's descendants.

80 College of Arms, MS F. 12, f. 294v; Bodleian Library, MS Ashmole 834, f. 14v.
81 Bodleian Library, MS Ashmole 834, ff. 68v–69v. I owe this reference and the Sadleir one to Nigel Ramsay.
82 College of Arms, MS L. 2, f. 349 (=291 in the original foliation).
83 College of Arms, MSS Grants 2/547; L. 6, f. 90; L. 9, f. 247; Misc. Grants 5, f. 72; Vincent 163, f. 18. British Library, MSS Add. 16940, f. 27; Harley 1359, f. 3v; Harley 1507, f. 443.
84 College of Arms, MSS G. 12, f. 242v; R. 21, f. 36; G. 10 (Visitation of London, 1568), f. 32.

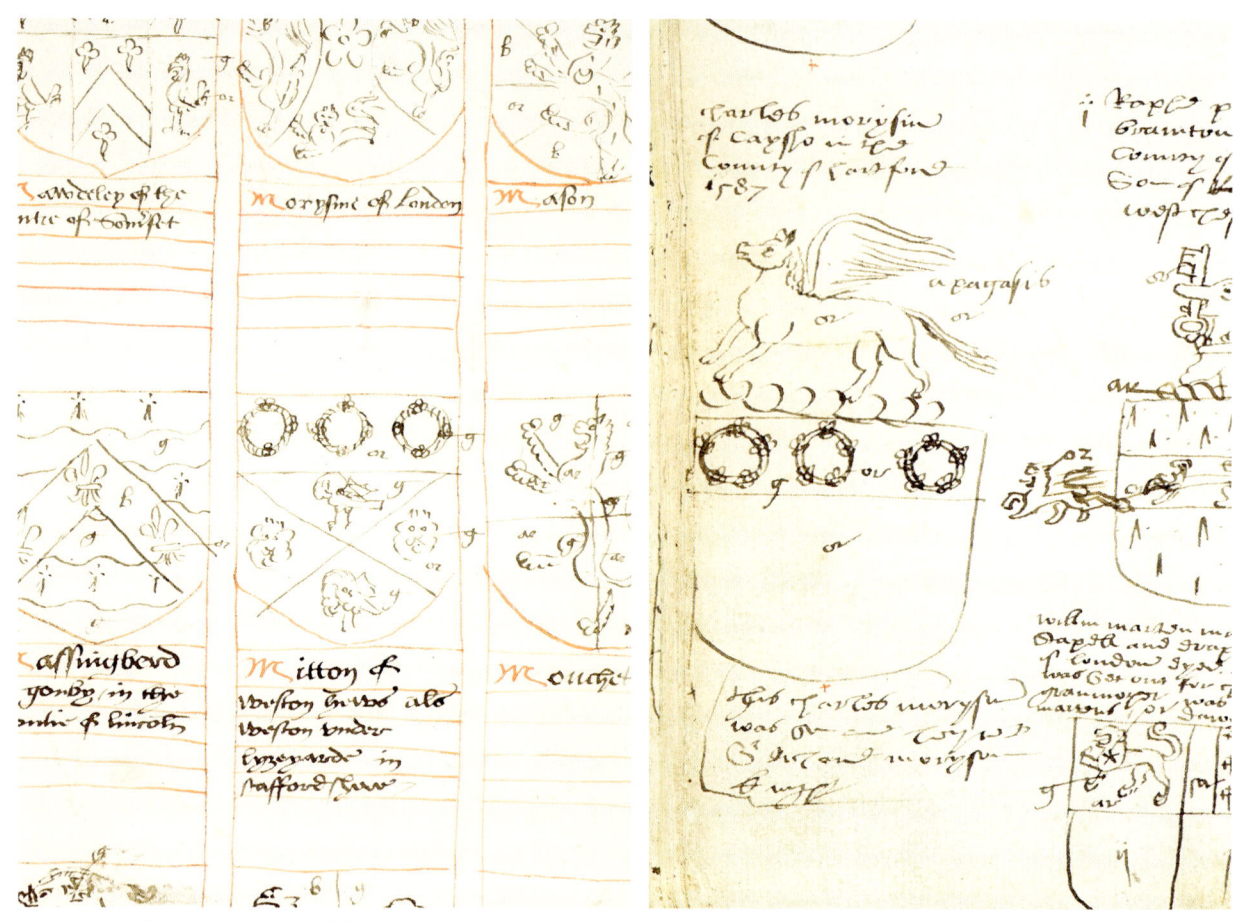

16a, b. Two versions of the arms of Morison:

(a). 'Morysine of London'; presumably arms granted to Sir Richard Morison (d. 1556). From a mid-sixteenth-century armorial. College of Arms, MS L.2, f. 349 (= 291).

(b). Arms and crest granted to Charles Morison of Cashiobury (Herts.) by Robert Cooke, Clarenceux King of Arms, 20 May 1587. From a seventeenth-century compilation entitled on the spine 'Cooke's Gifts'. College of Arms, MS F.13, f. 17.

Likewise, and also in 1559, Hervey granted James Baker of Bowers Gifford (Essex) a fairly complex coat of arms (*Ermine on a fess engrailed sable between three wolfs heads erased azure three fleurs-de-lys or*) and crest;[85] in 1574, in a patent to Baker's son Henry, Cooke simplified the arms by removing the wolf heads and replacing the crest altogether.[86] Nor were such changes always achieved by patent. In a very similar process, arms of *Argent on a fess engrailed gules between three eagles heads azure three fleurs-de-lys or* were granted (presumably by Hervey) in 1558 to John Leonard or Lennard of Chevening (Kent); in 1584, at the funeral of Lennard's wife, Cooke was happy to issue a certificate showing the much simpler coat *Or on a fess gules three fleurs-de-lys or*.[87]

[85] British Library, MS Add. 16940, f. 17; College of Arms, MSS L. 6, f. 90v, L. 9, f. 27a.
[86] Essex Record Office, Colne Priory Estate Papers, D/D Pr/558.
[87] British Library, MS Add. 16940, f. 8; College of Arms, MSS L. 6, f. 87, L. 9, f. 24b, B.EDN, f. 5.

GRANTS AND CONFIRMATIONS OF ARMS

Again, it was these simple arms that remained in use by relatives, including the original grantee's nephew Sampson Lennard, himself an officer of arms.

A slightly more complex case is that of Thomas Powle, a prominent and longstanding officer of the Elizabethan Court of Chancery. He was first granted arms as Thomas Powle, of Cranbrook (Essex), on 5 April 1556, by Thomas Hawley, Clarenceux, as follows:[88] arms: *Azure two bars wavy on a chief argent three martlets sable*; crest: *A red deer's head erased gules 'beryng his velvett hedd caulled a pollarde' gorged with a wreath linked or*. The crest clearly puns on the name Powle, and it is possible that the wavy blue and white lines of the shield do likewise (by way of 'powle' = 'pool'). But in 1557 Hawley died and on 10 May 1559 Powle was granted a replacement coat of arms by the new Clarenceux, William Hervey:[89] arms: *Per fess indented azure and gules three demi lions passant reguardant or armed and langued gules*; crest: *Standing on a dexter arm fesswise gules gloved argent purfled or a hawk proper beaked membered belled and jessed gules*.

The new coat of arms lasted a decade. But on 7 May 1569, Powle, by now Clerk of the Crown in Chancery, one of the Six Clerks in the court of Chancery and Controller of the Hanaper in the same court, as well as Steward of Waltham Forest, was granted new arms by Sir Gilbert Dethick, Garter, Robert Cooke, Clarenceux, and William Flower, Norroy, acting together:[90] arms: *Azure a fess engrailed ermine between three lions passant or*; crest: *A unicorn azure armed maned and unguled or gorged with a coronet argent*.

These arms were to endure, and when in 1588 Thomas Powle's youngest son (and successor in his Chancery posts), Stephen, received from William Dethick, Garter, a patent allowing his right to a quartering, it was the 1569 arms and crest that were confirmed to him (Fig. 17).[91]

The sequence of Powle's grants does not reflect a simple trend towards simplicity, it is true. The arms granted by Hervey in 1559 were no less busy or crowded than the canting design received from Hawley in 1556. However one should not rule out the possibility that aesthetic considerations played a part. Powle may simply have disliked the unmartial martlets and wanted to have lions – a timeless desire on the part of grantees, familiar to heralds of all eras. Hervey complied, with demi lions, but the new grant still did not satisfy. Cooke's grant of 1569 states that the previous version was 'not so well

---

[88] Original patent: British Library, MS Add. 37687G, summarized by Hope, *Proc., Soc. of Antiquaries*, 2nd ser., xvi (1895–7), p. 349.

[89] College of Arms, MSS Vincent 169, f. 102; Grants 2, f. 561. British Library, MSS Harley 1507, f. 373, Add. 16940, f. 37.

[90] College of Arms, MSS Old Grants [cross paty], f. 57 (draft by Glover); Misc. Grants 5, f. 148 (dated 23 June 1559); L. 9, f. 28b no 1; M. 11, f. 31. Original patent summarized by Hope, *Proc., Soc. of Antiquaries*, 2nd ser., xvi (1895–7), p. 351. On Powle and his grants, see Gwynn-Jones, 'Tudor Enigmas' (cit. in n. 14), pp. 77–8 (with note 19), 94–5 and plate 2 (= L. 9, f. 28b).

[91] Original patent (now in the Folger Library, MS Z.c.22 (41)) summarized by Hope, *Proc., Soc. of Antiquaries*, 2nd ser., xvi (1895–7), p. 353.

to be lyked of, for reasons to officers of armes well knowen'. The problem may have been the demi lions. Powle was not the only grantee of this period to have them excised from his arms. In 1559 Hervey granted the Lincolnshire gentleman Anthony Butler for his shield *Argent on a chevron between three demi lions passant guardant azure crowned or three covered cups or*. At some point after 1569 the lions disappeared, probably by means of a new grant or other instrument from Cooke.[92]

One analysis of the phenomenon seen here is that by Wagner, whose brief account of the turn towards less complex design in the later sixteenth century ran as follows: 'Elizabeth's reign ... saw a reaction towards simplicity in new grants, as looking more mediaeval and so nobler.'[93] The equation between simple heraldry and heraldry that is 'more mediaeval and so nobler' presupposes a relatively sophisticated degree of periodization in the way heraldry was viewed even by non-specialists, and an association between complexity and novelty. It is certainly clear that complex heraldic design was stigmatized by some as not only new, but purchased: think back to Sogliardo and the multi-coloured coat that earned his friends' scorn. In fact, the characterization of bought heraldry as overloaded was seriously out of date: the Sogliardo passage is thought in part to be Ben Jonson's way of poking fun at his most famous theatrical colleague over the arms granted to his father; but as we have seen the arms conferred on John Shakespeare in 1596 were of such simplicity that the king of arms who granted them was attacked by colleagues for granting to undistinguished persons coats of arms that too closely resembled those of old noble families.[94] But the perception that new heraldry was complex clearly persisted. And it is undeniably the case that the early part of the century had seen some designs of almost Sogliardic superabundance.

So were the Elizabethan grants and regrants the sign of a new gentry trying to pass itself off as long-established? Or was it merely a matter of taste – that they liked the antique style? Either way, the newly simplified heraldry might have implications for the history of the gentry in the Tudor period. And, one is prompted to wonder, why did early Tudor grantees accept complex Wriothesleyan designs? Were they glad to be distinguished as new? Was it, again, a matter of taste – but on this occasion a taste for 'modernizing' design? Or did it just boil down to the divergent business styles of two prominent heralds of different generations, each of them with a thriving practice?

There is a practical aspect to the situation: from the 1560s onwards, and particularly due to the industry of men like Robert Glover, heralds were able to avail themselves of 'ordinaries'. An ordinary, in this context, is a reference work gathering together and

---

[92] For the original grant (18 or 28 September 1559), see College of Arms, MS C. 23 (3), f. 3; British Library, MS Add. 16940, f. 12, and MS Harley 1116, f. 56v. At College of Arms, MS L. 9, f. 28b, the lions have been erased (see Gwynn-Jones, 'Tudor Enigmas' (cit. in n. 14), plate 2, for an illustration); at L. 6, f. 96v, they are simply crossed out.
[93] *Heraldry in England*, p. 27.
[94] For the suggestion that the design was that of William Shakespeare himself, perhaps initially drafted by his cousin Burbage, see Duncan-Jones, 'Shakespeare among the Heralds' (cit. in n. 65).

17. Original patent (in Latin) of Sir William Dethick, Garter King of Arms, confirming arms and granting a quartering to Stephen Powle, March 1588. The arms and crest are those granted to Powle's father in 1569. Washington (DC), Folger Shakespeare Library, MS Z.c.22 (41).

grouping coats of arms thematically rather than alphabetically by name; it makes it possible to search for all designs based around a chevron, for instance, or featuring a griffin. Intended partly to aid identification of unknown coats of arms, it is also invaluable to anyone designing a new one, since it allows the designer to check that his design does not conflict with existing heraldry. Lacking such resources, Wriothesley and other earlier kings of arms, it is argued, had to play safe by granting arms far removed from medieval heraldry in style; their successors could return to the classic design with greater security.[95]

This may very well explain, or contribute to, the simplifying turn in heraldic design style from the late 1560s on. But to account for the fact that grantees from earlier in the

[95] Ramsay, *Robert Glover*, forthcoming.

century returned to the College to be granted replacement arms in the new simple style (even if at the prompting of kings of arms like Cooke), one needs to look for a further element, and this is likely to be found somewhere in the fact that different design styles might, for contemporaries, have had both positive and negative connotations.

Conclusion
This survey has raised more questions than it has answered, but in addition to an overview of the area and the shortcomings of the surviving material, I have hoped to show that the subject can scarcely be tackled without sensitive awareness of two aspects that are not always given full or equal weight. One relates to the theory of the Early Modern grant of arms. The best way of understanding the doggedness with which the kings of arms defended their activities, the irony or outright ridicule with which those activities were viewed by outsiders – particularly for their financial aspects – and the severity with which monarchs and Earls Marshal tried to govern them, is to take seriously the language of the time, which represented a grant of arms as granting gentility too. Later doctrine – with reason, perhaps – abandoned this position. But it is clear that contemporaries regarded the grant as more than a recognition of status; it was a *conferment* of status. This one fact explains both the attempts made at controlling grants of arms, and the appeal of the alternative: the less closely regulated confirmation – which also flattered the recipient by representing his status as pre-existent.

But one should not forget that arms were to be seen, and the way they looked mattered too. There were aesthetic questions, which might affect their fitness for purpose; and their design might also make their newness all too apparent, in which case the newness of the armiger's gentility was also on display. The two aspects, independently significant, are thus intertwined; the historian of the gentry needs to *look* at the arms that men and women were granted, to see why it was so important to get them right.

'A herald, Kate? O put me in thy books' Shakespeare, the Heralds' Visitations and a New Visitation Address

ADRIAN AILES

One of the few facts we know for certain about William Shakespeare is that he was armigerous – that is to say, he bore an officially registered coat of arms.[1] In 1596 either his father John, then in his sixties, or, more likely, William himself on behalf of his father, had approached the heralds based at the College of Arms to acquire armorial bearings.[2] These were duly granted to John as head of the family, by the principal herald, Sir William Dethick, Garter King of Arms. Dethick was one of the thirteen English officers of arms whose role was to grant or confirm arms to suitable persons, to record armorial bearings, and to ensure that no duplication or wrongful assumption of such arms took place.[3] Heralds also compiled pedigrees, conducted elaborate heraldic funerals of the gentry and nobility, marshalled state occasions, and from time to time (principally in aLondon) read out important public proclamations. By 1600 their role as messengers or ambassadors had almost entirely come to an end.[4]

[1] I am grateful to Dr David Mateer and Dr Katherine Mair for having read a draft of this paper and for their helpful comments. I am also obliged to the Chapter of the College of Arms for permission to consult the Office copy of Raven's visitation.

[2] For Shakespeare's arms see Scott-Giles, *Shakespeare's Heraldry*, pp. 27–41; Charles Crisp, 'Shakespeare's Ancestors', *Coat of Arms*, 1st ser., vi (1960), pp. 105-8; R. C. Sutherland, 'The Grant of Arms to Shakespeare's Father', *Shakespeare Quarterly*, 14 (1963), pp. 379–85; Samuel Schoenbaum, *William Shakespeare: A Documentary Life* (Oxford, 1975), pp. 36, 166–73; G. Blakemore Evans and J. J. M. Tobin, 'Grant of Arms to John Shakespeare', in G. Blakemore Evans et al., *The Riverside Shakespeare*, 2nd edn. (Boston, 1997), Appx. C; Katherine Duncan-Jones, 'Shakespeare among the Heralds', *Coat of Arms*, new ser., xiii (2000), pp. 317–30, and eadcm, *Ungentle Shakespeare: Scenes from his Life* (London, 2001), pp. 82–103; James Kearney, 'Status' in *The Oxford Handbook of Shakespeare*, ed. Arthur F. Kinney (Oxford, 2011), pp. 182–201, at 182–4. See also *Heralds' Commemorative Exhibition Catalogue*, pl. XXXVIII, and Tarnya Cooper, *Searching for Shakespeare* (London, 2006), pp. 138–41. The transcript of the grant given in Scott-Giles, *Shakespeare's Heraldry*, pp. 36–7 is a composite of the first draft (College of Arms, Shakespeare Grants 1, formerly MS Vincent 157, article 23) and of a later intermediate stage (Shakespeare Grants 2, formerly MS Vincent 157, article 24) between that draft and the lost final fair copy given to John Shakespeare; Scott-Giles uses the intermediate as the basis for his composite transcript which is quoted in the present chapter.

[3] Technically only kings of arms (the three most senior heralds) could grant arms and then only on behalf of the Crown; cf. Gerard Legh, *The Accedens of Armory* (London, 1576), f. 115.

[4] For contemporary descriptions of the duties of a herald see: John Ferne, *The Blazon of Gentrie* (1586), p. 152; Francis Thynne, 'A Discourse of the Dutye and Office of an Herauld of Arms ... 1605 [1606]', and John Dodridge, 'A Consideration of the Office and Dutye of the Herauldes in

18. Sir William Dethick (d. 1612), Garter King of Arms from 1586 until his enforced departure in favour of William Segar in 1606. According to his opponents in the College, Dethick was a man of violent temper. He undoubtedly acted *ultra vires* by issuing patents purporting to grant arms when he was only a herald, and as Garter he incurred sustained criticism for allowing inappropriate arms to unsuitable persons. He was, however, a man of some erudition (being a mainstay of the Elizabethan Society of Antiquaries) and a methodical compiler and keeper of records, both in his own practice and in the management of the whole Office. College of Arms.

SHAKESPEARE AND THE HERALDS' VISITATIONS

From 1530 to 1687 another duty undertaken by the officers of arms was to go on heraldic 'visitation'. These were periodic surveys, undertaken usually every 20 to 30 years, each survey being conducted by one of the two senior heralds – the provincial kings of arms, Clarenceux, whose jurisdiction or 'heraldic march' extended across south Wales and England south of the river Trent, and Norroy, who looked after the northern province (north Wales and England north of the Trent); alternatively, they could depute the task to a junior officer of arms, who would journey in their stead. The main purpose of these visits was to register the descents of the local gentry in every county of England and Wales and to record their legitimate arms.[5] Only by this procedure could the heralds ensure that no duplication of arms took place, whether by separate families using the same or similar arms (a charge levelled at Shakespeare[6]) or by different branches within the same family. This was all the more necessary as some gentlemen 'refuse at the visitations to come to have their descentes entred, whereby they wronge their posterity and the heroldes, in that the haroldes cannot tell them their descentes and then they accompte the Haroldes ignorante fooles'.[7] Those gentry 'entering' their arms and pedigrees at the visitation were required to pay a fee set according to their status.

By Shakespeare's day visiting heralds were also required to justify the use of the styles 'esquire' and 'gentleman' by those registering, and they could publicly denounce

---

Englande, drawne out of sundrye observations ... 1600', both printed in Thomas Hearne, *A Collection of Curious Discourses* (London, 1720), pp. 230–68, 270–1; the relevant passages are quoted in full in Arthur Huntington Nason, *Heralds and Heraldry in Ben Jonson's Plays, Masques and Entertainments* (1907, reprinted New York, 1968), pp. 62–6. See also PRO, SP 14/44, f. 171 (*c.* 1604). For heralds in general at this time see Wagner, *Heralds of England*, and Wyman H. Herendeen, *William Camden: A Life in Context* (Woodbridge, 2007), pp. 375–424. Scotland and Ireland had separate heraldic authorities.

[5] For visitations during Shakespeare's lifetime see Wagner, *Heralds of England*, passim; A. Ailes, 'The Development of the Heralds' Visitations in England and Wales 1450–1600', *Coat of Arms*, 3rd ser., 5 (2009), pp. 7–23; A. E. Brown, 'Augustine Vincent, Herald, and his Projected History of Northamptonshire', *Northamptonshire Past and Present*, 52 (1999), pp. 21–31; Janet Verasanso, 'The Staffordshire Heraldic Visitations: Their Nature and Function', *Coat of Arms*, new ser., xv (2003), pp. 47–69; and the visitation procedure documents in *The Visitation of the County of Huntingdon ... 1613*, ed. H. Ellis (Camden Soc., 43, 1849), pp. 132–8. For later, but still relevant, material see Philip Styles, 'The Heralds' Visitation of Warwickshire 1682–3', *Trans., Birmingham Archaeological Soc.*, 71 (1953), pp. 96–134; P. L. Dickinson, 'Heralds' Visitation of Gloucestershire, 1682–83', *Bristol and Gloucestershire Archaeological Soc.*, 117 (1999), pp. 11–33; *The Visitation of London begun in 1687*, ed. T. C. Wales and C. P. Hartley, 2 vols (Harleian Soc., new ser., xv, 2004); and Adrian Ailes, 'Elias Ashmole's 'Heraldicall Visitacion' of Berkshire, 1665–66' (unpublished Oxford D.Phil. thesis, 2008).

[6] Shakespeare bore *Or, on a bend sable a spear or, the point steeled proper*, whereas the arms of Lord Mauley were *Or a bend sable*: Bodleian Library, MS Ashmole 846, f. 50r-v; College of Arms, MS WZ, f. 276v; Schoenbaum, *William Shakespeare: A Documentary Life*, pp. 172, 173; Duncan-Jones, *Ungentle Shakespeare*, p. 101; Scott-Giles, *Shakespeare's Heraldry*, p. 39.

[7] PRO, SP 14/44, f. 171 (*c.* 1604), quoted by P.H. Hardacre, 'The Earl Marshal, the Heralds, and the House of Commons, 1604-41', *International Review of Social History*, 2 (1957), pp. 106–25, at 109.

or 'disclaim' those who were unable to prove their gentry status or right to legitimate arms; if necessary, the visiting herald could deface or destroy any unlawful arms. Sometimes they would 'respite' an individual until such time as he could produce sufficient evidence of status or arms or simply provide the correct payment. This might necessitate a visit to the College of Arms in London after the visitation had taken place but hopefully before the final record had been submitted.

The itinerant herald could arrange for arms to be granted where appropriate. This did not automatically make the recipient a gentleman, though many thought this to be the case. Rather, as in the case of John Shakespeare, it confirmed and completed their existing gentle status.[8] Ben Jonson succinctly summed it up: a herald 'can give arms and marks, he cannot honour'.[9] The impressive body of records left behind by the visiting heralds consists today of many thousands of detailed pedigrees accompanied by finely tricked arms. These were carefully bound into volumes, county by county (the 'Office' or 'fair' copies'), and kept in the College of Arms.[10]

The first royal commission for a provincial king of arms to go on visitation was issued in 1530, although semi-official, so-called 'proto-visitations' stretched back to the 1480s.[11] By 1560 the time was ripe for a further round of nationwide surveys and a series of administrative and procedural reforms during the late 1550s and throughout the 1560s, coupled with a change in personnel at the College of Arms, resulted in a series of more regular, more sophisticated, more accurate, and more comprehensive visitations taking place. Between 1563 and 1585 practically the whole of the northern province was visited, and in the south, William Hervey, Clarenceux, personally or by deputy visited fifteen counties. These included Shakespeare's native county, Warwickshire, which was visited in 1563 by Hervey's deputy, Robert Cooke, then Chester Herald. Despite the Shakespeares' rise to gentry status, the family was never entered into a visitation. This was partly because William Shakespeare left no surviving sons to carry on his family name and arms, and partly because the county was not visited during his fifty-four-year lifetime.[12] It was Cooke who, as the new Clarenceux, later devised arms for John

[8] Sutherland, 'Grant of Arms to Shakespeare's Father', p. 382.
[9] *The Staple of News*, IV, I; quoted in Nason, *Heralds and Heraldry in Ben Jonson's Plays*, p. 73.
[10] For lists of visitations see C. R. Humphery-Smith, *Armigerous Ancestors: A Catalogue of Sources for the Study of the Visitations of the Heralds in the 16th and 17th Centuries with referenced lists of names* (Canterbury, 1997); G. D. Squibb, *Visitation Pedigrees and the Genealogist* (Canterbury, 1964); and Anthony Wagner, *Records and Collections of the College of Arms* (London, 1952), pp. 66–84.
[11] Compare N. Ramsay, 'Richard III and the Office of Arms', in *The Yorkist Age. Proceedings of the 2011 Harlaxton Symposium*, ed. H. Kleineke and C. Steer, Harlaxton Medieval Studies, xxiii (Donington, Lincs., 2013), pp. 142–63.
[12] Warwickshire was not visited again till 1619. For the heraldry of those married into the Shakespeare family and recorded in later visitations see 'Heralds' Visitations of Counties', in *Herald and Genealogist*, ed. J. G. Nichols, i (London, 1863), pp. 509–13; *The Visitation of the County of Warwick in the year 1619*, ed. J. Fetherston (Harleian Soc., xii, 1877); and Scott-Giles, *Shakespeare's Heraldry*, pp. 39–41.

SHAKESPEARE AND THE HERALDS' VISITATIONS

Shakespeare, probably sometime in the early 1570s (just as the young William, as the son of a burgess, was starting at grammar school), though, as we have seen, these were not granted until 1596; John's increasing financial difficulties were doubtless to blame for the postponement.

This dramatic revival in visitations was sadly not to last. Internal squabbles within the College,[13] the transfer of the Earl Marshalcy into commission,[14] the loss of revenue from fewer heraldic funerals with many now serviced by independent local painters and other 'mechanicks',[15] a decrease in both diplomatic missions abroad[16] and officially recorded grants of arms,[17] meant that the College went into something of a meltdown in the 1590s. Both Dethick and Cooke were accused of granting arms to all and sundry, including 'Shakespear the Player'.[18] If the mid-1590s were years of spectacular public acclaim and aristocratic patronage for the actor and playwright, then 1596, when arms were granted to his father, seems to have been particularly difficult for the College of Arms.[19] No royal commissions for new visitations were made in the 1590s, and officially recognised visitations virtually ceased.[20] The turn of the century witnessed the introduction of several badly needed reforms in the College, including the appointment of the great antiquary, William Camden, as Clarenceux King of Arms (1597), and of several other talented officers of arms. Nevertheless, despite the granting of a new

---

[13] See especially British Library, Cotton MS Faustina E. i, ff. 260–265v.

[14] Wagner, *Heralds of England*, p. 209; G. D. Squibb, *The High Court of Chivalry: A Study in the Civil Law in England* (Oxford, 1959), p. 231; letters patent creating the commissioners: British Library, MS Add. 6297, f. 3.

[15] British Library, Cotton MS Faustina E. i, ff. 97, 262v; Bodleian Library, MS Ashmole 840, p. 21; J. F. R. Day, 'Buried "The King's Trew Subject": The Late Medieval English Heraldic Funeral in Decline', *Coat of Arms*, new ser., 13 (2000), pp. 233–44; William Smith, Rouge Dragon Pursuivant, 'A Breff Discourse of the causes of Discord amongst the officers of Armes: and of the great Abuses and absurdities committed by Painters, to the great prejudice and hindrance of the same office', 1606, printed above, pp. 45–67.

[16] PRO, SP 14/44, f. 171; British Library, Cotton MS Faustina E. i, f. 271.

[17] Approximately 300 grants in the 1590s compared to about 700 in the 1580s: Edward Elmhirst, 'The Fashion for Heraldry', *Coat of Arms*, 1st ser., iv (1956–8), pp. 47–50, at 48. The probability is that this seriously underestimates the number of grants actually made by heralds, but many would have been unofficial and not entered into the College records: see Peter Gwynn-Jones, 'Tudor Enigmas', *Coat of Arms*, 3rd ser., i (2005), pp. 73-104. See also C. Cheesman, above, Ch. 3.

[18] The quotation is from the 1602 complaint by Ralph Brooke, York Herald, now Folger Shakespeare Library, MS V.a.350, p. 28 (see Cooper, *Searching for Shakespeare*, p. 141; Schoenbaum, *Shakespeare: A Documentary Life*, pp. 171–2); the arms were, of course, granted to Shakespeare's father. For the response of Dethick and Camden (as Clarenceux): College of Arms, MS WZ, f. 276v, and Bodleian Library, MS Ashmole 846, f. 50. See also Duncan-Jones, *Ungentle Shakespeare*, pp. 101–3; Schoenbaum, *Shakespeare: A Documentary Life*, pp. 172–3; and Scott-Giles, *Shakespeare's Heraldry*, p. 39.

[19] Duncan-Jones, *Ungentle Shakespeare*, pp. 83, 87; Wagner, *Heralds of England*, pp. 217–19.

[20] No records of visitations were deposited in the College: British Library, Cotton MS Faustina E. i, f. 260.

commission in 1603 by James I, regular visitations did not resume until 1610. When they did, it was along very much the same lines as the last round of surveys in the 1560s, '70s and '80s. Six years later the immortal bard was laid to rest in Trinity church, Stratford, his mortal remains eventually to repose beneath an impressive funerary wall monument decorated with his family's coat of arms.

The 1603 visitation commission to Camden as Clarenceux King of Arms, for him or his deputy to visit the southern province, differed little in detail from the last issued to his predecessor, Clarenceux Cooke in 1568.[21] It authorized Camden to enter churches, houses, and castles to record any arms displayed, to note the degree (status) and descents (ancestry) of the owners of arms (summoned to his visitation), to correct any unlawful or usurped arms and, if necessary, pull down them or deface them, to disclaim publicly those incorrectly using the titles 'esquire' or 'gentleman', to control the wearing of various mourning apparel at heraldic funerals (such as specific hoods and gowns), to prohibit any unauthorized heraldic work by painters, glaziers, engravers and others, to forbid anyone such as sheriffs, archdeacons, and clerks to add the styles 'esquire' or 'gentleman' to people's names unless they could justify this use, to command JPs, sheriffs, mayors, bailiffs and other local officials to assist Clarenceux in his visitation, and, finally, to command anyone finding fault with the visitation to appear before the Earl Marshal to present their case.

The mechanics and procedures of early seventeenth-century visitations differed little from those of Elizabeth's reign. Before the visitation the visiting herald compiled a list of the gentry and 'potential' gentry – those who might register and apply for arms – of the county. This initial 'catalogue' was based on previous visitations, funeral certificates, lists of JPs and civic corporations, tax lists, freeholders' books and lists of grand jurors, and any other relevant information gathered beforehand from local informants and officials, especially the undersheriffs. The herald then sent warrants of summons to the undersheriff for distribution to the high constables and bailiffs of each town and hundred together with a list (perfected catalogue) of names of persons whom each was to summon.[22] To assist in this process, the herald included many dozens, sometimes hundreds, of small blank tickets of summons, to be filled in by the constables and bailiffs and distributed to those persons; he may have filled in some of these himself. A schedule of where and when the gentry of each hundred were to meet was annexed. Those

---

[21] T. Rymer, *Foedera, Conventiones, Literae ...*, 20 vols (London, 1727–35), XV, p. 673, and XVI, p. 538. For a contemporary deputation visitation commission from Camden see *Visitation of the County of Huntingdon*, ed. Ellis, pp. 134-6.

[22] For the wording see *Visitation of the County of Huntingdon*, ed. Ellis, p. 137; and Bodleian Library, MS Ashmole 840, p. 665 (example of 1612). For a 1615 example see John Guillim, *A Display of Heraldry*, 6th edn. (London, 1724), Appendix: 'Observations on the Office and Officers of Arms', p. 51, where a further commendation is added by the bishop and chancellor of Durham and the visiting herald. See Brown, 'Augustine Vincent, Herald, and his Projected History of Northamptonshire', p. 25.

summoned (or their deputies) were to present themselves (with suitable evidences) at a local place of sitting (usually an inn situated in a market town) at a specified time; charges of contempt would be brought against any who refused to comply. The high sheriff would have sent a further warrant to the constables and bailiffs commanding them to deliver the warrants and assist the visiting herald. A letter from the Earl Marshal (or commissioners for his office) would be addressed to the knights and gentry of the county, recommending the visiting herald to their good consideration.[23] A second letter would go to the assize judges reminding them that the visiting herald was about to go on visitation, and entreating their assistance. It also requested that after the visitation commission had been read out at the assizes 'in the face of the countie', the judges should commend the commission to the knights and gentry present.[24] Another letter may well have been sent to the lord lieutenant and JPs warning them of the visit and likewise seeking their assistance; this was certainly the practice later in the century.

The visitation could now begin. The herald, armed with his commission and usually taking with him a junior officer of arms to act as an assistant or 'marshal', as well as a clerk and herald painter, journeyed to the county. He may well have taken a map and, with the permission of the College, copies of previous visitations. As already indicated, visits were often timed to coincide with the assizes, when the local gentry would already be gathered to meet the visiting judge and to serve on the grand jury. Amongst all the pomp and circumstance (and gossip) of such an occasion, the herald, dressed in his tabard of the royal arms, would read out his visitation commission; some of the summons tickets might be handed out at this point.[25] He might then take the opportunity of speaking to the assembled gentry, justifying his visit and exhorting them literally to sign up to his visitation – for it was in their interests and the interests of their progeny, as well as for the better stability of the social order and maintenance of the traditional hierarchy of civil society, to do so.

Over the following days and perhaps weeks, the visiting officer visited the various registration stations (usually a day or two apart), approving and recording the arms, pedigrees (including the name and age of the next heir), and status of those attending. The herald, his clerk, or the herald painter, would also make notes of documents, inscriptions, or seals, or any other 'evidences' (especially old grants or confirmations of arms) that had been brought or cited as proof. At the same time he would be compiling a list of those voluntarily disclaiming gentry status or who were disclaimed in their absence. Excuses for non-appearance were noted and those who could not provide

---

[23] For the wording, see Bodleian Library, MS Ashmole 840, p. 665 (example of 1612).

[24] For the wording, see Bodleian Library, MS Ashmole 840, p. 666 (example of 1612); cf. British Library, Cotton MS Faustina E. i, f. 147 (for 1622).

[25] *The Visitations of the County of Oxford taken in the Years 1566, 1574 and in 1634*, ed. W. H. Turner (Harleian Soc., v, 1871), p. x; Styles, 'The Heralds' Visitation of Warwickshire, 1682-3', p. 105. When the commission was not read out, it could result in a loss of local interest and respect: Styles, 'The Heralds' Visitation of Warwickshire, 1682-3', p. 98.

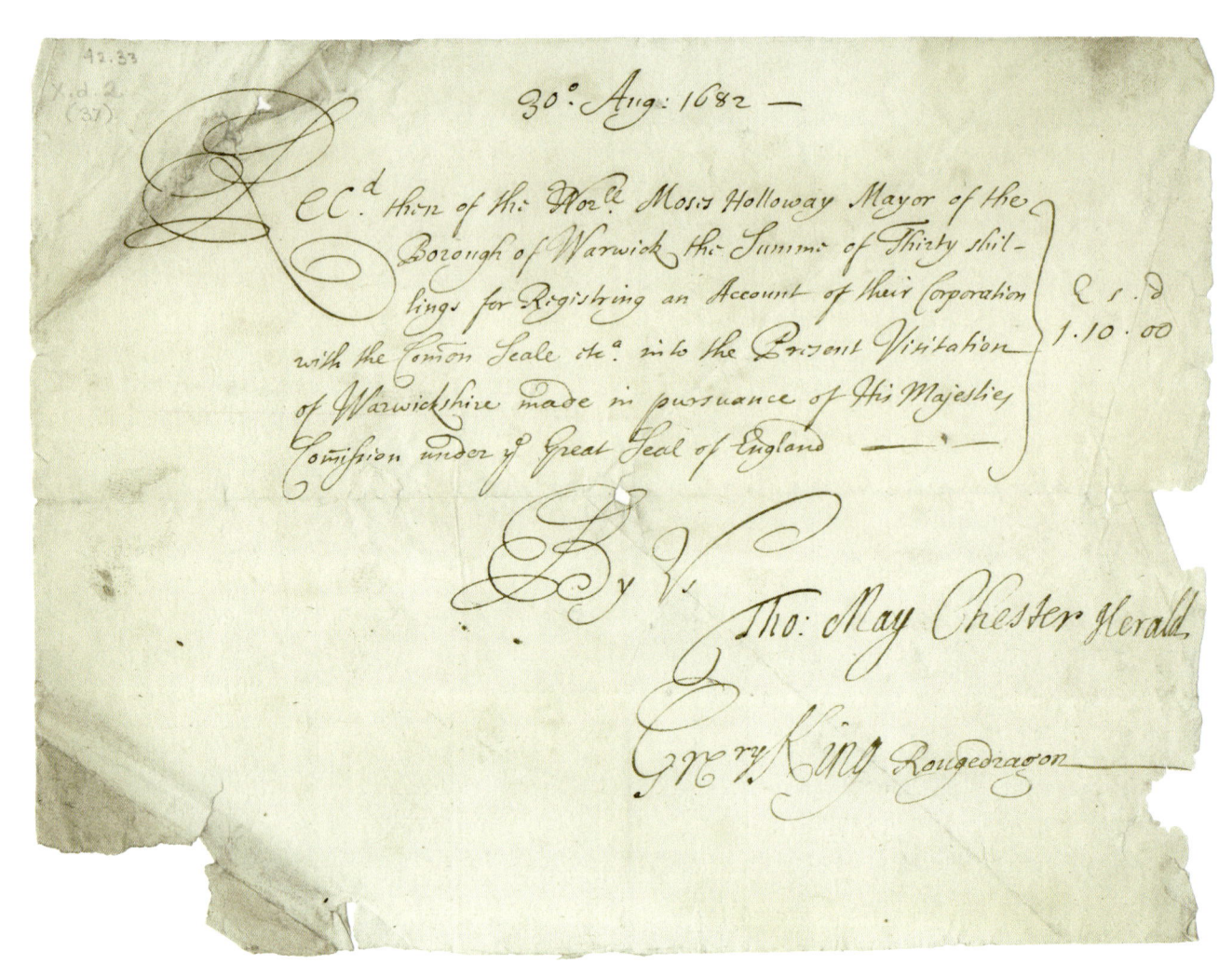

19. Receipt dated 30 August 1682 from Thomas May, Chester Herald, and Gregory King, Rouge Dragon Pursuivant, for 30 shillings received from the Mayor and Corporation of Warwick for having registered the borough seal in the visitation of Warwickshire.
Washington (DC), Folger Shakespeare Library, MS X. d. 2 (37).

sufficient proof for their arms were strictly commanded to cease using them.[26] The pedigrees and arms would be noted in narrative form or hasty family trees sketched and tricks made, though at some point the head of the family or his substitute would be asked to sign an agreed version; a registration fee would then be paid. The herald (or rather his accompanying artist) could also (for further payment) produce a signed certificate of the approved arms. Drawings of the common seal of the corporations of towns visited would be taken along with a list of corporation members and dignitaries (see Fig. 19).

After the initial visit a second round of summons tickets was sent out to pick up non-attenders or those previously missed, and, if necessary, a repeat visit was made.

[26] Brown, 'Augustine Vincent, Herald, and his Projected History of Northamptonshire', pp. 25–7.

Sometimes a local official or agent was deputed to gather outstanding fees or evidences, especially from those respited. Last-minute changes and payments could be made in London after the return of the herald to the capital but (hopefully) before the submission of the final record into the College library. Another letter addressed to the bailiff of each hundred listed those who, having ignored the summons, were to be directed to appear before the Earl Marshal (or the commissioners for the office of Earl Marshal) or else to forfeit a fine; individual summonses would then be issued to these renegades.[27]

Whilst travelling round the county the visiting herald (or his herald painter) might also take careful notes and drawings of any interesting remains of the past such as church monuments, sculptures, seals and stained glass, and would perhaps transcribe deeds, charters and earlier pedigrees; in many respects the heralds, and particularly those making such commissioned visits to the counties, were at the forefront of the first stirrings of the serious scientific study of English local history and topography.[28] At the very end of the visitation, often in the following year, the final list of disclaimers was prominently displayed (sometimes to the sound of trumpets) at the next assizes or general sessions. Those so named and shamed, nevertheless, often flouted the injunction and openly appeared again as gentry after the herald had left town.[29] Finally, fair copies of the approved and paid-for pedigrees and arms, duly signed by those registering them, along with any 'church notes' (as the arms and inscriptions noted from churches, manor houses and elsewhere were called), were bound and entered into the College collections (see Fig. 20).[30] The visiting herald could then claim his expenses and pay his herald painter. Such painters often kept their own drafts of the arms and pedigrees produced on

[27] For the preamble to the list sent to the bailiffs see Bodleian Library, MS Ashmole 840, p. 667 (example of 1612) and Guillim, *Display of Heraldry*, appendix, pp. 51–2; and *Visitation of Huntingdon*, ed. Ellis, p. 138, for an individual summons.

[28] T. D. Kendrick, *British Antiquity* (London, 1950), pp. 152–7; A. Ailes, '"To Search the Truth": Heralds, Myths and Legends in 16th and 17th-Century England and Wales', in *Genealogica et Heraldica: Proc., XXVIIth International Congress of Genealogical and Heraldic Sciences, St Andrews 2006*, 2 vols (Edinburgh, 2008), I, pp. 95–106; and Jan Broadway, '*No historie so meete*': *Gentry Culture and the Development of Local History in the Elizabethan and Early Stuart England* (Manchester, 2006), pp. 127–9, 239–40.

[29] For the preamble to a public list of disclaimers, see *Visitation of Huntingdon*, ed. Ellis, pp. 137–8, and Bodleian Library, MS Ashmole 840, p. 668 (for an example of 1612). See Verasanso, 'The Staffordshire Heraldic Visitations', pp. 61–2, for examples from 1619 of those ignoring an injunction. See also *Reports of Heraldic Cases in the Court of Chivalry, 1623–1732*, ed. G. D. Squibb (Harleian Soc., 107, 1956), pp. 3-4, and cf. pp. 20, 24; idem, *High Court of Chivalry*, p. 212; *Cases in the High Court of Chivalry, 1634–1640*, ed. R. P. Cust and A. J. Hopper (Harleian Soc., new ser. 18, 2006), pp. 171–2; and G. Grazebrook, 'The Earl Marshal's Court in England; Comprising Visitations and the Penalties Incurred by their Neglect', *Trans., Historic Soc. of Lancashire and Cheshire*, 45 (1894), pp. 99–140, at 133, 135–6. For another case, see Richard Cust, 'Sir Henry Spelman Investigates', *Coat of Arms*, 3rd ser., iii (2007), pp. 25–34, at 26.

[30] For church notes see Wagner, *Heralds of England*, p. 226; idem, *Records and Collections of the College of Arms*, pp. 17, 61–3; and Ailes, '"To Search the Truth": Heralds, Myths and Legends', p. 99.

20. The fair or 'Office' copy of the visitation of Norfolk taken by John Raven, Richmond Herald, in 1612–13, and deposited in the College of Arms in 1622. Entry for the family of Cobbe. College of Arms, MS C. 15 Part 1, f. 20 upper half.

visitation (including those not entered into the final Office copy) which they might over time add to as working tools of their own trade. Many of these unofficial hybrid versions have ended up amongst the Harley manuscripts in the British Library along with other background papers.[31]

Only one opening address given by a herald on visitation is known, having recently been discovered in the British Library. It can almost certainly be attributed to John Raven, Richmond Herald, and is found in a bound volume of heraldic papers amongst the Harley manuscripts.[32] These papers appear to be either the background notes assembled by Raven in preparation for his visitation of Norfolk in 1612 and 1613, or genealogies and other papers taken by him during that visit; Raven was deputed to visit

---

[31] See especially Squibb, *Visitation Pedigrees and the Genealogist*.
[32] British Library, MS Harley 1154, ff. 65v–61 (bound upside down, hence the backward foliation).

East Anglia by Camden who never went on visitation.[33] Not only is Raven's speech a unique record of what a visiting herald said on such an occasion but it also provides a valuable insight into how the heralds – those remembrancers of honour, guardians of chivalry, and arbiters of heraldic disputes – defined gentility and nobility and decided who, like Shakespeare's father, could legitimately bear arms.

By 1612 much had already been written on the right of the gentry to bear arms and, doubtless, Raven was familiar with most of these works. Sir Thomas Elyot's *The Boke Named the Governour* (1531) was particularly popular during Shakespeare's lifetime, running into several editions.[34] Other important heraldic works included Gerard Legh's *The Accedens of Armory* (1562), John Bossewell's *Workes of Armorie* (1572), and John Ferne's *The Blazon of Gentrie* (1586). The heralds themselves, not surprisingly, had written on the subject: most recently, William Wyrley, Rouge Croix Pursuivant, in his *The True Use of Armorie* (1592), and his successor as Rouge Croix, John Guillim, in his *Display of Heraldry* (1610), Francis Thynne, Lancaster Herald, in his 'Discourse of the Dutye and Office of an Heraulde of Arms' (1606), and the man who was to replace Dethick as Garter in 1607, Sir William Segar, in his *Booke of Honor and Armes* (1590) and *Honor Military and Civill* (1602). Special mention should be made of Sir Thomas Smith's influential *De Republica Anglorum* written at the time of Shakespeare's birth with its famous working definition of a gentleman that the heralds amongst others often used to their advantage: 'to be shorte, [one] who can live idly and without manuall labour, and will beare the port, charge and countenaunce of a gentleman, he shall be called master, ... and shall be taken for a gentleman'.[35]

Rather frustratingly, the various visitation commissions issued at intervals between 1530 and 1688 do not define who was gentry, and, therefore, eligible for entry into the hallowed pages of the final record. The first commission does, nevertheless, speak of granting arms to 'men of good honest Reputacyon', and from 1536 the letters patent appointing provincial kings of arms state that they could grant arms 'to distinguished [*claris*] men'; only gentlemen and above could bear arms.[36] Garter Kings of Arms, such as Dethick, did not normally travel on visitation but were allowed by the 1522 statutes of the Order of the Garter to give arms 'to those who by their valiant and laudable actions, their virtues, and honours of their degrees shall deserve them according to

---

[33] The fair or 'Office' copy is College of Arms, MS C.15 part 1, which was not handed in to the College until March 1622.

[34] Stuart Gillespie, *Shakespeare's Books: A Dictionary of Shakespeare's Sources* (London and New Brunswick, 2001), p. 140.

[35] *'De Republica Anglorum' by Sir Thomas Smith*, ed. M. Dewar (Cambridge, 1982), p. 72. Wyrley's authorship of *The True Use of Armorie* has been questioned.

[36] *Munimenta Heraldica: 1484–1984*, ed. G. D. Squibb (Harleian Soc., new ser. 4, 1985), p. 130. Legh provides a detailed checklist to determine who should be given arms: *Accedens of Armory*, f. 115r–v.

ancient custom'.[37] Francis Thynne, Lancaster Herald, wrote in 1606, that kings of arms could grant arms to 'persons of abilitye deserving well of the Prince and Commonwealth, by reason of Office, Authoritye, Wisdome, Learning, good Manners, and sober Governmente'. Financial guidelines produced in 1530 as to what was necessary to qualify for arms were soon outdated.[38] Otherwise, for the official College view on such matters one has to refer to the rather formulaic and anachronistic preamble of the heralds' grants of arms such as that given to Shakespeare's father.

Raven's address might, of course, simply reflect his own personal prejudices and not be typical of those of his visiting brother officers of arms, but it is all we have to go on and it would be fair to say that it does toe the party line; presumably it had been approved by his superior, Camden, who may have even have written it for his deputy. Raven himself was an East Anglian, having been born in Hadleigh (Suffolk); he was to die there in 1616. He had been an officer of arms since the Armada (1588), and in 1612, 1613 and 1614 he acted as Camden's deputy for the visitations of Norfolk, Suffolk, and Essex. The opening oration was almost certainly delivered at Norwich.

The probability is that Raven gave his address at the assizes, after the close of the judge's charge to the grand jury. The whole occasion was in effect a ritual display of the social and political order of the county – a captive audience for any visiting herald.[39] Raven begins his speech by reading out aloud the royal commission, thereby reminding the assembled gentry to participate in what is essentially a command from the king. Visiting heralds were, after all, legally appointed by the Crown and were members of the royal household; hence the king's rich coat upon their backs and collar of SS about their necks. Even so, it would be true to say they did not always receive the honour and respect that they believed was due to them. The recent dubious actions of some of their company can only have fuelled this prejudice; even the Queen was exasperated at some of their actions.[40] Small wonder that Ben Jonson could not only poke fun at Shakespeare's new arms and motto, 'NON SANZ DROICT' ('Not without right'), unfortunately granted by one of the more guilty College members, but also at all those who, 'so enamoured of the name of gentleman', had blatantly bought arms to prove their status. Such hostility and sometimes indifference to the Office of Arms meant that not all those who had been summoned turned up for visitations, and one cannot be certain that, despite the issue of summonses to appear before the Earl Marshal for contempt, this was ever enforced, since there are no surviving examples of fines being paid, though this may be due to loss of

---

[37] *Munimenta Heraldica*, ed. Squibb, pp. 73–4.
[38] Wagner, *Heralds of England*, pp. 165-7; Maurice Keen, *Origins of the English Gentleman: Heraldry, Chivalry and Gentility in Medieval England, 1300–c. 1500* (Stroud, 2002), pp. 109–10.
[39] Michael J. Braddick, *State Formation in Early Modern England, c. 1550–1700* (Cambridge, 2000), p. 38; Bodleian Library, MS Top.Yorks. c. 36, f. 29.
[40] British Library, Cotton MS Faustina E. i, f. 262v; Mary E. Hazard, *Elizabethan Silent Language* (Lincoln and London, 2000), pp. 214–15; J. H. Round, *Studies in the Peerage and Family History* (London, 1901), p. 293.

evidence.[41]

Having read the king's visitation commission, Raven then invited his audience to reflect upon the purpose (or 'end') of that commission, namely the consideration of peace and good order without which there is havoc and confusion. He says he is going to concentrate on 'gentleness and nobleness', which he sees as one.[42] The 1603 commission begins by stating that such visits take place 'for a due Order to be kept' regarding arms so 'that the Nobillity of this Realme maye be preserved in everie degree as apperteyneth, as well in Honor as in Worshippe; And that every Person and Persons, Bodies Politique Corporate and others, may be the better known in his and theire Estate Degree and Mystery withoute Confusion or Disorder'. Raven then notes that even base trades have rules, and that disorder has boldly hatched among the gentry. He adds that God created men in varying degrees of worth – that some have dominion over others just as the sun does over the planets. Some men are noble, others ignoble, some virtuous, others vicious, some bond, some free. After the Flood, as evil multiplied, so those more upright, just, valiant, and wiser than the rest were chosen to govern the others, to correct evil, defend the innocent, and advance the virtuous. Since in times past our ancestors did not know who was upright and just, they chose eminent persons descended from 'the best kynde' to rule over them; thus from the very beginning there was a distinction of persons and degrees. Those descended of the best families who and excel in virtue, valour, learning, counsel, wisdom and understanding deserve to have the rights of nobility including the most honourable ensigns attached to them and their posterity – for they have the best capacities and become notable examples to the ruder, ignoble, vulgar and base sort below. In short, Raven was arguing that from time immemorial there have been persons of different degrees and worth, some to govern and to safeguard order, and that those descended of the best families and who excel in certain qualities such as virtue and learning have the right to display arms betokening their noble status.

Shakespeare was well aware of the Tudor and early Stuart preoccupation with precedence[43] and social order whether in heaven or on earth. In *Troilus and Cressida*, Ulysses proclaims that the 'the heavens themselves, the planets, and this centre | Observe degree, priority, and place ... but when the planets | In evil mixture to disorder wander, | What plagues and what portents! What Mutiny' ... O, when degree is shaked, | Which

---

[41] *Visitation of Huntingdon*, ed. Ellis, p. 138, for a summons; Squibb, *High Court of Chivalry*, p. 35; Grazebrook, 'The Earl Marshal's Court in England', pp. 133, 135–6; Verasanso, 'The Staffordshire Heraldic Visitations', p. 63.

[42] For the relationship of gentility and nobility, see *Governour*, pp. 27–9. Garter Segar defines 'Gentleman or *Nobilis*' as the name given for pre-eminence, to distinguish men of virtue from base people: Sir William Segar, *The Book of Honor and Armes (1590) and Honor Military and Civil (1602)*: facsimile reproduction with an introduction by Diane Bornstein (New York, 1975), at *Honor Military and Civill*, p. 226.

[43] David Gelber, '"Hark, What Discord': Precedency among the Early Stuart Gentry', *Coat of Arms*, 3rd ser., iii (2007), pp. 117–44.

is the ladder to all high designs | Then enterprise is sick'. Shakespeare had very probably read Elyot's *The Governour*, which ran into many editions during the sixteenth century. In this work the author emphasized the need for order in heaven and on earth; how one sun rules over the day and one moon over the night. This order, he maintained, contains degrees high and base.[44] The writer John Ferne, who likewise had very probably studied *The Governour*, spoke in his own influential work, *The Blazon of Gentrie* (1586), of hierarchies both in heaven and on earth, as well as amongst the planets where the sun is the most noble; John Bossewell's *Workes of Armorie* (1572) also refers to the heavenly hierarchy.[45] Nor were precedence and order confined to the stratosphere, as Raven's audience was soon to discover. In 1619 James I was forced to intervene in the civic affairs of Norwich, urging the authorities there to adhere to a rigid code of seniority.[46]

Raven continues his speech by asserting that many gentlefolk are ignorant of their family arms usurping those of others, that sons do not know how to differentiate or 'difference' their father's arms (usually by adding a small charge such as a crescent). Others quarter their arms with several other coats not belonging to them, to give the impression that they are of a great and ancient family. Some are ignorant of their arms and ancestors and yet argue with the visiting herald that they are of an honourable descent, although they have no proof. What could be more dishonourable than for a professed gentleman to be ignorant of his ancestors' arms? Raven entreats the gentry of Norfolk – those that are honourably minded – to gather together as much evidence as possible – testaments, evidences (presumably he here meant grants of arms, armorial seals, stained glass and so on), deeds, offices, inquisitions (post mortem), epitaphs and funeral monuments, for he is ready with all willingness to receive and record; at this juncture Raven tactfully omits to mention his fees for this service.

It would be fascinating to know whether Shakespeare's three brothers knew how to difference correctly their father's arms during his lifetime; for William, as the first-born son, this would have entailed adding a label – a narrow band with three tags pendant from it – across the top of the shield, to be discarded on the death of his father. Multiple quarterings, like pretentious pedigrees, were a common conceit amongst aspiring Tudor gentry eager to show off their supposed ancestry; all too often, venal heralds responded with a patchwork quilt of dubiously legitimate coats. Indeed, Raven's reference would have struck a chord in the Shakespeare household. In 1599 William sought a confirmation of the ancestral arms of his mother, Mary Arden.[47] This would have

---

[44] Quoted in Gillespie, *Shakespeare's Books*, p. 140.
[45] Ferne, *Blazon of Gentrie*, pp. 5–6; Elyot, *Governour*, p. 31, note (a); Bossewell, *Workes of Armorie*, f. 10. For degrees even within the category of mere gentleman, see Segar, *Honor Military and Civill*, pp. 228–9.
[46] John Pound, *Tudor and Stuart Norwich* (Chichester, 1988), p. 87.
[47] College of Arms, Shakespeare Grants 3, formerly MS R. 21, p. 347; Scott-Giles, *Shakespeare's Heraldry*, pp. 38–9; Schoenbaum, *Shakespeare: A Documentary Life*, Fig. 130. For quarterings in Shakespeare's plays, see Scott-Giles, *Shakespeare's Heraldry*, p. 103.

allowed both John Shakespeare to *impale* his own arms with those of Mary side by side on the same shield, and, because Mary would be confirmed as an armorial heiress, it would have permitted William and his descendants permanently to *quarter* the two coats in the same way that the Tudor royal arms quartered those of France and England; to quote *A Midsummer Night's Dream*, 'an union in partition … | like coats in heraldry, Due but to one, and crowned with one crest'. Shakespeare knew his heraldry and was obviously keen to exploit its potential as a clear visual indicator of his status as a gentleman, successful playwright, and property owner.

Raven then returns in his oration to that multi-faceted quality, virtue, commonly regarded by humanists and heralds alike as an essential prerequisite for nobleness and gentility – the subjects of the herald's speech. To proceed from ancient stock, he tells his audience, is not enough: they should live uprightly and entertain virtuous actions which are profitable for all. If the country is invaded or there is civil disorder, an ancient coat of arms is of little use. It is much better to rely on virtue, wisdom, counsel, advice and courage! All the power of Caesar cannot make someone lacking virtue become a gentleman.

Here again, Raven closely follows Ferne, who notes that without virtue it is impossible to be a perfect gentleman, that virtue can make the ungentle gentle, and that the heralds prefer those who have been made new gentlemen by the industry of their virtues to those of ancient stock who lack this qualification.[48] For him virtues were 'the right colours of a Gentlemans coat-armor' to be preferred above the proud empty boast of some vain peacock-tail arms of a distant ancestor.[49] The best type of gentleman is he who combines ancient blood with merit, a view repeated by Segar and echoed in Raven's earlier statement that it was those of the best families (that is of ancient descent) *and* who have excelled in virtue, valour, learning and so on, who deserve the rights of nobility and the honourable ensigns attached to them.[50] Ferne also notes that not even the Emperor Sigismund could make a man lacking virtue a gentleman.[51]

But what was virtue? From the point of view of heralds, such as Raven, their grants and confirmations of arms from the mid-sixteenth century onwards had defined virtue in terms of commendable or meritorious service, usually in civilian actions or martial prowess. Segar summed it up well when he wrote in 1590 that 'it therefore behove the

---

[48] Ferne, *Blazon of Gentrie*, sig. Aiii, pp. 18, 27, 227; cf. Legh, *Accedens of Armory*, sig. A.iii, and Bossewell, *Workes of Armorie*, fos. 4, 13v–18; and for the necessity of virtue see also: Felicity Heal and Clive Holmes, *The Gentry in England and Wales 1500–1700* (Basingstoke, 1994), p. 9; J. P. Cooper, *Land, Men and Beliefs: Studies in Early Modern History*, ed. G. E. Aylmer and J. S. Morrill (London, 1983), pp. 50, 54–5; and Mervyn James, *English Politics and the Concept of Honour, 1485–1642* (Past and Present Soc., 1978), pp. 3, 22. For the value (or otherwise) of lineage, see Heal and Holmes, *Gentry in England and Wales*, pp. 33–7.

[49] Ferne, *Blazon of Gentrie*, pp. 15–16, 28.

[50] Ibid., pp. 14-15, 23, 29; cf. Segar, *Honor and Armes*, p. 50, repeated in *Honor Military and Civill*, p. 113.

[51] Ferne, *Blazon of Gentrie*, pp. 61–2.

verie Gentleman well borne to imbrace the love of vertue, and in the *actions* thereof to employ the course of his whole life'.[52] A note at the foot of one of the two drafts of the grant of arms to John Shakespeare (the original does not exist) states that he was 'A Justice of the Peace and was Baylife the Q. officer and cheffe of the towne of Stratford uppon Avon xv or xvi years past'; the 1599 exemplification of the same arms repeats this information within its main text. When Dethick and Camden were forced to defend Shakespeare's arms (as too close to the design of another and apparently on the grounds they had been granted to an unworthy family), they included the fact that John 'hath borne magestracy and was Justice of peace at Stratford upon Avon'.[53] John's grant and exemplification of arms also notes the martial service of his ancestors to Henry VII. There is an emphasis here on a knowledge of the law, being a servant of the commonwealth, and, by dint of ancestry, possessing martial achievement. Ferne and Raven would have approved of John's candidature.[54]

Honour and an honourable reputation were the due rewards, perhaps the inevitable consequences, of such virtue and meritorious service. As Segar had written, 'Honor is the recompence of vertue, it may not be looked for untill some vertuous testimonie bee first shewed'.[55] Again, Shakespeare's grant is typical of its day in stating that the heralds have been reliably informed that the grantee is 'of good reputacion and credit'.[56] Honour might be 'air' and 'a mere scutcheon' to Falstaff, but it was highly prized by those, like John and William Shakespeare, who earnestly sought formal acceptance into the honour community. At the end of the day an honourable reputation is what mattered; even the courts agreed.[57] Modern historians have concluded that, despite all the contemporary commentaries, rhetoric, and lawsuits in the Court of Chivalry, 'the gentry were that body of men and women whose gentility was acknowledged by others'; in short, those *reputed* to be gentlemen and gentlewomen.[58]

[52] Segar, *Honor and Armes*, 5th Book, p. 72; my italics. Note too the combination of well-born and virtue.
[53] Schoenbaum, *Shakespeare: A Documentary Life*, pp. 171, 172; Duncan-Jones, *Ungentle Shakespeare*, p. 101; Folger Shakespeare Library, MS V.a.156; Scott-Giles, *Shakespeare's Heraldry*, p. 39.
[54] Scott-Giles, *Shakespeare's Heraldry*, pp. 38–9; Ferne, *Blazon of Gentrie*, pp. 58–60, where he includes bailiffs amongst those eligible for arms. See also see Cooper, *Land, Men and Beliefs*, p. 50. The letters patent creating the first commissioners for the earl marshalcy in 1592 state that arms should be given to those of birth and lineage who should receive honour 'for service in Politick government or in Martial Actions': British Library, Add. MS 6297, f. 3.
[55] Segar, *Honor and Armes*, 5th Book, p. 74.
[56] The link between an honourable reputation and gentility and the ability to grant arms on the basis of repute stems back to the 15th century: see Cooper, *Land, Men and Beliefs*, pp. 48–9, 68–9; James, *English Politics and the Concept of Honour*, pp. 3, 5.
[57] O. Barron, 'The Gentility of Richard Barker', *Ancestor*, ii (1902), pp. 48–53; Squibb, *High Court of Chivalry*, p. 172; Heal and Holmes, *Gentry in England and Wales*, p. 7; Cooper, *Land, Men and Beliefs*, p. 74.
[58] Heal and Holmes, *Gentry in England and Wales*, p. 19.

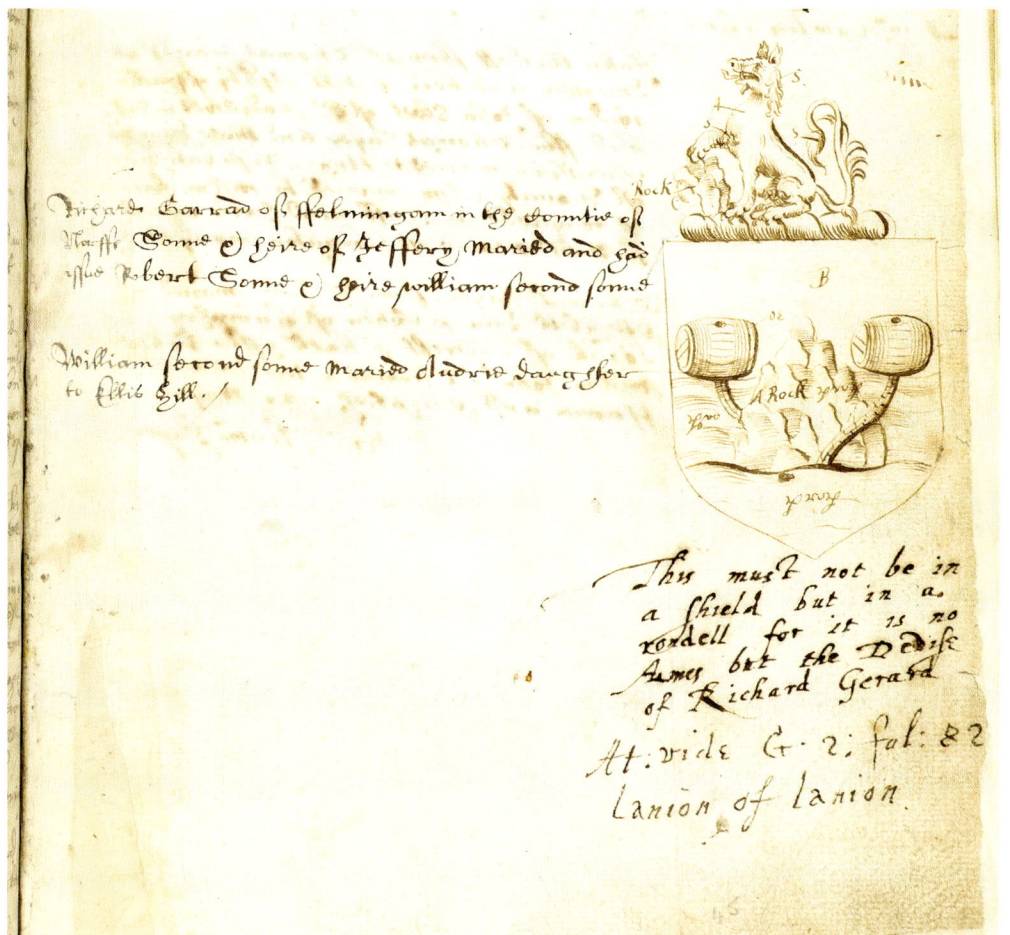

21. Visitation of Norfolk, by John Raven, Richmond Herald, 1612–13. Entry for the family of Garrard, with added comments by other heralds. College of Arms, MS C. 15 Part 1, f. 42 lower two-thirds of page.

Raven draws his thoughts to a close with what he claims is an afterthought but is actually the climax of the whole speech and the primary reason why he finds himself in Norwich talking to the gentry of the county. He notes that there are some who usurp the titles of gentility, emboldened as they are by their wealth and substance, and yet have no descent or arms. This is a great and punishable offence! 'Noe man can Appropriate unto himselfe, the state and title of generositye, without he beare tharmes, as ensignes, and especiall markes of honour, and as tokens, and signes of his gentle estate'. He continues that if riches suffice to make a man noble, then pirates and usurers could claim nobility: you do not choose a captain for a ship because he is wealthy but for his knowledge, wisdom and understanding. And marrying an armigerous woman does not automatically make you gentle, though a woman of ungentle blood can enjoy her husband's gentry status.

Raven is now able to focus on the crux of the matter – the ancient bond between gentility and arms. A gentleman must have a coat of arms to be recognised officially as such (at least in the heralds' eyes; and this after all was *their* survey) and, therefore, able to enter the forthcoming visitation. His remarks that those deserving of nobility (in which

121

he includes the gentry) not only have the right to arms but must also bear those arms to prove their estate (position in society), again echo Ferne. Raven's definition of arms appears to be lifted almost directly from *The Blazon of Gentrie*, as does his remark that marrying into the gentry does not make the husband a gentleman (unfortunately for John Shakespeare, who had allegedly married into the Ardens, an ancient Warwickshire family).[59] Ferne realised that there were those 'gentlemen' who, whilst commonly regarded as such, did not bear arms. This he believed was due to slothful heralds in times past, and he calls upon the heralds to denounce such imposters – which, as Raven was well aware, was an important part of the visitational process.[60]

Shakespeare too was very conscious of the close correlation between arms and gentility. In *The Taming of the Shrew* Petruchio boasts to Kate: 'I am a gentleman'. To test this assertion she strikes him. Petruchio responds he will cuff her if she does so again, to which she replies: 'So may you lose your arms: | If you strike me, you are no gentleman; | And if no gentleman, why then no arms'. Petruchio retorts: 'A herald, Kate? O put me in thy books'. In *Hamlet*, the two comic grave diggers inform us that Adam was a gentleman for he bore arms; how else could he dig?

Shakespeare may have made light of the ambiguous meaning of 'arms' but he, or his father, was sufficiently concerned about worldly recognition and social ascent to formalise the gentry status of his family and part with something like £30 for a grant of arms and later to try and get them quartered. Moreover, by having the arms granted to John Shakespeare they would not only fulfil a long-held wish of his aging father but would also lay to rest any doubt over the old man's gentle status.[61] They would also carry

---

[59] Ferne, *Blazon of Gentrie*, pp. 61–2, 82; Cooper, *Land, Men and Beliefs*, pp. 46–7, 66–7; Heal and Holmes, *Gentry in England and Wales*, p. 7 (quoting the contemporary lawyer, John Selden); but cf. Squibb, *High Court of Chivalry*, p. 171–2. For the gentry status of the Ardens see Mark Eccles, *Shakespeare in Warwickshire* (Madison, 1963), pp. 12–23; I am grateful to Dr David Mateer for bringing this work to my attention. Shakespeare's father-in-law was a husbandman and may not have been related to the ancient Ardens of Park Hall, but the grant and exemplification of John Shakespeare's arms make specific reference to Mary as an heir to Robert Arden (of Wilmcote), and Dethick's and Camden's defence of the arms notes that John 'maried the daughter and heire of Arderne', the implication being that John had married into the gentry family: Scott-Giles, *Shakespeare's Heraldry*, pp. 37, 38, 39.

[60] Ferne, *Blazon of Gentrie*, p, 91; Cooper, *Land, Men and Beliefs*, p. 66. Where pedigrees exist in the visitational record without arms it is generally assumed that the head of the family had been respited to find further proof of his family's arms or that he had agreed to apply for arms.

[61] For some 20 years John had been variously described as 'yeoman' and 'Mr', i.e. Master or gentleman: Schoenbaum, *Shakespeare: A Documentary Life*, pp. 34, 37, 38 and cf. 171; Eccles, *Shakespeare in Warwickshire*, pp. 28, 31, 32–3, 35, and cf. 85. According to the contemporary Cater's Case (1583), a 'Yeoman by his birth yet commonly called gentleman ... he may have the Addition of Gentleman although in Truth he is not a Gentleman, but only by Vulgar reputation': Edward Coke, *Reports*, Part VI, f. 67, quoted in Cooper, *Land, Men and Beliefs*, p. 62. Since John Shakespeare had once been bailiff of the town and served for many years as an alderman, claimed a certain degree of wealth and lineage (however much exaggerated in his grant of arms), and had

for William and his son Hamnet a patina of antiquity, since, in the case of the boy, they would be seen to span three generations – though sadly Hamnet was to die before the grant was issued. Furthermore, by having the arms granted to John Shakespeare, William was avoiding what the Fool in *Lear* was later to say: 'It's a mad yeoman that sees his son a gentleman before him'.[62] And if, as seems likely, it was William Shakespeare rather than his father who revived the application for arms, and if, as some claimed, 'the stage doth stain pure gentle blood', then officially acknowledged arms were a permanent and relatively cheap way of expunging (to borrow from *Macbeth*) that 'damned spot' on his family's honour.[63]

The turn of the sixteenth century was an age greatly concerned with lineage and degree, especially amongst those, who, like Shakespeare and his father, had risen through the social hierarchy and avidly sought to establish their family fortunes on a permanent basis. Such *arrivistes* – the new Tudor gentry – were eager to record their ancestry and arms and pass them on, along with their new found riches, property rights and social standing, to their heirs and assigns. As was noted by Robert Glover, Somerset Herald from 1570 to 1588, coat armour could confer hereditary gentle status.[64] This determination to achieve some form of security and posterity for the family name, arms and estate must have been particularly acute when plague had recently been so rampant and when succession to even the highest family in the land, that of the virgin queen, Elizabeth I, lay in doubt. Shakespeare would have sought to ensure not only that his son inherited his name and arms but also that his armigerous daughters would automatically be regarded as gentryfolk when it came to their chances in the marriage stakes: 'And nothing 'gainst Time's scythe can make defence | Save breed, to brave him when he takes thee hence' (Sonnet 12). By approaching the heralds, demonstrating his family's worth, and paying the appropriate fees Shakespeare (or his father) had followed correct heraldic protocol and gentlemanly procedure; John and William had gained their arms, 'Not without right'.

Raven had already noted that lineage on its own was not enough, and for his closing words he turned to those who, emboldened by their wealth alone, claimed gentility. That riches alone did not make a man noble was a commonplace among heraldic commentators of the day, including Segar, although it is true to say that property and wealth certainly helped support the claims of those seeking confirmation of their gentility (such as the Shakespeares) or who were eager to enter gentry ranks for the first time and

---

married into a gentry family, it would not have been unusual for others to have continued to have addressed him as 'Mr' even after his suffering some decay. Moreover, yeomen were often summoned to visitations, doubtless as potential gentry: Ailes, 'Elias Ashmole's 'Heraldicall Visitacion' of Berkshire', p. 62.

[62] Quoted in Duncan-Jones, *Ungentle Shakespeare*, p. 102.
[63] John Davies of Hereford, *Microcosmos* (Oxford, 1603), p. 215, quoted in Duncan-Jones, *Ungentle Shakespeare*, p. 103.
[64] Cooper, *Land, Men and Beliefs*, p. 69.

be included in the heralds' visitations.[65] In short, Raven is reminding his gentry audience, whilst also sending out a message to those who perhaps were not present but were keen to join their ranks, that it did not matter if you were of little or no ancestry (many visitation pedigrees consist of only three generations)[66] or of comparatively small wealth. What mattered was virtue, as borne out by meritorious service and public or martial actions, and the rewards of that virtue, namely honour and an honourable reputation by which one gained acceptance into the honour community.

By allowing for such a broad church when it came to defining the gentry, visiting heralds like Raven opened wide the doors of their visitations and invited in a relatively diverse community of gentlefolk. But as far as the heralds were concerned, there was still one more necessary qualification, namely arms: the tokens and ensigns of that virtue and honour. If this was a problem, then – Raven reassures his audience – they now have their chance to put the armorial matter straight: to formalise, regularise and register their heraldic status. Now they can discover their 'precedency' (presumably, gentry status), what their true unadulterated arms are, and whether they need to have those arms differenced. All heraldic offences can be remedied; the officer [of arms], Raven tells them, is here to help them. 'God Save the King!'

Raven could almost have ended his oration with an invitation to those gentry whose gentle and noble conscience have been sufficiently moved by his speech and whose armorial propriety has been quickly stirred, to step forward immediately and sign up to his visitation. Such a commendable response – duty, indeed, in the herald's eyes – would, however, have to wait for the coming days when Raven and his entourage would journey round the county to specific stations to register the arms and pedigrees of the local gentry and carefully examine the proofs laid before them. In the event, 169 Norfolk families were accepted into his visitation.[67] Had the same speech taken place a couple of decades earlier across the country in Warwickshire, then a certain John Shakespeare or his eldest son, might well have been amongst the first to step forward and petition the visiting herald: 'O put me in thy books'.

---

[65] Segar, *Honor Military and Civill*, pp. 209, 228; Heal and Holmes, *Gentry in England and Wales*, p. 9. The use of fiscal records to draw up lists of gentry to be summoned and the fact that new arms cost £30 suggests an assumption of some wealth. A note written at the foot of John Shakespeare's grant of arms states (albeit with some exaggeration) 'That he hath lands and tenements of good wealth and substance 500 li'. Garter and Clarenceux's defence of the same grant adds he had married an heiress of the Ardens 'and was able to maintain that estate': Scott-Giles, *Shakespeare's Heraldry*, pp. 38, 39.

[66] The signatory, usually the head of the family, his parents and in-laws, and his children especially the heir. Instructions to visiting heralds in 1634 specified that, to maintain accuracy, descents should not normally exceed 3 or 4 generations: PRO, SP 16/360, f. 236.

[67] Mark Noble, *A History of the College of Arms* (London, 1805), Appendix, p. xxix.

Tudor Pedigree Rolls and Their Uses

JOHN BAKER[1]

The pedigree rolls which became a common class of manuscript in Tudor England have received very little attention from historians. Most of them are to be found in record offices and in private possession rather than in public libraries,[2] and since there is no inventory of them it is impossible at present to make final judgments about their evolution and character. Yet a start must be made somehow. The intricate and elaborate rolls found in the sixteenth century have no direct parallel in the medieval period, though there was nothing new about the preservation of genealogies in written form. The narrative genealogy was the oldest and perhaps the commonest medieval type,[3] and it persisted into the sixteenth century, when it was still used by some heralds when making records on their travels. But the diagrammatic pedigree was easier for the eye to take in, and a roll was more convenient than a book with stems continued from page to page, especially if many generations were to be set down. The origin of the genealogical roll was doubtless the biblical genealogy, especially the *Compendium Historiae et Genealogia Christi* compiled by Peter of Poitiers in the later twelfth century, which was intended as an aid to interpreting the scriptures and in establishing the chronology of the world from the time of Adam.[4] By the end of the thirteenth century, rolls were also regularly used for royal pedigrees, and a particularly English form was the royal pedigree with a marginal commentary summarising events in national history, a genre probably inspired by the illustrated versions of Matthew Paris's chronicle (*c.* 1250).[5] At least forty

---

[1] I wish to acknowledge the generous help given to me in writing this chapter by Dr Nigel Ramsay, who placed his extensive knowledge freely at my disposal.

[2] Cf. M. Maclagan, 'Genealogy and Heraldry', in *English Historical Scholarship in the Sixteenth and Seventeenth Centuries*, ed. L. Fox (Dugdale Soc., 1956), pp. 31–48, at 47 ('now so often relegated to the billiard rooms or attics of country houses'). A few, indeed, are so large that they could not easily be examined in library conditions: below, p. 135 n. 45.

[3] The first detailed genealogies of the Anglo-Norman aristocracy were produced, in narrative form, around 1139: E. M. C. van Houts, 'Robert of Torigni as Genealogist', in *Studies in Medieval History presented to R. A. Brown*, ed. C. Harper-Bill, C. J. Holdsworth and J. Nelson (Woodbridge, 1989), pp. 215–33.

[4] At least 29 rolls survive with Poitiers's genealogy of Christ, and twice as many more in book form: Holladay, 'Charting the Past' (below, n. 7), at p. 122.

[5] O. de Laborderie, 'La Mémoire des origines Normandes des rois d'Angleterre dans les généalogies en rouleau des xiiie et xive siècles', in *La Normandie et l'Angleterre au Moyen Âge*, ed. P. Bouet and V. Gazeau (Caen, 2003), pp. 211–32; A. Bovey, *The Chaworth Roll: A Fourteenth-Century Genealogy of the Kings of England* (London, 2005); Laborderie, 'A New Pattern of English History: the First Genealogical Rolls of the Kings of England', in *Broken Lines: Genealogical Literature in late Medieval Britain and France*, ed. R. L. Radulescu and E. D. Kennedy (Turnhout, 2009), pp. 45-63; Holladay, 'Charting the Past' (below, n. 7).

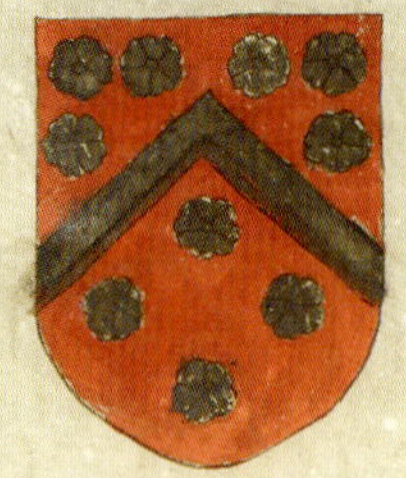

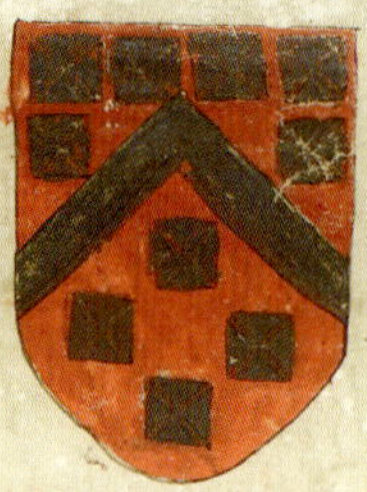

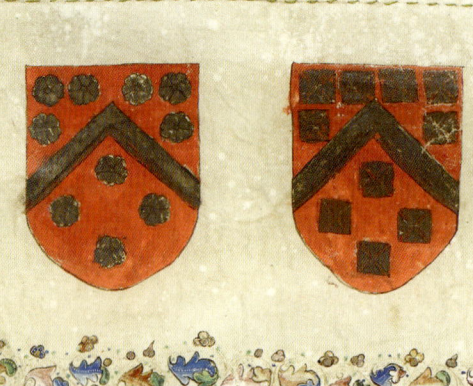

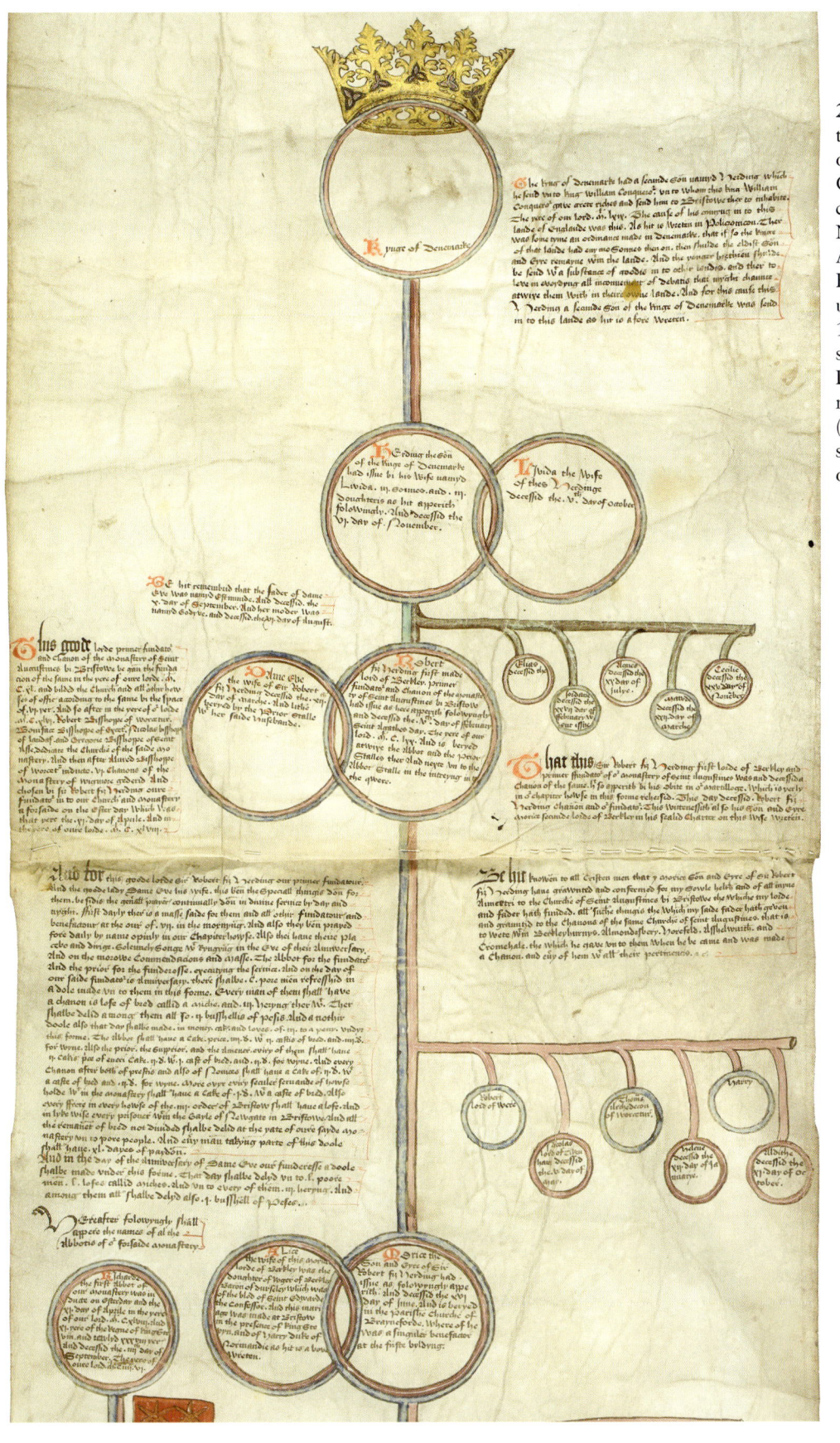

22 a and b. History of the Berkeley family, of Berkeley in Gloucestershire, compiled by John Newland, abbot of St Augustine's abbey, Bristol, from 1481 until his death in 1515. Gloucestershire Record Office, D 471/Z5. Head of roll (opposite), and (this page) detail showing the start of the pedigree.

examples have survived from the time of Edward I to that of Henry V (1272 to 1422), indicating a very wide contemporary circulation, and they continued to be produced throughout the fifteenth century.[6] They were not primarily designed as detailed genealogical studies, to prove or challenge title to the throne,[7] but rather as accessible works of history for lay consumption. Awkward breaks or kinks in the royal line of descent were simply omitted. In the fifteenth century some noble families commissioned their own versions, with their family line traced in parallel with that of the monarchy.[8] Again, it seems more likely that the purpose was to instruct or gratify the family rather than to provide the kind of record which might be useful in case of litigation over disputed inheritances. For practical purposes a cartulary containing genealogical information would be more useful, and examples of that kind of family record also survive from the late medieval period.[9] Monasteries seem to have been particularly keen to produce documentation of this type, with genealogies of their founders.[10] Private

[6] There is a list of such rolls from Henry VI to Henry VIII in S. Anglo, 'Early Tudor Propaganda', *Bull., John Rylands Library*, 44 (1961), pp. 17–48. There are numerous examples in the College of Arms.

[7] Some of the earliest ones may have been intended to clarify Edward I's title to the Scots throne: see W. H. Monroe, 'Two Medieval Genealogical Roll-Chronicles in the Bodleian Library', *Bodleian Library Record*, 10 (1978–82), pp. 215–21, at 219–20; J. A. Holladay, 'Charting the Past: Visual Configurations of Myth and History and the English Claim to Scotland', in *Representing History, 900–1300*, ed. R. A. Maxwell (Philadelphia, 2010), pp. 115–32, 233.

[8] E.g. the pedigree of Boteler of Sudeley (1448), Phillipps MS 26448; Sotheby's, 21 Nov. 1972, lot 556; now New York Public Library, MS Spencer 193 (commemorating the marriage of Ralph Boteler, Lord Sudeley, lord treasurer of England 1443–7, and Eleanor, daughter of the earl of Shrewsbury); pedigree of the Percy family (c. 1483/5), Bodleian Library, MS Pedigree Roll 5. See also *Handbook to the Maude Roll, Being a XVth-Century Manuscript Genealogy of the British and English Kings from Noah to Edward IV, with a Marginal History*, ed. A. Wall (Auckland, New Zealand, and London, 1919); this has a parallel genealogy of Monthault of Yorkshire. A late and very amateur example, with rustic painted portraits and arms, is the Ellerker genealogy with the 'Discente of all the Kinges and Queenes of Ingland since the Conquest until the quenes majestie that now is, with al ther ishews, what notable deds in their reinges or whow long thei lived' (College of Arms, MS 12/42/01).

[9] See J. Spence, 'Genealogies of Noble Families in the later Middle Ages', in *Broken Lines*, ed. Radulescu and Kennedy, pp. 63–77. As an early example, Spence instances the Pedwardine cartulary (1395) (British Library, MS Add. 32101), which commences with a genealogy and coats of arms in colours. Note also the Woodford cartulary (c. 1450) (British Library, Cotton MS Claudius A. xiii) and the Newton cartulary (c. 1500) (British Library, MS Add. 42134A).

[10] See E. Jamroziak, 'Genealogies in Monastic Chronicles in England', in *Broken Lines*, ed. Radulescu and Kennedy, pp. 103–22. Examples from the late 14th century are the history of Wigmore abbey, which includes a Mortimer genealogy (University of Chicago, MS 224) and the chronicle of Alnwick abbey, which includes a genealogy of the Percy family and its predecessors (British Library, MS Harley 3897; printed from MS Harley 692 by W. Dickson, 'Cronica Monasterii de Alnewyke', *Archaeologia Aeliana*, 1st ser., iii (1844), pp. 33–44. From the 15th century, the author notes the Tewkesbury abbey chronicle, with a history of the Clare, Despencer and Nevill families, with portraits and arms of the founders (Bodleian Library, MS Top. Glouc. c. 2). Note also the Clare Roll, College of Arms, MS 3/16 (formerly 16/21) (lords of Clare as founders of 'the Freeris in the

families may have relied largely on memory, unless there was some particular reason to write down the details. A notable example was that of Thomas Cave, who in the 1450s prepared a 'bill of remembrance' with a genealogy of the Fielding family, fearing that he might be killed in battle and the information lost for ever.[11] Genealogies must have been regularly needed for legal purposes. Pedigrees were certainly compiled in connection with claims to inherited property.[12] They would also have been needed in planning marriages which would not offend the canonical rules.[13] In the records of litigation they were set out in narrative form, but it would have been more helpful to jurors to see a diagram and it may well be that workaday ephemeral pedigrees were produced for such purposes. Although the relevant files of the central royal courts have long since disappeared, there survive among the archives of the county palatine of Lancaster a number of paper pedigrees from the early sixteenth century which were used in establishing consanguinity with sheriffs or coroners in order to challenge juries.[14] Even longer pedigrees would have been needed in actions of formedon, in the Common Pleas, which might be founded on grants made as much as two centuries earlier; a notorious Elizabethan example of this will be considered later.[15] But workaday scrowets were a far cry from the Tudor pedigree rolls with which we are concerned.

In the sixteenth century the production of elaborate pedigree rolls on vellum (or parchment), with painted coats of arms and various forms of decoration, became common practice.[16] No doubt there were a number of reasons for this. First, there were

---

same Honoure', 1456); illustrated in *Heralds' Commemorative Exhibn., 1484–1934*, pl. XLII; Bodleian Library, MS Pedigree Roll 33 (descendants of Robert le Brus as patrons of Gisburn priory, Yorks.; written *c.* 1470); Glos. Record Office, D471/Z5 (Berkeley family, patrons of St Augustine's monastery near Bristol, written in 1490 by John Newland, the abbot); for which see I. H. Jeayes, 'Abbot Newland's Roll', *Trans., Bristol & Glos. Archaeological Soc.*, xiv (1889–90), pp. 117–30, and Figs 22a–b, above.

[11] J. Denton, 'Genealogy and Gentility', in *Broken Lines*, ed. Radulescu and Kennedy, pp. 143–58, at 151.

[12] E.g. the 14th-century century pedigree of three generations of the Bereford family (College of Arms, MS 12/51E) and the early 15th-century pedigree of Latimer and Foliot (transcript ibid., MS 12/27A), written in Anglo-French, entitled: 'Coment poet Latymer ou ses heres [estre] despoille hors del dit manoir de Sutton ...'.

[13] A royal example in the College of Arms (MS 20/16) is a bundle of paper pedigrees showing Lady Margaret Beaufort's relationship 'within degree of marriage' to the royal houses of Denmark, Spain, Portugal, Burgundy, Scotland and Brittany. The first has the title: 'This pedegree shewith how my lady grace is within degre to this noble house off England and heir to the said auncient realme to Lancastre to Somersett and to many other roiall housis etc.'

[14] PRO, PL 21/2. One of these pedigrees sets out six degrees of kinship, though most were shorter. By Elizabethan times such questions would be resolved by calling heralds to give evidence based on their books: see below, p. 164 n. 169.

[15] Hugh Fitzwilliam's claim (1566–72) to property in Yorkshire depended on a grant made in the time of Edward II (1307–27): below, pp. 149–63.

[16] F. Heal and C. Holmes, *The Gentry in England and Wales, 1500–1700* (Basingstoke, 1994), at p. 35, said they were 'the growth area for the heraldic industry from the late sixteenth century'.

questions of genealogy affecting national politics. Although the old-style royal pedigree went out of fashion, in its place are to be found more complex pedigrees relating to the dynastic disputes and uncertainties which arose in the mid-fifteenth century in the conflict between York and Lancaster and continued under the Tudors.[17] These are well illustrated by the pedigrees of the Nevill family, beginning in the fifteenth century.[18] A fragmentary pedigree of around 1540, identified on the verso in a later hand as 'Genealogia Comitum Warwici et aliorum', focuses on the Nevills, deducing a descent from John Nevill (d. 1388), Lord Nevill.[19] It shows principally the issue of John and of his eldest son Ralph (d. 1425), first earl of Westmorland, and Ralph's second wife, Joan Beaufort (d. 1440), legitimated daughter of John of Gaunt; the issue of Ralph's first wife, Margaret (Stafford) are only partly shown and originally continued on the missing portion to the left.[20] The issue of Joan by her first husband, Sir Robert Ferrers (d. before 1396), are also included, ending with their granddaughter Joan (Greystoke), wife of Lord Darcy. The missing portion to the right evidently included (*a*) John of Gaunt (d. 1399), duke of Lancaster, half of whose arms remain at the right-hand side, and whose son Henry (d. 1447), Cardinal Beaufort, is shown at the bottom; (*b*) King Henry IV, whose son Thomas (d. 1421), duke of Clarence, is shown at the bottom right, with half of the arms of another son in a Garter; and perhaps (*c*) King Edward III, whose daughter Isabel is represented by a shield at the bottom of the present portion with the arms of her husband Ingelram de Coucy (d. 1397), earl of Bedford. The missing portion at the bottom continued with the earls of Warwick, descending from the Nevills via Richard Nevill (d. 1460) and his wife Alice Mountagu (d. 1460×2), whose shield is cut off at the bottom left, and presumably ended with the last of the Plantagenets, Margaret Plantagenet (1473–1541), widow of Sir Richard Pole (d. *c*. 1505), countess of Salisbury and Warwick *suo jure*. A descender to the left of Cardinal Beaufort's arms indicates that there was also

---

[17] See A. Allan, 'Yorkist Propaganda: Pedigree, Prophecy and the British History', in *Patronage, Pedigree and Power*, ed. C. Ross (Gloucester, 1979), pp. 171–92; A. F. Sutton and L. Visser-Fuchs, 'Richard III's Books', *The Ricardian*, ix (1992), pp. 343–58; R. L. Radulescu, *The Gentry Context for Malory's* Morte Darthur (Cambridge, 2003), pp. 62–7. E.g. College of Arms, MS 3/16 (roll showing the lords of Clare and the Yorkist title to the throne; written in the time of Edward IV).

[18] The Salisbury Roll (1463) is the best known of them, with full-length figures of the earls in robes and their wives in heraldic mantles: British Library, Loan MS 90; MS Add. 45133, f. 53 (fragment of 3 ff. with figures); A. Payne, 'The Salisbury Roll of Arms, *c*. 1463', in *England in the Fifteenth Century*, ed. D. Williams (Woodbridge, etc., 1987), pp. 187–98. The Rous Roll (British Library, MS Add. 48976; printed as *The Rous Roll*, intro. C. D. Ross [Gloucester, 1980]) also includes a Nevill pedigree. A book pedigree of the earls of Warwick and Leicester by Robert Cooke, *c*. 1565, in 18 ff., was sold at Sotheby's, 11 July 1960, lot 124.

[19] JHB, MS 947. Unusually, it originally comprised several membranes in width as well as in length.

[20] The earlier details correspond with those in the pedigree of Nevill, dating from the time of Henry VII, found in Bodleian Library, MS Ashmole 831 and MS Dodsworth 81, p. 154, the latter copied by Roger Dodsworth from an old roll ('Out of my antient rolle of petegrees which are very autenticall and cited by Mr Camden'); printed in *Visitations of the North*, Pt. III, ed. C.H. Hunter Blair (Surtees Soc., 144, 1930), pp. 23–31.

a continuation of John of Gaunt's issue, probably with John Beaufort (d. 1410), marquess of Dorset, whose daughter Margaret (d. 1509), countess of Richmond, was mother of Henry VII. The entire pedigree may therefore have been designed to show the relationship between the countess of Salisbury and King Henry VIII, and it may date from around the time of her attainder in 1539 on a charge of treason. A more ephemeral pedigree of 1562 shows the ancestry of Queen Elizabeth I, the earl of Huntingdon (Henry Hastings), and the children of the duke of Buckingham (d. 1521), traced back to the Clare family. It was probably a draft, being written on a paper roll with some roughly painted shields of arms.[21] There are marginal historical memoranda of a biographical nature, in the manner of the medieval royal pedigrees, but the object seems to have been to clarify the possibilities of succession if the Queen died; during the Queen's illness in 1562 the earl of Huntingdon had been spoken of as the probable heir.[22] The Queen herself was glorified in a huge pedigree roll of 1558, now displayed at Hatfield House, with a genealogy starting from Adam (and therefore, necessarily, including Noah), via King Arthur, King Lear, Julius Caesar and other historic figures.[23] Though there are some artistic similarities with the Nevill roll, this was a different kind of production. It must be considered more as a flattering *jeu d'ésprit* than a serious guide to history.[24]

But the growth area was in the production of private rather than royal pedigrees. For private persons, there were a number of reasons for producing formal pedigrees. One was to mark the union of two families on marriage, in which case the two lines might be set out in parallel. Another was to show the connection between different branches of a family sharing the same surname.[25] But perhaps the principal motive behind the burgeoning production of pedigrees was the desire to demonstrate the antiquity and gentility of the family, and to establish its right not only to its own chief coat of arms but to the arms of past heiresses which could be quartered with it. Although this exercise

[21] This belonged to J. P. Brooke-Little (d. 2006), Clarenceux King of Arms; his sale, Bloomsbury Auctions, 29 Nov. 2011, lot 380 (part); now JHB, MS 1346. It is undated, but Hastings is described as an earl (created 1560/1) and Henry Stafford (d. 1563), Lord Stafford, is shown as living.

[22] Another draft pedigree ending with the earl of Huntingdon is on the dorse of the Seylyard pedigree roll (JHB, MS 1349; below, p. 148), for which the paper was reused.

[23] Hatfield House, Cecil Papers 357. Cf. College of Arms, MS 3/53, a simpler pedigree of Elizabeth I in the form of a rose tree with red and white buds.

[24] According to an inscription near the end, the pedigree was commissioned by Edmund Brudenell, son and heir of Sir Thomas Brudenell [d. 1549], who caused it to be compiled at his home at Deene in 1558. Edmund was admitted to the Inner Temple the following year (Baker, *Men of Court*, I, p. 386) and was probably therefore aged around 20 when he caused the pedigree to be made.

[25] The Chamberlayne pedigree roll of 1552 (Christie's, 17 Nov. 2004, lot 13) was expressed to have been made for Leonard Chamberlayne [d. 1561] of Woodstock and his brother Edward to establish their connection with Sir Thomas Chamberlayne [d. 1580] of Prestbury, the King's ambassador in Flanders. Note also the Fitzwilliam pedigrees below, pp. 150–62, showing the relationship between different branches of the Fitzwilliam family; one of them (p. 154) was designed to show the family's relationship with Sir Nicholas Bacon, Lord Keeper of the Great Seal, and Sir William Cecil, Principal Secretary.

might also have a bearing on property ownership, the chief concern in many cases was the armigerous status which the roll reinforced. The older the arms, and the more numerous the quarterings (indicating past matches with armigerous families), the more worthy the blood.[26] This tendency to amass quarterings was not universally approved, and indeed the College of Arms ruled in the 1560s that a person was not entitled to quarter every coat which had descended to him.[27] But the decision made a significant exception for pedigree rolls, in which the practice continued without stint, artificially attaching impalements and quarterings and indeed armorial bearings to ancestors who never themselves used them.

In order to achieve these objectives, the typical Tudor pedigree set out not merely the lineal ancestry of the person for whom it was produced, starting in early medieval times, preferably at the Norman Conquest,[28] but also – in varying detail – the forebears of the heiresses, whether sole heirs or coheirs, who brought in their paternal arms. These latter were often shown in parallel to the main line. It was also desirable, if the present representative of a family descended from a younger son, to trace the parallel senior lines and show how they had become extinct. If a royal connection could be made as well, so much the better.[29] Every person in the pedigree was furnished with a shield of arms, distinguished where necessary with a due mark of cadency,[30] usually quartering the arms of previous heiresses – real or imaginary[31] – and impaled with the arms (where known)

[26] Cf. Wagner, *Heralds of England*, p. 208, who said of the Elizabethan new men: 'Their fathers under Henry VIII had been content with grants of pompous new arms; but the sons would, if possible, have old coats and pedigrees to justify them.'

[27] College of Arms, MS WC, f. 100v (referring to an undated ruling made about sixteen years before 1580/84); printed in Ramsay, *Robert Glover*, Ch. 2. In 1575 a coat of arms with 30 named quarters was confirmed to Thomas Penyston by Robert Cooke, Clarenceux King of Arms (patent at College of Arms, with 13 shields of arms in the margins; above, Fig. 13), but this was highly unusual.

[28] For the perceived desirability of tracing a descent from Norman times, see W. Wyrley, *The True Use of Armorie* (London, 1592), p. 24 (victorious Normans seen as more worthy than defeated Saxons); Heal and Holmes, *The Gentry*, at pp. 34-6 (where there are also examples of pedigrees deduced from Anglo-Saxons); J. Broadway, *'No Historie so Meete': Gentry Culture and the Development of Local History in Elizabethan and Early Stuart England* (Manchester, 2006), pp. 155–7. For the merits of Anglo-Saxon ancestry see also Simon Adams, above, pp. 1, 5, 6. Heal and Holmes cite a 17th-century Mostyn pedigree beginning with 'Adam, son of God', but most substantial rolls began in the Norman or Angevin period.

[29] The Sackville pedigree (1599) in the Victoria & Albert Museum (National Art Library, MS L.1981/41) showed how both Robert Sackville, son of Lord Buckhurst, and his wife Margaret (née Howard), daughter of the duke of Norfolk, were related to the Queen by descent from Anne Boleyn. A descent from Henry VIII and Anne Boleyn was also shown in the pedigree of Sir John Scott of Scott's Hall in Smeeth (Kent) (*c.* 1605×10) (JHB, MS 515).

[30] I.e., a small crescent for a second son, a mullet for a third son, and so forth. This system was not used before the Tudor period, but the pedigree rolls anachronistically assigned marks of cadency to earlier generations. It was an exercise in armorial logic, or law, rather than in history.

[31] Older quarterings were often of dubious authenticity. See the comments of Wyrley, *True Use of Armorie*, p. 6, where he praises Lord Stafford for using his single coat, 'far differing from a number of meaner persons, who if they possess any mannor or lands by descent, albeit their ancestors

of his or her own spouse. The roll commonly ended with an achievement of arms of the head of the family, showing all the quarterings which had been amassed, surmounted by a helm and crest.[32] The individuals in the pedigree were represented not only by shields of arms but also by circular medallions, often ringed with green, containing their names and occasionally other details.[33] Connections between the medallions might take the form of branches issuing from the main trunk of the family tree,[34] depicted as a natural tree with leaves. But this was not an ideal scheme, given that trees grow upwards whereas English pedigrees nearly always went downwards, with the *propositus* at the top and the living descendants at the foot. It was therefore more common to use connecting pedigree lines, at first often radiating – the eponymous *pied de grue* or 'crane's foot' – or meandering in all directions, with the blood-lines sometimes distinguished by different colours.[35] In the second half of the Tudor period the rectilinear pedigree became the norm,[36] although the natural foliate tree might still be used for artistic effect in the more elaborately worked rolls.[37] Occasionally other formats are found, such as the radial or

---

married the heire of the same many hundred yeers since, and whose parents peradventure never did beare any marke [*i.e., arms*], or if they did (time having obscured the same) it remaineth unknowen: yet shall you have them run to an Herald or painter, as busily as if the matter were of weight, and there make search they know not for what, and the herald or painter (on the other side) to draw some small peece of silver from them, will find out the badge [*i.e., arms*] of some one or other of the same name' to whom they were not related, which gave rise to much confusion; 'and yet into this quartering (being a very fountaine of errors) many both Noble men and Gentlemen, and the officers of Armes themselves, do oftentimes very rashly enter ...' The surviving rolls amply bear out this observation.

[32] Crests were rarely depicted before Tudor times, when it became usual to include them in an achievement of arms at the foot of the pedigree. The Nevill pedigree (above) is unusual in this respect; it shows an otherwise unrecorded crest for Nevill of Bulmer, apparently a moldwarp.

[33] Circles were not very convenient for fitting in writing, but they had been in almost universal use since medieval times.

[34] For earlier use of a natural tree in pedigrees see C. Klapisch-Zuber, *L'Ombre des ancêtres: Essai sur l'imaginaire médiéval de la parenté* ([?Paris], 2000), passim; M. A. Norbye, 'Genealogies in Medieval France', in *Broken Lines*, ed. Radulescu and Kennedy, pp. 79–101.

[35] JHB, MS 947 has an elaborate scheme of colour coding for the various lines of descent: the Nevill line is red, Mountagu green, Ferrers and Greystoke pale green with white roundels, King Edward III's descendants blue, and John of Gaunt's descendants blue intertwined with red, with red and white, and with white.

[36] A. R. Wagner, *The Records and Collections of the College of Arms* (London, 1952), pp. 58, 80, notes that Robert Glover was using 'the modern rectilinear tabular form' by 1569, and that it was adopted by William Flower for the visitation of Cheshire in 1566 and by Robert Cooke for the visitation of Essex in 1570. However, he was referring only to the form used in visitation books. The Chamberlayne pedigree by William Hervey (1552) is more or less rectilinear: roll sold at Christie's, 17 Nov. 2004, lot 13. And the form was not unknown to Sir Thomas Wriothesley in the first quarter of the century: A. R. Wagner, *English Genealogy*, 3rd edn. (Chichester, 1973), p. 372.

[37] E.g. the Sackville pedigree (1599) in the Victoria & Albert Museum (MS L.1981-41). The Cornwallis pedigree (1560) in the Essex Record Office (D/DBy F39) has branching vines with leaves and grapes intertwined with wild roses.

'target' pedigree,[38] or the upside-down pedigree with the living generations at the top and the ascent to ancestors going downwards.[39] A striking example of the latter is the tree of the Bacon family (1578) at Raveningham Hall (Norf.), which portrays Sir Nicholas Bacon standing on the ground with his wives, all full length, and their progeny (including the young Francis Bacon) blossoming from flowers on the branches of the family tree growing upwards.[40]

Book pedigrees for single families continued to be produced in the Tudor period,[41] with painted arms, and some of them were highly finished.[42] These usually run from left to right, sometimes with branches extending over several pages, and with parallel descents following sequentially. Also continuing, as a distinct genre, were volumes of documentary family history which could be used to support genealogies.[43] But the roll format enabled both the descent and the accumulation of coats of arms over the

[38] These were a speciality of the arms-painter Jacob Chaloner in the early 17th century: M.P. Siddons, *Welsh Pedigree Rolls* (Cardiff, 1996), p. 12; and see W. J. Hemp, 'Two Welsh Pedigrees', *Y Cymmrodor*, 40 (1929), pp. 207–25.

[39] E.g. the draft pedigree roll of Sir Thomas Egerton (1598) in Northants. Record Office, E(B) 627 ('Arbor Genealogica originem exprimens de progeniem Egertonorum'); this is on vellum, with tricked arms, and begins with five achievements of arms for different living branches of the family. A more extreme example is a slightly later Beaumont pedigree, on paper, dating from 1621–3, which is very broad collaterally (56 inches wide, but only 15 inches deep); more precise detail is given than is usual in pedigrees of this period, including dates of birth and death (JHB, MS 223, once owned by John Anstis).

[40] It is illustrated in R. Tittler, *Nicholas Bacon* (Ohio, 1976), facing p. 129. This type of pedigree has a medieval origin. A 15th-century example is the pedigree of King Edward IV in British Library, MS Harley 7353, which has a tree growing from a recumbent King Henry III at the bottom, and portraits emerging from flowers. Cf. College of Arms, MS 3/53, a pedigree of Elizabeth I (1577 or later) on a tree growing from William the Conqueror at the base.

[41] These are to be distinguished from books containing collections of pedigrees, usually copied from heraldic visitations, plainly written on paper and with uncoloured arms. These were made in large numbers as works of reference, the early-modern equivalents of Burke's *Peerage* and Burke's *Landed Gentry*.

[42] E.g. Philadelphia (Penn., USA), University of Pennsylvania, MS Codex 1070 (Robert Dudley, earl of Leicester, *c.* 1572×3); Northants. Record Office, Finch-Hatton 271 (Sir Christopher Hatton, 1577); the Lumley Inventory, Sandbeck Park (Yorks.), at ff. 18v–23v (Lord Lumley, 1586), printed in facsimile as *The Lumley Inventory and Pedigree*, ed. M. Evans (Roxburghe Club, 2010); College of Arms, MS Vincent 49 (Lord Vaux, *c.* 1600; attributed to Camden). A royal example is British Library, MS King's MS 396 (Elizabeth I, *c.* 1568×70). A plainer example, on paper, is JHB, MS 855 (Dyve pedigree, 1562×87, perhaps made in connection with the visitation of Bedfordshire in 1566 or 1582, when similar pedigrees were recorded). See also above, p. 130, n. 18 (earls of Warwick, *c.* 1565).

[43] E.g., Huntington Library, MS HM 160 (Dudley family, by William Bowyer, 1567); JHB, MS 1038 (Zouch family, by St Loe Kniveton, 1592); College of Arms, MS Vincent 3, and British Library, MS Harley 4840 (earls of Arundel, by Kniveton, undated); for other collections by Kniveton see R. T. Spence, 'Clifford, Anne (*known as* Lady Anne Clifford)', in *ODNB*, 12, pp. 79–81. Heralds such as Glover also made such books in connection with their preparation of pedigree rolls: e.g. College of Arms, Glover MSS A and B.

generations to be followed with greater ease. Such rolls are rare for the early Tudor period,[44] but hundreds of them must have been produced in the second half of the sixteenth century. They were usually engrossed on vellum (or parchment), though paper was used for drafts and copies. Usually it was necessary to join several sheets together, to make rolls which were five, ten or even twenty feet in length,[45] with the ends attached to wooden rollers. Since they were normally held together solely by glue, without stitching, some rolls have become dismembered over the centuries. The coats of arms were painted in colours, and for the better pedigrees gold and silver paint was used for metals; the silver has often oxidised to black, causing occasional armorial misunderstandings in later generations.[46] Added embellishments usually took the form of portraits, representations of significant supporting documents, with their seals, and occasional drawings of monuments.[47] Portraits are found even in the earliest Tudor pedigree rolls, though they were never common.[48] In some rolls the pictures of recent

[44] Two early examples are the Berkeley pedigree (1490) in the Glos. Record Office (D471/Z5) and the Denys roll (*c.* 1522) (below, n. 48; and Figs 20a–b). Sir Thomas Phillipps owned a Thimbleby pedigree roll, with arms painted on vellum, said to date from the time of Henry VII; but it sold in 1936 for only £1, suggesting that the claim was not accepted by the trade: Phillipps MS 13981; sold at Sotheby's, 30 June 1936, lot 281, to Walford.

[45] The enormous Seymour pedigree (1604), made from 26 parchment membranes glued together, is 6 feet 2 inches wide and 22 feet 5 inches long (Chippenham, Wilts. and Swindon Archives, 1300/376). It mentions 750 people and contains 35 portraits. It has been little studied in the past because it is too large to unroll in any ordinary room: but see now G. Bathe and A. Douglas, 'Forging Alliances: The Life of Edward Seymour, Earl of Hertford, and His Commissioning of the Great Illuminated Roll Pedigree of the Seymours and Monumental Tombs in Wiltshire and Westminster', *Wilts. Archaeological &Natural History Mag.*, 105 (2012), pp. 182–218. Probably the largest Early-Modern pedigree is that of the Shirley family (1632), which is 11 feet 9 inches wide and 29 feet 1½ inches long: Wagner, *Records and Collections* (cit. in n. 36), p. 16.

[46] Oxidisation is presumably the explanation for the appearance in the Halswell pedigree (1591) of a Tremayle quartering with a fess gules upon a field sable, which should have been argent (JHB, MS 1510). This was even approved by Ralph Brooke, Rouge Croix Pursuivant.

[47] The Hesketh pedigree (1594) ends with paintings of monuments formerly in Rufford church (British Library, MS Add. 44026). That of Oxenbridge (1600) in the E. Suss. Record Office (Acc. 7007; formerly Phillipps MS 26054) has a drawing of a monument in Brede church. That of Griffith of Burton Agnes (1604), compiled by Francis Thynne, has three knights at the head and several monuments in the body of the roll; there is a manuscript description (1948) in Society of Antiquaries, MS 774. The Philipot pedigree (1620) in the Hants. Record Office (93M86 W/1) has an armoured figure in a tabard of arms, and his wife in an armorial mantle, taken from a church window. The Byron pedigree (1627) in the Schøyen collection (MS 557; formerly Phillipps MS 24987) has five drawings of tomb-chests with effigies painted in life-like colours. There are also sketches of monuments in the pedigree of Charles Moore, Viscount Moore, copied by Randle Holme from the work of John Philipot (1632), in College of Arms, MS 9/34.

[48] The Denys pedigree in the College of Arms (MS 3/54), apparently dating from 1522 or shortly thereafter, has numerous demi-figures all wearing the civilian dress of the period and holding the shields with their arms; a portion is illustrated in the *Heralds' Commemorative Exhibn.* catalogue, pl. XLIV, and below, Fig. 24. Another early example is the Nevill pedigree of *c.* 1540 (JHB, MS 947) which contains four imaginary portraits in roundels with inscriptions in Lombardic lettering.

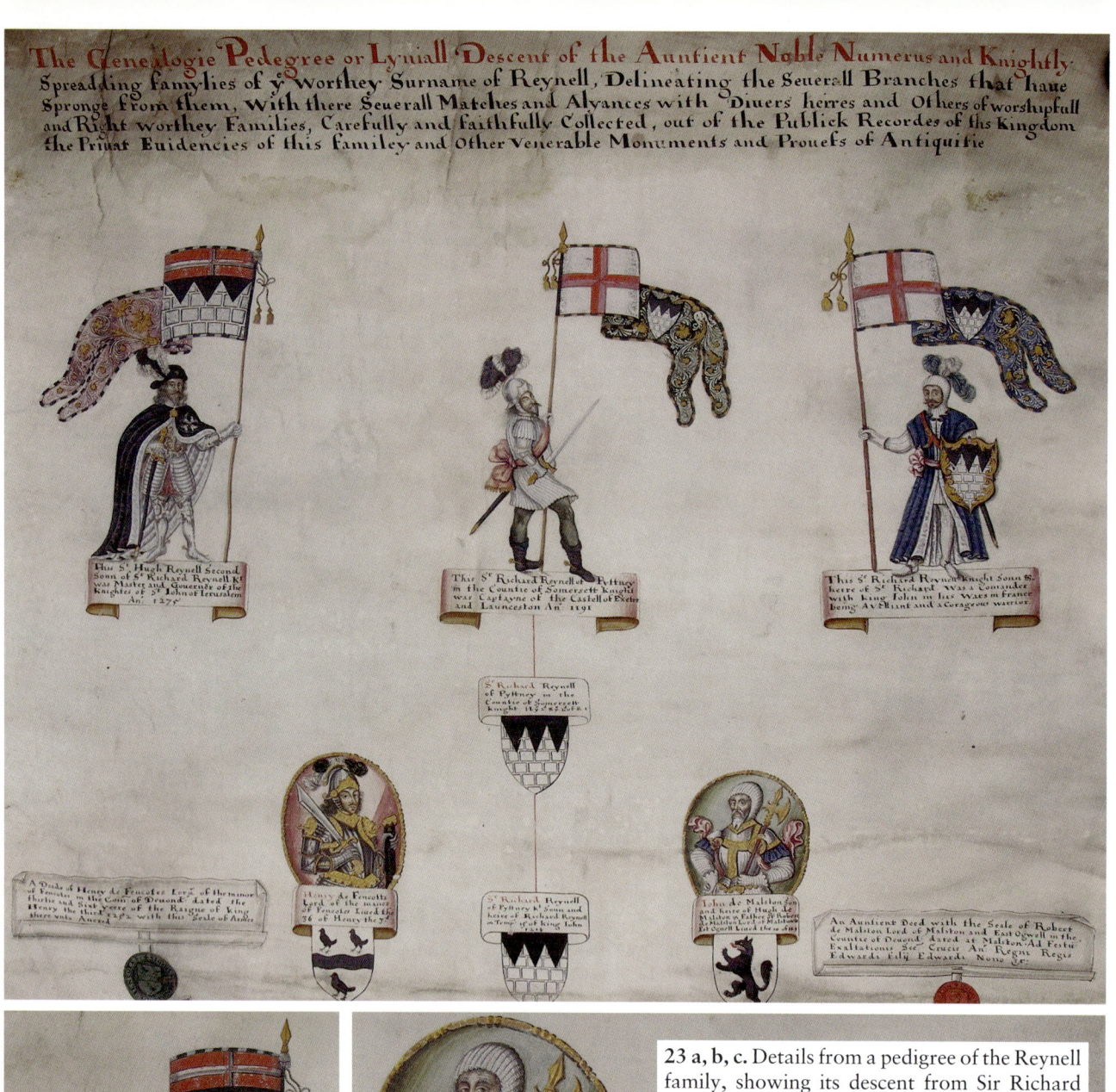

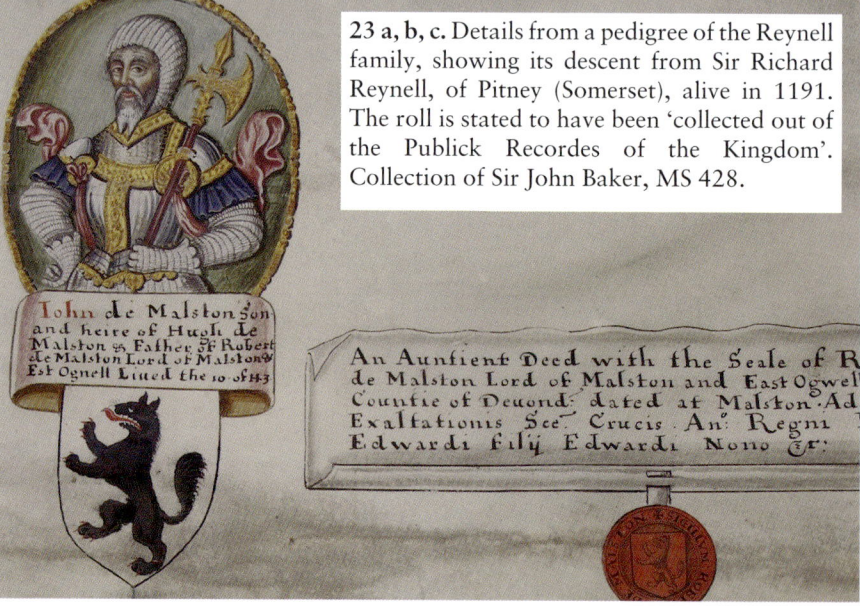

The Genealogie Pedegree or Lyniall Descent of the Auntient Noble Numerus and Knightly Spreadding famylies of ye Worthey Surname of Reynell, Delineating the Seuerall Branches that haue Spronge from them, With there Seuerall Matches and Alyances with Diuers heires and Others of worshipfull and Right worthey Families, Carefully and faithfully Collected, out of the Publick Recordes of this Kingdom the Priuat Euidencies of this Familey and Other Venerable Monuments and Prouefs of Antiquitie

23 a, b, c. Details from a pedigree of the Reynell family, showing its descent from Sir Richard Reynell, of Pitney (Somerset), alive in 1191. The roll is stated to have been 'collected out of the Publick Recordes of the Kingdom'. Collection of Sir John Baker, MS 428.

members of the family appear to be real likenesses, perhaps copied from oil paintings.[49] Others are fanciful, as in the Hatfield pedigree of Queen Elizabeth I (1558), which includes a mounted figure of William the Conqueror and six other imaginary portraits, not to mention Noah in his ark.[50] By the end of the Tudor period the fashion had begun of depicting the principal founders of the family as full-length figures in armour, holding pennons, guidons or shields with their arms. This may have been one of Robert Glover's inventions, since the pedigree which he prepared on behalf of Robert Cooke for Lord Burghley in 1580 has a figure in mail (representing James Sitsilt, living 1142) and two mounted knights in tournament order, wearing Tudor armour and holding shields of arms, with crests on their helms, their horses with armorial caparisons.[51] A book-pedigree of Elizabeth I, compiled about ten years earlier, in which Glover probably had a hand,[52] also has careful drawings of seals, a figure of William the Conqueror in chain mail and a cloak standing on a tomb,[53] and twenty-nine other figures, including realistic portraits of Henry VIII and his wives.[54] Such paintings have not as yet received any

---

The women – Margaret (d. 1390), daughter of Hugh, earl of Stafford, and Joan (d. 1440), daughter of John of Gaunt – are shown wearing the female dress of the second quarter of the 16th century. The two men – Sir Robert Ferrers (d. before 1396) and Ralph Nevill (d. 1425), first earl of Westmorland – are in fanciful antique costume, Ferrers with a turban.

[49] E.g. the pedigree of Hesketh of Rufford (1594), British Library, MS Add. 44026; illustrated in the *Heralds' Commemorative Exhibn.* catalogue, pl. XLV (dated *c.* 1615); R. Marks and A. Payne, *British Heraldry from its Origins to c. 1800* (London, 1978), p. 148; fully illustrated (in black and white) in W. G. Procter, 'Notes on the Hesketh Pedigree', *Trans., Historic Soc. of Lancs. & Ches.*, 62 (new ser., 26) (1911), pp. 58–66. In the Cornwallis pedigree (1560) in the Essex Record Office (D/DBy F39) are two realistic miniature portraits of Thomas and Anne Cornwallis. A Fitzwilliam pedigree (1564) in the Cambs. Record Office (R52/24/44/2; see below, n. 119) has a miniature portrait of Hugh Fitzwilliam as well as an imaginary portrait of Robert, duke of Normandy. The Sackville pedigree (1599) in the Victoria & Albert Museum (National Art Library, MS L.1981/41) incorporates a finely painted full-length portrait of Thomas Sackville, Lord Buckhurst, in Garter robes, with Lady Buckhurst, and at the head a portrait of Queen Elizabeth I flanked by two smaller ones of Thomas's son Robert and his first wife Margaret (née Howard).

[50] Hatfield House, Cecil Papers 357. The other figures are King Arthur, King Egbert, Clovis (king of the Franks), Incelgerius (Ingelger, count of Anjou), Arthgal (legendary earl of Warwick in the time of King Arthur) and Maud, daughter of William I. A little pedigree roll of Fitzwilliam of Gaynes Park (Essex), *c.* 1565×70, begins with a fanciful demi-figure of Robert, duke of Normandy (Northants. Record Office, Fitzwilliam (Milton) archive, F(M), Roll 452).

[51] Hatfield House Archives, Cecil Papers, 224/1. The Dudley book-pedigree of *c.* 1572×73 (University of Pennsylvania, MS Codex 1070) begins (f. 2) with two semi-recumbent figures in mail, holding shields, representing the earls of Leicester and Chester in the time of William the Conqueror.

[52] It has plausibly been attributed to the office of Robert Cooke, Clarenceux, on the ground that the fanciful royal coat of arms with Saxon and British quarterings is paralleled in several manuscript versions of Cooke's *Baronage*.

[53] Possibly a representation of the tomb at Caen, which was destroyed by Huguenots in 1562.

[54] BL, MS King's 396. The page with William the Conqueror (f. 3v) is illustrated in S. Doran, *Elizabeth: The Exhibition at the National Maritime Museum* (Greenwich, 2003), p. 105. Another page (f. 14), with fanciful demi-figures of Charlemagne and Luderick, forester of Flanders, is illustrated in Marks and Payne, *British Heraldry*, p. 115.

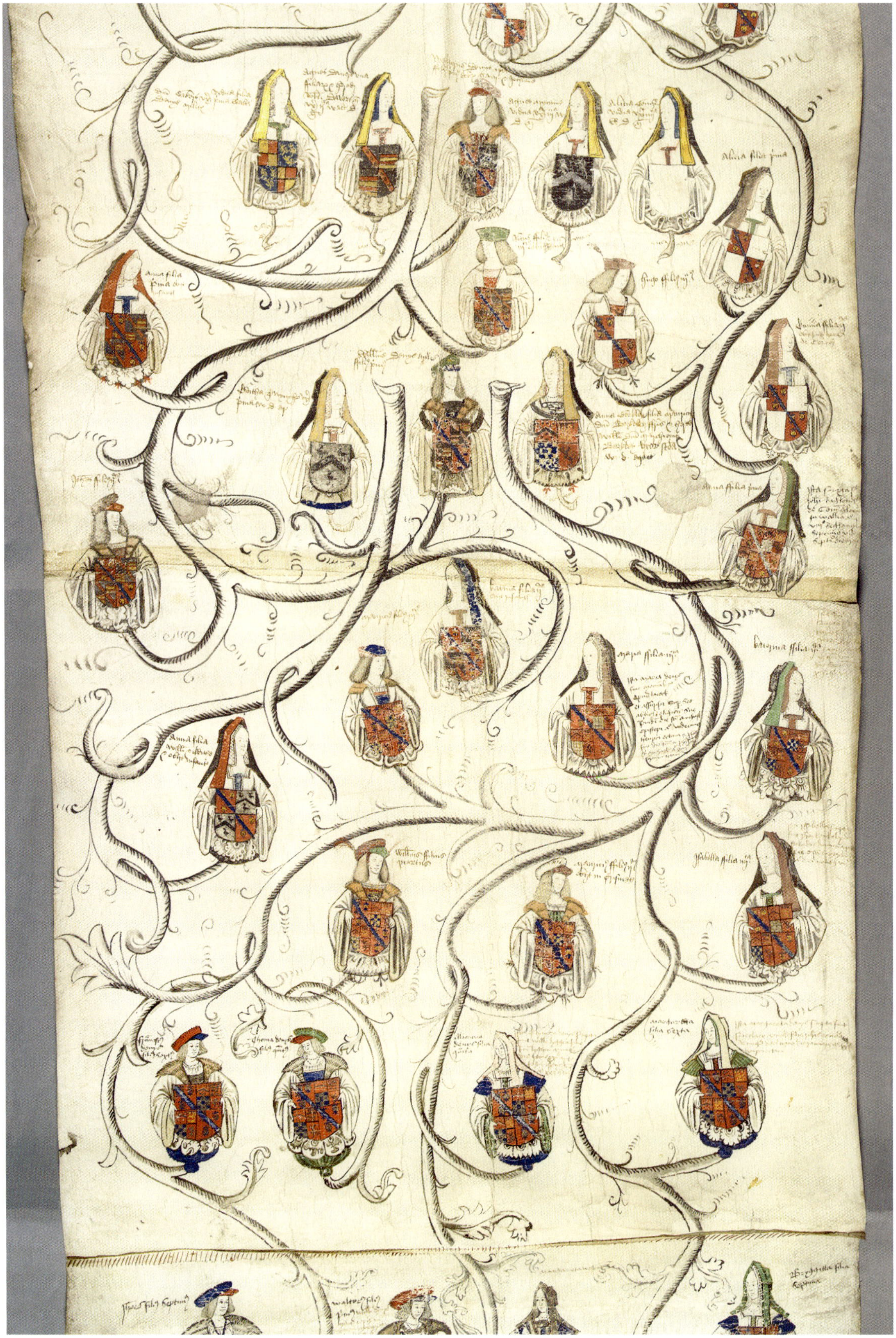

TUDOR PEDIGREE ROLLS AND THEIR USES

detailed attention from art historians. Sometimes, as in the case of James Sitsilt, they were an attempt to represent medieval military dress as seen on monuments and in church windows,[55] sometimes they were unashamedly contemporary,[56] even showing the recently introduced officers' red sash over the armour,[57] and sometimes purely fanciful.[58] Occasionally, where appropriate, official robes were shown,[59] and these might be equally anachronistic.[60] Pictorial embellishments such as these were more common in the

24 (opposite). Pedigree roll of the Denys family of Dyrham (Gloucestershire), probably made to commemorate the marriage of Walter Denys (d. 1571), the infant son of Sir William Denys and Anne (née Berkeley), to Margaret, daughter of Sir Richard Weston of Sutton Place (Surrey), in 1522. The pedigree takes the form of overlapping vines with sprouting demi-figures representing all the named individuals, each of whom holds a shield with their (or their father's) arms. Each new vine begins between the portraits of the parents whose issue descend from it. College of Arms, MS 3/54.

[55] The Reynell pedigree of 1595 belonging to Thomas Woodcock, Garter King of Arms, has a single knight in a coat of mail, surcoat, shield and guidon. A later Reynell pedigree, dated 1649, has three-full length armoured figures, one in a black mantle (see above, Fig. 23a), another in mail and surcoat, and the third in mail with an anachronistic officer's sash, besides two half-length figures in fanciful antique dress (JHB, MS 428). The pedigree of Sir Anthony Aucher (1621) begins with three figures in mail with shields of arms, holding guidons, one with a surcoat and one with an armorial tabard: Bonhams, 19 March 2013, lot 39 (19th-century copy). A Bamfylde pedigree of 1624 has two figures in mail and surcoats, with shields and standards (Phillipps MS 6351, now JHB, MS 640). There are clear artistic similarities between the figures in some of these rolls.

[56] A Fitzwilliam pedigree of 1565 (Northants. Record Office, F(M) Roll 434) begins with a half-length figure of William Fitzwilliam, supposedly earl marshal to William the Conqueror, in Tudor armour and ruff, with an antique coronet worn over a black bonnet, holding a sword and a small shield with the arms of Fitzwilliam. The Oxenbridge pedigree (1600) in the E. Suss. Record Office (Acc. 7007) is headed by five mounted knights in Tudor plate armour holding lances with guidons, their horses with armorial caparisons. A Scott pedigree of *c.* 1605×10 has a single figure in contemporary armour holding a guidon (JHB, MS 515).

[57] E.g. the pedigree of Arundell of Trerice (1604), which has three full-length figures standing together in profile in contemporary armour with red sashes over their shoulders and laurel wreaths on their heads (JHB, MS 518, a facsimile copy made *c.* 1810). These were supposed to represent Sir Ralph, Sir Oliver and Sir Remfry ('Reynfredus') de Arundell. Note also the 1649 Reynell pedigree (above, n. 55). The red shoulder-sash, designed for carrying wounded or slain officers from the field, remained part of the dress of British infantry officers until Victorian times, and is still worn by officers of the Royal Regiment of Scotland in full dress.

[58] The Sackville pedigree of 1599 (above, n. 29) has four figures at the foot in fanciful antique costume, two of them seated on the ground, holding armorial guidons or banners.

[59] The Bacon pedigree (1578) at Raveningham Hall (Norf.) includes a demi-figure of Francis Wyndham in the scarlet robes of a serjeant at law. A pedigree of the Pigott family (1598) has figures representing Richard Pygot (d. 1483) in a judge's robes and of Thomas Pygot (d. 1520) in a serjeant's scarlet robes: the finished roll belongs to Christopher Prideaux, of Doddershall Park, Quainton (Bucks.); there is a draft on vellum in the College of Arms, MS 3/57. The Sackville pedigree (1599) (above, n. 29) shows the contemporary Lord Buckhurst in Garter robes.

[60] E.g. the scarlet parliamentary robes worn by peers since the 15th century. The Seymour pedigree (1604) (above, n. 45) shows several supposedly Norman peers in parliamentary robes, holding their patents. The undated Griffin pedigree belonging to Lord Braybrooke begins with four figures in peers' robes and a mounted knight: [F.W. Steer and others], *Heraldry in Essex* (Chelmsford, 1953),

seventeenth century than in the sixteenth.[61]

Reliability of the Rolls

A considerable influence in developing this classical form of pedigree must have been the reorganisation of the heralds in the later fifteenth century and their practice, which became common in the sixteenth century, of holding visitations throughout the realm to verify and record the coat armour used by the gentry. The gentry were thereby familiarised with the need to prove their pedigree in order to justify their title to the ancient arms found on seals or monuments, or to prove their suitability for a grant of new arms. As early as 1476 Thomas Andrewes of Charwelton (Northants.) prepared a genealogical dossier – beginning with some family mythology – in support of his successful application for a grant of arms.[62] Another fifteenth-century manuscript shows the connection between a genealogy, in narrative form, and the various coats of arms quartered by the Woodford family.[63] By this time the heralds were beginning to collect pedigrees as well as rolls of arms for their own reference, and by the time of Henry VIII it was said to be part of the sworn duty of a king of arms to take notes of 'descents'.[64] After the College of Arms acquired a permanent home in 1565, the visitation books and other records were kept in the college for future consultation by the officers of arms and to warrant the preparation of pedigrees for the families mentioned in them.

It is noteworthy, however, that relatively few Tudor pedigree rolls are recorded as having been prepared in direct consequence of a visitation, authenticated by the officer of arms responsible for it.[65] It is even more notable that the majority of Tudor pedigrees

---

      p. 26. The Philipot pedigree in the Hants. Record Office (93M86 W/1), composed in 1620 by John Philipot, Rouge Dragon Pursuivant, has a single figure in parliamentary robes, holding his patent, and another with the mantle and collar of a lord mayor over plate armour. The 1649 Reynell pedigree (JHB, MS 428) shows Sir Hugh Reynell (fl. 1275) in the black mantle of a knight of St John, as 'master and governer' of the order, with a feathered bonnet, over 17th-century armour. The figures have hair and beards of the 17th-century fashion.

[61] There are numerous similar examples in local record offices. A pedigree of Fitch (1636) in the Essex Record Office (D/DDs F2) has a figure in plate armour with an armorial tabard and guidon. The great Vaughan pedigree of 1641, now in the Dyfed Record Office (Cawdor collection, Acc. 5309) is 4 feet 9 inches wide and has ten full-length figures at the top holding banners, including King Hywel Dda, King Louis of France and William the Conqueror; it is illustrated in the *Heralds' Commemorative Exhibn.* catalogue, pl. XLVI.

[62] College of Arms, MS Vincent 88, ff. 16–19; MS Vincent 4, ff. 25–28; Denton, 'Genealogy and Gentility', at 152. Thomas heads the later visitation pedigrees of the family: Baker, *Men of Court*, I, p. 216.

[63] College of Arms, MS B. 28.

[64] Wagner, *Heralds of England*, pp. 132–3, 161. It has nevertheless been suggested that genealogy did not much concern most heralds until well into the reign of Elizabeth: *ibid.*, p. 205. Indeed, William Dethick asserted that it was not part of their public duty and that a better repository for pedigrees would be the Court of Wards: *ibid.*, p. 206.

[65] Examples are (i) College of Arms, MS 9/17 (pedigree of Done, from the 1566 visitation of Cheshire, signed by William Flower, Norroy King of Arms); (ii) ibid., MS 9/29 (pedigree of Claxton, signed

are not authenticated at all, or even dated.[66] One explanation may be that many were drawn up by arms-painters, or local antiquaries, without official sanction. By the end of the sixteenth century there were numerous arms-painters' shops in London and elsewhere, where pedigrees might be obtained;[67] the painters were employed by the heralds themselves, and proficiency in that line was considered a qualification for becoming an officer of arms.[68] But the signatures of painters were hardly likely to lend authenticity to their products, at least until the practice began of giving them formal deputations by patents from the kings of arms.[69] An equally plausible explanation is that even the officers of arms who prepared pedigrees were not at first accustomed to sign

---

by Flower, and by Robert Glover as his marshal, 1576, presumably from the 1575 visitation of Durham); (iii) manuscript sold at Sotheby's, 28 March 1983, lot 4, now belonging to Thomas Woodcock, Garter King of Arms (pedigree of Legh of Booths with the same two signatories, 1580, presumably from the visitation of Cheshire); (iv) JHB, MS 1510 (pedigree of Halswell of Halswell (in Goathurst, Som.), signed 'p[er] Rouge Croix Marshall for Clarencieulx Kinge of Armes 1591'; Ralph Brooke, Rouge Croix Pursuivant, conducted the visitation of Somerset on behalf of Robert Cooke, Clarenceux King of Arms, in 1591).

[66] This is in contrast to Welsh pedigree rolls, which were commonly signed and dated by the gentlemen antiquaries who produced them: Siddons, *Welsh Pedigree Rolls* (cit. in n. 38), lists a large number. The first compiler of Welsh pedigrees in English was Thomas Jones (d. 1609) of Tregaron: *ibid.*, pp. 40–3; F. Jones, 'The Dynevor Heraldic Pedigrees', *Coat of Arms*, xi (1970), pp. 116–21; one of his rolls is cited in a grant of arms, below, p. 164 n. 170. An English example is the rough pedigree of Loundes of South Repps (Norf.) compiled by James Strangeman, 'student in antiquetyes', in 1595: College of Arms, MS 3/29.

[67] Wagner, *Heralds of England*, p. 238; for local pedigree-makers see also William Dakins's evidence of 1598, below, pp. 143–4. In 1618 the commissioners for the office of Earl Marshal forbade painters to make pedigrees without licence from the kings of arms: A. R. Wagner and G. D. Squibb, 'Deputy Heralds', in *Tribute to an Antiquary*, ed. F. G. Emmison and R. Stephens (London, 1976), pp. 229–64, at 236.

[68] Wagner, *Heralds of England*, p. 200, instances Humphrey Hales, who was so recommended in 1581 and was appointed Bluemantle Pursuivant in 1583. Hales had previously studied law in Staple Inn and Gray's Inn.

[69] This practice has not been traced before the 1560s: Wagner and Squibb, 'Deputy Heralds', at p. 233. An example of a pedigree roll authenticated by a deputy is JHB, MS 166, made for Sir Nicholas Lower and his wife in 1621 by Thomas Dade, 'under-herald for Cornwall' serving under Camden: 'Quaedam Stem[m]ata Antiqua Generositatem ac insignia Illustris illius Familiae de Lowers et praecipue Nicolai Lower iam in Comitatu Cornubiensi remanentis ejusdem Familiae Militis praeclarissimi approbantia una cum Geneologia Excellentissimae istius Dominae Dominae Elisabethae uxoris suae filiae Henrici Killegrewe Militis iam defuncti, omni cum fide ac dilligentia perscrutata prout per diversas chartas et earum Familiarum evidencias authentice datas et sigillatas plenius liquet et apparet, me Thoma Dade gen[eroso] subfeciali Cornubiense sub Willi[el]mo Cambdeno Armigero, principali Rege Armorum Angliae, Confirmante et delineante ut sequitur Quinto die Martii Anno incarnationis Domini 1620'. This was a direct result of the visitation of Cornwall by heralds acting for Camden the previous year. It is the only known reference to Dade: Wagner and Squibb, 'Deputy Heralds', at p. 254. He cannot be the Thomas Dade of Tannington (Suff.), who had died in 1619. An equally obscure signatory is William Lowther, who produced a Gawdy pedigree in 1611: British Library, MS Add. 37535.

their work, or were not permitted to do so.[70] The first known to have signed pedigree rolls was William Hervey, as Norroy King of Arms in the early 1550s,[71] but it was not until the last quarter of the sixteenth century that a signature became common.[72] Sealed pedigrees were even less common.[73] In the same period Robert Glover introduced the

[70] The Earl Marshal's Orders of 1568 forbade pedigrees to be made in the Office without the consent of Garter and one other king of arms, save that either of the two provincial kings could 'make or sett forth in paper only such matches of discents of any Gentleman as they shall take notes of in their Visitations, soe that to the same discents they nor either of them shall not subscribe their names': *Munimenta Heraldica*, ed. G. D. Squibb (Harleian Soc., New Ser., iv, 1985), p. 100. In other words, all pedigree rolls on vellum produced by heralds after 1568 should bear the signatures of at least two kings of arms. The purpose was to preserve the perquisites of the kings of arms after their records were made available to the other heralds: Wagner, *Heralds of England*, p. 192. The evidence set out in n. 72, below, shows that the order was not generally observed. But it was a ground of complaint in 1595 against Ralph Brooke, York Herald, that he daily drew pedigrees for his own profit contrary to the order: *ibid.*, p. 215.

[71] Four instances are (i) Chamberlayne roll (1552) sold at Christie's, 17 Nov. 2004, lot 13; (ii) copy pedigree of Hastings (1553), College of Arms, MS B. 19, ff. 30–34; (iii) Dudley roll (1553), ibid., MS 16/5 ('travayled and set furth' by Hervey, but also signed by his fellow kings of arms), below, Fig. 26; (iv) Penyston (Cornwall) roll (1564), College of Arms, MS 8/24. Note also the Fitzwilliam pedigree roll dated 1564, which was sealed by Hervey with his official seal as Clarenceux King of Arms (Cambs. Record Office, R52/24/44/2; below, n. 119).

[72] The earliest example known to the writer of an original pedigree roll signed by Robert Cooke is that of Southcote (1572), JHB, MS 102 ('This pedegree or descent was examined, regestred and allowed in the yere of owre Lord God 1572 by ... Robert Cooke Alias Clarencieulx Roy Darmes); this was doubtless an outcome of Cooke's visitation of Essex in 1570. But note also a copy roll of 28 Feb. 1572 in College of Arms, MS Philipot 75, ff. 110v–112v (pedigree of Thomas Wentworth, signed by Cooke and Flower, kings of arms, and three other officers). There are two rolls signed by Cooke in 1573 and 1575 in the College of Arms, MSS 9/2B and 2C (Penyston). There are several examples, signed by different officers of arms, from 1576: e.g. the Fane pedigree, Northants. Record Office, Westmorland (Apethorpe) MSS, 1/1/6 (Robert Cooke; additionally signed by William Dethick, Garter, in 1588); Seymour pedigree, Longleat House (Wilts.), Seymour Papers vol. 6 (William Dethick, York Herald, 20 July 1576); Claxton pedigree, College of Arms, MS 9/29 (William Flower, Norroy, and Robert Glover, his marshal); Warren pedigree, ibid., MS 12/50e (Flower, Norroy); Talbot pedigree sold at Mallam's, Oxford, 6 Oct. 2000, lot 264, and now in the Fiske Collection (Robert Glover, Somerset Herald, *c.* 1576/7). Note also the Legh of Booths pedigree sold at Sotheby's, 28 March 1983, lot 4, now belonging to Thomas Woodcock, Garter King of Arms (Flower and Glover, 1580); and the Macwilliam pedigree, Society of Antiquaries MS 572 (Cooke, *c.* 1580). Examples of pedigree rolls signed by all three kings of arms are (i) Dudley, 1553, in the College of Arms, MS 16/5 (with a cartouche explaining that 'This pedegree hereabove declared was travayled and set furth by Willyam Harvey alias Norroy King of armes and corrected, controled and oversene' by the two other kings) (see Fig. 26); (ii) Fitzwilliam, 1565 (below, p. 153); (iii) Newport of Ercall (Salop.), also of 1565, in the College of Arms, MS 3/34; (iv) Repps of Norfolk, 1599, described in by C. L. S. Linnell, 'A Roll of Arms [*sic*] of the Repps Family', *Norfolk Archaeology*, 33 (1965), pp. 310–17.

[73] For the Fitzwilliam pedigrees of 1565 and 1568 see below, pp. 153, 157. A pedigree of Fulwer, signed by the three kings of arms and with the common seal of the College of Arms, was in the College of Arms (MS 9/40) but has been missing for some time. A pedigree of Fisher of Alrewas, sealed by William Segar *c.* 1615, is now JHB, MS 1350.

practice of heading pedigree rolls with an elaborate title in Latin asserting that they had been compiled from books and records in the College of Arms and elsewhere.[74] That authentication by an officer of arms was seen as desirable is demonstrated by the fact that an impostor called William Dakins established a local practice, masquerading variously as a king of arms or herald, conducting a visitation and supplying pedigrees, when he was not an officer of arms at all. For this fraud he was in 1580 sentenced by the Star Chamber to stand in the pillory and lose one of his ears.[75] This disgrace did little to diminish his practice, which continued actively until 1596, when he was imprisoned; even while in gaol he produced five pedigrees, and in the year after his release at least ten more.[76] One of his rolls, signed 'William Dakins Ali[a]s Lancaster Harrauld at Armes', is in the writer's possession.[77] Evidently made in the 1590s for Edmund Bagshaw (born 1545×6) of Stevenage and Berkhamsted (Herts.), it begins with a fictitious Sir Gregory Bagshaw in the time of Henry VI; the artwork is crude and the writing none too literate,[78] but the later part, presumably based on information received, is probably as accurate as any real herald would have made it.[79] Dakins nevertheless confessed that his pedigrees were for the most part false, and that they were made 'without any good proofes and most part of his owne head'.[80] He was not alone in his shady practices, and on his examination in 1598 he named seven others, including Edward Waterhouse 'that taketh

---

[74] Earlier pedigrees rarely have a title of any kind. Glover's practice was taken up by other officers. For example, the Repps pedigree roll (1599), mentioned in n. 72, is headed: 'Hoc stemma familiae de Repps de Westwalton in com. Norffolciae tam ex evidentiis quam ex diversis libris et recordis penes nos in officio Armorum remanentibus quanta fieri potest diligentia et veritate elaboratum est ...'.

[75] British Library, MS Harley 1070, f. 86v; J.S. Burn, *The Star Chamber* (London, 1870), p. 66 (says one ear); Lambeth Palace Library, Talbot Papers, MS 3197, f. 325; Wagner, *Heralds of England*, p. 237. The charge was impersonating Norroy and forging pedigrees. He had conducted a visitation of Cheshire in 1579 under his bogus authority: *Acts of the Privy Council, 1578–80*, p. 141. For his forging of arms and pedigrees, see also College of Arms, MSS Vincent 110, ad finem (Constable of Cattfoss pedigree, cancelled by Richard Lee, Richmond Herald), and Vincent 150, p. 162 (Goodhall pedigree, cancelled by the officers of arms).

[76] College of Arms, MS Vincent 430, pp. 1–8 (account of an inquiry into his misdeeds in 1598); Wagner, *Heralds of England*, p. 237. He is not to be confused with the Cambridge academic of the same name (d. 1607), one of the translators of the Bible.

[77] Bloomsbury Book Auctions, 13 Dec. 2002, lot 22; now JHB, MS 214. It is probably the pedigree of 'Mr Bagshott' which heads Dakins's list of pedigrees produced in 1596–97: College of Arms, MS Vincent 430, p. 2. If so, it was drawn up with six others while Dakins was staying at Edward Brockett's house in Hertfordshire. By the Earl Marshal's warrant of 26 March 1598, pedigrees written by Dakins were supposed to be brought in to the College of Arms for inspection and correction, and this may explain why no others have come to light.

[78] In one place Christopher is abbreviated as 'expfer', and the signature uses 'Alis' for 'Alias'.

[79] It is close to that recorded in the 1634 Visitation of Bedfordshire, when Edmund was aged 68: *Visitations of Bedfordshire*, ed. F. A. Blaydes (Harleian Soc., xix, 1884), p. 79. A Henry Bagshawe was involved in a Chancery suit in 1580 which seems indirectly to have concerned Dakins: letter from the Earl of Shrewsbury to the Lord Chancellor, Derbys. Record Office, D258/39/20.

[80] College of Arms, MS Vincent 430, pp. 2, 4.

upon him to be Mr Clarenceux his man ... and gatherith fees as an Herald', and John Scott, 'servant to one Hurte a scryvenour in Cambridge'.[81]

If the Bagshaw pedigree had been signed by the real Lancaster Herald it would presumably have carried more clout than a purely private production. Dakins would not otherwise have had to put his ears in jeopardy by signing his productions. But it is important to notice the distinction between a pedigree roll and a grant of arms. A king of arms had but to point his wand and a coat of arms came into existence.[82] His patent of grant operated in the same way as a charter, or deed of confirmation, and his signature and seal provided authentic proof that the grant had been made. Patents of grant were always accepted by the heralds in their visitations as conclusive proof that the arms belonged to the grantee and his issue. A pedigree, on the other hand, was a series of conclusions based on historical evidence which might or might not be reliable or correctly interpreted. Pedigrees were only as good as the evidence on which they rested. Some heralds may have seen their function as being merely to register what information the family provided, with a modicum of critical examination;[83] but, even if they conducted a thorough examination of the evidence, as duty required, they could not by their signature make something true which was not true. With respect to more recent information, the signature of the head of the family or a prominent member of it – which came to be required for the registration of visitation pedigrees – was more important than that of any herald.[84] In practice, successive pedigrees produced for the same family often contained amendments as more information came to light. In a remarkable instance of 1579, the conscientious Glover even made a client covenant under seal to allow a pedigree to be altered if a somewhat conjectural assertion turned out on further investigation to be wrong.[85]

Most of the pedigree rolls found in archives relate to established gentry, and that is presumably why they have been preserved. But a few rare survivals show that pedigrees were also made for some very obscure people who do not feature in the heraldic visitations. One is a modest paper roll of about 1580, with five crudely painted shields of arms, for the Seymans of Knoddishall (Suff.), a place better known for the seat of the

---

[81] John Scott was the author of 'Foundation of the University of Cambridge' (1615), the first commercial guide book to the univerity, which was published in manuscript, usually with painted arms of the colleges and founders. JHB, MS 179, is an example made for Sir Miles Sandes, Bt., which also includes paintings of arms in the Old Schools.

[82] Many Tudor patents granting arms include a miniature painting of a king of arms pointing his wand towards the arms depicted in the left-hand margin.

[83] When William Dethick was charged with exemplifying a false pedigree of Rotheram in 1595, his defence was that he had merely exemplified what he was shown: Wagner, *The Heralds of England*, pp. 205, 206. See also Wagner, *English Genealogy*, pp. 313–18.

[84] See *Pitton* v. *Walter* (1719) in Viner's *Abridgment*, tit. 'Evidence', T.b.87.5; *Blount's Case* (1737) 1 Atk. 295 at 297; G. D. Squibb, *The High Court of Chivalry* (Oxford, 1959), p. 210.

[85] Bodleian. Library. MS Ashmole 840, pp. 697–700; Ramsay, *Robert Glover*, Ch. 7 (the client being William Brereton).

Jenneys.[86] The Seyman family is not mentioned in the visitations and none of the arms in the roll are to be found in the *Dictionary of British Arms* or the very full ordinary of Suffolk arms.[87] A more extreme example is the vellum pedigree of Langhorne of Lastingham (Yorks.), compiled in the 1580s.[88] It traces the descent from a Hamond Langhorne in the reign of Henry II to a Robert and Henry Langhorne in the time of Richard III; it would have continued on another skin which is no longer present. The family was so obscure that it has left no trace in the visitations or even in the registers of wills proved at York or Canterbury, and yet the compiler managed to connect it by marriage with many well-known Yorkshire families and adorned the roll with no less than forty-five coats of arms. Nearly all of it is completely fictional, including the supporting citations, such as a visitation by one Blackburn Herald in 10 Edward II, another by one 'Beawe James heraulde at arms' in 2 Richard II, and a 'Hawley heraulde at armes' in 13 Henry VI. On a separate membrane there is even a facsimile painting of a patent of 'Richard Halley Principall Kinge at Armes' granting a crest to Henry Langhorn on 10 January 1484. Although this is an outrageous example, it seems that dubious pedigrees were commonplace, even if the deception was usually more subtle.[89] And they were not confined to the socially obscure. For example, the Pigott family founded by Thomas Pigott or Pygot (d. 1520), serjeant at law, son of a Berkshire attorney of lowly origins, on achieving social prominence asserted a spurious connection with the armigerous Pygots of Yorkshire and had it embodied in a roll of 1598.[90] Some of the greatest men in the land employed heralds or arms painters to search out some connection with a major medieval family whose arms they might adopt. The Spencers of Northamptonshire, who had originated as sheep-farmers and would be raised to the baronage in 1603, linked themselves quite unwarrantably with the medieval Despencer family and assumed their arms.[91] Lawyers such as Sir Anthony Fitzherbert (d. 1538), justice of the Common Pleas, and Sir Nicholas Bacon (d. 1579), Lord Keeper of the Great Seal,[92] and even statesmen of the eminence of Sir Walter Mildmay, likewise adopted

---

[86] JHB, MS 1347. This probably belonged to Augustine Vincent (d. 1626), Windsor Herald, whose manuscripts passed to Ralph Sheldon (1623–84); inscribed on the dorse 'Ex dono Rad: Sheldon'; it later belonged to J. P. Brooke-Little (1927–2006), Clarenceux King of Arms; his sale, Bloomsbury Auctions, 29 Nov. 2011, lot 380 (part).

[87] J. Corder, *A Dictionary of Suffolk Arms* (Suff. Records Soc., 7, 1965).

[88] Christie's, 4 June 2008, lot 23; now JHB, MS 746. Since the lower part is lost, it is not possible to discern for whom it was prepared, but a likely culprit is the attorney William Langhorne.

[89] See Wyrley, *True Use of Armorie* (cit. in n. 28), p. 20.

[90] Baker, *Men of Court*, II, pp. 1276–9; the roll is mentioned in n. 59, above.

[91] J. H. Round, *Family Origins and Other Studies* (London, 1930), pp. 33–4.

[92] Bacon's supposed descent from one William Bacon in the time of Edward II was recited in his grant of arms (1569) (British Library, MS Add. 39249) and in a pedigree roll (College of Arms, MS 12/51E). It was also set out in a pedigree made for his grandson Edmund Bacon: British Library, MS Add. 39251. For its falsity see W. Rye, *The False Pedigree and Arms of Bacon of Suffolk* (Norwich, 1919). He was granted the ancient arms of Bacon in 1568: Baker, *Men of Court*, I, p. 253.

ancient arms on the strength of spurious pedigrees.[93]

The production of the Mildmay pedigree affords a striking example of the deception, perhaps even self-deception, which these exercises involved.[94] Mildmay was the youngest son of a Chelmsford mercer and the grandson of an Essex yeoman. His father, perhaps at his instance, had been granted a coat of arms in 1542, and he (Walter) had in 1546 and 1552 obtained further grants of two entirely different coats.[95] All three coats were distinctively Tudor, and by the 1580s – when fellow statesmen such as Bacon and Cecil were acquiring new pedigrees – they had come to seem unfitting for someone of Mildmay's importance. What was required was a medieval ancestry and a medieval-looking coat of arms. This would require heraldic cooperation. But the officers of arms, unlike the country painters, did require some written evidence before they would lend their name to such discoveries. So proof was duly found. A series of charters and other documents, stretching back to a Hugh Mildeme in the time of King Stephen, and equipped from the thirteenth century with armorial seals, was conveniently discovered so that Robert Cooke, Clarenceux, could prepare an engrossed pedigree roll showing how the arms on the seals had descended to Sir Walter, and then issue a confirmatory grant (or 'restitution') of these arms on 12 June 1583 to Sir Walter, adding the tinctures (*Argent, three lions rampant azure*) not found on the seals,[96] and a proper mark of cadency (a martlet), with permission nevertheless to quarter the 1542 coat.[97] The supporting documents were copied in facsimile in a vellum roll signed by the Earl Marshal and Cooke on 20 August 1583, and a summary of their contents was engrossed on an illuminated vellum roll signed by Cooke without date.[98] The documents were still

[93] Baker, *Men of Court*, I, p. 47, II, p. 1098; J. H. Round, *Peerage and Pedigree*, 2 vols (London, 1901), II, pp. 134–213; Maclagan, 'Genealogy and Heraldry' (cit. in n. 2), pp. 38–42; M. Keen, *Origins of the English Gentleman* (Stroud, 2000), pp. 18-19.

[94] Round, *Family Origins*, pp. 62–72. Round left open the question whether the evidence was genuine, since it was not accessible when he wrote.

[95] Baker, *Men of Court*, II, p. 1098. The 1542 coat alone is carved on the father's tomb in Chelmsford Cathedral. In June 1567 a 'Mr Myldemaye' paid two French crowns for an escutcheon of his arms: College of Arms, MS Vincent 502(ii), f. 5 (heralds' waiting book).

[96] Round was no doubt correct in supposing that the arms were granted on the negative argument that all other combinations of common tinctures and metals were already in use and therefore Mildmay must have borne blue lions on a silver field. The only occurrences of these arms in *Dictionary of British Arms: Medieval Ordinary*, vol. I, ed. D. H. B. Chesshyre and T. Woodcock (London, 1992), p. 282, are for Geoffrey de Camville [d. 1308], though the tinctures were usually reversed: G.J. Brault, *Rolls of Arms of Edward I*, 2 vols (London, 1997), II, p. 91.

[97] Pedigree roll: Northants. Record Office, W(A) box 1/parcel I/4 (signed by Cooke but undated). Grant of restitution: ibid., 15A. The full arms authorised by Cooke were Mildmay (ancient) quartering Rouse, Cornish and Mildmay (modern). The restitution was retrospective, and the quartered arms (but with the 'ancient' coat in the fourth quarter as well) occur in a stained glass panel of *c.* 1600×20 belonging to the writer, impaled by Waldegrave (quarterly of ten), for the daughter of Thomas Mildmay, MP (d. 1566), who would himself have used the 1542 coat.

[98] 'Briefe notes howe to prove the Pedigree of the famylie of Mildmay, by the Evidence inclosed', Northants. Record Office, W(A) box 1/parcel I/15B; roll of facsimiles, ibid., 15D (also signed by

under scrutiny in September 1585, when one of the armorial seals is said to have crumbled in Cooke's hands.[99] These unusually elaborate preparations may have been designed to ward off previous scepticism about the Mildmay claims. In commenting on the variation in spelling from Mildeme to Mildmay, Cooke observed that 'there is no more cause of scruple or doubte to bee conceived in this sirname of Mildemay ... beinge a very rare name I finde them onlie in Essex, North[amptonshire] and Glouc[estershire] and theie be all extracted of one famely ...'.[100] The discovery of the medieval evidence might well have seemed too good to be true, in that what had just come to light provided Mildmay with a pedigree stretching over more than four centuries, without any troublesome gaps, a pedigree which entitled him to an ancient coat of arms previously unknown to heraldry and which was clearly unknown to the family itself in the 1540s and 1550s. In fact the evidence was a bundle of very proficient forgeries. It is difficult not to believe that both the revered Mildmay and the less scrupulous Cooke were parties to this victimless fraud, though it has been charitably supposed that the prime culprit here was not Sir Walter but his eldest son Anthony.[101]

The consequence of such fabrications is that the pedigree rolls of ascendant families may be more interesting now for what they tell us about a family's claims and pretensions than for factual information about a family's remoter origins. On the other hand, it may be assumed that the more recent information which they contain was in general correctly recorded, because it was intended to be of practical use, and it is often the best or only evidence we have for collateral relations or children who did not survive. Moreover, there is no doubt that a long-established family which was content with its real pedigree might commission genealogical research of a high order so that the details might be preserved for posterity in a pedigree roll. This would usually involve studying the family's deeds, with particular attention to armorial seals, and distilling further information from wills, inquisitions and monumental inscriptions. Robert Glover (Somerset Herald 1570–88) was a particularly careful genealogist, and sometimes included copies of seals and documents in his pedigrees. In the pedigree which he prepared for the Dudley family in the mid-1570s he claimed to have consulted public records in the Tower, six abbey cartularies, several chronicles, two old pedigrees belonging to the Earl of Leicester, and

---

George, earl of Shrewsbury). The bundle of evidences is ibid., 15C. These were formerly kept in the leather-covered box containing the grant of 1583: ibid., 15.

[99] One of them, W(A) box 1/parcel I/15C, was endorsed by Cooke: 'This peece of Evidence did we se fayre sealed with a Seale of Armes in white waxe bearinge in the Scutchin Three Lyons rampant But being unce a lyttle handled through age and evill keping the said waxe mouldred in oure handes a peeces Anno Domini 1585 Et mense Septembris'.

[100] 'Briefe notes howe to prove the Pedigree of the famylie of Mildmay' (previous note).

[101] L. L. Ford, 'Mildmay, Sir Walter (1520/21–1589)', in *ODNB*, 38, pp. 119–26, at 124. Cooke certainly used at least four forged charters, which still survive, to support the earlier part of his pedigree of Sydney: see C. L. Kingsford, 'On Some Ancient Deeds and Seals belonging to Lord De L'Isle and Dudley', *Archaeologia*, lxv (1914), pp. 251–68, at 253–6.

records in the College of Arms.[102] Other heralds were equally assiduous. The pedigree of the relatively minor Seylyard family of Delaware (Kent), compiled between 1585 and 1591, relied in part on the transcription of a quantity of local archival material, including manorial court rolls. The results were set out in a large paper pedigree, with transcripts of the supporting documents in their proper places, and the coats of arms in written blazon.[103] From this an engrossment on vellum, which cannot at present be traced, was presumably prepared.[104] Whether research in such detail was normal can only be a matter of conjecture, but where it was carried out the result is of historical value in preserving information which would otherwise have been lost.[105] Sir Kenelm Digby is said to have spent £1,500 on researching his ancestry, though the result was tainted by an anxiety to stretch it back to the Anglo-Saxon period.[106]

In evaluating a pedigree roll for present historical purposes it is obviously necessary to try to place it in context. This requires, firstly, that it should be assigned a date, even if only approximate. Very few Tudor pedigree rolls are formally dated, since they rarely have headings or official subscriptions, though in some cases the date is disclosed near the foot of the text when someone is described as 'now living' in a given year. In the absence of an explicit date, it is necessary to study the last rows in the roll and engage in some independent genealogical research. The latest marriage in the main line, as indicated by an impalement, will often be that of the person commissioning the pedigree.[107] The approximate date of that marriage will provide the *terminus a quo*,

---

[102] College of Arms, MS 13/1. Cf. the letter to John Cotes, College of Arms, MS Vincent 92, ff. 15–16, 19–20, in which he informed a client that he had inspected three documents in a black box, two old pedigrees, and an inquisition *post mortem*, and sent his notes for the client's comments.

[103] JHB, MS 1349 ('The pedygre of William Seylyard of Delaware in the parishe of Brasted in Kent esquire taken owte of recordes and also owte of his owne evydences remayninge at Delaware in Kent and <finished [added]> the xx daye of September anno Elizabethe xxxiii° et anno Domini 1591'). One of the supporting notes begins: 'Yt apperethe in the courte roulles of the manor of Brasted in Kent nowe in anno Domini 1585 in the possession of ... Lord Stafford ...' It seems not to be in the autograph of Robert Cooke (d. 1593), who signed the vellum roll of 1578 (next note).

[104] A vellum pedigree was in the possession of C. R. C. Petley (1807–90), who also owned the paper roll, but it may have been earlier in date. It was cursorily described by G. Leveson-Gower in *Proc. Soc. Antiquaries*, 2nd ser., ix (1883), pp. 335–42, and exhibited by Mrs Petley at Burlington House in 1894 (when it was said to be for *William* Seylyard). It was 7 feet long, with 43 painted shields of arms and an achievement (not in the paper roll); according to the inscription, it was 'travailed and sett forth aswell by sondry evidences and court rolles as also by the records of the Office of Armes and allowed to John Seyliard of London Gentilman in Anno Domini 1578 by me Rob[ertu]s Cooke alias Clarensieux Roy Darmes'.

[105] This particular example has been used by local historians. It was referred to in T. Philipott, *Villare Cantianum; or, Kent Surveyed and Illustrated*, 2nd edn. (Lynn, 1776), p. 137, and was printed in full [by J. J. Howard] in *Miscellanea Genealogica et Heraldica*, 2nd ser., i (1886), pp. 7–20; reprinted in *Some Pedigrees from the Visitation of Kent, 1663–68*, ed. J. J. Howard and R. Hovenden (London, 1887), pp. 64–77.

[106] Heal and Holmes, *The Gentry*, p. 36.

[107] This is not universally true. The Heigham pedigree in Suff. Record Office (Ipswich) (HD 2418/57)

while details of the couple's children, or their absence, may provide the *terminus ad quem*. Then it is necessary to assess how far the pedigree was intended to record factual knowledge and how far (if at all) to buttress a legend based on fiction. Quite often it will do both, the earlier part being different in character from the later. The assessment, again, will usually depend on the compatibility of the pedigree with surviving record sources, always bearing in mind that contemporaries sometimes had less at their disposal than we do – though sometimes more – and that the line between fiction and bold conjecture may be a faint one. Doubtless no one at the time was misled by the falsities of the obviously false pedigrees. Like legal fictions, they were designed to achieve a result which was widely accepted as more or less legitimate but which could not otherwise be achieved. The historical research which was commissioned to support them was not aimed at uncovering the unvarnished truth, however inconvenient, but to provide as many of the available facts as suited the case to be made, to suppress those which did not, and to invent what was necessary to fill the gaps. It was objectionable, no doubt, when the ingenuity extended to the alteration or fabrication of historical documents, or even of funeral monuments in churches.[108] But using historical skills to bolster a family's vanity was not seen as seriously dishonest, at any rate by the upwardly mobile, and it generally did no one any harm. It was another matter entirely if a pedigree was falsified in order to support a claim to property, since that had the object of depriving someone of their lawful inheritance by fraud. And that brings us to a *cause célèbre* concerning pedigree rolls, a case which was of enormous importance and interest in the 1570s but has largely escaped the notice of historians.[109]

The Fitzwilliam Case (1567–72)

The Fitzwilliam family of Sprotborough (Yorks., West Riding) was genuinely ancient and could plausibly justify its claim to a pedigree beginning in the time of William the Conqueror;[110] but the main line had ended on the death of William Fitzwilliam without issue in 1517. The Yorkshire estates had then been divided between his two aunts and

---

ends with an achievement of arms impaling Teringham for John Heigham (d. 1522), great-uncle of Sir John Heigham for whom the pedigree was made; it shows Sir John's marriage to Anne Wright [1562], but no children.

[108] As to which see Heal and Holmes, *The Gentry*, p. 34.

[109] It is not mentioned in the monumental history of the College of Arms by Sir Anthony Wagner. There is a mention of Hugh Fitzwilliam's pedigree in *Collins's Peerage of England*, ed. E. Brydges, 9 vols (London, 1812), IV, p. 374, but no indication there that it was contentious. There is a brief mention in M. E. Finch, *The Wealth of Five Northamptonshire Families* (Northants. Record Soc., xix, 1956), pp. 100–2, 188–9; but this is based on the Fitzwilliam evidence, and the author thought it 'impossible to establish' whether Hugh Fitzwilliam's researches were 'partisan'.

[110] So thought F. M. Stenton, *Anglo-Saxon England* (Oxford, 1943), p. 675, quoted by Wagner, *English Genealogy*, 3rd edn., pp. 54–5. The family in fact began with William Fitzwilliam, son of William FitzGodric and Albreda de Lisoures, the heiress of Sprotborough, early in the 12th century: see J. Hunter, *South Yorkshire: Deanery of Doncaster* (London, 1828), I, pp. 332–5; J. W. Clay, *The Extinct and Dormant Peerages of the Northern Counties of England* (London, 1913), p. 76.

25. Pedigree roll of the Fitzwilliam family of Emley and Sprotborough (Yorkshire), one of many commissioned by Hugh Fitzwilliam (d. c. 1575) to support his case against the Copley family for the Fitzwilliam estates. It begins by stating that William Fitzwilliam came over with William the Conqueror, and traces the descent of Hugh, and of Philip Copley's mother Dorothy Fitzwilliam, from Sir John Fitzwilliam in the reign of Edward III. Datable to c 1571. College of Arms, MS 12/48s: whole roll displayed in two halves (upper half at left, lower half at right).

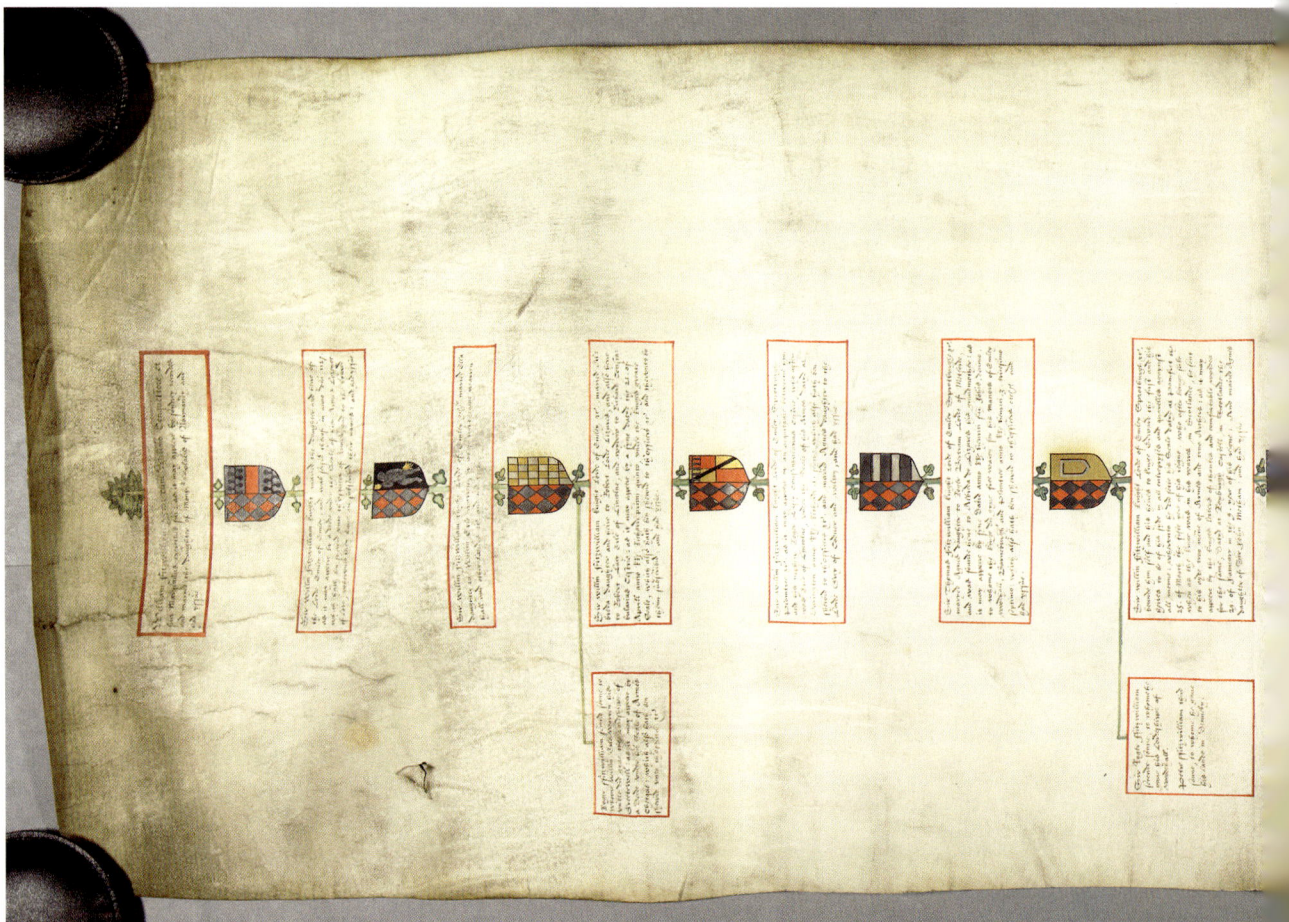

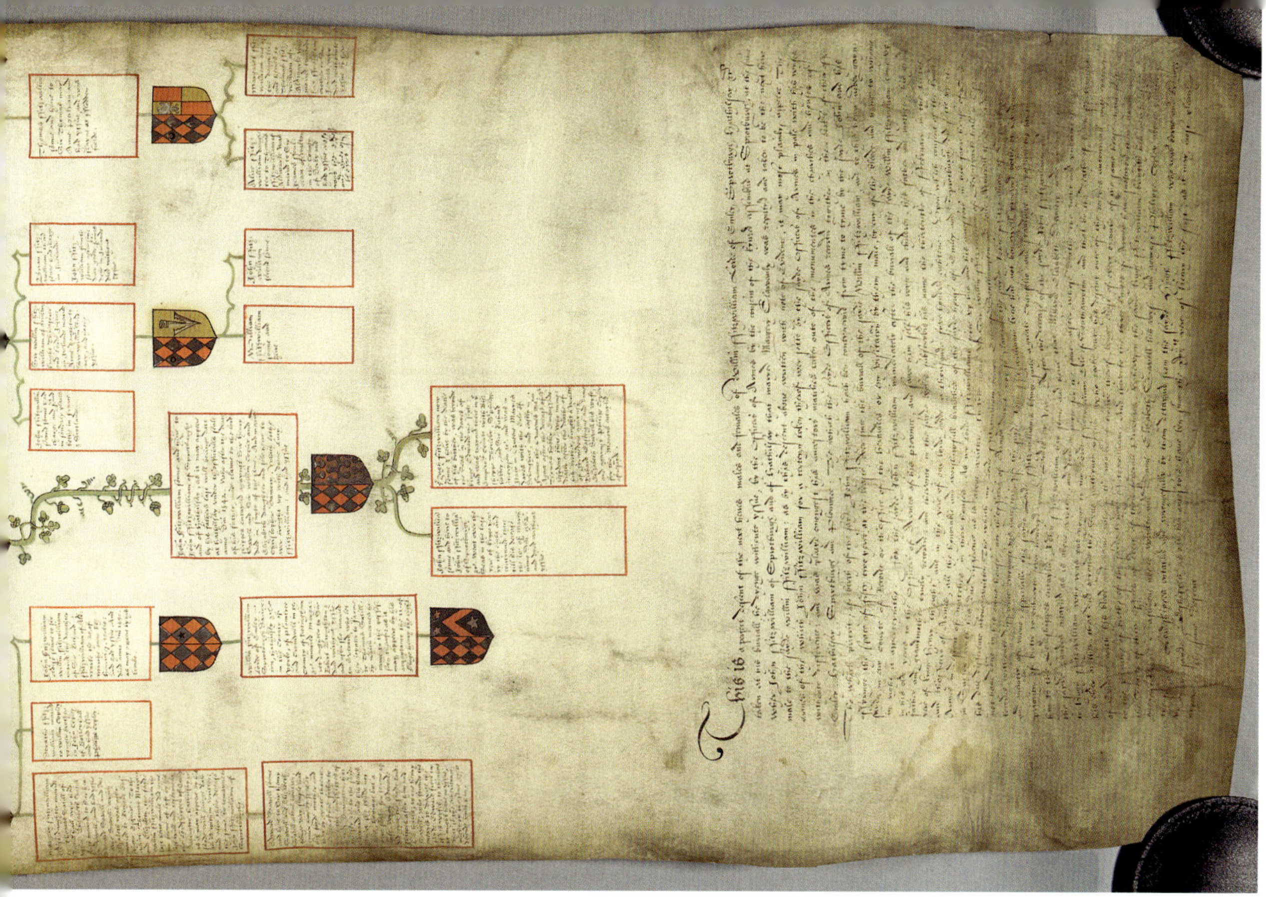

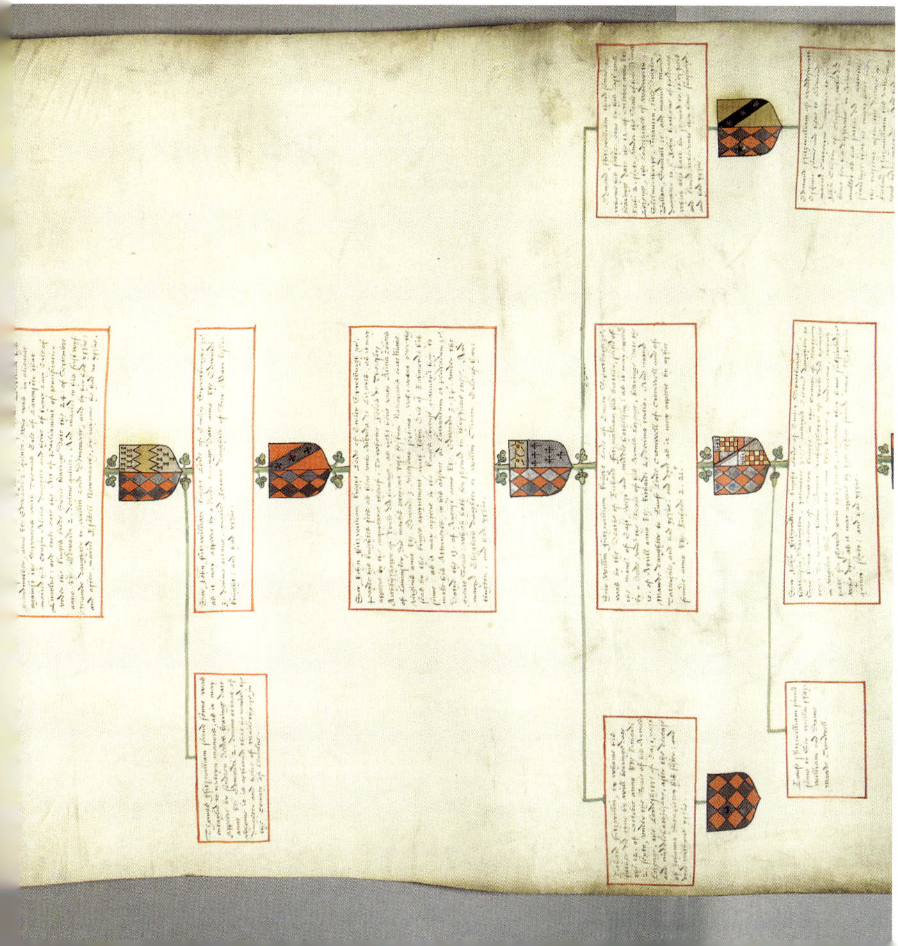

coheirs. Sprotborough went to Dorothy, wife of Sir William Copley; Emley and Darrington (formerly Darthington) went to Margery, wife of Thomas Suthill. But there were still many Fitzwilliams around in the sixteenth century. One of them, Hugh Fitzwilliam, the only surviving son of John Fitzwilliam of Haddesley (formerly Hathilsey), who claimed to have spent his early years in the household of William Fitzwilliam (d. 1542), earl of Southampton,[111] and to have been engaged on diplomatic missions in the mid-sixteenth century, believed himself the chief representative and male heir of the ancient line and therefore entitled to the estates under an ancient settlement in tail male.[112] By his own account his father had laid claim to the estates of Fitzwilliam of Sprotborough but had died while the suit was pending.[113] Hugh was to spend much of his later life pursuing this ancestral claim with vigour, collecting historical evidence from the Tower of London, the College of Arms and elsewhere. He represented in 1565 that he was motivated in part by the 'burning of three great Bagges of evidence of the Fitz Williams by Sir Henry Savell of Tankersley', whose wife was the sole heiress of Margery Suthill, 'meaninge thereby to deface the bloode and name forever ...', as also by the biblical injunction 'to mayntayne antiquity, nobility and birthright'.[114] He probably acquired a genuine taste for antiquities, and his collection of manuscripts included an important thirteenth-century roll of arms, later known as the Dering roll – probably the one sold in 2007 for £192,000[115] – as well as Cotgrave's Ordinary of *c.*

[111] Inscription around his portrait in the pedigree roll dated 1564, Cambs. Record Office, 52/24/44/2: 'put yong to my Lord Fitzwilliams erle of S[out]ha[m]p[ton]'; repeated in College of Arms, MS 12/48S (*c.* 1571). This is not easy to square with his having been a scholar at Winchester in 1544, unless he was with the Earl in his early infancy. There was a fuller account of his life in the lost book which he compiled: Hunter, *South Yorkshire*, I, pp. 340–1.

[112] William Fitzwilliam referred in his will of 1516 to an ancestral entail, saying that God had so blessed his family with worship and ancestry that he had given nothing away at all: *Testamenta Vetusta*, ed. N. H. Nicolas, 2 vols (London, 1826), I, pp. 545–6. Hugh's claim, according to the pleadings in the Common Pleas, was as great-great-grandson of Sir John Fitzwilliam, great-great-great-grandfather of the William Fitzwilliam who died in 1517.

[113] Fitzwilliam pedigree roll, College of Arms, MS 12/48S. This was in Sotheby's sale of 22 February 1833, lot 684, and subsequently with John Cochrane (1837), Evans (1838) and Rodd (1839) before being acquired by Sir Thomas Phillipps (MS 29177); it was purchased at the 1899 Phillipps sale (lot 553) by W. A. Lindsay (d. 1926), Clarenceux King of Arms. In F(M) Roll 435, the last entry in the pedigree is: 'Hugh Fitzwilliam now sonne and heire dothe claime the foresaide manours to him intailed as his father did against Dame Elizabeth Savell and Philipp Copley 1570'.

[114] *Collins's Peerage of England*, ed. Brydges, IV, p. 374, citing a book pedigree in the possession of Earl Fitzwilliam (see below, pp. 153–4).

[115] Sotheby's, 4 Dec. 2007, lot 46; now British Library, Add. Roll 77720. It includes a shield with the arms borne since the 13th century by Fitzwilliam (*Lozengy argent and gules*) but there attributed to William Crepin (Bec-Crispin): Brault, *Rolls of Arms Edward I* (cit. in n. 96), I, p. 166, no. 296 (corrected by Glover to FitzWilliam), and II, pp. 176–7. For Hugh Fitzwilliam's ownership, see A. R. Wagner, *Catalogue of English Mediaeval Rolls of Arms* (Oxford, 1950), pp. 14, 142. Wagner pointed out that Hugh Fitzwilliam may have owned the 15th-century copy of the Dering roll, now British Library, MS Add. 38537. Glover saw one or other of them in Fitzwilliam's possession in 1563: Oxford, Queen's College, MS 158, p. 434.

1340.[116] Some of his claims, however, were based on oral or lost evidence,[117] and we shall see that some of this was spurious. He was supported in the claim by all his kinsmen, and when he made his will in 1563 he appointed his patron Sir William Fitzwilliam of Milton (Northants.) as his principal executor, leaving him all his writings and evidence 'wheresoever they be'.[118] The documents are still preserved in the Fitzwilliam (Milton) archives in the Northamptonshire Record Office.

No one was more devoted to pedigree rolls than Hugh Fitzwilliam, who commissioned more than twenty in ten years. In 1564 he obtained from William Hervey, Clarenceux King of Arms, a sealed pedigree setting out his descent at length and displaying the ancient Fitzwilliam arms without any mark of cadency.[119] It was scarcely adequate for legal purposes, since it was purely lineal and did not show the parallel lines of descent and how they had come to an end. By May 1565 he had commissioned a much more elaborate roll, which is quite remarkable in being signed not only by the three kings of arms (including Hervey), with their seals appended in wooden skippets, by Robert Cooke (then Chester Herald), and by three pursuivants of arms, but also by twelve principal representatives of all the current branches of the Fitzwilliam family.[120] Hugh transcribed it into a book, which had drawings of seals and a title-page with the figure of a woodman, from whose mouth issued a scroll inscribed: 'No marvell though I be

[116] Wagner, *Cat. English Mediaeval Rolls of Arms*, p. 60. The Cotgrave manuscript, now in the College of Arms, has a heading which mentions Hugh Fitzwilliam's ownership; it was printed in *Rolls of Arms of the Reigns of Henry III and Edward III*, ed. N. H. Nicolas (London, 1829), pt. 2. This also included the Fitzwilliam arms (blazoned as *Masclé argent and gules*, which is to be interpreted as *lozengy* rather than *masculy* as now understood). In 1562 Fitzwilliam showed Hugh Cotgrave an ancient roll of arms 'which was many yeares kept by his auncestors' and asked Cotgrave to copy it out, 'beinge soe auncient that it was very hard to be read': College of Arms, RR 38F/d.

[117] He claimed to have received much of his information from his father's elderly cousin Margery Holmes, daughter of Ralph Fitzwilliam (who lived in the time of Henry VI): Hunter, *South Yorkshire*, I, p. 339.

[118] PRO, PCC 3 Langley (PROB 11/60), dated 14 Oct. 1563, proved 26 Jan. 1577; printed in *North Country Wills*, vol. II, *1558–1604*, ed. J. W. Clay (Surtees Soc., 121, 1912), pp. 40–1.

[119] Cambs. Record Office, R52/24/44/2. It is signed: 'In verefiing of this decent to be trewe I have therunto set my hand and seall 1564 | W. Hervy alias Clarencieulx King of Armes'. Another linear pedigree of small dimensions (4 inches wide, but trimmed at the margins with the loss of some notes) is Northants. Record Office, F(M) Roll 450, which also begins with William Fitzwilliam, who came with the Conqueror, but it lacks the end. A third (3¾ inches wide, and only 1¾ inches thick when rolled) is F(M) Roll 452, which ends the Fitzwilliam line with Sir William, of Gaynes Park (in Theydon Garnon, Essex), and continues with the descent of his wife Anne Sapcote from the Nevills.

[120] Northants. Record Office, F(M) Roll 434 (dated 3 May 1565); the seal of Garter is now detached. The roll is headed: 'This is the lineall descent of the Fitzwilliams of Sprotburgh, Lordes of Emley, with certayn notes of Evidens, declaringe the tyme perticulerly wherin thei lyvid, as yow shall perceive by figures answeringe to the mayne Lyne of the same. Hugh F.' It may, therefore, have been drawn by or on the instructions of Hugh Fitzwilliam, rather than being an independent production by the officers of arms. The 'notes of Evidens' are the transcriptions of documents, some of them seemingly spurious, set down in the margins of the roll: for these see also the next note.

wode [*i.e.* mad] | Which am berevid of lande and goode'.[121] For good measure, Hugh also procured a pedigree designed to show the family's rather distant relationship with Sir Nicholas Bacon, lord keeper of the Great Seal, and Sir William Cecil, secretary of state.[122]

Thus equipped with pedigree rolls authenticated on the highest heraldic authority, Hugh commenced three lawsuits to recover the family's estates. On 12 February 1566 he sued out a writ of formedon in the descender for the manor of Sprotborough against Philip Copley, son of the coheiress Dorothy and currently in seisin,[123] basing his claim on a gift in tail male by Edmund Deyncourt in the time of Edward II.[124] He made out his descent from Ralph Fitzwilliam, second son[125] of the great-great-great-grandfather of the William Fitzwilliam who died without issue in 1517, alleging that he was the next heir male. The complex pleadings which followed in the Common Pleas were thought worthy of publication by Sir Edward Coke,[126] and the case was reported by Sir James Dyer, chief justice of the Common Pleas.[127] They may be summarised as follows.[128] As to one moiety of the manor of Sprotborough, Copley vouched to warranty one Thomas Barnby, and as to the other he pleaded in bar that William and Dorothy Copley had been seised (in Dorothy's right), that they levied a final concord in 1525×6, and that he was Dorothy's son and heir.[129] Hugh counterpleaded the voucher on the ground that Barnby's ancestor

---

[121] Hunter, *South Yorkshire*, I, pp. 334 n. 1, 341. This was the version used by Collins (above, n. 109). Dr Ramsay has suggested that this book may have contained some transcripts of charters, not all authentic, which Glover saw in the 1580s: Bodleian Library, MS Eng. misc. c. 121, ff. 121–124. The woodman was doubtless taken from the supposed arms of 'Sir John, lord of Emley', which occur in the second row of several Fitzwilliam pedigrees (including F(M) Roll 434).

[122] Northants. Record Office, F(M) Roll 442 (a paper draft). Sir William Fitzwilliam of Gaynes Park (Essex), was related to them both through the marriage of Anne Fitzwilliam to Sir Anthony Cooke of Gidea Hall (Essex).

[123] According to his own account, he was seised as tenant for life under a family settlement made on 3 July 1547: PRO, KB 27/1240, m. 226.

[124] PRO, CP 40/1282, m. 1256 (three membranes). The action of formedon in the descender enabled the heir to entailed property to recover the property if it had been alienated. In such an action the tenant (defendant) could 'vouch to warranty' the person from whom he had obtained the property, and (assuming the vouchee was legally bound to warrant the title) he had to take over the defence. If the vouchee took on the defence and failed, the demandant (plaintiff) recovered the entailed property, but the tenant was entitled to recover property of equal value against the vouchee as compensation.

[125] He was in fact the third son, as will appear below.

[126] PRO, CP 40/1298, m. 1953 (four membranes); E. Coke, *A Booke of Entries* (London, 1614), ff. 317–319v.

[127] J. Dyer, *Ascun Novel Cases* (London, 1581), f. 290. There is also a report in Dalison 75.

[128] There was another plea as to a moiety of some messuages and land which were parcel of the manor, as to which Copley pleaded that he was joint tenant with his wife. This was the only plea on which issue was joined (for trial by jury), but there is no record that it was ever tried; the plea roll ends with a continuation of process against the jury until Trinity term 1572.

[129] An entail could be 'barred' by a final concord, with proclamations for interested parties to intervene, by virtue of a statute of 1489.

had nothing except as a feoffee (trustee) of the last William Fitzwilliam, and that he had died before the other feoffees; to this Copley demurred in law.[130] As to the plea in bar, there were lengthy further pleadings which it is unnecessary to go into, culminating in a demurrer by Hugh to Copley's rejoinder. The legal interest of the case lay not in the substance of the factual claim but in the legal complexities of pleading a final concord and counterpleading a voucher.[131] In Hilary term 1571 the court formally decided both demurrers in Hugh's favour.[132] He was awarded seisin of the second moiety, which was delivered to him by the sheriff on 9 March; as to the first moiety, the vouchee was ordered to answer, and he in turn vouched John, Lord Darcy, who seems never to have appeared. The record ends inconclusively, as records often did.

Around the same time Hugh commenced another action of formedon in the Common Pleas against Richard and Elizabeth Gascoigne (daughter of the coheiress Margery), claiming the manors of Emley and Darrington, and counting on the same gift by Edmund Deyncourt in the reign of Edward II.[133] The tenants vouched Edward Savell, who in Trinity term 1568 vouched Elizabeth (wife of Thomas Darcy), and Katherine (wife of Francis Savell), daughters of John, Lord Conyers, and Henry Kempe, their nephew, as coheirs of Sir John Conyers, great-grandfather of John, Lord Conyers. Since these heirs were under age, the court awarded a parol demurrer, that is, a stay until they came of age. On 12 February 1571 Hugh reported to the court that they were all of full age, and a resummons was awarded.[134] The outcome is not known. The third suit concerned the manor of Plumtree (Notts.), and that came to trial at Nottingham assizes in 1571.[135]

The net result of this prolonged litigation was that Hugh recovered a moiety of the manor of Sprotborough, in consequence of legal defects in the pleading, but none of the facts alleged on either side in relation to the descent came to trial before a jury.[136] The pedigree rolls therefore had no direct effect on the outcome. They were, however, considered highly significant and were the subject of a very revealing collateral dispute while the Common Pleas actions were depending. In 1568 Savile and Copley joined in a petition to the Duke of Norfolk, as Earl Marshal, reciting that they had 'made earnest sute and labor to the fellowshippe and companye of herrauldes for a true pedegre and

---

[130] By entering a demurrer in law a party confessed all that had been pleaded but challenged its legal effect.

[131] A writ of error was brought on the latter point but disallowed because it was a side issue and not a final judgment.

[132] According to Dyer's report, the decision was reached in Trinity term 1570, but judgment was not entered on the record till later.

[133] PRO, CP 40/1263, m. 1850.

[134] PRO, CP 40/1272, m. 1107.

[135] This is recited in Northants. Record Office, F(M) Roll 437. The record has not yet been found. According to the roll, Copley in this action pleaded nontenure, which Hugh Fitzwilliam treated as a confession of the pedigree.

[136] A demurrer had the effect in law of confessing all the facts alleged by the other side.

discent to be made unto them of the lyne of Fitzwilliams of Sprotbrughe', whose heirs they claimed to be,

> which pedegre and discent the heraludes could not trulye set fourthe unto your said oratours for that their bookes and recordes of theire office are so uncerten and untrue, by reason the leaffe wherein the said true pedegre was set fourthe ys cut out of the said booke and another leaffe placed in the roume therof, wherein an untrue discent ys made and declared, which discent the said heraldes have delivered under their handes to one Hughe Fitzwilliams, who by having of the said descents so chaunged and corrupted and thereby conveying hymselfe as heire male of the same lyne of Fitzwilliams hathe broughte a formedon in the descender against your said orators.

Hugh's pedigree, they said, had been brought to examination before the Earl of Leicester (Robert Dudley) and Sir William Cecil, as the Earl Marshal's deputies, when the books and records were produced and the excision of the leaf proved. They had proffered a true pedigree, but the deputies were unwilling to determine the matter without the Earl Marshal's consent. The petitioners therefore sought the revocation of the untrue descent, that they might have their true descent 'set out according to the truethe' on the Earl Marshal's authority, and that the heralds' books might be 'perfyted and reformed'.[137] At some point the officers of arms reported to the Earl Marshal that they could not with a clear conscience justify the pedigree made by Hervey, whereupon the matter was referred (or referred back) on 16 May to the Earl of Leicester and Cecil.[138] On the same day the Earl Marshal ordered Hugh to appear and deliver up the Hervey pedigree, which he declined to do.[139] Hugh also declined to produce his other evidence.[140] On 6 July following, an enquiry was held before the three kings of arms at the College of Arms, and evidence was taken from three of Hervey's servants.[141] Thomas Drury deposed that he had written out the pedigree from the instructions of Rouge Dragon, receiving a fee of six shillings from Hugh Fitzwilliam, and Robert Greenwoode deposed that he had limned and painted the escutcheons.[142] Edmund Knight, appointed

---

[137] Contemporary copy in Sheffield Archives, CD 477/2 (undated; signed 'Tho. Grenewood'); there is another copy in Doncaster Archives, DD/CROM/9/1.

[138] Copies in College of Arms, MS WC, f. 122; British Library, MS Add. 6297, f. 8; Bodleian Library, MS Rawlinson B. 146, f. 89; cf. Squibb, *High Court of Chivalry* (cit. in n. 84), p. 32 (giving the date as 1567).

[139] Copy of the summons in Lambeth Palace Library, MS 3513, f. 68.

[140] According to a note in the visitation book for Yorkshire (presumably College of Arms, MS D.2), 'Hugh Fitz William dyd promesse by his faith unto the thre Kinges of Armes that he wolde bring unto thame as good proffe for his grand father by Avedence as he had donne for his father, but when thaye dyd demande the same he denayed altogether unjustelly': *The Visitation of Yorkshire in the Years 1563 and 1564, Made by William Flower*, ed. C. B. Norcliffe (Harleian Soc., xvi, 1881), p. 126.

[141] British Library, MS Add. 10110, f. 270 (among the papers of Sir William Dethick, Garter King of Arms at the time). Dr Ramsay, who discovered these depositions, has identified the hand as that of Robert Glover.

[142] The roll of 1564 in the Cambs. Record Office is not in fact illuminated, yellow paint being used to

Rouge Dragon in 1565, stated that the pedigree had been made by Hervey but that he laid it out ('which he him self did couche').[143] This offers us a rare glimpse into the manner of producing an official pedigree. But the next part of Knight's evidence was more to the point, and was seemingly damning to Hugh. He admitted that Hervey had cut a leaf out of the records and had commanded Knight to replace it with an amended version, because it was 'untrue'. Although Knight had retained the excised leaf 'for his dischardge', he had later delivered it to Hugh at his request. Given Hugh's refusal to appear, the Earl Marshal had little choice but to decide against him, which he did the same month. The sentence recited that Hugh had unjustly practised with Hervey to disinherit the petitioners,

> and for that cause did winne the sayde Clarencieulx not onely to cutte owte and alter sondry leaves of his aunceyent recordes, but also in lieu of them to put into the sayde bookes of recorde other new leaves, wherin such mater was by him registrid as might best serve to justifye the same faulse descent and pedigree. After the makinge wherof the sayde Clarencieulx did not onely sette his hande and seale therunto for the further justifyenge of the same but also did practyse with dyvers other of the Officers of Armes to do the like.

The Hervey pedigree was thereupon condemned as false and untrue, and the officers of arms were commanded to prepare a true and perfect pedigree. This was duly drawn up, signed by the Earl Marshal, and sealed with the College of Arms seal on 20 July 1568.[144] The new version made no mention of Hugh at all.

The result did not, as we have seen, affect the outcome of Hugh's litigation, which was at least partly successful. Nor did it dampen his genealogical claims. The Earl Marshal's sentence was expressed to be provisional, 'untill further and better mater may be shewid to the contrary', and that effectively gave Hugh leave to press on with the gathering of information – or misinformation. On 8 July 1570 Hugh signed another pedigree, apparently intended to be sealed by the officers of arms (but with blank seals), insisting on the correctness of his version:[145]

---

represent *or*; but this, though signed and sealed, is longer (21 feet 5 inches) and narrower than that mentioned in evidence (where it was said to be two or three yards long and 18 inches wide). The 1565 pedigree in the Northants. Record Office [F(M) Roll 434] is 14 feet 2 inches long. In his will, dated 15 Oct. 1585, Grenewood described himself as a painter-stainer of London (PRO, PROB 11/68, fof. 372); his executors were Cooke, Knight and Glover.

[143] In signing the 1565 roll he had written: 'For as mouche as I have ben clarke under Master Clarencieulx in his office and have bene alwais an ernest searcher out of the truthe of this famely, and have diligently examyned this boke with all the bokes of the offyce, and also the evidences menscioned in the same with the originall and do finde it to agree in everie particular ... in the veryfyeng of the truthe herof I have subscribed my name ...' (Northants. Record Office, F(M) Roll 438). The word 'book' was used in this period for all written documents, including rolls.

[144] Original sealed version, Cambs. Record Office, R52/24/44/3; copy of sentence only, Hale MSS, Lambeth Palace Library, MS 3513, f. 67.

[145] Northants. Record Office, F(M) 435. There are six pendent seals, of which only the first and third have impressions (the arms of Fitzwilliam).

> Wher as I Hugh Fitzwilliam sonne and heire to John Fitzwilliam the yonger of Sprotburgh and of Hathilsay in the countie of Yorke have upon the sight of myne evidence and by th'advyse of my learned counsell caused by descent and pedegree to be sette foorth aswell to showe my right and title: as how the houses of the Fitzwilliams of Aldwerke, Adwyke, Bentley and Geynsparke[146] ar descended of the house of Sprotburgh and of Hathilsay. Which pedegree and descent is brought downe with the date of the yeres of our Lorde and of the reignes of the kinges and sette out in blazon with every their due differences warranted by the monumentes in the churches and houses of every their severall dwellinges, and by the conference and showe of every theire particuler evidence certyfienge their continuance since they came out of the sayd house, tyll now within the memory of man. And for the confirmation of every particuler therof, the eldist of every braunche of the sayd howses to the number of twelve, have subscribed therunto their names. All which evidence I shewed after that to the Officers of Armes, and conferred my descent and pedegree with them, aswell with my sayd evidence, as also with a descent tripartite of the sayd houses recorded in their Office the xiij[th] day of February in the tenth year of Kinge Henry the eight set out in blazon with every of their due differences. To the which entry of the tripartite in the heraldes bookes, John Fitzwilliam of Sprotburgh my graundfather subscrybed his name. To the which my descent and pedegree so conferred with myne evidence and the tripartite set owte under the handes and seales of the same bloode and name recorded in their Office, the three Kinges of Armes with other other Officers have subscrybed, and to the briefes of myne evidence of every particuler therof with the kynred and for the confirmation of the truth therof they have sette therunto the seales of their office of every their severall provinces autenticall, with their severall declarations, the third of May in anno Domini 1565.

The main purpose of this roll, it seems, was to confirm the connection between the Sprotborough branch and the Fitzwilliams of Mablethorpe (Lincs.), who had used different arms.[147] Hugh admitted that the former pedigree was defective in this connection:

> And at the traveylinge and setting foorth of my sayd pedegree I could not bringe downe in descent the issue and lyne of the sayde Thomas Fitzwilliam with the reste, by reason that my cousyn William Fitzwilliam now of Mablethorpe was then within age, and the Queenes Majesties warde: duringe whose minorytie aswell for the lacke of the sight of his evydence as wanting his necessary conference, nothing could then be don therin. But now of late havinge traveylid in the same, beinge by him ernestly requestyd, I have seene and perused sondrey evidences and recordes with dyvers other prooves of credence, wherby I fynde how he is lyneally deryved from the sayd Thomas Fitzwilliam, as it is exactly and perfectly sette owte in this pedegree, with his armes and due differences accordingly. The which armes, although that house of Mablethorpe hath of longe tyme ... omitted, as meny other famelyes of antiquytie and fresh memory have don, bearinge the armes onely of them by whome their enherytance doth growe, leavinge owte their owne armes of their surname: Neverthelesse seinge my sayd cousyn doth require his Armes of his owne family with his due difference, it can not be denyed him.

[146] Aldwark, Adwick, and Bentley (near Emley) (Yorks.), and Gaynes Park (in Theydon Garnon, Essex).
[147] Baker, *Men of Court*, I, pp. 682–3. In Northants. Record Office, F(M) Roll 435, the arms of this branch are shown as *Lozengy argent and gules, in dexter chief a crescent sable for difference*, quartering the earlier Fitzwilliam coat and another.

TUDOR PEDIGREE ROLLS AND THEIR USES

On 16 November 1570 another addition was made to the collection, this time a pedigree of Lionel Fitzwilliam of Sprotborough by Edmund Knight, Chester Herald.[148] None of these rolls, as we have seen, had to be produced in evidence in the Common Pleas case; but, in the context of Hugh's partial success in that suit, the mass of 'evidence' was beginning to seem very weighty. Hugh had evidently become 'the historian of the family', and his rolls were of value to its other branches, particularly Sir William Fitzwilliam of Milton.[149]

Hugh's opponents were, however, about to devise a less technical way of proceeding, and of getting their complaints before a jury, and their stratagem has provided us with another useful corrective to the Fitzwilliam archive. In Trinity term 1571 Copley brought an action on the case for deceit against Hugh in the Queen's Bench, alleging that he had himself been taken in by the deception and that this was the reason why he had not defended the Common Pleas action effectively.[150] The plaintiff's bill set out the gift in tail by Deyncourt in the time of Edward II and the pedigree as alleged by Hugh, but asserted that Hugh's ancestor Ralph had had an elder son Nicholas, that Nicholas's grandson Jervaise was the next heir male, and that Jervaise (who was still alive) had released to Copley all his right on 20 May 1564. According to Copley,

> ... the aforesaid Hugh Fitzwilliam, being not unaware of the foregoing but craftily compassing to be held, reputed and accepted as the kinsman and next heir male of [the donee], and falsely and craftily scheming to recover the aforesaid manor [of Sprotborough] ... by undue ways and means, on the twentieth day of June [1565] at Westminster in the county of Middlesex[151] practised and conspired with a certain William Harvye *alias* Clarencieulx, then king of arms, now deceased, to corrupt, alter and change the true degree or line of consanguinity or descent derived from [the donee] in a certain book or commentary of him the said late king of arms, being then truly inscribed and anciently noted;[152] and the same Hugh and William, by this practice and conspiracy of theirs, then and there tore a whole leaf out of the book or commentary aforesaid in which was the true line and degree of consanguinity ... and craftily inserted another leaf [with the false lineage] in the place of the same leaf so torn out ... and to the intent that greater faith would be placed in the aforesaid false lineage and degree of consanguinity the same Hugh on the said twentieth day of June at Sprotborough aforesaid obtained and procured from the said William Harvy *alias* Clarenseulx, late king of arms, a certain instrument or exemplification of the aforesaid leaf which was

---

[148] See also Cambs. Record Office, R52/24/44/1.
[149] Hunt, *South Yorkshire*, I, p. 334; Finch, *Five Northamptonshire Families*, p. 188.
[150] PRO, KB 27/1240, m. 226 (enrolled at the time of the defendant's plea in Hilary term 1572); reported in Cambridge University Library, MS Hh. 2. 9, f. 19v; Harvard Law School, MS 5048, f. 12v; translated (from the Harvard MS) in *Sources of English Legal History*, ed. J. H. Baker, 2nd edn. (Oxford, 2010), p. 673.
[151] Probably a legal fiction, so that the case could be tried in Middlesex. It is later stated that the parties were at Sprotborough on the same day.
[152] It is not clear to what this refers. In the pedigrees recorded at the visitation of 1573–4, Nicholas is shown as the second son of John and Ralph as the third: *Visitation of Yorkshire, 1563 and 1564*, ed. Norcliffe (cit. in n. 140), pp. 124, 125.

newly inserted, as mentioned above, made and sealed under the seal of him the said late king of arms,[153] comprising in itself that the aforesaid John, grandfather of the aforesaid Hugh, was the elder son of the aforesaid Ralph ... and thereafter frequently showed, published and disclosed it to the said Philip and many other lieges of the lady Queen as the true lineage and degree of consanguinity ... [whereby] both the same Philip and many other faithful lieges of the present lady Queen thought and believed for certain that he the said Hugh was the kinsman and next heir male of the body of [the donee], after which practice, conspiracy and publication [Hugh sued out the writ of formedon in the descender on 12 February 1566], and because the aforesaid Philip, by reason of the aforesaid false practice, conspiracy and publication, and putting his trust in them, did not dare to plead to the writ aforesaid that the aforesaid Hugh was not the next heir kinsman and heir of [the donee], and having no other sufficient matter to plead in bar, pleaded to the writ another plea which was insufficient [so that Hugh recovered seisin].[154]

Copley laid his damages as £1,000. In Michaelmas term 1571, before Fitzwilliam entered a plea, there was a discussion in open court which was briefly noted by a law reporter. The judges expressed the preliminary view that the action would not lie, and urged Hugh to demur. This advice puzzled the reporter and in the event was not followed. But the main point of interest in the report of the case is the remark: 'The justices said that the book of Clarenceux King of Arms is not a record and is of no force in our law; but he could have this pedigree made by Clarenceux King of Arms disproved, if he will and can, for it is not conclusive against him.'[155] We may suppose the gist of the remark to have been that, if Copley was prepared now to prove to a jury that the evidence had been falsified, he could have done the same in the Common Pleas and avoided the alleged damage. At the same time, the judges appeared to be saying that all the trouble taken by Hugh in procuring a pedigree authenticated by officers of arms was legally in vain because the courts would look beyond it to the supporting evidence.

Hugh's response, after pleading Not Guilty in Hilary term 1572, was to commission yet more pedigree rolls. One of them was a copy of the 1565 roll prefaced by an assertion that Copley and Savell had, by their pleading in the two formedon actions, confessed the descent to be true.[156] This is perhaps stretching the logic of pleading a little far. It is correct that, since the plea in bar did not deny the pedigree, the pedigree had to be taken as confessed for the purpose of the proceedings; but the vouchers to warranty were not outright confessions, since their object was to hand over the defence of the action to

---

[153] This has not been found. The version mentioned opposite is dated 1573.
[154] Abridged and translated from the Latin record.
[155] '... les Justices dirent que le liver Clarentius Roy des armes nest record ne de nul force in nostre ley, mes il poet aver disprove cest pedigree fayt per Clarentius sil voet et poyet car nest conclusion vers lui' (CUL MS). The word 'record' is here used in its technical sense of an indisputable record, such as a plea roll, and 'conclusion' in the technical sense of an estoppel (by record). Matters of record were evidentially superior to matters of writing, even sealed writings. The report ends: 'Et puis ne fuit dit de ceo cest jour.'
[156] Northants. Record Office, F(M) 438. This gives the roll references for both suits.

someone else.[157] Moreover, Copley had explained that his ineffective pleading was a result of Hugh's deception. Another roll, made around the same time, was prefaced with a declaration by Hugh as to the falsity of the complaint made before the Earl Marshal.[158] A third roll was made by Edmund Knight, Chester Herald, with a preface questioning both the relevance of the allegations against Hervey and the validity of a claim apparently being set up through the Fitzwilliams of Bentley:[159]

> This discent of John Fitzwilliam of Sprotborough granfather to Hugh Fitzwilliam was sett downe in severall aunscient books in the iij. severall offices of Armes, in Garters, Clarentiaux, and Norroys, Kings of Armes ... This is to be notid that in no one of the aunscient books in the offices of the iij. Kinges of Armes neither the discent of the Fitzwilliam of Bentley nor the name of Bentley is onse menscioned in writing or blason, and therefore this discente of the Fitzwilliam of Bentley is sett downe by their evidens and monument, this is further to be notid that William Harvye the late Clarenciaux did not damnifye any of the Fitzwilliam of Bentley by cuttinge outt of leaves out of his aunscient books whearyn non of the Fitzwilliam of Bentleys discente was to be founde, and no man havinge cawse to complayne of the saide leaves but Hugh Fitzwilliam sonn and heyre to John Fitzwilliam the younger of Sprotborough, the sayde aunscient leaves makinge for the saide Hughs tytell beyng subscribed the 10th of Henry the 8th by John Fitzwilliam of Sprotborough the elder grandfather to the sayde Hugh and confyrmed by xiiij of the blood and name and vij of the offycers of Armes before the cuttynge out of the saide leaves as hearunder written maye appeare.

Then, on 16 May 1573, a copy of a pedigree belonging to Lord Lumley was signed and sealed by Sir Robert Tyrwhit and five other witnesses: this traced the descent of Hugh's mother Margery Clervaux from Ralph Nevill, earl of Westmorland.[160] The purpose was to show that the arms of Hugh's father were represented without any mark of cadency, which was considered to be evidence that he was the heir male of Fitzwilliam of Sprotborough.[161] Two days later, on 18 May 1573, Hugh approved yet another pedigree roll, reciting the document of 1519, various depositions in the Chancery and Star Chamber, the confessions of Savell and Copley in the Common Pleas suits, and the

---

[157] They were preceded by the formal words of 'defence', *Et defendit jus suum* ('And he denies their right').

[158] Doncaster Archives, DD/CROM/9/2. It has not been possible to examine this roll.

[159] Northants. Record Office, F(M) 438. This mentions a 'tripartite' document, a pedigree supposedly signed by John Fitzwilliam and two other members of the family on 13 Feb. 1519, which is also referred to in subsequent rolls as 'folio 82' in a book belonging to the College of Arms. In his memorandum book he gave an account of John Fitzwilliam's visit to the College of Arms to subscribe it in a herald's book: Hunter, *South Yorkshire*, I, p. 340. This has a very dubious ring to it, and it has not been found. Hugh made a certified copy of it, which he signed in autograph on 22 April 1572: F(M) Roll 440 ('a true and perfite discent according to my parte tripertite').

[160] Northants. Record Office, F(M) Roll 454. Note also F(M) Roll 455, which shows the relationship between Hugh Fitzwilliam, the Earl of Southampton, and William Fitzwilliam of Milton, 'by the mariage with Nevile'.

[161] This claim is made in the inscription at the foot. It was not unknown, however, for marks of cadency to be dropped when arms were impaled with those of a wife (as here).

Lumley pedigree.[162] At around the same time the mysterious missing leaf removed by Hervey seems to have reappeared in some form or other.[163] Hugh caused multiple copies to be made of it, with the object of showing that it was not adverse to his case. On the contrary, it had the same effect as the Lumley pedigree in showing that Hugh's father was the heir male:[164]

> This is a coppie of one of the leaves cut oute of an aunsciente booke in the Office of armes by William Harvy the late Clarencious surmised by the procuremente of one Hewgh Fitzwilliam in a instrument sett owte by Thomas the late Duke of Norfolke as Earle marshall of Englande, bearinge date the xix[te] of July 1568. The whiche is kepte in the Office of Armes under three lockes and three keys: the whiche coppie was examined and subscribed unto by dyvers of the blood and name in hec Verba. (Vide.) This pedegree is verbatim, as touching the discente from William Fitzwilliam qui venit cum Conquestor[e], to John Fitzwilliam and Margaret sonne and doughter to John Fitzwilliam that mared Margerye Clarvaux and that Fitzwilliam that marred Clarvaux standeth without differance. Thes beynge Witnesses to the same, and so subscribed, that is to saye, William Fitzwilliam, Humphery Fitzwilliam, Thomas Fitzwilliam, Henry Fitzwilliam, and John Fitzwilliam in the office of Armes the xxvi[te] of Maye 1573, then preasent Gilbarte Dethicke Knight alias Garter Kinge of Armes, Robarte Cooke alias Clarentius Kinge of Armes, Ritchmonde, Lanckaster, Rouge dragon, Haroldes of Armes. The whiche leafe sheweth that the sayde John Fitzwilliam that mared Margerye Clarvaux beyng grandfather and grandmother to the sayde Hughe Fitzwilliam was cossen and the next heyre male to William Fitzwilliam that maried Margaret Broughton dyenge without issue beynge the laste heyre male of the eldest brother of the house of Sprotburgh contrarye to the purporte of the sayde instrumente.

If this were our only evidence, it would be impossible at this distance of time to be absolutely sure that Hugh had forged this document. But it must be held heavily against him that he did not give evidence to the Earl Marshal's enquiry in 1568; that the missing leaf was only produced as a last resort, without explanation, and that it turned out to be in his favour; and that most of the officers of arms seem to have withdrawn their support. The Queen's Bench judges also gave up their opposition to the action and allowed it go to trial. They wrote to the officers of arms, ordering them to bring in their books and records, and the Earl of Shrewsbury (appointed Earl Marshal in 1572) wrote to the officers to same effect, indicating that the matter was to be tried in Trinity term 1573.[165]

---

[162] Northants. Record Office, F(M) Roll 437.

[163] Northants. Record Office, F(M) Roll 447. This is the principal version, with six autograph signatures on the reverse. The endorsement was summarised in the copies (next note).

[164] Northants. Record Office, F(M) Rolls 444–6. All the copies have at top left a heading 'Fitzwilliam de Sprotborough Fol. xxii' and kneeling figures representing the second row in the pedigree, one in armour with a tabard of Fitzwilliam, and the other of a woman in a Fitzwilliam mantle over a kirtle of Warenne; in Roll 444 this is in colours. Roll 445 is endorsed with an address to Sir William Pykering at York.

[165] The judicial letter was in the Bacon-Frank MSS formerly at Campsall Hall, quoted in Hist. MSS Commn., *Sixth Report* (1874), appendix, pp. 453–4; the sender is not identified but was presumably Chief Justice Catlyn. A draft of the Earl of Shrewsbury's letter, dated from Sheffield

The trial duly took place, at Westminster, and the jury found for the plaintiff with £20 damages. This was considerably less than Copley had claimed, but the verdict settled decisively that Hugh had falsely manufactured his evidence and that he was not the heir male of Sprotborough.

This was the end of Hugh's campaign. He had never married, and he was no doubt acutely aware that his own line, for all its antiquity, was soon to end. In 1572 he had embarked on a brief public career as member of Parliament for Peterborough, probably through the influence of Sir William Fitzwilliam, but by February 1576 he was dead without issue.[166] At the next visitation of Yorkshire, by Robert Glover in 1584–85, the Fitzwilliams of Sprotborough were treated as extinct.[167] It had all been in vain.

Conclusion

Hugh Fitzwilliam's case illustrates both the importance of pedigree rolls and their evidential limitations. They were a convenient and visually impressive way of making a permanent record of family history, less likely to be thrown away by future generations than the files of photocopies created by today's amateur genealogists. Expenditure on the research and artwork must have varied enormously, and yet, whatever its level of sophistication, every pedigree roll provided an opportunity to commission something worth keeping. In setting out connections which might otherwise have been forgotten, particularly when this was based on recent memory, they served and still serve a valuable historical purpose. Hugh, of course, had a more focused objective. Rolls had obviously been used in litigation before, and their imposing physical appearance may sometimes have been intended to impress a jury. Hugh saw them as central to the preparation of his case. And yet, as it turned out, even when a roll was signed by seven officers of arms, and by the heads of all living branches of a family, it was still not legally conclusive because it was not a 'record'. Indeed, even after the same roll had been corrected following a quasi-judicial enquiry, and approved in its revised form by the earl marshal and six officers of arms, it still served only as evidence 'untill further and better mater may be shewid to the contrary'. This has remained the law ever since. The courts require the best available evidence of any fact, and therefore will not accept in evidence a pedigree based on sources which could themselves be produced.[168] But, *faute de mieux*, they have allowed old pedigrees to be put in evidence, albeit usually taken from visitation books

---

Castle, 26 May [?1573], is in the Sheffield Archives, BFM/2/112; this date was in vacation, so 'to be tried this term' must refer to the coming Trinity term. George Talbot, earl of Shrewsbury, became earl marshal after the attainder of the Duke of Norfolk for high treason in Jan. 1572.

[166] Hasler, *Commons, 1558-1603*, II, p. 127.
[167] *The Visitation of Yorkshire, made in the Years 1584/5, by Robert Glover*, ed. J. Foster (London, 1875), p. 7.
[168] *King v. Foster: the Earl of Thanet's Case* (1682) T. Jones 224, where the King's Bench declined to accept in evidence a pedigree 'map' – despite the sworn testimony of Dugdale and others that it was prepared in the College of Arms – but required the production of the books and records on which it was based.

rather than rolls.[169] Even a roll might be the best evidence in the absence of a visitation pedigree or relevant records,[170] and it was the opinion of Lord Mansfield in the eighteenth century that a pedigree roll bore especial weight if it had been displayed for many years in the family mansion and accepted without correction by those who saw it.[171] For most purposes, though, a pedigree roll is no more than a template to be tested against other available evidence.

The cautious approach of the law is a helpful guide to historians and others in assessing the genealogical and armorial information set out in pedigree rolls. But the interest of these rolls is not limited to the factual information which may be extracted from them. As essays in local and family history in an age when historical research of any kind was still rudimentary, as exercises in conveying complex information visually, as works of art, or simply as mundane artefacts widely owned and appreciated in their day, they deserve much more attention than they have received.

26 (opposite). Section of the 1553 Dudley pedigree roll, from College of Arms MS 16/5. The roll has a cartouche explaining that 'This pedegree hereabove declared was travayled and set furth by Wyllyam Hervey alias Norroy King of armes and corrected, controled and oversene' by the two other kings.

[169] *Vernon* v. *Manners* (1572) Plowd. 425 at f. 426 ('... les triours [*of the challenge*] fueront assigne, a queux evidence fuit done per les Heraldes del armes, et testimony hors de lour lieurs fuit monstre en proufe que le cosinage fuit voier, pur que les triours trovont le cosinage'). Cf. *Steyner* v. *Droitwich (Burgesses)* (1695) Skin. 623 ('though the Heralds Books are allowed to prove a Pedigree, yet this is because they have not better Evidence; and this is their proper Business about which they are employed, and therefore there is some credit given to them, but they do not deserve much, because they are negligently kept'). No mention of such pedigrees is to be found in the plea rolls of the courts, but that is because the rolls did not record evidence.

[170] The heralds themselves were certainly willing to rely on their predecessors' pedigree rolls, which were cited in 17th-century visitation books. For instance, Cooke's pedigree of the Southcote family (1572), now JHB, MS 102, was produced at the 1634 Visitation of Essex (Harleian Soc., xiii (1878), at p. 491); and William Segar's sealed pedigree of Fisher of Alrewas (*c.* 1615), now JHB, MS 1350, was produced at the visitation of London 1633–5 (Harleian Soc., xv (1880), p. 275). Robert Cooke's grant of arms to Thomas Penyston (1575) recited 'two auncient petigries the one made ... in the tyme of King Henry the sixt, the other ... by Sir Thomas Holme knight alias Clarencieulx Kinge of armes in the tyme of Kinge Henrry the seventh', as well as family muniments and the pedigree compiled by Cooke himself, in support of its antiquity: framed patent in the College of Arms (MS 9/2A; the pedigree roll is ibid. MS 9/2C). William Dethick's grant of arms with three quarterings to Walter Jones (1603) even recited a private pedigree roll 'made and collected out of sundry evidences by Thomas Jones of Tregaron, a gentleman industrious and scienced in the antiquities and genealogies of the worshipful gentlemen in her Majesty's principality of Wales': British Library, MS Add. 5524, f. 206 (spelling modernised); printed with the original spelling in *A Collection of Miscellaneous Grants ... of Arms*, ed. W. A. Littledale (Harleian Soc., 76, 1925), p. 121. Welsh genealogy had been somewhat beyond the active purview of the English officers of arms, but there was an active trade in pedigree rolls in Wales: see Siddons, *Welsh Pedigree Rolls* (cit. in n. 38), mentioning Jones's pedigree (1602), at p. 42, no. 199.

[171] *Goodright* v. *Moss* (1777) 2 Cowp. 591, at p. 594. This would be particularly important after visitations ceased in the 1680s. But public display was later held not to be essential: *Monkton* v. *Att.-Gen.* (1831) 2 Russ. & Mylne 147, at pp. 161-3.

Wyllm Beauchamp lorde of Elmesley and Erle of warwyke
Ysabell dowghter and heyre to Wyllyam Maudyt Erle of warwyke
Maude dowghter to Sir John
Guy Beauchamp Erle of warwyke
Alyce dowghter to Sir Raffe Tony.
Katheryn lady lovell dowghter to the lorde Clyntone. 2a
Thomas lorde Barkley
Margaret dowghter to the Erle of Marche 1a
John Barkeley lord of Beuyshorne
Alyce dowghter and heyre of Beuyshorne
Thomas Beauchamp erle of warwyke
Katheryn Countes of warwyke dowghter to therle of marche.
James Barkeley knyght of this lyne is descendid the lorde Barkley

Colours of Continuity: the Heraldic Funeral

ROGER KUIN

It was a chilly Friday, October 24, 1572, in Lathom Hall, the vast manor house in Lancashire that was known as 'the palace of the North'. A particularly cold winter was just beginning, but the Master would not live to see it. Around noon, Edward Stanley, third earl of Derby, died: he was 63, and had had a complex life, close (sometimes too close) to the centres of power. From being cup-bearer at Anne Boleyn's coronation to being High Steward at Queen Mary's, from being Wolsey's ward to being Lord Lieutenant of Lancashire, Derby – often underestimated as 'half a fool', but always both grand and cautious – is very properly listed in the *Oxford Dictionary of National Biography* as a 'magnate'. He had bought Lathom Hall as a suitable place for someone of his grandeur to live and receive in, and now he lay dying there.

The household knew that, apart from their feelings, there was urgent work to be done in order that the Earl's last journey might be arranged with due magnificence. The very first thing, which may in fact have been set in hand earlier, as soon as his death was certain, was to send to London for a herald to take charge of the ceremony. For someone as grand as Derby, one of the kings of arms was suitable, and in the event all three – Norroy, Clarenceux and Garter – attended, as well as Lancaster Herald. One of their colleagues (perhaps Robert Glover, Somerset Herald), fortunately for us, decided to describe the proceedings in great detail, and it is his description that I will quote in what follows.[1]

'First after his departure his Body was well seared, wrapte in leade and chestid.' The first job, after his laying-out, was to send for the local surgeons to come and embalm the body. This was part of their regular work, and they would be paid about £2 each, with the spices and perfumes that they used costing another £9 or so.[2] Embalming was essential, as a grand funeral could take a month or more to organize. Having been embalmed, the Earl's corpse was properly 'cered' or 'seared,' i.e. wrapped in seven ells (just over 26 feet) of wax-covered and thus waterproofed canvas. Meanwhile, a local blacksmith had made a more or less form-fitting inner coffin of lead, into which the 'cered' corpse was placed. The lead coffin was then sealed and placed inside a more elaborate chest-shaped wooden outer coffin.

---

[1] The description exists in several manuscripts; I have used that in College of Arms, MS I. 14, ff. 145–148v, which is in Robert Glover's hand.

[2] Clare Gittings, *Death, Burial and the Individual in Early Modern England* (London and Sydney, 1984), pp. 166–7. It is extremely hard to establish a correspondence between 16th-century currency and its modern equivalent. A foot-soldier in Ireland around the time of the Earl's death earned £14 a year.

COLOURS OF CONTINUITY: THE HERALDIC FUNERAL

> Then the Chappell, the Howse, with the two Courtes, was hanged with blacke clothe and garnished with Escucheones of his Armes.

The chief outward sign of mourning was black cloth, which could vary from simple buckram to the finest sarcenet and velvet. It was the most expensive item in the heraldic funeral, typically making up between two-thirds and three-quarters of the total cost; at Sir Robert Cecil's funeral, it accounted for £1,544 of the total £1,977 bill. In the present case Lathom Hall's private chapel was hung with large black stretches of cloth around the walls, as were also some public spaces in the house itself (typically, the Great Hall and perhaps one or two other rooms), and some black cloth was hung in the courtyards between the Hall's central building and its two wings (one of which is now the only remnant). Upon this cloth were hung 'escutcheons': shields of varying sizes, painted on paper, on buckram, or on metal, with the Earl's arms: *argent, on a bend azure three bucks' heads caboshed or*. These were the first signs of the heraldry that was to pervade the entire ceremony: they were ordered literally by the dozen, and painted by whatever painters could be sub-contracted by the heralds.[3]

Meanwhile, the heralds themselves were busy organizing the procession in all its details. We do not know which of the four did the actual work, but all three kings and Lancaster were present (which means that all were paid, at rates suited to their rank[4]). Lancaster may well have ridden up to Lathom ahead of the kings, or sent someone, as much of the organizing had to be done locally. It had been decided that the Earl would be buried in the church at Ormskirk, about three miles from Lathom, and the date was set for Thursday, December 4.

> And on Saturday before the funerall the Bodye was brought in to the Chappell where it was coverid with a Palle of blacke velvet garnished with escucheons of his Armes, and theron was sett his Coate of Armes, Heaulme, and Creast, Sword and Targe, and about him were placid the Standerd, great Banner and vi Bannerolles.

This was the chapel of the Hall, and the body in its double coffin was set up on a simple catafalque. It was then covered with a large cloth, the pall, of costly black velvet[5]. Before the Reformation and in the reign of Queen Mary, this would have had a white cross on the centre, lying on top of the coffin; but now the pall was decorated only with

---

[3] Individual heralds often worked with a specific and trusted painter: so Robert Glover had much of his work done by Richard Scarlett. (Nigel Ramsay in a private communication.)

[4] In 1463, at the funeral of the Earl of Salisbury and his son, Garter and Clarenceux Kings of Arms received £3 each plus 10s. per day; the heralds £2 each and 5s. per day; and the pursuivants £1 and 2s. 6d per day (Wagner, *Heralds of England*, p. 107).

[5] The Pall, when ordered especially, became the perquisite of the Heralds after the funeral. Often, though, it was hired from the College, and could be part of an overall fee: at the funeral of Sir James Deane, merchant and former alderman, the heralds' bill was £54 16s. 4d, for assistance of 2 heralds, each with an attendant, and dressing all 4 in black; hire of hearse and pall; and the painters' bill of £18 6s. for standard, pennon, coat of arms, helm, crest, mantle, wreath, target, 8 dozen scutcheons painted on metal, paper or buckram, and 4 more pennons (Vanessa Harding, *The Dead and the Living in Paris and London, 1500–1670* [Cambridge, 2002], p. 222).

heraldry. The parts hanging down had escutcheons sewn on; and on top of the coffin and pall were placed the central elements of heraldry, the 'Achievements.'[6] The first of these was the 'Coat of Arms,' also known as the 'Coat of Name', a tabard with the Earl's full arms embroidered; then came the Helm, with its Crest; the Sword, and the Targe or shield (Fig. 27). All these elements of arms were made specially for the occasion, of lightweight materials, and were not the same as those used in battle. It will be noticed that the Coat of Arms contains eight quarterings. The first of these, on the top left for the spectator, is the device of the Stanley family. It is followed by the Lathom arms, which Isabel Lathom had brought into the family when she married Sir John Stanley in 1385. (All such quartered arms came from heraldic heiresses[7] who had married into the family.) The next one, *gules a triskele argent garnished and spurred or*, represents the Isle of Man, of which the Stanleys had been Lords since 1405. Then come the Goushill arms, belonging to Joan Goushill, who had married Thomas, the first Lord Stanley in the fifteenth century. These four are followed on the lower level by the arms of Warenne, Strange or Lestrange, Woodville and Mohun: again, all belonging to heraldic heiresses who had married Stanleys.

The same arms appear again in the targe or heraldic shield, on the right, surrounded this time by the Garter: the defunct Earl had been received into the Order in 1547, like many of his forefathers ever since Sir John Stanley I, Lord of the Isle of Man, had received the Garter *c.* 1405.

Placed around the coffin were the flags. First of all the Standard: this was based on the standards carried on the battlefield. All heraldic standards in England had, closest to the staff, the Cross of St George, followed by the owner's device (not his arms) and his motto. In the Earl's case the motto was 'SANS CHANGER' and the crest of *an eagle, or, preying on a child proper, swaddled in a basket, or and gules*. Beyond that on the standard is the Earl's badge or device of a stag's head, and near the fabric's point (always split, except for royalty) is another badge that looks like a mailed glove holding an eagle's wing.

After the standard comes the Great Banner. This – allowed only to peers and their ladies – is the central heraldic statement of a funeral procession, containing as it does the defunct's principal arms and quarterings. It has the same arms, in the same order, as the coat of name, which we have seen above. With the great banner are the Bannerols. In the procession, as we shall see, these are carried around the coffin, and represent the family's alliances with other prominent armigerous dynasties. Their number was regulated: an earl was allowed six bannerols, while a monarch would have twelve and a baron only

---

[6] This term sometimes gives rise to confusion. As a plural, it refers to the heraldic accoutrements of the deceased. In the singular (often abbreviated to 'Hatchment') it designates a heraldic device, larger and more solidly made than an escutcheon, that in a funeral could be fastened to the hearse's 'Majesty' and in later years often remained in the church.

[7] A heraldic heiress is a woman who inherits her family's arms, having no brothers. Such an inheritance has nothing to do with inheriting land or property.

27. Funeral hearse of Sir Edward Stanley, KG, earl of Derby, 1572. College of Arms, MS Vincent 151, Part 1, p. 366.

four. In Derby's case the bannerols were simple and clear, which was not always so: below, we shall see that Sir Philip Sidney's funeral bannerols contained up to twenty-four quarterings. Derby's bannerols celebrated marital alliances with the Nevilles, the Stranges, the Hastings, the Howards, the Barlows and the Cottons.[8]

> And on Sundaye in the morninge before the sermon, the Erle of Derbye his sonne, beinge present with a great number of esquyers and gentlemen and the three cheife Officers of his house, viz. the Steward, Thresorer and Comptroller, standinge about the bodye with whyte staves in their handes, Clarentieulx Kinge of Armes with his riche coate on his backe published this thanckes gyvinge and style of the defunct in forme folowinge.
>
> 'All honor, laude and prayse to almighty god who throughe his devyne mercy hath taken out of this transitory lyfe to his eternall ioye and blisse, the right Honorable Edward Erle of Derby, Lord Stanley, Straunge and of Man, one of the Quenes Maiesties most honorable prevy Counseill, and knight and companion of the most noble Order of the Garter.'

Note that we are now still at Lathom Hall, in the chapel. What is here described is not part of the funeral, though in a number of cases it was conflated with the Offering (described below). The Earl's eldest son Henry, who is now the Fourth Earl and Chief Mourner, is present, with the three chief officers of his father's extensive household bearing their white staves of office. But first Clarenceux King of Arms, dressed in his tabard of office, solemnly proclaims the 'style and title' of the deceased.[9]

We next move to Ormskirk, whither the procession was to go and where in the church the craftsmen are building the 'hearse' or grand catafalque.

> At Ormskirke ii myles from Lathum was a stately hearsse erected of fyve principalles, xxxtie foot of height xii foot of length and ix foot of breadth, double raylid, all garnished in this order and manner folowinge. ¶ First the toppe part and the Rayles couered with blacke clothe, the valence and the principalles coverid with velvet: to the valence, a fringe of silke, the maiestye beinge of tafeta lyned with buckram, had theron curiouslye wrought in gold and siluer a hachement of his Armes with his healme, creast, supporters and worde, and iiii other buckram escucheones in metall, the toppe garnished with escucheons and pencils in metall, and six great buriall paste scucheones at the iiii corners and the uppermost toppe, the valence sett forth with small scucheones of his Armes, on buckram in metall within the Garter, the rayles and postes also garnished with escucheons wrought with gold and siluer on paper royal. ¶ The which Hearsse was placid betweene the Quyre and the bodye of the Church, the which church was also hangid throughout with blacke cloth, scucheones also beinge sett theron, not only of his owne Armes within the Garter: but also empalid with the three Countesses his wifes.

---

8   These last two appear to have been brought in at the last moment in a policy change: the illustrations in the College of Arms MS show the Stanley arms impaled with the Lathoms and the Goushills. The Earl's last two wives were Margaret Barlow and Mary Cotton.

9   It should by rights have been Norroy King of Arms, who dealt with the North as Clarenceux dealt with the South; that it is the latter who proclaims the Earl's style perhaps indicates that he was the first to arrive – we are still four days away from the funeral proper. The tabard of office, or 'rich coate of arms', was, and is, embroidered with the royal arms, signifying that the heralds were servants of the Crown.

COLOURS OF CONTINUITY: THE HERALDIC FUNERAL

Some technical terms: the principals were the vertical posts, the 'Majesty' is the canopy, with the 'valences' hanging down from it on all four sides. The 'word' is the motto; 'penciles' are penoncelles or small pennons of arms, 'buriall paste' was probably some kind of papier-maché. The hearse was placed between the choir and the body of the church, i.e. at the point where the transepts of a cross-shaped church would branch. Ormskirk did not have transepts, so the hearse would have been set up between the fifth pillars from the West. What perhaps strikes modern readers most is the impressive height of thirty feet.

When the hearse was ready, the funeral proper could begin: 'And this beinge finished by Wensday at night before the Buriall, the order of proceedinge on Thursdaye beinge the daye appointid for the funeralle was in manner folowinge.'

The MS now describes the funeral procession, which departed from Lathom Hall and marched slowly and solemnly the three miles to the church. We should imagine a considerable number of spectators: not only the many local people who were so largely dependent on the Earl and his family, but gawkers from many miles around. The funeral procession of an earl was a spectacle not often seen, and word had been going around for more than a month. It began, as always, with a large number of 'the poor' who had received or were receiving largesse, in the form of warm robes, food and drink, and money.

> First two yeomen conductors with blacke staves to lead the waye. (Morgan ab Robert, Thomas Botell.) Then all poore men in gownes ii and ii to the number of an hundrith. Then the Quyre and singinge men to the number of xl^{tie} in their surplesses.

For such a procession (and this is only the beginning), considerable organization was required: this was the heralds' work. They marshalled the procession at the Hall and sent the head of it on its way before (as we shall see) taking their own place in it.

> Then an Esquyre bearinge the Standert with his hoode on his head and his horsse trapte to the grounde, garnished with a Shaffron of his Armes within the garter on his forehead and iiii scucheons of buckram in metall one eche side two. (Peter Stanley.)
>
> Then the defunctes gentlemen, mountid on comly geldinges in their gownes, and hoodes on their shoulders, ii and ii to the number of lxxx.
>
> Then the two Secretaries of the defunct rydinge togither as the other gentlemen aforesayd. (Gilbert Moorton, Gabriell Mason.)
>
> Then the Esquires and Knightes in lyke order ii and ii to the number of .l.
>
> Then the Defunctes ii Chappellaynes with hoodes on their shoulders according to their degrees. (John Sherborne Bachelor of diuinity, Christopher Thomson Maister of Arte.)
>
> Then the Preacher beinge the Deane of Chester his horse trapt and a doctores hoode on his shoulder (Doctor Longworth.)
>
> Then the Defunctes three cheif Officers that is to saye, the Steward, Threasorer, and Comptroller, with whyte staves in their handes and hoodes on their shoulders, their horsses trapte (William Masey, Sir Richard Sherburn, Henry Stanley).

Some more terms: the horse is 'barbed' or 'trapt' to the ground, i.e. hung with black cloth decorated with escutcheons, including one on the 'shaffron' or 'chamfrain,' the

171

horse's frontlet between the eyes. After the Standard come the deceased's 'gentlemen' or gentlemen servants. Gowns with hoods, or even just with tippets, were grander than those without, as they took up more yardage and cost more. After the gentlemen and knights of the Earl's household and staff come two chaplains, accompanying the preacher for the occasion, who in this case was Dr Richard Longworth, formerly Master of St John's College, Cambridge.[10] And following the preacher, the three household officers we have already met back in Lathom the previous weekend.

Now there follows the heraldic heart of the procession, immediately preceding the coffin itself:

> Then an Esquyre bearinge the great Banner of his Armes, his hoode on his head, his horsse trapte, and garnishid with escucheones in manner aforesaid. (Edward Norryce)
> Then a Herauld of Armes, with his hood on his head, his horsse trapte as is afore mencionid, wearinge the defunctes coat of Armes of damaske, did beare his heaulme of steele parcell guilt with mantles of blacke veluet the knopes guilt, and on a wreath of his colores stood his creast curiouslye payntid and wrought in gold and silver. (Lancaster.)
> Then a Kinge of Armes with his hoode on his heade wearinge his Coate of Armes, richly embroderid with the armes of England, his horse trapte and garnished as is aforesayd, bearinge the shylde of Armes of the defunct within the Garter and theron a coronet. (Norroy).
> Then another Kinge of Armes rydinge in like order bearinge the defunctes sworde, with the pomell upward, the hilt and chape guilt with a Scabberd of velvet. (Clarentieulx).
> After theim another Kinge of Armes rydinge as the other bearinge another of the defunctes coates of Armes, beinge wrought as the other was, and one the left syde of him rode a gentleman huisher with a whyte rod in his hand, his horse trapte and his hood on his head. (Garter principall king of Armes. George Leigh, hussher).

The Great Banner was, as noted above, the essence of a man's heraldic identity. Here it is being borne by Edward Norris, a well-connected young man of twenty-two (his father was Henry, Baron Norris, and his mother was an old friend of the Queen's) who had just been made a Member of Parliament.

After him follow the officers of arms themselves, in ascending order of rank. In the procession, which they have organized and marshalled, their specific task is to bear the Achievements: so John Cocke, Lancaster Herald, wears the Earl's coat of arms, and carries the helm, the wreath and the crest. Then comes William Flower, Norroy King of Arms (whose province was the North), carrying the targe or shield, with the Earl's arms surrounded by the Garter and surmounted by a coronet. He is followed by Robert Cooke, Clarenceux King of Arms (who dealt with the South of England), carrying the Earl's Sword, point downwards, with its velvet scabbard. And finally Sir Gilbert Dethick, Garter King of Arms (chief of all the heralds), carrying another copy of the Earl's coat of arms, and accompanied by an usher bearing a white rod. It should be noted that all these personages were mounted on horseback: another sign of this funeral's magnificence.

[10] The choice of Longworth, a Puritan, to preach at the funeral of the more or less recusant Earl of Derby indicates that the funeral was organized by the heralds in consultation with the heir: Henry, the Fourth Earl, was a convinced Protestant with Puritan sympathies.

COLOURS OF CONTINUITY: THE HERALDIC FUNERAL

And now, at last, we come to the Earl himself, or at least his earthly remains in their coffin with the pall over it, the whole mounted on a carriage:

> Then the Chariot wherin the bodye laye was coverid with blacke velvet garnishid with escucheones, drawen by iiii horses trapte with blacke and one eche horse was placid iiii escucheones and a shaffron of his armes and also on each horse sat a page in a blacke coat and a whode on his head, on the foreseat of the said Chariot sate a gentleman huisher in his gowne and his hoode on his heade, and a whyt rod in his hand. (Edward Scasbricke gentleman husher).
>
> And next about the bodye, beinge in the sayd Chariot, rode iiii Esquyres, beinge assistantes to the bodye, their hoodes on their heades, and their horses trapte to the grounde. (Robert Barton, Robert Dalton, Roger Bradshaw, John Preston.)

The main point to make about this is the mention of the mounted 'assistants to the body.' In a normal heraldic-funeral procession conducted on foot, these four would each have held a corner of the Pall (hence the term 'pall-bearers,' nowadays used for those carrying the coffin on their shoulders). In a royal funeral, the coffin on the chariot would have had a recumbent effigy of the deceased on its top.

Outside the coffin and the Assistants to the Body, there was another heraldic unit:

> And one the out syde of theim about the sayd chariot rode six other Esquyres, in their hoods on their heades, their horses trapte, eche of theim bearinge a Banneroll, not only of the defunctes armes, but also of the armes of suche noble houses whereof he was descendid, viz.
>
> The Armes of Thomas first Erle of Derbye of that name, Lord Stanley and of Man, empallid with the Armes of Elenor his wyfe, daughter of Richard Nevill Erle of Salsbury and sister to Richard Neuill Erle of Warwick and Salsbury. (Edward Terbucke.)
>
> The second Banneroll was the Armes of George Lord Stanley and Strange, the sonne and heyre of the sayd Thomas, impallid with the Armes of Jane, his wyfe, daughter and heyre of John Lord Strange of Knokinge. (Edward Leigh.)
>
> The third Banneroll was the armes of Thomas the 2. Erle of Derby of that name, Lord Stanly, Strange and of Man, impallid with the Armes of Ann his wyfe daughter of Edward Lord Hastings and sister to George Lord Hastinges, the first erle of Huntingdon of that name. (William Stanley.)
>
> The 4. Banneroll was the armes of the defunct empalid with the Armes of Darothy his first wyfe, daughter of Thomas Duke of Norfolk, Erle of Surrey and Erle Mareshall of England, Lord Mowbray Segrave and Bruse. (Charles Holt.)
>
> On the 5. Banneroll was also the defunctes Armes, empallid with the armes of Margaret his 2. wyfe daughter of Ellys Barlowe Esquyre. (George Midleton.)
>
> One the sixt Banneroll was empallid with the Armes of the defunct: the Armes of Mary his third wife, daughter of Sir George Cotton knight, vicechamberlayne to Kinge Edward the sixt. (Francis Holt.)

Earls were allowed six bannerols. They were more or less square flags, like the Great Banner but sometimes wider if many quarterings were to be displayed. It is interesting to see that in Derby's case each bannerol showed only one 'affinity'[11]: it was usual to gather more details of that link into the space.

---

[11] 'Affinity,' in heraldry, is used in the ancient sense of a relationship through marriage, as opposed

173

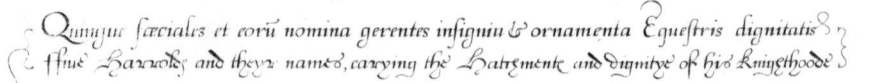

28. The heralds at the funeral of Sir Philip Sidney, 1587. Detail from engraving of Sidney's funeral procession by Theodore de Bry, made after a drawing by Thomas Lant, who was subsequently appointed Portcullis Pursuivant of Arms.

In a pre-Reformation heraldic funeral, the bannerols of arms would have been carried at the beginning of the Achievements, while their place around the coffin would have been occupied by religious banners, of the saints, the Trinity, the Sacred Heart, etc. So it is here that we can see condensed the replacement of religious images by heraldry, that was also evident in the royal arms' replacing of the Rood on the rood-screens of churches.[12]

After the coffin come the mourners: that is, the heir, followed by other prominent mourners related to the deceased by blood or friendship.

> Next after the Chariot proceedid the Cheif mourner in the morninge robes of an Erle and on eche syde of him rode a gentleman huissher with whyt rodes in their handes, their hoodes on their heades and their horses trapte. (Richard Ashton gentleman huisher, Henry Erle of Derby, Marmaduke Newton gentleman huisher.)
>
> One the left syde of him and somethinge behynd, rode the gentleman of the horsse of the defunct, his hoode on his head and his horsse trapte and leadinge in his hand the horse of estate, all coverid and trapte with blacke velvet. (John Ormston.) [see Fig. 28, from Sir Philip Sidney's funeral roll]
>
> Next after rode viii other morners beinge assistantes to the cheif mourner, their hoodes on their heades their horsses trapte with fyne clothe to the grounde (John Lord Sturton, Sir Rowland Stanley, Sir Peires Leigh, Mr Butler Esquyre, Mr Ratcliffe Esquyre,

---

to 'consanguinity'. It may still be seen in the 'Tables of Kindred and Affinity' displayed in the porch of a few English country churches, detailing which persons one may not marry because of the degree of relationship of either sort.

12 Cf. Jennifer Woodward, *The Theatre of Death: The Ritual Management of Royal Funerals in Renaissance England, 1570–1625* (Woodbridge, 1997), pp. 39–40.

COLOURS OF CONTINUITY: THE HERALDIC FUNERAL

> Alexander Barlowe, Alexander Rigby, William Stopforth). Then a yeoman in a blacke coat, bareheadid, on foot.
> Then ii sonnes of the Principall Mourner in gownes and hoodes on their shoulders, either of them havinge a gentleman to leade their horsses. (William Stanley esquyre, Francis Stanley esquyre.)

Henry Stanley, the Chief Mourner, was now the Fourth Earl.[13] He was forty-one, and had recently, as a widower from an unhappy first marriage, taken a local woman to common-law wife. He was constantly in debt, and this funeral must have been a heavy burden: a full heraldic funeral of this kind cost between £1,000 and £3,500.

Other mourners assisted the heir, their number, like that of the bannerols, determined by rank. The total number was always odd, comprising the Chief Mourner and a number of pairs. An earl could have nine: the heir and eight others. In this case, they are listed – as they doubtless rode – by rank: a baron, two knights, two esquires, and three gentlemen.[14] Henry's two sons, William and Francis, were boys: William, eventually the Sixth Earl, was eleven, Francis, who died shortly afterwards, was a year younger.[15]

The part of the procession that followed the Chief and Principal Mourners was sometimes composed of interested parties not linked to the family or the household; but in the Earl's case it comprised the lower-rank members of the household and entourage:

> Then two yeomen huishers with whyt rodes on foote.
> Then the Defunctes Yeomen ii and ii to the number of fyve hundrith.
> Then all gentlemens servantes ii and ii.

The procession moved slowly between Lathom Hall and Ormskirk. Considering the number of people involved, it must at its full length have filled up a considerable part of the distance. But the Heralds were taking no chances and had installed black-coated yeomen 'whifflers' – armed attendants wearing a chain of office, employed to clear the way – along the way. Eventually the huge cortège arrived at the church.

> And thus beinge whifled all the waye by certayne yeomen in blacke coates on foote with blacke staves in their handes proceedid to the Church doore, where ther servantes attendid to receyve their horses, then beinge dismounted all the gentlemen that proceedid

[13] Shakespeare-lovers may recall that the Fourth Earl, like his father, was a patron of the group of players to which the dramatist belonged: under Henry's son Ferdinando Lord Strange, it became 'Lord Strange's Men,' and at his accession in 1593, and later under his son, the 6th Earl, 'the Earl of Derby's Men'.

[14] The ones we know about are John, 9th Baron Stourton (d. 1587); Sir Rowland Stanley of Hooton (1518–1614), head of the Stanley family's senior branch; Sir Piers Legh VII (d. 1589), builder of Lyme Hall in Cheshire and High Sheriff of Lancashire. Of the others, Alexander Barlow was certainly a relative of the deceased Earl's second wife.

[15] The reason that Ferdinando Stanley, born c. 1559 and eldest surviving son, is not listed as present is probably that he was in the process of entering St John's College, Oxford at this time. His father's accession to the earldom made him Lord Strange. In 1593 he succeeded as 5th Earl. He was a major literary and theatrical patron.

175

> before the corps entrd into the Church and receyvid their places, according to their degrees, leavinge the c. poore men without the Churche on eche syde the way.
>
> Then the bodye was taken out of the Chariot by viii gentlemen in gownes, with hoodes on their heades, assistid by iiii yeomen in blacke coates and borne into the hearse wher he was orderly placid uppon a table, beinge iii foote highe coverid with blacke clothe, and uppon him was not only laid a pale of blacke velvet, but also his coate of Armes, sword and targe, healme and creast. (William Orall, Jaspar Worth, Francis Banes, John Meare, Thomas Storkey, John Byrom, Edmond Winstanly, James Bradshawe).
>
> And thus the bodye beinge placid the principall mourner entrid the Hearse, wher was preparid for him at the head of the defunct a stoole with a carpett and ii quishiones of blacke velvet to kneele and leane upon.
>
> Then entrid the other viii mourners and tooke their places whithin the outermost part of the hearsse one eche syde of the bodye, havinge eche of theim a quisheon of blacke velvet to leane upon, their stooles coverid with blacke clothe and a cusheon of the same to kneele uppon.
>
> And at the feet of the defunct without the raile, stode the two esquyres, holdinge the Standert and great Banner and on eche syde of the hearse stoode the other six esquyres, with the Bannerolles, and behynde the principall mourner stoode three kinges of Armes and the 4 gentlemen huishers, and betwene the Standerd and the great Banner stoode Lancaster herauld of Armes, wearinge the defunctes coat of Armes.

The participants are now taking their places for the second and greatest heraldic moment of the funeral: the Offering.

The illustration (Fig. 27) shows the Earl's hearse with the coffin on its table inside. It does not show the stools, which were placed one at the head of the coffin and four down either side. These were covered in rich velvet and furnished with cushions for kneeling. It also does not show the Achievements, which were laid (for the moment) upon the coffin's pall. We need to imagine also, outside the Hearse proper, at the foot end of the coffin, the Esquires holding the Standard and the Great Banner, with Lancaster Herald wearing the Earl's Coat of Arms, between them; at the head of the coffin, behind the Chief Mourner, the three Kings of Arms; and down each side three esquires each with a bannerol.

> And thus the body beinge placid and every other estate according to their degrees, Norroy Kinge of Armes pronounced the style of the defunct as before is mencionid, which endid the Deane of Chester began his sermon, and after the sermon the vicare began the commemoracion and after the Epistle and Ghospell the offringe was commenced in manner and forme folowinge.

As we see, the proclamation of the deceased's 'style' (his rank and titles), was made twice: once at Lathom Hall, and now once more in the public context of the funeral itself. This time, moreover, it was made by Norroy, the king of arms in whose province lay Lathom and Ormskirk.

Following the proclamation came, as was usual, a funeral sermon. Such sermons were cast in a standard mould, the first half being a meditation on life's brevity and vanity, and the second a eulogy of the departed. We may assume that Dean Longworth's

sermon dwelt upon the first with the proper zeal of his Puritan outlook, and upon the second with the presence of the heir in his mind.

Now it was the turn of the Vicar of Ormskirk to begin the Commemoration, during which a Psalm was said or sung and the Epistle and Gospel read. After this the whole company turned to the heraldic climax of the entire funeral: the Offering. The Offering was climactic because it incarnated the passing of the Earldom – as, in other heraldic funerals, of every degree of nobility or gentry – from the deceased to his heir. Originally, in pre-Reformation funerals, it was connected with prayers for the soul of the deceased, which gave it a great religious solemnity; now, in Protestant England, this solemnity was transferred to the social continuity of which heraldry was the symbol.

> First Henry Erle of Derby beinge principall morner did offere for the defunct a peice of gold havinge before him Garter Clarentieulx and Norroy Kinges of Armes and Lancaster Herauld of Armes, and one eche syde of Garter a gentleman huisher and an esquyre to beare the cheif mourners trayne. And after him did proceed the other viii mourners ii and ii according to their degrees.

The beginning of the heraldic ceremony saw the Chief Mourner, surrounded by the full complement of Heralds, coming up to the altar or communion table to offer a piece of gold on behalf of the deceased. Then the other principal mourners came up and did the same. The offerings were laid in a dish held by the officiating clergyman, in this case the Vicar of Ormskirk.

> And in lyke order he with the other morners repayrid to their places, wher he remayninge a smale tyme went to offere for him self, havinge Clarentieulx and Lancaster only before him, and thus havinge offrid, stayed betweene the vicaire and Lancaster Herauld of Armes, to receyve the honorable hachmentes of his father, offrid up by the other viii mourners in manner and forme folowing.

We should remark here that the Chief Mourner offered twice: once for the deceased, and then once more, but with less pomp, for himself. After which he remained at the altar, flanked by the Vicar, representing divine grace, and the Herald, representing earthly rank. For now, as the beginning of the actual transfer of nobility, it is the symbols thereof, the Achievements of Arms, that are offered up.

> First the Lord Sturton and Sir Rowland Stanley offrid up the coate of Armes, having before theim Clarentieulx Kinge of Armes.
> Secondly Sir Peirce Leigh knight and Thomas Butler esquyre, offrid the Sword bearinge the pomell forewarde, havinge before theim Norroy Kinge of Armes.
> Thirdly John Ratcliffe and Alexander Barlowe esquyres offrid the targe of his Armes and before theim went Clarentieulx Kinge of Armes.
> Fowethly Alexander Rigby and William Stopforth esquyres offrid the Heaulme and Creast, havinge before theim Norroy Kinge of Armes.
> Which endid, the principall mourner repayred to his place and one eche side of him a gentleman huisher and his trayne borne by an esquyre and before him Clarentieulx King of Armes, wher he remainid vntill the offringe was endid.

Here we can see that Garter King of Arms, as the grandest of the officers of arms, was not involved in the physical offering, but remained in his place outside the hearse, at the head end of the coffin.

> Then offrid the other viii morners for theim selves, viz., The Lord Sturton and Sir Rowland Stanley havinge before theim Clarentieulx Kinge of Armes. Then Sir Peirs Leigh knight and Thomas Butler esquyre and before theim Norroy kinge of Arms. Then Alexander Rigbye and William Stopfoorth esquyres hauinge before theim Blewmantle Pursuivant of Armes.

Here there are two curiosities. In the first place, John Ratcliffe and Alexander Barlow have disappeared from the scene, although 'the other eight mourners' are mentioned; secondly, a new heraldic figure appears who has not been previously mentioned: Bluemantle Pursuivant, the lowest in rank of those present. (The College of Arms was composed of three Kings of Arms, six Heralds, and four Pursuivants.) The likeliest explanation is that both Lancaster and Bluemantle accompanied one of the kings of arms (probably either Garter as the principal king or Norroy as the locally responsible one): the heralds' Chapter orders of 20 February 1565 stipulated that each king should be accompanied by one herald and one pursuivant when taking a funeral.[16]

> Thus when the Principall Morner and the eight mourners assistantes had offrid and placid agayne as aforesayd, then offered the 4 Esquyres assistantes to the defunct, havinge before theim Lancaster Herald of Armes.
> Then the Standerd offrid by an esquyre that bare it and before him Blewmantle Pursuivant of Armes.
> Then the great Banner offrid by the esquyre that bare it and before him Blewmantle Pursuivant of Armes.
> Which standerd and Banner beinge offrid by the esquyres that bare theim, [they] did put of their hoodes and tooke their places emongest the rest of the mourners beinge gentlemen.
> Then offrid the Steward, Treasorer and Comptroller with whyte staues in their handes and Lancastre Heraulde of Armes before theim.
> Then offrid all other Knightes esquyres and gentlemen, wearinge blacke, proceedinge in order ii and ii according to their degrees.
> Then offrid the yeomen huishers, and after theim the defunctes yeomen ii and ii.

At this point, after the four assistants 'pall-bearers' have offered, the heraldic aspect of the offering is completed by the offering of the Standard and the Great Banner, Bluemantle in each case accompanying the bearer. It is interesting that the Esquires that bore them now 'put off their hoods.' The hood was worn during the procession, and worn on the head only by certain participants: the bearers of the various flags, the heralds and their ushers, those accompanying the corpse in its coffin, the Master of the Horse leading the Horse of State, the Chief Mourner and his companions and the other principal mourners. There are various possible explanations for this: some writers say it denotes

---

[16] College of Arms, Partition Book I, 1527–83, f. 281r–v.

COLOURS OF CONTINUITY: THE HERALDIC FUNERAL

those most intimately connected with the defunct,[17] but one could also suggest that it is connected with the heraldic function. What unites all those wearing the hood on their heads is their closeness to, and importance in, the ceremony's heraldry; and when the bearers of the standard and the great banner have offered these and left them at the altar, they put off their hoods.[18] (Note that the three main household officers do not offer their white staves of office: they will need them later.)

The Offering is the principal ceremony of the heraldic funeral. What is omitted from the 1572 narrative is the precise role of the Chief Mourner with respect to the achievements. Once he has offered for himself, he remains at the altar. As the achievements are brought up, each is offered to the clergyman, *who then gives it to the heir*, who passes it to the senior herald (in this case Garter), who lays it on the altar: 'And that his heire, if he have any, or next of whole blood, or some one for him (which commonly is the chief mourner) may publickly receive in the presence of all the mourners, the coate armour, Helme, Creast, and other Achievements of honour belonging to the defunct; whereof the King of Armes of the Province is to make record, with the defuncts match, issue and decease for the benefit of posterity.'[19]

The Offering, in other words, is the ceremony of transfer: the transfer of the deceased person's nobility and rank to his heir, and therefore of the continuity of that nobility. Once this has happened, the official and symbolic attention is focused on the heir, and the body of the defunct loses much of its importance.

> And thus the offringe endid, the .C. poore men were placid to proceed homewarde on foote, and after theim the knightes esquyres and gentlemen on horsback. Then garter principall King of Armes, then the principall mourner with the other viii mourners, ii and ii, and then the yeomen on foote ii and ii.

At this stage, it is the Principal Mourner – the Heir – who is at the centre of the homeward procession, as the corpse on its chariot had been in the procession to the church. It is the Heir who is now preceded by Garter King of Arms, as the corpse had been previously.

What, then, became of the defunct?

> After whose departure presently the body was by the viii gentlemen and 4 yeomen aforesayd caried to the grave, and before it Clarentieulx and Norroy Kinges of Armes and Lancaster Herauld of Armes and about the bodye went the 4 Esquyres assistantes and the vi other esquyres bearinge the Bannerolles, and after the bodye went the Steward, treasorer and comptroller with iiii gentlemen huishers and two yeomen huishers, who when the bodye was buried, kneelinge on their knees with weepinge and teares, brake their white staves and rodes over their heades and threw the shyvers of the same into the grave. That donne, the six Esquyres delyuerid vp the six bannerolles, which were

---

17 Cf. Woodward, *Theatre of Death*, pp. 20–1.
18 There are complex rules about the wearing of hoods and tippets by both men and women, and of their permitted fabric, length and width by rank.
19 Woodward, *Theatre of Death*, p. 31, citing Sir William Segar, *Honor Military and Civill* (London, 1602), §IV, p. 254. The 'record' is the Funeral Certificate, for which see below.

179

> presently with the rest of the Hatchementes placed orderly over and about him, and so the said officers departed to Lathum Hall, where before dinner they receyuid their offices and staves agayne of the new Erle their Lord and Master.

As we can see, the actual Burial was a relatively small and intimate affair, without the presence of the heir and the other principal mourners. The participants are chiefly the officiating clergyman, the remaining heralds (we may presume that Bluemantle had accompanied Garter) and the three main officers of the Earl's household. It is at this stage that the Book of Common Prayer's Burial Service is used.

What remains of the heraldic ceremony is this. The achievements, we remember, were those of the late Earl personally: the Heir will have his own. So they will not return with what is now the heir's procession, back to Lathom Hall: instead they are reverently laid over the coffin in the open grave. When the grave is filled, the achievements will be recovered and hung in the church, together with the bannerols (Fig. 29).[20] The officers of the household, meanwhile, break their staves of office and throw the fragments into the grave, as a sign of mourning, and of their personal loyalty to the deceased. Technically, they were his servants, and with his death their position is terminated. The modern equivalent would be a formal letter of resignation. And as we have seen, once they return to the Hall they receive their offices again – with new staves as a sign of them – from the new Earl.

This happens, says the manuscript, 'before dinner.' The heralds, although they doubtless enjoyed a splendid feast as much as all who were present, were not professionally concerned with it, and therefore do not describe it in their professional account. The dinner, however, was almost invariably lavish to the highest degree. For it was the heir's first occasion to show both his grandeur and his generosity. At the funeral feast for the Earl of Shrewsbury in 1560, 320 'messes' (1,280 servings) were served: the venison alone accounted for 50 does and 29 red deer.[21] It was *de rigueur* to serve quantities far greater than needed for those present: at Lady Katherine Berkeley's funeral in 1596, 'the excesse herein appears, when with suche dishes as for most part passed untouched at former tables, more then one thousand poore people were plentifully fed the same afternoone.'[22] The excess, in other words, was not wasted: it went to the poor. The poor, many of whom as we have seen marched in the procession, obtained several perks from a great lord's or lady's funeral: a warm gown, an excellent meal, and usually also 'a dole of money'.[23]

[20] Obviously, such textiles are more or less ephemeral, and few survive today. Some rare remnants can be seen in the Sackville family chapel of the church of St Michael and All Angels in Withyham (Suss.).

[21] Cf. D. Cressy, *Birth, Marriage and Death: Ritual, Religion and the Life-Cycle in Tudor and Stuart England* (Oxford, 1997), p. 445.

[22] Woodward, *Theatre of Death*, p. 36, citing *Records of Early English Drama: Coventry*, ed. R. W. Ingram (Manchester, 1981), pp. 512–13.

[23] This could be considerable: at Sir Nicholas Bacon's funeral the dole given to the poor was £193 6s. 8d. (Cressy, *Birth, Marriage and Death*, p. 443).

29. Funeral achievements in Aldershot church (Hants.) of Sir John White (d. 1573), alderman of London. His arms are visible on the shield, 'coat of arms' or tabard, and a bannerol: *six pieces azure and or, with three roundels argent each having two waves vert upon it in the azure and three lions' heads razed in the or*. His motto, IN D[OMI]NO CONFIDO ('My trust is in the Lord') is on the standard. Engraving by J. Cleghorn, jun., 1848, in the collection of Julian W. S. Litten.

Properly speaking, the heralds' job was now nearly over. However, one of those present at the actual interment had to act as the College's official witness, and draw up and sign the Funeral Certificate. This document, crucial to both family and College of Arms, began by stating the identity of the deceased, the date and place of death, and the date and place of burial. After that was mentioned the defunct's marriage, issue and sons-in-law (where appropriate), the executor(s) of the will, and sometimes the principal mourners. After stating which Officer of Arms had been present, the certificate concluded with the executors' signatures.[24]

[24] See College of Arms, MS. Vincent 90, for examples.

It has seemed both interesting and appropriate to follow in some detail this funeral of the Third Earl of Derby, if only because its description is so often cited but rarely quoted. It was a characteristic funeral for its time and for the rank of the defunct. Now, however, we need to look at some of the other examples of heraldic funerals, as they fill in some gaps.

One well-documented heraldic funeral adds several elements to those discussed above: that of the national hero Sir Philip Sidney. Sidney had been military governor of Flushing, one of the cautionary towns granted to Elizabeth in return for her military aid to the Netherlands in their struggle against Spain; he had been mortally wounded by a ball in the thigh at the Battle of Zutphen in September 1586; and he died of gangrene at Arnhem in October of that year, at the age of 31.

On his staff in the Netherlands had been a draftsman who later became a herald, Thomas Lant, who made annotated drawings of Sidney's funeral procession, which form one of our sources for the event and its details (see Fig. 28, above). The other source is a manuscript by Richard Lee, Richmond Herald; we may assume that it was he who organized what was to be done with Sidney's remains.[25] In the first place his body was of course embalmed. Secondly, a decision had to be made when and where to have his funeral. For whatever reason, the date decided upon was in February, 1587. The heralds organized the transport of the body: in this case a ship, hung – as would have been a chariot on land – with black cloth and escutcheons, and known as the Black Pinnace. This brought the body – presumably in its two coffins – to the Port of London, where it was laid in the Minories, a 'liberty' near the Tower, which also housed the Office of Ordnance, of which Sidney had been Joint Master, and the Worshipful Company of Grocers, with which he may have had some connection.[26]

The funeral, organized by the heralds, was sponsored and paid for by Sidney's father-in-law, the Queen's Principal Secretary, Sir Francis Walsingham. It was clearly intended to make a particularly brave show: partly because Sidney had caught the public's imagination as a young and brilliant hero, courtier and poet, diplomat and commander, fallen on the battlefield; partly also perhaps as a counterweight to the execution of Mary Queen of Scots just over a week earlier. In spite of Sidney's being a knight, the funeral was that of a baron: perhaps because he held a French barony, conferred by King Charles IX in 1572, or perhaps as a posthumous promotion for honour's sake.[27] Thomas Lant drew the entire procession – there were around 700

---

[25] See his detailed list of participants, drawn up for the College of Arms, in Bodleian Library, MS Ashmole 818, §IX, ff. 40–41.

[26] My thanks to Dr Kate Mould, of the University of Sydney, who has shared with me her valuable research on the Minories and their relation to Sidney's funeral. It used to be said that Sidney had the freedom of the Grocers Company; but there is no evidence for this. However, a detachment of Grocers marched in the tail of the funeral procession; and Dr Mould believes that this may originate in a link between the Company's old patron St Anthony and the church adjoining the Sidney family's London residence in Threadneedle St.

[27] Sir Henry Unton, a knight, was buried as a baron in 1596 'because he died ambassador leger for

participants – and had it engraved by Theodore de Bry, with the result that we have a complete record of the procession in 30-odd plates, of which a number of copies remain: the Folger Shakespeare Library has a photocopy, but it is the only one mounted on cloth and spindles, as Aubrey tells us the originals often were.[28]

What is notable about the Sidney funeral procession is, first of all, the military element: representatives were included of both the infantry and the cavalry under his command in the Netherlands, the former with 'fyffes and drommes playing softly' and a trailed Ensign [the infantry banner]; the latter with trumpeters and a trailed Guidon [the smaller cavalry banner]. There was, unusually, both a Standard and a Pennon, and between the latter and the Great Banner two horses: the 'horse for the field, with imbrodred furniture' ridden by a page trailing a broken lance, and the 'barbed horse (whose Caparizen was with cloth of goulde)' led by a footman and ridden by a page carrying a reversed battleaxe. Apart from these military reminders, the procession also comprised a number of representatives of the Estates of the Netherlands, who were in London for diplomatic negotiations at the time.

Another unusual element, though becoming more common at this time, was the number of the 'poor' being that of the defunct's age at death. Heraldically, the curiosities were that the pennon carried Sidney's arms rather than devices; that he had a great banner and four bannerols (showing his funeral to be a baron's), and that the bannerols – unlike those of the Earl of Derby – displayed a great many quarterings, not all beginning with his own arms: the first bannerol impaled the Sidney arms with those of Pakenham, thus representing Philip's paternal grandfather Sir William and his wife; the second impaled the Dudley arms with those of Guildford, representing Philip's maternal grandfather John, duke of Northumberland, and his wife Jane Guildford; the third impaled the Sidney arms with those of Walsingham, representing Philip himself and his wife Frances Walsingham; while the fourth Bannerol shows Sidney impaling Dudley and thus represents Philip's parents, Sir Henry and Mary Sidney. In all cases except Pakenham, the quarterings are quite full, ranging from six per side to a maximum (in the case of Dudley) of fifteen: this last undoubtedly an affirmation of the Dudleys' standing and noble connections in the face of criticisms such as those contained in the libellous pamphlet *Leicester's Commonwealth* which Philip had himself refuted in his manuscript *Defence of the Earl of Leicester*.[29]

France', i.e. on a diplomatic mission to that country. Cf. J. F. R. Day, 'Death Be Very Proud: Sidney, Subversion, and Elizabethan Heraldic Funerals,' in *Tudor Political Culture*, ed. D. Hoak (Cambridge, 1995), pp. 179–203, at 194.

[28] John Aubrey, *Brief Lives*, ed. O. L. Dick (Ann Arbor, 1957), p. 280. Excellent reproductions of the Brown University copy are available on a University of Maryland website titled 'The Sidney Funeral Project.' (http://wiki.umd.edu/psidney/index.php)

[29] Cf. *Leicester's Commonwealth*, ed. Dwight C. Peck (Athens, Ohio, and London, 1985. Sidney's *Defence* – very heraldic in nature – is printed in *Miscellaneous Prose of Sir Philip Sidney*, ed. Katherine Duncan-Jones and Jan van Dorsten (Oxford, 1973), pp. 59–122.

30. Drawing of a funeral, unidentified and perhaps imaginary; mid-sixteenth century. College of Arms, MS M.6, f. 74.

The engravings also contain an image of the dressed hearse in the choir of Old St Paul's, awaiting the procession, which marched from the Minories along Cheapside to the cathedral. Since Philip had no children other than a baby girl, the Chief Mourner at the funeral was his younger brother Robert. He did have an unusually large number of heralds: Clarenceux King of Arms (Robert Cooke, who had a few years earlier drawn up the Sidney Pedigree which is now in the Bodleian Library, Oxford), Somerset Herald (Robert Glover), Richmond Herald (Richard Lee, who seems to have been the main organizer of the funeral), and three pursuivants: Rouge Dragon, Bluemantle, and Portcullis. This enabled the achievements to be extended, adding the gauntlets and the spurs to the usual coat of arms, targe, and helm; while the sword was carried together with the targe (Fig. 28).

Sidney's heraldic funeral, then, was one in which nobility and military glory were combined, and in which the heraldry was employed to emphasize certain aspects of family standing.

What happened at a heraldic funeral when the defunct was a woman? We may take as an example the 1596 funeral of Lady Katherine Berkeley *née* Howard, daughter of the poet Earl of Surrey, the first wife of Henry Berkeley, Seventh Baron Berkeley, Lord

31. Woodcut showing a French noblewoman in mourning clothes. From Cesare Vecellio, *Degli habiti antichi et moderni di diverse parti del mondo* (Venice, 1590), f. 273. Vecellio comments that a French noblewoman does not go to the burial of her husband, although she is involved in planning the funeral. She wears this form of dress for a full year: it includes an overgarment of black, and a veil of either black or white, of which part comes down to her feet.

32 (below). The hearse and funeral effigy of Elizabeth I, 28 April 1603. Four horses, trapped in black and bedecked with penoncelles (or pencels), draw the hearse, beside which twelve bannerols are carried by noblemen. The image of the Queen atop her coffin was made by John Colt. Detail from a drawing of her funeral procession in British Library, MS Add. 5408, as engraved in *Vetusta Monumenta*, III (1796), Plate XXIII.

Lieutenant of Gloucestershire. In this case, the "poor" heading the procession were seventy poor women. Following them were gentlemen servants and gentlemen of the household; but following the coffin, the arrangement was different. First came Garter King of Arms, flanked by the defunct's chief usher and the chief mourner's; then came Lady Strange, the Earl of Derby's daughter, 'for this day principal mourneresse, in her gown, mantle, train, hood, and tippet of black, and in her Paris head [hood], tippet, wimple, vaile and barbe of fine lawn,' flanked by the deceased's son and brother-in-law who supported her by her arms, and followed by 'Mrs Audley Denis, bearing the train of the principal mourneress, apparelled as an esquiresse, in her gown, and lined hood of blacke, with a plaited kerchief, and barb of lawn'. Then there followed, by rank: two baronesses (including the deceased's daughter-in-law) and four knights' wives, all distinguished by details of dress. 'Which seven were called the seven principal mourneresses, and estates of the funeral.' After them followed four 'esquiresses,' then 'the late Lady's gentlemen, the principal mourneress's two gentlewomen,' and the gentlewomen of the other principals, 'to the number of fourteen.' Then came eight chambermaids, after whom the tail of the procession was formed, as it often was, by civic and municipal dignitaries.

We have seen that in the procession, Lady Strange took the part of the Chief Mourner, because at a woman's funeral, in the heraldic rules, all the principal mourners should be women. At the offering, however, it was the heir, Thomas Berkeley, who was presented with the achievements.

So far we have followed the funerals of very grand nobles, and in the country. Heraldic funerals, however, reached down into another world: that of London municipal notables. Here the great documentary source is the diary of Henry Machyn, clerk of the parish of Holy-Trinity-the-Less and furnisher of funeral necessities.[30] For thirteen years, between 1550 and 1563, Machyn recorded many London funerals, for several of which he furnished trappings such as escutcheons and hearse cloths. His descriptions are a great deal more terse than that of the Earl of Derby's funeral, but they give an interesting insight into the world of London aldermen, Lord Mayors, and other prominent citizens. Here is an example from 1560:

> The xxiii day of July was bered my good lade [Chester,] the wyff of ser Wylliam Chester knyght and draper and altherman and marchand of the stapull, and the howse and the cherche and the strette hangyd with blake and armes, and she gayff to xx pore women good rossett gownes,[31] and he gayff unto iiii althermen blake gownes and odur men

---

[30] *The Diary of Henry Machyn, Citizen and Merchant-Taylor of London, from A.D. 1550 to A.D. 1563*, ed. John Gough Nichols (Camden Soc., original ser., 42, 1848). A scholarly electronic version is *A London Provisioner's Chronicle, 1550–1563, by Henry Machyn: Manuscript, Transcription, and Modernization*, ed. Richard W. Bailey, Marilyn Miller and Colette Moore, at http://quod.lib.umich.edu/m/machyn/. It is admirably searchable by year and date.

[31] 'Russet' was a coarse woollen cloth of a reddish-brown color. A russet gown was not as elegant (or as expensive) as a gown of 'blacke', but it may have been warmer.

> gownes and cottes to the nombur of a C. and to women gownes ... and ther was ii harold[s] of armes; and then cam the corse and iiii morners beyryng of iiii pennon of armes abowtt, and cam morners a-for and after, and the clarkes syngyng; and master Beycon dyd pryche over nyght; and the morow after to the howse to dener; vi dosen of skochyons and a d' [a half dozen] of bokeram.

We notice here that there were two heralds present; and that the flags were limited to pennons, which were not restricted to the nobility. Elizabeth, Lady Chester, was not a nobody: her husband, Sir William Chester of Lombard Street (1509–?95), was one of the great Tudor merchants, who traded to Ethiopia, the Barbary Coast and Persia. Elizabeth's funeral took place at the high point of his fortunes, which declined from 1573 onwards. The singing 'clarkes' were a remnant of Catholic funerals revived in Mary's reign, and are more often met with in London funerals than in country ones. Machyn himself clearly furnished the 'skochyons' and possibly the pennons as well. We notice, too, that the company repaired to 'the howse' for the funeral feast, on the following day: in many London funerals, these feasts were held in the hall of the deceased's (or her husband's) livery company. Almost all the leading London citizens and aldermen 'saw their company hall as the best location for this (the feast), aiming to involve the company in the funeral and remembrances.'[32]

Machyn's diary spans both the Marian Counter-Reformation and the Elizabethan Re-Reformation, and he seems to have absorbed these with some equanimity. In the Marian Catholic period, the banners of saints around the coffin were revived, as was the cross on the pall and the bearing of candles and tapers in the funeral procession. Here is Machyn's account of a Catholic funeral from 1556:

> [The ... day of July was buried the lady Seymer, wife of sir Thomas Seymer knight, late lord mayor; with ... ...] armes; with ii whyt branches, xx torchys, and xx men [had] xx gowne of sad mantyll fryse, and xx women [xx gowns] of the sam frysse, and iiii baners of emages, and iiii grett [tapers] apon iiii grett candyll-stykes gylted, and a vi dosen skochyons; and the strett hangyd with fyn brod clothes, and the chyrch [hung with] armes; and after durge they whent home to her plasse. [On the] morow iii masses songe, on of the Trenete, and on of owr Lade, the thurd of requiem, and a sermon; and after masse hard [to] her plasse to dener, for ther was mony mornars, and a grett mone mad for her for her deyth, and gyffen money ... wardes in London.

No herald is mentioned here, though there may have been one. We notice the two 'white branches,' great candlesticks or candelabra; the gowns of 'mantle frieze,' a coarse woollen cloth with a nap on one side; the 'banners of images,' often of saints or of the Trinity; the 'great tapers' as in the illustration above; the 'dirge' or Office for the Dead;[33] the masses sung 'on the morrow,' the next day, and the feast on that day; and 'a great money made,' i.e. a great distribution of money to the poor.

---

[32] Harding, *The Dead and the Living*, p. 216.
[33] The word comes from the first word of the Latin antiphon: '*Dirige, Domine, Deus meus, in conspectu tuo viam meam*' ('Direct, O Lord, my God, my way in thy sight').

In many ways, the Elizabethan Re-Reformation, doing away with these specifically Catholic elements, replaced the religious imagery and ceremony with heraldry. This, of course, had wide-ranging consequences. It meant that the officers of arms became much more important; and that the Offering became, not so much an act of solidarity with – and care for – the defunct as a celebration of worldly continuity of family and rank. In fact, the whole funeral became such a ceremony. Several historians have, in the manner of the New Historicism, seen this development as an affirmation of political power;[34] but as Jennifer Woodward has shown, what was affirmed in the heraldic funeral was something shared between the grand and the simple.[35] It was, in the best sense of the term, perhaps the feudal spirit. The grand make a show of elements that concern them, to celebrate the continuity and the network of relationships that characterizes their family; the simple support this, some by simply lining the route and pondering on the passing of worldly things, some by presenting themselves for a role in the company of the 'poor' (or, perhaps, the higher-ranked one of a municipal dignitary) and obtaining the gift of a gown, a dole of money, and a splendid dinner.

The heraldry itself – which Edmund Bolton in 1597 called 'the Hieroglyphics of Nobility' – is the language of this spirit. Even at the time, some non-experts considered it arcane: William Wyrley wrote, in his 1592 *The True Use of Armorie*, 'How is it possible for a plain unlearned man ... to discerne and know asunder six or eight ... sometimes thirtie or fortie severall marks clustered together on shield or banner ...?'[36] However, we should not exaggerate the impenetrability of heraldry's language. In a funeral procession with four or six bannerols of several quarterings each, it is more than likely that spectators of the deceased's own class, or even of the class of their servants, would spot several coats of arms they recognized, and say something like, 'Goodness: I never knew old So-and-So was related to the Mortimers! Fancy that.' It is a language, not just a code: a language of continuity, both in time and space. The heraldic funeral, then, is a text in that language: a text of celebration of the deceased, a text of consolation for the living who were linked to him or depended on him, and a text of continuity of the very fabric of society.

In the course of the seventeenth century it became clear that the grand heraldic funeral such as described above had had its day. Ways were sought to make the occasion less cripplingly expensive: one such expedient, that also carried a certain glamour of its own, was the nocturnal funeral, conducted by torchlight. This, being simpler, could be done quickly and thus avoid embalming; it also avoided vast and costly processions, which took time to organize; and it obviated the complex choice of official mourners, replacing this with the voluntary attendance of those who felt closest to the deceased.[37]

---

[34] E.g. Ronald Strickland, 'Pageantry and Poetry as Discourse: the Production of Subjectivity in Sir Philip Sidney's Funeral,' *ELH (Journal of English Literary History)*, 57 (1990), pp. 19–36.
[35] Cf. Woodward, *Theatre of Death*, p. 28.
[36] Cited *ibid.*, p. 26.
[37] See especially Gittings, *Death, Burial and the Individual*, ch. 9, pp. 188–215.

COLOURS OF CONTINUITY: THE HERALDIC FUNERAL

Another was the heralds' offering complete packages: this began quite early as, the heralds' specific functions and actions being many and varied, it was easier for the Officers of Arms to negotiate an all-in fee with the family. A sum of £100 was not unusual for a grand funeral: added to this, the hearse and its rich trappings were perquisites for the heralds.[38] In the seventeenth century, competition in certain areas began to thrive – painters of heraldry increasingly went into business on their own, competing with the heralds' official subcontractors. This led to some surrealistic situations: 'one Leigh went to a painter in Silver Street to search for arms. The painter showed him sixteen different coats for Leigh and marshalled them all for him in one escutcheon.'[39] And eventually, of course, came the specialist undertakers who would dominate the field until our own day.[40]

In its heyday – chiefly from the mid-fifteenth century to the mid-seventeenth – the heraldic funeral furnished an incomparable spectacle, as well as being one of the staples of heraldry itself, and of the Heralds' activity and influence. It is, of course, not unconnected with the rapid social and political change that marked the Tudor period, and the equally rapid rise to power of a class of 'new men.' These new men did not so much create new standards as seek to be recognized by the old ones, even as they modified these by their adherence. Within the ritual of the grand funeral, such a modification was effected by the replacement of religious imagery and prayers for the dead by heraldic imagery and ceremonies of secular continuity; and the fact that it was enacted in such a very public and colourful spectacle gave it a wider currency than it might otherwise have had. The Hieroglyphics of Nobility had truly become the Colours of Continuity.

---

[38] *Ibid.*, p. 182.
[39] Wagner, *Heralds of England*, p. 238; above, p. 56. Eventually, in 1618, a general order was made forbidding 'ceremonious funerals' without the presence of a herald, insisting on a proper funeral certificate, and forbidding painters to provide heraldic material without a licence from a king of arms and a fixed price (Wagner, pp. 238–9).
[40] See Julian Litten, *The English Way of Death: the Common Funeral Since 1450* (London, 1992), ch. 1 'The Trade', and p. 194.

Heraldry and Gentry Communities in Shakespeare's England

RICHARD CUST

In 1581, when Thomas Legh refurbished the Great Hall of his manor house at Adlington in Cheshire, he followed the fashion popularized at around this time by Lord Burghley at Theobalds and installed a massive display of the coats of arms of local families. Only part of the original display survives, at the west end of the hall. But it does give a sense of how imposing the whole array must have been. The initial ordering was probably based on the roll of arms of county families which Legh had copied into a large historical scrapbook, showing the families in their order of precedence at this time, with the Savage, Booth, Brereton and Warburton arms at its head. Thirty years later, when a visitor came to the house, the ordering had been changed. The Savages were still at the head, but the Cholmondeleys had now moved into second place and gratifyingly the Leghs of Adlington were now in the top ten, along with their cousins the Leghs of Lyme, and just outside the most upwardly mobile of all Cheshire families in this period, the Grosvenors of Eaton.[1] The rejigging of the order of precedence was made possible by the use of wooden frames for the shields, which could be moved around and inserted in the appropriate place as notions of local ranking were revised. However, even this did not satisfy the visitor who gave it as his opinion that as a representation of the 'gentlemen of Cheshire according to their degrees' it was misleading: 'divers ancient houses of good account are omitted and many other misplaced here.'[2] (See Figs 33–4.)

The Adlington display touches on a number of interesting aspects of heraldry and gentry honour in this period. It demonstrates the fascination that English contemporaries had with heraldic display and genealogy which, amongst other things, led to the

[1] G. Nares, 'Adlington Hall, Cheshire – II', *Country Life*, cxii (Jul.–Dec. 1952), no. 2916 (5 Dec. 1952), pp. 1828–32; Manchester, Chetham's Library, Mun.E.8.22, 'The Adlington Manuscript', ff. 29–34, 39. 186 coats of arms in the Great Hall were recorded in 1611, whilst the current display at the west end consists of 60. It is not clear when the current arrangement of shields dates from. When Nares visited in 1952 he dated the arrangement to 1744; but since then the shields have been rearranged, possibly exposing an earlier version of the arrangement, although this does not correspond to either the Adlington roll or the 1611 layout.

[2] Cheshire Record Office, CR63/2/22, 'Cheshire pedigrees written c.1633 by Mr Will Davenport', unpaginated, 'A note of the gentlemen of Cheshire according to their degrees A.D.1611 (viz as they are ranked at Adlington Hall). But they are not rightly placed as I thinke.' The unidentified visitor may have been William Davenport himself, who resided nearby at Bramall Hall, and whose family had a strong interest in heraldry, illustrated by the armorial window glasses installed by successive generations in the hall and church: J. S. Morrill, 'William Davenport and the "Silent Majority" of Early Stuart England', *Jnl. Chester Archaeological Soc.*, lviii (1975); *Corpus Vitrearum Medii Aevi, Great Britain. Summary Catalogue, 9: The Medieval Stained Glass of Cheshire*, ed. P. Hegbin-Barnes (Oxford, 2010), pp. 35–42.

33. The display of coats of arms of Cheshire families at the west end of the hall at Adlington Hall (Ches.), set up by Thomas Legh in 1581.

proliferation of such displays in manor houses up and down the country during the 1570s and 1580s. It also illustrates the growing consciousness of the existence of distinctive county elites, each of which had its own sense of identity and which individuals like Legh could take pride in belonging to. This gave rise to another phenomenon of the period: the emergence of the first county histories which in their early incarnations were often a record of the distinguished achievements of elite local families. There is also the intriguing evidence that the arrangements made for periodically updating the display offers for the contemporary preoccupation with notions of precedence within gentry communities; and the sense that was apparent from the comments of the visitor that this was something fluid, changing and open to constant competition and negotiation. We can start by looking at the wider evidence for these displays of gentry coat armour. What has survived from this period; what different forms does it take; and, in particular, why was there a sudden flowering of such displays in the 1570s and 1580s.

The most renowned of these displays, and the probable inspiration for others, was the presentation installed by Lord Burghley in the Green Gallery at Theobalds, probably soon after the building of this was completed in 1573. Here the character of the display was rather different, consisting of a painted array of trees hung with the coats of arms of gentry from every one of English counties, with paintings in between showing the principal towns, landscape and produce of each. The herald Robert Glover recorded the

34. The Adlington Manuscript, drawn up at the behest of Thomas Legh of Adlington (Ches.), showing the coats of arms of Cheshire gentry families in order of precedence. Manchester, Chetham's Library, Mun. E.8.22, f. 29.

arms depicting Staffordshire, twenty coats shown in rough order of precedence, with the four baronial families of Lord Stafford, the earl of Essex, Lord Audley and Lord Paget at their head.[3] The sources used for this presentation are unknown, but the style and approach of depicting local elites shire by shire follows the practice of medieval rolls of arms, such as the Parliamentary Roll which showed the arms of gentry from all the counties of England *c.* 1312. This particular roll was much copied in the Elizabethan period and Burghley may have been familiar with it through his office as deputy Earl Marshal during the 1560s. He may also have received guidance from individual heralds,

[3] J. N. Summerson, 'The Building of Theobalds 1564–1585', *Archaeologia*, xcvii (1959), pp. 107–26, at 117; J. M. Sutton, 'The Decorative Program at Elizabethan Theobalds: Educating an Heir and Promoting a Dynasty', *Studies in the Decorative Arts*, vii (1999–2000), pp. 38–42; *The Visitacion of Staffordschire made by Robert Glover, al's Somerset Herald*, ed. H. S. Grazebrook (London, 1883) (also issued as *Collections for a History of Staffordshire*, William Salt Archaeological Soc., iii [1882], pt. 2), pp. 26–7. The first surviving reference to the display dates from 1583.

192

such as Robert Cooke, Clarenceux, who copied the entire roll, or, more likely, his client Robert Glover, Somerset Herald, who copied sections of it.[4]

Most of the other displays that we know about from this period show the arms of nobles and gentry in one particular shire rather than all the counties. When, in 1585, Sir Christopher Hatton completed the building of his great house at Holdenby in Northamptonshire, which was modeled on the ground plan at Theobalds, he provided a unique installation in the central hall consisting of three huge stone pyramids, 'depainted' with coats of arms. These showed the coat armour of the entire baronage of England, but alongside this he contented himself with depicting the arms of his fellow Northamptonshire gentry.[5] The Earl of Shrewsbury's magnificent house at Worksop, again built in the 1580s, had a renowned long gallery painted with the arms of English and foreign nobles and then in a 'lower roome' the gentry of his native Derbyshire.[6] The painted frieze installed by Sir William Fairfax in the Great Chamber at Gilling Castle, north Yorkshire, between 1582 and 1585 gives us a good sense of what the Theobalds display must have looked like. It consists of 22 trees hung with armorial shields with various animals at their foot. But this time the shields showed the arms of 443 Yorkshire families, arranged according to their wapentakes. Again, we have good evidence for the source of this arrangement: it was based on Fairfax's surviving 'Book of Arms of Yorkshire', arrayed wapentake by wapentake and once more, probably, compiled by Robert Glover. Here, however, the sense of precedence was less pronounced than elsewhere. Coats of arms were arranged across the trees, apparently in no particular order, although the primacy of baronial families such as the Manners, earls of Rutland, was maintained by inscribing their arms on the trunk of the tree (see Fig. 35).[7]

[4] P. R. Coss, *The Knight in Medieval England, 1000–1400* (Stroud, 1993), pp. 78–81; A. R. Wagner, *A Catalogue of English Mediaeval Rolls of Arms* (Harleian Soc., 100, 1950, for 1948), pp. xiii–xv, xx–xxi, 42–50, 140, 143; J. F. R. Day, 'Cooke, Robert (d. 1593)', in *ODNB*, 13, pp. 160–1; Nigel Ramsay, *Letters and Papers of a Tudor Herald and Scholar: Robert Glover, Somerset Herald* (Harleian Soc., forthcoming). The Parliamentary Roll belonged to the genre of local rolls of arms – as distinct from the general rolls or occasional rolls – which became popular from the 1270s onwards, in imitation of the Dering roll which showed the knightly families of Kent and Sussex. (I am grateful to Nigel Ramsay for the suggestion of Glover's involvement.)

[5] John Bridges, *The History and Antiquities of Northamptonshire*, 2 vols (London, 1791), I, p. 525; N. Pevsner, *The Buildings of England: Northamptonshire*, revised B. Cherry (Harmondsworth, 1973), pp. 261–3. A section of one of these pyramids still survives at Holdenby, although the original house has long since been demolished.

[6] M. Girouard, *Robert Smythson and the Elizabethan Country House* (London, 1983), pp. 110–15; University of Birmingham, Cadbury Research Library, MS 544/1, f. 52, William Wyrley's notebook.

[7] H. Murray, *The Great Chamber at Gilling Castle*, Saint Laurence Papers VIII (York, 1996), pp. 4–13, plate opp. p. 29; J. Bilson, 'Gilling Castle', *Yorkshire Archaeological Jnl.*, xix (1907), pp. 105–92, at 137–77; H. Shaw, *Details of Elizabethan Architecture* (London, 1839), pp. 23–4 and plate XV; T. Mowl, *Elizabethan and Jacobean Style* (London, 1993), pp. 18–23; *The Visitation of Yorkshire, made in the Years 1584/5, by Robert Glover, Somerset Herald*, ed. J. Foster (London, 1875), pp. 639–51. The painted trees show frequent changes in the depiction of the arms listed in the roll which Murray suggests are to be accounted for by repainting in the Victorian period.

35. Detail of the heraldic frieze in the Great Chamber at Gilling Castle, Yorkshire, set up by Sir William Fairfax, c. 1582×5, showing the coat armour of the gentry of the wapentake of Rydale cum Pickering. The arms of Edward Manners (d. 1587), earl of Rutland, are on the trunk of the tree. Henry Shaw, *Details of Elizabethan Architecture* (1839), Plate xv.

County displays came in various shapes and sizes, and appeared in a variety of locations. Those in houses were generally displayed in the more public parts of the building where they would be seen by visitors: galleries, halls, chambers or the parlours used for entertaining guests. The display of 109 coats of arms of Staffordshire gentry that Sampson Erdeswicke set up at Sandon, probably in the 1590s, was located in the gallery. This may have again taken the form of painted trees hung with shields, a familiar motif that he used for displaying his family's arms in the parish church; and once more Glover, who was his client and whom he much admired, probably provided information for the display, although Erdeswicke's own antiquarian researches would have sufficed for much of this.[8] The display of painted shields of Northamptonshire gentry set up by Erasmus Dryden at Canons Ashby, where he undertook extensive refurbishment of the house after succeeding his father in 1584 was located in the Winter Parlour which he used for entertaining his gentry neighbours (Fig. 36).[9] On the other hand Sir William Brereton's massive display of 330 painted shields and window glasses (some surviving examples dated 1577) was scattered around his newly built house at Brereton Hall (Ches.), appearing in his drawing room, on the staircases and in the first floor windows. This showed the arms of Cheshire gentry and was again based on research by Glover, who supplied him with a parchment roll showing the county's heraldry.[10]

Others chose different venues for their displays, but, invariably, the emphasis was on using public spaces for this. During the early 1580s Robert Ryece, a Suffolk gentleman with antiquarian interests, installed a display of 160 coats of arms (of which 46 still survive) in the window glasses of his parish church at Preston. This was another display where there was a clear order of precedence. The senior knightly families of Jermyn, Rookwood and Wingfield had their arms set up in the chancel, alongside those of the premier local peer, the earl of Oxford. Other senior knightly families took pride of place in the nave alongside the bulk of what Ryece described as the 'ancient and grounded' families of the shire; while the county's newly risen common lawyers had their coats relegated to the west window (Fig. 37).[11] Sir Thomas Tresham chose the very different public venue of the market house at Rothwell (Northants.), which he himself commissioned in 1578. On the outside, carved in a stone frieze above first floor level he

---

[8] M. W. Greenslade, *The Staffordshire Historians* (Staffordshire Historical Collections, 4th ser., xi, 1982), pp. 22–36; Staffordshire Record Office, D240/J/48/18. Erdeswicke was in and out of custody during the 1580s, because of his recusancy; but in the 1590s his antiquarian researches blossomed.

[9] [Oliver Garnett], *Canons Ashby*, National Trust Handbooks (London, 2001), pp. 8–9, 34–5.

[10] Hegbin-Barnes, *Stained Glass of Cheshire*, pp. 271–8.

[11] D. MacCulloch, *Suffolk and the Tudors: Politics and Religion in an English County, 1500–1600* (Oxford, 1986), pp. 119–20; *Suffolk in the XVIIth Century. The Breviary of Suffolk by Robert Reyce, 1618*, ed. Lord Francis Hervey (London, 1902), pp. 172–88; G.C. Harlow, 'Robert Ryece of Preston, 1555–1638', *Proc., Suffolk Institute of Archaeology*, 32 (1970), pp. 43–70, at 56, 58. The arms were first recorded by the Essex antiquary, James Strangman, in 1586–9, and it seems improbable that they were installed much earlier, since Ryece was only thirty in 1585 and did not inherit the manor until 1589.

36. The Winter Parlour at Canons Ashby (Northants.), decorated by Erasmus Dryden in the late 1580s with the coats of arms of Northamptonshire families.

displayed 90 coats of arms showing the gentry families of Rothwell hundred and the wider county, intended, he declared in a Latin inscription, as 'a tribute to his sweet fatherland and county of Northampton' (Fig. 38).[12] This display made a lasting impression within the shire. In 1635, when Sir Christopher Hatton (III) proposed paying for the rebuilding of the county gaol through a subscription, he suggested that the JPs emulate Tresham's example. The idea was to display the coats of arms of all those who subscribed, 'so that posterity might see', as he put it, that it was 'wholly performed by the liberality of the nobility and gentry resident within our own county.'[13]

The period from the 1570s to the 1590s, then, was a golden age for setting up these displays of county heraldry. But the practice was by no means novel. The earliest displays of armorial glass and carvings can be traced back to the mid thirteenth century, about the same time as rolls of arms were also becoming popular. Henry III and Edward I set

[12] J. A. Gotch, *The Buildings of Sir Thomas Tresham* (London, 1883), pp. 15–20.
[13] J. Wake, *The Brudenells of Deene* (London, 1953), p. 113.

up large displays in Westminster Abbey and York Minster respectively, arraying the arms of the baronial families of England. During the fourteenth century the practice spread to parish churches and the great halls of manor houses, with more localized displays often being exhibited alongside royal and baronial arms.[14] An early example was the coat armour set up by Sir William de Etchingham in the mid 1370s in window glass at his newly built parish church. This showed members of the royal family in the east window, the earls of England in the chancel and his knightly neighbours in east Sussex in the nave.[15] Such displays often revealed a strong sense of identity with the local county elite. In the 1420s or 1430s, John Pympe installed window glass in Nettlestead church (Kent), showing the arms of some 35 of the more ancient families among his east Kentish neighbours; and in his will he ordered that his tomb chest display his similarly ancient lineage.[16] Around the same time the Archbishop of York installed the arms of twelve leading Nottinghamshire families in the window glass of his palace at Southwell.[17] Similar displays of armorial glass showing the leading families of Lancashire and Cheshire were set up set up by the Davenports in the Great Hall at Bramhall (Ches.) in the late fifteenth century and by Sir William Norris at Speke Hall, near Liverpool between the 1530s and '40s.[18] Arrays of county coat armour, then, were a regular feature of medieval churches and manor houses. But this does not explain why they suddenly proliferated from the 1570s onwards.

The answer lies primarily in the growth of heraldry and antiquarianism during the early part of Elizabeth's reign. This was in part a reaction to contemporary alarm about widespread social dislocation and the threat to order and degree in the mid-sixteenth century. Amongst other responses, this prompted efforts to achieve greater certainty and fixity when it came to defining who was a gentleman, which led to the heralds taking on the prime responsibility for policing the honours system and authorizing claims to status and titles. There was a rapid expansion in their role once the Office of Arms was newly incorporated in 1555. Fresh measures were introduced to register and record gentry pedigrees and coats of arms in the Earl Marshal's reforms of the 1560s; and by the 1570s the process of county visitations – with heralds going into the shires to inspect and validate claims to gentility – had been extended to cover the whole country. These initiatives led to the production of what was, in effect, a new generation of local rolls of arms, with gentry pedigrees and coat armour being grouped together county by county

---

[14] Coss, *Knight in Medieval England*, pp. 86–91; R. Marks, *Stained Glass in England during the Middle Ages* (London, 1993), pp. 87, 92–7.

[15] N. Saul, *Scenes from Provincial Life: Knightly Families in Sussex, 1280–1400* (Oxford, 1986), pp. 148–53.

[16] Coss, *Knight in Medieval England*, p. 91; W. E. Ball, 'The Stained-Glass Windows of Nettlestead Church', *Archaeologia Cantiana*, xxviii (1909), pp. 157–282, at 239–41.

[17] S. J. Payling, *Political Society in Lancastrian England* (Oxford, 1991), pp. 16, 218.

[18] Hegbin-Barnes, *Stained Glass of Cheshire*, pp. 35–42; *Corpus Vitrearum Medii Aevi, Great Britain. Summary Catalogue, 8: The Medieval Stained Glass of Lancashire*, ed. P. Hegbin-Barnes (Oxford, 2009), pp. 135–46.

37. One of the nave windows of Preston St Mary (Suffolk), showing part of the display of the arms of Suffolk gentry set up by Robert Ryece in the 1580s.

38 (opposite). Rothwell Market House, commissioned by Sir Thomas Tresham in 1578, showing the arms of the families of Rothwell Hundred (Northants.) and an inscription in which the building is presented as a 'tribute to his sweet fatherland and county of Northampton'. J. A. Gotch, *The Buildings of Sir Thomas Tresham* (London, 1883), Rothwell Plate 2.

and then copied and recopied by heralds and antiquarian scholars.[19]

At the same time as this was happening there was a great leap forward in what contemporaries called the new 'genealogical science'. Led by Glover, the doyen of Elizabethan antiquaries, heralds and antiquarian scholars began to research the pedigrees and descents of gentry families far more systematically than before, to ascertain whether they qualified under the new gold standard for gentility, the ability to demonstrate a noble descent through at least three generations. This led to a renewed fascination with coats of arms, which were one of the principal means of ascertaining a descent. Heralds and antiquarian scholars scoured through charters, deeds, seals and medieval rolls of arms, and visited parish churches to note down the arms on monuments and in window glasses, all in order to trace gentle status through past generations. Out of this there again developed updated versions of the local rolls of arms, to supplement the copies being made of medieval rolls. William Wyrley, for example, who acted as assistant to Sampson

[19] R. P. Cust, *Charles I and the Aristocracy, 1625–42* (Cambridge, 2013), pp. 7–11; A. Ailes, 'The Development of Heralds' Visitations in England and Wales', *The Coat of Arms*, 3rd ser., 5 (2009), pp. 7–23. For an example of the visitation records of this period, see Glover's 1583 visitation of Staffordshire, which incorporated all sorts of other evidences alongside the visitation itself and was much copied: *Visitacion of Staffordshire*, ed. Grazebrook, passim.

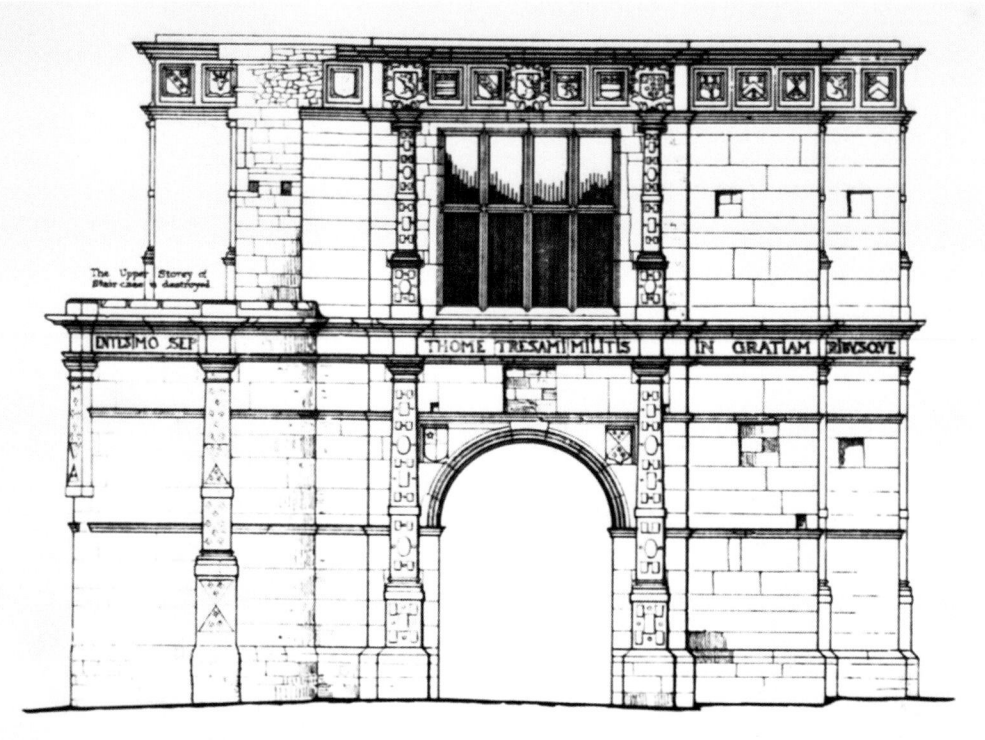

East Elevation.

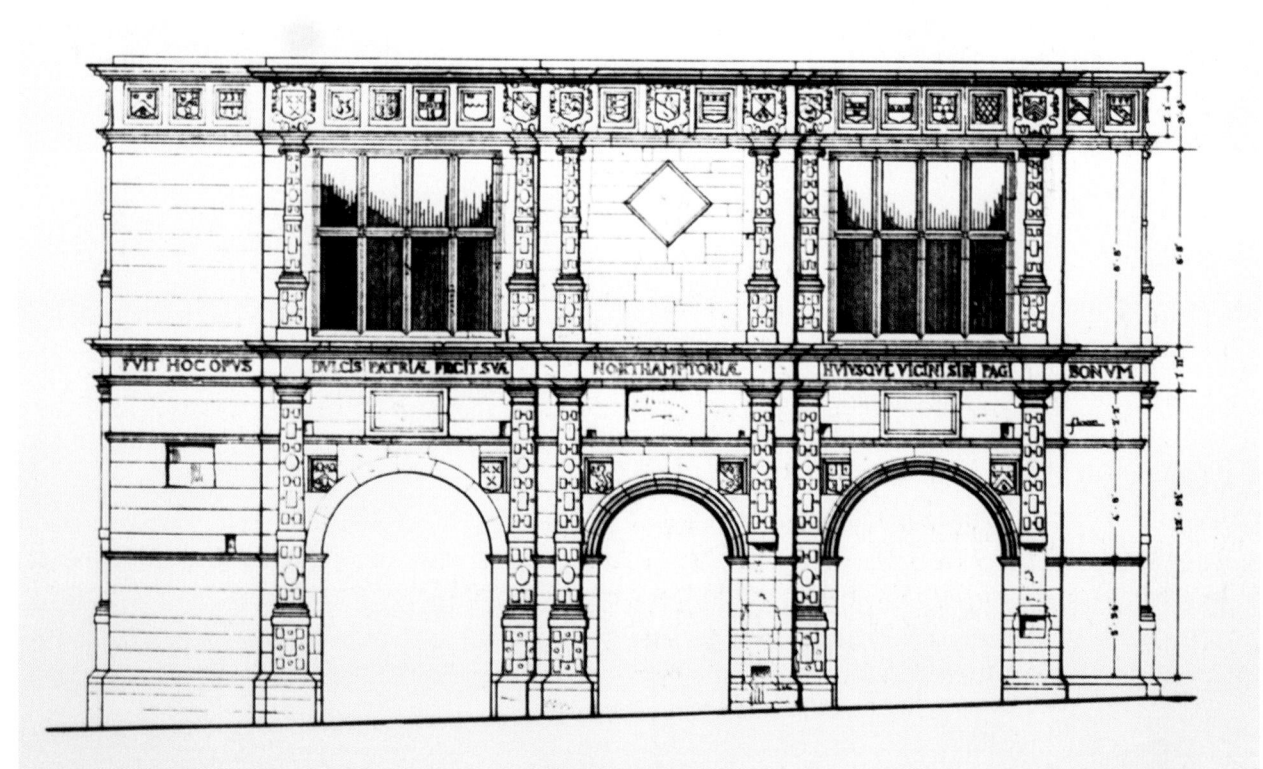

North Elevation.

Erdeswicke in his antiquarian researches, compiled rolls for Derbyshire, Leicestershire, Northamptonshire and Nottinghamshire, often accompanied by potted commentaries on local families in the style which was emerging in county histories and chorographies.[20] As we have seen, these were then passed on to gentlemen such as Sir William Brereton, Sir William Fairfax and Thomas Legh. All of this helped to stimulate a rapidly growing interest among the gentry in researching their ancestral heritage and recording the coat armour of their native county elites. It was this flowering of heraldic and antiquarian studies, then, that provided the tools and much of the stimulus for the county displays. At the same time there was a further source of encouragement for gentlemen to set up these displays, in their growing sense of pride in, and identity, with their native counties. One of the most obvious manifestations of this was the emergence of county histories and chorographies around the same time as the county displays were becoming popular. William Lambarde's *Perambulation of Kent*, setting out the defining features and 'singularities' of his native shire, was published in 1576. In 1586 the first edition of William Camden's *Britannia* appeared in print, covering every county in England and providing a framework and, in many cases, an inspiration to others. Richard Carew in his *Survey of Cornwall* and Sampson Erdeswicke in his *Survey of Staffordshire*, both begun in the late 1580s, acknowledged their debt to Camden. But they went much further by incorporating extensive genealogies and family histories of the gentry of their shires, parish by parish.[21] Robert Ryece, whose *Breviary of Suffolk*, was in turn inspired by the publication of Carew's work in 1602, summed up the primary purpose of this genealogical history as 'to perpetuate the reverend estimation and continuation' of his own ancestors and those of his friends and neighbours. This was partly intended as an act of pious remembrance; but also, as he explained, to provide a source of inspiration to the current generation, 'to excite the regarders to all honourable endeavours and piety of life.'[22] Allied to this was an evident sense of pride in the county and the unity and harmony of its gentry. Diarmaid MacCulloch has identified this as a particular feature of late-Tudor Suffolk. The aggressive self-assertiveness which characterized the dealings of local magnates in the early sixteenth century was gradually overlaid by a concern to promote harmony and establish the shire's reputation for orderliness and agreement. He points to several influences at work here, mostly grounded in Protestant and humanist notions of good fellowship and unity. But among these he highlights the work of local antiquaries who encouraged the gentry to associate themselves with the corporate entity of their native shire. Ryece's oft-quoted description of his gentry neighbours

---

[20] Cust, *Charles I and the Aristocracy*, pp. 12–16. For Wyrley's rolls of arms, see University of Birmingham, Cadbury Research Library, MS 544/1, 2; College of Arms, MS Vincent 197. For another example, see the Gloucestershire roll compiled by the local antiquarian Roger Kemys: Gloucestershire Record Office, D885 (I am grateful to Jan Broadway for this reference).

[21] J. Broadway, *'No Historie so Meete': Gentry Culture and the Development of Local History in Elizabethan and Early Stuart England* (Manchester, 2006), pp. 28–34.

[22] *Ryece's Breviary*, ed. Hervey, pp. 2, 157–8.

encapsulated this communal ideal:

> If differences doe arise which are very seldome, such is the great discretion ever tempered with love and kindnes among them, that these devisions are soon smothered and appeased ... such is the religious unitie wherewith in all good actions they doe concurre, that whatsoever offendeth one displeaseth all, and whosoever satisfieth one contenteth all.[23]

Similar sentiments fed into the displays of county heraldry. Heraldry was an emblematic language which to the initiated could convey the whole history of a family and its associations. The early Stuart antiquary Sir Thomas Shirley described coats of arms as 'little mappes' which 'make us know in epitomie all the qualities, offices and most famous acts of persons which have bin of any consideration in the world.' Because of this they could act as an inspiration to later generations which 'must needs be spurred on to the same actes which had beene honored with soe noble a remuneration.'[24] This made the coat of arms a particularly potent symbol for gentry families. Arms were in effect miniature repositories of the family's honour, while at the same time proclaiming their membership of the exclusive upper class of the virtuous and well born. Just as the accounts of genealogies and families in the county survey announced membership of what Ryece called the 'ancient and grounded gentry' of one's native shire, so the inclusion of one's coat armour amongst a larger display clearly asserted that one belonged to a select social elite.[25]

This was a particular concern in late-sixteenth-century England because of the prevailing sense of flux and change amongst the upper classes. As newcomers flooded into the ranks of the gentry, and established families rose and fell, there was intense competition for status. The Shakespearean era became the great age of genealogical invention, as old families with perfectly respectable pedigrees felt the need to push their descents back to the Norman conquest and newly risen families were desperate to disguise their origins with the appearance of antiquity. Sir Christopher Hatton, for example, commissioned extensive researches from Laurence Bostock, a Cheshire antiquary, to disguise the fact that he was a relative newcomer to the ranks of the upper gentry. These equipped him with a new coat of arms and led to the production of an elaborate pedigree, sanctioned by Glover in 1580, which traced his descent back to Ivon,

---

[23] MacCulloch, *Suffolk*, chapters 2–3; *Breviary of Robert Reyce*, ed. Hervey, p. 60. Similar sentiments were expressed by Thomas Wotton in his introduction to the *Perambulation of Kent*. Addressing his fellow gentry, he referred to 'the general coniunction and association of your mindes and your selfes in good amitie and familiaritie, one toward another': cited in J. Broadway, 'A Convenient Fiction? The County Community and County History in the 1650s', in *The County Community in Seventeenth- Century England and Wales*, ed. J. Eales and A. J. Hopper, Explorations in Local and Regional History, 5 (Hatfield, 2012), pp. 39–55, at 39.

[24] R. P. Cust, 'Catholicism, Antiquarianism and Gentry Honour: The Writings of Sir Thomas Shirley', *Midland History*, xxiii (1998), pp. 40–70, at 50–1.

[25] This theme is explored in relation to William de Etchingham by Nigel Saul, who points out that he was able to 'bask in the reflected splendour of his superiors' by setting his own family's arms in the chancel windows of Etchingham church, alongside those of the earls of England: Saul, *Scenes from Provincial Life*, pp. 150–1.

a Norman peer who came over with the Conqueror, and thus established his equality with several of the premier noble families of England. The new coat of arms was a feature of Hatton's house at Holdenby (Northants.). We do not know whether he arranged it alongside those of other noble families on the armorial pyramids, in the same way as in his new pedigree; but the very fact of being able to display his arms in close proximity would have implied a claim to parity of status.[26] One man's coat armour was, after all, as honourable as another's. To a much greater extent than in other forms of heraldic display – on funeral monuments or personalised pedigrees, for example – the marshalling of arrays of coat armour brought home the essential equality of the gentry classes, as was, perhaps, best illustrated by the cheerful intermingling of the coats of earls and mere gentlemen in the display at Gilling Castle.

Alongside this desire to assert one's own family status there was also evidence of the strong and growing sense of gentry community identified by MacCulloch. This could be portrayed more immediately and more graphically through a marshalling of coat armour than any by other medium that was available to contemporaries. It depicted the local elite, in a way that they themselves were best equipped to understand, as an association of armigerous gentlemen, equal and united in their heraldry. This was made explicit in the display set up by Sir Robert Jermyn at Rushbrooke Hall (Suff.) late in Elizabeth's reign. Alongside a display of the coat armour of 139 Suffolk families – from both the east and the west of a county that was often seen as divided into two halves – he wrote the inscription 'qui sumus', 'who we are'. Then to underline the historical continuity of this body he set up the shields of 109 extinct local families, which he labelled 'qui fuimus', 'who we were'.[27] This sense of pride in the harmony, unity and enduring continuity of local elites was also evident in Sir Thomas Tresham's inscription on the market house at Rothwell. This described the building and the armorial frieze as 'a tribute to his sweet fatherland and county of Northampton', an acknowledgement of the gentry's devotion to 'the public good' and a monument to 'the perpetual honour of his friends'. The effect was to blend together some of the common themes around which identification with one's county was constructed: loyalty, fellowship, generosity and honourable service to the common weal.[28]

This discussion of the motives for creating county displays has tended to emphasise the way in which they represented the essential equality of the armigerous elite. But, of course, they were not necessarily read in this way, as the reaction of the visitor to Adlington in 1611 illustrated. Precedence was a constant preoccupation of late Tudor and early Stuart England, again a product of the fierce competition for social status driven by the sense of social upheaval and change. Gentry heads of families measured their standing and reputation within their shire by where they appeared in the pecking

---

[26] E. St John Brooks, *Sir Christopher Hatton* (London, 1946), pp. 73–81; Northamptonshire Record Office, Finch-Hatton MS 271.
[27] MacCulloch, *Suffolk*, p. 119.
[28] Gotch, *Buildings of Sir Thomas Tresham*, pp. 15–20.

orders of county ranking illustrated in commissions of the peace, public processions, seating arrangements on county occasions and so on. Relative status was also demonstrated in these displays of coat armour. The messages were often quite subtle, conveyed through the order in which arms were displayed, the grouping together of particular family coats and the position of displays relative to each other. But their implications were readily apparent to contemporaries. The significance of the way in which Ryece arranged his display in Preston church was certainly not lost on Sir Simonds D'Ewes when he visited in the early seventeenth century. He was disappointed to see his own arms marshalled in the west window, alongside the progeny of other Suffolk lawyers, and made a point of insisting that they be moved into the nave alongside those of his wife's family, the Cloptons.[29] As the Adlington display illustrated – with its delineating of the steady advance of the Leghs up the ranks of the local gentry – a further motive of these presentations was to assert and advertise the patron's relative status within the local gentry community.

The fashion for setting up these displays of county coat armour appears to have been a relatively short-lived phenomenon. The display at Adlington was periodically updated well into the eighteenth century[30]; and gentry families continued to add heraldic decoration to their houses into the nineteenth century and beyond. But what has survived suggests that after the start of the seventeenth century the heraldry – whether it be on funeral monuments, fire places, window glasses or display pedigrees – was designed to celebrate the patron's own family and kin rather than the wider body of the local gentry community.[31] Other forms of representation took over this latter function, most notably the county histories which proliferated in the seventeenth century.[32] The county displays were the product of a particular moment when local gentlemen were becoming particularly conscious of the need to define and assert gentry status, and were being provided with the means to do this by heralds and antiquaries. It was their work – and, in particular, that of the pivotal figure of Robert Glover – drawing up visitation records, compiling church notes, collating the evidence of deeds and charters, and out of this producing up-to-date versions of the local rolls of arms, which provided the tools and much of the stimulus for creating these displays. This was also a moment which coincided with the gentry's wider absorption of humanist and Protestant ideals of harmony, good fellowship, and loyalty and service to one's 'country'.[33] Together these aspirations and concerns gave rise to one of the most intriguing by-products of the Shakespearean age's fascination with heraldry.

[29] MacCulloch, *Suffolk*, p. 120.
[30] Nares, 'Adlington Hall' (cit. in n. 1).
[31] This is apparent, for example, from the survey of heraldry in National Trust houses: T. Woodcock and J. M. Robinson, *Heraldry in National Trust Houses* (London, 2000).
[32] Broadway, *'No Historie so Meete'*, passim.
[33] R. P. Cust, 'The "Public Man" in Late Tudor and Early Stuart England', in *The Politics of the Public Sphere in Early Modern England*, ed. P. Lake and S. G. Pincus (Manchester, 2007), pp. 116–43.

SPECIMEN OF THE STAINED GLASS, IN THE DINING ROOM

IN ONE OF THE BAY-WINDOWS, AT GILLING CASTLE, YORKSHIRE.

Drawn by T. Willement. Engraved by Henry Shaw.

London, Pub.d Nov.r 1834, by W.m Pickering, Chancery Lane.

'Wanting Arms': Heraldic Decoration in Lesser Houses

TARA HAMLING

Imagery derived from heraldry was ubiquitous even in lesser houses during Shakespeare's lifetime. Arms, crests and badges were a common feature of the large-scale wall and ceiling decoration that became fashionable in the houses of the gentry and the wealthier among the 'middling sort' in Elizabethan and Jacobean England. Interior decoration was not an optional luxury for people of status during this period; it was an essential and expected element in the fashioning of identity and lifestyle. It contributed to improved living conditions (in insulating and ornamenting the interior) while also providing a medium for the public demonstration of wealth and social position. This combination of practical and social considerations in the use of decoration is described by the Puritan commentator Philip Stubbes in 1583: 'cloth of gold, arase,[1] tapestrie, and other riche ornaments, pendices, and hangings in a house of estate serve not onely to manuall uses and servile occupations, but also to decorate, to bewtifie, and become the house, and to showe the riche estate and glorie of the owner.'[2] Heraldry was an essential ingredient of this domestic display, but not all owners who had the financial means to beautify their homes with rich decorations could legitimately claim to be entitled to a coat of arms. There was, however, a range of design options for householders in want of arms, including the appropriation of para-heraldic motifs and the invention of pseudo-heraldic emblems to reflect their status and character, using a visual language that relied on the heraldic tradition.

Viewing Arms in Windows and Walls

A character in Henry Peacham's 'Dialogue tending to the Blazon of Arms', printed in 1612, explains his desire to be instructed in heraldry: 'the principal use I would make of this skill is, that when I come into an old decayed Church or Monastery ... or Gentelmans house, I might busie myself in viewing Armes, and matches of Houses in the windows or walls.'[3] This reflects the fashion in the later sixteenth century to adorn the main reception rooms of gentry houses with displays of family lineage and alliances in large-scale surface decoration such as painted schemes, carved chimneypieces and painted glass. A supreme example of this vogue for heraldic display is the great chamber of Gilling Castle (Yorks.), created in the 1580s by Sir William Fairfax as part of an extensive rebuild and development of an existing fourteenth-century manor house.[4] Every part of the

---

[1] I.e. arras: tapestry wall hanging of Flemish origin.
[2] Philip Stubbes, *The Anatomie of Abuses* (London, 1583), p. 34.
[3] Henry Peacham, *The Gentlemans Exercise* (London, 1612), p. 141.
[4] See also Richard Cust, above, pp. 193, 202 and Figs 35, 39; and Timothy Mowl, *Elizabethan and Jacobean Style* (London, 1993), pp. 19–23, for photographs.

---

39 (opposite). One of the heraldic stained glass windows in the Great Chamber at Gilling Castle, Yorkshire, commemorating the marriages of the family of Sir William Fairfax; created in the 1580s.
From Henry Shaw, *Details of Elizabethan Architecture* (1839), Plate xiv.

decorative scheme demonstrates the familial and local connections of the owner; the chimneypiece has the Fairfax achievement of arms in the central panel with four coats of arms below representing Sir William's four sisters and their husbands (Bellasis, Curwen, Vavasour, and Roos, each impaled with Fairfax). Another panel above the entablature has the royal arms of Elizabeth I. Depicted within a deep frieze on painted boards above the wainscot of the room is a series of twenty-one trees in a landscape intended to represent the parishes of Yorkshire, and hanging on the branches are 433 coats representing all the gentlemen then living in each area. The heraldic extravaganza continues in the painted glass. The south window, which survives almost intact, is devoted to the heraldry and genealogy of the family of Sir William's second wife, the Stapletons. The main bay window (altered in the eighteenth century) was dedicated to the Fairfax family. These two windows are the work of one Bernard Dininckhoff, who has left his signature, with the date 1585, in the bottom right-hand light of the south window. The east window was apparently painted slightly later, and shows the arms and connections of the Constables, in celebration of the marriage of Sir William's son Thomas to Catherine Constable. Even the plasterwork ceiling exploits heraldic references: its relief decoration includes the lions of the Fairfax coat with goats and talbots as the Fairfax and Stapleton supporters. Such a complex system of heraldic display worked on several levels. It could operate on purely visual terms to impress by evoking a sense of antiquity, pedigree and magnificence, but it could also be perused in detail; inventories indicate that in the 1590s there was a book to which visitors could refer in order to identify the various arms in plasterwork, paint and glass.[5]

A display of heraldry also formed part of the remodelling and decoration of Canons Ashby (Northants.). The decoration of the ground-floor parlour was carried out in the 1590s by Sir Erasmus Dryden, with a series of painted crests and devices in the panels of the wainscot to celebrate his ancestral heritage and local connections (Fig. 36, above). These references to important Northamptonshire families were presumably intended to honour Dryden's peers when he received and entertained them in this room; as Nicholas Cooper has observed about the decoration of gentry houses more generally, 'Heraldic references were statements of status and an acknowledgement of affinities, both self-advertisement and courtesy'.[6] This sort of display might also usefully serve to intimidate any visitor from outside this circle of powerful landowners and thus reinforce the authority of the county elite.

Gilling Castle and Canons Ashby were older properties that were extended and redecorated by well-established members of the gentry. But this fashion was also embraced enthusiastically by the newly elevated, such as Sir Edward Phelips, whose brand new mansion built *c.* 1600 at Montacute (Som.) was adorned with armorial

[5] Nicholas Cooper, *Houses of the Gentry, 1480–1680* (New Haven and London, 1999), p. 320, citing E. Rebecah, 'Inventories made for Sir William and Sir Thomas Fairfax', *Archaeologia*, xlviii (1885), pp. 121–56.
[6] *Ibid.*, p. 320.

40. Stained glass with coats of arms in a bay window in the Library at Montacute House (Somt.). This colourful display of Phelips family connections is in what was once the 'great chamber' – the principal and grandest room of an Elizabethan country house.

decoration including a stained glass window in the great chamber (now called the Library) with 42 painted shields representing the arms of the Phelips family, their neighbours and allies (Fig. 40). Following his purchase of a string of titles in 1624, Richard Robartes embellished his new house at Lanhydrock (Cornw.) with a finely carved front door displaying his baronial arms. Around the same time he commissioned an impressive, although largely fictional, family pedigree roll which traced his family lineage back to the medieval Earls of Cornwall. This suggests that such extravagant pomposity might have resulted from the insecurities of recent advancement, which required adamant and ostentatious proclamation. The carved chimneypiece in the great chamber of Chastleton House (Oxon.), which was built c. 1607–12 by Walter Jones, a clothier, to establish himself as a country gentleman, bears his arms impaling those of Pope for his wife, but there is no evidence that his bride – apparently the daughter of an émigré settler from the duchy of Cleves – had any right to arms, so these must be

'borrowed' or fictional. Jones had previously had to justify his right to use a coat of arms very similar to that borne by the Talbot earls of Shrewsbury, *a lion rampant within a border engrailed or*. The heralds decided that both parties were entitled to use it: Walter was acknowledged to have already established 'by one scienced in the antiquities and genealogies' his own right to a coat of arms.[7] This dispute and the display of apparently bogus Pope arms in the most showy of the reception rooms at Chastleton demonstrates the importance of heraldic display, even if contested or unsubstantiated, in the homes of upwardly mobile members of society. It indicates how a display of arms could be somewhat contrived and deployed for general effect rather than being intended for careful perusal by knowledgeable, possibly critical, eyes.

The prominent display of arms was also an important aspect of civic and mercantile self-fashioning among the urban elite. At Strangers' Hall, a large merchant's house in Norwich, a collection of arms (now incorporated within the hall screen) exhibits various aspects of the identity of its owner, Nicholas Sotherton, in the 1530s: the arms of the Merchant Adventurers' company, his personal arms, the arms of the Grocers' Company impaling his own 'merchant's mark', and the arms of the City of Norwich.[8] A stained glass window in the great parlour at Suckling House also depicted the arms of Norwich with the arms of two subsequent owners, Geoffrey Steward and John Clerk (impaling the Mercers' arms). Clerk acquired the property through marriage to Steward's widow and it seems he retained or had painted the Steward arms to represent the descent of the property: a version of the genealogical displays found in country houses but in this instance celebrating forebears in public life and civic leadership.[9]

Personal coats of arms also adorned a range of moveable household items and were especially prominent in decorative textiles. In the greater houses of the elite, arms were often woven within the fabric of extortionately expensive imported tapestries in response to a specific commission. This stamp of ownership did not, however, preclude resale. In 1592 Elizabeth, countess of Shrewsbury, purchased for the gallery of her new Hardwick Hall a second-hand set of tapestries with the story of Gideon that had belonged to Sir Christopher Hatton. She craftily used painted woollen patches with her shield of arms, to cover over the Hatton arms.[10] Embroidered cushions provided an affordable way to display arms in lesser houses and could be produced at home by gentlewomen, such as the early (*c.* 1540) example with the arms of Warneford-Yates, now in the Victoria and Albert Museum, London (Fig. 41). Family arms and crests were especially common on

---

[7] Hilary L. Turner, 'Walter Jones of Witney, Worcester, and Chastleton: Rewriting the Past', *Oxoniensia*, lxxiii (2008), pp. 33–44, at 39.

[8] Chris King, 'The Interpretation of Urban Buildings: Power, Memory and Appropriation in Norwich Merchants' Houses, *c.* 1400–1660', *World Archaeology*, 41 (2009), pp. 471–88, at 479–80.

[9] The window was recorded in antiquarian sources but is no longer extant. I am very grateful to Chris King for sharing all his information on Suckling House.

[10] Santina M. Levey, *An Elizabethan Inheritance: The Hardwick Hall Textiles* (London, 1998), p. 23, Fig. 16.

41. Embroidered cushion cover, *c.* 1540, linen canvas, embroidered with silk in tent stitch. Victoria and Albert Museum, T.120–1932. Long cushion covers were made to size to furnish wooden benches, but were primarily for display rather than comfort. The arms at the centre of this design celebrate the marriage of John Warneford and Susanna Yates.

objects associated with inheritance, including textiles, but also bedsteads, plate and books (especially religious texts). These items represented a considerable financial and symbolic investment and were indissolubly associated with notions of legacy. The dual significance of arms, as a claim to status in the present but with an eye to posterity, is also represented by their presence as a standard element of the vocabulary of portraiture, an art form increasingly embraced by members of the provincial and minor gentry in the second half of the sixteenth century.

Royal Arms

In great houses such as Gilling Castle and Hardwick Hall, the personal coats of arms of the owner were exhibited in decorative schemes which also displayed the royal arms. In some lesser houses, however, the depiction of the royal arms could serve in place of personal arms.

From 1561 the royal arms were set up in parish churches to represent the role of the monarch as head of Church as well as State. The new, assertive presence of the royal arms in local communities might have encouraged an associated trend in domestic space. The presence of the royal arms as a feature of domestic decoration during this period has often resulted in mistaken assumptions about a direct royal connection with a given property. An oak overmantel carved with the arms of James I in high relief (now in the Victoria and Albert Museum) originally decorated the ground-floor parlour of a house in Bromley-by-Bow, to the east of London, which was built around 1606. It was no doubt

42. Carved wood overmantel with the arms of James I as kingt of England, from 'The Old Palace', Bromley-by-Bow, *c.* 1606. Victoria and Albert Museum, no. 248–1894. The ornate decoration of the ground-floor parlour was acquired by the museum in *c.* 1900 and is now displayed as a 'period room' in the British Galleries.

these arms that prompted a tradition that the house had been used by the King as a hunting lodge, and by the time the house was demolished in 1894 it was called 'The Old Palace'. It is, however, far more likely that the house was built for a wealthy London merchant; the royal arms may have served in place of personal arms or to signal some working connection with the Court. Some familiarity with the approved iconography for James is indicated by the figures of Peace and Plenty set in niches on each side of the arms (Fig. 42).[11] Elsewhere it seems highly unlikely that the arms of James I represented anything other than an attempt to aggrandise the owner. The elaborate display of the royal arms as the centrepiece of an embellished plasterwork ceiling at 'The Old Merchant's House' in Great Yarmouth (Norfolk), seems incongruous in what was a relatively modest merchant's house, containing only two rooms on the ground floor (Fig. 43). The presence of this fashionable decoration and the inclusion of the royal arms was

[11] James Doelman, *King James I and the Religious Culture of England* (Woodbridge, 2000), p. 91.

43. Old Merchant's House, Great Yarmouth (Norf.). Interior of ground floor, showing windows and Jacobean plaster ceiling. This new town house was embellished with highly fashionable, but relatively inexpensive, decorative plasterwork – reflecting the owner's middling status. The presence of the King's arms as the centrepiece to the design may also reflect a prevailing trend. English Heritage.

probably a strategic move on behalf of a middling-level townsman to appropriate a higher authority and bolster his identity and role in the local community. Such work was also carried out during major renovations to upgrade an older property, as for example with the arms of Charles I that were painted onto the chimneybreast of a ground-floor parlour as an extension to a medieval property at 17, Palace Street in Canterbury (Kent). This sort of home improvement often coincided with the elevation of the owner to some public office.[12]

Similarly, the popular claim that 'Queen Elizabeth I slept here' may in some cases have been assumed because of the presence of her arms in domestic decoration, common in town as well as country houses. Colourful wall paintings in the parlour at Pittleworth Manor (Hants.) include as the centrepiece the royal arms of Queen Elizabeth I with the

[12] This link between public office and urban rebuilding is identified by King, 'Interpretation of Urban Buildings'.

44. Wall paintings at Pittleworth Manor (Hants.), dated 1580.
The decorative scheme combines the Royal Arms, at centre, with scenes representing the story of Dives and Lazarus (cf. Luke 16, vv. 19–31) and inscribed texts on spiritual matters.

motto 'God preserve in health oure noble Queene Elizabeth Amen ANO DOMI 1580' (Fig. 44). On either side of these arms are two pictorial scenes from the Parable of Dives and Lazarus, illustrating Luke chapter 16, while in a frieze around the top of the walls is a narrow band of inscription identifying the story along with moral texts such as: 'Repent amend and synn no more: aske grace and mersye and pittey the poore'.[13] In this way the scheme of decoration constructs an identity appropriate for the ideal householder: patriotic, pious and charitable. The royal arms of Elizabeth I adorned several chimneypieces at 229 High Street in Exeter, a massive townhouse largely rebuilt in 1584 by George Smith, a former mayor, and demolished in 1930.[14] One example in plasterwork was salvaged and is now installed in the parlour at St Nicholas Priory in Exeter (Fig. 45). Another overmantel with Elizabeth's arms, at no. 196 High Street, Exeter, is all that remains of the large merchant's house that was built there in the 1580s.

[13] For further discussion see Tara Hamling, *Decorating the Godly Household: Religious Art in Post-Reformation Britain* (New Haven and London, 2010), pp. 132–4.
[14] D. Portman, *Exeter Houses 1400–1700* (Torquay, 1966), p. 31.

45. Plasterwork overmantel with Royal Arms of Elizabeth I. From 229 High Street, Exeter, reinstalled at St Nicholas Priory, Exeter. One of several elaborate chimneypieces from a grand town house that was demolished in 1930. At least one other also contained the arms of Queen Elizabeth.

Inventories of grand town properties sometimes list royal arms in 'maps', 'tables' or pictures, as part of (re)movable household decorations.[15] Many surviving examples of contemporary cast iron fire-backs – another fashionable interior design item – include royal arms or badges, far more than could possibly have been intended for the Crown.[16] It is clear therefore that displaying the royal arms contributed towards social capital, as a sign of good citizenship and possibly also of authority in some local office. That no direct connection with the Court can be inferred simply from the presence of royal arms in interior decoration is also supported by the appearance in the later sixteenth century of printed sheets of paper incorporating the arms of England and the Tudor Rose, which could be used to adorn a range of surfaces; one surviving fragment, removed from Besford Court (Worcs.) and now in the Victoria and Albert Museum, is still attached to a section of the wattle and daub wall (Fig. 46). Similar printed paper dating from the 1580s was used to line a fine inlaid wooden box in the collection of the Shakespeare Birthplace Trust, which was probably used to store expensive ingredients for medicinal purposes.

[15] For example, an inventory of the Canterbury residence of John Semark, gent. and alderman, records in the hall a "map of the queens arms set in wainscot"; inventory of John Semark, 3 Feb. 1585, Maidstone, Kent History & Library Centre, PRC 10/14, f. 152v. My thanks to Catherine Richardson for this information.

[16] Jeremy Hodgkinson, *British Cast-Iron Firebacks of the 16th to Mid 18th Centuries* (Crawley, 2010), pp. 141–53.

213

46. Print from wood block on paper, pasted onto wattle and daub, removed from Besford Court; *c.* 1550×75. Victoria and Albert Museum, E.2431–1918. The arms of England and the Tudor rose feature as repeated motifs within a pattern, but do not indicate a direct royal connection. Such paper was expensive as wall decoration and adorned larger houses; another similar example in the Victoria and Albert Museum was removed from Howbridge Hall (Essex).

In just a few cases, however, it is possible that the royal arms were depicted as a result of some direct connection with the monarch. Painted decoration in a ground floor room at Little Gaddesden Manor (Herts.) appears to commemorate a specific episode in the life of Elizabeth I. A painted overmantel has at the centre the royal arms and ER with scenes on either side thought to depict the arrest of Elizabeth when princess, following Wyatt's rebellion in 1554. The arrest took place just two miles away at Ashridge House, a dissolved monastery converted to use as a royal residence, where Elizabeth lived for several years during the reign of Mary I. Another large painted timber panel found in the cellar in the 1890s also depicts Elizabeth with figures in the background and is described as another depiction of her arrest, but it is possible that the original decoration of the room had a wider scheme of imagery in celebration of her life and reign. Edward VI had granted the manor of Little Gaddesden to his sister while princess, and in 1576 it was leased out by the Queen for twenty-one years to Henry, Lord Cheney; this is presumably when the present house was first built, because a plaque on the west front bears the same

date.[17] It seems very possible, therefore, that the decoration of the house reflects its credentials as part of the Queen's property portfolio.

Paintings in the building now known as The Forge in Much Hadham (Herts.), once part of a medieval hall house on an H-plan, may reflect an attempt on behalf of a local dignitary to court the favour of his monarch. In a small room in the south wing fronting the street in this relatively modest building is painted a particularly elaborate representation of the royal arms of Queen Elizabeth paired with a depiction of the biblical story of the Judgement of Solomon (Figs 47–8).[18] Judging from the evidence of the costumes, the paintings appear to date from the mid 1570s. The royal arms on the west wall have as additional supporters two yeomen of the guard holding halberds, and throughout the background there are little white and red roses to represent the Tudor union of Lancaster and York. This depiction of royal heraldry is unusually sophisticated for wall painting in a domestic context and the quality of the painting of the biblical scene is also especially fine and detailed, with the action set in a contemporary courtly context. The choice of this particular scene as part of a scheme with the royal arms may have been intended as a compliment to the Queen: in state propaganda, Elizabeth was sometimes compared to Solomon, to support her identity as a wise and godly Protestant ruler. Indeed it is possible that the wall painting was intended to be seen and admired by the Queen herself. Elizabeth stayed at nearby Hadham Hall, the seat of Henry Capell, from the 13th to 16th of September 1578, as part of her planned route back to London from the summer progress to Norfolk.[19] There is no record of her activities in the area during her stay but it is certainly possible that the owner of this property hoped to receive her and carried out decorative work accordingly. The painted decoration in black and white on the east wall with its window onto the street includes two shields with the Newce coat of arms, and so we are able to associate the work with either Clement Newce (d. 1579) or his son William (d. 1610/11). Clement Newce is described on his funerary brass in the parish church 'as of Muche Hadham in the Counttye of Hertford esquier somtymes Cyttezin and Mercer of London'. He acquired manorial lands and was confirmed in his elevation to the gentry by being granted arms in 1549. It is, therefore, quite plausible that Newce commissioned these paintings with a view to receiving the Queen during her 1578 visit.[20]

[17] 'Topography: Little Gaddesden', in VCH *Herts.*, II (London, 1908), pp. 208–14, at 209.
[18] The paintings are described in Muriel Carrick and Charlotte Ryder, *The Forge, Much Hadham, Hertfordshire: 16th & 17th Century Wall Paintings* (Hertford, 2000). The story of their discovery and unconventional conservation history is recounted by Jane Rutherford, 'Sixteenth-Century Wall Paintings at The Forge, Much Hadham, Hertfordshire', in *All Manner of Murals: The History, Techniques and Conservation of Secular Wall Paintings*, ed. Robert Gowing and Robyn Pender (London, 2007), pp. 121–31.
[19] Zillah Dovey, *An Elizabethan Progress: The Queen's Journey into East Anglia, 1578* (Stroud, 1996), pp. 130–7.
[20] The paintings are associated with the Queen's 1578 visit to the area by Carrick and Ryder, *The Forge*, p. 23.

47. Royal Arms of Elizabeth I. Detail of wall paintings of *c*.1572 at 'The Forge', Much Hadham (Herts.). One of the most elaborate displays of the arms of Elizabeth, complete with additional supporters in the form of Yeomen of the Guard. The imagery seems out of all proportion to its modest domestic setting.

48. Judgement of Solomon, detail of wall paintings of *c*.1572 at 'The Forge', Much Hadham (Herts.). Might this depiction of the biblical King Solomon's wisdom have been intended as an allusion to the court of Queen Elizabeth?

'WANTING ARMS': HERALDIC DECORATION IN LESSER HOUSES

Wanting Arms

But how might householders who lacked the right to bear arms participate in the fashion for heraldic imagery in domestic decoration? As we have seen, some interior decoration from the period incorporates royal badges and emblems; these could be cast in plaster readily and repeatedly from moulds, and thus were inexpensive to manufacture. The lion, fleur-de-lis and Tudor rose, for example, are depicted on shields in plasterwork on the chimneybreast at the building known as 'Harvard House' in Stratford-upon-Avon in work carried out *c.* 1596 by Thomas Rogers, a local butcher. Henry Peacham's treatise describes another alternative, as one of his characters observes:

> Excellent have beene the conceipt of some Citizens, who wanting Armes, have coined themselves certaine devises as neere as may be alluding to their names, which wee call Rebus. Master Bishoppe caused to be painted in his glasse windowes the picture of a Bishop in his Rochet, his square cappe on his head, by which was written his Christen name George. One Foxe-craft caused to be painted in his Hall & Parlour a Foxe, counterfeiting himselfe dead upon the Ice, among a company of ducks and Goslings. These and a thousand the like, if you bee a diligent observer you shall finde both in City and Country, especially in Towne halls, Churchwalls, and Windowes, olde Monasteries and such places, which many a time and often I have enquired after as the best receipt against Melancholy.[21]

An example of this sort of rebus in domestic decoration adorned the chimneybreast in a first-floor room at Creswells Farm, Sible Hedingham (Essex). The painting included two images from classical mythology depicted within a diptych-style frame: a scene of Aeneas escaping from the burning city of Troy, carrying his father Anchises on his back, and a depiction of the three-headed giant called Geryon. The apparent lack of accompanying text leaves the meaning of the imagery unclear, but the authors of a report on the paintings point to the possibility that Geryon was considered a rebus of Jegon, the name of the family in possession of the property from 1592 through the greater part of the seventeenth century.[22] The Creswells Farm wall paintings appear to have been derived from woodcuts in Andrea Alciati's emblem book, *Emblemata*, published in various editions from 1531 onwards; clearly, the reproduction of emblems from printed books could serve in place of heraldic decoration for those householders 'wanting arms'. A wall painting discovered in 1956 at 25 Buttermarket, Bury St Edmunds (Suff.), is similar to the Creswells Farm example, with just two adjoining emblems separated by a decorative pilaster on a large chimneybreast in a first-floor room. These emblems were copied from Thomas Combe's translation of Guillaume de la Perrière, *The Theater of Fine Devices*, and so the wall paintings must postdate the year of Combe's publication, 1614.[23]

---

[21] Peacham, *Gentleman's Exercise* (cit. in n. 3), pp. 166–7.
[22] M. Carrick, P. M. Ryan and M. C. Wadhams, 'Wall Paintings at Creswells Farm, Sible Hedingham, Essex', *Archaeological Jnl.*, 144 (1987), pp. 328–39.
[23] Michael Bath and Malcolm Jones, 'Emblems from Thomas Combe in Wall Paintings at Bury St Edmunds', *Emblematica*, 10 (1996), pp. 195–203.

Finally, it is worth pointing to another iconographic type in domestic decoration of Shakespeare's time which involved heraldic display: the Nine Worthies. These heroes from the Ancient World were depicted in stone sculpture on the exterior facade of Montacute House in Somerset (*c.* 1600) and in the plasterwork frieze of the great chamber at Aston Hall in Birmingham (*c.* 1635). The nine figures were also depicted in an early seventeenth-century wall painting in a ground-floor room of a relatively modest town house in the High Street of Amersham (Bucks.).[24] At Aston and the house in Amersham, each figure holds a standard with his identifying symbol. The iconography of the Worthies as a subject for interior decoration was obviously well known to Shakespeare and his contemporaries, because a gag in *Love's Labour's Lost* relies on familiarity with Alexander the Great's symbol in the painted hangings that adorned domestic walls: "O, sir, you have overthrown Alisander the conqueror! You will be scraped out of the painted cloth for this: your lion, that holds his poll-axe sitting on a close-stool, will be given to Ajax: he will be the ninth Worthy."[25] The great illustrated manuscript of popular iconographies compiled by Thomas Trevelyon in 1608 also includes the Worthies in the same format as at Aston and Amersham, informed by the same printed source.[26] Trevelyon's drawing of Alexander includes on the standard an image of a lion sitting on a chair, which could be interpreted as a close-stool (lavatory) (Fig. 49). This imagery and the wider heraldic tradition to which it refers must therefore have been common enough for Shakespeare to expect his audience to be able to visualise this specific component, and so we can assume that a wide range of people was able to appreciate the power of its visual language.

To conclude, it is clear that heraldic imagery offered a particularly rich and versatile vocabulary for use as domestic decoration. The display of arms could be encyclopaedic and arcane, pragmatic or pretentious, personal or corporate; it could signal affiliation and allegiance to family, neighbours, monarch, city, trade or locality. The use of heraldry in domestic decoration to proclaim or claim status within specific communities was a serious business, while for those in want of arms the display of feigned pseudo-heraldic alternatives could at least amuse, offering a 'recipe against melancholy' for visitors to houses and theatres alike.

49 (opposite). Alexander the Great, from the Nine Worthies. Page from Thomas Trevelyon's Miscellany, 1608. Folger Shakespeare Library (Washington, DC), MS V.b.232. The pseudo-heraldic emblem associated with Alexander appealed to William Shakespeare's sense of humour.

[24] John L. Nevinson, 'A Show of the Nine Worthies', *Shakespeare Quarterly*, 14 (1964), pp. 103–7.
[25] Act V, Scene II.
[26] As identified by Anthony Wells-Cole, *Art and Decoration in Elizabethan and Jacobean England: The Influence of Continental Prints, 1558–1625* (New Haven and London, 1997), pp. 118–19. The Miscellany is sumptuously published as: *The Trevelyon Miscellany of 1608. A Facsimile Edition of Shakespeare Folger Library Ms V.b.252*, ed. Heather Wolfe (Washington; Folger Shakespeare Library, 2007) and is reviewed in *Journal of the Early Book Society*, 12 (2009), 317–19.

Alexander Macedon, A Pagan
2

My name is Alexander kynge of Macedon, who in my tyme
did overcome the worlde, which being done, J wept for that
J hearde there was not a-nother worlde to overcome, Darius
and the Percians can saye, soe can the Greekes, the Indi-
ans, and the Moores, that Alexanders valour hath obtay-
ned, Eternall memory, most meete for my deserts: yet should
my dutye drawe me to this homage, to honor thee fayre
Albions maiestye, And so of me being ded fame sounds her trumpe

Heraldry in Tudor and Jacobean Portraits

KAREN HEARN

The display of heraldry played a central part in allowing a viewer to identify the descent, rank, connections and power of individuals and families.[1] Accordingly, in surviving early English portraits, the inclusion of the sitter's arms became common. They were often painted onto a plain background, from which they stood out clearly; and they were most commonly placed at the upper right or upper left of the picture area. In London, although there was much institutional competition between the members of the Painter-Stainers' Company and the heralds of the College of Arms, in practice both groups had to collaborate in the painting of heraldic material on a broad range of objects and surfaces, including, we must presume, portraits.[2] A few painters were able to conduct simultaneous careers as heralds and portraitists. The most high-profile of these was Sir William Segar (*c*. 1564–1633), a client of the Earl of Leicester, and trained as a scrivener, who was appointed Portcullis Pursuivant in 1585 and rose to become Garter King of Arms in 1604.[3]

Very few portraits painted in England survive from before the beginning of the sixteenth century, and it is accordingly difficult to draw many general conclusions about the earliest images. There are, however, many similarities of format and content between early English and early Netherlandish and German portraiture. Heraldic elements had long been included in early northern European portraits, such as the small portrait by the Bruges-based painter Petrus Christus (active 1444, died 1475/6) of an English diplomat in Flanders, *Edward Grimston*, in 1446 (private collection; on loan to the National Gallery, London).[4] Grimston was an ambassador for Henry VI and is known to have visited Calais and Brussels; he holds a Lancastrian chain or collar of SS while, behind him, his arms are depicted twice, as if carved in stone, on a fictive stone wall.

The names of most of the portraitists of the English elite are now unknown, but it is clear, from the styles and techniques of the surviving images, that the painters were

---

[1] Maurice Howard and Tessa Murdoch, "Armes and Bestes': Tudor and Stuart Heraldry', in *Treasures of the Royal Courts: Tudors, Stuarts & the Russian Tsars*, ed. Olga Dmitrieva and Tessa Murdoch, exhibition catalogue (London: Victoria and Albert Museum, 2013), pp. 56–67. For examples of heraldry on gentry and merchant portraits, see Tarnya Cooper, *Citizen Portrait* (New Haven and London, 2012).

[2] Robert Tittler, 'Regional Portraiture and the Heraldic Connection in Tudor and Early Stuart England', *British Art Jnl.*, 10, no. 1 (Spring/Summer 2009), pp. 3–10; subsequently expanded as chapter 6, 'Heraldry and Portraiture', in Robert Tittler, *Portraits, Painters and Publics in Provincial England 1540–1640* (Oxford, 2012), pp. 102–24.

[3] Curiously, the *ODNB* entry on William Segar does not address his work as a painter; for this, see, currently, Erna Auerbach, *Nicholas Hilliard* (London and Boston, Mass., 1961), pp. 271–81.

very often incomers who had been born and – most importantly – *trained* in northern Europe, where highly developed workshop systems turned out many accomplished practitioners.

From the outset, it is important to be aware that some of the pigments that were used in early paintings may have faded or changed colour over time. This, of course, can be crucial in interpreting the 'tinctures' of the arms depicted in images. Plant-derived reds, such as madder, can fade away almost completely, for instance, while smalt – an (initially) rich blue pigment – tends to alter permanently, through interaction with the paint medium and exposure to light, to brown or grey.[5] Until the final decade of the sixteenth century (when canvas started to be favoured as a support) English portraits were generally painted on wooden panel, usually composed of vertical joined boards of (almost always) imported Baltic oak.[6]

Merchants' marks were only very occasionally included in English portraits (unlike in Flemish portraiture). A rare example of this for an English sitter is the full-length of *Thomas Gresham*, 1544, by an unidentified Netherlandish artist (London, Mercers' Company) (Fig. 50).[7] Almost a century later, the (by then old-fashioned) portrait of the merchant venturer *William Windover* of New Sarum, Wiltshire, of about 1633, the year of his death, includes not only the sitter's arms but also what is presumably his merchant mark.[8]

At upper right in the *c.* 1564 portrait by an unknown artist of *Robert Dudley, 1st Earl of Leicester, with a Dog*, Dudley's arms are shown encircled by the collar of the Order of the Garter, to which he had been appointed in 1559; well balanced within the composition, they appear to be original to the portrait (Fig. 51).[9] Subsequently, in January 1566, the French king, Charles IX, conferred on him the Order of St Michael, and Dudley's arms – encircled by this French order – seem then to have been squeezed in on this portrait, at upper left, to mark this later honour.

Sometimes such painted-on arms can, however, be misleading, and can turn out to have been added long after the original date of painting. When this is the case, it may

---

[4] See Joel M. Upton, *Petrus Christus: His Place in Fifteenth-Century Flemish Painting* (University Park [Pennsylvania] and London, 1990), pp. 22–32; and Maryan W. Ainsworth, *Petrus Christus: Renaissance Master of Bruges*, exhibition catalogue (New York: Metropolitan Museum of Art, 1994), pp. 62–3, Fig. 65.

[5] On smalt, see http://www.tate.org.uk/about/projects/changing-properties-smalt-over-time.

[6] For an up-to-date survey, see Karen Hearn, 'Panel-painting and Portraiture', in *The Cambridge World Shakespeare Encyclopedia*, vol. 1, *Shakespeare's World*, ed. Bruce R. Smith (Cambridge University Press, online; forthcoming).

[7] Cf. discussion of portraiture of Gresham by Karen Hearn, *Dynasties. Painting in Tudor and Jacobean England, 1530–1630*, exhibition catalogue (London: Tate Gallery, 1995), pp. 57–8.

[8] http://www.bbc.co.uk/arts/yourpaintings/paintings/william-windover-of-new-sarum-d-1633-merchant-adventurer-064976 ; I am grateful to Timothy Duke, Chester Herald, for suggesting this.

[9] Unknown artist, *Robert Dudley, 1st Earl of Leicester with a Dog*, *c.* 1564, oil on panel, 110×80 cm. (private collection), reproduced in Hearn, *Dynasties*, pp. 96–7, cat. no. 49.

50. Netherlandish School, *Sir Thomas Gresham*, 1544, oil on panel. London, Mercers Company. Gresham's merchant mark is shown at upper left; 1544 was the year of his marriage.

51. Unknown artist, *Robert Dudley, 1st Earl of Leicester with a Dog, c.*1564, oil on panel. Waddesdon, The Rothschild Collection. At right are Leicester's arms encircled by the Order of the Garter; at left, added, are the same arms within the Order of St Michael; 110 × 81 cm.

ÆTATIS X
M·D·LXV

HERALDRY IN TUDOR AND JACOBEAN PORTRAITS

well be that they do not actually relate to the person depicted. Such an example is Hans Eworth's spectacularly attired *Unknown Lady, c.* 1565×8, which was formerly at Wentworth Castle (Fig. 52).[10] Although her rich dress and copious jewellery indicate that the sitter is of extremely high rank, the large and elaborate coat of arms at upper left was, in fact, added as much as a century later, and cannot refer to the sitter herself. The arms had been borne by Henry Clifford, 2nd Earl of Cumberland, and by his wife Eleanor Brandon, the daughter of Henry VIII's sister Mary – who accordingly was for many years thought to be the subject of the portrait. Eleanor, however, died in 1547, about twenty years before the date of this painting. Subsequently, it was suggested that the sitter might be the Cumberlands' only child, Margaret Clifford (1540–96), who in 1555 married Henry Stanley, Lord Strange, later 4th earl of Derby. Margaret would have been aged twenty-five to twenty-eight during these years, although, as a married lady, one would expect her to have used not her parents' arms but her own combined with those of her husband. Lorne Campbell has, however, shown that in sixteenth- and early seventeenth-century English portraits, married women sometimes were represented by their maiden (or parental?) coat of arms, surmounted by helmet and crest.[11]

The panel on which it is painted is made up from three vertical oak boards, the right-hand one having been cut down as described in footnote 9. An unfaded strip of paint, which had long been protected by the frame along the bottom, shows that the present pink of the pearl-studded dress was originally a much deeper shade of rose madder, or red. The background of the portrait, on the other hand, was probably originally lighter in colour, but seems to have been covered by a layer of dark brown paint quite early in the painting's history. Interestingly, it appears that a space for a coat of arms was reserved in the original background, where it can be now seen, in X-ray, as a smaller, blank shield shape under the present elaborate cartouche.

The Wentworth Castle collection also contained another portrait by Eworth: an unknown lady, aged twenty-four, dated 1563 and of similar size. In that, the Wentworth arms are placed at the left-hand edge, as if to match those in a now-lost pendant portrait of a husband, whose arms would have been painted at the right-hand edge of *his*

---

[10] Hans Eworth (active 1540–74), *Unknown Lady, c.* 1565×8, oil on panel, 99.8×61.9 cm. (Tate Gallery, T03896), reproduced *ibid.*, pp. 71-3, cat. no. 28. At some time prior to 1866, a strip 7.5 cm. (3 in.) wide was removed from the right-hand side of the painting and part of the inscription was consequently lost. So, while the truncated Roman numerals – 'ÆTATIS X[...] M.D.LXV [...]' at top right – can refer only to a painting date of 1565×8, the age of the sitter is now unknown. The approximate original proportions were reconstructed (during conservation at the Tate Gallery during the 1980s) by placing a loose strip of wood in the frame to represent the missing section.

[11] L. Campbell, 'Holbein's Miniature of Mrs Pemberton: The Identity of the Sitter', *Burlington Magazine*, cxxix (1987), pp. 366–71, at 368–9. The miniature of *Jane Pemberton, Mrs Small*, of about 1540, bears on the back of its case what seems to be her own coat of arms in what is presumed to be a faithful 17th-century copy of a 16th-century original.

---

52 (opposite): Hans Eworth, *Unknown Lady, c.*1565–8, oil on panel, 99.8×61.9 cm. London, Tate Gallery. The elaborate but misleading coat of arms (upper left) was added many years later.

53. Hans Eworth, *Thomas Howard, 4th Duke of Norfolk*, 1563, oil on panel, 108.6 × 81.3 cm. Private Collection.

54. Hans Eworth, *Margaret Audley, duchess of Norfolk*, 1562, oil on panel. Collection of Lord Braybrooke, on display by English Heritage at Audley End House (Essex).

55. Gerlach Flicke, *Archbishop Thomas Cranmer*, 1545×6, oil on panel, 98.9 × 76.2. National Portrait Gallery. Cranmer's armorial finger-ring is carefully painted to be clearly legible to viewers of this portrait.

56. Cornelius Johnson, *Susanna Temple*, 1620, oil on panel, 67.9 × 51.8 cm. London, Tate Gallery.
A martlet – the heraldic bird that is the Temple family crest – can be seen in Susanna's earring, above the rectangular black diamond.

portrait.[12] Sir Roy Strong suggested that the ladies portrayed might be two of the three daughters of Thomas, 1st Baron Wentworth of Nettlestead (1501–51): Jane (d. 1614), Margaret (d. 1587) and Dorothy.[13] Each married advantageously more than once, although their exact wedding dates are not known.

Arms in portraits might also be depicted as embroidered or woven into fictive textiles (just as they were in real textiles). An exceptional example of the representation of heraldic textiles is Hans Eworth's visually linked pair of portraits of *Thomas Howard, 4th Duke of Norfolk*, 1562, and his second wife, *Margaret Audley, Duchess of Norfolk*, 1562 (Figs 53–4).[14] In the Duke's portrait, the post-Flodden Howard arms, supported by the Duke's Howard lion, which is stitched into the background hanging on the right, correspond with those of Audley (supported by the 'Audley Beast') in the hanging that continues behind the Duchess, on the left-hand side, in her portrait.

Items of jewellery that bear heraldic elements might be included in portraits, affirming the identity of the sitter. Tudor and early Stuart heraldic seal rings, moreover, survive in considerable numbers.[15] In Gerlach Flicke's signed portrait of *Archbishop Thomas Cranmer* (Fig. 55), painted in 1545 or 1546, the sitter wears such a ring on the forefinger of his left hand, carefully positioned to be clearly legible to someone viewing the portrait at close quarters. The arms are those of Cranmer, quartered with those of Cranmer impaled by the arms of Aslacton.[16] At some point prior to 1539, the Cranmer arms had apparently been changed, on the instructions of Henry VIII, from three cranes between a chevron to three pelicans between a chevron, as shown in the portrait.[17]

Heraldic elements in portraits, whether shown in jewellery or textiles, can sometimes moreover become crucial aids in recovering the identity of a sitter. This was the case with Cornelius Johnson's 1620 portrait of *Susanna* (or Susan) *Temple* (Fig. 56),

---

[12] Art Institute of Chicago; see Roy Strong, *The English Icon: Elizabethan & Jacobean Portraiture* (London and New York, 1969), p. 96, no. 38.

[13] Sir Roy Strong, letter of 7 January 1986, Tate Gallery files.

[14] Hans Eworth, *Thomas Howard, 4th Duke of Norfolk*, 1562, oil on panel, 108.6 × 81.3 cm. (private collection) and *Margaret Audley, Duchess of Norfolk*, 1562, oil on panel (Lord Braybrooke; on display at Audley End, Essex); both reproduced in Hearn, *Dynasties*, pp. 70–2, no. 27 and Fig. 31, and in *Elizabeth I & Her People*, ed. Tarnya Cooper and Jane Eade, exhibition catalogue (London: National Portrait Gallery, 2013), pp. 80–2, nos 17a and 17b.

[15] For example, the Boteler Ring, England, *c*. 1580, gold, engraved and cast (London, Victoria and Albert Museum, M.99–1984), illustrated in Dmitrieva and Murdoch, *Treasures of the Royal Courts* (cit. in n. 1), p. 152, Fig. 193.

[16] For a detail of this ring, see http://images.npg.org.uk/MATBimg/std/6/3/535_2007_micro09.jpg

[17] Gerlach Flicke, *Archbishop Thomas Cranmer*, 1545 or 1546, oil on panel, 98.9 × 76.2 cm. (London, National Portrait Gallery); see entry by Catharine MacLeod in Hearn, *Dynasties*, pp. 48–9, cat. no. 12; for the Cranmer arms, see Ralph Morice, 'Anecdotes and Character of Archbishop Cranmer', in *Narratives of the Days of the Reformation*, ed. J.G. Nichols (Camden Soc., orig. ser., 77, 1859), pp. 234–72.

57. George Gower, *Self-portrait*, 1579, oil on panel, 56.4 × 49.6 cm. Private Collection.
Photography by Chris Titmus, © copyright Hamilton Kerr Institute.
In the metal balance below the lines of verse, Gower has depicted a pair of dividers,
representing his profession as a painter, as outweighing his family coat of arms.

58. Attributed to John de Critz, *Robert Cecil, 1st Earl of Salisbury*, *c.*1602, oil on panel, 90.2 × 73.4 cm. National Portrait Gallery. The heraldic seal-bag on the table indicates Cecil's post as the Queen's Principal Secretary.

59. Robert Peake, *Henry, Prince of Wales and Sir John Harington*, 1603, oil on canvas. New York, Metropolitan Museum of Art. Photo. © SCALA, Florence. The two youths are identified by the small heraldic shields that are painted as though suspended from tree-twigs above their heads, and by their inscribed ages.

the only daughter of Sir Alexander Temple (1583–1629).[18] Her own date of birth is not recorded, but was probably between September 1603 and June 1607.[19] By July 1626, she had married Sir Gifford Thornhurst of Agnes Court (Kent), who died in December 1627.[20] In 1633 she remarried, to Sir Martin Lister of Thorpe Arnold (Leicestershire), by whom she had five daughters and five sons.[21]

Susanna is depicted wearing a drop earring, of which the central element is a martlet – a bird that is part of the Temple coat of arms. When a group of family portraits at Harlaxton (Lincolnshire) was published in 1888, this work was erroneously described as 'A Lady of the De Ligne Family', while a different portrait was identified as being of Susanna Temple.[22] Meanwhile, a copy or second version of the present portrait – one that seems largely to have been repainted after a fire in 1878 – had acquired the later (inaccurate) inscription: 'Eliz. dau. of Wm L. Petre & wife to Wm Sheldon AD 1621'.[23] The original portrait had, however, been engraved in the late seventeenth century by Robert White (1645–1703) and captioned with Susanna's name and titles,[24] and this, confirmed by the sitter's martlet earring, secures the identification of the sitter as Susanna Temple.

Heraldry could also interact with the emblems and visual devices that so often appear in sixteenth-century English portraits. A particularly sophisticated example is in the only known large-scale sixteenth-century self-portrait by a British artist – that of George Gower (Fig. 57), who came from a Yorkshire gentry family. Neither Gower's date of birth nor where and with whom he trained as a painter is known. The painting, dated 1579, shows Gower holding a brush and palette (with carefully arranged, differently coloured, reserves of paint set out on it) in his left hand. Above, in the pans of a finely delineated metal balance, a pair of dividers (representing the artist's trade) is shown ostensibly outweighing his family's coat of arms.[25] Over this device, an eight-line verse expresses Gower's pride in his professional skill, which he compares to the military

---

[18] Cornelius Johnson (1593–1661), *Portrait of Susanna Temple*, 1620, oil on panel, 67.9 × 51.8 cm. (Tate Gallery, T03250).

[19] Information kindly supplied by John Matthews, August 2003; see also his essay 'The Temple Family Portraits by Cornelius Johnson and Others', *Genealogists' Magazine*, 31, no.1 (March 2013), pp. 5–13.

[20] *Ibid.*; Matthews notes that there is a memorial in Etchingham church (Suss.), dated 1626, to an unnamed son of the couple.

[21] Her second son, the zoologist Martin Lister (born 1639), later became physician to Queen Anne; see J. D. Woodley, 'Lister, Martin (*bap.* 1639, d. 1712)', in *ODNB*, 33, pp. 986–7, and online.

[22] H. Walpole, *Anecdotes of Painting in England*, with additions by J. Dallaway, ed. R. N. Wornum, 3 vols (London, 1888), I, p. 212 n. 4.

[23] Now at the Petre family home, Ingatestone (Essex).

[24] The engraving includes the caption: 'C: Iohnson pinxit 1620. R: White Sculp: Susanna Temple. The only daughter of Sr. Alexander Temple Knight. Ladie Thornhurst. Ladie Lister.'

[25] E. K. Waterhouse, 'A Note on George Gower's *Selfportrait* at Milton Park', *Burlington Magazine*, xc (1948), p. 267.

achievements that had in the past gained his family its gentry status:

> Thogh youthfull ways me did intyse, From armes and vertew e[ke]
> yet thanckt be God for his god gift, w[hi]ch long did rest as slepe
> Now skill revyves with gayne, and lyfe to leade in rest
> by pensils [*that is, 'brushes'*] trade, wherefore I must, esteem of it as best
> The proof wherof this balance show, and armes my birth displays
> what Perents bare by just re[n]owme, my skill mayntenes the prayes
> And them whose vertew, fame and acts, have won for me this shield
> I reverence muche w[i]th servyce eke, and thanks to them do yield.[26]

The portrait, nevertheless, still ensures that viewers know that Gower comes of an arms-bearing family. Two years later, in 1581, Gower was appointed Serjeant Painter to Elizabeth I, and from then until his death in 1596 his name appears regularly in the royal accounts, for both decorative and heraldic painting.[27]

These few examples serve not only to illustrate the widespread inclusion of heraldry in portraits during the sixteenth and early seventeenth centuries – the 'age of Shakespeare' – but should also act as reminders of the need to be attentive to the material considerations of dealing with fragile and mutable pigments, wooden panels and canvas, which may have undergone many interventions and changes over the four hundred or more years since they were painted.

---

[26] See Hearn, *Dynasties*, pp. 107–8, cat. no. 57, and *Elizabeth I and Her People*, ed. Cooper and Eade, p. 174, no. 67.

[27] See K. Hearn, 'Gower, George (d. 1596)', in *ODNB*, 23, pp. 103–4, and online. The role of the Serjeant Painter was a managerial one, including responsibility for carrying out painting at, and of, royal properties, and it also gave rights in the purveying of art materials.

Heraldic Language and Identity in Shakespeare's Plays

BEATRICE GROVES

In Shakespeare and Fletcher's *All is True* (1612–13), Queen Katherine laments that 'like the lily | That once was mistress of the field and flourished, | I'll hang my head and perish'.[1] It is an image in which natural imagery is given depth through both a biblical echo and a heraldic pun.[2] 'Field' is the heraldic name for the surface or background of a shield, and lilies (in the form of fleurs-de-lis) were a prominent part of the royal arms of England – arms that Katherine will no longer own when she ceases to be Queen. The underlying heraldic meaning of the image, therefore, gives its elegiac beauty a political edge. In *All is True* Katherine fights boldly to preserve her royal status, and ten lines earlier she has declared to Wolsey that "nothing but death | Shall e'er divorce my dignities" (3.1.140–1). The heraldic undertow of her plaintive image reflects on the idea that it is only in death that she will cease to be royal.

Shakespeare's unobtrusive, thoroughgoing heraldic imagery is one understudied aspect of his reflection of, and participation in, the visual culture of his time.[3] Shakespeare's heraldic language often (as in the above example) portrays the visual mode as something which accurately reflects deeper truths. *All is True* – as the name suggests – is attentive to visual modes of apprehending truth, and it is this concern which lies behind Shakespeare's creative engagement with heraldic language. It has been influentially argued that the social and religious upheavals of the early modern period 'provoke a keen, apparently nearly universal suspicion of "appearances" ... [which] produces a distinctive way of thinking about human subjectivity that emphasizes the disparity between what a person is and what he or she seems to other people'.[4] Shakespeare's heraldic language, however, challenges this position for it implicitly accepts a non-ironic relation between appearance and reality. In the early modern theory of heraldry, outward signs are accurate signifiers of inner worth. Heraldry was then understood to give people a fixed and visible identity: a person was who his armorial bearings proclaimed him to be.

This essay argues that, for all the subtlety and complexity with which Shakespeare employs heraldic language, at its heart this language marks an acceptance of visual modes of apprehending truth and identity. Arms are intimately linked with identity: one modern

---

[1] *Henry VIII*, 3.1.150–2. All references to Shakespeare's works are to: *William Shakespeare: The Complete Works*, ed. Stanley Wells and Gary Taylor (Oxford, 1986).
[2] See: Hannibal Hamlin, *The Bible in Shakespeare* (Oxford, 2013), pp. 114–15.
[3] For an overview of this field, see Chloe Porter, 'Shakespeare and Early Modern Visual Culture,' *Literature Compass*, 8 (2011), pp. 543–53.
[4] Katharine Eisaman Maus, *Inwardness and Theater in the English Renaissance* (Chicago, 1995), p. 210.

specialist has written that 'arms represent people or groups of people as though they themselves were present. The presence of a coat of arms acts as a substitute for the person even after his death'.[5] Heraldic language is particularly important for theatrical characters who are trying to forge their identities. In John Ford's *Perkin Warbeck* (1634), the young pretender to the throne proudly proclaims himself 'lion-hearted' and compares himself to 'sunbeams':[6] images that link him to heraldic badges of royalty. In different ways the Bastard (in *King John* (c. 1592)) and Hal (in the second tetralogy (c. 1595–9)) are likewise trying to prove themselves to be royal, and for them also the heraldic images of the lion and the sun are crucial to their self-presentation. Heraldic imagery is also important in Shakespeare's presentation of female identity, and this essay will explore this aspect of his language in two of his most richly heraldic texts: *The Rape of Lucrece* (1593–4) and *Cymbeline* (1609–10). These texts share a climactic scene in which a man describes a sleeping, naked woman – and in these scenes poetic blazon (a mannered evocation of feminine beauty rendered in its constituent parts) interacts with heraldic blazon (the verbal description of a coat of arms). Jonathan Sawday has argued for the essentially homosocial nature of poetic blazon – 'competing males exercising their wit at the expense of partitioned females'[7] – and in heraldry likewise women are very much the second sex.[8] Shakespeare uses this fundamental inequality to invest his heroines with power as they commandeer the male world of blazon. Olivia not only mockingly takes over Cesario's poetic blazon of her beauty (*Twelfth Night*, 1.5.233-8) but also performs her own blazon of him: '"I am a gentleman." I'll be sworn thou art. | Thy tongue, thy face, thy limbs, actions and spirit | Do give thee five-fold blazon' (1.5.281-3).[9] The language of armory in *Lucrece* and *Cymbeline*, like Olivia's blazon, creates a playful yet non-satiric correspondence between apparent and inner worth. Olivia uses a heraldic term – her 'five-fold blazon' refers to the five generations of arms needed to create a 'Gentleman perfect'[10] – but Viola's gentility is proved instead through her own self: her speech, action, spirit and physical beauty. Viola's worth can be seen through her disguise: she is her own coat of arms. Women are not treated as equals by the law of arms, but the

5 Ottfried Neubecker with J. P. Brooke-Little, *Heraldry: Sources, Symbols and Meaning*, 2nd edn. (Twickenham, 1997), p. 7.
6 *The Dramatic Works of John Ford*, ed. Henry Weber, 2 vols (Edinburgh, 1811), vol. I, pp. 195 (Act 5, scene 4), 210 (Act 5, scene 3).
7 Jonathan Sawday, *The Body Emblazoned: Dissection and the Human Body in Renaissance Culture* (London, 1995), p. 201.
8 For example women are unable to transmit their arms to their children unless their husband is likewise armigerous.
9 Other blazoning heroines include: Cleopatra (*Antony and Cleopatra*, 5.2.78–89), Beatrice (*Much Ado*, 1.1.65-66, 2.1.274-7), Juliet (*Romeo and Juliet*, 2.5.24-34) and Katherina (*Taming of the Shrew*, 2.1.219-25).
10 'To the making of a Gentleman perfect in his bloud, it is required, that he can lay five discents successively and lineally, on the part of his father, as, that his first Auncestor, that obtained the coat, was in degree above him, five steps ascending': John Ferne, *Blazon of Gentrie* (1586), p. 87. See also Guy Cadogan Rothery, *The Heraldry of Shakespeare* (London, 1931), p. 79.

heraldic language surrounding Shakespeare's heroines makes their virtue the vouch of their nobility. Characters such as Imogen, Viola and Lucrece blazon their true virtue through their outward appearance: a correspondence of sign and signified that the law of arms itself desires, but does not fully realise.

The Moral Symbolism of Heraldry

Popular sixteenth-century heraldic works – such as Gerard Legh's *Accedens of Armory* (first published in 1562), John Bossewell, *Workes of Armorie* (1572), John Ferne's *Blazon of Gentrie* (1586) and William Wyrley's *True Use of Armorie* (1592) – encouraged a new approach to heraldry by creating a complex system in which colours and charges are suffused with symbolic meaning. Legh, for example, gives a moral significance to every combination or colour and metal in a coat of arms. He writes that the joining of sable with gold on a shield means that the bearer will be 'constant in eyerye thynge, also in love' or that silver alone 'signifieth to the bearer thereof Chastitie, virginitie, cleare conscience, & Charitie'.[11] Although inimical to professional heralds, this desire to read meaning into the language of armory is clear from an early period. Henry VI's grant of arms to King's College, Cambridge, for example, described the arms thus: 'In a black field three silver roses, having in mind that our newly founded college enduring for ages to come, whose perpetuity we wish to be signified by the stability of the black colour, may bring forth the rightest flowers redolent in every kind of sciences'.[12] In the early Elizabethan period, elaborate arms became the norm, and these 'overcrowded'[13] shields seem to have been linked with their bearer's desire to read meaning into their arms. The 1561 grant of arms to Dr John Caius, for example, notes the symbolism of its many charges: 'betokening by the boke lerning: by the ii serpentes resting upon the square marble stone, wisdom with grace founded & stayed upon vertues sable stone: by sengrene & flower gentle, immortality y^t [that] never shall fade'.[14]

Heraldry carried a mystique in the early modern period which gave it additional power as a literary language: it combined descriptive clarity with an implication of hidden, arcane mysteries. While medieval armory had prioritised clarity, the heraldic textbooks of the Elizabethan and Jacobean period cultivated an air of mystery – to the extent that one twentieth-century heraldic writer has complained that 'heraldic language has not always been mystifying ... It was owing to the decadence of heraldry during the Tudor period that the Elizabethan heralds, most of whom cared little and understood less about the subject, began to mask their ignorance with a needless elaboration of heraldic nomenclature'.[15] One of the sections of Edmund Bolton's *Elements of Armories* (1610)

---

[11] Gerard Legh, *The Accedens of Armory* (London, 1576), ff. 3v, 5. The 1576 edition is cited throughout this chapter.
[12] W. H. St John Hope, *A Grammar of English Heraldry*, 2nd edn., revised by A. R. Wagner (Cambridge, 1953), p. 66.
[13] *Ibid.*, p. 72.
[14] *Ibid.*, p. 72.
[15] *Ibid.*, p. 78.

is entitled 'The mysteries',[16] and Legh's *Accedens of Armory* hints likewise at heraldry's 'misteries' and states that he has taken an oath not to reveal them.[17] Ferne's *Blazon of Gentrie* highlights this aspect of heraldic language and writes that the 'secret emblems' on coat-armour – 'The *hieroglyphics* of Nobility' – are comparable to the Egyptian practice of using 'holy, and sacred sculptures, or ingravings, to signify the hidden or secret conceit of their mind'.[18] This tension between the visible and the mysterious invested heraldic language with a peculiar power. As the language of power and display it would have been comprehended to some extent by everybody, but it was also an enigmatic and specialized dialect that retained the prestige of mystery.

For poets and playwrights of this era, heraldry offered a means of representing social and moral values in a way that medieval heralds could never have envisioned. Spenser used heraldic symbolism to give an additional layer of meaning to the decorative accoutrements of his faerie knights: the lions and fleurs-de-lis embossed on Mercilla's throne (5.9.27) recall the royal arms of England, 'gules three lions passant guardant or, quartering azure three fleurs-de-lis or'.[19] Elizabeth is clearly figured in *The Faerie Queene* (1590–6) in characters such as Britomart and Belphoebe, but the poet tells us that she can be found 'in mirrours more than one' (3.proem.5). In the description of Mercilla, one of the less flattering images of the Queen is subtly expressed through heraldic images. In another passage, Spenser describes Arthur's shield as being made of diamond and having no charge. The diamond indicates his adamantine purity – 'this ston is called of the Greekes, by the name of a vertue, as may not be daunted' – and the lack of a charge signifies a young knight who has not yet proven himself.[20] Spenser is highlighting that part of the Arthurian legend which is his own construct: not the boy or king of legend, but as a young prince learning the virtues of good governance. This kind of symbolic heraldic imagery is of particular interest for Spenser, as he is writing an allegorical poem: a work intent on exploring the relationship between appearance and reality. Braggadochio's shield 'bore the Sunne brode blazed in a golden field' (5.3.14). One of the heraldic conventions which keeps the language succinct is that charges (for which the tincture is not given) have a default colour. In the case of the sun, its proper colour is gold. Not only do Braggadochio's arms disobey the primary rule of heraldry, that a metal

---

[16] Edmund Bolton, *The Elements of Armories* (London, 1610), sig. A3.
[17] Legh, *Accedens*, f. 110v. For the secret signs of bastardy, see f. 65.
[18] Ferne, *Blazon*, p. 26, sig. A1v, p. 148.
[19] Edmund Spenser, *The Faerie Queene*, ed. A. C. Hamilton, H. Yamashita and T. Suzuki (Harlow, 2001), p. 573. All references are to this edition.
[20] Legh, *Accedens*, f. 8. There may also be a specific reference to Perseus, whose 'Christiline shielde' had no charge until he had killed the Medusa (f. 16v). Spenser may also be also excising a traditional Marian aspect of Arthur's shield to create his Protestant prince. Juliana Berners gives a traditional blazon of Arthur's arms as 'a Crosse of silver in a fielde of vert, and on the right side an Image of the virgin Mary with her Sonne in her armes': G[ervase] M[arkham], *The Gentlemans Academie* (1595), f. 59r–v.

must not be put on a metal,[21] but by putting the same metal against itself they mark a particularly extreme flouting of this rule. Braggadochio's arms – a gold sun on a gold field – declare him to be the sham knight that he is.

In the late sixteenth century, the martial function of heraldry was decreasing in importance and the ornate, precise and highly prestigious language of armorial bearings gained a wider, and more metaphorical, function. Heraldry was fashionable in the sixteenth century, but more crucially it was the language of power.[22] As such it was both highly visible and widely comprehensible.[23] In Shakespeare's *Rape of Lucrece* the heroine believes that her face, like a blotted escutcheon, will reveal her rape:

> Yea, the illiterate that know not how
> To cipher what is writ in learned books,
> Will cote my loathsome trespass in my looks.[24]

Lucrece's face is described as a coat of arms throughout this poem and hence 'cote' here (an archaic spelling of 'quote', meaning to 'notice, observe, mark [or] scrutinize'[25]) carries a pun on the 'coats' that even the illiterate could decipher. Armorial bearings and badges were prominent on buildings, tombs, stained glass, seals, coins, chimney-pieces, wall-hangings and banners. In many churches the royal arms were displayed where Doom paintings once had been.[26] The thriving trade in heraldic books likewise expresses its popularity in the period: there were at least forty-six heraldic works published during Elizabeth's reign.[27]

---

[21] Hope, *Grammar of Heraldry*, p. 14.

[22] In keeping with the connection between heraldry and power, Shakespeare sometimes uses the language of armory to impart grandeur – as in Constance's 'for my grief's so great | That no supporter but the huge firm earth | Can hold it up. Here I and sorrows sit; | Here is my throne; bid kings come bow to it' (*King John*, 2.2.71–4). A supporter is 'a figure of an animal, mythical creature, human being, etc., represented as holding up or standing beside the shield': *Oxford English Dictionary*, XVII, pp. 260-1, §4, s.v. 'Supporter'

[23] The in-depth knowledge that Shakespeare might have expected from his audience is suggested not only by the number of heraldic references, but also by the fact that some call for somewhat arcane knowledge: for example, in *Richard II* the Black Prince is described as one who 'In war was never lion raged more fierce, | In peace was never gentle lamb more mild' (2.1.174–5). This description would have been particularly resonant for those who were aware of his unusual practice of having one armorial shield in battle, and another for times of peace: Scott-Giles, *Shakespeare's Heraldry*, p. 59.

[24] *The Rape of Lucrece*, ll. 810–12.

[25] *Oxford English Dictionary*, XIII, p. 53, s.v. 'Quote', as verb, §5.b. The meaning of 'cipher' here ('to decipher') is the only example given by the *OED*.

[26] W. H. St John Hope, *Heraldry for Craftsmen & Designers* (London, 1913), pp. 52–62, 319–46 and passim; Michael P. Siddons, *Heraldic Badges in England and Wales*, 3 vols (London: Society of Antiquaries, 2009), I, pp. 21–161; H. Munro Cautley, *Royal Arms and Commandments in Our Churches* (Ipswich, 1974), pp. 27–8, plates 4, 55.

[27] See: Thomas Moule, *Bibliotheca Heraldica Magnae Britanniae* (London, 1822), pp. 16–56.

HERALDIC LANGUAGE AND IDENTITY IN SHAKESPEARE'S PLAYS

Touchstone's declaration that 'we quarrel in print, by the book, as you have books for good manners' (*As You Like It*, 5.4.88–9) may be a direct reference to one of these works: William Segar's *Booke of Honor and Armes* (1590), which lays out in painstaking detail exactly how knights should take offence.[28] The prime authority of Shakespeare's era was Legh's *Accedens of Armory*[29] and there are a striking number of parallels to this text in Shakespeare's works. Sir Nathaniel explains in the Pageant of the Nine Worthies: 'my scutcheon plain declares that I am Alisander' but Costard mocks 'your lion, that holds his pole-axe sitting on a close-stool, will be given to Ajax. He will be the ninth worthy'.[30] The performers have accurately copied Legh's blazon of Alexander's shield – 'Geules, a Lion Or, seiante in a Chayer, holdyng a battayle Axe Argent'[31] – and Costard's witticism may have been inspired by Legh's 'chair' (which like Ajax ['a jakes'] was slang for a privy), leading him to suggest (via canting heraldry) that Alexander's arms would be more suitable for Ajax.[32]

Much of Shakespeare's animal lore, likewise, finds a parallel in Legh, for whom the characteristics of animals are crucial for their suitability as charges. Hamlet's air-eating Chameleon[33] and backwards-walking crab are both in Legh and in the latter case give an added barb to Hamlet's comparison of Polonius to a crab by suggesting what this unusual movement might signify: 'yet where all other go forwarde, this goeth sidelong, or backewarde, The crabbe getteth his living by pollicy'.[34] Likewise Legh gives the 'temple-haunting martlet' (*Macbeth*, 1.6.4) which nests in Macbeth's battlements a possibly pertinent armorial significance. Legh, like Banquo, notes that 'the Martilet breedeth and dwelleth in aunceint houses of honour, as Castelles, and Towers' and gives this as one reason that the martlet is the symbol worn on the shield of the fourth son as a mark of cadency (each son bore a different mark to signify where they lie in the succession). Legh argues that the martlet is the mark of cadency of the fourth brother 'because he is so far from the house of inheritaunce, he must be a travayler on the sea, a horseman in fielde, or a worthy captaine of a Castel, and so to live gentleman like, & aspire to honour'.[35] The martlet symbolizes the unlikelihood of the person who bears it ever succeeding to the title, and reminds them to live a virtuous life without expectation. Macbeth is unlikely to lawfully inherit the throne (as Duncan has two sons) but has not

---

[28] Ibid., pp. 37–8.
[29] Oswald Barron, 'Heraldry,' in *Shakespeare's England*, ed. S. Lee and C. T. Onions, 2 vols (Oxford, 1916), II, pp. 74–90, at 78.
[30] *Love's Labour's Lost*, 5.2.561, 572–4.
[31] Legh, *Accedens of Armory*, f. 23. Legh's book also gives a detailed account of Lear's story: f. 96r–v.
[32] *Oxford English Dictionary*, I, p. 288, and II, pp. 1069–71, *s.v.* 'Ajax', 'Chair.' Canting heraldry – heraldry that punned on the bearer's name – was very popular: Hope, *Grammar of Heraldry*, pp. 32, 59.
[33] "Excellent, i'faith, of the chameleon's dish. I eat the air, promise-crammed" (*Hamlet*, 3.2.90–1); 'his lyving is onely of the Ayer, and never eateth anye thinge': Legh, *Accedens*, f. 83.
[34] Legh, *Accedens*, f. 86. Hamlet says to Polonius "if, like a crab, you could go backward" (2.2.205).
[35] Legh, *Accedens*, f. 108v. See below, Fig. 60.

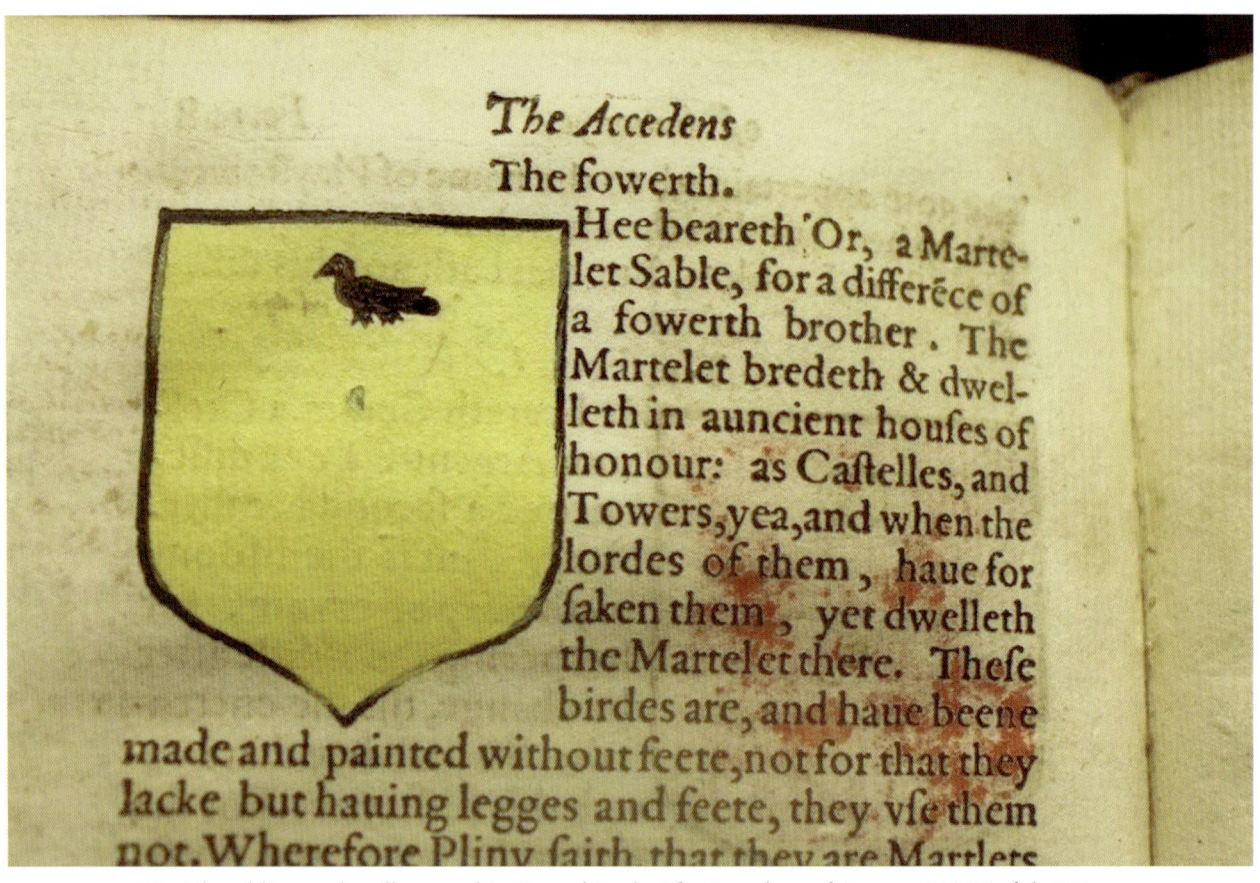

60. A heraldic martlet, illustrated in Gerard Legh, *The Accedens of Armory* (1568), fol. 108v. Bodeian Library, 4° A.13 Art.

learnt the virtue of living without expectation. Banquo's long speech about the martlet – observing that its presence means 'that the heaven's breath | Smells wooingly here' (1.6.5–6) – is pregnant with dramatic irony, which is further strengthened by the bird's heraldic import.

Cadency was part of the system of differencing, which made it possible for a son to bear his ancestral arms while his father was still alive, and yet not be mistaken for him, by the addition to the coat of a small distinguishing sign, a *brisure* or a mark of difference.[36] When Beatrice says of Benedict – "if he have wit enough to keep himself warm, let him bear it for a difference between himself and his horse" (*Much Ado*, 1.1.64–6) – she transforms even Benedict's wit (proof of his difference from his horse, in a non-heraldic sense) into an heraldic mark of 'difference' which actually serves to

[36] For a very unusual example of a literary use of marks of cadency, see the heraldic description of a hanging in Robert Wilson's play *The Three Ladies of London*: '2. trees rampant, | And then over them lay a sower tree parsant, | With a man like you in a greene field pendant, | Having a hempen halter about his necke, | With a knot under the left eare because | You are a younger brother': R. W., *Three Ladies of London*, Old English Drama: Students' Facsimile Edition (London, 1911), sig. E4.

connect them. Benedict is being described as the son of a horse (hence his need for a mark of 'difference') and – given the insulting context – Beatrice presumably intends an allusion to one of the famously stupid scions of horses: asses or donkeys.

When Ophelia distributes her rue she says "there's rue for you, and here's some for me. We may call it herb-grace o' Sundays. O, you must wear your rue with a difference" (4.5.180-2). In the theatre Ophelia generally gives this rue (the flower of repentance) to Gertrude. However, as women did not bear any differencing on their arms, it is perhaps more likely that she presents the rue to Laertes (the brother who would naturally bear the same arms – rue – as herself).[37] The cadency of Laertes' arms would have disappeared on Polonius's death (as he would now be the inheritor of his father's full armorial bearings), so it seems possible that the mark of difference that Ophelia has in mind is the mark of bastardy. Laertes claims that 'that drop of blood that's calm proclaims me bastard' (4.5.116), and Ophelia could be likewise implying that as Laertes has not yet revenged himself, his sorrow cannot by any means be compared to hers; he cannot be Polonius's true son.

Heraldry and Double Meanings

These marks of difference are potent examples of the creative possibilities of heraldic language. Heraldry made identity visible and its pedantry over minutiae – such as marks of cadency – gave it a technical precision which Shakespeare could use creatively. Heraldic terminology is also rife with words – such as 'coat', 'colours', 'herald', 'stain', 'difference', 'arms', 'crest', 'shield', 'blazon', 'field', 'charge', 'cognizance' – which were specific heraldic terms and yet also bear a wider meaning. Legh tells of a gentleman who is scornful about the whole concept of armory and insists on misunderstanding when a herald asks to see his coat, sending for his overcoat instead. The herald is offended by this joke and repeats that he would like to see the gentleman's coat of arms: "Armes, quod he, I would have good leggs, for myne armes are indifferent."[38] Shakespeare frequently uses such heraldic puns: in *Henry VI Part 2* the field vert of Cade's supposed arms denotes an actual field – green as the grass on which he was born – and as Dick claims, "the field is honourable" (4.2.51), because armorists considered ancient, plain arms (such as a field vert) as honourable. *The Merry Wives of Windsor* (1597) opens with Sir Hugh Evans demonstrating his heraldic ignorance: he uses 'passant' when he means 'passing well' and he thinks that to 'quarter' a coat means to cut it up (1.1.17, 25). He also mishears the 'dozen white luces' (pike fish) on Shallow's arms as 'louses' (1.1.14,

---

[37] Women did not bear marks of cadency, because as they would not inherit (or take part in combat) it did not matter whether their arms were unique: 'Gentlewomen maye beare there fathers cotes whole without defference. For if a Gentilman have twenty daughters, and mo, yet they shall all beare there fathers Armes without difference. But there is an order of bearing the same, which while the gentlewoman is a mayd, she must beare the same in losinge [lozenge] wise': Legh, *Accedens*, f. 97v. See also: Hope, *Grammar of Heraldry*, p. 22.

[38] Legh, *Accedens*, sigs. A3v–A4.

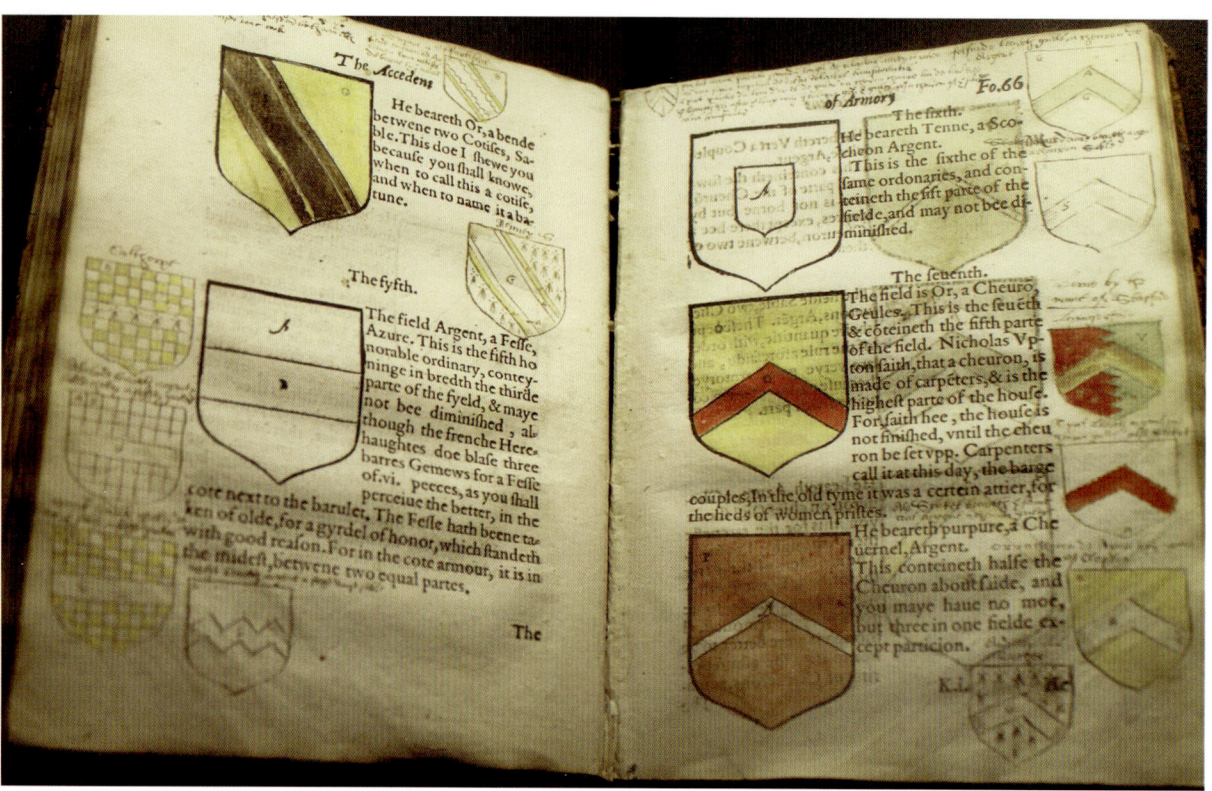

61a. Detail from Gerard Legh, *Accedens of Armory* (1568), with some of its shields painted in, and others added in the margin, by an early owner. Bodleian Library, 4° A.13 Art.

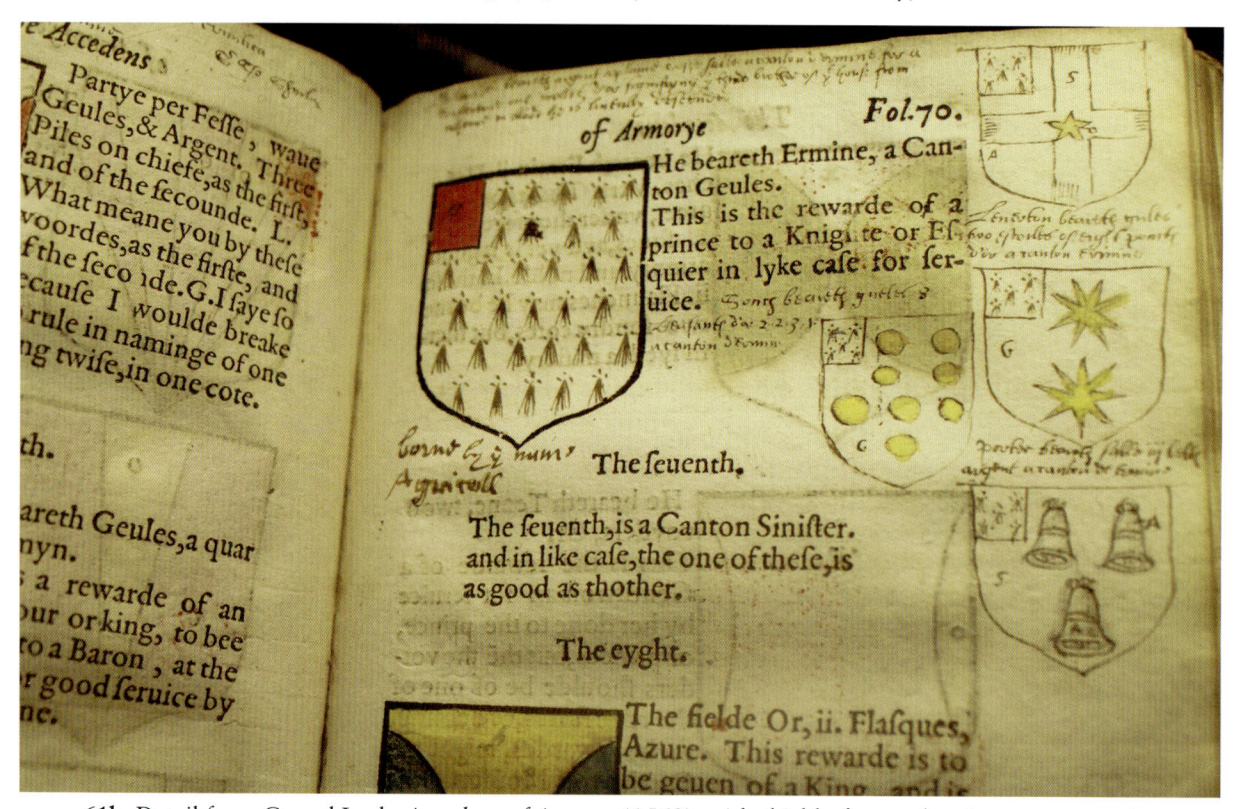

61b. Detail from Gerard Legh, *Accedens of Armory* (1568), with shield of arms showing a canton gules given as an augmentation of honour. Bodleian Library, 4° A.13 Art.

16), which means that this 'old coat' grows shabbier with age rather than more honourable. The punning display of heraldic pretension with which the play starts creates a comic foil to the luminous description of armorial bearings with which it ends. In the final scene Mistress Quickly sends the fairies to bless the armorial bearings in Windsor Castle: "each fair instalment, coat, and sev'ral crest | With loyal blazon evermore be blessed" (5.5.62–3).[39] Both the puns at the start of the play and the solemnity of its conclusion take heraldry seriously, however, for the jokes at the beginning hold up heraldic illiteracy as something for the audience to mock.

Shakespeare's heraldic punning indicates the currency of armorial language, as a pun relies on being widely and immediately recognised to work. But the capability of heraldic language to carry double meanings was also used by Shakespeare in more creative ways. The double meanings common to many heraldic terms allow an unobtrusive heraldic layer of meaning to be present throughout Shakespeare's plays. One example is Iago's role as Othello's 'ensign'. An ensign meant 'heraldic arms or bearings' but it also had two specifically military usages: 'a military or naval standard; a banner, flag' and – the primary meaning it carries in Iago's case – 'the soldier who carries the ensign; a standard-bearer'.[40] Iago is 'his Moorship's ensign' (1.1.32) and in Shakespeare's main source, Cinthio's *Gli Hecatommithi* (1565), Iago's character is fact simply designated 'The Ensign'. Because 'ensign' means both the banner and the man who holds that banner, the honourable associations of heraldic insignia are implicitly transferred to the man who carries them. Iago's standing with Othello is enabled, and to some extent expressed, through the fact that he is Othello's ensign: 'for as nothing is more dishonourable and shamefull to a Captain or general then the losse of his Banner, Standarde, or Guydon, &c. so no service in fielde of greater worship, and better worthye of rewards, then to preserve the same from the hands and dishonour of the enemy'.[41] As Othello's ensign – the one who carries the banner of his arms – Iago literally holds Othello's honour in his hands. An ensign was entrusted with the protection of the regiment's honour (he defended the flag from falling into enemy hands) and this gives a specific context for the trust that Othello places in Iago's suggestion that his honour has been betrayed. Othello's honour as a soldier is under Iago's protection and so he is more liable to believe him when he presents himself as the protector of Othello's honour in another sphere. In the law of arms, honour is embodied by a banner and a man who lets his banner fall into another man's hands has lost his honour. Iago transfers the conduct of the battlefield into

[39] *Merry Wives* was commissioned – shortly after John Shakespeare's acquisition of arms in autumn 1596 – by Shakespeare's patron, the new Lord Chamberlain, Sir George Carey, Lord Hunsdon, to be played before the Queen at the Garter Feast on 23 April prior to his installation to the Order of the Garter: Katherine Duncan-Jones, *Shakespeare: An Ungentle Life*, 2nd edn., The Arden Shakespeare (London, 2010), p. 112.
[40] *Oxford English Dictionary*, V, pp. 280–1, *s.v.* 'Ensign', §§4 and 7.
[41] John Ferne, *The Blazon of Gentrie: Devided into two parts* (London, 1586), p. 101 (misprinted 111).

peacetime and plays on Othello's military understanding of honour as embodied by a piece of cloth. When Othello's ensign – the keeper of his honour – shows him his handkerchief in another man's hands he is quick to believe that his honour has been sullied.

The Blazon of Royalty: the Lion and the Sun in *King John* and *Henry IV Part I*

Richard I's lion-skin is presented in *King John* as a version of a heraldic badge – a 'distinctive device, emblem or figure assumed as the mark or cognizance of an individual or family'.[42] It is linked to the lion which Richard bore on his shield and which was to become part of the royal arms of England.[43] The lion-skin was won by Richard for a great feat of arms (killing the Libyan lion) and, like a canting coat of arms, it plays on his name: Richard Lionheart. The Duke of Austria wears the lion-skin as a trophy[44] but it is an implicitly unchivalric gesture (as Henry Peacham notes 'no Christian may directly beare anothers Coat by his sword'[45]) and he is challenged for this action by Richard's bastard son:

> *Constance.* Thou wear a lion's hide! Doff it, for shame,
>   And hang a calf's-skin on those recreant limbs.
> *Austria.* O, that a man should speak those words to me!
>   *Bastard.* And hang a calf's-skin on those recreant limbs.
> *Austria.* Thou dar'st not say so, villain, for thy life.
>   *Bastard.* And hang a calf's-skin on those recreant limbs.   (3.1.54–9)

Austria is a coward who thinks he is safe in claiming a desire to defend his honour against Constance's accusations (for, as a woman, she cannot answer a challenge). But Austria's blustering creates the opportunity for the Bastard's simple, but highly effective, wit. Austria then implies that it would be beneath the dignity of his ducal status to challenge the Bastard (by calling him 'villain'), but the Bastard simply ignores the implication and repeats the insult.

In the source for *King John* (the anonymous play *The Troublesome Raigne of King John* (1591)), the Bastard explicitly challenges Austria to a duel and Lymoges declines, using Fauconbridge's base birth as the cover for his cowardice: 'let it suffice, I scorne to joyne in fight with one so farre unequall to my selfe'.[46] King John responds:

---

[42] Hope, *Heraldry for Craftsmen*, p. 165.
[43] Lions were a badge of Richard I and have ever since been regarded as royal beasts: Siddons, *Heraldic Badges* (cit. in n. 26), II, pt. 1, p. 157.
[44] Shakespeare has combined the Duke of Austria (whom Richard humiliated at Acre, and who later imprisoned him) with the Vicomte of Limoges (whose castle Richard died besieging).
[45] Henry Peacham, *The Compleat Gentleman* (London, 1627), p. 149.
[46] *The Troublesome Raigne of John, King of England*, ed. J. W. Sider (New York, 1979), Act 3, ll. 34–5. For further discussion of this scene, and the evidence it provides that the *Troublesome Raigne* was Shakespeare's source, not vice versa, see: Beatrice Groves, 'Memory, Composition and the Relationship of *King John* to *The Troublesome Raigne of King John*', *Comparative Drama*, 38 (2004), pp. 277–90.

> *K. John*: *Philip*, we cannot force the Duke to fight,
> Being a subject unto neither Realme:
> But tell me *Austria*, if an English Duke
> Should dare thee thus, wouldst thou accept the challendge?
> *Lymoges*. Els let the world account the *Austrich* Duke
> The greatest coward living on the Earth.
> *K. John*. Then cheere thee *Philip*, *John* will keepe his word,
> Kneele down, in sight of *Philip* King of *Fraunce*
> And all these Princely Lords assembled here,
> I gird thee with the sword of *Normandie*,
> And of that land I doo invest thee Duke. (3.38–48)

The comic 'trick' has the same form in both versions (Austria is wrong-footed out of his assurance that he cannot challenge an inferior or a woman); in Shakespeare's version, however, the hierarchy of the moment is different, for it is not the king who causes Austria to lose face (as in the source) but the Bastard.

Although the challenge is less conspicuous in Shakespeare's version, the knightly context remains present in the word 'recreant'. 'Recreant' designates 'a person who admits to having been defeated or overcome; that yields or surrenders ... (hence) cowardly, faint-hearted, craven, afraid'.[47] The word – like many heraldic terms – is of Anglo-Norman origin, and a recreant knight was one who had the ignominy of having his shield defaced or reversed.[48] In *The Faerie Queene*, Burbon – a figure of Henri de Bourbon (Henri IV, king of France) who, in Spenser's eyes, had abandoned the 'shield' of his faith in his conversion to Catholicism – abandons his shield in the heat of battle and 'from the day that he thus did it leave, | Amongst all Knights he blotted was with blame, | And counted but a recreant Knight, with endless shame' (5.11.46). The Bastard's use of the word 'recreant' carries the implication that, as Austria is a coward, he cannot bear the arms of a lion and should rather bear a calf (which would accurately express his stupidity).

The royal lion is instead associated in *King John* with Richard's bastard son, who is closely allied with his father: he is rechristened Richard in his father's honour – "Arise Sir Richard and Plantagenet!" (1.1.162) – carries 'a trick of Coeur-de-lion's face' (1.1.85), shares his military prowess and is identified with his arms. In the English law of arms a bastard could wear his father's arms: 'we in England allow the base sonne his Fathers Coate, with the difference of a bend Batune, sinister, or bordure engrailed, or the like'.[49] Therefore, on stage, the Bastard should bear Richard's arms (at the time of his birth) with the baton sinister of bastardy across them: '*Gules, a gold lion rampant to the sinister, [...] a baston azure*'.[50] The lion is the king of beasts and is perhaps the oldest

---

[47] *Oxford English Dictionary*, XIII, p. 371, s.v. 'Recreant.'
[48] Rothery, *Heraldry of Shakespeare*, pp. 37–8.
[49] Peacham, *Compleat Gentleman*, p. 155. For some historical indications of bastardy on arms, see: Hope, *Grammar of Heraldry*, pp. 61, 63; A. R. Wagner, 'Heraldry', in *Medieval England*, ed. A. L. Poole, 2 vols (Oxford, 1958), I, pp. 338–81, at 366–8.
[50] Scott-Giles, *Shakespeare's Heraldry*, pp. 46–7.

charge associated with English royalty – the first heraldic shield of English royalty is generally considered to be Richard's rampant gold lion – and he was the first king to bear the royal arms of England (*gules, three lions passant guardant or*).[51] The willingness of English heralds to allow a bastard son to bear his father's arms is both supported by, and lends support to, the royal temper of the Bastard in *King John*.

Richard's greatest military triumph was the siege of Acre (1191), and it is a siege recalled by the central action of *King John*: the siege of Angiers (Angers, in western France). At Acre the besieging parties (like at Angiers) included the English king, Philip of France and the Duke of Austria. At Acre (as at Angiers) these parties united to attack the city.[52] At Acre Richard humiliated the Duke of Austria (as his son does at Angiers). This humiliation had been a heraldic one: '[Richard] had cast downe his [Austria's] ensignes pitcht up in a turret at Acres... and trode under his feet'.[53] This event became part of Richard's myth: 'thus did *Richard* take | The coward *Austrias* colours in his hand, | And thus he cast them under *Acon* walles, | And thus he trod them underneath his feete'.[54] When the Bastard takes back the famous lion-skin from Limoges, Duke of Austria, he erases the ignominy of the memory (perpetuated by that trophy) of Richard's death at Limoges's hands. He also supports the image of himself as Richard's son – both in his reprise of his father's action of shaming Austria (the taking of the lion-skin is cast as a version of the shaming of Austria's arms that occurred at Acre) and through his acquisition of the royal lion (which, in some productions, he wears throughout the rest of the play). The lion theme is strikingly present in *King John* but is only once applied to the king. It is instead the Bastard who inherits Richard's royal lion.

[51] These were first used by Richard I and remained the royal arms until 1340 when Edward III quartered them with the Ancient Royal Arms of France: W. M. Ormrod, 'A Problem of Precedence: Edward III, the Double Monarchy, and the Royal Style', in *The Age of Edward III*, ed. J. S. Bothwell (York and Woodbridge, 2001), pp. 133–53, at 133–4. The only shield which appears in Henslowe's diary as a stage property was presumably the royal coat of arms: 'One shield with three lions': *Henslowe's Diary*, ed. Walter W. Greg (London, 1904), Appx. II, p. 80.

[52] Raphael Holinshed, *Holinshed's Chronicles of England, Scotland, and Ireland*, ed. H. Ellis, 6 vols (London, 1807-8), III, pp. 230, 235. For more on this siege, see John Stow, *A Survey of London: Reprinted from the Text of 1603*, ed. Charles Lethbridge Kingsford, 2 vols (Oxford, 1908), II, p. 203.

[53] Richard 'had cast downe his ensignes pitcht up in a turret at Acres, which he had woone at the verie time when that citie was delivered by the Saracens: for while they were in tretie on the one side, the duke on the other, not knowing anie thing therof, gave the assault unto that part of the towne which was appointed unto him to besiege. And so being entred the towne, and perceiving that by treatie it was to be delivered, he retired into the turret which he had first woone and entred, and there set up his standard and ensignes, which king Richard (as the Dutch writers affirme) coming thither, threw downe and trode under his feet': *Holinshed's Chronicles*, III, p. 235.

[54] Anthony Munday, *The Downfall of Robert Earl of Huntingdon (1601)* (Oxford: Malone Soc., 1964), ll. 1926–9. See also: 'Consider in what despite, the Duke of Austriche tooke the treading of his banner under foote, which was of meere chaunce, but king Richarde the firste, might saye of evill happe': Legh, *Accedens*, f. 134; John Gillingham, *Richard I* (New Haven and London, 1999), pp. 224–6.

HERALDIC LANGUAGE AND IDENTITY IN SHAKESPEARE'S PLAYS

In *Henry IV Part I* (*c.* 1596–7), Hal – like the Bastard – is trying to prove his essential royalty. Unlike in the Bastard's case it is not that his paternity is in question; what Hal needs to prove is that he is truly of royal blood, and not simply the son of a usurping father. One of the ways he achieves this is through co-opting through his language and self-presentation the heraldic badges of Richard II, the man his father deposed.[55] The sun was one of the badges that the historical Richard II wore most frequently and this choice was part of his propensity to use heraldry to indicate the holiness of the king.[56] Richard impaled his arms with those of Edward the Confessor (*Azure, a gold cross flory and five gold doves*) and in doing so proclaimed heraldically a special kinship with England's sainted king.[57] He also used the badge of 'the pelican in her piety' – suggestive of sacrificial kingship modelled on that of Christ.[58] The analogy of divinity and majesty is an ancient and thoroughgoing one, and in Elizabethan royal panegyric the monarch was 'the Image of God on Earth'.[59] The strikingly Christological comparisons that Richard II draws in Shakespeare's play – calling his detractors Judases and Pilates (3.2.128, 4.1.158–62, 4.1.229–32)[60] – have some historical heraldic parallels. Richard was one of the first to employ supporters in his arms, and – fittingly – he chose angels as his supporters. It is possible that Shakespeare knew of this (he could have seen them in the roof of Westminster Hall)[61] and it is tempting to speculate that this piece of heraldic self-glorification is one reason for Richard's assertion that 'God for his Richard hath in heavenly pay | A glorious angel' (3.2.56–7) – an allusion to Christ's words: 'thinkest thou, that I can not nowe pray to my Father, and he wil give me mo then Twelve legions of Angels?' (Matthew 26, 53).

In the Wilton Diptych (the late fourteenth-century panel painting in which Richard II is presented to the Virgin and Child), the angelic hosts which surround the Blessed Virgin wear one of Richard's badges, the white hart, on their clothes.[62] Badges are a particularly ancient and visible branch of heraldry (Richard III, for example, had 13,000

---

[55] It is arguable that Henry IV's cavalier attitude to the royalty expressed through his coat-armour is a mark of his usurped and insecure position. At Shrewsbury he uses heraldry to conceal rather than reveal his identity: 'The king has many marching in his coats' (*I Henry IV*, 5.3.25).

[56] Siddons, *Heraldic Badges*, II, pt. 1, pp. 230–1, 234–5.

[57] Scott-Giles, *Shakespeare's Heraldry*, pp. 62–3. Henry V flew the flag of Edward the Confessor (which Richard II had impaled with his own arms) at Agincourt.

[58] Siddons, *Heraldic Badges*, II, pt. 1, p. 194.

[59] Charles Merbury, *A Briefe Discourse of Royall Monarchie, as of the Best Common weale: Wherin the subiect may beholde the sacred Maiestie of the Princes most Royall Estate* (London, 1581), p. 43.

[60] See *King Richard II*, ed. Peter Ure, The Arden Shakespeare (London, 1994), pp. xlviii, lxii; Naseeb Shaheen, *Biblical References in Shakespeare's Plays* (Newark, New Jersey, 1999), pp. 374-5, 380-3.

[61] Scott-Giles, *Shakespeare's Heraldry*, p. 64. See also Guy Cadogan Rothery, *Concise Encyclopedia of Heraldry* (London, 1931), pp. 244–5, 249.

[62] See *The Regal Image of Richard II and the Wilton Diptych*, ed. Dillian Gordon, Lisa Monnas and Caroline Elam (London, 1997), plate 3.

representations of his famous white boar badge painted on fustian for his coronation[63]). They were often worn by retainers and embroidered on the sleeves or chests of family members and became the distinctive mark of family, house or individual. Three of Richard II's badges include the sun (a symbol of divine status of a king): a sun in splendour, a sunburst (the sun appearing from behind clouds) and a rose *en soleil*.[64] Two centuries later, Ferne notes that the royal crown is set with stones, one of which is the colour of 'sunne beames' to show that the monarch 'should shine in devine and celestiall vertues'.[65] The historical Richard II wore sumptuous clothes emblazoned with his sun badge on public occasions: when jousting, for example, he wore cloth of gold woven with golden suns or red silk stamped with golden suns.[66] Shakespeare clothes his Richard II with words that gleam with the same sun imagery. Richard descends 'like glist'ring Phaethon' (3.3.177) and he has an extended metaphor comparing himself to the 'eye of heaven' (3.2.32–48) on his return from Ireland (historically, Richard II's ship on his return from Ireland bore a sail painted with a large golden sun in splendour (Fig. 69)).[67] During the deposition scene Richard transfers this image to Bolingbroke, wishing him 'many years of sunshine days' (4.1.211) and praying 'O, that I were a mockery king of snow, | Standing before the sun of Bolingbroke' (4.1.250–1).[68] Richard's attempted sublimation of his identity through deposition is expressed by Shakespeare as a transfer of heraldic symbolism as he rhetorically confers his 'badge' on his rival.

It is, however, not Bolingbroke but his son who takes up Richard's holy, heraldic imagery of kingship. Unlike his father, who intends a pilgrimage to the Holy Land but never sets out, Hal becomes 'the mirror of all Christian Kings' and scatters 'a largess universal like the sun' (*Henry V*, 2.0.6, 4.0.43). Once again this has some historical precedent: Henry V made striking use of the sun badge – sending a thousand red gowns to France in 1421 bearing the cross of St George 'in the manner of a sun'.[69] Hal revives Richard's heraldic imagery to imbue himself with his charisma of sanctity and a legitimating aura of divinity. He combines the politically astute rule of his father with the sacral kingship of the man his father deposed, and by so doing creates a brilliantly effective form of government that portrays him as the true heir to each of these kings.

Henry IV believes that the parallels between his son and the man whose throne he usurped are not auspicious – he complains that "for all the world, | As thou art at this hour was Richard then" (*I Henry IV*, 3.2.93–4). But in fact Hal is making strategic use of this appearance of Ricardian dissipation:

[63] Siddons, *Heraldic Badges*, II, pt. 1, p. 52.
[64] *Ibid.*, pp. 234–8, 230–3.
[65] Ferne, *Blazon*, p. 143.
[66] Lisa Monnas 'Fit for a King: Figured Silks Shown in the Wilton Diptych,' in *Regal Image*, ed. Gordon, Monnas and Elam, pp. 165–78, at 167.
[67] Siddons, *Heraldic Badges*, II, pt. 1, p. 231.
[68] See also: 3.2.214.
[69] Siddons, *Heraldic Badges*, II, pt. 1, pp. 231–2.

62. Ship bringing Richard II back to England in 1399, with his badge of a sun on its sail. Engraving in *Archaeologia*, xx (1824), Plate vii, after British Library, MS Harley 1319, f. 18.

> Herein will I imitate the sun,
> Who doth permit the base contagious clouds
> To smother up his beauty from the world ...
> [so that] My reformation, glitt'ring o'er my fault,
> Shall show more goodly, and attract more eyes
> Than that which hath no foil to set it off. (1.2.194–212)

Richard had himself been likened by Bolingbroke to just such an image of a sun appearing from behind the clouds:

> See, see, King Richard doth himself appear,
> As doth the blushing discontented sun
> From out the fiery portal of the east
> When he perceives the envious clouds are bent
> To dim his glory and to stain the track
> Of his bright passage to the occident. (*Richard II*, 3.3.61–6)

Bolingbroke's metaphor alludes to the general association of the king with the sun, but more specifically it recalls one of the historical Richard II's favourite badges: the sunburst (a sun partially obscured by clouds) (Figs 63–5).[70]

In the jousts of 1386 Richard II wore this badge embroidered on his short gown as well as on the coverings of his war horse and he wore a large gold sun and a silver cloud

---

[70] This sunburst badge can be seen on the effigy of Richard II at Westminster which is pounced all over with badges, including this one: Hope, *Heraldry for Craftsmen*, Fig. 92.

251

after hym his brother kyng Richard the thryde whiche beyng
will conceyued disenherited his nevewes kyng Edward the v.th and
Richard duc of york vnder whome also they died whiche Richar-
he was kyng and did that foule de- de was preysed for a
coragious knyght he was Sleyne at the bataple
of Rede more and is buryed at the grey ffrers
of Ley- of
cestre

64–5 (above). Sunbursts used in Tudor royal badges.

All three images on these pages are from 'Prince Arthur's Book', produced for Sir Thomas Wriothesley (d. 1534), Garter King of Arms. College of Arms, MS Vincent 152, pp. 54, 60 and 84.

63 (opposite). An array of royal badges includes a white rose *en soleil* and a white boar, for Richard III (upper left), and a sunburst beside a portcullis, for Henry VII (lower left). An achievement of each king's arms is shown at right.

as a crest atop his helmet.[71] Richard often wore this badge (presumably intended to symbolize royal invincibility) on his military garments, as, for example, on the journey to Scotland in 1385.[72] The symbolic potential of the sunburst image was exploited by the Kirkstall Chronicler when he described Richard's triumph over his opponents in 1397: 'the wonderful and persistent royal patience, once a sun that was covered with cloud ... has scattered the clouds and revealed the sun's light more clearly'.[73] Like *Richard II*, and the historical Richard II, Hal connects his royalty with the quasi-divine power of the sun through the image of the sunburst.[74] In the crucial soliloquy in which Hal announces that his dissipation is merely a cloak for his royalty, he employs this Ricardian trope of sacral kingship.

It is at Shrewsbury that Hal is recognised as the true heir, and Vernon describes him in a speech in which the Ricardian insignia of angels and the sun return:

> Glittering in golden coats like images,
> As full of spirit as the month of May,
> And gorgeous as the sun at midsummer ...
> I saw young Harry with his beaver on,
> His cuishes on his thighs, gallantly armed,
> Rise from the ground like feathered Mercury,
> And vaulted with such ease into his seat
> As if an angel dropped down from the clouds
> To turn and wind a fiery Pegasus.   (4.1.101–10)

'Glittering' and 'sun' recur from Hal's soliloquy and express the fulfillment of his vision of a reformation that 'shall show more goodly, and attract more eyes | Than that which hath no foil to set it off'. The golden hue with which Hal is suffused here, is likewise the colour of royalty: 'For looke how much this metall excelleth all others in the kinde thereof, as in finesse and puritie: So muche shoulde the bearer therof, excel all other, in prowes and Vertue. Therefore, saith Christyne of Pice, no man should beare this mettal in armes, but Emperours & kinges or of the blood royall'.[75] Tarquin's 'golden coat'

---

[71] Siddons, *Heraldic Badges*, II, pt. 1, p. 235; Kay Staniland, 'Extravagance or Regal Necessity? The Clothing of Richard II,' in *Regal Image*, ed. Gordon, Monnas and Elam, p. 91.

[72] Staniland, 'Extravagance,' p. 91. For the use of the sunburst on other military garments, see: Monnas 'Fit for a King,' p. 168.

[73] 'admirabilis et diuturna regalis paciencia olim quidam sol erat tectus nube... nubes et sole ventulavit et solis lucem clarius demonstravit': in M. V. Clarke and N. Denholm-Young, 'The Kirkstall Chronicle, 1355–1400,' *Bulletin of the John Rylands Library*, xv (1931), pp. 100–37, at 131, ll. 1-4).

[74] In addition to the general quasi-divine import of the sun, Richard II specifically linked himself through this badge with a saint, by having it depicted on St Edmund's tunic in the Wilton Diptych: Shelagh Mitchell, 'Richard II: Kingship and the Cult of Saints,' in *Regal Image*, ed. Gordon, Monnas and Elam, p. 118 and plate 2. For more on the heraldic expression of Richard's devotion to England's royal saints, see *ibid.*, pp. 115–24.

[75] Legh, *Accedens*, sig. B1. Christine de Pizan (1365–*c.* 1430), whom Legh cites here, was author of a popular guide to heraldry, the *Livre des faits d'armes et de chevalerie*, which Caxton had published in English as *The Book of Fayttes of Armes and Chyvalrye*.

HERALDIC LANGUAGE AND IDENTITY IN SHAKESPEARE'S PLAYS

(*Lucrece*, l. 202) is a reminder that he is a king, and perhaps there is latent pun relating Hal's military wear, his 'golden coat', to the royal arms.

The royal arms of England were gold lions set on a red field (*gules, three lions passant guardant or*) and at Shrewsbury Hal becomes associated with both colours.[76] Vernon describes him as 'Glittering in [a] golden coat', and Hal promises his father:

> I will redeem all this on Percy's head,
> And in the closing of some glorious day
> Be bold to tell you that I am your son;
> When I will wear a garment all of blood,
> And stain my favours in a bloody mask,
> Which, washed away, shall scour my shame with it.   (3.2.132–7)

There is a messianic aspect to the heraldic imagery here (Hal's speech draws linguistic parallels between his 'garment all of blood' and the blood-stained 'red garments' of the redeemer in Isaiah 63, 1–4).[77] Legh likewise notes that gules is a particularly honourable heraldic colour because 'God the father, promising Redemption to the people, by the passion of Christ, saieth what is he that commeth from Edom, with red coloured clothes of Bosra'.[78] The imagery here proclaims Hal's royalty (through connecting him with the royal colours) but also alludes, more specifically, to Richard's method of imbuing his kingship with holy imagery. Shakespeare expresses through heraldic imagery – the 'gules' and 'or' of Hal's blood-spattered armour and the language of Richard's badges (the angels, the sun and the sunburst) – both Hal's incipient royal status and his political ability to align himself with Richard II's own self-presentation. The hiatus of the usurpation is rhetorically smoothed over by Hal's astute performance of his transformation from a prodigal into an inheritor of Richard's heraldic imagery of sanctification.

Blazon and Heraldic Female Bodies

Spenser opens *The Faerie Queene* with the promise to:

> … sing of Knights and Ladies gentle deeds;
> Whose prayses having slept in silence long,
> Me, all too meane, the sacred Muse areeds
> To blazon broad emongst her learned throng.   (1.proem.1)

The general and specific sense of blazon – 'to proclaim (as with a trumpet), to publish, divulge, make known' and 'to describe esp. virtues and excellencies' – are both present in Spenser's opening words. (Ferne gives the etymology of blazon from the French

---

[76] Richard II seems to have often worn the sun and sunburst badges on red silk or red-painted armour (Siddons, *Heraldic Badges*, II, pt. 1, pp. 230, 235) presumably to echo the gold-on-red of the royal arms.
[77] For more on this parallel (and the messianic imagery of Richard and Hal in general), see: Beatrice Groves, *Texts and Traditions: Religion in Shakespeare 1592–1604* (Oxford, 2007), chapter 5.
[78] Legh, *Accedens*, f. 6.

255

'blazonner: that is to say, to spread out, or lay open, ones name'.[79]) But blazon in its technical sense of expressing heraldry in verbal form, is also present – and as the *Oxford English Dictionary* notes, the proper senses of blaze and blazon 'acted and reacted on each other' in the sixteenth century.[80]

Heraldic imagery is central to Spenser's poem, and the language of armory sometimes overlaps with the poetic sense of blazon (the description of female beauty through minute renderings of its constituent parts). For instance, when the false and the true Florimell appear together, it is as if 'two sunnes appear in the azure skye,' (5.3.19). Azure is the heraldic term for blue, and the sun in the context of a heraldic charge had just appeared (in the description of Braggadochio's shield five stanzas earlier). The underlying heraldic diction is suitable for this moment of mistaken identity: it is as though both women have the same coat of arms and cannot, therefore, be told apart. In Shakespeare likewise the two senses of blazon interact – Romeo offers a blazon of Juliet's face in heraldic terms: 'beauties ensign yet | Is Crimson in thy lips and in thy cheeks, | And Deaths pale flag is not advanced there' (*Romeo and Juliet*, 5.3.91–3). The blazon has in fact told Romeo something true about Juliet's identity – that she still belongs to Beauty's lists and has not defected to the side of Death (she is not dead) – but he is tragically inattentive to his own blazon.

The thirteenth sonnet of Sidney's *Astrophil and Stella* (1591) expresses this intersection between the poetic and heraldic senses of blazon:

> Phoebus was judge between Jove, Mars, and Love,
>   Of those three gods, whose arms the fairest were.
>   Jove's golden shield did eagle sables [*sic*] bear,
> Whose talents held young Ganymede above:
> But in vert field Mars bare a golden spear
>   Which through a bleeding heart his point did shove.
>   Each had his crest: Mars carried Venus' glove,
> Jove on his helm the thunderbolt did rear.
> Cupid then smiles, for on his crest there lies
>   Stella's fair hair, her face he makes his shield,
>   Where roses gules are borne in silver field.
> Phoebus drew wide the curtains of the skies
>   To blaze these last, and sware devoutly then,
>   The first, thus matched, were scarcely gentlemen.[81]

Stella's beauty, as in the judgment of Paris, outshines that of her competitors, but it also makes her face and hair into the most honourable of heraldic arms and crests.

---

[79] Ferne, *Blazon*, p. 164.
[80] *Oxford English Dictionary*, II, p. 27, *s.v.* 'Blazon.'
[81] *Sir Philip Sidney: The Major Works*, ed. Katherine Duncan-Jones (Oxford, 2002), pp. 158–9. Duncan-Jones notes that there is a further pun in the word 'blaze' here (as it is the appropriate action of Phoebus), and that Stella's face may be intended to recall the Devereux arms: *argent a fesse gules in chief three torteaux* (p. 359).

HERALDIC LANGUAGE AND IDENTITY IN SHAKESPEARE'S PLAYS

Blazoning, in both its poetic and heraldic senses, was a predominantly male activity in the sixteenth century. Sawday claims that poetic blazon 'was a form of homosocial mediation amongst men, in which the female body was ... the circulating token, but it was male desire which valorized the currency'.[82] Heralds were primarily interested in the male line, the line down which arms passed.[83] The misogyny inherent to the inferior status of women in heraldry is expressed by Ferne when he explains why a woman can be ennobled by her husband but not vice versa: 'this is, the ordinaunce of the laws: wherein is secreatlye set foorth, of how much more excellencye and worthynes, is nobleness in man, then when it falleth in the other sexe, which as shut up or rather extinguished, can not communicate, the brightnes and virtue thereof, to an other'.[84] A modern encyclopedia expresses it thus: 'in Western culture the family is patrilineal and inheritance is by male primogeniture; hence, property descends from father to son. A patent of arms states that the grant is made to a man and his heirs and descendants forever; therefore a coat of arms is an incorporeal hereditament the possession of which, and the right and power of its transmission to offspring, is vested in heirs-male'.[85] In the early modern period women bore their father's arms on a lozenge rather than a shield to distance their coats from the bearing of arms on the battlefield.

In Shakespeare's plays, however, the inferiority of women in the law of arms is inverted. The heraldic language that surrounds heroines such as Lucrece, Viola, Ophelia and Imogen expresses the way that they embody (just as a coat of arms was meant to) a perfect correspondence between inner and outward virtues. In the 'Argument' to Shakespeare's *Rape of Lucrece* the heroine is portrayed as one who embodies the virtue that has been proclaimed of her: 'in their discourses after supper every one commended the virtues of his own wife; among whom Collatinus extolled the incomparable chastity of his wife Lucretia. In that pleasant humor they all posted to Rome, and intending by their secret and sudden arrival to make trial of that which every one had before avouched, only Collatinus finds his wife (though it were late in the night) spinning amongst her maids; the other ladies were all found dancing and reveling, or in several disports; whereupon the noblemen yielded Collatinus the victory, and his wife the fame'. Lucrece lives up to her report, her virtue is equal to the claims made about her, and as such she is yielded 'the fame'. Lucrece's inner and outer virtue, public and private fame, are in perfect synchrony.

---

[82] Sawday, *The Body Emblazoned*, pp. 202, 192. For the argument that poetic blazoning was a homosocial activity, see pp. 191–206.
[83] At the same time, the fact that the coats of arms of heraldic heiresses would pass down to their descendants was of immense interest to heralds, especially in the later sixteenth century and subsequently, as it enabled quarterings to be added to coats of arms.
[84] Ferne, *Blazon*, p. 62.
[85] Julian Franklyn and John Tanner, *An Encyclopaedic Dictionary of Heraldry* (Oxford, 1970), s.v. 'Heraldic heiress.'

Lucrece's husband blazes her beauty abroad: 'the clear unmatched red and white | Which triumph'd in that sky of his delight; | Where mortal stars as bright as heaven's beauties, | With pure aspects did him peculiar duties' (ll.11–14). Tarquin likewise blazons the red and white of Lucrece's face as outdoing the lily and the rose: 'the colour in thy face, | That even for anger makes the lily pale, | And the red rose blush at her own disgrace' (ll. 477–9). These prominent heraldic flowers form part of the shared terminology of the blazon of arms and the blazon of beauty and the narrator describes Lucrece likewise as a lily and a rose. He describes the red and white in her cheeks as 'this silent war of lilies and of roses' (l. 71) and 'her lily hand her rosy cheek lies under' (l. 386).

Lucrece's face is, in fact, most consistently blazoned not by Tarquin or her husband, but by the narrator. In a long and complex conceit, Virtue (whose arms are white) and Beauty (whose arms are red) compete over to which of them Lucrece belongs:

> When virtue bragg'd, beauty would blush for shame;
>   When beauty boasted blushes, in despite
>   Virtue would stain that o'er with silver white. (ll. 59–61)

Lucrece's blushes prove her to belong to Beauty but her maidenly paleness when shamed by her own blushes puts Virtue in the ascendant, and the heraldic terminology of 'stain' and perhaps even 'o'er' ('or' is the heraldic name for gold, which is often linked with red) strengthens the trope.[86]

> But beauty, in that white entituled
> From Venus' doves, doth challenge that fair field;
> Then virtue claims from beauty beauty's red,
> Which virtue gave the golden age to gild
> Their silver cheeks, and call'd it then their shield,
>   Teaching them this to use it in the fight,
>   When shame assail'd, the red should fence the white.
>
> This heraldry in Lucrece's face was seen,
> Argued by beauty's red and virtue's white;
> Of either's color was the other queen,
> Proving from world's minority their right;
> Yet their ambition makes them still to fight,
>   The sovereignty of either being so great
>   That oft they interchange each other's seat. (ll. 52–70)

The Rape of Lucrece is an insistently heraldic text.[87] Lucrece speaks of 'my sable ground of sin' (l.1074), using the heraldic term for black, and both she and Tarquin are

---

[86] For an excellent discussion of this passage, see: William Shakespeare, *The Complete Sonnets and Poems*, ed. Colin Burrow (Oxford, 2002), notes to ll. 55–72.

[87] Nancy J. Vickers notes, among many other heraldic insights into this text, that the word colour appears more often in *Lucrece* than in any other Shakespearean text: 'This Heraldry in Lucrece's Face', *Poetics Today*, 6 (1985), pp. 171–84.

profoundly concerned about the consequences of the rape for their arms. Lucrece sees suicide as means by which 'to clear this spot by death (at least) I give | A badge of fame to slander's livery' (ll.1053-4), and Tarquin believes that his crime will be visible on his face as well as his escutcheon:

> True valor still a true respect should have;
> Then my digression is so vile, so base,
> That it will live engraven in my face.
>
> 'Yea, though I die, the scandal will survive,
> And be an eye-sore in my golden coat;
> Some loathsome dash the herald will contrive,
> To cipher me how fondly I did dote'   (ll. 201–7)

Critics have tended to be rather dismissive of the idea of abatement (a dishonourable mark added to a coat of arms for a base action), calling it 'an elaborate make-believe' that 'seems to have existed only in the fancy of heralds and writers on heraldry'.[88] One commentator goes so far as to write of the 'preposterous system of abatements, which will be found set out in full in the old heraldry books, but which have yet to be found occurring in fact. The subject of abatements is one of those pleasant little insanities which have done so much to the detriment of heraldry'.[89] Sixteenth-century heraldic writers were nonetheless enthusiastic about detailing such marks – Legh writes, for example, that dismembering the charge was a punishment for adultery.[90] Ferne spells out in detail 'the nine vices, that a Gentleman must eschew (as rebatements of his honour, and staynes, to his coat-armor of Gentlenes)'.[91]

Such marks of abatement are crucial for those who wish to believe in the correspondence between the dignity of a coat of arms and the honour of its bearer. Heraldry proclaims that those who wear coat armour are honourable – someone who bears arms is meant not only to be of a particular family but to embody the ideals of chivalry for which a forebear won the right to bear arms: '*Armes* are tokens or resemblances, signifying some act or quality of the bearer'.[92] Such a belief is only tenable, however, if there is some way to signify dishonour. Ferne is convinced that vile actions will be punished with marks of abatement: 'and those whose actions are more vile in blemish of their name | Have coats reverst, for honor longs to none but vertues deedes | As gardens are preserv'd for hearbes, when fieldes are fit for weedes'.[93] *The Rape of*

---

[88] Rothery, *Heraldry of Shakespeare*, p. 37; M. C. Bradbrook, *Shakespeare and Elizabethan Poetry: A Study of his Earlier Work in Relation to the Poetry of the Time* (London, 1951), p. 258.
[89] Arthur C. Fox-Davies, *The Complete Guide to Heraldry* (London, 1909), p. 72.
[90] Legh, *Accedens*, f. 48v.
[91] Ferne, *Blazon*, p. 96.
[92] John Guillim, *A Display of Heraldry: Manifesting a more easie access to the knowledge thereof then hath hitherto been published by any through the benefit of method* (London, 1660 [first published in 1610]), p. 2.
[93] Ferne, *Blazon*, sig. A7v.

Lucrece seems to accept this system – both protagonists believe their escutcheons will be soiled by the rape – but Shakespeare may perhaps have reflected that he had never seen any such marks on the numerous heraldic insignia displayed in churches or at court.[94] The fact that no marks of abatement (beyond, sometimes, a mark for bastardy) ever seem to have actually been used serves to undermine the equation between arms and honour – as each new generation will inherit unblemished arms whatever their merit. The heraldic reality in which abatements do not exist destabilises the belief in the correspondence between visible and hidden virtue which was proclaimed by early modern heraldic writers.

In reality Tarquin's escutcheon will bear no blot, and the poem suggests likewise that his and Lucrece's belief that their faces will reveal the rape (ll. 201–3, 755–6, 807–12) is also inaccurate. Lucrece sees her groom blush and 'thought he blush'd to see her shame' (l.1344), but she is wrong. The poem explains at some length that the groom has no knowledge of what has happened and blushes from mere bashfulness at her gaze (ll.1338–58). Shakespeare suggests that Lucrece's belief is naïve – she trusts Tarquin because his 'inward ill no outward harm express'd' (l.91) – but the heraldic language brings to the surface the complexity of the relationship between how things seem and how they are. Lucrece laments:

> O unseen shame, invisible disgrace!
> O unfelt sore, crest-wounding private scar!
> Reproach is stamp'd in Collatinus' face,
> And Tarquin's eye may read the mot afar.   (ll. 827–30)

This speech declares that Collatine will be heraldically – and hence visibly – wounded by the rape: his crest (the most honourable and visible part of the heraldic achievement, originally worn on the top of the helmet)[95] will be lopped and his motto ('mot') changed.[96] Yet the disgrace that Lucrece believes Collatine to have suffered is also 'unseen', 'private' and 'invisible'. This speech embodies the tension inherent in the relationship between sign and signified explored throughout the poem and embodied by heraldic language.

The depiction of Troy in *The Rape of Lucrece* functions as a parallel for the poem itself – a work of art about the suffering caused by a rape, symbolised as the siege and

---

[94] One recent dictionary notes that 'no examples of arms rebated can be found in the records': Franklyn and Tanner, *Encyclopaedic Dictionary of Heraldry*, s.v. 'Rebatements of honour.'

[95] 'Heraldic crests are the true outcome of chivalry, the sign of the fighting gentleman, for though a yeoman might wear his leader's insignia on his coat, he could not wear the crested helm': Rothery, *Heraldry of Shakespeare*, p. 44. The honour of the crest is strikingly and ironically expressed by Salisbury at the death of Prince Arthur: 'This is the very top, | The height, the crest, or the crest unto the crest, | Of murder's arms' (*King John*, 4.3.45–7).

[96] The awkward relationship between heraldry and femininity is expressed by the fact that heraldry's highest honour (the crest) cannot be borne by a woman: 'as it represents the ornament worn on the knight's helmet, it cannot properly be borne by a woman': *Oxford English Dictionary*, IV, p. 12, s.v. 'Crest', §3a.

fall of a city. Lucrece (who believes in a perfect correspondence between sign and signified) describes the accurate fit between faces and natures in the painting: 'the face of either cipher'd either's heart, | Their face their manners most expressly told: | In Ajax' eyes blunt rage and rigor roll'd, | But the mild glance that sly Ulysses lent | Showed deep regard and similing government' (ll. 1396–1400). But Lucrece is disturbed by the face of the treacherous Sinon who has been painted with a 'saint-like' face (l.1519). Sinon's face draws attention to the way that the correspondence between inward and outward virtue observed in the previous characters is the product of artistic licence rather than reality – just as Lucrece's own perfect embodiment of the virtue she possesses, expressed through the heraldic descriptions of her beauty, is the product of Shakespeare's own artistic creation.

Cymbeline

The plot of *Cymbeline* contains two main strands – the story of Imogen and the war between Rome and England. The heraldic punning of the wager story (likewise a contest between Italy and Britain) synthesizes these two threads. Cymbeline rejects paying the Roman tribute because, like Posthumus, he is too concerned with the preservation of his own honour: 'thy Caesar knighted me; my youth I spent | Much under him; of him I gathered honour, | Which he to seek of me again perforce | Behoves me keep at utterance' (3.1.69–72). Cymbeline believes that it would derogate from his honour as a knight to pay tribute but, as with Posthumus, the play presents him as mistaken in the position his pride leads him to take. The fact that Posthumus is wrong to enter the contest with Giacomo, wrong to doubt his wife and wrong to think that his honour is increased by this conduct, underlines the fact that chivalric courtly pride (embodied by Cloten[97]) is likewise wrong to seek war against Rome. Shakespeare's deployment of armorial language in *Cymbeline* recognises the innate worth of Imogen and her brothers, but works to divorce true chivalric values from an honour-politics which it depicts as self-regarding. The play tacitly undermines those English aristocrats who were eager for a more bellicose foreign policy against Roman Catholic enemies (against the quiescent tendencies of James I).

Lucrece's story is replayed in *Cymbeline* in which a husband likewise blazes his wife's perfections to other men, and by so doing spurs another man to enter her bedroom in pursuit of her honour.[98] Once again heraldic puns are present in the description of the wife's perfections – Posthumus vows 'I would abate her nothing' (1.4.66) – and, as in *The Rape of Lucrece*, her sleeping body is described in heraldic terms. Giacomo calls her a

[97] Cloten stands on his status and it mocked for it through heraldic punning. When he asks (about going to look at a visitor to court) 'is it fit I went to look upon him? Is there no derogation in't?' the Second Lord mockingly replies (with a pun on a grant of arms) 'you are a fool granted, therefore your issues, being foolish, do not derogate' (2.1.40–5).

[98] Giacomo makes the parallel with Lucrece explicit as he steals towards Imogen with the words 'our Tarquin thus | Did softly press the rushes ere he wakened | The chastity he wounded' (2.1.12–14).

'fresh lily'[99] and says that:

> The flame o' the taper
> Bows toward her, and would underpeep her lids,
> To see the enclosèd lights, now canopied
> Under these windows, white and azure-laced
> With blue of heaven's own tinct. (2.2.19–23)

'Tinct' recalls the heraldic term for colours and metals ('tinctures'),[100] and the deep blue of Imogen's irises (described with the heraldic term 'azure') is veined with a lighter blue ('blue of heaven's own tinct') which alludes to a much rarer heraldic shade 'bleue celeste'.[101] The mole under her breast (Giacomo's knowledge of which is accepted by Posthumus as evidence for her adultery) is a 'stain' (2.4.139, 140). Later in the play we discover that this is a birth mark she shares with her brother Guiderius, who has 'upon his neck a mole, a sanguine star' (5.6.366). Sanguine is a rare heraldic colour known properly as a 'stain'.[102] Neither the words 'sanguine' or 'stain' are used of Imogen's birthmark in the scene in which Giacomo watches her sleeping, but the heraldic implications of stains are present. Sanguine was associated with signs of abatement, and heraldic writers claimed that it was used to indicate adultery.[103]

The heraldic language in this passage (and the underlying menace of the 'stain') highlights Giacomo's intrusive and objectifying male gaze (and our own voyeurism) but it also critiques this gaze. A shield is presented to the view of the world, but Giacomo has no right to be looking at Imogen's naked, sleeping body. But, as with *The Rape of Lucrece*, the armorial language associated with Imogen's body is also defiant evidence of her virtue. The blazon of Imogen and Lucrece – which draws attention to the objectifying gaze of the men who observe them – speaks likewise to their essential honour. These women are their own arms: their bodies and actions speak the virtue that arms promised the bearer to possess. Like Ophelia – 'whose worth … | Stood challenger, on mount, of all the age | For her perfection' (4.7.27–9) – Imogen is her own champion. The heraldic descriptions of her beauty declare that this beauty reflects her inner virtues.

When later in the play Imogen's unconscious body is once again displayed to our view, heraldic language also recurs. Her brother carries her body out of the cave, and the delicate bluish tint of her skin is once more blazoned as azure ('the azured harebell, like thy veins' (4.2.223)) and she is again compared to a lily – 'O sweetest, fairest lily!' (4.2.202). Lilies were the most prominent heraldic bloom (along with the rose) and, in

---

[99] 2.2.15. For the heraldic significance of the lily, see further pp. 236 and 262–3.
[100] 'Some one Tincture, as when *Coat*-Armour consists of any one of the *Metals, Colours,* or *Furres* onely': Guillim, *Display of Heraldrie*, p. 48.
[101] Rothery, *Heraldry of Shakespeare*, p. 16.
[102] Ferne, *Blazon*, p. 163.
[103] Fox-Davies, *Complete Guide to Heraldry*, p. 72. Burrow writes that 'a reversed inescutcheon sanguine … was in theory used to indicate a rapist': Shakespeare, *Complete Sonnets and Poems*, p. 255, note to l. 206.

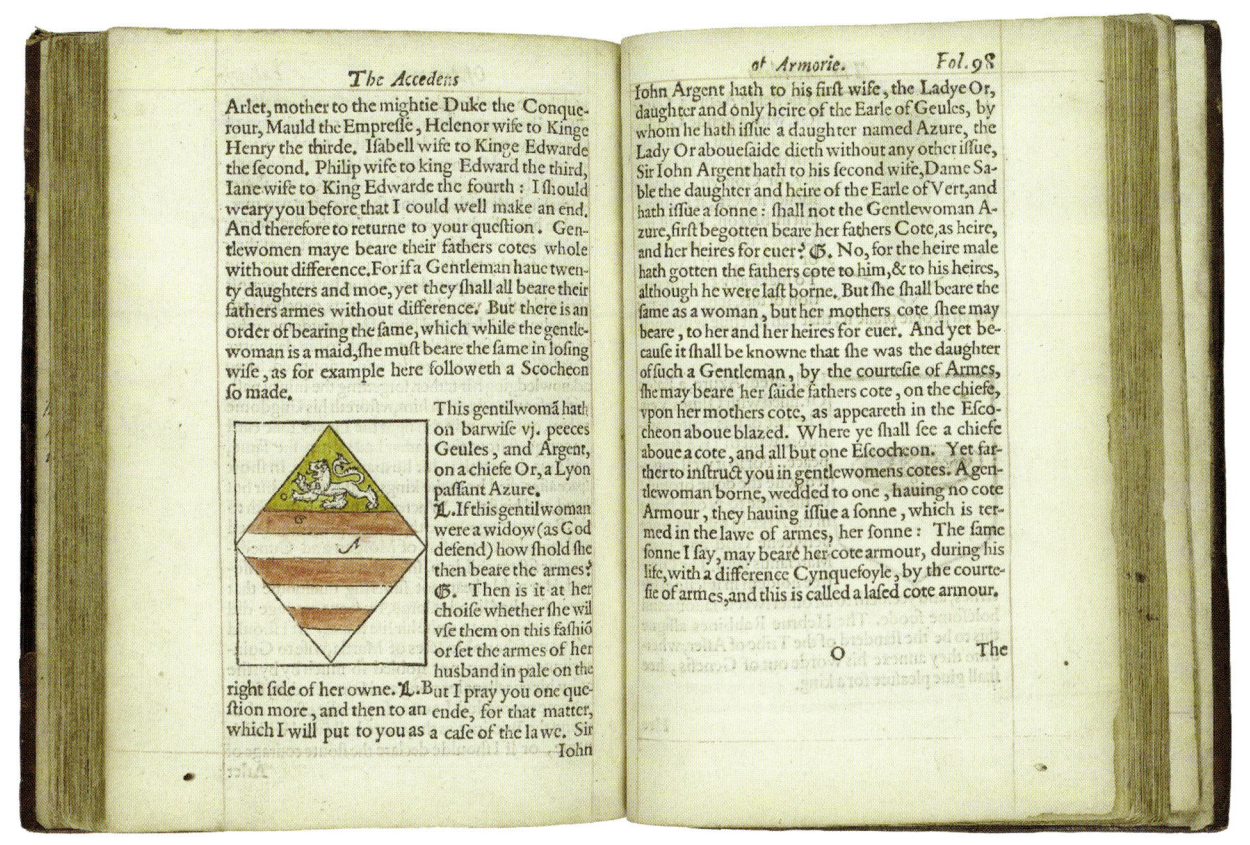

66. A woman's coat of arms (imaginary), in the characteristic shape of a lozenge; in Gerard Legh, *Accedence of Armorie* (1591), with colours added at an early date. Washington (DC), Folger Shakespeare Library, STC 15391 copy 2, ff. 97v–98.

addition to symbolizing Imogen's purity, it also represents her hidden royalty: Edward III had quartered the fleurs-de-lis of France with the lions of England, so for Shakespeare's audience the lily was a symbol of English royalty. The hidden royalty of her brothers is likewise declared through heraldic language. Belarius describes how the nobility of their nature is visible in their valour: 'O thou goddess, | Thou divine Nature, how thyself thou blazon'st | In these two princely boys!' (4.2.170–2).

Cymbeline is saturated with heraldic language. It concludes with the Soothsayer's vision – of an eagle disappearing into sunbeams (4.2.349) – which is finally understood once its heraldic imagery is recognised:

> [It] foreshowed our princely eagle,
> Th'imperial Caesar, should again unite
> His favour with the radiant Cymbeline,
> Which shines here in the west. (5.6.475–8)[104]

[104] Anachronistically, the traditional badge of English royalty – the sun – is already Cymbeline's symbol (the first probable evidence for its use as a royal badge is under Richard I: Siddons, *Heraldic Badges*, II, pt. 1, p. 230).

263

Cymbeline is the sun: the badge which, as we have seen above, will be worn by English royalty a thousand years later. *Cymbeline*'s anachronistic heraldic imagery fits with the way in which this history of first century England is peopled by medieval knights. Belarius, Guiderius and Arviragus are created knights on the battlefield (the most heroic of honours) and Cymbeline tells proudly how 'thy Caesar knighted me' (3.1.69). The anachronistic use of chivalry and heraldry in *Cymbeline*, do, however, link with the myths of sixteenth-century armory, as these claimed that England's history in the first century had a crucial relation with its heraldry. Cymbeline was the king who reigned in England while Christ lived, and the shield known as the cross of St George – 'a field of silver with a plaine Crosse of gules'[105] – was believed to have been brought to England at this time: 'Harding doth write, that Ioseph of Aramathia, whoe came into this realme with Vespasian the Emperour, and instructing Arviragus, (then the king of this land) in the faith, Christened him, and gave unto him this shield: which was 200 yeres before Saint George was borne'.[106] The climactic 'peace' of the play (it is *Cymbeline*'s final word) relates to the play's implicit Christian context, heraldically expressed through this banner which was both the flag of England given to Arviragus and that of Christ's Resurrection.

In *Cymbeline*, as in other late plays, Shakespeare seems to have been particularly interested in the relationship between appearance and reality. Shakespeare's mature plays have a non-satiric engagement with spectacle and participate in 'a rehabilitation of ... the visual'.[107] Heraldry – like theatre – is invested in the power of the visual: John Beaumont (the elder brother of the playwright) went so far as to claim that heraldry had made his eyesight more valuable to him: 'our sight (which of all senses wee hold ye derest) you haue made more precious unto us, by teaching us the excellent proportions of our visible objects'.[108]

Shakespeare sought his own grant of arms and in his plays he took heraldic imagery seriously. Popular sixteenth-century heraldic writers believed that a coat of arms enabled the onlooker to 'knowe and discerne' not only a knight's 'deedes of Armes' but also 'their excellent valiantnesse'.[109] Outward signs, according to these early modern theorists of heraldry, were accurate signifiers of inner worth. Shakespeare's plays implicitly accept

---

[105] Berners, *Gentlemans Academie*, f. 60v.
[106] Legh, *Accedens*, f. 28. The flag of St George was (mistakenly) believed to have been due to Richard I's devotion to the saint; but St George's cross was certainly worn by Edward I's troops in his Welsh campaigns. See O. de Laborderie, 'Richard the Lionheart and the Birth of a National Cult of St George in England: Origins and Development of a Legend', *Nottingham Medieval Studies*, xxxix (1995), pp. 37–53; D. A. L. Morgan, 'The Banner-bearer of Christ and Our Lady's Knight: How God became an Englishman Revisited', in *St George's Chapel, Windsor, in the Fourteenth Century*, ed. N. Saul (Woodbridge, 2005), pp. 51–61.
[107] Arthur F. Marotti, 'Shakespeare and Catholicism', in *Theatre and Religion: Lancastrian Shakespeare*, ed. Richard Dutton, Alison Findlay and Richard Wilson (Manchester, 2003), pp. 230, 232.
[108] A commendatory epistle to: Edmund Bolton, *Elements of Armories* (London, 1610), sig. A1.
[109] Richard Robinson, *The Auncient Order, Societie, and Unitie Laudable, of Prince Arthure, and his Knightly Armory of the Round Table* (London, 1583), sig. A1v.

both this moral reading of heraldic language and heraldry's own dependence on visual modes of apprehending identity. This, does not, however prevent him using it flexibly in characters (such as Richard II and Hal) who manipulate heraldic meaning for their own political ends or in creating heroines whose perfect embodiment of the correspondence between inward and outward virtue could be read as casting an ironic shadow on a system in which women were usually considered an inferior partner. Above all, given Protestantism's distrust of visual culture, there is perhaps something radical in staging characters (such as Imogen and Queen Katherine) who are exactly what their heraldic imagery claims them to be. Shakespeare's drama, like heraldry, was part of the visual culture of early modern England, and his thoughtful engagement with the moral potential of heraldic language is part of his dramaturgy's championing of the visual as a medium of truth.

Literary and Dramatic Heraldry

KATHRYN WILL

In late sixteenth- and early seventeenth-century England, people across the economic and social spectrum helped shape heraldry's symbolic meanings. Heraldic imagery was ubiquitous, appearing in the stained glass windows of parish churches and cathedrals, at funerals, on the uniforms of servants, and in the halls of the companies and guilds of London and the provinces. The level at which a person understood heraldry's technicalities constituted what might be characterized as *heraldic literacy*. Like its textual counterpart, heraldic literacy depended on a variety of factors, including social status, education and occupation. Broadly speaking, however, heraldic literacy differed in degree rather than kind: most people understood that a coat of arms marked familial identity and some degree of social status. The walls of one Derbyshire church bore illustrated shields supposedly belonging to the tribes of Israel, so that even illiterate parishioners might infer that heraldic bearings had been marks of distinction since pre-Christian times.[1] *The Gentleman's Academie*, Gervase Markham's 1595 adaptation of the *Boke of St. Albans*, presents this same argument in textual form. But instead of images, it provides the reader with Biblical details, explaining that Adam and Eve produced the first 'gentleman and churls,' and positing that Jesus was not only divinely blessed, but also held earthly distinction as a 'gentleman by his mother Mary princesse of coat armor.'[2]

Citing Biblical and classical precedent, many early modern writers on heraldry insisted that only virtuous men could bear arms. But in spite of their moral exactitude, the only *de facto* qualification for bearing a coat was a pedigree of sufficient repute. At court and among arms-bearing gentry, heraldry became a symbol of both a person's pedigreed status – an accident of birth – and their inherent fitness for that status. Given this fraught burden, heraldic imagery at these levels often highlighted bearers' social insecurities rather than alleviating them. For example, at Queen Elizabeth's Accession Day tournaments, courtiers placed their heraldic prowess on full display in hopes of gaining favour with the Queen. In addition to showcasing their familial coats of arms, they presented the Queen with *imprese*—single-use shields displaying personalized emblems accompanied by clever mottoes.[3] Impressing the Queen with one's wit was a

---

[1] Clare Tilbury, 'The Heraldry of the Twelve Tribes of Israel: An English Reformation Subject for Church Decoration,' *Jnl. of Ecclesiastical History*, 63 (2012), pp. 274–305.

[2] *The Gentlemans Academie. Or, The Booke of S. Albans: Containing Three Most Exact and Excellent Bookes: the First of Hawking, the Second of All the Proper Termes of Hunting, and the Last of Armorie: All Compiled by Iuliana Barnes, in the Yere from the Incarnation of Christ 1486. And Now Reduced into a Better Method*, by G.M. (London, 1595), sig. M3v.

[3] Alan Young, *Tudor and Jacobean Tournaments* (New York, 1988), pp. 123, 125ff.

difficult task, so many competitors hired poets to create *imprese* for them.[4] Both William Shakespeare and Ben Jonson were involved in this process: records show that Shakespeare was paid 44 shillings for creating a device for the Earl of Rutland,[5] and several of Jonson's *Epigrams* mock the recipients of his witty creations.[6] The fact that such creative outsourcing occurred is evidence that heraldry could easily conceal disparities between noblemen's aspirations and their actual abilities.

Though the heralds at the College of Arms were tasked with maintaining heraldry's aura of ancient privilege, their regulatory authority was a relatively recent phenomenon. The Crown had taken until the middle of the fifteenth century to allow heralds the authority to grant arms, and its financial support of the College was erratic.[7] As a consequence of its constantly shifting institutional role, the College's evidentiary standards were unclear and inconsistent, and its records were private, lending an air of secrecy to its proceedings. Most troublingly, the officers' genealogical principles were occasionally undercut by pressure from upwardly mobile customers – aspiring gentlemen who had questionable pedigrees but deep pockets.

The insular nature of the College, the heralds' perceived self-importance, and their vulnerability to strivers made them easy fodder for satirical critique. *Microcosmographie* (1628), John Earle's popular book of characters, includes a characteristic portrait of a greedy herald. Earle likens the herald to a travelling salesman, calling his grants of arms 'a kind of Pedlery ware, Scutchions, and Pennons and little Daggers, and Lyons, such as Children esteem and Gentlemen.' Indeed, he says the herald's fancy language is no more than a sales pitch: 'He seemes very rich in discourse, for he tels you of whole fields of gold and silver, Or & Argent, worth much in French, but in English nothing.'[8] In an early version of the text, Earle's herald also elevates undeserving men purely for profit: while 'he seemes to deale onely with Gentry … his cheifest purchases are from those that are newe.'[9] Other writers extended their critiques to heraldry's upwardly mobile customers. In *Picturae Loquentes* (1631), Wye Saltonstall disparages the 'young heir' who 'takes Armes afresh of the Herauld, and payes for crest, and Motto.'[10] Thomas Overbury

---

[4] *Ibid.*, p. 129.
[5] Scott-Giles, *Shakespeare's Heraldry*, pp. 19–20. He cites 'an entry in the accounts of the steward to the Earl of Rutland in connection with the celebrations on the King's accession day, 1613,' which reads, 'To Mr. Shakespeare in gold about my Lord's impresa 44 *s.*; to Richard Burbage for painting and making it, in gold 44 *s.*', p. 20. This transaction is also noted in Young, *Tudor and Jacobean Tournaments*, p. 129.
[6] See Epigram 29, 'To Sir Annual Tilter', and Epigram 73, 'To Fine Grand', in *Ben Jonson*, ed. Ian Donaldson (London, 1985), pp. 231, 246–7.
[7] Wagner, *Heralds of England*, pp. 29–30, 39; and the same author's *Heraldry in England* (London, 1946), p. 22.
[8] John Earle, *Micro-cosmographie. Or, A Peece of the World Discovered; in Essayes and Characters* (London, 1628), sig. I9.
[9] John Earle, *The Autograph Manuscript of Microcosmographie* (London, 1966), p. 137.
[10] Wye Saltonstall, *Picturae Loquentes* (London, 1631), sig. C11r–v.

mocks the Welsh's alleged obsession with armory in *A Wife* (1614), asserting that 'A Welchman' 'loves a Herrald, and speakes pedigrees naturally.'[11] Many Welsh living in England held ancestral titles and spoke proudly of their lineage, even if they lacked land or other accoutrements of wealth traditionally associated with English gentility.

Though mockery was the norm, some writers acknowledged that heralds could have a positive impact when they acted as guardians of social welfare. In *The Holy State* (1642), Thomas Fuller insisted that heralds could promote the honourable elements of English society by respectfully linking past and present. Fuller models the ideal herald after William Camden,[12] the former Clarenceux King of Arms and well-respected historian, describing him as a 'Warden of the temple of Honour … grave and faithfull in discharging the service he is imployed in,' who 'carefully preserveth the memories of extinguish'd Families' and 'is more faithfull to many ancient Gentlemen then their own Heirs were.'[13] In Fuller's view, the good herald helps memorialize history; he also preserves and applies its standards in order to ensure the moral purity of the English gentry. Rather than distributing coats with unprincipled abandon, he considers the qualifications of each individual applicant, refusing to 'favour [the] wealthy unworthinesse' of 'rich Clown[s],' but gladly granting 'honourable Arms to such as raise themselves by deserts.'[14]

Fuller's idealistic portrait, though atypical, was not mere fantasy. Many heralds had strict personal standards and were quick to cry foul if they suspected their colleagues of selling bad grants or falling short in their genealogical research. This internal policing stemmed partly from interpersonal conflict, but the heralds were also conscious of the high stakes attached to their activities and felt compelled to defend their institution's public image. Accordingly, some of their quarrels were aired in print and took place over a span of decades. Ralph Brooke, York Herald, attacked William Camden's genealogies in *A Discoverie of Certaine Errours Published in Print in the Much Commended Britannia* in 1596, and Camden's friend Augustine Vincent published a response criticizing Brooke's work in 1622.[15] While the average Londoner may not have had

---

[11] Thomas Overbury, *A Wife now the Widdow of Sir Thomas Overburye. Being a Most Exquisite and Singular Poem of the Choice of a Wife. Whereunto are Added Many Witty Characters, and Conceited Newes, Written by Himselfe and Other Learned Gentlemen His Friends* (London, 1614), sig. F2.

[12] Florence Sandler, 'Thomas Fuller,' in *The Dictionary of Literary Biography*, vol. 151: *British Prose Writers of the Early Seventeenth Century*, ed. Clayton D. Lein (Detroit, Mich., etc., 1995), pp. 157–69, at 161.

[13] Several decades later, Samuel Butler would approach this trait from a less complimentary angle, writing in his *Characters* that the herald 'is a kind of a necromancer and can raise the dead out of their graves to make them marry and beget those they never heard of in their lifetime.' *Characters*, ed. Charles W. Daves (Cleveland and London, 1970), pp. 115–18, at 116–17.

[14] Thomas Fuller, *The Holy State* (Cambridge, 1642), sig. T3–T4v.

[15] Ralphe Brooke, *A Discoverie of Certain Errours, Published in Print in the Much Commended Britannia in 1594* (London, [1596]), and Augustine Vincent, *A Discouerie of Errours in the First*

access to these tomes, the quarrel was familiar to educated men like Ben Jonson,[16] who may have owned both texts.

Because the system for granting arms was ubiquitous yet hotly contested, highly coveted yet easily abused, early modern writers found it both a useful symbolic social referent and a ready target. Balladeers and playwrights employed armorial allusions and jokes that spanned multiple social registers, and they highlighted heraldry's superficial elements in order to take aim at con artists and pretenders both rich and poor. These writers were attuned to the ways in which heraldry's specialized language and imagery could be marshalled for political and social commentary, particularly of the satirical variety. Anonymous composers of verse and well-known dramatists alike used heraldry's distinctive vocabulary and symbolism to represent the ethical poles that structured communal experience. While their attacks on heralds and pretenders could be severe, most writers ultimately upheld heraldry as a system that justly celebrated honour and exposed corruption.

Local Devices

In or around 1580, the brothers John and Lawrence Dutton, players in the Earl of Warwick's drama company, quit acting for Warwick and took up as players for the Earl of Oxford.[17] Though such transfers were far from unheard of, records suggest that the Dutton brothers were notorious for being fickle, volatile, and generally reprehensible. Rumour had it that Lawrence was a brothel keeper who let his customers avail themselves of his own wife's sexual services. Records from the Court of Exchequer suggest that he may have been involved in illegal money-changing activities,[18] and he was once jailed for committing 'disorders and frays' upon gentlemen at the Inns of Court.[19] He would eventually go to prison for defaulting on a loan, jump bail, and leave his brother to pay his debts.[20]

Edition of the Catalogue of Nobility, Published by Raphe Brooke, Yorke Herald, 1619 (London, 1622).

[16] According to David McPherson, 'In 1614 Jonson's personal library was called 'well-furnisht' by the great scholar John Selden, who would not use the term lightly,' in 'Ben Jonson's Library and Marginalia: An Annotated Catalog,' *Studies in Philology*, 71, no. 5, Texts and Studies (Dec. 1974), p. 5. The entries for Brooke's and Vincent's books are at pp. 32 and 106, respectively, although the latter is listed as a spurious attribution.

[17] W. Ingram, 'Laurence Dutton, Stage Player: Missing and Presumed Lost,' in *Medieval and Renaissance Drama in England*, 14, ed. John Pitcher (Cranbury, NJ, 2001), pp. 122–43, at 124–5; Edwin Nungezer, *A Dictionary of Actors And of Other Persons Associated With the Public Representation of Plays In England Before 1642* (New Haven, 1929), p. 123.

[18] Ingram, 'Laurence Dutton', pp. 123–5 ff.

[19] A. H. Nelson, *Monstrous Adversary: The Life of Edward De Vere, 17th Earl of Oxford* (Liverpool, 2003), pp. 240–1.

[20] Ingram, 'Laurence Dutton,' pp. 138–40; D. Kathman, 'Grocers, Goldsmiths, and Drapers: Freemen and Apprentices in the Elizabethan Theater,' *Shakespeare Quarterly*, 55 (2004), pp. 1–49, at 25.

The Duttons' transgressions, besides incurring reprimands from the authorities, also caught the attention of their contemporaries. In *The Elizabethan Stage*, E. K. Chambers cites a manuscript poem that lambastes the brothers for their behaviour. Angered at being called 'chameleons' for swapping employers, the Duttons had 'compared themselves to any gentleman.' An anonymous verse writer responded with vicious sarcasm, attributing to the brothers a vulgar coat of arms and describing it at length. The poem is four stanzas long and takes the form of an extended *blazon*—the formalized idiom used to describe the positions of the symbols on a heraldic shield. Its first eight lines are sufficient to convey its satirical tone and heraldic formula:

> The fyeld, a fart durty, a gybbet crosse-corded,
> A dauncing Dame Flurty of all men abhorred
> A lyther lad scampant, a roge in his ragges,
> A whore that is rampant, astryde wyth her legges,
> A woodcocke displayed, a calfe and a shepe,
> A bitch that is splayed, a do[r]mouse asleepe;
> A vyper in stynch, *la part de la drut*,
> Spell backwarde this Frenche and cracke me that nut.[21]

The verses' biting tone is characteristic of many libellous texts during the period, but its use of quasi-heraldic imagery is particularly creative. The writer convincingly parodies heraldic jargon and even uses a smattering of French, the technical language of blazon. The *fyeld*, or shield background, is not given a traditional metal or colour like *argent* (silver) or *gules* (red); instead, it's described as 'a fart durty,' a synesthetic image that combines sight with smell. The word *rampant* normally refers to an animal, usually a lion, rearing up with its forelegs raised. Readers familiar with the term could easily picture a 'whore that is rampant, astride with her legges.' Those aware of Lawrence's rumoured side business would have found the image particularly apropos, though any reader could appreciate its generic shock value. In folk tradition, the animals attributed to the shield possess unflattering traits, while *drut* (spelled backward as the poem suggests) constitutes a scatological joke. The remainder of the poem completes the device with 'three mynstrellmen pendent on three payre of gallowes,' and tops it with a bird bearing goat's horns – the trademark symbol of a cuckold.

This graphic ditty reveals that heraldry could be used in local culture as a means for characterizing persons and influencing public opinion. Heraldry's association with identity meant that it could be used ironically, for insult instead of commendation. Just as importantly, the idiosyncratic terminology of blazon provided a recognizable framework, one easily converted into memorable rhyming verse that could be written down or performed orally. The anonymous writer of the Dutton verses appropriates traditional blazon not to honour the brothers, but to condescendingly skewer them –and,

---

[21] British Library, MS Harley 7392, f. 97, printed in E. K. Chambers, *The Elizabethan Stage*, 4 vols (London and New York, 1923), II, p. 98.

if the poem was circulated among mutual acquaintances, to embarrass and admonish them. Adam Fox has explained that 'extempore rhymes, verses and ballads which ordinary men and women frequently composed themselves and sang or recited among their neighbours' circulated in both printed and oral form. Though both the high and lowbrow used verse to critique their fellows, 'the practice of inventing ballads and songs in order to ridicule and shame a rival or adversary' was 'most familiar … to the various peoples of the 'middle sort' who comprised urban or parish elites.'[22] Indeed, though the author of the Dutton libel could have been a spiteful neighbour or fellow actor, the poem's erudition suggests that it may have been the work of a social superior. Perhaps it was written by a bitter gentleman at the Inns of Court, still smarting from the 'disorders and frays' that Dutton had committed upon the writer and his friends.[23]

In print and song, mock heraldry was useful not just for publicly slighting immoral behaviour, but also for criticizing undeserved honour and its common counterpart, arrogant pretension. Some broadside ballads made these themes openly political by expressing nostalgia for an era when heraldic distinction belonged to an elite few. *Time's Alteration*, thought to have been published near the end of King James' reign, is one such lament. 'When this old cap was new,' its speaker declares, 'Good Hospitality, was cherishe[d] then of many, | Now poore men starve and dye, and are not helpt by any.' In this distant past, order and degree were properly respected; although the wealthy enjoyed better lives, they also took care of the poor:

> The Nobles of our Land,
>   were much delighted then,
> To have at their commaund
>   a crue of lusty men.
> Which by their Coats were knowne,
>   of tawny, red, or blue,
> With Crests on their sleeves showne,
>   When this old Cap was new.[24]

---

[22] Adam Fox, 'Ballads, Libels and Popular Ridicule in Jacobean England,' *Past & Present*, no. 145 (Nov. 1994), pp. 47–83, at 48, 57. For libels of notable court figures, see Alastair Bellany and Andrew McRae's online database of manuscript libels and anti-libels from the Stuart era, 'Early Stuart Libels: an edition of poetry from manuscript sources,' ed. Alastair Bellany and Andrew McRae, Early Modern Literary Studies Text Series I (2005), <http://purl.oclc.org/emls/texts/libels/>. One poem in the database is a defence of the Earl of Essex, who as Earl Marshal held jurisdiction over the royal heralds from 1597 until his execution in 1601 ('Admir-all weaknes wronges the right', Bodleian Library, MS Rawl. poet. 26, f. 20^v). Essex was publicly criticised for a number of political missteps, including the dubbing of dozens of knights against Queen Elizabeth's wishes. See Paul E. J. Hammer, *The Polarisation of Elizabethan Politics: The Political Career of Robert Devereux, 2nd Earl of Essex, 1585–1597* (Cambridge and New York, 1999), pp. 115, 222–5, 231.

[23] Nelson, *Monstrous Adversary: The Life of Edward De Vere*, pp. 240–1.

[24] Martin Parker, 'Time's Alteration; Or, The Old Man's rehearsall, what brave dayes he knew, A great while agone, when his Old Cap was new,' in *The Roxburghe Ballads*, II, ed. W. Chappell (Ballad Society, 1874), pp. 581–6, at 583.

Though its schema is more poetic than historically accurate, the ballad recalls a time when noblemen paid retainers who fought on their behalf and wore their livery. Liveries were distinctive uniforms in colours associated with a nobleman's family, often the ones used in his coat of arms. In addition to these colours (e.g. 'tawny, red, or blue'), the servants' garb might feature familial icons or badges. The ballad refers to these badges as 'Crests on their sleeves,' alluding to the fact that they frequently corresponded with images used in the family arms. During this era of proper order, the speaker continues, 'None under a degree of a knight, | in Plate dranke beere or Wine,' but now 'eache Mechanicall man, | hath a Cupboord of Plate for a [shew].'[25] That is, in the medieval past, only men of a certain income displayed their prominence in the form of silver or gold plateware, including items engraved with their coat of arms.[26] In the present day, by contrast, even 'mechanicall men' – i.e., artisans and craftsmen – can attain luxury goods that feature their ill-gotten heraldic devices.[27] The suggestion that lowly labourers were able to buy such valuables is poetic hyperbole, since poor men remained unable to afford arms. The speaker is actually caricaturing upstart gentlemen who brazenly flaunt their recently acquired titles.

This ballad was probably marketed to, read by, and sung for a whole range of people—not only gentlemen but also the very 'mechanicall men' it disparages.[28] Its complaints about middle-class pretension reflect a broad ambivalence about the changing nature of social and economic distinction in early modern England. But the song's sense of recent decline ignores the fact that such changes had been occurring for decades, and that heraldry in particular had long been used for pedestrian purposes. By the late sixteenth century, for example, most London guilds were using a corporate coat of arms. The earliest such coat was granted to the Drapers' Company of London in 1439, and other London companies or guilds had applied for and received coats during the following decades.[29] This meant that individual craftsmen and merchants could share in a communal heraldic identity. While the speaker of *Time's Alteration* bemoans a perceived shift away from rigid distinctions between labour and honour, other ballads – including one called *The Honourable Prentice* – do the opposite by openly trumpeting

---

[25] *Ibid.*, p. 585.

[26] In Ben Jonson's *Volpone* (1606), the title character receives one such plate from a flatterer hoping to inherit Volpone's wealth. Volpone's servant Mosca describes the plate as 'Massy, and antique, with your name inscribed, | And arms engraven' (1.1.93–4); *Ben Jonson's Plays and Masques*, ed. Richard Harp (New York, 2001), p. 11.

[27] In using the word 'mechanicall', the speaker probably also intends an additional, disparaging connotation of vulgarity or coarseness. When applied to persons, the *OED* defines it as 'Engaged in manual labour; belonging to the artisan class,' with the additional (now obsolete) connotation 'characteristic of this class, mean, vulgar,' *The Oxford English Dictionary*, 2nd edn., ed. J.A. Simpson and E. S. C. Weiner, 20 vols (Oxford, 1989), IX, p. 534, *s.v.* 'Mechanical', §2.a.

[28] Tessa Watt, *Cheap Print and Popular Piety 1550–1640* (Cambridge, 1991), pp. 1–8.

[29] J. Bromley and H. Child, *The Armorial Bearings of the Guilds of London* (London and New York, 1960), especially pp. vii and xviii; Wagner, *Heralds of England*, p. 126.

the virtues of the humble craftsman.[30] Indeed, guild members in London could find their work extolled in graphical format as well as in song. A broadside sheet engraved and printed by Benjamin Wright in 1596 displays the shields and mottoes of 60 London corporations, from the armourers to the watermen, surrounded by the coats of the English counties.[31] With its vivid illustrations and eye-catching layout, it demands to be coloured and displayed on the walls of guild halls, taverns, and craftsmen's homes. Highlighted in cheap ballads and printed broadsides, heraldic imagery could act as a badge of contemporary craft identity rather than an accoutrement of elite heritage.

Heraldry on the Popular Stage
Through verse, print, and song, the middling sort and those who plied trades could claim their own brand of heraldic privilege. Still, while those on the cusp of gentility could hope to ascend the social ladder, the actual chasm between working people and aristocrats remained vast. In fictional accounts, heraldry often highlighted that gap rather than bridging it. English writers had long used heraldic imagery satirically, as a way to denigrate the pretensions of the lowly. A fifteenth-century poem called *The Tournament of Tottenham* depicts peasants participating in a community joust; in addition to laughing at their cowardly behaviour, the writer also mocks their pedestrian heraldry. One man's crest is a sieve and a rake, 'poudred with … iii cantell [slices] of a cake.' Rather than evincing solidarity with its subjects, Victor Scherb observes, the poem comically 'ridicules rural and village occupations, and the socially inappropriate imitation of noble practices.'[32]

Likewise, early modern dramatists used heraldic signification to both celebrate and rebuke social strivers. With varying degrees of irony, they staged lowly workers rising to improbable glory, heralds conning customers for profit, and newly-minted gentlemen insisting that their lineages could be traced back to Noah's flood. Thomas Heywood's *The Foure Prentises of London, With the Conquest of Ierusalem* (*c.* 1594) is a genuine celebration of its titular chivalric apprentices. The four men are brothers; though they were born French nobles, their father's fall from royal grace has forced them to become artisans in London. The young men work as a mercer, a goldsmith, a haberdasher and a grocer, and despite the circumstances, their father observes, 'of the City-trades they have no scorne.'[33] Indeed, although the brothers express the desire to be soldiers, it is as

---

[30] *Thomas Heywood's* The Four Prentices of London: *A Critical, Old-Spelling Edition*, ed. Mary Ann Weber Gasior (New York and London, 1980), p. xxiv.

[31] Benjamin Wright, *The Armes of All the Cheife Corporatons* [sic] *of England wt. the Companees of London Described by Letters for Ther Seuerall Collores* (London, 1596), STC 26018.

[32] Victor I. Scherb, 'The Tournament of Power: Public Combat and Social Inferiority in Late Medieval England,' in *Studies in Medieval and Renaissance History*, xii (Old Ser., xxii) (1991), pp. 105–28, at 113.

[33] *Thomas Heywood's* The Four Prentices of London: *A Critical, Old-Spelling Edition*, ed. Mary Ann Weber Gasior (New York and London, 1980), 8, 1.1.35.

THE
Foure Prentises of London:
With the Conquest of Ierusalem.

As it hath bene diuerse times Acted, at the Red Bull, by the Queenes Maiesties Seruants.

written by THOMAS HEYWOOD.

67. The title-page of Thomas Heywood's *The Foure Prentises of London. With the Conquest of Ierusalem* (1615). The woodcut identifies the four brothers by using the arms of the London livery companies to which they belonged: the Grocers, Mercers, Haberdashers, and Goldsmiths.

artisans that they head to Jerusalem on a crusade, defeat their enemies, and earn crowns for their achievements.

Heywood's audience at the Rose Theatre ranged from guildsmen to the well-to-do. Despite the main characters' noble origins, the play takes a favourable view of merchants and of upward mobility more generally, making it closer in spirit to ballads like *The Honourable Prentice* than *Time's Alteration*.[34] The play's use of heraldry reflects its ultimately positive message about craft identity: the young men proudly bear their corporations' arms on pennons and shields throughout the crusade, using heraldic guild imagery to link their artisan labours with their chivalric aspirations. When the play was printed in 1615, the title page featured an illustration of the apprentices accompanied by their respective London companies' actual coats of arms. By prefacing the play-text with images familiar to all London residents, not just to the heraldically literate, the printer marked *The Four Prentices* as a vehicle for labour-based civic pride (Fig. 67).

Like Heywood, William Shakespeare – himself the belated acquirer of a coat of arms – generally declined to mock heraldic pretension. William's father John had begun the process of applying for a coat after becoming Bailiff of Stratford-Upon-Avon in 1568. He ran into financial troubles, however, and no grant was made until 1596, after William had revived the application process. Even then, the award emphasized the family's ancestral support for Henry VII while glossing over John Shakespeare's recent civil service.[35] The grant would also be challenged by Ralph Brooke, the contentious York Herald. Brooke accused his colleague William Dethick of making nearly two dozen grants to 'mean persons' 'for lucre.'[36] One of these grants was the Shakespeare arms, a shield that featured a diagonal spear and the phrase 'NON SANZ DROICT', meaning 'not without right.' Fittingly in light of its adamant motto, the grant was ultimately upheld (Figs 68a, b).

Given the circumstances, Shakespeare's status as an arms bearer was relatively fragile. As a result, he may have felt a personal, familial stake in maintaining heraldry's reputability, or at least in not diminishing it.[37] Despite the fact that he had never attended university, he had read the chronicle histories of Edward Hall and Raphael Holinshed, and through these sources he learned about the heraldic badges used by medieval kings. While his characters rarely blazon complete coats of arms, his history plays highlight heraldic icons in medieval contexts and emphasize their royal role. The plays refer to the

---

[34] See Fenella MacFarlane, 'To 'Try What London Prentices Can Do': Merchant Chivalry as Representational Strategy in Thomas Heywood's *The Four Prentices of London*,' in *Medieval and Renaissance Drama in England*, vol. 13, ed. J. Pitcher (Madison, NJ, 2001), pp. 136–64, especially 147–8.

[35] Samuel Schoenbaum, *William Shakespeare: A Documentary Life* (Oxford, 1975), pp. 36–8; Scott-Giles, *Shakespeare's Heraldry,* pp. 28–9.

[36] A. Wagner, *Heralds of England*, p. 188; Katherine Duncan-Jones, *Shakespeare: An Ungentle Life* (London, 2010), p. 116.

[37] See Duncan-Jones, *Shakespeare: An Ungentle Life*, pp. 94–119, and Scott-Giles, *Shakespeare's Heraldry*, p. 25.

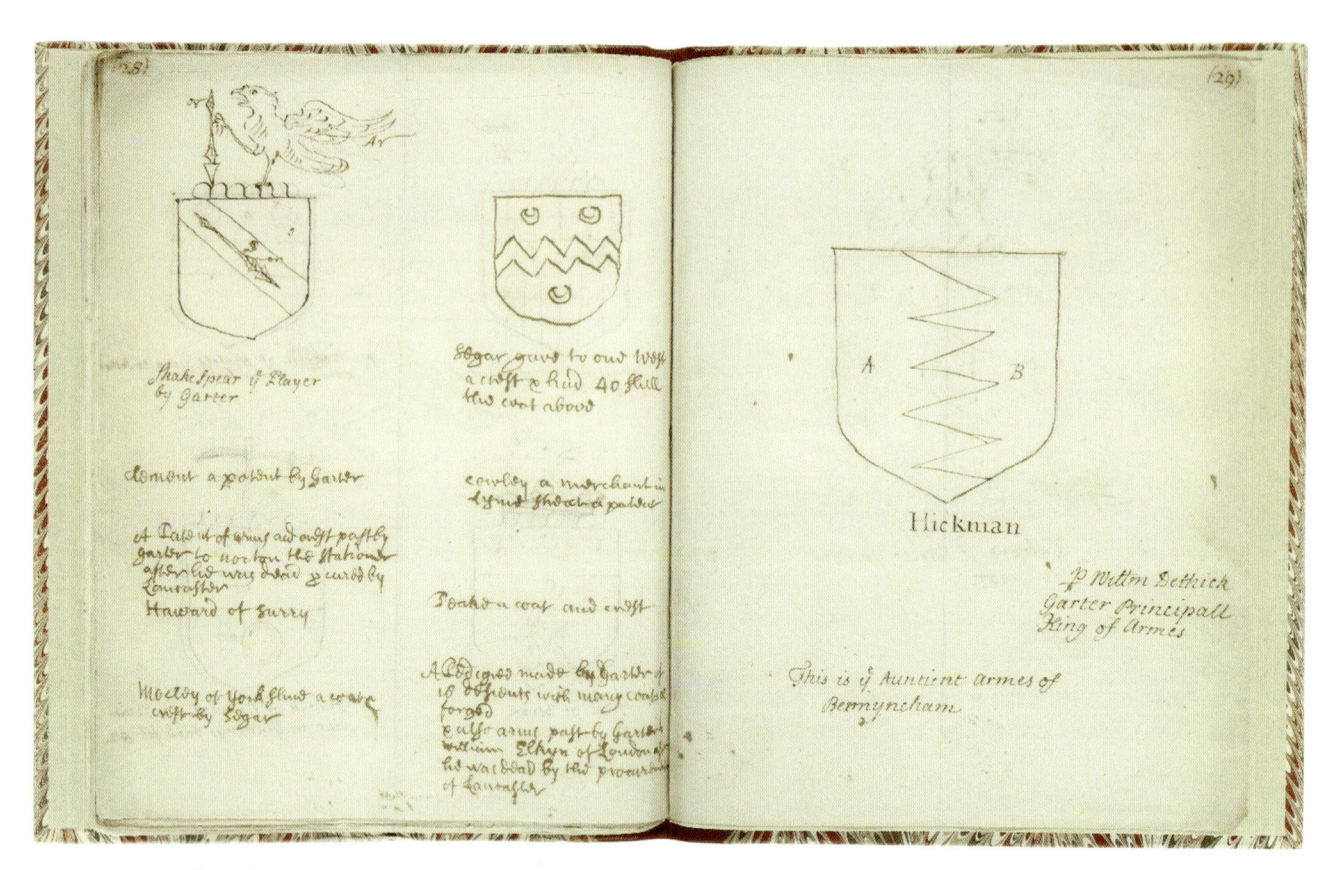

red and white roses of the Lancastrians and Yorkists, the sun of Richard II, and Richard III's tusked boar.[38] Having designed a tournament *impresa* for the Earl of Rutland, he was also familiar with heraldry's ongoing role in courtly contests. He incorporates this knowledge into the second act of *Pericles*, in which six knights present their heraldic *imprese* to a king and his daughter prior to a competitive tilt.[39] The characters discuss each image and motto in enough detail to suggest that Shakespeare consulted emblem books before writing the scene.[40]

Rather than satirizing such moments of heraldic display, Shakespeare presented them as evocative theatrical spectacles. He also turned heraldic language into poetry, weaving blazon into his dialogue as verbal ornamentation. Listeners familiar with heraldry's colours may have detected subtle commentary on war in Hamlet's Pyrrhus

---

[38] Scott-Giles, *Shakespeare's Heraldry*, pp. 18–20.

[39] William Shakespeare, *Pericles, Prince of Tyre*, ed. Hallett Smith, in *The Riverside Shakespeare*, 2nd edn., ed. G. Blakemore Evans et al. (Boston and New York, 1997), pp. 1531–64, at pp. 1539–40, 2.2.1–59.

[40] 'The author was of a certainty acquainted with more than one Emblem writer, in more than one language, and Paradin, Symeoni, and our own Whitney may be recognised in his pages. We conclude that he had them before him, and copied from them when he penned the second scene of the Second Act of Pericles,' Henry Green, *Shakespeare and the Emblem Writers* (London, 1870), p. 158.

68. Shakespeare's arms, as drawn in a copy, partly written by Peter le Neve (d. 1720), Norroy King of Arms, of Ralph Brooke's manuscript, 'A note of some coats and crests lately come to my hands given by William Dethick when he was York herald'. This latter manuscript, evidently, was part of Brooke's campaign against Dethick.

Folger Shakespeare Library (Washington, DC), MS V.a.350, p. 28: (a) with facing page (opposite), and (b) enlarged detail of the Shakespeare arms (above).

speech, which uses the genteel vocabulary of heraldry to evoke a graphically violent battle:

> The rugged Pyrrhus, he whose sable arms,
> Black as his purpose, did the night resemble
> When he lay couched in th'ominous horse,
> Hath now this dread and black complexion smear'd
> With herald[r]y more dismal: head to foot
> Now is he total gules, horridly trick'd
> With blood of fathers, mothers, daughters, sons … (2.2.452–8)[41]

Though the allusions deepen its meaning, the passage was presumably comprehensible even to the heraldically illiterate. Those unfamiliar with the words *sable* (black), *gules* (red), or *trick* (to draw a coat of arms in outline and name its component colours) could still visualize the image of a blood-soaked warrior, thanks to the accompanying imagery of black arms and slaughtered innocents.

Though he often uses heraldic imagery to describe the exploits of noblemen, Shakespeare also invokes it to contextualize quotidian experiences and emotions. In *A Midsummer Night's Dream*, for instance, a distraught Helena uses heraldic metaphor to reflect on her failing friendship with Hermia. She muses that the two women have always been close – like twin cherries on a single stem, or

> …with two seeming bodies, but one heart,
> Two of the first, [like] coats in heraldry,
> Due but to one, and crowned with one crest. (3.2.212–14)[42]

Early critics of the play professed difficulty parsing the passage's meaning, noting that it fails to follow the formal rules of blazon.[43] Modern editors agree that Helena is describing a bifurcated shield topped with a single figure – perhaps a 'hart,' punningly suggested by the phrase 'one heart.'[44] Such shields normally belonged to married couples, so Helena is suggesting that she and Hermia are as intimately bound as a husband and

---

[41] William Shakespeare, *The Tragedy of Hamlet, Prince of Denmark*, ed. Frank Kermode, in *The Riverside Shakespeare*, 2nd edn., pp. 1189–245, at 1206.

[42] William Shakespeare, *A Midsummer Night's Dream*, ed. Anne Barton, in *The Riverside Shakespeare*, 2nd edn., pp. 256–83, at 270.

[43] For early debates about the passage, see Joseph Ritson, *Cursory Criticisms on the Edition of Shakspeare published by Edmond Malone: 1752–1803* (London, 1792), pp. 44–5; and *The Plays and Poems of William Shakspeare*, ed. Edmond Malone and James Boswell (London, 1821), V, p. 272(–3) n. 2. The latter is known as the 'Third Variorum' edition of Shakespeare's plays. Malone left his materials to Boswell, who published the new edition after Malone died.

[44] R. A. Foakes writes: 'Helena's image is of a shield divided into halves of the same color ('Two of the first'), and thus in effect not differentiated. This coat-of-arms is granted by right to one person ('Due but to one') and surmounted by a single crest (a hart or heart).' *The New Cambridge Shakespeare* (Cambridge and New York, 2003), p. 102. Russ McDonald, editor of the Penguin edition, adds that read this way, the image becomes 'analogous to the *double cherry* on *one stem*' referred to earlier in the passage (New York, 2000), p. 50.

wife.[45] The passage is both heraldically literate and emotionally impressionistic: Shakespeare heightens Helena's sense of fragility by comparing her estrangement to marital strife. And although the analogy displays his familiarity with an armorial rule, his main goal is to elicit the audience's compassion – and perhaps empathy – for a character who has lost a dear friend.

In *The Merry Wives of Windsor* (*c*. 1597), his sole play set in Elizabethan England, Shakespeare engages in a rare moment of middle-class heraldic satire. At the play's opening, several characters, including a Welsh parson named Evans, converse punningly about a local Justice's armorial device. The justice, Sir Robert Shallow, boasts that his lineage stretches back three hundred years, and notes that his coat of arms features a dozen white luces, a type of small fish (1.1.16–17).[46] Responding to Shallow's blazon, Evans inadvertently refers to the fish as 'louses'; then, in a comical misunderstanding of conventional heraldic attitudes, he describes them as *passant* (walking): 'The dozen white louses do become an old coad [*sic*] well. It agrees well passant: it is a familiar beast to man and signifies love' (19–21). In an attempt to display his heraldic aptitude, Evans instead reveals his ignorance. The scene is not meant to satirize arms ownership or heraldry as a whole; instead, Shakespeare is poking fun at the Welsh by alluding to their reputed love of heraldic pomposity.[47] Here and throughout his oeuvre, Shakespeare references heraldry not to critique the system's foibles, but to reveal the social bonds that underpin its presence in everyday life. Both personally and professionally, he viewed heraldry as a symbolic medium that illuminated personal relationships and communal histories.

In contrast to Shakespeare's sympathetic approach, Ben Jonson openly disdained heraldry's use in contemporary culture. A voracious reader with a 'literary man's library',[48] he owned Brooke's and Vincent's sparring genealogy texts but not the popular heraldic manuals of the day, such as Gerard Legh's *Accedens of Armory* (1562) or John Guillim's *Display of Heraldry* (1610). Still, Jonson was clearly familiar with heraldic rules and terminology: one early-twentieth-century critic observes that his citations of

---

[45] Valerie Traub contends that Helena's reflections 'ask us to recognize female unity as analogous in its emotional intensity and physical closeness to marriage. [...] like the separate coats of arms of a marital pair, [Helena] and Hermia have been not only emotionally unified, but materially and symbolically conjoined, 'crowned with one crest''; *The Renaissance of Lesbianism in Early Modern England* (Cambridge and New York, 2002), pp. 171–2.

[46] William Shakespeare, *The Merry Wives of Windsor*, ed. Anne Barton, in *The Riverside Shakespeare*, 2nd edn., pp. 324–60, at p. 324.

[47] Similarly, although a mock ceremony at the play's conclusion seems to critique the ritual admission of knights to the Order of the Garter, the scene lampoons the 'devolution of chivalric principles' in Elizabethan culture rather than the Order itself; James N. Ortego II, 'Seeking the Medieval in Shakespeare: The Order of the Garter and the Topos of Derisive Chivalry,' *Fifteenth-Century Studies*, 35 (2010), pp. 80–104, at 97. For an explanation of the Garter context, see David Crane's introduction to the play in The New Cambridge edition (Cambridge and New York, 2010), pp. 1–3.

[48] McPherson, 'Ben Jonson's Library and Marginalia', p. 6.

heraldry are 'far more numerous and technical' than Shakespeare's.[49] They are also almost exclusively satirical, a paradox that reflects Jonson's ambivalent attitude toward social climbing and genteel pretension. The playwright had famously fraught relationships with his heritage and his multiple occupations. During his childhood, his family was poor; like Shakespeare, he missed out on a university education, and he was a dues-paying member of the Bricklayers' Company for a good part of his adult life.[50] Yet he claimed armigerous status as an adult, telling his friend William Drummond that his arms were 'three spindles or rhombi; his own word about them, *percontabor* or *perscrutator*.' These had been the arms of the Johnstones of Annandale, his Scottish ancestors.[51] Indeed, Jonson eventually surpassed his humble origins. Having earned renown as an actor and a playwright, in 1616 he was awarded the position of court poet, and he published his works in folio that same year.[52]

While Jonson considered writing an intellectual endeavour, he saw theatrical spectacle as a kind of fraud. Throughout his career, he privileged poetry and maligned theatre's 'mighty shows', deriding its visual displays as mere 'painting and carpentry.'[53] Still, Jonson found theatre useful for venting his annoyance with social deception, particularly among the middling sort. He was highly attuned to heraldry's superficial appeal, and many of his plays portray the system as a tool misunderstood by ignoramuses and misused by charlatans. In *The New Inn* (1629), he pokes fun at middle- and lower-class characters who consider heralds' quarrels the height of scholarly debate. The New Inn's host tells a visiting lord that his son's nurse is well-versed in genealogy and 'studies Vincent against York' (2.6.28).[54] The lord responds with sarcastic admiration, remarking, 'She'll conquer if she read Vincent' (28–9). Then, in an aside to his audience, he snickers, 'A bawd, I hope, and knows [how] to blaze a coat' (31). His pun on 'blaze' links *blazon* (heraldic description) and the burning sensation that accompanies a sexually transmitted disease.[55] Instead of respecting the nurse's genealogical aptitude, the lord turns it into evidence of her sexual promiscuity.

---

[49] A. H. Nason, *Heralds and Heraldry in Ben Jonson's Plays, Masques and Entertainments* (New York, 1907), p. 3.

[50] Jonson may have attended Cambridge for several weeks, but no official records of his time there survive. Ian Donaldson, *Ben Jonson: A Life* (Oxford and New York), pp. 85–90; David Riggs, *Ben Jonson: A Life* (Cambridge, 1989), pp. 4–5.

[51] London Consistory Court records also refer to Jonson as 'Armiger'. Donaldson, *Ben Jonson: A Life*, pp. 163, 56–7.

[52] *Ibid.*, pp. 322, 324–31.

[53] Ben Jonson, 'Expostulation with Inigo Jones': *ibid.*, pp. 462–5, lines 39, 50. Inigo Jones, Surveyor of the King's Works, was the stage designer for many of Jonson's Stuart court masques. Jonson's open feud with his artistic collaborator eventually cost the poet his court position. See *ibid.*, pp. 422–5.

[54] Ben Jonson, *The New Inn*, ed. Michael Hattaway (Dover and Manchester, 1984), p. 114.

[55] *Ibid.*, p. 114, n. 31.

LITERARY AND DRAMATIC HERALDRY

In *The Staple of News* (*c.* 1624), Jonson portrays heraldry as a farcical status system easily manipulated by the venal and disingenuous. The play features a character named Piedmantle, whose name is a parody of the title 'Bluemantle Pursuivant,' one of the junior officers in the College of Arms (*pied* is French for 'foot', emphasizing his lowly status). Like several other characters, Piedmantle hopes to win the favor of Lady Pecunia, the play's personification of money. He claims that he has traced Pecunia's lineage 'From mans creation' (2.2.15), a feat that is sure to flatter her and win her affection.[56] Pecunia is indeed eager to hear his findings, as she knows she is descended from royalty: 'By the Fathers side, I come from *Sol* [the sun],' she boasts; 'My Grandfather was *Duke* of *Or* [gold]' (4.4.11–12). To her delight and the other characters' confusion, Piedmantle displays her coat of arms and blazons it in all its complicated glory. In honour of Sol, it includes 'In a field azure, a sun proper, beamy' (15–16), as well as a multitude of other symbols:

Piedmantle	She bears (an't please you) *Argent*, three *Leeks vert*, In *Canton Or,* and *tassel'd* of the *first*.
Pennyboy Canter	Is not this *Canting?* do you understand him?
Pennyboy Junior	Not I; but it sounds well, and the whole thing Is rarely painted: I will have such a Scroll, What ere it cost me. (25–30)

In heraldic usage, 'canting arms' are coats that make a visual pun on the bearer's name. The device that Piedmantle gives Pecunia is full of such puns: the 'beamy' sun references Sol; the *Canton Or* honours her grandfather, the Duke of Or; and leeks, the national badge of Wales, represent Pecunia's 'Welsh blood' (24). But when Pennyboy Canter calls the blazon 'canting',[57] his apparent confusion suggests that he also intends the word in its non-heraldic sense, meaning 'pretentious jargon.' Piedmantle's obscure terminology only 'sounds well' to Pennyboy Junior because of its obscurity. More importantly, it describes an impressively illustrated heraldic device. The combination of linguistic and visual magnificence intrigues the eager young man enough to make him covet his own (unmerited) heraldic shield.

With this scene, Jonson displays his erudition alongside his disdain. One scholar observes that 'every technical term in the passage … contributes directly and materially

---

[56] In another of Jonson's allusions to heraldic texts, Piedmantle brags that he has 'read *The Elements* / And *Accidence* and all the leading books' (21–2). Ben Jonson, *The Staple of News*, ed. Anthony Parr (Manchester and New York, 1988), pp. 117–18. All subsequent references to the play are to this edition.

[57] 'Canting' has many connotations, several of which are relevant here. Its heraldic definition, 'allusive arms,' appears under the *OED*'s participial adjective entry (*The Oxford English Dictionary*, 2nd edn., ed. J. A. Simpson and E. S. C. Weiner, 20 vols (Oxford, 1989), II, p. 848, *s.v.* 'Canting', as participial adjective, §5). Pennyboy Canter's meaning is as a verbal substantive: 'the use of the special phraseology of a particular class or subject (always *contemptuous*); jargon, gibberish, *ibid.*, p. 847, *s.v.* 'Canting', as verbal substantive, second entry, §1.2. The *OED* quotes his question as an illustrative example of this usage.

to Jonson's satirical allegory.'[58] The exchange demonstrates Jonson's frustration with the fact that heraldic rhetoric was often used deceptively, to impress the ignorant and flatter the wealthy. Given his own hard-earned success as a writer, he may have resented the tendency of the heraldic economy to reward lying heralds and uninformed, mercenary climbers. The latter paid for undeserved coats in order to hear themselves called gentlemen in lofty terms, while the former used their cunning to exploit heraldry's surface appeal and make a quick material profit. Jonson's public condemnation of buyers and sellers of heraldry is likely to have stemmed from his private conviction that heraldic distinction should be earned rather than bought. As an upwardly mobile poet, Jonson only respected arms that reflected their owner's hard work and intellectual prowess.

Heraldry, particularly its imagery, was a quotidian component of life in late sixteenth and early seventeenth century England. Edmund Bolton, the author of a 1610 treatise called *The Elements of Armories*, complained that with arms 'occurring every-where, in seales, in frontes of buildings, in utensils, in all things,' few people bothered to learn anything about their history or proper use, 'sildome [going] any farther then to fill up a wide Wardrobe with particular Coates.'[59] In Bolton's eyes, heraldry's increased availability had caused a shameful indifference to its precepts. Social strivers simply acquired heraldic imagery for their own gain and failed to respect it as a historical framework for gentility. While Heywood and Shakespeare might have taken issue with this cynical characterization, Jonson would surely have agreed: very few people were familiar with the obscure details of blazoning or pedigree research, and heraldry was often used for personal advancement. But this perspective disregarded the fact that heraldic imagery and language had *always* been manipulable. From the Court to the city streets, heraldry's meanings varied widely depending on the prejudices and predilections of those who created and consumed it. Now, thanks to the circulation of printed verses, illustrations and plays, it was being exploited in new contexts, bringing its idiosyncrasies to the attention of a wider public than ever before. The writers of popular print and drama were expanding heraldry's versatility as social commentary. On stage and in verse, they deflated heraldry's puffed-up airs while simultaneously expanding its cultural relevance.

---

[58] Nason, *Heralds and Heraldry in Ben Jonson's Plays, Masques and Entertainments*, p. 115.
[59] Edmund Bolton, *The Elements of Armories* (London, 1610), sig. A4.

Heraldry and Alternate Emblematic Forms in the Age of Shakespeare

ALAN R. YOUNG

As historians of heraldry have often noted, certain features of an achievement of arms, such as crests, mottoes, charges, and supporters, appear to have migrated from a rich and varied body of mottoes and visual devices commonly used by their bearers to provide signs of identity. Because such verbal and visual devices contributed to the early development of heraldry, they were understandably often of considerable interest to heralds and others who later studied and wrote about heraldry. Even after heraldry had become a well-defined system of hereditary visual signs that served to mark an individual bearer's social rank, ancestry and family identity, that same individual – in addition to a coat of arms – might choose some other form of alternate identification. What follows here is a discussion of two of the most common of these: the impresa and the badge. A concluding section will then examine how some authors of English emblem books used heraldic arms and badges as the basis for some of their designs.

The *impresa* (plural: *imprese*) was the most notable and complex counterpart to heraldry. During the fifteenth and sixteenth centuries, the impresa, a carefully crafted combination of motto and emblematic image, became a highly regarded art form in Europe and especially in Italy. For the most part, an impresa was created by an individual (for himself or a third party) to express his or her circumstances, state of mind, or immediate or lifelong goal. It was commonly designed for display in connection with a particular situation or occasion, such as a courtship, tournament, pageant, masque, or specific military endeavour. Accordingly it was frequently valid only for a limited time and context. When Shakespeare composed an impresa for Francis Manners, earl of Rutland (for which the playwright was paid forty-four shillings in gold), the impresa was placed on a shield and specifically designed for presentation to James I at the Accession Day tournament on 24 March, 1613.[1] An impresa might also be created for fictive characters in plays or literary romances, familiar examples being found in Shakespeare's *Pericles* and Sidney's *Arcadia*.[2] It should be noted, however, that imprese were also often used to express the collective concerns and identity of a group or organization.

The Heraldic Badge

This latter use of the impresa to express a collective identity would appear to overlap somewhat with the role played by the heraldic badge, the history of which may have

---

[1] See Alan R. Young, *Tudor and Jacobean Tournaments* (London, 1987), pp. 72, 207.
[2] For detailed discussions on the use of imprese in both works, see A. R. Young, 'A Note on the Tournament Impresas in *Pericles*,' *Shakespeare Quarterly*, 36 (1985), pp. 453–6; and 'Sir Philip Sidney's Tournament Impresas,' *Sidney Newsletter*, 6, no. 1 (1985), pp. 6–24.

preceded the development of both the impresa and heraldry itself.[3] The badge was an identification device, generally consisting of a visual image to which occasionally was added a motto or a cypher. In its developed form, it tended not to be borne by the person to whom it belonged,[4] but instead was worn by that individual's followers and retainers. As one modern herald explained, the badge was 'a mark of ownership or allegiance, whose most important and distinctive use was for display on a lord's standard in the field and on the livery of his retainers, but which was also borne on belongings and decorations.'[5] Tombs, monumental brasses, buildings and stained glass windows were also places where badges were displayed. Sometimes a visual device on a badge would match part of its owner's achievement of arms, whether a supporter, or part of a crest, or a charge upon the shield. It might also appear on its owner's standard or banner.[6] Among examples of badges derived from their owner's arms were the hart's head of Sir William Stanley, the martlets on the standard of Sir John Wogan, the lion and cinquefoils of Sir William Pierrepoint,[7] and the white hart of Richard II, whose achievement of arms included two white harts as supporters. Similarly, Richard III's badge of a white boar, famously mocked in Shakespeare's *Richard III*, reflected his achievement of arms, the supporters of his coat of arms being two white boars.

At other times, badges appear to have existed quite independently of their owners' arms. A number of royal badges provide examples of this kind, among them the *planta genista* (broom cod) attributed to Henry II, the star and crescent of Richard I, the sun-in-splendour of Richard II, the white rose-en-soleil and the falcon with fetterlock of Edward IV,[8] the swan of Henry V and Henry VI, and the crowned portcullis of Henry VII (a badge inherited from his mother, Margaret Beaufort). Henry VII, the first Tudor monarch, also had a hawthorn bush and crown with the cypher 'HR'.[9] His son Henry

---

[3] On the origin of badges, see Michael Powell Siddons (Wales Herald Extraordinary), *Heraldic Badges in England and Wales*, 3 vols in 4 parts (Woodbridge, 2009), I, pp. 13–15. Siddons's monumental work provides a compendious annotated catalogue of badges. For two earlier illustrated accounts, together with lists of badges, see Mrs Bury Palliser, *Historic Devices, Badges, and War-Cries* (London, 1870), pp. 268–353; and Arthur Charles Fox-Davies, *Heraldic Badges* (London, 1907), pp. 74–161. For an illustrated discussion of a number of surviving English royal badges from the medieval period, see John Steane, *The Archaeology of the Medieval English Monarchy* (London, 1999), pp. 131–4, 152, 161, 176 and *passim*.

[4] Arthur Charles Fox-Davies, *A Complete Guide to Heraldry* (New York, 1909), p. 454.

[5] Hugh Stanford London (Norfolk Herald Extraordinary), *Royal Beasts* (London: The Heraldry Society, 1956), p. 4.

[6] On this point, see Siddons, *Heraldic Badges*, I, p. 2. See also Woodcock and Robinson, *Oxford Guide to Heraldry*, p. 107.

[7] See Siddons, *Heraldic Badges*, I, p. 3.

[8] See Woodcock and Robinson, *Oxford Guide to Heraldry*, pp. 107–8. These authors cite the records of badges in three College of Arms manuscripts: M 3; L 14 pt. 2; and Vincent 172.

[9] Henry VII's badge has been much discussed. It does not, it would appear, allude to the place where legend has it that Richard III's crown was found prior to Henry's crowning following the Battle of Bosworth in 1485. See Virginia Kay Henderson, 'Retrieving the 'Crown in the Hawthorn Bush':

VIII created one of his various badges by taking his father's Tudor rose (itself a combination of the red rose of Lancaster and the white rose of York) and dimidiating it with the pomegranate of his first wife, Catherine of Aragon.[10] Queen Anne (Boleyn) had a crowned falcon and sceptre, and another wife, Queen Jane (Seymour), had a badge depicting a castle surmounted by a crowned phoenix.[11] Henry's daughter Mary I kept her father's Tudor rose but replaced the pomegranate with a sheaf of arrows, in acknowledgement of her marriage to King Philip of Spain, while Henry's other daughter, Elizabeth I, used her mother's crowned falcon and sceptre unaltered as one of her badges.[12] At various times, Elizabeth also used a sieve, and a crowned rose with the motto 'Rosa sine spina' (Rose without a thorn) (Fig. 69).[13] As many commentators have noted, large numbers of badges, including some of those referred to here, are still to be seen on English inn signs.[14]

The Impresa

The badge may often appear to be emblematic in some way.[15] Fierce beasts, such as the boar of Richard III or the rampant bear of Richard Neville, earl of Warwick, might

---

The Origins of the Badges of Henry VII,' in *Traditions and Transformations in Late Medieval England*, ed. Douglas Biggs, Sharon D. Michalove and A. Compton Reeves (Leiden, 2002), pp. 237–60.

[10] The history of the Tudors' rose badges is explored by S. Anglo, *Images of Tudor Kingship* (London, 1992), chapter iv. Anglo argues at p. 35 that for the Tudor monarchs, beasts and badges 'became symbols not of pedigree but of the dynasty itself'.

[11] Thomas Evelyn Scott-Ellis, Lord Howard de Walden, reproduced this in *Banners, Standards, and Badges, from a Tudor Manuscript in the College of Arms* (London, 1904), p. 19. Scott-Ellis notes that the badge was emblazoned on a grant of land to Jane Seymour by Henry VIII in 1536. Later, the badge was granted by Edward VI to his maternal relatives. For another depiction of the phoenix badge, see Ottofried Neubecker's *A Guide to Heraldry* (London, 1979), p. 198.

[12] An example of Elizabeth's use of the badge is to be found on her virginals, now in the Victoria and Albert Museum, London. Three examples of Anne Boleyn's crowned falcon are to be found in the letters patent creating Anne Boleyn marquess of Pembroke in her own right, issued 1 September 1532 at Windsor Castle (British Library, MS Harley 303, f. 1); in a design for a table fountain by Hans Holbein the Younger, *c.* 1533, now in Basel, Kunstmuseum, Kupferstichkabinett; and in Anne's copy of Clément Marot's *Le Pastor évangélique*, in which the falcon badge is displayed below her coat of arms. This beautifully illuminated manuscript was probably presented to her by the French ambassador, Jean de Dinteville, on the occasion of her coronation, the festivities for which started in late May 1533 (British Library, Royal MS 16 E. xiii). Jane Seymour, Henry's third wife, used a somewhat different falcon badge, which derived from the Seymour family badge.

[13] The sieve, symbol of the Vestal Virgin Tuccia, was appropriated by Elizabeth. Camden in *Remaines* claims it was one of Elizabeth's most commonly-used devises (p. 182). It appears in three of her painted portraits, one of which is in the collection of the Folger Shakespeare Library (Fig. 69). The motto 'Rosa sine spina' was used on the coinage of Henry VIII and his successors (including James I and Charles I). Elizabeth on her coinage added the image of the rose.

[14] On this topic, see Jacob Larwood and John Camden Hotten, *English Inn Signs* (London, 1951), especially the chapter on 'Heraldic and Emblematic Signs', pp. 64–97. See also Palliser, *Historic Devices*, pp. 2–3.

[15] Siddons has argued that the supposed 'meanings' of badges were often 'made up at a later date in

TVTTO VEDO &
MOLTO MANCHA

E R

SANCHO RIPO
SO & RIPOSATO
AFFANO 1579

HERALDRY AND ALTERNATE EMBLEMATIC FORMS

appear to be emblematic of the warlike qualities desirable in a warrior, while combined white and red roses emblematize the union of the formerly warring houses of York and Lancaster. However, the badge functioned primarily as a mark of identification, fealty, and ownership, and its emblematic qualities (if any) were of secondary significance. This was not the case with the impresa. As noted above, the impresa was largely for occasional use or the expression of some personal lifelong aspiration; it was supposed to be somewhat obscure in meaning, thereby wittily challenging those who sought to interpret it; and it was used only by its owner, though institutional imprese appear to have been a departure from this. Because the impresa was intended to be difficult to interpret, as an identification device it was very different from both the badge and the coat of arms.

Among the earliest examples of imprese are those to be found in medieval France and the court of Burgundy in the late fourteenth century. In England, probably in imitation of French practice, they were first employed in tournaments during the reign of Edward III (1327–77).[16] The publication much later of Paolo Giovio's *Dialogo dell'imprese militari et amorose* (1555),[17] Ludovico Domenichi's *Ragionamente* (appended to Giovio in 1559), Girolamo Ruscelli's *Discorso* (appended to Giovio in 1556), and Claude Paradin's *Devises héroïques* (Lyons, 1557) gave added impetus to a growing fascination with imprese throughout Europe. In England these works quickly became familiar, as is evident from the records of a tournament in 1559 (or possibly 1560). On this occasion, Robert Dudley (the future earl of Leicester) and seven others appeared in the tiltyard bearing imprese copied from three of the writers just named (Figs 70a–b).[18] By the time of Shakespeare, the impresa was ubiquitous in England. It was

69 (opposite). Portrait of Queen Elizabeth with Sieve, by George Gower, 1579 or later. Folger Shakespeare Library (Washington, DC). The sieve was the symbol of the Vestal Virgin, Tuccia; Camden mentions it as a favourite device of Elizabeth's.

---

order to explain their origin.' Among the examples he cites are Henry V's fiery cresset badge, the Lancastrian red rose, Edward IV's sun, the Pelhams' buckle, and the crampet of the Wests, Lords de la Ware (*Badges*, I, pp. 16–17).

[16] On the history of early examples of English imprese, see Alan R. Young, *English Tournament Imprese* (New York, 1988), pp. 7–8.

[17] Giovio's work was subsequently published with illustrations in a variety of editions. In England, Samuel Daniel published an unillustrated translation of it in 1585, entitled *The Worthy Tract of Paulus Iovius*. As Michael Bath has pointed out, N.W.'s prefatory epistle to Daniel's work employs unacknowledged material from Claude Mignault's 'Syntagma de symbolis, stemmatum et schematum,' the preface which Mignault composed for the 1573 edition of Alciati's emblem book. In addition, Daniel's own epistle makes use of Girolamo Ruscelli's *Discorso* (1556), while his appended 'notable devises' were taken without acknowledgement from Lodovico Domenichi's *Ragionamento* (1556) and Gabriello Simeoni's *Le imprese heroiche et morali* (1559), both of which were appended to editions of Giovio. See M. Bath, *Speaking Pictures: English Emblem Books and Renaissance Culture* (London, 1994), pp. 132–3, 136–7.

[18] College of Arms, MS M. 6, ff. 56v–57. For a discussion of the eight imprese and the drawings of them in the manuscript, see Young, *Tudor and Jacobean Tournaments*, pp. 125–7; and Young, *English Tournament Imprese*, pp. 4, 34 note 9, and Nos. 59, 250, 307, 383, 412, 445, 471, 503.

70a–b. Details from the top of the pages showing tournament *imprese* in College of Arms, MS M.6, ff. 56v–57.

familiar from tournaments, court and civic entertainments, literary romances, and plays. Examples in material culture are abundant. The impresa was to be found, for example, in painted portraits, ship decorations, jewelry, wall and ceiling decorations, needlecraft, and decorated fireplaces.[19]

In its fully-fledged form, the impresa combined a motto and a symbolic image. Sixteenth-century theorists, of whom Giovio was probably the best known, liked to affirm that strict rules governed its composition. Supposedly, for example, neither motto (the soul) nor picture (the body) should be comprehensible without the other; the impresa should be neither too obscure nor too obvious in its meaning; human forms should not be depicted; the language of the motto should differ from the native tongue of the bearer; and the motto should be very succinct, although short verses were permitted. However, theorists often disagreed among themselves about such rules, which in any case were frequently ignored. Today, this once flourishing and fashionable word-image genre has largely vanished, apart from scattered examples in such places as certain American state flags and seals, certain American paper money bills, the national flags of certain countries, and certain military flags such as the United States Navy Jack.[20] Vestiges of the genre are found today in some advertisements, trademarks, and corporate logos.[21]

A key source for our understanding and knowledge concerning English imprese is the antiquary and herald William Camden. In the year following his appointment in 1597 as Clarenceux King of Arms, he and his fellow members of the nascent Society of Antiquaries met one afternoon in Derby House (the same building that housed the College of Arms) to present papers on the 'Antiquity of Arms in England.' Two years later, on 28 November 1600, the Antiquaries met to discuss the 'Antiquity, Variety, and Reason of Motts, with Arms of Noblemen and Gentlemen in England.' Camden again presented a paper, as did his senior colleague at the College of Arms, William Dethick, Garter King of Arms. The main purpose of the Antiquaries' deliberations at both meetings was to explore the history and origins of heraldry and indirectly to separate what was strictly to be considered heraldic from the other verbal and visual matter that often appeared to serve a somewhat similar function.

Substantial portions of the papers Camden presented to the Society of Antiquaries were published in his *Remaines of a Greater Worke Concerning Britain* (1605). This work and its voluminous predecessor *Britannia* (1586), together with several other

---

[19] For a detailed survey and commentary regarding the presence of emblematic content, including imprese, in material culture during the early modern period, see Peter M. Daly, 'The Emblem in Material Culture', in *Companion to Emblem Studies*, edited by Peter M. Daly (New York, 2008), pp. 411–56 and 584–93.

[20] On this topic, see A. R. Young, 'The Emblem and Flags,' in *Companion to Emblem Studies*, pp. 457–76 and 593–5.

[21] Peter M. Daly, 'The European Imprese: From Fifteenth-Century Aristocratic Device to Twenty-First-Century Logo,' *Emblematica*, 13 (2003), pp. 303–32; and the same author's 'The *Nachleben* of the Emblem in Some Modern Logos, Advertisements, and Propaganda,' in *Companion to Emblem Studies*, pp. 489–517 and 597–9.

works by Camden, attempted collectively to offer a ground-breaking history that would demonstrate that Britain had as worthy and as significant a culture as any other major European nation. Camden's lengthy and detailed section on imprese in the *Remaines* should be read in this light. In his 1598 paper to the Antiquaries on mottoes,[22] he had been at pains to emphasize that in Britain 'Impreses without Motts as bodies withoute soules weare in use aunciently among us.' Later, the use of the impresa had 'beene derived from the Italians by the French unto us, when they beganne to take up Impreses, which was in the Neapolitan warres about the yeare 1460.'[23]

For Camden, mottoes on their own could often be thought of as imperfect imprese, but unlike one of his fellow Antiquaries, he did not explore how a motto added to coat armour and linked with a crest could—as Sir James Whitelocke argued in his paper— 'have an analogie and reference between them and the creast to which they are added, like to that which is between the body and soule of an impresse, as for instance, a clubb with an olive branch wreathed about yt, and this mott underneath, *Pax vi potior* (Peace is better than force).' The motto, Whitelocke further argued, was added to coat armour 'in order to give some shew of the mind and affection of the bearer. Thus the coate and mott together, described the giver of them, both in body and mynd.'[24] In Whitelocke's opinion, then, the impresa and the combined crest and motto of an heraldic achievement could have a very similar function. Perhaps to reinforce his point, Whitelocke did not sign his name to his paper, but instead playfully employed his alternate method of identification by supplying his impresa-like crest and motto: 'My crest is a falcon raysing herself upward toward the sky from a high tower – My word under it is, *Oculis in solem, alis in Coelum* (Looking to the sun, flying to heaven).' Though both Camden and Whitelocke are aware of the links between imprese and heraldic arms, neither discusses how imprese could be derived from arms, a process that Ruscelli seems to have approved of.[25]

---

[22] Camden's interest in mottoes was anticipated by Christopher Barker (Suffolk Herald, 1517–22, then Richmond Herald, 1522–36, and Garter from 1536 until his death in 1550), who compiled two lists, each of about eighty mottoes (College of Arms, MSS 2 M. 6, f. 105v; and M. 4, f. 2). See Woodcock and Robinson, *Oxford Guide to Heraldry*, p. 113.

[23] British Library, Cotton MS Faustina E. v, f. 19.

[24] Thomas Hearne, *A Collection of Curious Discourses Written by Eminent Antiquaries upon Several Heads in our English Antiquities*, 2 vols. (London, 1771), I, p. 171.

[25] See Ruscelli, *Discorso*, appended to Giovio's *Ragionamento de Monsignor Paolo Giovio sopra i motti et disegni d'arme et d'amore che comunemente chiamano imprese* (Venice, 1556), pp. 158, 190, 205, 230. On this topic Mason Tung cites Henri Estienne's much later *L'art de faire les devises* (Lyons, 1645), a work translated into English by Thomas Blount as *The Art of Making Devises* (London, 1646). Referring to Ruscelli, Blount's translation states: 'Those figures of *Devises* are excellent, which are taken from the Armes of some Family; to which, something is either added, diminished or changed, according to the subject that is in hand, and in pursuance of the designe we have, in favour of the person that bears that kind of Blazon' (p. 24; sig. D4v). Cf. Blount, p. 62 (sig. I3v). See Mason Tung, 'From Heraldry to Emblem: A Study of Peacham's Use of Heraldic Arms in *Minerva Britanna*', *Word and Image*, 3, pt. 1 (1987), p. 94.

71. Part of the account of English tournament *imprese* given by William Camden in his *Remaines* (1614), pp. 218–19.

In his 1600 paper at the Antiquaries' meeting, Camden also gave some examples of the use of mottoes in coat armour. However, in the section on imprese in his *Remaines* he makes a clear distinction between heraldic forms and imprese (Fig. 71). Whereas arms 'were devised to distinguish families, and were most usuall among the nobilitie in warres, tiltes and tournaments in their coates called *Coate-armours, Shields, Standards, Banners, Pennons, Guydons*',[26] an impresa 'is a devise in picture with his Motte, or Word, borne by noble and learned personages, to notifie some particular conceit of their owne.'[27]

In his *Remaines*, Camden then gives a quick history of the impresa, the essentials of which appear to be based on Giovio's *Dialogo*. About a hundred years ago, he suggests, 'the French and Italian in the expedition of Naples, under *Charles* the eight beganne to leave Armes, happly for that many of them had none.' Instead of bearing into battle their

[26] William Camden, *Remains Concerning Britain*, edited by R. D. Dunn (Toronto, 1984), p. 178. All references to the *Remaines* will be to this edition. Camden's statement is consistent with an earlier comment in his section on 'Armories', and a matching statement in his 1598 paper, that 'Armes are ensigns of honour borne in banners, shields, coates, for notice and distinction of families one from the other, and descendable, as hereditary to Posteritie' (p. 156).

[27] *Remains*, p. 177.

heraldic arms, many of the participants in this military affair bore 'their mistresses colours, or these Impreses in their banners, shields, and caparisons.' Thereafter, according to Giovio (though this is not mentioned by Camden), those in Italy who followed the military profession embroidered imprese on the breast and back so that in battle one company could be distinguished from another.[28] Another factor that Camden does not mention is that there may have been an additional explanation for the shift away from displaying coat armour in time of war. As Gervase Markham explained a number of years later, he 'that in his Colours shall carry full Coate-Armour, doth indiscreetly; for he puts that honor to hazard, which he may with more honor keepe in safetie, and inticeth his enemie by such ostentation to darre beyond his owne nature.'[29] It should also be noted that as the use of long guns became prevalent among infantrymen, those who displayed their coats of arms on the battlefield exposed themselves to being shot at from afar. Indeed, it could be argued that they invited such a fate. But very much earlier than this, as Robert W. Jones has recently argued regarding the medieval battlefield, once coat armour became more complex and the numbers of those bearing arms increased, 'it must have become increasingly difficult for anyone to remember all of the arms of one's friends on any particular campaign, particularly as one's friends might become one's foes.' The use of heraldic arms, rather than providing a means whereby 'the individual could be recognized by his friends and distinguished from his foes, preventing him from being attacked in error,' had thus become a potential source of battlefield confusion and error.[30]

In character with his goal of extolling British prestige, Camden then says that the use of imprese in Europe was imitated in England: 'albeit a few have borrowed somewhat from them, yet many have matched them, and no few surpassed them in wittie conceit.'[31] Then follows discussion of a number of examples used by English royalty. Initially, these consisted only of emblematic visual devices. For Camden, they are 'imperfect Devises,' and he deems them 'livelesse bodies, for that they have no word [i.e. motto] adjoyned' (p. 178). From the examples he gives, however, it is clear that Camden is talking about badges, which, as has been noted above, are quite distinct in function from imprese. What comes next, and in imitation of Giovio's list of 'imprese militari et amorose,' is a long descriptive list of fully formed English imprese going back to the time of Henry VIII, when 'English wits beganne to imitate the French and Italian in these devises, adding the Mots'.[32]

---

[28] Paolo Giovio, *Dialogo dell'Imprese militari e amorose* (Lyons, 1559), p. 8.
[29] *The Sovldiers Accidence* (London, 1635), 32. Markham's work was first published in 1625. Thomas Venn, writing after the Restoration, echoed the same sentiment in *Military & Maritime Discipline* (London, 1672), p. 178.
[30] *Bloodied Banners: Martial Display on the Medieval Battlefield* (Woodbridge, 2010), pp. 11–12.
[31] *Remains*, p. 178. 'Caparisons' were the cloth coverings spread over the saddle or harness of a horse. Like the bard (horse armour, often consisting of quilted cloth) or trapper (a covering for a horse, made of cloth), caparisons were often elaborately decorated, often with a rider's impresa.
[32] *Remains*, p. 182. Camden's view that 'perfect' imprese (i.e., those employing both motto and visual device) appeared in England only after Henry VIII's accession is neat and tidy but does not take account of the earlier examples, from the thirteenth century onwards.

Camden describes, for example, one of the imprese that Henry VIII used during the meeting he had with the French king, Francis I, at the Field of the Cloth of Gold in 1520. The elaborate pomp and circumstance of this state event included a major tournament, for which a number of imprese were composed. Camden selects one of Henry's as an example: the device of an English archer in green, 'drawing his arrow to the head,' with the accompanying motto 'Cui adhaereo, praeest' ('He whom I follow triumphs'), an implicit warning to Francis.[33] He also lists imprese used by two of Henry's wives and by his successors – Edward VI, Mary I, and Elizabeth I. That for Mary, for example, depicted a winged figure of Time drawing Truth out of a pit. It had the motto 'Veritas temporis filia' ('Truth is the daughter of time').[34] The impresa appears to have been adopted by Mary at her accession and was designed (Camden says 'by perswasion of her Cleargie') to refer to her goal of returning England to the Catholic faith. The motto was especially familiar because she used it on her coinage. Her Protestant sister Elizabeth herself used the motto during the celebrations at her accession, ironically making clear her view of what she intended to do about the religious faith that Mary had imposed upon her subjects.

Following his brief historical list of royal imprese, Camden continues with a much longer list of the imprese employed by 'noble and gentlemen of our nation, in our age.' Many but by no means all of the imprese that he lists were devised for use in tournaments. As was the case with others who made similar lists, or authors like Henry Peacham who wrote about imprese, Camden's chief source was the gallery close to the tiltyard in Whitehall. Here on permanent display were hung the imprese shields that tournament participants had presented when they competed in the annual Accession Day tournaments held during the reigns of Queen Elizabeth and James I. The Shield Gallery was open to the public, and various visitors wrote descriptions of it, often listing details

---

[33] *Remains*, p. 182. Camden's most likely sources were Edward Hall's *The Union of the Two Noble and Illustre Famelies of Lancaster and Yorke* (1542, with revised and augmented editions in 1548 and 1550); College of Arms, MS M. 6, ff. 7v–12v, 67–73; and British Library, Cotton MS Caligula D. vii. To all of these he would have had easy access. Camden mistakenly claims that Charles V, the Holy Roman Emperor, was also present and that Henry was using his impresa to warn both Francis and Charles, each of whom sought alliances with Henry to gain advantage over the other. Henry did, however, meet with Charles a month before the Field of Cloth of Gold and again shortly afterwards at Calais.

[34] I have been unable to locate Camden's exact source for the visual image he describes. There is a considerable literature concerned with the 'Veritas filia temporis' motif, including Fritz Saxl, 'Veritas filia Temporis', in *Philosophy and History. Essays Presented to E. Cassirer*, ed. Raymond Klibansky and H. J. Paton (Oxford, 1936), pp. 197–222; D. J. Gordon, "Veritas filia temporis': Hadrianus Junius and Geoffrey Whitney,' *Jnl. of the Warburg and Courtauld Institutes*, xxvii (1940), pp. 228–40; Samuel C. Chew, *The Virtues Reconciled: An Iconographic Study* (Toronto, 1947), pp. 69–77; and Antonio Bernat Vistarini and Tamás Sajó, 'Veritas filia Dei. The Iconography of Truth Between Two Cultural Horizons in the *Ithika hieropolitica*', in *In Nocte Consilium. Studies in Emblematics in Honor of Pedro F. Campa*, ed. John T. Cull and Peter M. Daly (Baden-Baden, 2011), pp. 291–322.

of the shields themselves.[35] The fact that in many instances Camden is unable to identify the original inventors of the imprese that he describes strongly suggests that his information often came from the Shield Gallery rather than directly from the tiltyard ceremonies, even though from 1597 he attended tournaments in his official capacity as Clarenceux King of Arms. Often the original bearers of impresa shields, Camden says, can only be ascertained 'at Tiltes and else-where' when they 'adjoined after the olde and most laudable Italian manner, their Armes withal.'[36] So much for the imprese, then, as a means of identification.

Among the limited number of examples of imprese for which Camden was able to identify their bearers, three may be cited here. Two were fashioned by the ill-fated Robert Devereux, earl of Essex. The first was presented when Essex was 'cast Downe with sorrow.' It consisted of a black shield, devoid of any graphic figure, with the motto 'Par nulla figura dolori' ('Nothing can represent [my] sorrow') (Fig. 72).[37] The other contained the image of a diamond. Around it was the motto 'Dum formas minuis' ('While you form it, you diminish it').[38] As Camden suggests, this latter impresa alludes to the manner in which diamonds 'are impaired while they are fashioned and pointed.' As applied to Essex's situation at the tournament when this was presented to Queen Elizabeth in the tiltyard, the diamond presumably alludes to Essex and the 'you' to Elizabeth. But the full significance of the impresa and how it relates to the complex relationship between Essex and the Queen will forever be elusive since we do not know precisely when this impresa was composed.

Interpretations of other tournament imprese of participants such as Sir Philip Sidney, Henry Howard, earl of Surrey, and Sir Henry Lee, who are named by Camden, also remain somewhat elusive since no exact dates are available. Among those bearers of imprese who are identified, however, are two close acquaintances of Camden: Richard

---

[35] Young, *Tudor and Jacobean Tournaments*, pp. 131–4; and Young, *English Tournament Imprese*, pp. 11–12, 29–33.

[36] *Remains*, p. 183. When Camden wrote the relevant section of the *Remaines*, most of the shields he saw were those that had been presented to Queen Elizabeth. Having published his *Remaines* in 1605, Camden never developed further his interest in imprese. However, in a document he compiled that contains a list of participants at various tournaments between December 1613 and March 1622, he did give the impresa mottoes for twelve men who took part in the tournament held on James I's Accession Day, 24 March 1614: British Library, MS Harley 5176, f. 218v.

[37] *Remains*, p. 184. Henry Peacham, who knew Camden's *Remains* and who visited the Shield Gallery, included a woodcut of Essex's impresa in his *Minerva Britanna* (1612) and commented 'where the minde's with deadly sorrow wounded, | There no proportion, can effect delight.' The black shield ('the face of night') represents chaos, since all within Essex is confounded. This was the shield which 'this noble *Earle* did beare, | The last *Impresa*, of his greife, and care' (p. 114).

[38] *Remains*, p. 190. A full-length watercolour portrait of Essex attributed to Nicholas Hilliard shows this impresa embroidered on the bases of his armour (National Portrait Gallery, London). Essex was Earl Marshal from 1597 to 1601 and hence had governing authority over the heralds and College of Arms. There are extant a small number of other impresa portraits recording their subjects' participation in tournaments. See Young, *English Tournament Imprese*, pp. 26–7.

72. Emblem 114, 'Par nulla figura dolori', in Henry Peacham's *Minerva Britanna* (1612).

Carew and Abraham Hartwell. Neither was a tournament participant, but both were fellow members of the Society of Antiquaries. Hartwell's impresa may serve here as a second example, but it is different from those of Essex in that it was not designed for a tournament or for military use. Instead, it appears to make a statement about the bearer's lifelong religious commitment. Camden, coyly and perhaps with intended humour, introduces the impresa as though the inventor were unknown to him: 'His conceit was godly and correspondent to his name, who made an Hart in his race to a fountaine and over it, VT CERVVS FONTEM' ('Like a deer to a spring'), and 'under it, SIC ABRAHAMVS CHRISTVM' ('So Abraham to Christ').[39] As Camden knew, Hartwell was a cleric and had been Rector of Toddington (Beds.) and later secretary to the Archbishop of Canterbury, John Whitgift. Leaving aside all this, Camden comments: 'The meaning is plaine to all which know Scriptures, and I take the Gentlemans name to be *Abraham Hartwell*.' The

[39] *Remains*, 173.

Biblical reference that Camden expects his readers to recognize is to Psalms 42:1: 'As the hart panteth after the water brooks, so panteth my soul after thee, O God' (King James Version). This appears to be an expression of Hartwell's piety suitable to his service to the Church of England. Hartwell was present at the meeting of Antiquaries when Camden first presented the material that became the discussion of imprese in *Remaines*, and one may speculate that Hartwell himself told Camden about his impresa, aware of the latter's interest in the topic.[40]

Following the publication of Camden's book, imprese continued to excite the interest of Shakespeare's contemporaries. James I maintained the custom of celebrating Accession Day (his being on March 24) with a tournament in the Whitehall tiltyard. Other important occasions were often also celebrated with tournaments, usually at Whitehall or some other suitable venue such as Hampton Court or Greenwich. As in the reign of Queen Elizabeth, participants continued to be expected to present newly-invented imprese. Other court entertainments, particularly masques, might also involve the designing of imprese. Following the accession of Charles I in 1625, tournaments came to a halt; however, imprese underwent a revived interest at the time of the Civil War, when individual captains of units of cavalry, both Royalist and Parliamentarian, each had cornets (approximately two feet or 0.6 meters square) on which they displayed an impresa. As Thomas Blount remarked in 1646, whereas the ongoing civil war had led to 'Tiltings, Tournaments, and Masques' being 'for the present laid aside', there remained a role for imprese: 'as those Justing or jesting Wars are disused, so have we now an earnest, though much to be lamented Warre, which renders them more usefull then ever.'[41] (Fig. 73 shows the title-page of his book.)

The Emblem

Often mentioned alongside discussions of the impresa was another popular Renaissance art form—the emblem. Typically, the emblem, like the impresa, employed both a motto and emblematic visual material, but it differed from the impresa in two important ways. Generally it contained a third part, in the form of a poem. In addition, it differed from the impresa because it had a different function. Whereas the impresa was concerned with the expression of the thoughts and feelings of an individual (or group), often in relation to a specific occasion, the emblem tended to express a general truth.[42] One would thus

---

[40] Like a number of imprese, Hartwell's involves an obvious pun, the same as that employed in the heraldic crest of another Hartwell (see James Fairbairn, *Fairbairn's Crests of the Families of Great Britain and Ireland*, revised by Laurence Butters (London, 1986), p. 230). Puns have also been common in so-called 'canting' heraldry, the spear in the Shakespeare shield and crest being a familiar example.

[41] *The Art of Making Devises*, sig. A4. For a full account of the imprese used on Civil War flags, many of which, along with the arms of their bearers, were recorded by heralds, see Alan R. Young, *Emblematic Flag Devices of the English Civil Wars 1642–1660* (Toronto, 1995).

[42] At the opening of the section on imprese in *Remaines*, Camden pointed out (with examples) the distinction between an impresa and an emblem (*Remains*, p. 177).

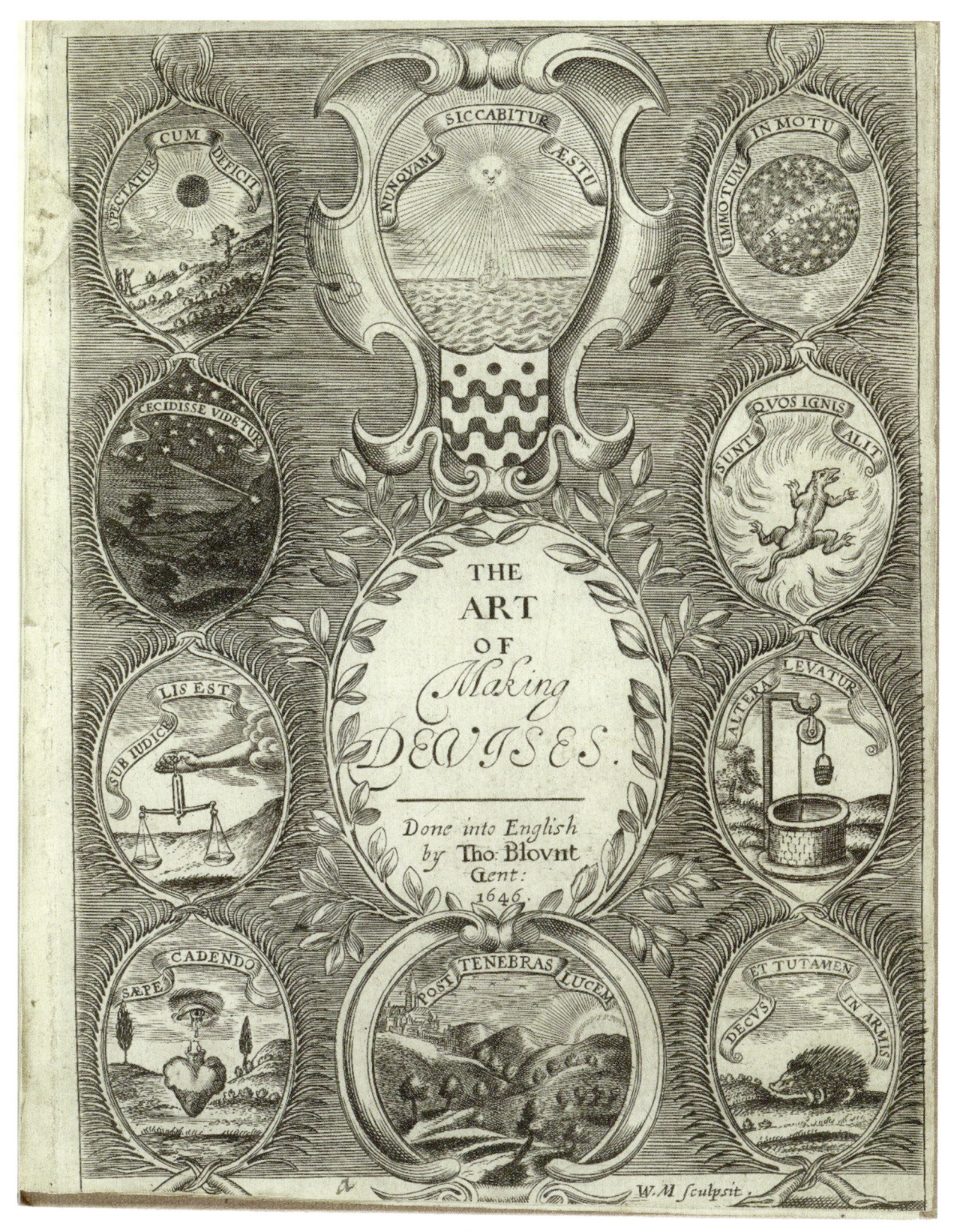

73. Engraved title-page of Thomas Blount, *The Art of Making Devises* (1646), showing Civil War flag *imprese*.

expect the emblem to be farther removed than the imprese from coat armour, since it did not act as a means of identification. However, at least two English emblem composers deliberately blurred this distinction and created a hybrid genre by using heraldic materials in the pictures of their emblems. While the poems offered readers generalized lessons in a manner typical of the emblem, such compositions could at the same time be personalized as in an impresa by referring to the bearers of the heraldic motifs, and applying the 'meaning' of the combined motto and picture to the named individuals.

Henry Peacham, a writer with a particular interest in heraldry, was one author who composed such heraldic emblems.[43] These can be found in his three manuscript emblem books based on King James I's *Basilikon Doron* (the book of advice James composed for his son Prince Henry), and in his printed emblem book *Minerva Britanna* (1612).[44] Many of the heraldic emblems in *Minerva Britanna* are derived from Peacham's *Basilikon Doron* emblems. Aware that his printed book was not confined to emblems in their 'purest' form, Peacham's sub-title for his work was *A Garden of Heroical Deuises, furnished, and adorned with Emblems and Impresa's of sundry natures, Newly Devised, moralized, and published*. Two examples from *Minerva Britanna* will be briefly considered here.[45]

Emblem 11, dedicated to '*IAMES*, King of greate Britaine,' is typical in that it does not use James's complete coat armour. Instead, the picture makes use of parts of James's full armorial achievement and depicts two lions rampant acting as supporters to a royal crown that would normally be placed below the crest.[46] As the poem explains, one lion

---

[43] In his *The Art of Drawing* (1606), Peacham announced that he would publish 'a discourse of Armory.' This essay first appeared in *Graphice, or The Gentleman's Exercise* (1612). Thereafter, he steadily expanded this material on heraldry in succeeding editions of the *The Compleat Gentleman* (1622, 1627, 1634). See Alan R. Young, *Henry Peacham* (Boston, 1979), pp. 68–9, 81–2. Among the writings on heraldry that Peacham draws upon are Iehan le Féron's *De la Primitive Institution des Roys, Heravldz & Poursuivans d'Armes* (1555) and *Le Simbol Armorial des Armoiries de France, & d'Escoce, & Lorraine* (1555), Gerard Legh's *The Accidens of Armorie* (1562, etc.), John Ferne's *The Blazon of Gentrie* (1586), Camden's *Remaines* (1605), and John Guillim's *A Display of Heraldrie* (1610). Peacham appears to have been a friend of William Segar, who provided a laudatory poem addressed to Peacham in this latter's *Minerva Britanna* (1612), sig B3ᵛ. Segar had been a herald since 1585, and in 1612 was Garter King of Arms. He was himself author of *The Booke of Honor and Armes* (published anonymously in 1590). Later he issued this in an expanded, illustrated form as *Honor Military and Civill* (1602). Segar was also a very accomplished portrait painter.

[44] For discussions of Peacham's heraldic emblems see Alan R. Young, *Henry Peacham's Manuscript Emblem Books* (Toronto, 1998), pp. xv, xvi–xix; Young, *Henry Peacham*, pp. 47–9; and Tung, 'From Heraldry to Emblem,' pp. 86–94.

[45] Other examples in *Minerva Britanna* of emblems employing heraldic materials are those numbered 1, 12, 19, 30, 31, 45, 82, 101, 102, 107, 124, 137, 160, 171.

[46] The crown is accurately represented as being double-arched, with a circlet of alternating crosses formy and fleurs-de-lys, and surmounted by an orb ensigned with a cross formy (this last is partially cut off by the ornamental border in the editions of *Minerva Britanna* that I have consulted).

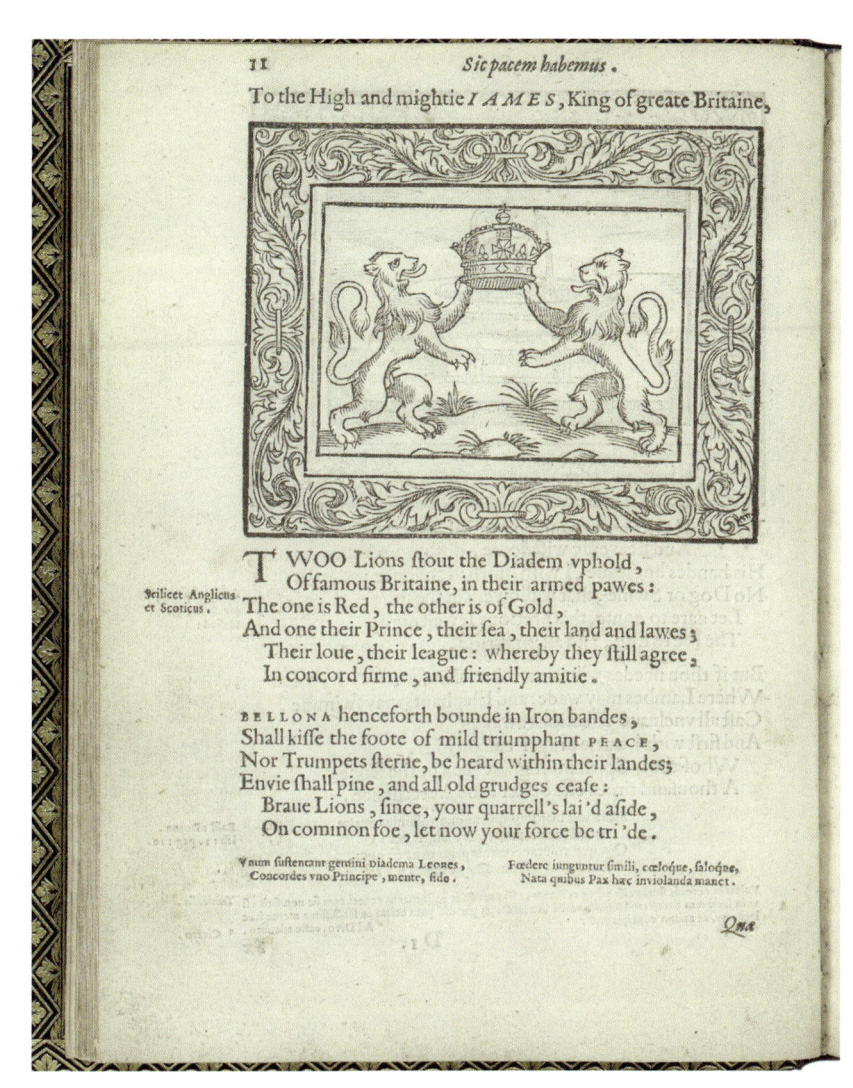

74. Emblem 11, 'Sic pacem habemus', in Henry Peacham's *Minerva Britanna* (1612).

is red and the other gold, something that Peacham is not able to show in this printed version of the emblem.[47] Peacham's readers, even without his marginal explanatory note, would have recognized that the gold lion derives from one of the supporters of the English arms and that the red lion comes from the shield of the Scottish arms, then quartered with the English arms and those of Ireland in James I's royal arms. Combined with the motto 'Sic pacem habemus' ('Thus, we have peace'), the emblem becomes a paean to James, the poem offering thoughts on the unity and peace brought about by the union of England and Scotland that occurred in 1603 when James VI of Scotland succeeded Queen Elizabeth of England (Fig. 74). Below Peacham's poem is a Latin verse quatrain that further emphasizes the theme of union. As Peacham well knew, the concept of

---

[47] In the one earlier *Basilikon Doron* manuscript that employed painted images, Peacham was able to use colours that were heraldically correct. For this example, see British Library, MS Royal 12 A. LXVI, Book 2, Emblem 2.

75. Emblem 15, 'Auspice caelo', in Henry Peacham's *Minerva Britanna* (1612).

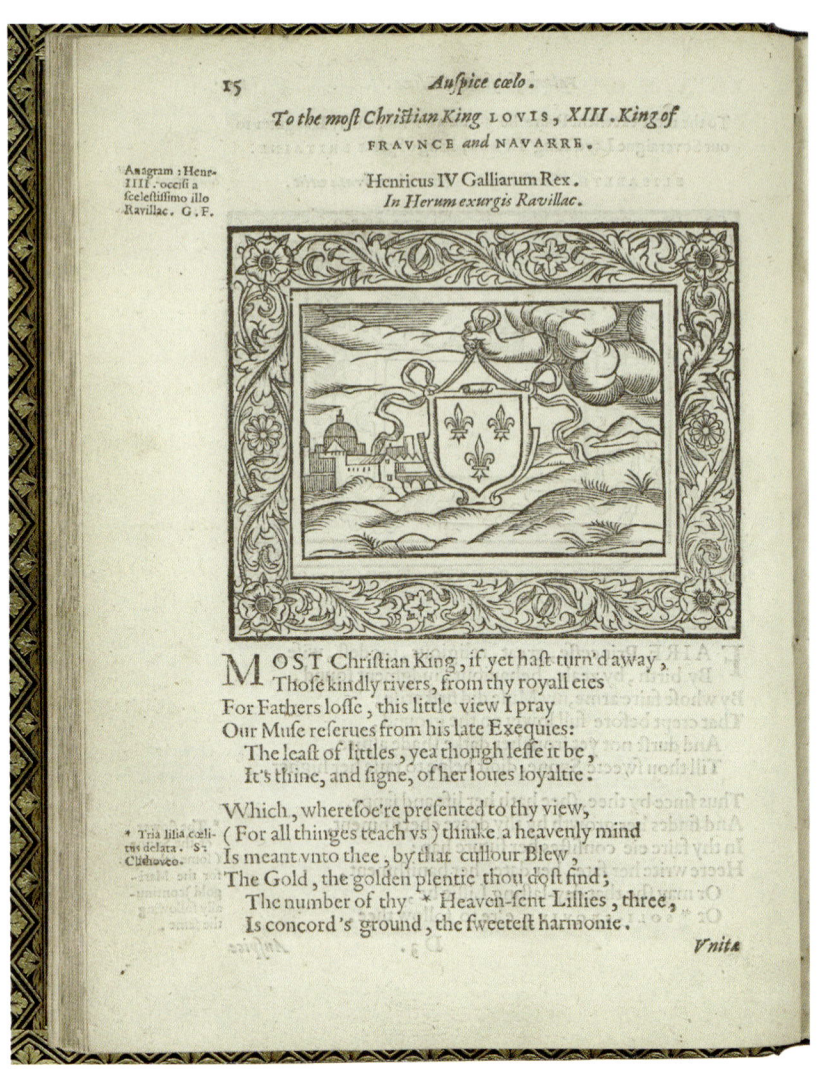

Anglo-Scottish unity was dear to James I's heart. That James was now 'King of Great Britain' mattered greatly to him,[48] for the king believed that through him the fabled sovereign unity of ancient times could be restored. As Peacham clearly realized, James's claim to sovereignty could be asserted—and his role in the creation of British unity expressed—through the official, sanctioned symbolism of the armorial code. In its expression of the King's political aspirations, the emblem takes on the qualities of an impresa, but in its more general expression of thanks for peace, Peacham's composition functions more like an emblem.

[48] Upon his accession, James had styled himself as 'King of England, Scotland, France, and Ireland.' However, on 20 October 1604, he issued a proclamation that stated: 'we do … assume by the clearness of our right the name and style of King of Great Britain, France, and Ireland', an expression of his intense desire for the closest possible union between England and Scotland, a union heraldically signalled in the new royal arms.

HERALDRY AND ALTERNATE EMBLEMATIC FORMS

A few pages later, Peacham provides a composition dedicated to the French king, Louis XIII. At its head, it has the motto 'Auspice caelo' ('By the favour of heaven'), together with an anagram on the name of Louis's father, 'Henricus IV Galliarum Rex' – 'In Herum exurgis Ravillac' ('From these Ravillac rises up') (Fig. 75). As a marginal note reminds Peacham's readers, Henry IV was assassinated by the Catholic zealot François Ravaillac, on 14 May 1610.[49] Peacham's picture depicts a hand issuing from a cloud and holding a ribbon from which hangs a shield with the French arms, three fleurs-de-lys. As Peacham was able to show in his original watercolour version, the fleurs-de-lys were gold in colour placed upon a blue field, the same configuration and colours as those quartered in the British royal arms.[50] In the first stanza of the accompanying poem, Peacham commiserates with Louis's grief for his murdered father, while in the second stanza he provides emblematic interpretations for the heraldic colours (blue and gold) and for the number (three) of fleurs-de-lys. The blue, according to Peacham, represents Louis's 'heavenly mind' and the gold signifies 'the golden plenty thou dost find.' The number three of the 'Heaven-sent Lillies' is a sign of concord as in 'the sweetest harmonie' to be found in music.[51] Again, what superficially looks like an emblem makes use of heraldic motifs to form something like an impresa that expresses the personal and particular situation of a single individual.

A number of other emblems in *Minerva Britanna* are based on well-known heraldic badges, some of which have already been referred to above.[52] As his frontispiece and as part of the material addressed to his dedicatee and heir to the throne, Henry Prince of Wales, Peacham depicted the three-feather badge of the Black Prince that had become associated with the title of Prince of Wales. He added the cypher HP (i.e., Henricus princeps) and surrounded his image with intertwined Scottish thistles and English roses to symbolize the unity of Scotland and England.[53] Below this he added a two-line Latin epigram, part of which was an anagram on the royal motto 'Ich dien' ('I serve'). Emblem

---

[49] Prince Henry, James I's son, was the dedicatee of *Minerva Britanna*. As Mason Tung points out, the murder had special significance for the Prince since it ended his plan to accompany the French king in his march on Cleves in June of 1610. See Tung, 'From Heraldry to Emblem', pp. 90–1.

[50] Edward III, who claimed the French throne, quartered the French royal arms with his own. The arms of France were *azure, semy of fleurs-de-lys or*. Charles V reduced the number of fleurs-de-lys to three, and this was followed by Henry IV. The French fleurs-de-lys remained part of the British royal arms until 1801, when they were dropped by George III.

[51] On Peacham's knowledge and use of colour symbolism in his emblems and in his writings on armory, see Young, *Henry Peacham*, pp. 40–1, 64, 65; and Young, *Henry Peacham's Manuscript Emblem Books*, p. xix.

[52] In his epistle 'To the Reader', Peacham refers to a number of royal imprese and heraldic badges, among them imprese of the Scottish kings James III and James IV (sig. A3r–v). In 'The Authors Conclusion' at the end of *Minerva Britanna*, he refers to various 'Impresa's, and Devises rare,' including the heraldic badges of Henry IV and Henry V (p. 211).

[53] This motif can be found as early as 1502 in the marginal decorations of the illuminated copies of the Treaty of Perpetual Peace drawn up by James IV of Scotland and Henry VII. See PRO, E39/58, E39/59, E39/81; and Edinburgh, National Archives of Scotland, SP6/31.

76. Emblem 31, 'Protegere Regium', in Henry Peacham's *Minerva Britanna* (1612).

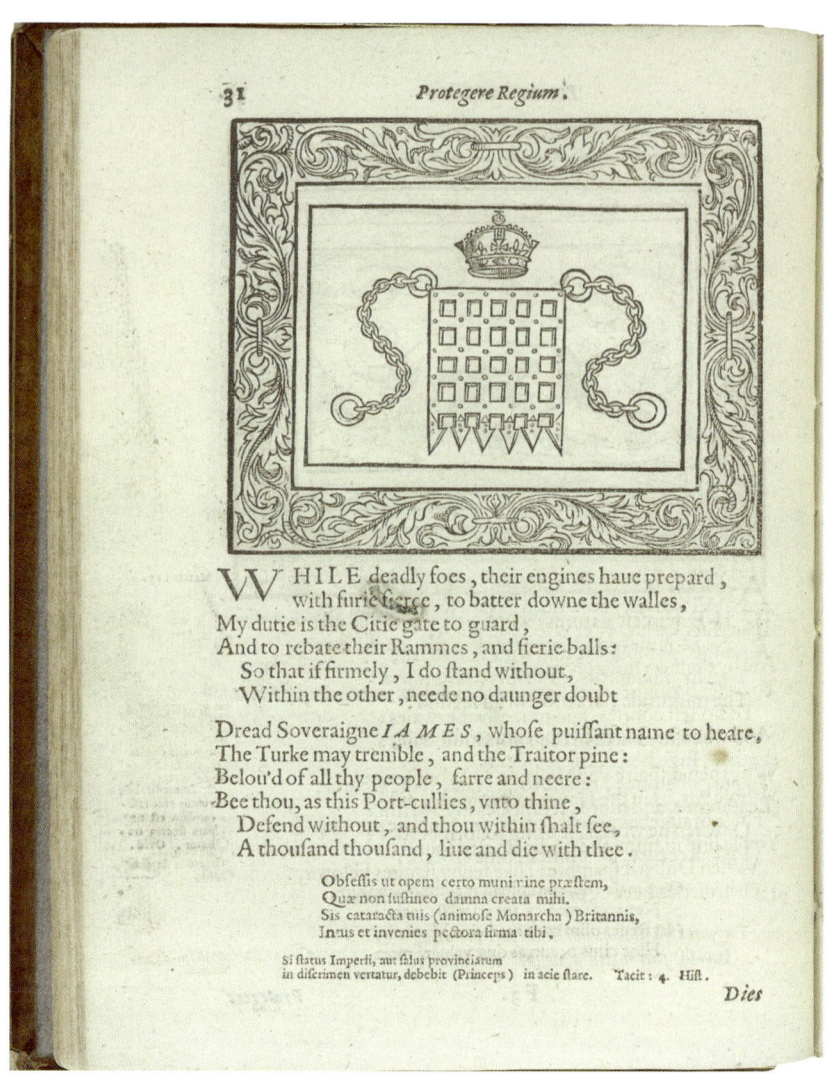

77 (opposite). Doors of Henry VII's Chapel (the Lady Chapel), Westminster Abbey, *c.* 1510. Oak, entirely plated with bronze openwork panels, with royal badges such as the portcullis, fleurs-de-lis, falcon and fetterlock.

31 offers another example of his use of an heraldic badge. Beneath the motto 'Protegere Regium' ('To protect the realm') (Fig. 76), Peacham depicts Henry VII's crowned portcullis, a badge that he might have seen on the bronze doors of the King's funeral chapel in Westminster Abbey (Fig. 77). The accompanying poem applies the emblem to King James and expresses the hope that James will be like the portcullis and defend his people from all external enemies. As Emblem 90, Peacham has an emblem based on another badge of Henry VII, a badge that he saw, according to his marginal note, in a window in Westminster Abbey. Beneath the motto 'Tyranni morbus suspicio' ('The disease of a tyrant is suspicion'), Peacham depicted a hawthorn tree, in the branches of which is a crown.[54] The accompanying poem first recounts the standard Tudor-biased

---

[54] Henry's crown and hawthorn badge also appears a number of times on the bronze doors to his Westminster chapel.

302

legend about the 'valiant' earl of Richmond (the future Henry VII) overthrowing the 'usurping Richard' at Bosworth and finding the crown in a hawthorn bush. A second stanza balances this with the new king's inner guilt about the way he himself gained the crown and the feeling that he faces a future beset with 'greife, and thornes of heavie care.'

A few years after the publication of *Minerva Britanna*, the as yet unidentified 'H. G.' authored *The Mirrour of Maiestie: Or, The Badges of Honour Conceitedly Emblazoned With Emblemes Annexed, Poetically Unfolded* (London: W[illiam] J[ones], 1618).[55] This rather rare volume contains images of the shields from the coats of arms of thirty-three 'Noble Personages', first among them being King James I, Queen Ann, and the then heir to the throne, Prince Charles.[56] Twelve of those represented were Knights

---

[55] It seems likely that 'H. G.' pirated material originally composed by the Italian refugee Ludovico Petrucci, who was in prison at the time. See Martin R. Smith, 'The *Apologia* and Emblems of Ludovico Petrucci', *Bodleian Library Record*, viii (1967–72), pp. 40–7.

[56] In the case of Prince Charles, the author chose to depict the heraldic badge of three ostrich plumes

of the Garter, their shields surrounded by the garter with its distinctive motto, 'Honi soit qui mal y pense' ('Evil be to him who evil thinks'). These images of heraldic shields, except for that of James, were placed on the left hand side of every page opening, with the bearer's name above. Below each image were verses that typically commented upon some feature of the arms to provide an emblematic interpretation in praise of the bearer. The arms and accompanying verses thus became akin to an impresa, expressing the character and aspirations of their bearer. Building upon this foundation, on the right side of each page-opening is a fully-formed emblem/impresa (with two for the King), with motto, emblematic picture, and verses. Each of these compositions is further designed to praise the bearer of the arms named on the facing page to the left. Two examples from *The Mirrour of Maiestie* must here suffice to illustrate the phenomenon described as follows by the 1870 editor of the work: 'The paths of the Herald and of the Emblematist, even if they do not run into one another and cross and double, are so close together as not to be distinguishable in all instances.'[57]

The first example is dedicated to the Earl of Southampton (Henry Wriothesley), a participant in the rebellion led by his friend the Earl of Essex in 1600 (Fig. 78). Lucky not to be executed along with Essex (his initial death sentence was commuted), Southampton was imprisoned in the Tower of London until the accession of James I in 1603. That year he returned to full favour and was made a Knight of the Garter and had all his rights and privileges restored. His heraldic shield displayed a cross between four seabirds.[58] Referring indirectly to Southampton's earlier difficulties (his 'storme of troubles' and the 'cold frosts of Friends'), the author stresses his current 'free state' and interprets the birds, which are used by seamen to predict storms, as representing how wise forethought can prevent problems. The matching composition on the facing page has the motto 'In utraque perfectus' ('Perfect in both') and has a picture depicting a man. His right side is dressed in armour and in his right hand he holds a lance and shield. His left side is in normal clothing. In his left hand he holds Mercury's caduceus, and his left ankle and the left side of his headpiece are winged in the manner of Mercury. He thus emblematically represents perfection both in military pursuits and in the arts.[59] The motto and image form a fitting tribute to Southampton. He had served with distinction during Queen Elizabeth's reign in the military expeditions to Cadiz and the Azores and

---

with the motto 'Ich Dien' ('I serve') rather than the Prince's coat of arms. Copies of *The Mirrour of Maiestie* can be found in the British Library, the Huntington Library, and the Houghton Library at Harvard. In 1870, the Holbein Society published a facsimile edition containing commentaries and notes by Henry Green and James Croston.

[57] Henry Green, Introduction to *The Mirrour of Maiestie*, pp. 78–9.

[58] In the comments provided in the 1870 facsimile edition, James Croston identifies the birds as hawks (p. 128).

[59] In Greek mythology, the caduceus was the staff carried by Hermes (Mercury in Roman mythology) and by heralds in general. The Roman figure of Mercury was considered to be the messenger of the gods. In the Renaissance, Mercury was often associated with the arts since, among other things, he was considered to be the patron of orators, wit, literature, and poets.

56.

To The Earle Of Sovth-hampton.

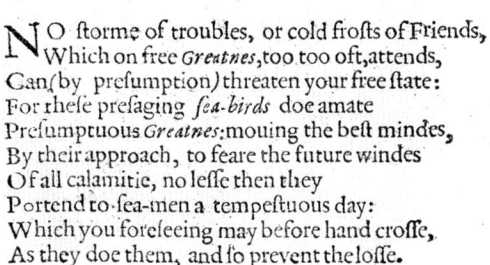

N O ſtorme of troubles, or cold froſts of Friends,
Which on free *Greatnes*, too too oft, attends,
Can (by preſumption) threaten your free ſtate:
For theſe preſaging *ſea-birds* doe amate
Preſumptuous *Greatnes*; mouing the beſt mindes,
By their approach, to feare the future windes
Of all calamitie, no leſſe then they
Portend to ſea-men a tempeſtuous day:
Which you foreſeeing may before hand croſſe,
As they doe them, and ſo prevent the loſſe.

27.

EMBLEME 13.

W Hat coward *Stoicke*, or blunt captaine will
Diſ-like this *Vnion*, or not labour ſtill
To reconcile the *Arts* and *victory*?
Since in themſelues Arts haue this quality,
To vanquiſh errours traine: what other than
Should loue the Arts, if not a valiant man?
Or, how can he reſolue to execute,
That hath not firſt learn'd to be reſolute?
If any ſhall oppoſe this, or diſpute,
Your great example ſhall their ſpite confute.

E 2

78. Pages 26 and 27 "To the Earle of Southampton" from *The Mirrour of Maiestie*.

in the campaign in Ireland. In James I's reign in 1614, he was a volunteer on the Protestant side in Germany. However, he had also been a noted patron of letters,[60] and he may even have been a patron of Shakespeare, who dedicated both *Venus and Adonis* and *Lucrece* to him.[61] The verses that accompany this device decry those who do not endeavor to reconcile arts and arms, lauding Southampton as an exemplary model for those who have failed to unite the two.

A second example from *The Mirrour of Maiestie* is provided by the composition dedicated 'To the Lord Chancellor' (Sir Francis Bacon) (Fig. 79).[62] His heraldic shield is

---

[60] Among those in his patronage were John Florio, George Chapman, Samuel Daniel, Thomas Heywood, and the composer Alfonso Ferrabosco the younger.

[61] That Southampton was a patron of Shakespeare and that he was the 'Mr W. H.' of the *Sonnets* has long been a subject for speculation.

[62] Bacon had a meteoric rise in status. Having written in favour of the union of England and Scotland (*A Brief Discourse touching the Happy Union of the Kingdoms of England and Scotland*), he was rewarded with a knighthood following James I's accession. In 1607 he was appointed Solicitor-

TO THE LORD CHANCELLOR.   11.

EMBLEME 6.

THe *North* and *Southerne Poles*, the two fix'd Starres
Of worth and dignitie, which all iuſt warres,
Should ſtill maintaine, together: be here met
And in your ſelfe as in your Scutchion ſet:
The *halfe Moone* 'twixt, threatens as yet no change,
Or if ſhe doe, ſhe promiſes to range,
Till ſhe againe recouer what ſhe loſt:
Your endleſſe fame, (ſo) gaines your *Bounties* coſt.

NEuer ſhould any thinke himſelfe ſo ſure
Of friends aſſiſtance, that he dares procure
New enemies: for vnprouok'd they will
Spring out of forg'd, or cauſeleſſe malice ſtill.
Elſe, why ſhould this poore creature be purſu'd,
Too ſimple to offend, a beaſt ſo rude.
Therefore prouide (for malice danger brings)
Houſe-roome to find vnder an *Eagles* wings.
You are this *Eagle*, whcih ore-ſhades the *ſheepe*
Purſu'de by *humane wolues*, and ſafe doth keepe
The poore mans honeſt, though might-wronged cauſe,
From being cruſhed by oppreſſious pawes.
Faire Port you are, where euery *Goodneſſe* findes
Safe ſhelter from ſwolne *Greatneſſe*, ſtubborne winds
Eager to drench it: but that feareleſſe reſt
Dwels in your harbour, to all good diſtreſt.
I bid not you prouide, you are complete,
The good for to protect, or bad defeate.

C 2

79. Pages 10 and 11 "To the Lord Chancellor" from *The Mirrour of Maiestie*.

quite plain except for a chief (the band across the top part of the shield) charged with two mullets (five-pointed stars). Between the mullets is a mark of cadency, a crescent with both horns upright to denote that Bacon was a second son. The verses below interpret Bacon's mullets emblematically as the North and South Pole Stars. They are 'fix'd' and hence represent the 'worth and dignitie' of the bearer, a notion supported by what the author describes as the 'halfe Moone,' which 'threatens as yet no change.' The facing page provides an impresa-like emblem with the motto 'Sub umbra alarum tuarum' ('Beneath the shadow of thy wings'), words derived from Psalm 17, 8.[63] The Psalm is a plea to

General, and in 1613 he became Attorney-General. In 1616 he became a member of the Privy Council, and the following year he became Lord Keeper of the Great Seal, and, very shortly after, Lord Chancellor of England. In the same year that *The Mirrour of Maiestie* was published, Bacon was ennobled, with the title Baron Verulam. In 1627 he became Viscount St Albans.

[63] The Vulgate text (Psalm 16, 8) reads: 'a resistentibus dexterae tuae custodi me ut pupillam oculi sub umbra alarum tuarum protege me.' In the King James version of the Bible (Psalm 17, 8), this

306

HERALDRY AND ALTERNATE EMBLEMATIC FORMS

Jehovah for protection from worldly evils and the enemies that assail us. In accord with this, the accompanying picture depicts an eagle with outspread wings. A sheep, pursued by a fierce wolf, races to shelter beneath the eagle's wings. In the verses below, Bacon is likened to the eagle. As Lord Chancellor, he provides refuge to the innocent and the poor from the malice and oppression of those with more power ('Safe shelter from swolne *Greatnesse*'). Thus, starting with Bacon's heraldic shield, 'H. G.' has fashioned a two-part emblematic composition that, though it may have some general application in the manner of an emblem, is more like an impresa in its application to a particular individual and his office at a particular time in his life.

* * *

Heraldry, then, with its formal code of hereditary visual signs served a valued function in identifying an individual's family, social rank, and genealogy – or in identifying a collective enterprise, as in the case of arms associated with a college, a city, or ecclesiastical establishment. However, for those individuals wishing to identify themselves in some more personal way that displayed their particular aspirations or character, another whole code of visual signs was available, in the form of the emblem and the impresa. Heraldry as it developed in the sixteenth and early seventeenth centuries often imported emblematic signage; but the emblem and impresa themselves often reworked heraldic materials in a striking variety of fascinating ways.

---

reads: 'Keep me as the apple of the eye, hide me under the shadow of thy wings.' There is no equivalent in the King James Bible for the first phrase in the Vulgate text of this verse, 'a resistentibus dexterae tuae custodi me' ('From those who resist thy right hand, preserve me').

Afterword: From the Late Seventeenth Century to the Present Day

PETER O'DONOGHUE

Despite the chronological, technological and cultural distances that separate us from the England of Shakespeare, heraldry remains a part of our visual vocabulary; and the superstructure which depends upon it, that of the College of Arms and its heralds, continues to offer ceremonial, heraldic and genealogical services which would have been recognisable to the Elizabethan. New coats of arms are granted by the kings of arms, using powers delegated to them by the Sovereign, in numbers that are comparable to the annual figures for the reign of Elizabeth I. The heralds continue their practices in heraldic research, in genealogy, and in the various related fields that have always fallen to them. If their activities are less well-known in Britain than their Tudor counterparts might have imagined, yet their geographical reach is vastly extended, with coats of arms regularly being granted to citizens of Her Majesty's overseas Realms and Territories, as well as to Americans. In this afterword I shall chart briefly how heraldry and the heralds have weathered the storms of change, and consider the present day activities of the College of Arms.[1]

The later seventeenth century saw the heralds facing difficult times. The county-by-county visitations had for a century and a half given them opportunities to examine and regulate heraldic practice throughout England and Wales. These provincial appearances had served to enhance the authority and reputation of the College of Arms, and to remind gentry families that the use of coats of arms was restricted. Each heraldic funeral had likewise been an opportunity for the heralds to display their power. Both visitations and funerals were reliant upon the culture and cooperation of the nobility and gentry and of those who aspired to those ranks: armorial display, as part of the wider culture of chivalry, had remained for much of the Tudor and Stuart period an important means of constructing and expressing the social identity of the upper ranks of society.[2]

In the mid and late seventeenth century, social and political changes saw the gradual eclipse of this aspect of English culture. Chivalric norms which were at least theoretically rooted in military service and the display of prowess on the battlefield, came to be replaced by those of the Enlightenment. Heraldry itself therefore seemed less relevant and its regulation became more difficult: the visitations came to an end, the last one being in

---

[1] The central text for the history of the College of Arms, upon which much of what follows must depend, is Sir Anthony Wagner, *Heralds of England* (London, 1967).

[2] Richard C. McCoy, *The Rites of Knighthood. The Literature and Politics of Elizabethan Chivalry* (London, 1989), pp. 157–61.

AFTERWORD: FROM THE LATE SEVENTEENTH CENTURY TO THE PRESENT

1687–9. Not unconnected were the repeated and successful challenges mounted against the legal authority of the Court of Chivalry, upholder of the law of arms.[3] With the power to punish transgressors seriously diminished, the authority of the College of Arms was declining and the activities of the heralds reducing in significance.[4] They were cast uncomfortably as the policers of social boundaries in which few outside the Court could believe. In the early eighteenth century the College risked becoming little more than a venue for sinecurists and placemen.[5]

The history of heraldry in England would have been very different had this trend continued. In France, for example, more than one attempt to bring armorial display under the control of the authorities had foundered. In 1615, with the heralds themselves powerless, a *juge d'armes* was appointed with full power to regulate heraldry; he failed to impose conformity. In 1696 commissioners were appointed by Louis XIV to the same end, but they used their power to register coats of arms only as a mechanism to generate revenue, with the registers being filled by fictitious designs.[6]

The early eighteenth century saw few new grants of arms being made in England, yet the heralds persisted in their professional activities. The designs of such arms as were granted were simple and effective; and coats of arms continued to be deployed as a part of gentry identity, albeit on a less exuberant scale. Those seeking to position themselves as gentlemen rather than yeomen remained keen to use armorial display, even if they had no lawful right to what they claimed. Rather than seek new arms, they assumed existing designs. Shields of arms continued to be depicted on funerary monuments and on personal property (such as coaches). The energy that in an earlier era might have been directed towards regulation, now found its outlet in scholarship: the great historians and antiquaries William Dugdale, Elias Ashmole, Gregory King, Peter Le Neve, John Anstis and Stephen Martin Leake were all based at the College of Arms for part or all of their careers. Moreover, the other roles of the heralds – as experts on court ceremony, precedence, orders of knighthood, and genealogy – continued and developed during this period. As new orders of knighthood were established and reformed over the coming centuries, each would have its own Genealogist, nearly always a herald, responsible for

---

[3] G. D. Squibb, *The High Court of Chivalry* (Oxford 1959), pp. 92–9; see also Wagner, *Heralds of England*, pp. 314–16.

[4] For the decline in this period see Wagner, *Heralds of England*, pp. 314–18. The cultural background is discussed in Felicity Heal and Clive Holmes, *The Gentry in England and Wales, 1500–1700* (Stanford, 1994), pp. 38–40. This may also have been part of another broad pattern: the decline in authority as exercised by chartered London monopoly bodies, such as the Livery Companies. See Ronald F. Homer, 'The Pewterers' Company's Country Searches and the Company's Regulation of Prices', in *Guilds, Society & Economy in London, 1450–1800*, ed. Ian Anders Gadd and Patrick Wallis (London, 2002), pp. 101–13, at 102, 105, 107; and John Forbes, 'Search, Immigration and the Goldsmiths' Company: A Study in the Decline of its Powers', in *ibid.*, pp. 115–26.

[5] Wagner, *Heralds of England*, pp. 394 et seq.

[6] Michel Pastoureau, *Traité d'Héraldique*, 4th edn. (Paris, 2003), pp. 68–9.

80. Sir John Anstis, painted while he was Garter King of Arms (1719–44). Attributed to Thomas Hudson. Given to the College of Arms in 1951 by a descendant.

The COLLEGE of ARMS or HERALD'S OFFICE.

81. The College of Arms in the mid-eighteenth century. Engraving by Benjamin Cole for William Maitland's *History of London From its Foundation to the Present Time* (London, 1753–6).

establishing and recording the coats of arms and sometimes the pedigrees of members; these roles continue today.[7]

The later decades of the eighteenth century saw an improvement in the fortunes of the members of the College of Arms and a resurgence of popular interest in heraldry. In part this was because the heralds themselves were now exploring new directions. Heraldry and genealogy had always been intimately connected, but the study of the history of families had tended to be bound up with the descent of dignities and property: in other words, with the stories of noble and gentle landowning families. Tudor and Jacobean heralds were often genealogists, and some were expert in the use of documentary sources for the elucidation of these descents. The later eighteenth century saw heralds for the first time consider the investigation of family histories as an activity worthwhile for its own sake.[8] Those with quite humble backgrounds turned to the

[7] Sir John Anstis was instrumental in the establishment of the Order of the Bath in 1725, and Sir George Nayler later acted as its Genealogist, not without controversy – see Wagner, *Heralds of England*, pp. 433–49.

[8] Of considerable interest in this regard is the publication by the herald Ralph Bigland in 1764 of his *Observations on Marriages, Baptisms and Burials as preserved in Parochial Registers* (London, 1764). This work was in part an extended advertisement for the genealogical services offered by

TO ALL AND SINGULAR
to whom these Presents shall come Sir Isaac Heard Knight GARTER Principal King of Arms

heralds as professional genealogists who could shed light on their ancestry. One example of the new directions being explored by the heralds was the establishment in 1747 of a single central registry of births for dissenters. Some ninety years before the civil registration of births in England, this registry, run by the heralds, provided an official record of birth for all, including dissenters, Jews and other non-Christians, regardless of religion. Sadly it did not become a success, largely because of an over-hasty launch.[9]

The reign of George III (1760–1820) also saw a significant rise in the demand for grants of new coats of arms. In the three years 1700–2 a mere 29 grants of arms by the Kings of Arms had been registered, but the equivalent figure for 1770–2 was 79 grants.[10] The reasons for this revival – which demonstrates yet again the flexibility and persistence

---

the heralds, and in part a disquisition on the variety of sources that could usefully be employed in the course of research, together with a series of recommendations as to how the parochial and other records then being created in England might be improved.

[9] Wagner, *Heralds of England*, pp. 381–3.
[10] M. P. D. O'Donoghue, 'Grants of Arms in the Early Eighteenth Century', *The Coat of Arms*, 3rd ser., iii (2007), pp. 145–58, at 148.

83 (left). Arms granted in 1803 to Sir Brook Watson, Bt. (1735–1807). The shield and crest both include allusions to the shark attack by which he lost his right leg, aged 14: an event made famous by the painting by John Singleton Copley (1778). College of Arms, MS Grants 22/363.

82 (opposite). Grant of an Honourable Augmentation to the arms, crest and supporters, made by letters patent dated 30 September 1806 by Sir Isaac Heard, Garter King of Arms, to William (Nelson), Earl Nelson, sole brother and heir of Horatio, late Viscount Nelson, deceased. College of Arms, MS Grants 24/281. A further augmentation to the arms was made the following year.

of this medieval system of signs – are related. A movement away from chivalric forms in the seventeenth century had left heraldry and its administrators, the heralds, without a significant part of their influence. The eighteenth century saw this process reversed. Historians now focused their interest on the late Middle Ages as the period when the national characteristics and institutions of England were established.[11] The same period was found attractive for popular culture, as expressed in the growing vogue in the arts for the 'gothick' and picturesque, and for medieval portrayals of chivalry and courtly love. The late Middle Ages had an imaginative appeal for the educated of the late eighteenth and nineteenth centuries, resulting in a great growth of interest in heraldry, grants of arms, and armorial display.[12] Genealogy gained an impetus from the same source, and perhaps also from the Enlightenment wish to categorise and classify.

If a romantic interest in the past was one force driving this growth, another was a development in the concept of what a shield of arms could do: in other words, in the

[11] Rosemary Sweet, *Antiquaries* (London and New York, 2004), p. 262.
[12] Mark Girouard, *The Return to Camelot: Chivalry and the English Gentleman* (London and New Haven, 1981).

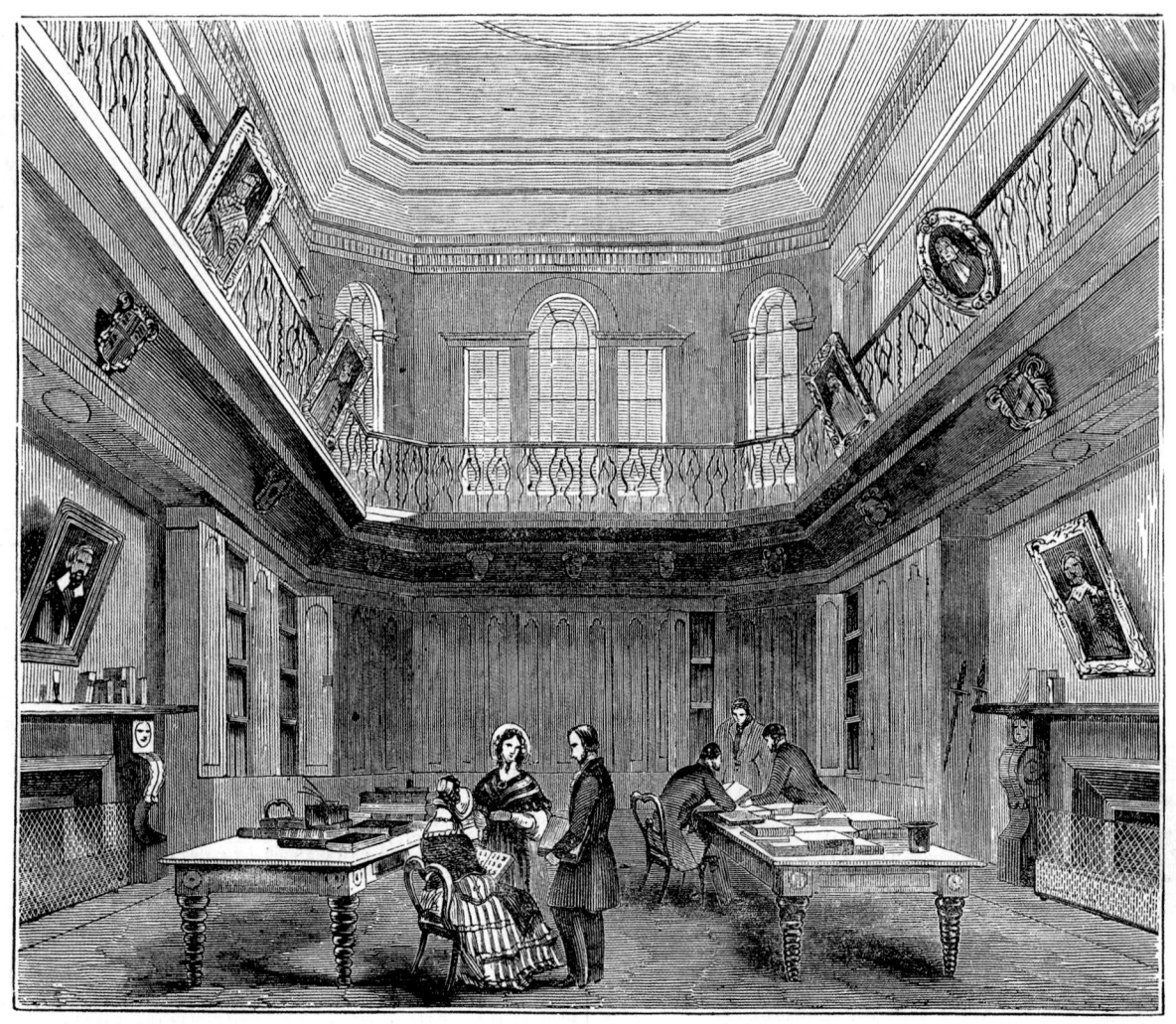

THE NEW RECORD-ROOM, HERALDS' COLLEGE.

84. The Record Room at the College of Arms when first opened, as shown in *The Illustrated London News*, 20 April 1844. The fireplaces have since been replaced by more presses for the College's manuscript records.

power of heraldic design. Whereas medieval and early modern coats of arms were primarily marks of membership of a particular social and cultural group, they now became in addition a means of making statements or narratives about personal as well as group identity.[13] The designs of newly granted coats of arms could now express something of the personal history of the recipient, figuring forth critical moments that

[13] In this they may have been more like *imprese*. Cheesman notes in his discussion of *imprese* and devices that 16th- and 17th-century heraldry frequently deploys 'static, repeated, and often non-figurative charges, whilst devices and emblems ... create (or artfully allude to) narratives'. See Clive Cheesman, 'Some Aspects of the "Crisis of Heraldry"', *The Coat of Arms*, 3rd ser., vi (2010), pp. 65–80, at 79. For the emergence of the 'modern self' in relation to the development of personal narratives, see Charles Taylor, *Sources of the Self: The Making of the Modern Identity* (Cambridge, 1989), cited in Rosemary Sweet, *Cities and the Grand Tour* (Cambridge, 2012), p. 272.

85. Letters Patent of Garter and Clarenceux Kings of Arms, granting arms, crest and badge to Sir Gary Hickinbottom. As with all such documents, the patent is headed by the royal arms, with those of the Earl Marshal and the College of Arms. It includes an exemplification of the standard which can be borne by Sir Gary, and it has a decorative floral border that also includes the Arms of Office of the two granting kings.

both created and expressed the essence of the individual. In this period of constant and worldwide war, the moments in question frequently were military; but they could also be moments of danger or salvation encountered in ordinary life. Coats of arms could thus fuse romantic notions of the self with an idealizing interest in the medieval. The resulting designs, often called 'landscape heraldry' by heraldic textbooks, were quite different in appearance from what had gone before, with the heraldic aesthetic self-confidently rejecting the subtle and symbolic in favour of the literal. Subsequent heraldists have

consistently denigrated the designs of this period as being debased, and they are only now being reassessed, as constructs expressive of their time.[14] The philosophy that underlay this kind of heraldry is still with us, moreover, since modern designs consistently seek to express allusively the critical essence of a grantee's life, career and personality.

With the heralds finding new roles, heraldry finding itself popular once more, and heraldic design again deemed relevant to the culture of the times, the nineteenth century was a comparatively prosperous one for the College of Arms. The heralds were in the main capable and active. Their ceremonial roles at Court, even though much reduced from the Stuart period, nonetheless continued, as the British tradition of formal royal pageantry was developed. Ever since the beginnings of the empire in America and the Indies, the heralds had granted arms to residents of the colonies; as the British Empire grew, so the reach of the College overseas developed. Approximately 75 to 80 grants of arms were made each year during the reign of Queen Victoria, with recipients now including people living in India, Canada and Australia as well as in the Caribbean and in Africa.[15]

At home, there were practical challenges: the accommodation and preservation of the College's growing and immensely valuable archive proved to be a constant and growing area of concern. It had become clear that the College, enmeshed as it was in dingy lanes and alleys between St Paul's Cathedral and the river Thames, was an inconvenient distance from the West End of London, where the heralds' clients were likely to be. Relocation to a more suitable site was after much discussion rejected; the College instead invested in a large specially-designed Record Room, completed in 1844.[16] The College buildings were later truncated by the development of a new Victorian street, which had, however, the beneficial effect of opening up and improving the area.

Perhaps surprisingly, and certainly unusually for so old an institution, the English heralds escaped parliamentary intervention and reform. Until 1867 the office of Lyon King of Arms, heraldic authority for Scotland, had been sustained by payments of fees; it had by the 1860s fallen to a low ebb, and the professional practices of the Scottish heralds were insufficient to support them. A perceived need for reform led to an Act of Parliament reforming that office, directing all fees to the Treasury, and setting salaries for the heralds.[17] The Court of the Lord Lyon continues on this basis in Scotland to the present day, overseeing all heraldic matters within that country. A similar system of

---

[14] For forthright criticism of this style of design see C. W. Scott-Giles, *The Romance of Heraldry* (London, 1940), pp. 201–2.

[15] Woodcock and Robinson, *Oxford Guide to Heraldry*, p. 36. Slightly lower annual figures are given in Michael Maclagan, 'Activities and Rewards of the Officers of Arms in the Mid-Nineteenth Century', *The Coat of Arms*, 1st ser., vi (1960), pp. 146–7.

[16] Wagner, *Heralds of England*, pp. 472–88.

[17] Lyon King of Arms Act 1867, c. 17. See Wagner, *Heralds of England*, p. 513, and Woodcock and Robinson, *Oxford Guide to Heraldry*, p. 155.

AFTERWORD: FROM THE LATE SEVENTEENTH CENTURY TO THE PRESENT

salaries and government control was introduced for the Irish heraldic authority, headed by Ulster King of Arms, in 1871. This latter body came to an end in 1940, with some of its functions later being taken over by a new body, the Office of the Chief Herald of Ireland. Heraldry in the Republic of Ireland comes under the authority of this office, now part of the National Library of Ireland.[18]

The reformist atmosphere might have threatened the College of Arms too, had it not already demonstrated its perennial flexibility by reforming itself. Grants of arms continued to be made in reasonable numbers; and associated functions, such as peerage claims, genealogical research, and the administration of part of the growing honours system, meant that the heralds were in some cases as busy and prosperous as they had ever been. As before, the heralds found that new opportunities presented themselves, even though other areas of activity were declining. For example, the demographic fragility of gentry families in the eighteenth and early nineteenth centuries, had led to a large number of changes of arms and surname by royal licence, as families sought to perpetuate their lineage in the face of failure in the male line; the heralds administered the process.[19] By the end of the nineteenth century, however, such forms of adoption into established lineage were becoming scarcer.

On the rise, by contrast, was the granting of coats of arms to corporate bodies, and in particular to local authorities. Some cities and boroughs had been using arms for centuries, but the Victorian sense of municipal pride expressed itself in the pursuit of grants of coats of arms for many other and newer places. Such municipal coats of arms were displayed on the amenities of the place and on insignia, as an expression of civic pride; like all arms, they assisted in the development and expression of a sense of corporate and geographical identity. In the twentieth and twenty-first centuries such grants of arms would grow still more popular, with the boundary revisions and structural reorganizations of the past sixty years seeing many local authorities established as well as abolished. Today, grants of arms are made each year to a number of local authorities, large and small, ranging in size from parish, town and community councils to those for entire counties or large cities.

Such grants are also made by the kings of arms at the College of Arms to municipal bodies in Australia, New Zealand and the other overseas Realms and Territories of which

---

[18] The Office of Ulster King of Arms had a ceremonial role which ended with the establishment of the Irish Free State in 1922; but as a Crown official appointed for life, Sir Neville Wilkinson continued as Ulster until his death in 1940, retaining the role of heraldic authority for the whole island of Ireland. The heraldic functions of Ulster King of Arms as regards Northern Ireland were transferred to the College of Arms in 1943. The standard history of the Genealogical Office and Office of the Chief Herald of Ireland is Susan Hood, *Royal Roots, Republican Inheritance* (Dublin, 2002). For the history of the transfer of authority, see especially chapters 4 and 5. See also Andrew Lyall, 'Irish Heraldic Jurisdiction', *The Coat of Arms*, new ser., x (1993–4), pp. 134–42, 179–87, 238–44, 266–75.

[19] Lawrence Stone and Jeanne C. Fawtier Stone, *An Open Elite? England 1540–1880*, abridged edition (Oxford, 1986), pp. 82–9.

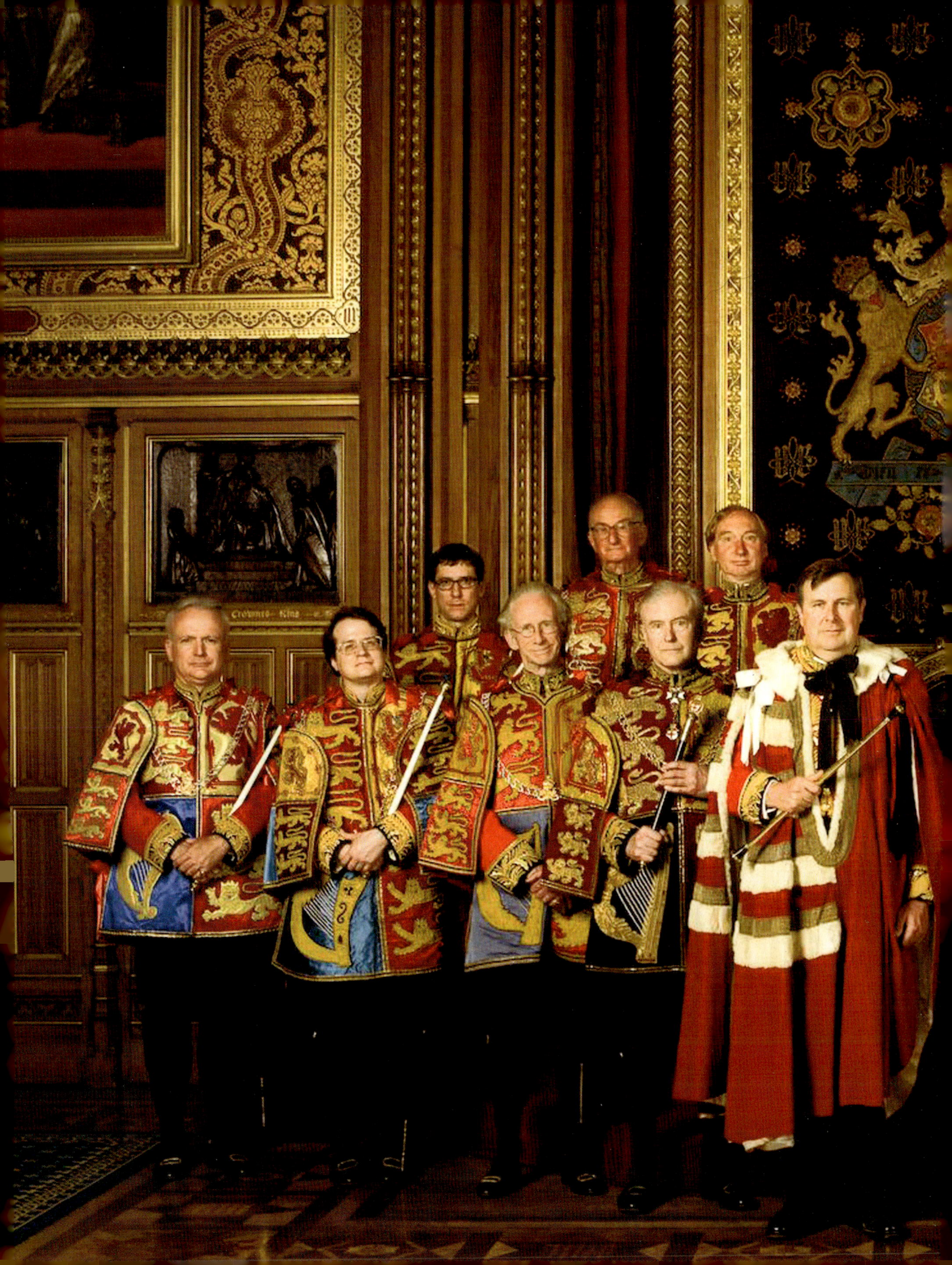

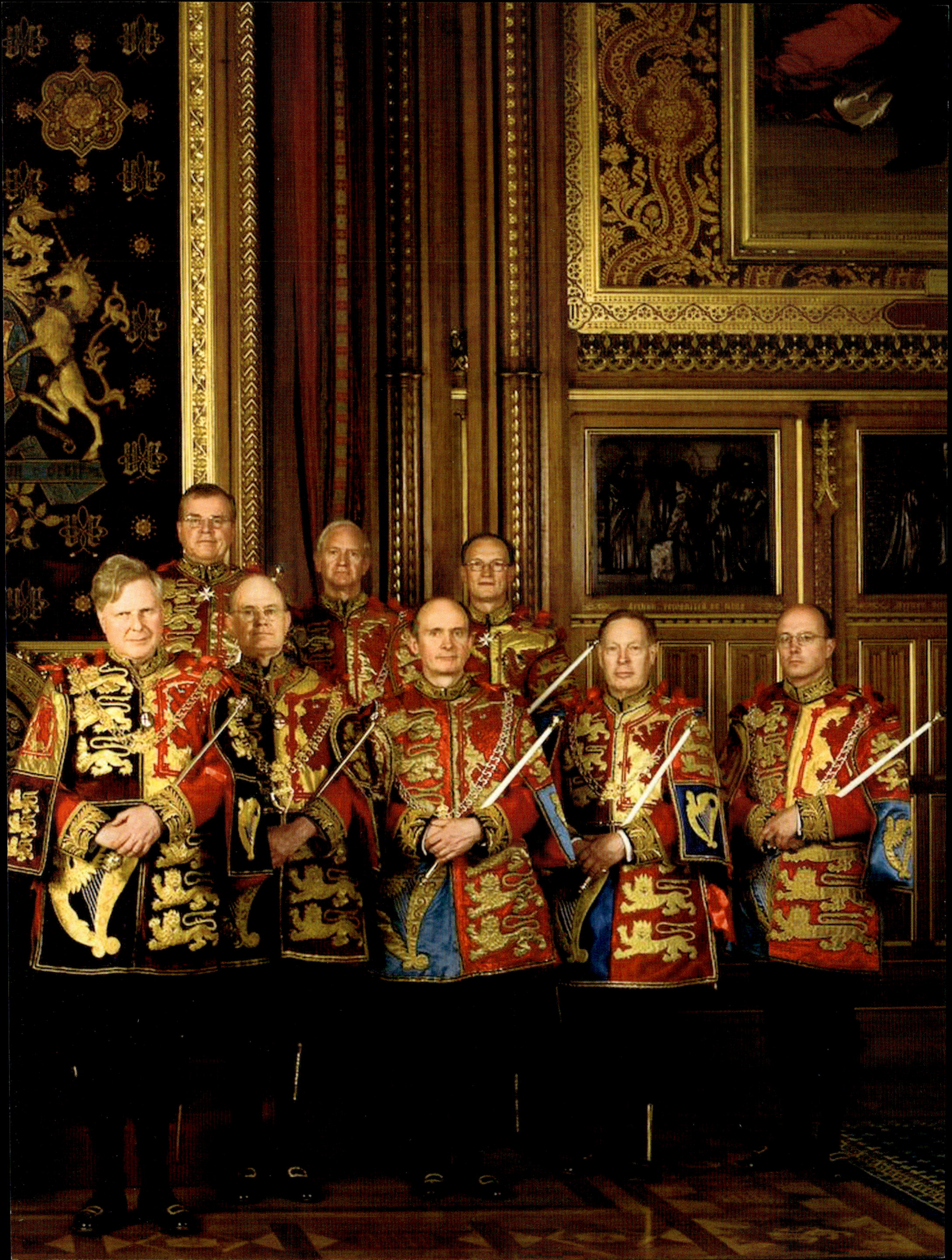

the Queen is the head of state. For almost all of them, the College of Arms is the heraldic authority for grants of arms. The exception is Canada, where in 1988 the Queen issued letters patent delegating her royal prerogative power over coats of arms to the Governor General of Canada, who then established a Canadian Heraldic Authority. This active body, presided over by the Chief Herald of Canada, is now responsible for overseeing the law of arms in Canada and for granting new coats of arms to Canadian citizens.[20]

Later nineteenth- and twentieth-century heraldic design was influenced by the scholarly study of medieval heraldry and its sources. Heralds and heraldic writers sought a return to the context and design of the earliest coats of arms, valuing clarity and simplicity, and emphasizing heraldry's origins as a system for identification. This tendency persisted throughout the twentieth century. Developments in the fine and applied arts, including abstract art, pop art, and commercial graphic design, have all also had more or less unacknowledged impacts on what is now considered to be a satisfactory or at least a possible design for a coat of arms. These influences, like those of the eighteenth century, have enabled heraldic design to remain in touch with its contemporary cultural environment.

The post-War years saw a rise in the popular awareness of heraldry in the English-speaking world, associated in part with the accession of Queen Elizabeth II and her coronation in 1953. Large numbers of new grants of arms to corporate bodies were made in this period; a second peak in annual numbers came with the legislative changes of the 1970s. Personal grants of arms continue, of course, to be made by the English kings of arms, whose jurisdiction ranges over so much of the world, as well as England, Wales and Northern Ireland: the numbers of such grants made each year have continued to fluctuate, currently standing at about 140. The grants include those of Honorary Arms made to US citizens. By special agreement with the US Government, the English kings of arms are permitted to make such grants to those US citizens who can demonstrate genealogical descent of any kind from a subject of the British Crown. Those with an ancestor who was British, Irish, Canadian or from a British colony, territory or dominion, for example, or whose ancestor lived in an American colony prior to Independence, are able to petition. There is thus a genealogical aspect to this process. The heralds of the eighteenth century developed professional practices in genealogical research; this activity continues to grow and develop today, with the heralds of the

---

86 (previous two pages). The Earl Marshal surrounded by the Officers of Arms in their uniforms (which consist of tabards bearing the Royal Arms), as present at the State Opening of Parliament at the Palace of Westminster on 25 May 2010.

[20] The letters patent are printed in 'The Canadian Heraldic Authority', *The Coat of Arms*, new ser., vii (1989), pp. 176–80. For a summary, see Stephen Slater, *The Complete Book of Heraldry* (London 2002), pp. 230–1. See also the website of the Canadian Heraldic Authority: http://www.gg.ca/document.aspx?id=2, accessed 11 January 2013.

modern College of Arms participating in the great explosion of interest in genealogy that the last half-century has witnessed.

As well as grants of Honorary Arms, the English kings of arms are also able to make formal devisals of coats of arms to institutions and corporate bodies in the USA and elsewhere in the world, provided permission is granted by the appropriate state or national government. Such devisals are not grants in the legal sense, because they are outside the Kings' jurisdictions, but they are otherwise identical to grants of arms, being made by letters patent, scrivened and illuminated by hand on vellum.[21]

In Scotland, grants of arms continue to be made by Lord Lyon King of Arms, and in Ireland by the Chief Herald of Ireland. There is no equivalent to the heralds of the United Kingdom and Canada elsewhere, although heraldic regulation is not unknown. In several countries a degree of legal protection is afforded to coats of arms, particularly where they are borne by municipal bodies.[22] The College of Arms is unique in its size, the number of heralds and staff who work there, and the scale and significance of its archives. Although an official body, it retains its independence, answering to no particular government department but working closely with several of them as well as with Buckingham Palace. Over the heralds, who are members of the Royal Household, is placed only the authority of the Earl Marshal, and the Sovereign, by whom all heralds are directly appointed under the Great Seal.

But it is above all heraldry itself that sustains the College: a system which has proved capable of communicating differing, related meanings for different times and cultures, which can convey all the value of anachronism and the attraction of elitism; and which can provide an effective statement of identity for a modern entrepreneur, a democratically elected local council, or an ambitious international business corporation.

---

[21] See Woodcock and Robinson, *Oxford Guide to Heraldry*, pp. 169–70. Two examples of recent devisals are: that to Kent School, Connecticut, in 2007 (see http://www.college-of-arms.gov.uk/Newsletter/014.htm); and that to Sunway University College, Malaysia in 2006 (see http://www.college-of-arms.gov.uk/Newsletter/012.htm, and http://sunway.edu.my/university/why-sunway/the-university/grant-of-arms), all accessed 11 January 2013.

[22] A useful summary of the variety of forms of registration and protection in different countries is provided at: http://www.americanheraldry.org/pages/index.php?n=Registration.Foreign; accessed 8 December 2012.

Further Reading

This list comprises publications that either are the basic works of reference or are recent contributions to the subject; it therefore overlaps with those works that are cited above, in the various chapters. For the fullest coverage of early publications there is still nothing to match Thomas Moule, *Bibliotheca Heraldica* (London, 1822; reprinted, London, 1966). For more recent works it is best to turn to the Bibliography of British and Irish History, set up by the Royal Historical Society and now available online through the website BREPOLIS.

General

J. S. A. Adamson, 'Chivalry and Political Culture in Caroline England', in *Culture and Politics in Early Stuart England*, ed. K. Sharpe and P. Lake (Basingstoke, Hants., and London, 1994), pp. 161–97, 349–57 [chivalry and mock chivalry, 1620s–1640s].

O. Barron, 'Heraldry', in *Shakespeare's England*, ed. Sidney Lee and C. T. Onions, 2 vols (Oxford, 1916), II, pp. 74–90.

W. Dugdale, *The Antient Usage in Bearing of such Ensignes of Honour as are Commonly Call'd Arms* (Oxford, 1682); 2nd edn. (Oxford, 1682).

P. C. Franke, 'The Heraldry of *The Faerie Queene*', *Coat of Arms*, new ser., iv (1980–1), pp. 317–23 [drawings of the coats of arms blazoned by Spenser].

D. Gelber, "Hark, What Discord': Precedency among the Early-Stuart Gentry', *Coat of Arms*, 3rd ser., iii (2007), pp. 117–44.

J. Good, 'London Guild and Diocesan Heraldry during the Reformation', *Coat of Arms*, new ser., xii (1997–8), pp. 96–102 [changes to arms of livery companies at the Reformation and subsequently].

Felicity Heal and Clive Holmes, *The Gentry in England and Wales, 1500–1700* (Basingstoke and London, 1994) [incl. discussion of gentry concern with lineage (pp. 20–47)].

Mervyn [E.] James, *Family, Lineage, and Civil Society. A Study of Society, Politics, and Mentality in the Durham Region, 1500–1640* (Oxford, 1974) [the 'lineage society'].

M. E. James, *English Politics and the Concept of Honour, 1485–1642, Past & Present Supplement*, no. 3 (1978) [reprinted in his *Society, Politics and Culture. Studies in Early Modern England* (Cambridge, etc., 1986), pp. 308–415].

C. D. Liddy with C. Steer, 'John Lord Lumley and the Creation and Commemoration of Lineage in Early Modern England', *Archaeological Jnl.*, 167 (2011, for 2010), pp. 197–227 [retrospective funerary monuments].

M. Maclagan, 'Genealogy and Heraldry in the Sixteenth and Seventeenth Centuries', in *English Historical Scholarship in the Sixteenth and Seventeenth Centuries*, ed. L. Fox (London, etc.: Dugdale Soc., 1956), pp. 31–48.

R. Marks and Ann Payne, comp. and ed., *British Heraldry, from its Origins to c. 1800*, exhibition cat. (London: British Museum, 1978).

Alfred J. F. von Mauntz, *Heraldik in Diensten der Shakespeare-Forschung* (Berlin, 1903).

Arthur H. Nason, *Heralds and Heraldry in Jonson's Plays, Masques and Entertainments* (New York, 1907).

M. P. Siddons, *The Development of Welsh Heraldry*, 4 vols (Aberystwyth: National Library of Wales, 1991–2006).

[A. R. Wagner and others], *Heralds' Commemorative Exhibition, 1484–1934, Held at the College of Arms. Enlarged & Illustrated Catalogue* (London, 1936).

A. R. Wagner, 'Heraldry and the Historian', in his *Pedigree and Progress. Essays in the Genealogical Interpretation of History* (London and Chichester, 1975), pp. 34–49.

FURTHER READING

A. R. Wagner, *English Genealogy*, 3rd edn. (Chichester, 1983).

Thomas Woodcock and John Martin Robinson, *Oxford Guide to Heraldry* (Oxford, etc., 1988).

T. Woodcock and J. M. Robinson, *Heraldry in National Trust Houses* (London, 1999).

Coats of Arms and Grants of Arms

A. Ailes, 'Signets and Scutcheons: James I and the Union of the Crowns', *Coat of Arms*, 3rd ser., i (2005), pp. 15–21 [signet with royal arms designed in 1603].

W. Paley Baildon, 'Heralds' College and Prescription', *The Ancestor*, VIII (1904), pp. 113–44, and IX (1904), pp. 214–24 [incl. numerous excerpts from texts of grants of arms].

C. H. Hunter Blair, 'Armorials on English Seals from the Twelfth to the Sixteenth Centuries', *Archaeologia*, lxxxix (1943), pp. 1–26 and plates.

J. Cherry, 'Seals and Heraldry, 1400–1600: Public Policy and Private Posts', in *The Age of Transition: The Archaeology of English Culture, 1400–1600*, ed. D. Gaimster and P. Stamper, Soc. for Medieval Archaeology Monograph 15 (Oxford, 1997), pp. 251–63 [replacement of religious imagery by heraldry at the Reformation; royal, episcopal and hospital seals].

E. Elmhirst, 'The Fashion for Heraldry', *Coat of Arms*, 1st ser., iv (1956), pp. 47–50; replied to by A.R. Wagner, 'The Fashion for Heraldry. Dr Elmhirst's View Reviewed', *ibid.*, pp. 119–20. [Numbers of coats of arms granted in later 16th century.]

J. A. Goodall, 'Heraldry Depicted on Brasses', in *Monumental Brasses as Art and History*, ed. Jerome Bertram (Stroud, Glos.: Alan Sutton Publishing, in association with the Monumental Brass Soc., 1996), pp. 47–55. [See also C. Humphery-Smith, 'Genealogy from Brasses', *ibid.*, pp. 56–61.]

P. Gwynn-Jones, 'Tudor Enigmas', *Coat of Arms*, 3rd ser., i (2005), pp. 73–104 [numbers of coats granted in the later sixteenth century; grants made by William Hervey, Clarenceux; arms of the College of Arms].

M. Howard and Tessa Murdoch, "Armes and Bestes': Tudor and Stuart Heraldry', in *Treasures of the Royal Courts: Tudors, Stuarts & the Russian Tsars*, ed. Olga Dmitrieva and Tessa Murdoch (London, 2013), pp. 56–67 [heraldic decoration; heraldic beasts].

J. Hunter, 'Heraldry of the Monument of Queen Elizabeth, at Westminster', *Archaeologia Cambrensis*, new ser., i (1850), pp. 194–9 [funerary monument, erected by James I, showing her descent from William I, through Edward III].

A. Kwan, 'John Dee's Crest, and Arms in his 'Mathematical Preface'', *Coat of Arms*, 3rd ser., i (2005), pp. 9–13 [grant of crest, 1576].

W. A. Littledale, ed., *A Collection of Miscellaneous Grants, Crests, Confirmations, Augmentations and Exemplifications of Arms*, 2 parts (Harleian Soc., lxxvi–lxxvii, 1925–6) [full texts of over 220 grants etc., 15th to 17th cent.].

Nigel Llewellyn, 'Claims to Status through Visual Codes: Heraldry on Post-Reformation English Funeral Monuments', in *Chivalry in the Renaissance*, ed. Sydney Anglo (Woodbridge, 1990), pp. 145–60.

Jean-Claude Loutsch, 'Généralités sur les brisures des bâtards. Conceptions suivant les pays d'après la littérature héraldique. Théorie et réalité', in *Académie internationale d'héraldique. VIII Colloquium. Canterbury. 29th August – 4th September 1993. Proceedings*, ed. C. R. Humphery-Smith (Canterbury, 1995), pp. 7–14.

Neil MacGregor, *Shakespeare's Restless World* (London, etc., 2012), Chapter 15 (pp. 202– 14), 'The Flag That Failed: Flags for Great Britain' [six designs for the Union Flag of 'Great Britain', *c.*1604, drawn in Edinburgh, National Library of Scotland, MS 2517, f. 67].

W. H. Rylands, ed., *Grantees of Arms Named in Docquets and Patents to the End of the Seventeenth Century* (Harleian Soc., lxvi, 1915). [The fullest list of grants that has been printed.]

M. P. Siddons, *The Heraldry of Foreigners in England, 1400–1700* (Harleian Soc., new ser., 19, 2010) [texts of grants of arms and augmentations of arms].

Clare Tilbury, 'The Heraldry of the Twelve Tribes of Israel: An English Reformation Subject for Church

HERALDS AND HERALDRY IN SHAKESPEARE'S ENGLAND

Decoration', *Jnl. of Ecclesiastical History*, 63 (2012), pp. 274–305 [theological genealogies; arms of the Twelve Patriarchs, as painted in Burton Latimer parish church (Northants.), 1630s].

Draft Grants of Arms to Shakespeare (1596 and 1599)

E. K. Chambers, *William Shakespeare*, 2 vols (Oxford, 1930) [incl. discussion of the grants of arms (II, pp. 18–32)].

K. Duncan-Jones, *Ungentle Shakespeare. Scenes from his Life* (London, 2001) [incl. discussion of the grants of arms (pp. 91–103)].

Sidney Lee, *A Life of William Shakespeare*, enlarged version, 2nd edn. (London, 1916), pp. 281–8.

B. Roland Lewis, *The Shakespeare Documents: Facsimiles, Transliterations, Translations & Commentary*, 2 vols (Stanford, Calif., and London, [1940–1]) [incl. illustrations and texts of both the 1596 and the 1599 drafts (vol. I, pp. 208–17, 299–306) and material from the disputes as to Shakespeare's eligibility for arms (vol. II, pp. 336–46)].

Samuel Schoenbaum, *William Shakespeare: A Documentary Life* (Oxford, 1975), pp. 36, 166–73 [incl. illustrations of all three grants].

C. W. Scott-Giles, *Shakespeare's Heraldry* (London, 1950), chapter ii (pp. 27–41): 'Shakespeare's Arms' [incl. composite version of the 1596 grants].

Heralds

B. Borukhov, 'Sir William Segar: Nine Additions to his Biography', *Notes and Queries*, 252 (2007), pp. 328–31 [addenda to *ODNB*].

A. E. Brown, 'Augustine Vincent, Herald, and his Projected History of Northampton-shire', *Northamptonshire Past and Present*, no. 52 (1999), pp. 21–31.

D. Carlson, 'The Writings and Manuscript Collections of the Elizabethan Alchemist, Antiquary, and Herald Francis Thynne', *Huntington Library Quarterly*, 52 (1989), pp. 203–72.

J. P. Cooper, 'Ideas of Gentility in Early Modern-England', in his *Land, Men and Beliefs. Studies in Early-Modern History*, ed. G. E. Aylmer and J. S. Morrill (London, 1983), pp. 43–77 [heralds' views on social status].

Richard Cust, *Charles I and the Aristocracy, 1625–1642* (Cambridge, etc., 2013) [incl. discussions of 'Heralds and Earl Marshals in Late Tudor England' (pp. 7–22) and 'Heralds and the Court of Chivalry' (pp. 156–71)].

B. Danielsson, *John Hart's Works on English Orthography and Pronunciation [1551, 1569, 1570]*, Pt. 1 (Stockholm, 1955) [incl. biographical material about Hart, Chester Herald from 1567 to 1574].

J. F. R. Day, 'Gentlemen "Made good cheap": A Character of a Seventeenth-Century Herald', *Coat of Arms*, new ser., iv (1980–1), pp. 290–7 [characterisation in John Earle's *Micro- cosmography* (1628)].

Rodney Dennys, *Heraldry and the Heralds* (London, 1982).

M. A. Fitzsimons, 'Money and the Degrees of Being. A Note on English Heraldry', *Review of Politics*, x (1948), pp. 332–45 [heralds' venality].

A. K. Fursey, 'A Note on Deputy Heralds, the Holme Family and the *Academie of Armory*, 1688', in *Tribute to an Armorist*, ed. J. Campbell-Kease (privately printed, 2000), pp. 131–7 [Randle Holme I (1571–1655), and his descendants, deputy heralds].

W. H. Godfrey, assisted by A. R. Wagner, *The College of Arms, Queen Victoria Street; with A Complete List of the Officers of Arms*, by H.S. London, London Survey Committee, Monograph 16 (London, 1963).

P. H. Hardacre, 'The Earl Marshal, the Heralds and the House of Commons, 1604–1641', *International Review of Social History*, ii (1957), pp. 106–25.

Wyman H. Herendeen, *William Camden: A Life in Context* (Woodbridge, 2007) [incl. discussion (pp. 353–96, 410–24) of Camden's activities as Clarenceux King of Arms, and the writings of Sir John Ferne, Sir William Segar and John Selden].

T. D. Kendrick, *British Antiquity* (London, 1950) [incl discussions of the dispute between Camden and

FURTHER READING

Ralph Brooke (pp. 148, 152–5) and of heralds' church-notes (pp. 156–7)].
H. Stanford London, 'John Philipot, M.P., Somerset Herald, 1624–1645', *Archaeologia Cantiana*, 60 (1948, for 1947), pp. 24–53, 134.
H. Stanford London, 'John Hart, Orthographic Reformer and Chester Herald, 1567–74', *Notes & Queries*, cciii (1958), pp. 222–4.
Richard C. McCoy, *The Rites of Knighthood. The Literature and Politics of Elizabethan Chivalry* (Berkeley, Los Angeles and London, 1989) [incl. discussion of role of Earl Marshal].
S. Piggott, 'William Camden and the *Britannia*', *Proc., British Academy*, xxxvii (1951), pp. 199–217.
F. R. Raines, ed., 'Letters on the Claims of the College of Arms in Lancashire, in the Time of James the First: by Leonard Smethley and Randle Holme, Deputy Heralds', in *Chetham Miscellanies*, V (Chetham Soc., xcvi, 1875).
W. Rockett, '*Britannia*, Ralph Brooke, and the Representation of Privilege in Elizabethan England', *Renaissance Quarterly*, 53 (2000), pp. 474–99.
P. Selwyn, 'Heralds' Libraries', in *Cambridge History of Libraries in Britain and Ireland*, I: *To 1640*, ed. E. Leedham-Green and T. Webber (Cambridge, 2006), pp. 472–88.
R. Tittler, *Portraits, Painters, and Publics in Provincial England, 1540-1640* (Oxford, etc., 2012) [deputy heralds, such as the Randle Holme dynasty, as provincial portraitists]
A. R. Wagner, *Heralds of England. A History of the Office and College of Arms* (London, 1967).
A. R. Wagner and G. D. Squibb, 'Deputy Heralds', in *Tribute to an Antiquary. Essays Presented to Marc Fitch by Some of his Friends*, ed. F. Emmison and R. Stephens (London, 1976), pp. 229–64.
R. Tittler, *Portraits, Painters, and Publics in Provincial England, 1540-1640* (Oxford, etc., 2012) [deputy heralds, such as the Randle Holme dynasty, as provincial portraitists]

Heraldry and the Law: The Law of Arms
Richard P. Cust and A. J. Hopper, ed., *Cases in the High Court of Chivalry, 1634–1640* (Harleian Soc., new ser., 18, 2006). [Summaries of all cases in this period; see also: www.court-of-chivalry.bham.ac.uk]
R. P. Cust, *Charles I and the Aristocracy, 1625–1642* (Cambridge, etc., 2013) [incl. discussion of 'The Court of Chivalry and the Defence of Honour' (pp. 140–71)].
R. P. Cust, 'Sir Henry Spelman Investigates', *Coat of Arms*, 3rd ser., iii (2007), pp. 25–34 [case brought in Court of Chivalry against Thomas Tuckfield, 1635, for using arms that had been disclaimed in a visitation].
C. D. I. Forrester, 'The Independent Rights of Married Women in the Law of Arms', *Coat of Arms*, new ser., ii (1976–7), pp. 70–6 [incl. discussion of heralds' chapter ruling of 1561×2].
Peter R. Moore, 'The Heraldic Charge against the Earl of Surrey, 1546–47', *English Historical Review*, 116 (2001), pp. 557–83.
G. D. Squibb, *The High Court of Chivalry: A Study of the Civil Law in England* (Oxford, 1959).
G. D. Squibb, *The Law of Arms*, revised edn. (London: The Heraldry Soc., 1967) [Pamphlet].
G. D. Squibb, ed., *Reports of Heraldic Cases in the Court of Chivalry, 1623–1732* (Harleian Soc., cvii, 1956). [Summaries of selected cases, incl. those involving heralds.]
Richard P. Cust and A. J. Hopper, ed., *Cases in the High Court of Chivalry, 1634–1640* (Harleian Soc., new ser., 18, 2006). [Summaries of all cases in this period.]
Richard Cust, *Charles I and the Aristocracy, 1625–1642* (Cambridge, etc., 2013) [incl. discussion of 'The Court of Chivalry and the Defence of Honour' (pp. 140–71)].

Heraldic Manuscripts and Early Books on Heraldry
John Bossewell, *Workes of Armorie* (London, 1583; reprinted 1597).
William Camden, *Remains Concerning Britain*, ed. R.D. Dunn (Toronto, 1984).
Louise Campbell and F.W. Steer, *A Catalogue of Manuscripts in the College of Arms: Collections*, vol. I (London, 1988).

Matthew Carter, *Honor Rediuiuus* [sic] *or an Analysis of Honor and Armory* (London, 1655); 3rd edn. (London, 1673).

J. F. R. Day, 'Primers of Honor: Heraldry, Heraldry Books, and English Renaissance Liter- ature', *Sixteenth Century Jnl.*, 21 (1990), pp. 93–103.

John Ferne, *The Blazon of Gentrie* (London, 1586).

I. A. Gadd, "'Ornamental for Closet or House': Printed Catalogues of the Arms of the London Livery Companies, 1596–1677', *Coat of Arms*, 3rd ser., iii (2007), pp. 55–66.

John Guillim, *A Display of Heraldrie* (London, 1611); 2nd edn. (London, 1632); 3rd edn. (London, 1638); etc., to '6th edn.' (London, 1724).

Randle Holme, *The Academy of Armory, or, A Storehouse of Armory and Blazon ...* (London, 1688) [Books I and II, and Book III, chapters 1–13.]

Randle Holme, *The Academy of Armory, or, A Storehouse of Armory and Blazon ...*, ed. I. H. Jeayes (Roxburghe Club, no. 144, 1905). [Book III, chapters 14-22, and Book IV, chapters 4-13, printed from British Library, MSS Harley 2033–5.]

J. A. Lawson, 'This Remembrance of the New Year. Books Given to Queen Elizabeth as New Year's Gifts', in *Elizabeth I and the Culture of Writing*, ed. P. Beal and G. Ioppolo (London, 2007), pp. 133–71 [incl. 'Heraldry and Armoury' (pp. 152–4)].

Gerard Legh, *The Accedens of Armory* (London, 1562; and several later editions).

Thomas Milles, *The Catalogue of Honor, or Tresury of True Nobility ...* (London, 1610).

J. Murrell, 'John Guillim's Book: A Heraldic Painter's *Vade Mecum*', *Walpole Soc.*, 57 (1993–4), pp. 1–51.

William Segar, *The Booke of Honor and Armes* (London, 1590). [Published anonymously.]

William Segar, *Honor Military, and Civill* (London, 1602).

John Selden, *Titles of Honor* (London, 1614); 2nd edn. (London, 1631); 3rd edn. (London, 1672).

A. R. Wagner, *A Catalogue of English Mediaeval Rolls of Arms*, Aspilogia I (Oxford, 1950) [also issued as Harleian Soc. Publications, vol. 100]; additions and corrections in *Rolls of Arms: Henry III*, ed. T. D. Tremlett and H. S. London, Aspilogia II (Oxford, 1967) [also issued as Harleian Soc. Publications, vols 113–114], pp. 255–81.

Cyril E. Wright, *English Heraldic Manuscripts in the British Museum* (London, 1973) [scholarly booklet].

A. R. Young, 'Alciato, Paradin and John Bossewell's *Workes of Armorie*', *Emblematica: An Interdisciplinary Jnl. for Emblem Studies*, 3 (1988), pp. 351–76 [Bossewell's derivation of material from Andrea Alciato and Claude Paradin].

A. R. Young, *Henry Peacham* (Boston, 1979).

Pedigrees and Pedigree Rolls

G. Bathe and A. Douglas, 'Forging Alliances: The Life of Edward Seymour, Earl of Hertford, and his Commissioning of the Great Illuminated Roll Pedigree of the Seymours and Monumental Tombs in Wiltshire and Westminster', *Wiltshire Studies (Wilts. Archaeol. & Natural History Mag.)*, 105 (2012), pp. 182–218 [1604 and later; roll measures 22 ft. 5 in. × 6 ft. 2 in. (6.83×1.88 m.)].

Oliver D. Harris, 'Lines of Descent: Appropriations of Ancestry in Stone and Parchment', in *The Arts of Remembrance in Early Modern England. Memorial Cultures of the Post Reformation*, ed. Andrew Gordon and Thomas Rist (Farnham, Surr., and Burlington, Vermont, 2013), pp. 85–102 [John, Lord Lumley (d. 1609); the Carew family, of Devon; and Sir Edward Dering (d. 1644)].

W. J. Hemp, 'Two Welsh Heraldic Pedigrees, with Notes on Thomas Chaloner of Denbigh and Chester, Ulster King of Arms', *Y Cymmrodor*, xl (1929), pp. 207–25. ['Target' pedigree designs.]

Brendan Kane, *The Politics and Culture of Honour in Britain and Ireland, 1541–1641* (Cambridge, 2010), at pp. 146–90 [Irish pedigrees and pedigree-rolls].

Ann Payne, 'Heraldry and Genealogies', in *Art Collecting and Lineage in the Elizabethan Age: The Lumley Inventory and Pedigree*, ed. Mark Evans (Roxburghe Club, 2010), pp. 20–7.

FURTHER READING

M. P. Siddons, *Welsh Pedigree Rolls* ([Aberystwyth:] National Library of Wales, 1996). [Incl. list of over 400 rolls dating from before *c*. 1700.]

M. P. Siddons, 'Printed and Manuscript Pedigrees', in *Welsh Family History. A Guide to Research*, ed. John and Sheila Rowlands, 2nd edn. (Birmingham, 1998), pp. 211–29.

Visitations

A. Ailes, 'The Development of the Heralds' Visitations in England and Wales, 1450–1600', *Coat of Arms*, 3rd ser., 5 (2009), pp. 7–23.

P. O'Donoghue, 'Visitation Instructions, 1634', *Coat of Arms*, 3rd ser., vi (2010), pp. 17–22 [printed from College of Arms, MS 1 B. 5, ff. 31v–32v].

M. P. Siddons, ed., *The Visitation of Herefordshire, 1634* (Harleian Soc., new ser., xv, 2002).

G. D. Squibb, *Visitation Pedigrees and the Genealogist*, 2nd edn. (London, 1978) [incl. assessment of reliability of many editions of visitation records.]

Janet Verasanso, 'The Staffordshire Heraldic Visitations: Their Nature and Function', *Coat of Arms*, new ser., xv (2003), pp. 47–69.

A. R. Wagner, *Records and Collections of the College of Arms* (London, 1952) [incl. authoritative list of visitation records].

D. R. Woolf, *The Social Circulation of the Past: English Historical Culture, 1500–1730* (Oxford, 2003), chapter 4, 'The Genealogical Imagination' (pp. 99–137) [visitations and pedigrees].

Funerals

I. W. Archer, 'City and Court Connected: The Material Dimensions of Royal Ceremonial, ca. 1480–1625', *Huntington Library Quarterly*, 71 (2008), pp. 157–79 [coronations and funerals].

J. T. Brighton, 'The Plantagenet Arms in Bakewell Church', *Coat of Arms*, new ser., iii (1978–9), pp. 102–4 [wooden shield, perhaps from funeral of Sir John Manners, 1611, or his son George, 1623].

D. Cressy, 'Death and the Social Order: The Funerary Preferences of Elizabethan Gentlemen', *Continuity and Change*, 5 (1990), pp. 99–119.

J. F. R. Day, 'Death Be Very Proud: Sidney, Subversion, and Elizabethan Heraldic Funerals', in *Tudor Political Culture*, ed. D. Hoak (Cambridge, 1995), pp. 179–203.

J. F. R. Day, 'Buried "the King's True Subject": The Late Medieval English Heraldic Funeral in Decline', *Coat of Arms*, new ser., xiii (1999–2000), pp. 233–44 [incl. discussion of funeral of George Talbot, earl of Shrewsbury, 1590].

Clare Gittings, *Death, Burial and the Individual in Early Modern England* (London and Sydney, 1984), chapter 8 (pp. 166–87).

Vanessa Harding, *The Dead and the Living in Paris and London, 1500–1670* (Cambridge, etc., 2002), chapter 8 (pp. 208–33).

Anthony Harvey and Richard Mortimer, *The Funeral Effigies of Westminster Abbey* (Woodbridge, 1994).

R. Houlbrooke, 'Civility and Civil Observances in the Early Modern English Funeral', in *Civil Histories. Essays Presented to Sir Keith Thomas*, ed. P. Burke, B. Harrison and P. Slack (Oxford, 2000), pp. 67–85, at 79–82.

M. E. James, 'Two Tudor Funerals', *Trans., Cumb. & Westmld. Antiquarian & Archaeo- logical Soc.*, new ser., lxvi (1966), pp. 165–78 [William Dacre, Baron Dacre of Gilsland, 1563, and Thomas Wharton, Baron Wharton, 1568].

T. W. King and F. R. Raines, ed., *Lancashire Funeral Certificates* (Chetham Soc., lxxv, 1869) [1568–1601].

J. W. S. Litten, 'The Heraldic Funeral', *Coat of Arms*, 3rd ser., i (2005), pp. 47–67.

Nigel Llewellyn, *The Art of Death. Visual Culture in the English Death Ritual, c. 1500 – c. 1800* (London, 1991), pp. 65–72: 'Heraldic Displays' [at funerals].

J. P. Rylands, ed., *Cheshire and Lancashire Funeral Certificates, AD 1600 to 1678* (Lancs. & Ches. Record Soc., vi, 1882).

HERALDS AND HERALDRY IN SHAKESPEARE'S ENGLAND

Lawrence Stone, *The Crisis of the Aristocracy, 1558–1641* (Oxford, 1965), pp. 572–81.
Peter Summers and John E. Titterton, *Hatchments in Britain*, 10 vols (Chichester, 1984–94). [Nationwide survey of extant hatchments; general account of hatchments in vol. 10.]
Clodagh Tait, *Death, Burial and Commemoration in Ireland, 1550–1650* (Basingstoke and New York, 2002), pp. 39–48.
A. R. Wagner, 'A Note on Hatchments', *Antiquaries Jnl.*, xxxvi (1956), pp. 71–3.
W. Walters-DiTraglia, 'Death, Commemoration and the Heraldic Funeral in Tudor and Stuart Cheshire', 2 parts, *Coat of Arms*, 3rd ser., iii (2007), pp. 35–54 and 103–16.
Jennifer Woodward, *The Theatre of Death: The Ritual Management of Royal Funerals in Renaissance England, 1570–1625* (Woodbridge, 1997), especially chapter 1 (pp. 15–36).

The Order of the Garter
John Anstis, ed., *Register of the Most Noble Order of the Garter, from its Cover in Black Velvet, Usually Called the Black Book*, 2 vols. (London, 1724). [Incl. biographical accounts of numerous heralds.]
Peter J. Begent and Hubert Chesshyre, *The Most Noble Order of the Garter: 650 Years* (London, 1999).
Richard Cust, 'Charles I and the Order of the Garter', *Jnl. of British Studies*, 52 (2013), pp. 343–69.
Richard Cust, *Charles I and the Aristocracy, 1625–1642* (Cambridge, etc., 2013) [incl. discussion of 'The Order of the Garter' (pp. 119–39)].
L. Jefferson, 'A Garter Installation Ceremony in 1606', *The Court Historian*, vi (2001), pp. 141–50.
L. Jefferson, 'Gifts Given and Fees Paid to Garter King of Arms at Installation Ceremonies of the Order of the Garter during the Sixteenth Century', *Costume*, 36 (2002), pp. 18–35 [down to 1594; list based on Paris, Bibl. Nat. de France, MS anglais 107].
J. N. Ortego, 'Seeking the Medieval in Shakespeare: The Order of the Garter and the Topos of Derisive Chivalry', *Fifteenth-Century Studies*, 35 (2010), pp. 80–104.
D. Starkey, ed., *Henry VIII. A European Court in England*, exhibition cat. (London, 1991) [incl. section on 'The Orders of the Garter and St Michael', by D. Starkey and others (pp. 94–9)].
R. C. Strong, 'Queen Elizabeth I and the Order of the Garter', *Archaeological Jnl.*, cxix (1964), pp. 245–69. [Reprinted with slight revision in Strong, *The Cult of Elizabeth: Elizabethan Portraiture and Pageantry* ([London], 1977), pp. 164–85, 203–6 and 212-13, and in Strong, *The Tudor and Stuart Monarchy. Pageantry, Painting, Iconography*, 3 vols (Woodbridge, 1995–8), II, pp. 55–86.]
R. B. Waddington, 'Queen Elizabeth and the Order of the Garter', *Sixteenth Century Jnl.*, 24 (1993), pp. 97–113.

Paraheraldry: Badges, Devices, Mottoes, Imprese and Flags
S. Anglo, *Images of Tudor Kingship* (London, 1992). [Tudor badges and emblems.]
M. Bath, *Speaking Pictures: English Emblem Books and Renaissance Culture* (London and New York, 1994).
M. Bath, 'Ben Jonson, William Fowler and the Pinkie Ceiling', *Architectural Heritage (Jnl. of the Architectural Heritage Soc. of Scotland)*, xvii (2007), pp. 73–86 [Long Gallery at Pinkie (in Perth) with painted inscriptions and emblems, mentioned by Ben Jonson, 1619].
Peter M. Daly and Mary V. Silcox, *The English Emblem: Bibliography of Secondary Literature* (Munich and London, 1990).
P. M. Daly and M. V. Silcox, *The Modern Critical Reception of the English Emblem* (Munich and London, etc., 1991). [English authors, especially before 1700; emblems and the emblematic in late 16th – early 17th century painting, tapestry, carving, jewellery, funerary monuments and *imprese*.]
P. M. Daly, 'Paradin in Sixteenth-Century England: An Aspect of the Reception of Continental Imprese', in *Emblematic Perceptions: Essays in Honor of William S. Heckscher*, ed. P. M. Daly and D. S. Russell (Baden-Baden, 1997), pp. 61–91 [Paradin's *Devises héroïques*: 1551, 1557; and Latin version, as *Symbola Heroica*, 1562 and many later editions).
P. M. Daly, 'The European Imprese: From Fifteenth-Century Aristocratic Device to Twenty-First-Century Logo,' *Emblematica*, 13 (2003), pp. 303–32.

FURTHER READING

P. M. Daly, ed., *Companion to Emblem Studies* (New York, 2008) [collection of studies].

I. Gentles, 'The Iconography of Revolution: England 1642–1649', in *Soldiers, Writers and Statesmen of the English Revolution*, ed. I. Gentles, J. Morrill and B. Worden (Cambridge, 1998), pp. 91–113 [flags and mottoes].

C. S. Knighton and T. Wilson, 'Serjeant Knight's Discourse on the Cross and Flags of St George (1678)', *Antiquaries Jnl.*, 81 (2001), pp. 351–90 [incl. account of 'Debates about St George and his Cross in Tudor and Stuart England' (pp. 355–9)].

H. Stanford London, *Royal Beasts* (East Knoyle, Wilts.: The Heraldry Soc., 1956) [incl. the Tudor red dragon and, from 1603, the Scottish unicorn of James I].

Averill Lukic, 'The Same Anticipation of Resurrection: Paradin in North Wales?', *Emblematica*, 17 (2009), pp. 229–38 [tomb at Conwy, 1586, with design apparently derived from Paradin's *Devises héroïques*].

Neil MacGregor, *Shakespeare's Restless World* (London, etc., 2012), chapter 15 (pp. 202–14), 'The Flag That Failed: Flags for Great Britain' [six designs for the Union Flag of 'Great Britain', *c.* 1604, drawn in Edinburgh, National Library of Scotland, MS 2517, f. 67].

K. Sharpe, *Image Wars. Promoting Kings and Commonwealth in England, 1603–1660* (New Haven, Conn., and London, 2010) [incl. Civil War flags (pp. 364–9); Commonwealth and Protectorate seals (pp. 505–7)].

Michael Powell Siddons, *Heraldic Badges in England and Wales*, 3 vols in 4 parts (Woodbridge, 2009) [largely medieval, but comes as late as Elizabeth I (II, pt. 1, pp. 10–11) and her time].

Mason Tung, 'From Heraldry to Emblem: A Study of Peacham's Use of Heraldic Arms in *Minerva Britanna*', *Word & Image*, 3 (1987), pp. 86–94.

F. Whigham, 'Elizabethan Aristocratic Insignia', in *Texas Studies in Literature and Language*, 27 (1985), pp. 325–53 [mottoes, badges, *imprese*, etc.].

Alan R. Young, 'Sir Philip Sidney's Tournament Impresas,' *Sidney Newsletter*, 6, no. 1 (1985), pp. 624.

A. R. Young, 'A Note on the Tournament Impresas in *Pericles*', *Shakespeare Quarterly*, 36 (1985), pp. 453–6 [sources of the *imprese* of Pericles and the five knights in *Pericles*].

A. R. Young, assisted by Beert Verstraete, *The English Tournament Imprese* (New York, 1988) [list of all 521 identified *imprese*, 1494–1622].

A. R. Young, *Emblematic Flag Devices of the English Civil Wars, 1642–1660* (Toronto, 1995).

Tournaments: Tilts

S. Anglo, 'Archives of the English Tournament: Score Cheques and Lists', *Jnl., Soc. of Archivists*, ii (1960–4), pp. 153–62.

S. Anglo, 'Financial and Heraldic Records of the English Tournament', *Jnl., Soc. of Archivists*, ii (1960–4), pp. 183–95.

S. Anglo, intro., *The Great Tournament Roll of Westminster: A Collotype Reproduction of the Manuscript* (Oxford, 1968).

R. C. Strong, 'Elizabethan Jousting Cheques in the Possession of the College of Arms', 2 parts, *Coat of Arms*, v, no. 34 (April 1958), pp. 4–8, and no. 35 (Jul. 1958), pp. 63–8. [Reprinted in Strong, *The Tudor and Stuart Monarchy. Pageantry, Painting, Iconography*, 3 vols (Woodbridge, 1995–8), II, pp. 101–9].

R. C. Strong, 'Fair England's Knights: The Accession Day Tournaments', in *The Cult of Elizabeth: Elizabethan Portraiture and Pageantry* ([London], 1977), pp. 129–63, 201–3, 206–12.

F. A. Yates, 'Elizabethan Chivalry: The Romance of the Accession Day Tilts', *Jnl., Warburg & Courtauld Institutes*, xx (1957), pp. 4–25. [Reprinted in her *Astraea: The Imperial Theme in the Sixteenth Century* (Harmondsworth, Middx., 1977), pp. 88–111.]

Alan Young, *Tudor and Jacobean Tournaments* (London, 1987).

Illustration Credits

Illustrations have been reproduced by kind permission of the following institutions and individuals:

Frontispiece: The Worshipful Company of Painter-Stainers, London.
1: The Marquess of Bath, Longleat House, Warminster (Wilts.).
2a–b: The Huntington Library, San Marino (Calif., USA).
3, 41, 42, 46: The Trustees of the Victoria and Albert Museum, London.
4, 5, 6: The British Library Board.
7, 9a–b, 17, 19, 49, 66, 67, 68, 69, 71, 72, 73, 74, 75, 76: Folger Shakespeare Library, Washington (DC, USA).
8, 10, 12, 13, 14, 15a–b, 16a–b, 18, 20, 21, 24, 25, 26, 27, 28, 30, 63–5, 70, 87: The Corporation of Kings, Heralds and Pursuivants of Arms, London.
11, 55, 58: The Trustees of the National Portrait Gallery, London.
22: Gloucestershire Archives, Gloucester.
23a–c: Sir John Baker.
29: The Julian W. S. Litten Collection.
33, 34, 37: Photographs by Prof. Richard Cust, no. 34 being by permission of the Trustees of Chetham's Library, Manchester.
35, 39: Publisher's Collection.
36, 40: National Trust Images.
43, 44: English Heritage.
45: Exeter Museums; photograph by Dr Tara Hamling.
47, 48: Much Hadham Forge Museum; photographs by David Calvert.
50: The Worshipful Company of Mercers, London; photograph copyright Louis Sinclair.
51: Waddesdon Manor (Bucks.), The Rothschild Collection (Rothschild Family Trust; on loan); photograph copyright The National Trust.
52, 56: The Trustees of the Tate Gallery, London.
53: Private Collection; photograph copyright.
54: Collection of Lord Braybrooke, on display at Audley End House, Essex; photographed by English Heritage.
57: Private collection. Photograph by Chris Titmus, copyright The Hamilton Kerr Institute.
59: The Trustees of the Metropolitan Museum of Art, New York; photograph copyright © Art Resource / Scala, Florence.
60, 61a–b: Bodleian Library, Oxford; photographs by Dr Beatrice Groves.
88, 89, 90, 91: M. P. D. O'Donoghue, York Herald of Arms.
92: Sir Gary Hickinbottom.
93: The Corporation of Kings, Heralds and Pursuivants of Arms; photograph by Julian Calder.

Index

Adlington Hall (Ches.) 190, 203 and Fig. 33
Alciato (Alciati), Andrea, *Emblemata* 217
Aldershot (Hants.), parish church Fig. 29
Altensteig, Veronica 28
Amersham (Bucks.), town-house 218
Andrewes, Thomas, arms 140
Anglo-Saxon period 1, 5, 6, 132, 148
Anstis, Sir John, Garter King of Arms 28, 309, 311 n. 7 and Fig. 80
Antiquaries, gathering or Society of 33, 289, 290, 291, 295, 296
Anyson, Richard, herald-painter 62
Apsyne, Melchior, and Samuel his son, funeral undertakers 64
Arden family 118–19, 122
Armada, Spanish 6
Arms, Office of: *see* London, College of Arms
Arms: abatement 259–60; achievement(s) 168, 176, 177, 179 and Fig. 29; augmentation of honour Fig. 61b; of bastards 247; Biblical 266; 'borrowed' or fictional 207–8; certificates or declarations 81–2; cost 77; differencing 241, 242–3; displays 190–203, 204–18; grants and confirmations 41, 49, 56, 66, 67, 68–104, 105, 109, 144, 146, 238, 308–13, 314–15 317, 320–1 and Fig. 10; and honour 259–60; impaled 119; law of 257; moral symbolism 218–43; ordinaries of arms 103; patents 77–84; on portraits 220–35; quarterings 81, 119, 132, 168, 173, 183 and Fig. 10; repeat and replacement grants 98–104, 267; rolls of arms 40, 152, 192, 198, 203; royal arms 209–15, 240, 255 and Figs 44, 45, 47; supporters 67, 240 n. 22, 249; women's arms 96, 97, 225, 257; *see also* badges, crests
Arms-painters 141
Arundell family, of Trerice (Cornw.), pedigree 139
Ashmole, Elias, Lancaster Herald 309
Aston Hall (Birmingham) 218
Aylworth, John, arms 73
Babthorp, Sir William, heraldic funeral 62
Bacon family, pedigrees 13, 139 n. 59, 145–6, 154
Bacon, Sir Francis, Lord Chancellor, emblem with his arms 305–7 and Fig. 79
Bacon, Sir Nicholas, pedigree 145–6, 154; funeral 180 n. 23; grant of arms 145 n. 92
Badges and devices: 283–5, 292; bear and ragged staff, of earls of Warwick and of Robert Dudley, earl of Leicester 13 and Fig. 2a; castle surmounted by crowned phoenix, of (Queen) Jane Seymour 285; collar of SS 116, 220; falcon and sceptre, of (Queen) Anne Boleyn 285; lion, of Richard I and his son and Richard II 246; pelican in her piety, white hart, etc., of Richard II 249–51, 254–5 and Fig. 62; pomegranate, of (Queen) Catherine of Aragon 285; red and white roses, for Lancaster and York 215, 285, 287; sewn on sleeves 272; stag's head, of Edward Stanley, earl of Derby 168
Bagshaw, Edmund, pedigree 143
Baker, Henry, arms 100
Baker, James, arms 100
Balgay, Dr Nicholas, heraldic funeral 57
Bamfylde family, pedigree 139 n. 55
Barker, Sir Christopher, Garter King of Arms 37 n. 37, 71, 73, 80, 96, 98, 290 n. 23
Barnes, Richard, heraldic funeral 64
Beauchesne, John de 21
Beaufort, Henry, duke of Somerset 4
Beaufort, Lady Margaret, pedigree 129 n. 13
Bekwith, Lady, heraldic funeral 62
Benolt, Thomas, Clarenceux King of Arms 71, 94–5
Bereford family history 129 n. 12
Berkeley (née Howard), Lady Katherine, 15–16; funeral 180, 184, 186
Berkeley family 14–15, 128 n. 10; history and pedigree Figs 22a–b
Berkeley, Henry, Lord Berkeley 15–16, 184, 186
Bertie, Peregrine, Lord Willoughby d'Eresby 20, 24
Besford Court (Worcs.), heraldically decorated paper 213 and Fig. 46
Bigland, Ralph, Garter King of Arms 311 n. 8

331

Bincks, Edward, deputy herald 62
Blackwell, William, arms 96
Blount, Thomas, *Art of Making Devises* 290 n. 25, 296 and Fig. 73
Board of Green Cloth 7
Bointon, Sir Thomas, heraldic funeral 62
Boke of St Albans 266
Boleyn, Anne, wife of Henry VIII, badges 285
Bolton, Edmund 188; *Elements of Armories* 238-9, 264, 282
Booth, Sir William, heraldic funeral 59
Bossewell, John, *Workes of Armorie* 115, 118, 238
Bostock, Jane 27; Ralph 27
Bostock, Laurence 201
Boteler family, pedigree 128 n. 8
Bowyer, William 16 and Figs 2a and b
Bramall Hall (Ches.), 197
Brandon, Charles, duke of Suffolk, Earl Marshal 8; orders by (1524×33) 77
Brandon, Gregory, arms 95
Brereton Hall (Ches.) 195
Brereton, Sir William 195, 200
Bridges, John, arms 81
Bristol, plan of (1568) 28
Bromley-by-Bow (near London), 'Old Palace' 209-10 and Fig. 42
Brook, Roger, heraldic monument 58
Brooke, Ralph, York Herald: 37 n. 37, 58, 94, 95, 275; *Discoverie of Certaine Errours* 268, 279; pedigree by 140 n. 65
Brudenell, Edmund 24
Bruges, Louis de, earl of Winchester, arms 77-8
Brus family, pedigree 128 n. 10
Bry, Theodore de, engraver 183 and Fig. 28
Burton, William 29
Bury St Edmunds (Suff.), emblematic wall-painting 217
Butler, Anthony, arms 102
Bysshe (or de la Biche), Sir Edward, Garter King of Arms, 79 n. 38
Caius, Dr John, arms 238
Cambridge, King's College, arms 77, 238
Camden, William, Clarenceux King of Arms 24, 33, 57, 109, 268, 289 and Frontis. and Fig. 15b; grants of arms 79, 88, 120; visitations 93, 110, 116; his *Britannia* 31, 200, 289; *Remaines* 285 n. 13, 289-90, 291-6 and Fig. 71
Canada: Canadian Heraldic Authority 320

Canons Ashby (Northants.) 195, 206 and Fig. 36
Canterbury, bird's eye drawing by William Smith Fig. 5
Carew, Richard 200; *impresa* 294-5
Carey, George, Lord Hunsdon 34, 36, 58 n. 93
Carey, Henry, Lord Hunsdon 4
Carlos, Col. William, arms 78 n. 33
Catholicism 2
Cave, Thomas 129
Cawthorne, William, arms 84
Cecil, Robert, earl of Salisbury, heraldic funeral 167; portrait Fig. 58
Cecil, Sir William 58
Cecil, William, Lord Burghley 2, 5, 10, 24, 31-2, 47, 75, 156, 190, 191; pedigree 137, 154
Chaloner, Jacob 134 n. 38
Chaloner, Thomas, deputy herald 59
Chamberlayne family, pedigree 131 n. 25
Charles I, arms (when Prince of Wales) 303
Charles IX, king of France 182
Chastleton House (Oxon.) 207-8
Cheney, Henry, Baron Cheney 214-15
Cheshire, account and map 29-30; heraldic funerals in 58-62
Chester, drawing and plan 29-30
Chester, Elizabeth, wife of Sir William, heraldic funeral 186-7
Chivalry, Court of 8, 22, 120, 309
Cholmley, Sir Richard, heraldic funeral 64
Cholmondleigh (Cholmley), Sir Hugh, heraldic funeral 59
Christus, Petrus 220
Church Notes 113, 203 *and see* Pedigrees
Clare family (lords of Clare), history 128 n. 10, 130 n. 17; pedigree 131
Claxton family, pedigree 140 n. 65, 142 n. 72
Clerk, John, of Norwich 208
Clifford (née Brandon), Eleanor, wife of Henry Clifford 225
Clifford, Henry, earl of Cumberland 225
Clifton, Sir John, heraldic funeral 65
Clough, Garret 63
Coach-painters 57, 58
Coke, Sir Edward, *Boke of Entries* 154
Combe, Thomas, *Theater of Fine Devices* 217
Constable family, armorial glass 206
Constable of England 7-8
Constable, Sir Marmaduke, heraldic funeral 62
Cooke, Robert, Clarenceux King of Arms 1, 12, 16, 22, 24, 49, 192-3; involvement in

INDEX

funerals 170, 172, 184; grants of arms 41, 67, 75, 79, 80, 94, 95, 98, 100, 101, 102, 109 and Figs 13, 16b; pedigrees by 16, 137, 142 n. 72, 146–7, 153, 184; visitation 110
Copley family, of Sprotborough (Yorks. W.R.), dispute involving 152–63
Copley, Philip 154–5
Cornwall, earls of 207
Cornwallis family, pedigree 137 n. 49
Cotgrave, Hugh, Richmond Herald 153 n. 116
Coxe (or Cockes), John, Lancaster Herald 22, 172
Cranmer, Thomas, archbishop of Canterbury, portrait 230 and Fig. 55
Crests, heraldic 56, 66, 75, 133, 145, 168 172, 179, 260, 267, 272, 290, 296 and Fig. 10
Criche, Edmund, arms 84
Critz, John de, portrait attributed to Fig. 58
Cuerdley (Lancs.) 34, 39
D'Ewes, Sir Simonds 203
Dade, Thomas, deputy herald 141 n. 61
Dakins, William, 'counterfeit herald' 58 n. 94, 59, 62, 143
Dalton, Lawrence, Norroy King of Arms, grant of arms Fig. 12
Danby, Sir Thomas, heraldic funeral 64
Daniel, Samuel, *Worthy Tract of Paulus Iovius* 287 n. 17
Darcy, Thomas, Baron Darcy 4
Davenport, William 190 n. 2
Dawney (Dawnay), Lady, heraldic funeral 62
Dawney, Sir Thomas, heraldic funeral 62
Deane, Sir James, funeral 167 n. 5
Denys family, of Dyrham (Glos.), pedigree 135 n. 48 and Fig. 24
Denys, Sir Robert, heraldic funeral 65
Dering Roll of Arms 152
Despencer family, history 128 n. 10
Dethick, Nicholas, Windsor Herald 11, 18–19, 20
Dethick, Sir Gilbert, Garter King of Arms 11, 18, 19, 20, 49, 73, 94, 172; grants of arms 78, 81, 97, 98, 101
Dethick, Sir William, Garter King of Arms 11, 18, 20, 33, 59 n. 101, 140 n. 64, 289 and Figs 15a–b, 68; grants of arms 78, 81 n. 45, 88, 95, 101, 105, 109, 120, 164 n. 170 and Fig. 17; opponent of Robert Glover 20; pedigree by 142 n. 72; portrait Fig. 18
Devereux, Robert, earl of Essex, Earl Marshal 24, 36; *imprese* 294; warrant about pedigrees (1598) 143 n. 75
Digby, Sir Kenelm, pedigree 148
Dininckhoff, Bernard 206
Dives and Lazarus, parable 212 and Fig. 44
Domenichi, Ludovico, *Ragionamente* 287
Done family, pedigree 140 n. 65
Drury, Thomas, servant of William Hervey 156
Dryden, Sir Erasmus 195, 206 and Fig. 36
Dudley family, Barons Dudley and earls of Warwick 13, 14; pedigrees 16, 147–8 and Fig. 26
Dudley, Ambrose, earl of Warwick 14
Dudley, John, duke of Northumberland, Earl Marshal 9, 13, 14, 15
Dudley, Robert, earl of Leicester, Deputy Earl Marshal 1–25 *passim*, 75, 156, 220, 287; portrait 221 and Fig. 51
Dugdale, Sir William, Garter King of Arms 1, 309
Dutton, John and Lawrence 269–70
Dyer, Sir James, reports 154
Dyson, Humfrey 43
Earle, John, *Microcosmographie* 267
Edulph, Simon, arms 98
Edward I 128, 196–7
Edward IV, badges 284
Edward VI 4, 9, 15; *imprese* 293
Edwards, Francis, funeral undertaker 64
Egerton, Sir Thomas, pedigree 134 n. 39
Elizabeth I 4, 5, 6, 8; arms and badges 211–12, 214, 215, 285 and Figs 44, 47, 69; funeral Fig. 32; *imprese* 293; legitimacy 3; pedigrees 131, 137; portrait Fig. 69
Ellerker family, pedigree 128 n. 8
Elmhirst, Edward 92–3
Elyot, Sir Thomas, *Boke Named the Governour* 115, 118
Emblems 296–307 and Figs 72–6, 78–9
England, 'Particular Description' of, by William Smith 31 and Fig. 5
Erdeswicke, Sampson 6, 195, 198, 200
Estgrigg, coachpainter 57
Etchingham (Suss.), parish church 197, 201 n. 25
Etchingham, Sir William de 197, 201 n. 25
Eton College, arms 77
Eworth, Hans, portraits: Unknown Lady 225 and Fig. 52; another Unknown Lady 225–6; Thomas Howard, duke of Norfolk 230 and

Fig. 53; Margaret Howard (née Audley), duchess of Norfolk 230 and Fig. 54
Exeter, town-houses 212–13 and Fig. 45
Eye (Suff.), arms 78
Fairfax, Sir William 193, 200, 205–6 and Figs 35, 39
Fane family, pedigree 142 n. 72
Fane, Sir Francis 58
Farebank, Robert, herald-painter 62
Farrand, William, arms 75
Ferne, Sir John, *Blazon of Gentrie* 115, 118, 119, 120, 122, 237, 239 245, 250, 255–6, 257, 259, 298 n. 43
Féron, Jehan le 298 n. 43
Field of the Cloth of Gold 293
Fielding family, pedigree 129
Fisher family, of Alrewas (Staffs.), pedigree 164 n. 170
Fitch family, pedigree 140 n. 61
Fitzalan, Henry, earl of Arundel, Lord Steward 5, 11
FitzGilbert (or Marshal), John, Marshal of England 8
Fitzherbert, Sir Anthon y 145–6
Fitzwilliam family, of Mablethorpe (Lincs.), arms 158
Fitzwilliam family, of Sprotborough (Yorks., W.R.), lawsuit concerning 149–63; pedigrees 131 n. 25, 137 n. 49, 139 n. 56 and Fig. 25
Fitzwilliam, Hugh 129 n. 15, 152–63
Flags, heraldic (standard, great banner, bannerol , penoncelle or pencil) 168, 170, 171, 172, 173–4, 176, 178, 180, 183 187, 296 and Figs 29, 30, 32; religious banners 174, 187
Flicke, Gerlach, portrait of Archbishop Cranmer 230 and Fig. 55
Flower, William, Norroy King of Arms 12, 18, 19, 37, 49, 73, 76, 79, 172; grants of arms 73, 80, 101; pedigree by 140 n. 65
Foliot family, pedigree 129 n. 12
Ford, John, *Perkin Warbeck* 237
Foster, Joseph 89, 92, 95
Foxe, John, arms 79
France, heraldry regulated by *juge d'armes* 309
Frederick II, king of Denmark 20
Frederick V, Elector Palatine 34
Fuller, Thomas, *The Holy State* 268
Funerals, heraldic: 6, 10, 109, 166–89, 308 and Figs 27–32; burial 179–80; cost 167, 175, 180, 188; dinner 180; funeral certificate 181; funerals of women 184, 186; funerals in London 186–7; hearse 170–1; laying-out, embalming and cering 166–7; offering 176–9; proclamation of deceased's 'style' 170, 176; sermon 176–7; *and see* flags
G., H. (unidentified), *Mirrour of Maiestie* 303–7 and Figs 78–9
Gargrave, Sir Thomas, and Sir Cotton his son, heraldic funerals 64
Garter, Order of 7, 8, 9–10, 115, 303–4
Gascoigne, Richard and Elizabeth 155
Gaunt, John of, duke of Lancaster 3, 14, 130–1
Gawdy, Sir Francis, heraldic funeral 66
Genealogies: *see* Pedigrees
Gerard, Thomas 31
Gilbert, Sir John, heraldic funeral 65
Gilling Castle (Yorks., N.R.) 193–4, 202, 205–6, 209 and Figs 35, 39
Giovio, Paolo, *Dialogo dell'imprese militari* 287, 289, 291–2
Gisburn priory (Yorks., W.R.) 128 n. 10
Glover, Robert, Somerset Herald 9, 11, 12 n. 64, 18, 20, 22, 24, 45, 79, 102, 154, 156 n. 142, 198, 203; cartographer 28; involvement in funerals 166, 167 n. 3, 184; involvement in grants of arms 75–6, 79, 84, 99; misc. MSS transcribed by 156 n. 141, 191–2, 193, 195, 198; ordinary compiled by 37, 102–3; pedigrees drawn by 16, 35, 137, 140 n. 65, 142–3, 144, 201;
Gower, George, portrait of Queen Elizabeth Fig. 69; self-portrait 234–5 and Fig. 57
Gower, Sir Edward, heraldic funeral 62
Gray (Grey), Sir Thomas, heraldic funeral 62
Great Yarmouth (Norf.), 'Old Merchant's House' 210–11 and Fig. 43
Grenewood (Greenwoode), Robert, arms-painter 156
Grenewood, Thomas 156 n. 137
Gresham, Sir Thomas 221 and Fig. 50
Grey family 4
Griffith family, of Burton Agnes (Yorks.) 135 n. 47
Grimston, Edward 220
Grove, Robert, arms 98
Guillim, John, Rouge Croix Pursuivant: *Display of Heraldry* 115, 279, 298 n. 43
Gwynn-Jones, Sir Peter, Garter King of Arms 94
Hadleigh (Suff.) 116
Hales, Humphrey, Bluemantle Pursuivant 19,

INDEX

141 n. 68
Halswell family, pedigree 140 n. 65
Hardcastle, of Newcastle, deputy herald 63
Hardwick Hall (Derbys.) 208, 209
Harington, Sir John, portrait Fig. 59
Harrison, William 68–9
Hart, John, Chester Herald 33
Hartwell, Abraham, *impresa* 295–6
Harvey, Sir George 40 n. 52, 66
Haselwood, Richard 63
Hastings, Henry, earl of Huntingdon, pedigree 131
Hatton, Sir Christopher (III) 196
Hatton, Sir Christopher 193, 201, 208
Hawkeslowe, William, Clarenceux King of Arms 78
Hawkins, Katherine, heraldic funeral 56
Hawkins, Sir John 56
Hawley, Thomas, Clarenceux King of Arms 101
Hayes, Sir Thomas 67
Heigham family, pedigree 148 n. 107
Hellard, Peter, arms 78 n. 31
Heneage, Sir Thomas 19, 22
Henry III 196–7
Henry V, badge 284
Henry VI, badge 284; grant of arms by 238
Henry VII, badges 284, 302 and Fig. 63
Henry VIII 3, 4, 8, 14, 131, 303; arms and badges 284–5; *imprese* 293
Henry, prince of Wales 301; portrait Fig. 59
Heralds: 116, 162, 184, 189 and Fig. 86; deputy heralds 141; diplomatic role 6, 105, 109; funeral turns 55; kings of arms 8, 45, 66, 68, 69–71, 76, 79–84, 92, 93, 97, 105–14, 141, 144, 156, 166–7, 170, 177, 178, 179 and Fig. 26; partitions (of monies) 49, 54; promotion 48, 55; tabard 168, 170 n. 9, Frontis. and Figs 7, 8, 28, 80, 86; Ulster King of Arms 317 *and see* London, College of Arms
Herick, Robert and William, arms 78, 79
Hervey, William, Clarenceux King of Arms 1, 14 n. 73, 18; grants of arms 73, 80, 81, 88–9, 94, 98, 101; pedigrees by 16, 133 n. 36, 142, 153, 156–7 and Fig. 26; visitations 108
Hesketh family, pedigree 137 n. 49
Heywood, Thomas, *The Four Prentises of London* 273, 275, 282 and Fig. 67
Hickinbottom, Sir Gary, arms Fig. 85
Hilton, William, deputy herald 63

Hoby, Edward, arms 78
Holdenby (Northants.) 193, 202
Holland, Philip, Portcullis Pursuivant 49
Holme, Randle, deputy herald 59
Holme, Sir Thomas, Norroy King of Arms, arms granted by 78 n. 31, 164 n. 170
Hondius, Jodocus 29 n. 12
Hooker (alias Vowell), John, self-styled Exeter Herald 64, 65
Howard (née Audley), Margaret, duchess of Norfolk, portrait 230 and Fig. 54
Howard family 4, 8
Howard, Henry, earl of Northampton, commissioner for the office of Earl Marshal 5, 24, 45, 47
Howard, Henry, earl of Surrey, *impresa* 294
Howard, Thomas, duke of Norfolk, Earl Marshal 2, 4, 5, 9, 10, 11, 12, 13, 15, 25, 76; orders to College of Arms (1561) 73, 75; orders to College (1565) 75; orders to College (1568) 10, 19, 24, 39, 75; portraits 230 and Figs 10, 53
Howard, Thomas, earl of Arundel, Earl Marshal 58
Hurte, scrivener, of Cambridge 144
Huys (or Hewes), Thomas, arms 96
Imprese 285–96 and Figs 70a–b, 71
Ireland: heraldic authorities (Ulster King of Arms; Chief Herald of Ireland) 317, 321
James I 283, 296; arms 298–300, 303
Jermyn, Sir Robert 202
Johnson, Cornelius, portrait of Susanna Temple 230, 234 and Fig. 56
Johnston, Nathaniel 1 n. 5
Jones, Thomas, of Tregaron 141 n. 66, 164 n. 170
Jones, Walter, arms 164 n. 170, 207–8
Jonson, Ben: 279–82; *Epigrams* 267; *Every Man out of his Humour* 69–70, 102, 116; *The New Inn* 280; *The Staple of News* 108, 280–2; *Volpone* 272 n. 26
Judgement of Solomon, wallpainting Fig. 48
Kays, —, serjeant porter, arms 96
Kemys, Roger 200 n. 20
King, Gregory, Rouge Dragon Pursuivant, later Lancaster Herald 309 and Fig. 19
Kitson, Thomas 75
Knight, Edmund, Norroy King of Arms 49, 156–7, 159
Knighthood, orders of 309

335

Lamb, Thomas, arms 96
Lambarde, William 200
Lancashire, map Fig. 4
Lancaster, noble house of 130
Langhorne family, of Lastingham (Yorks.), pedigree 145
Langhorne, William 145 n. 88
Lanhydrock House (Cornw.), 207
Lant, Thomas, Portcullis Pursuivant 22, 33, 36 n. 32, 174, 182 and Fig. 28
Lathom Hall (Lancs.) 166, 176
Latimer family, history 129 n. 12
Le Neve, Peter, Norroy King of Arms 47, 309 and Fig. 8
Leake, Stephen Martin, Garter King of Arms 309
Lee, Richard, Clarenceux King of Arms 19, 24, 49, 63, 76 n. 25, 77, 143 n. 75, 182, 184
Lee, Sir Henry, *impresa* 294
Legh family, of Booths (Ches.), pedigree 142 n. 72
Legh, Gerard, *Accedens of Armory* 57, 115, 238, 239, 241, 254, 259, 264, 279, 298 n. 43 and Figs 60, 61a–b, 66
Legh, Sir Piers (Peter), heraldic funeral 58–9
Legh, Thomas 190, 200, 203 and Figs 33, 34
Leicester's Commonwealth 3, 15
Lennard (or Leonard), John, arms 100
Lennard, Sampson, Bluemantle Pursuivant, arms 101
Lilly, Henry, Rouge Dragon Pursuivant 33
Lily (fleur-de-lis), heraldic 236, 239, 258, 261–2, 262–3, 301
lion, heraldic 246–8
L'Isle, Sir Arnulph, arms 78 n. 33
Lisle, barony of 13, 15
Lister, Sir Martin 234
Little Gaddesden Manor (Herts.) 214–15
London, College of Arms 6, 7, 8, 9, 10, 11, 12, 24, 25, 36, 39, 41, 70–1, 73, 84–9, 108–9, 113, 116, 132, 156, 157, 197, 220, 267, 281, 308–21 and Figs 14, 81; Chapter orders (1565) 178; records 148, 152, 156, 162, 267, 316 and Fig. 84
London, Haberdashers' Company 27, 41, 43
London, heraldic funerals of mayors and aldermen 186–7
London, livery companies: corporate arms 272, 273 and Fig. 67; halls 187; arms in halls 42, 67; descriptions of arms by William Smith 31, 42

London, Mercers' Company 42; portrait of Sir Thomas Gresham Fig. 50
London, Painter-Stainers' Company 41, 45, 220; *see also* Painters
London, St Alphege's church 42
London, Tower of London, records 152
London, Victoria and Albert Museum: cushion cover with arms of Warneford and Yates Fig. 41; drinking glass of William Smith Fig. 3; overmantel from Bromley-by-Bow Fig. 42; wallpaper from Besford Court 213 and Fig. 46
Longworth, Dr Richard 172
Louis XII, king of France 301
Louis XIV, king of France 309
Loundes family, of South Repps (Norf.), pedigree 141 n. 66
Low, Sir Thomas 42
Lower, Sir Nicholas 141 n. 69
Lowther, William 141 n. 69
Lumley, John, Lord Lumley 161, 162; pedigree 134 n. 42
Lynde, Cuthbert and Thomas de la, arms 81 n. 45
Macclesfield (Ches.) 60
Machyn, Henry 12, 186–7
Macwilliam family, pedigree 142 n. 72
Malory, Lady, heraldic funeral 62
Manners family, earls of Rutland, arms 193 and Fig. 35
Manners, Francis, earl of Rutland, *impresa* 267, 283
Manuscripts
  Arundel Castle (Suss.), MS Autograph Letters 1513–85, art. 103: 20
  Baker, Sir J. H., MS 102: 142 n. 72, 164 n. 170; MS 166: 141; MS 179: 144 n. 81; MS 214: 143; MS 223: 134 n. 39; MS 428: 139 n. 55, 140 n. 60 and Fig. 23; MS 515: 132 n. 29, 139 n. 56; MS 518: 139 n. 57; MS 640: 139 n. 55; MS 746: 145; MS 855: 134 n. 42; MS 947: 130, 133 n. 35, 135 n. 48; MS 1038: 134 n. 43; MS 1346: 131; MS 1347: 144–5; MS 1349: 148; MS 1350: 164 n. 170; MS 1510: 135 n. 46, 140 n. 65
  Birkenhead, Wirral Archives, Misc. Accessions, YPX/91/1: 39
  Birmingham, University of Birmingham, Cadbury Research Library, MS 544/1, 2:

INDEX

200 n. 20

Brighton, East Suss. Record Office, Acc. 7007: 135 n. 47, 139 n. 56

Bury St Edmunds Library, MS once in Milner-Gibson-Cullum collection 37

Cambridge University Library, MS Hengrave 65: 75

Cambridge, Cambs. Record Office, R52/24/44/1: 159; R52/24/44/2: 142 n. 71, 153 n. 119, 156; R52/24/44/3: 157 n. 144

Carmarthen, Dyfed Record Office, Cawdor collection, Acc. 5309: 140 n. 61

Chelmsford, Essex Record Office, D/D Pr/558: 100; D/DDs F2: 140 n. 61; D/DGe/F1: 81; D/Du/290/1: 81

Chester, Cheshire Record Office, CR63/2/22: 190

Chippenham, Wilts. & Swindon Archives, 1300/376: 135 n. 45

Doncaster, Doncaster Archives, DD/CROM/9/1: 156 n. 137; DD/CROM/9/2: 160–1

Gloucester, Glos. Record Office, D 471/Z5: 135 and Figs 22a–b; D 885: 200 n. 20

Hatfield House, Cecil Papers 224/1: 137; Cecil Papers 357: 131, 137

Hertford, Herts. Archives, D/ELW/F14: 79 n. 38

Ipswich, Suffolk Record Office, EE2/C/1: 78; HD 2418/57: 148 n. 107

Leicester, Leics. Record Office, DG9/2572: 78–9

London, British Library, Cotton MS Caligula D. vii: 293 n. 33; Cotton MS Faustina E. i: 109; Cotton MS Otho E. viii: 19; MS Harley 245: 40; MS Harley 692: 128 n. 10; MS Harley 1046: 30 n. 13; MS Harley 1154: 114–24; MS Harley 1319: Fig. 62; MS Harley 1349: 42 n. 56; MS Harley 2186: 39; MS Harley 3897: 128 n. 10; MS Harley 4628: 40; MS Harley 4840: 134 n. 42; MS Harley 5176: 294 n. 36; MS Harley 6159: 39 and Figs 4, 6; MS Harley 6363: 31 n. 18; MS Harley 6601: 36 n. 34; MS Harley 6860: 42 n. 56; MS Harley 7353: 134 n. 40; MS Sloane 2596: 31 n. 17 and Fig. 5; MS Add. 10110: 156; MS Add. 10620: 31 n. 17; MS Add. 16940: 89; MS 37535: 141 n. 69; MS Add. 37687A: 77; MS Add. 37687B: 78 n. 31; MS Add. 37687G: 101; MS Add. 38537: 152 n. 115; MS Add. 39249: 143 n. 92; MS Add. 44026: 137 n. 49; MS Add. 78167: 33 n. 20; MS Egerton 2830: 77–8; MS King's 396: 134 n. 42, 137; Add. Ch. 4115: 78 n. 33; Add. Ch. 8661: 73; Add. Roll 77720: 152 n. 115

London, College of Arms, MS 1/1: Fig. 12; MS 3/16: 128 n. 10; MS 3/34: 142 n. 72; MS 3/53: 131 n. 23, 134 n. 40; MS 3/54: 135 and Fig. 24; MS 3/57: 139 n. 59, 143; MS 8/24: 142 n. 71; MS 9/2 A: 164 n. 170; MS 9/2B: 142 n. 72; MS 9/2C: 142 n. 72, 164 n. 170; MS 9/17: 140 n. 65; MS 9/29: 140 n. 65, 142 n. 72; MS 9/34: 135 n. 47; MS 11/23: 80; MS 12/27A: 129 n. 12; MS 12/42/01: 128 n. 8; MS 12/48s 152 n. 113 and Fig. 25; MS 12/50e: 142 n. 72; MS 12/51e: 129 n. 12, 145 n. 92; MS 13/1: 16, 147–8; MS 16/5: 14 n. 73, 142 nn. 71, 72 and Fig. 26; MS C. 15, Pt 1: Figs 20, 21; MS F. 13 (Cooke's Grants): 86 and Fig. 16b; MS I. 14: 166–80; MS L. 2: 99 and Fig. 16a; MS L. 6: 89; MS L. 9: 88, 89; MS L. 10: 88 and Fig. 10; MS M. 6: 287, 293 n. 33 and Figs 30, 70a–b; MS M. 11: 89 n. 54; MS R. 21: 86; MS R. 22: 79; MS R. 36: 71, 77; MS Arundel 40: 36 n. 32, 95; MS Bysshe's Grants: 86; MSS Camden's Grants 1–3: 79, 86; MS Dethick's Gifts: 86; MS Dethick's Gifts X: 88, 96 and Fig. 15a; MSS Misc. Grants 2 and 3: 86; MS EDN 22: 37; MS EDN 56: 86; MS Philipot 3. 2. 1 Berks. & Beds.: 39; MS Philipot 34 Norfolk: 39; MS Philipot 41 Suffolk: 39; MS Philipot b. 42: 34; MS Philipot c. 16: 35; MSS Shakespeare Grants 1 and 2: 105 n. 2 MS Smith's Alphabet: 37; MS Vincent 3: 134 n. 43; MS Vincent 49: 134 n. 42; MS Vincent 76: 20 n. 100 MS Vincent 90: 181 n. 24 MS Vincent 92: 73; MS Vincent 151, Pt. 1: Fig. 27; MS Vincent 152: Figs 63–5; MS Vincent 161: 86, 89 n. 54; MS Vincent 197: 200 n. 20; MSS Vincent's Old Grants 1 and 2: 86; MS WZ: 88, 95, 109 n. 18 and Fig. 15b

London, Lambeth Palace Library, MS 508: 33 n. 20; MS 701: 19; MS 3198: 20
London, London Metropolitan Archives, CLC/262/MS 2077: 42 n. 56; CLC/262/MS 2463: 31; CLC/262/MS 2464: 42 n. 55
London, Society of Antiquaries, MS 429: 37–8; MS 572: 142 n. 72
London, Victoria & Albert Museum, L. 1981/41: 132 n. 29, 133 n. 37
Longleat House, Dudley Papers XX: 19 MS 249: 16 and Fig. 1
Manchester, Chetham's Library, Mun. E. 8. 22: 190 and Fig. 34
Manchester, John Rylands University Library, MS Eng. 6: 20 n. 101
Northampton, Northants. Record Office, E(B) 627: 134 n. 39; Fitzwilliam (Milton) Roll 434: 139 n. 56, 153 n. 120, 160, 161; F(M) Roll 435: 152 n. 113, 157–8; F(M) Roll 437: 161–2; F(M) Roll 438: 157 n. 143, 160 n. 156; F(M) Roll 440: 161 n. 159; F(M) Rolls 444–7: 162; F(M) Roll 450: 153 n. 119; F(M) Roll 452: 153 n. 119; F(M) Roll 454: 161 n. 160; F(M) Roll 455: 161 n. 160; MS Finch-Hatton 271: 134 n. 42; Westmorland (Apethorpe) 1/1/4, etc.: 146; W(A) 1/1/6: 142 n. 72; W(A) 1/1/15B, C, D: 146
Nuremberg (Germany), Stadtbibliothek, Nor. H. 1142: 33 n. 20
New York (USA), New York Public Library, MS Spencer 193: 128 n. 8
Oxford, Bodleian Library, MS Ashmole 765: 30 n. 13; MS Ashmole 831: 130 n. 20; MS Ashmole 840: 110, 111; MS Ashmole 846: 88 n. 50; MS Gough Berks. 12: 41; MS Pedigree Roll 5: 128 n. 8; MS Pedigree Roll 33: 128 n. 10; MS Rawl. B. 120: 34–5; MS Rawl. B. 141: 34; MS Rawl. B. 282: 30 n. 14; MS Rawl. B. 282*: 30 n. 13; MS Top. gen. e. 29: 34 n. 27, 42
Philadelphia (Pa., USA), University of Pennsylvania, MS Codex 1070: 134 n. 42, 137 n. 51
San Marino (Calif., USA), Huntington Library, MS HM 160: 16, 134 n. 43 and Figs 2a, 2b
Sheffield, Sheffield Archives, BFM/2/112: 162 n. 165; CD 477/2: 156
Washington (DC, USA), Folger Shakespeare Library, MS V. a. 156: 94; MS V.a.157: 45, 47; MS V.a.199: 45–66 and Figs 9a–b; MS V. a. 350: 109 and Fig. 68; MS V. b. 144: 37 n. 37; MS V. b. 194: 39; MS V. b. 217: 37 and Fig. 7; MS V.b.232: 218 and Fig. 49; MS X. d. 2 (37): Fig. 19; MS Z. c. 22 (41): 101 and Fig. 17
Winchester, Hants. Record Office, 93M86 W/1: 135 n. 47

Marblers 57, 66
Markham, Gervase, *Gentleman's Academie* 266; *The Souldier's Accidence* 292
Marshal, Earl: and College of Arms 7–8, 10, 19–20, 24, 49, 68, 73, 75, 93, 104, 156, 161, 162, 321 and Fig. 86; deputies 1, 156, 192; office placed in commission 24, 25, 36, 42, 75, 95, 109; orders of Earl Marshal or commissioners 141 n. 67, 142, 143 n. 77, 157, 186 n. 39, 197; petition to 155–6; texts relating to 6, 155–6; and visitations 110, 111, 113, 116–17; *and see* Brandon, Charles; Devereux, Robert; Dudley, John; FitzGilbert, John; Howard, Thomas; Talbot, George
Martlet, heraldic 234, 241, 284 and Fig. 60
Mary I, Queen of England 4, 10; badge 285; *imprese* 293
Mary, Queen of Scots 1, 3, 4, 12, 182
Mathew, —, heraldic funeral 56
Mathew, John, and Nathan his son, funeral undertakers 63, 64
Mauley, Piers (or Peter), baron(?) 95, 107 n. 6 and Fig. 15b
May, Thomas, Chester Herald Fig. 19
Merchants' marks 221
Mignault, Claude 287 n. 17
Mildmay Sir Walter, pedigree 145–7
Modus Tenendi Parliamentum 5–6
Montacute House (Somt.) 206–7, 218 and Fig. 40
Monthault family, pedigree 128 n. 8
Monuments and tombs 135 n. 47
Mortimer family, pedigree 128 n. 10
Morysin (or Morison), Charles, arms 99 and Fig. 16b
Morysin (or Morison), Sir Richard, arms 99 and Fig. 16a
Mottoes: 170–1, 266, 267, 285, 290, 291,

INDEX

296–307; William Partryche Fig. 12; Shakespeare 116, 275; Edward Stanley, earl of Derby 168, 170; Sir John White Fig. 29
Much Hadham (Herts.), The Forge 215 and Figs 47–8
Musgrave, Sir Richard 58
Nelson, William, Earl Nelson, granted an augmentation to his arms Fig. 82
Nettlestead (Kent), parish church 197
Nevill (or Neville) family, Lords Nevill 4; history and pedigree 128 n. 10, 130
Neville, Charles, earl of Westmorland 5
Newce, Clement and William 215
Newland, John, abbot of St Augustine's abbey, Bristol Fig. 22a–b
Newport family, of Ercall (Salop.), pedigree 142 n. 72
Nibley Green (Glos.), battle of 15
Nine Worthies 218
Nobility, 'ancient' 2, 3, 4, 25
Norden, John 29
Norfolk, visitation of (1612–13) 114, 116, 122 and Figs 19, 20
Norgate, Edward, Windsor Herald 33
Norman Conquest 132, 201
Norris, Sir William 197
Norwich 116, 118; city arms 208; Strangers' Hall 208; Suckling House 208
Nuremberg (Germany) 27, 28, 29, 31–2, 36
Ormskirk (Lancs.), parish church 167
Ortelius, Abraham 29
Overbury, Thomas, *A Wife* 267–8
Overton, Henry ('Harry Painter'), deputy herald 58
Oxenbridge family, pedigree 135 n. 47, 139 n. 56
Oxford university 27
Painters (Painter-Stainers), abuses of 48, 55–9, 66; *see also* London, Company of Painter-Stainers
Pantolf, —, heraldic funeral 56
Paradin, Claude, *Devises héroïques* 276 n. 40, 287
Paris, Matthew 125
Parker, Matthew, archbishop of Canterbury 2 n. 10, 6
Parliamentary Roll of Arms 40, 192–3
Parr, William, marquess of Northampton 4
Partryche, William, arms Fig. 12
Parys, John, arms (1468) 78

Patten, Mercury, Bluemantle Pursuivant Fig. 15a
Paulet, William, marquess of Winchester 12
Peacham, Henry: *The Gentleman's Exercise* 205, 217; *Minerva Britanna* 294 n. 37, 298–303 and Figs 72, 74, 75
Peake, Robert, portrait of Henry, prince of Wales, and Sir John Harington Fig. 59
Pedigrees and pedigree rolls 3, 10, 35, 39, 49, 66, 77, 113, 124, 125–65; book format 134; cited by heralds 164 n. 170; dated or datable 148–9; drawings of funerary monuments 135; evidentiary value 163–4; false 56, 62; headed with Latin titles 142–3; naturalistic trees represented 133; radial or 'target' form 133–4; rectilinear form 133; reliability 144, 147, 149; sealed 142, 153, 157, 161, 164 n. 170; signed 142, 144, 153, 157, 161, 162 n. 163; wavy lines to indicate illegitimacy 35; Welsh 141 n. 66
Pedwardine family, pedigree 128 n. 9
Peirson, Richard, arms 83–4
Penyston family (Cornw.), pedigrees 142 nn. 71, 72
Penyston, Thomas, arms 132 n. 27, 164 n. 170 and Fig. 13
Percy family, pedigrees 128 nn. 8, 10
Percy, Henry, earl of Northumberland 5
Percy, Thomas, arms 96
Perrière, Guillaume de la 217
Petrucci, Ludovico 303 n. 55
Pfinzing, Paul 29
Phelip, Sir William, Lord Bardolf, arms 58
Phelips family, armorial glass Fig. 40
Phelips, Sir Edward 206
Philipot family, pedigree 135 n. 47, 140 n. 60
Philipot, John, Somerset Herald 135 n. 47, 140 n. 60
Phillipps, Sir Thomas, MSS from collection 128 (MS 26448), 135 n. 47 (MSS 26054, 24987), 139 n. 55 (6351), 152 (MS 29177)
Phillips, Augustine 58
Pigott (or Pygot) family (Yorks.), pedigree 139 n. 59, 145
Pittleworth Manor (Hants.) 211–12 and Fig. 44
Pizan, Christine de 254
Plantagenet (later de la Pole), Margaret, countess of Warwick and of Salisbury, pedigree 130–1
Plantagenet, Arthur, Viscount Lisle 13
Poitiers, Peter of 125
Pope, Thomas 58

Portraiture, heraldry in 220–35
Powle, Stephen, arms 101 and Fig. 17
Powle, Thomas, arms 101
Preston St Mary (Suff.), parish church 195, 203 and Fig. 37
Pympe, John 197
Ratcliffe, Sir John, heraldic funeral 59
Ravaillac, François 301
Raven, John, Richmond Herald 114–24 and Figs 20–1
Raymond, John, arms 98 n. 74
Repps family, of Norfolk, pedigree 142 n. 72, 143 n. 74
Reynell family, pedigree 139 and Fig. 23
Richard I, arms and badges 246–8, 284
Richard II, arms and badges 249–51, 254–5, 284 and Fig. 62
Richard III 8; arms and badges 284 and Fig. 63
Richard Robinson, *The Auncient Order ... of Prince Arthur* 264
Robartes, Richard 207
Rolls of Arms: *see* Dering Roll, Parliamentary Roll of Arms
Rothwell (Northants.), market house 195, 202 and Fig. 38
Ruscelli, Girolamo, *Discorso* 287, 290
Rushbrooke Hall (Suff.) 202
Ryece, Robert 195, 200, 203 and Fig. 37
Ryley, William, Norroy King of Arms 84
Sackville family, pedigree 132 n. 29, 137 n. 49, 139 nn. 58, 59
Sackville, Thomas, Baron Buckhurst, earl of Dorset 4
Sadleir, Sir Ralph, arms 73, 99
St George, Sir Henry, Clarenceux King of Arms 93
St George, Sir Richard, Norroy King of Arms 41, 93
St George: heraldic cross of 264; cult of 10
St Michael (St-Michel), Order of 221
Salesbury, Sir Robert, heraldic funeral 59
Saltonstall, Wye, *Picturae Loquentes* 267
Sandon (Staffs.)
Savage, Sir John, heraldic funeral 59–62
Savell (or Savile), Sir Henry, of Tankersley (Yorks.) 152, 155–6
Saxton, Christopher 29
Scarlett, Richard 66, 167 n. 3
Scotland, Lyon King of Arms 316–17, 321
Scott family, pedigree 139 n. 56

Scott, John, deputy herald(?) 144
Seal-engravers 57, 58, 66
Seals, drawings of 147, 153
Segar, Sir William, Garter King of Arms 20, 22, 33, 59 n. 100, 220, 298 n. 43; grants of arms 79, 81–2, 84, 95; *Booke of Honor and Armes* 115, 119–20, 123–4, 241, 298 n. 43
Seylyard family, of Delaware (Kent), pedigree 148
Seyman family, of Knoddishall (Suff.), pedigree 144–5
Seymour family, pedigree 135 n. 45, 139 n. 60
Seymour, Edward, earl of Hertford 4
Seymour, Jane (wife of Henry VIII), badge 285
Shakespeare, John, arms 95–6, 102, 105, 107–8, 118, 120, 124 n. 65 and Fig. 15b
Shakespeare, William: arms 88, 102 n. 94, 107, 108, 118, 119–20 and Figs 15a, 68; *impresa* composed by 267, 276; motto 116, 275; heraldry in his plays 236–65, 275, 282; *All is True* 236; *Antony and Cleopatra* 237 n. 9; *As You Like It* 241; *Cymbeline* 237, 261–4; *Hamlet* 122, 243, 276, 278; *Henry IV Part 1* 250, 254–5; *Henry V* 250; *Henry VI Part 2* 243; *King John* 237, 246, 247–8, 240 n. 22; *King Lear* 123; *Macbeth* 241–2; *Merry Wives of Windsor* 243, 245, 279; *Midsummer Night's Dream* 119, 278–9; *Much Ado about Nothing* 237 n. 9, 242–3; *Othello* 245–6; *Pericles* 276, 283; *Rape of Lucrece* 237, 240, 257–61, 307; *Richard II* 240 n. 23; *Richard III* 284 *Romeo and Juliet* 237 n. 9, 256; *Taming of the Shrew* 122, 237 n. 9; *Troilus and Cressida* 117–18; *Twelfth Night* 237; *Venus and Adonis* 307
Sheldon, Ralph 145 n. 86
Shirley, Sir Thomas 201
Sible Hedingham (Essex), Creswells Farm 217
Siddenham, Sir George, heraldic funeral 65
Sidney, Sir Philip: *Arcadia* 283; *Astrophil and Stella* 256; funeral 6, 33, 182–3 and Fig. 28
Simeoni, Gabriello, *Le imprese heroiche et morali* 276 n. 40, 287 n. 17
Smith, George, of Exeter 212
Smith, Mary 43
Smith, Ralph 43
Smith, Randal 27
Smith, Sir Thomas, *De Republica Anglorum* 115
Smith, Sir Thomas, of Cuerdley (Lancs.), arms 39

INDEX

Smith, Wentworth 34
Smith, William, Rouge Dragon Pursuivant 27–45 *passim*, 98
Smyth, John, of Nibley (Glos.) 3, 14
Smythe, Thomas, 'customer of London', arms 96
Solomon, Judgement of, wallpainting Fig. 48
Somerset, William, earl of Worcester 4
Sotherton, Nicholas 208
Southcote family, pedigree 142 n. 72
Southwell (Notts.), episcopal palace 197
Speed, John 29
Speke Hall (Lancs.) 197
Spenser, Edmund, *Faerie Queene* 239–40, 247, 255–6
Sprotborough (Yorks., W.R.), lawsuit about 152, 154–5
Squibb, Arthur, Clarenceux King of Arms 42
Stanhope, Sir Thomas, heraldic funeral 63
Stanley (née Clifford) Margaret, wife of Henry Stanley, earl of Derby 225
Stanley, Edward, earl of Derby, funeral 166–80 and Fig. 27
Stanley, Ferdinando, earl of Derby 175 n. 15
Stanley, Henry, earl of Derby 4, 170, 174, 175
Stanysby, Robert, arms 73, 80
Stapleton family, armorial glass 206
Steward, Geoffrey 208
Stone, Lawrence 3
Strangeman (or Strangman), James 141 n. 66, 195 n. 11
Stratford-upon-Avon (Warws.), Harvard House 217
Stubbes, Philip 205
Sun, heraldic 250–1, 254–5, 263 n. 104 and Fig. 62; rose *en soleil* Fig. 63; sunburst 251, 254, 255 and Figs 63–5
Sutton family, Lords Dudley 1, 2, 5, 14
Talbot family, archives 1 n. 5; pedigree 142 n. 72
Talbot, Elizabeth (Bess of Hardwick), countess of Shrewsbury 208
Talbot, Francis, earl of Shrewsbury, funeral 180
Talbot, George, earl of Shrewsbury, Earl Marshal 1, 11–12, 18–20, 22, 24, 75, 146 n. 98, 162–3; house at Worksop (Notts.) 193
Tawney, Richard Henry 3
Temple, Peter, arms 80
Temple, Susanna, portrait 230, 234 and Fig. 56
Theobalds (Herts.) 190, 191
Thornhurst, Sir Gifford 234
Thynne, Francis, Lancaster Herald 41, 115, 116, 135 n. 47
Time's Alteration (ballad) 271–2, 275
Tournament of Tottenham (poem) 273
Tournaments 287, 293, 294, 296 and Figs 70a–b
Trafford, Sir Edmund, heraldic funeral 59
Trappes (or Trapes), Robert, arms 99
Tresham, Sir Thomas 195, 202 and Fig. 38
Treswell, Ralph 28
Treswell, Robert, Somerset Herald 28
Trevelyon, Thomas, iconographic compiler 218 and Fig. 49
Tromp, Sir Martin, arms 78 n. 33
Trystram, Matthew, arms (1467) 77
Turpin, Richard, Windsor Herald 18
Tyler, painter, of Ratcliff (Middx.) 66
United States of America: grants of Honorary Arms to US citizens 320; devisals of arms to institutions 321
Unton, Sir Henry, funeral 182 n. 27
Vaughan family, pedigree 140 n. 61
Vecellio, Cesare, *Habiti Antichi et Moderni* Fig. 31
Vere, Edward de, earl of Oxford 11
Vertue, George Fig. 8
Vincent, Augustine, Windsor Herald 145 n. 86; arms 78; *Discouerie of Errours* 268, 279, 280
Vincent, Sir Francis 78
Visitations, heraldic 6, 10, 18, 39, 93, 107–17, 122, 141 n. 69, 163, 197, 308 and Figs 4, 6, 19–21; spurious 143 n. 75, 145
Wagner, Sir Anthony, Garter King of Arms 92–3, 102
Walsingham, Sir Francis, Principal Secretary, Chancellor of the Order of the Garter 18, 22, 182
Warneford, John, arms 208 and Fig. 41
Warren family, pedigree 142 n. 72
Warwick, earls of, pedigree or succession 130
Waterhouse, Edward 143–4
Watson, Sir Brook, arms Fig. 83
Webster, George, arms 96
Wentworth, Thomas, Baron Wentworth, portraits of two of his daughters (Jane, Margaret and Dorothy) 229–30
Westminster Abbey: heraldry 196–7; dispute of Dean and Chapter with heralds 12; Henry VII's Chapel 302 and Fig. 77
Whetenhall, John, heraldic funeral 56
White, Sir John, funeral achievements Fig. 29

White, William Augustus 47
Whitehall, Shield Gallery 293–4
Whitelocke, Sir James 290
Wilkenson, Christopher, arms 81
Wilson, Robert, *The Three Ladies of London* 242 n. 36
Winchell, Robert 42
Windover, William 221
Wittewronge, Sir John, arms 79 n. 38
Women: arms granted to 96, 97; arms in shape of lozenge Fig. 66; did not bear marks of cadency 243 n. 37; did not bear crests 260 n. 96; inferiority in the law of arms 257; arms transmitted by heraldic heiresses 257 n. 83; use of parental arms even if married 225; role in heraldic funerals 184, 186
Wood, Anthony 27
Woodford family, narrative genealogy 140
Worksop (Notts.) 193
Wotton, Thomas 201 n. 23
Wray, Sir Christopher, arms 75
Wright, Benjamin, *Armes of All the Cheife Corporatons* [sic] 273
Wriothesley, Henry, earl of Southampton, emblem with his arms 304–5 and Fig. 78
Wriothesley, Sir Thomas, Garter King of Arms 71, 88, 92, 94–5, 97, 98, 102, 103, 133 n. 36 and Figs 10, 63–5
Wyrley, William, Rouge Croix Pursuivant 132 n. 31, 198; *True Use of Armorie* 115, 188, 238
Yates, Susanna, arms 208 and Fig. 41
York Minster, heraldry 196–7
York, house of 130
Zouch, Edward la, Lord Zouch 33

Printed and bound in the Republic of San Marino by Fotoedit s.r.l.